Invitation to

psychology

This is your **Invitation to Psychology,** the challenging and fascinating study of human behavior. Discover what psychologists have learned about why people do what they do. At the same time, make some discoveries about your **own** life and behavior.

The authors

Invitation to
psychology

Rachel G. Ragland
Burt Saxon

Second
Edition

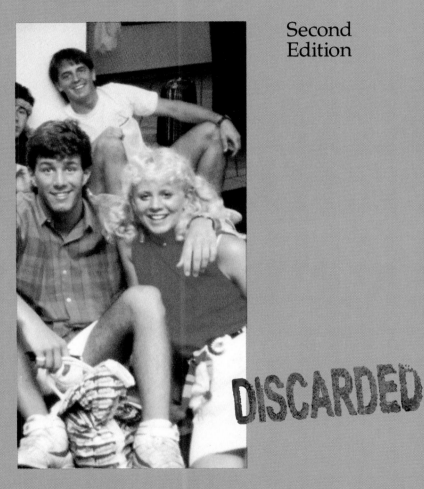

Scott, Foresman and Company

Editorial Offices: Glenview, Illinois
Regional Offices: Sunnyvale, California ○ Atlanta, Georgia
Glenview, Illinois ○ Oakland, New Jersey ○ Dallas, Texas

Authors

Rachel G. Ragland is a former psychology teacher at Norwalk High School, in Norwalk, Connecticut. Her experience includes instruction and development of curriculum for high school general psychology and social psychology courses. She has served as a member of the American Psychological Association Committee on Psychology in the Secondary Schools and as a consultant for development of teaching materials in psychology for WNET-TV. Ms. Ragland is currently a doctoral candidate in curriculum and teaching at Teachers College at Columbia University, where she is also Program Director for the Metropolitan School Study Council.

Burt Saxon has been a social studies teacher and curriculum developer in New Haven, Connecticut since 1970. Currently he teaches social studies at Hillhouse High School, in the talented and gifted program, which he also directs. Dr. Saxon has written extensively on adolescent development. He has also been a visiting instructor in urban education at Yale University.

ISBN: 0-673-35033-9

Academic Advisor

Philip G. Zimbardo is an award-winning, distinguished teacher who has taught introductory psychology for thirty years. He is well known as an active researcher with broad interests in psychology, and he writes extensively for magazines, newspapers, and professional journals. He is currently preparing a twenty-six-part television series, *Discovering Psychology*, which he will host for the Public Broadcasting System. Dr. Zimbardo is author of *Psychology and Life*, a college psychology text now in its twelfth edition; *Shyness: What It Is, What to Do About It*; and *The Shy Child*.

Acknowledgments for quoted matter and photographs appear on pages 532–534. These pages are an extension of the copyright page.

Commissioned Art
214–215 Ron Bradford
226, 290, 304 Pat Dypold
107, 148, 161 Jared D. Lee
52, 268 Diana Magnuson
40, 58, 81, 96, 117, 137, 172, 193, 223, 241, 245, 298, 315, 357, 390, 404, 461 Dick Martin
222 (bottom) George Suyeoka

Consultants

The authors and publisher would like to thank the following educators who read and critiqued *Invitation to Psychology* during its editorial development. They contributed valuable comments, chapter by chapter, on both the content and the level of difficulty. Their assistance has helped make *Invitation to Psychology* a practical classroom text.

Adele Livesay
Anderson High School
Austin, Texas

Sheila McCormick
William Aberhart Senior
High School
Calgary, Alberta
Canada

James McDonald
Assistant Principal
Mt. Tahoma High School
Tacoma, Washington

Jearlean Mills
Redan High School
Stone Mountain, Georgia

Dr. Stephanie Smith
Indiana University N.W.
Department of Psychology
Gary, Indiana

William Stepien
Chairman, Social Studies
Department
School District #300
Dundee, Illinois

Table of Contents

Unit 2 Discovering the World

Unit 4 Who Are You?

It's Your Turn

Charts, Graphs, and Tables

To the Student

Invitation to Psychology has been organized to make it easy to use. The book is divided into units and chapters, and they in turn are made up of sections—usually three to five per chapter. Regular features appear in both units and chapters. The **Table of Contents** and the **Index** will help you find what you need to know. Also note that the reference material at the end of the book includes an extensive **Psychology Skills Handbook** and a **Glossary** of psychology terms.

Units and Unit Features

The five units of *Invitation to Psychology* correspond to well-defined areas of psychological study. Each unit ends with a one-page **Experimenting with Psychology** feature describing real psychological experiments you can conduct yourselves, and an objective **Unit Test.** Also included in each unit is one or more **Case Studies.** These provide an in-depth look at an individual or group of individuals and illustrate some aspect of psychological research.

Chapters and Chapter Features

Each chapter includes an introduction, several numbered sections, and a two-page chapter review. The section and sub-section headings together make an outline of the main ideas in a chapter. By skimming a chapter, you will get a good idea of what you will be studying. Two kinds of special content features are found in each chapter. One, called **Close-Up,** focuses on an interesting example, news item, or research study that highlights a concept discussed in the text. The other, labeled **It's Your Turn,** gives you an opportunity to *apply* the skills and concepts you're learning at that point in the text.

Study Aids

Each **unit** begins with two pages that feature a photo, the unit title, and an introduction including a listing of the chapters covered. The **unit test** allows you to review the key terms and main ideas from that unit.

Each **chapter** introduction has an introduction with a list of the sections included and a **Chapter Review** with a section-by-section chapter **summary;** psychology skill **activities;** a **chapter test** with key terms and main ideas for each section; **critical thinking** questions; and a **skill exercise** to demonstrate your psychology skills. Both the activities and the critical thinking questions are labeled **easy** and **challenging,** so that you can select an appropriate level.

Every **section** in a chapter begins with a **Preview** feature in the yellow box in the margin. This will tell you what you will be learning from the section, the objectives of your study. Sections end with a set of **review questions.**

When this symbol appears, it signifies that the information that follows is quoted from another book. The end of the quotation is indicated by this symbol ■

Psychology Skills Handbook

As you read through the chapters in *Invitation to Psychology,* you will sometimes see this symbol **&&&.** This indicates that you are being referred to an Exercise in the **Psychology Skills Handbook**—the section at the back of your book with the green-tabbed pages. Exercises in the Handbook extend your knowledge of a topic you're studying by giving you descriptions of the methods psychologists use to arrive at their conclusions about behavior. Each Exercise in the Handbook gives you a step-by-step description of the different procedures psychologists follow in gathering and analyzing data. In addition, each Exercise includes an Application that allows you to try your hand at research and data analysis.

INTRODUCING
PSYCHOLOGY

"Why study psychology?" a friend might ask you. "It's nothing but 'common sense.' " "Common sense" ideas about human behavior *are* sometimes right, but just as often they are wrong. Below are fifteen "common sense" statements about human behavior. Some are supported by scientific evidence. Others are not. Test your knowledge by taking the *Common Sense* Psychology Test.

The *Common Sense* Psychology Test

Mark on a sheet of paper which statements are true and which are false.

1. You can tell how narrow-minded a person is by measuring the distance between his or her eyes.

2. Of all animals, only humans have the ability to reason.

3. The ability to withstand pain is different among different ethnic groups.

4. Opposites attract, so that people with different personalities tend to be attracted to one another.

5. Bright parents tend to have bright children.

6. The study of mathematics exercises the brain, helping the person to think better in other subjects.

7. People who are really suicidal don't talk about it, so you needn't take threats of suicide seriously.

8. A moderate amount of anxiety is good for you in that it often improves performance.

9. Very bright children are usually weak and in poor health.

10. People who can be hypnotized easily are generally weak-willed individuals.

11. With training, some animals can learn to communicate using abstract symbols.

12. Frustration builds character; the more of it children experience, the stronger they will be as adults.

13. Almost all of the U.S. astronauts have been firstborn children.

14. Shyness is a common adolescent experience we all outgrow.

15. Insanity is incurable, although its symptoms often disappear for long periods of time, then reappear later.

Compare your answers with those at the bottom of the opposite page. How good is your common sense psychology? Some of the answers were probably obvious to you. But some, no doubt, surprised you.

We'll be exploring these topics and more in the following pages. But first, let's see what we actually mean by "psychology."

1. Psychology Is . . .

Sports magazines carry interviews with athletes who talk about "psyching out" their opponents. Newspapers report stories of governments using "psychological warfare" on their enemies. Your friend tells you that the stomach flu you have the morning of your midterm exams is just "psychological." You want to get one of your friends to take your Saturday night work assignment—

Many tennis pros, like Boris Becker (above), John McEnroe, and Martina Navratilova, are famous for "psyching out" their opponents and making tennis as much a game of wits as skill.

for the *third* weekend in a row. You say to yourself: "I'm going to have to use a little 'psychology' to get Brian to work for me again." So you casually drop the information that you and Laurie are scheduled to work on Saturday night. (Laurie is a person Brian is *really* interested in getting to know better.) Later, you complain that you're going to have to miss some great fun Saturday night because you're scheduled to work—and Brian generously offers to switch nights with you.

Psychology is a term we encounter in some form every day. Yet few people would be able to give an accurate definition of it. Psychologists define **psychology** as the scientific study of the behavior of living things. Let's take this definition apart and see what it means.

Psychology Is Scientific

Psychologists try to approach their studies using the same methods as other sciences. Like other scientists, psychologists study natural events to learn how one force acts on another in bringing about an end result. (Specific methods used by psychologists are described at length in the following chapters and in the **Psychology Skills Handbook** section at the back of this book.) Unlike many chemists or physicists, however, psychologists are dealing with living things, and this complicates their work somewhat. Studying *human* subjects scientifically is an especially big order. We aren't the purely rational, thinking beings we often pretend to be. We are, in fact, bundles of emotions, feelings, prejudices, and anxieties. That's why psychologists focus their studies on behavior, which brings us to the second key word in our definition.

Thinking activity is one type of behavior studied by psychologists; emotional behavior, like love, is another.

Psychology Is the Study of Behavior

Psychologists cannot see into people's heads to understand why they do what they do. Instead, they must observe actions, or **behavior.** From their observations, they try to figure out *causes* of their subjects' behavior. When psychologists study behavior, they study the actions or activities of living things.

All physical and mental activity is behavior of some sort. So, to organize their work psychologists divide the study of behavior into four broad groups.

1. *Physical characteristics.* Things such as body size, sex, appearance, inborn drives, and inheritance contribute to the physical aspects of behavior.

2. *Cognitive activity.* **Cogni-** **tive** (intellectual or thinking) activity helps determine our ability to reason, to solve problems, to learn new behaviors, and to communicate with each other. These are examples of the *thinking* side of human behavior.

3. *Emotional states.* Things such as anger, fear, love, and other *feeling* states are types of emotional behavior.

4. *Social and environmental factors.* These shape behavior through our contacts with others, the kind of society we live in, family influences, and many other external forces. Because people are "social animals" these factors play an important role in our lives.

These four areas are not independent of each other. We feel and think at the same time. We do things with a physical body that operates in a social context. The psychologist's job is to investigate these relationships as systematically as possible.

Psychology Is the Study of Living Things

The other key words in the definition of psychology are *living things.* A psychologist's main aim is to study human beings. Sometimes, however, because of the nature of the study, it is not possible to do this directly. Occasionally, psychologists must study other animals in order to learn about people. You will see that a great amount of research in psychology is done with animals as subjects. In fact, human subjects often refer to themselves as "guinea pigs" when they volunteer for experiments, although the guinea pig itself is seldom used in psychology. Rats, cats, monkeys, and pigeons are much more common.

Animals make useful research subjects, for a number of reasons.

1. They can be studied under experimental conditions for much longer periods of time than human beings.

2. The shorter life span of animals helps the researcher to study the development of certain behaviors over many generations in a relatively short time.

3. The animal doesn't know it is part of an experiment, and is therefore a "good" subject.

4. Animals can be used in ways that would be unethical for human subjects. For example, animals can be punished, rewarded, and trained to do things that people would not do (running a maze, for instance).

5. Some psychological processes found in animals are remarkably similar to those of human beings.

Many psychologists believe that animal research is, at best, a "starting point" for learning about the complex forces that govern human action. When you read about animal experiments in the pages that follow, bear in mind that people might not react in exactly the same way. However, the reaction may be quite similar.

Section Review

1. Define psychology.
2. List the kinds of behavior psychologists study.
3. Give three reasons why animals make good subjects for psychology experiments.

Animals are used for research because they can be trained to do things humans wouldn't do. They can also be trained to do things humans can do. Using learning techniques, a Florida family trained a squirrel to water-ski!

2. Why Study Psychology?

When you flatter someone just before asking a favor, you are using a bit of "psychology" to get what you want. The soothing music you hear in the dentist's office is meant to put you in a better mood for what's coming. However, if results like these were all that psychologists could claim for their efforts, taking a course in the subject would hardly be worthwhile. Psychology has much broader and more meaningful purposes.

General Purposes of Psychology

Psychologists generally try to serve four important purposes. They are:

1. *To acquire basic knowledge about behavior for its own sake.* The job of research psychologists is to be curious. Among the kinds of things they want to know more about are: What drives and motivates people? How are attitudes formed? How can the effects of growing older change human beings? How is personality shaped? Psychologists always ask *what* and *how*, first rather than *why*. They look for significant relationships and causes in behavior. From this basic research have come several broad theories of behavior. Some of these will be discussed later in the text.

2. *To apply basic knowledge to specific situations.* Psychology is used in many ways in industry, education, and architectural design. For instance, architects are now designing buildings with behavior functions in mind, not just beauty and cost. Learning theories play an important part in the development of effective teach-

ing techniques. Research in developmental psychology has contributed to better child-rearing practices. The military services and some business corporations use psychological tests to try to match the right person with the right job.

3. *To apply basic knowledge to clinical situations.* Psychologists are concerned with many of the mental and emotional disorders that you hear about every day. **Clinical studies,** those based on observations of actual patients, provide improved methods for diagnosing and treating these disor-

ders. You may have mental or emotional problems some time in your life, as most people do, that might be solved with the help of a therapist, or counselor. People who have marriage problems often turn to psychologists who specialize in this type of help.

But the most important use of this area of psychology may be in providing an "early warning system" to prevent mental and emotional distress. School psychologists, for example, provide important help for students with behavior problems. "Hot lines" and cri-

sis intervention centers deal with on-the-spot situations that call for immediate action by trained volunteer helpers.

4. *To apply basic knowledge to social problems.* Psychologists are playing an increasingly important role in dealing with the problems of society. Important among these are crime and delinquency. Assume, for the sake of discussion, that you get into serious trouble with the law. If you are found guilty there's a good chance that you will be interviewed by a psychologist before sentence is passed. His or her report will probably influence the judge's decision. If you are unfortunate enough to be sent to prison, another psychologist will help prison officials determine how to rehabilitate you. Finally, whether or not you get probation will depend in part on the psychologist's evaluation of your progress and the likelihood that you will "go straight."

A great deal of research also has been done on the psychological factors that affect aggression and violence among people. In this respect, psychologists try to play a constructive role in resolving conflict and prejudice among different social groups.

Psychology and You

The popular interest in psychology that has grown up in the last few decades has made almost everyone an amateur psychologist. People read a

Major Fields in Psychology	
Developmental Psychology	Focus on individual growth and behavior change across the lifespan
Physiological Psychology	Focus on biological processes and how they affect behavior
Experimental Psychology	Focus on understanding basic behavioral processes such as sensation and perception, learning, and motivation
Social Psychology	Focus on the effect of social interaction and the social environment on the individual
Educational Psychology	Focus on understanding learning and memory and how they can be applied in real-life situations
Health Psychology	Focus on psychological factors that can affect one's physical health and well-being
Personality Psychology	Focus on individual traits and how people differ from each other
Clinical/Counseling Psychology	Focus on assessing and treating people with psychological problems
Industrial/Organizational Psychology	Focus on research and application of psychological principles in the workplace

book and think they have explanations for any human event. One reason for studying psychology is simply to unlearn incorrect popular notions about the causes of behavior. For example, a popular notion is that "human nature doesn't change." It can and does. Although psychologists don't have all the answers, they do have some specific ways of looking for them.

As you study psychology you'll learn about the various theories that psychologists have proposed to explain behavior in general. We'll also be looking at particular behaviors. How does human memory work? What is a conditioned response? Why do we change as we grow older? When is behavior "abnormal"? These, and other areas that psychol-ogy has selected for investigation, are considered in the chapters that follow. If nothing else, your study of psychology should make you a bit more "scientific," as well as sensitive, in understanding other people and the way they behave.

Studying psychology can also assist you in your future career. The development and expansion in "human service" occupations—such as nursing, law enforcement, community service, and sales—has opened doors for trained people in schools, hospitals, clinics, and social agencies. To be a "full-fledged" psychologist requires an advanced degree, usually a Ph.D. Many jobs are available, however, which require less formal training in psychology. (The young man or woman who works with street gangs, for instance, will almost certainly have had some background in psychology.) According to one estimate, the number of psychology-related jobs in this country will increase by 40 percent within the next ten years. In fact, you'll be more effective in any occupation, or future life-style, that involves dealing with people if you have some reliable knowledge of what makes them— and you—"tick."

Finally, perhaps the most important use you can make of psychology is to learn more about yourself. Psychology can help you take a better look at yourself and the unknown side of your personality. One of your objectives may be to discover how fascinating, unpredictable, heroic, and troublesome this self can be. Knowing this may help you understand why you are hard to get along with at times, or show you how to better handle your frustrations and worries. Knowing yourself better can help you to make the most of your abilities. Think of this practical "how to" aspect of psychology as a bonus. It won't solve all your problems, but it can help.

Section Review

1. List some of the general purposes of psychology.
2. How might psychology be useful to you?
3. Describe some careers in psychology.

3. Psychology Through History

Psychology, the scientific study of behavior, was just a hundred years old in 1975. Before that, for great periods in human history, people believed that it was impossible to study the "mind"—the thinking and feeling part of human nature—scientifically. Mental and emotional problems often weren't believed to have natural causes.

Early Ideas About Behavior

It wasn't that people weren't *interested* in finding out the causes of behavior. From earliest times, people have sought to explain behavior and to find remedies for behavior disorders. Archeological evidence shows that Stone Age people engaged in a practice called trephining to cure behavior disorders. Trephining involved chipping away a hole in the disturbed person's skull to allow the "evil spirits" inside to escape. This might have actually cured some types of disorders by relieving pressure on the brain. Some trephined skulls show growth over the wound indicating that some people miraculously survived this treatment.

The idea that supernatural forces, like "evil spirits," caused behavior disorders persisted among the ancient Chinese, Egyptians, and Hebrews. It wasn't until Greek and Roman times that the idea that mental disorders had natural causes gained wide acceptance. Hippocrates, the "father of modern medicine," was one of the first to argue that mental and emotional problems had natural causes. He proved that some disorders were caused by injury to the head. He also correctly observed that some physical and mental characteristics were inherited.

Unfortunately, the Greeks had little knowledge of biological processes. They had such reverence for the human body that they rarely did autopsies to try to discover the cause of illnesses. This led them to develop some inaccurate ideas about the biological processes. They believed, for example, that all things in the world were made up of a combination of four basic elements. These elements were fire, air, earth, and water. Each element had a quality associated with it. Fire was warm. Air was cold. Earth was dry, and water moist. In the human body, these elements were thought to exist in the form of the four "humors": blood (warm and moist); black bile (cold and dry); yellow bile (warm and dry); and phlegm (cold and moist).

In the second century A.D. Galen, a Greek physician, applied these elements to human personality. He thought that if a person had a great amount of one of these "humors" his

or her personality would be shaped in that direction. For example, an excess of blood caused a sanguine, or cheerful, warm-hearted person. A lot of black bile made the person melancholic, or sad. A person with too much yellow bile was thought to be *choleric,* or hot tempered. And an apathetic, or *phlegmatic,* person was the result of too much phlegm.

During the Middle Ages, the scientific study of behavior all but disappeared in Europe, although the scientific tradition of the Greeks and Romans survived in the Arab world. In Western Europe, people believed that behavior disorders were caused by possession by devils or witchcraft. Instead of being treated as if they were ill, mentally disturbed people often were imprisoned, tortured, or put to death.

The scientific revolution which began in Europe in the seventeenth century again brought about a search for natural causes of biological proc-

These medieval woodcuts represent the "four humors." Opposite: The choleric, or hot-tempered, personality; above, left to right: The lively, or sanguine, personality; the melancholic personality; the apathetic, or phlegmatic, personality.

esses. This led to attempts to find physical causes for psychological traits. Many of these attempts seem amusing today. One was the "science" of phrenology, which developed in the late 1700s.

Phrenologists believed that personality was made up of a certain number of "faculties." These were particular types of feelings or behaviors. Each faculty was located in a specific area of the brain. Phrenologists drew up "maps" of the brain, like the one below, showing the location of the faculties. A person who had a great deal of a particular faculty would have a bump on his or her head at the point where this trait was in the brain. An individual's personality could be discovered by studying the shape of the head.

Modern objections to the claims of phrenology are overwhelming. A comparison of a phrenologist's map of the brain with the actual findings of scientists shows that there is no correspondence whatsoever. When we stimulate the part of the brain thought by phrenologists to be the center of religiousness, for example, the subject twitches his leg. Modern research has found nothing to support the existence of the "faculties" discussed by the phrenologists.

Later Developments

This inadequate approach to our mental and emotional life lasted well into the nineteenth century. In fact, psychology did not become a true science until 1875 when Wilhelm Wundt, a professor in

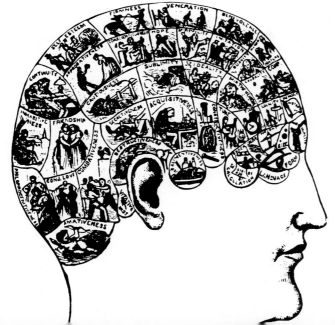

9

Germany, opened the first psychology laboratory.

A year earlier, Wundt had written a book, *Principles of Physiological Psychology,* which argued that the mind must be studied as scientifically as other "natural laws." Wundt's laboratory was intended for just this purpose. He studied the perception of objects as a clue to the processes of thinking and feeling. Wundt's method was based on **introspection,** a detailed examination of one's own thinking, or reflections. Meanwhile, others at the time were studying memory, sensation, and the perception of light and sound.

How Did Psychology Develop in the U.S.?

The new science spread quickly throughout the world. It made its most rapid progress, however, in the United States. It began with the work of Edward Bradford Titchener at Cornell University. Titchener emphasized the importance of how physical sensations, emotions, and images are combined in human consciousness. This approach to psychology, called **structuralism,** studied behavior as parts that fit together in a structure.

About the time that Titchener was developing his theories, a young physiology professor at Harvard, William James, came to somewhat different conclusions about the new science of behavior. He turned from physiology to philosophy and combined these subjects into a course in psychology in 1875. Out of this came his trailblazing book *The Principles of Psychology* in 1890. This book profoundly affected the course of psychology for many years to come.

James challenged some of Titchener's beliefs. According to James, events happened with a purpose. Life was a process of adapting to a confusing outer world. It had to be organized by each individual on the basis of experience. The organization of experience—making sense out of nonsense—was the mind's principal goal.

James' approach has been called **functionalism** (or, sometimes, associationism) because it emphasizes the function of associations in working toward a specific goal. James thought the value of an act was in how well it works, or functions.

Since James' time, an explosion in psychological research has resulted in many theories about human behavior. These theories will be the subject of the next section.

Section Review

1. What was the important advance in the study of mental disorders made during Greek and Roman times?
2. Tell when the science of psychology first began.
3. Discuss the contributions of Wundt, Titchener, and James.

4. Psychology: A Bunch of Theories?

"Why study psychology?" you sometimes hear people say. "It's nothing but a bunch of theories." There *are* a lot of theories in psychology. If there weren't there would be little progress in the study of behavior. Psychologists use theories, as one psychologist put it, "to acquire and organize information about behavior." Research is often done to prove or disprove theories, and theories are constantly being revised in the light of new evidence.

Major Approaches to the Study of Behavior

There are five major theories or approaches in modern psychology. They are listed below.

1. *Psychologists should study behavior from the outside.* The approach is called **behaviorism.** It is best shown by the work of B. F. Skinner, which will be discussed in Chapter 2. Behaviorists place their primary emphasis on experience, or learning. They analyze behavior experimentally. They limit themselves to studying those events they can see and measure. Behaviorism stresses the role of the environment in shaping behavior.

2. *Psychologists should study behavior from the inside.* According to this approach, psychologists should concern themselves with non-measurable as well as measurable processes. This is generally the viewpoint

of **cognitive psychology.** Cognitive psychologists go beyond behaviorists to state that experience affects the way we perceive new events, and that the thought processes determine behavior. Cognitive psychologists do not believe we are controlled by our environment. Instead, they believe we control our surroundings with our ability to reason and make decisions. A leader of this school was Jean Piaget, who studied the development of thinking ability in children. His theories are considered in Chapter 5.

3. *Psychologists should look at the "parts" of behavior and from these draw conclusions about the whole.* This is the method of the physical psychologist and some learning theorists. They try to break down experience into its simplest parts and to study these parts individually. An example of the type of research carried out by physical psychologists would be to measure your reaction time in releasing a switch when a light is beamed at you.

4. *Psychologists should look at the whole of behavior, and from this draw conclusions about the "parts."* This holistic ("whole") approach has been stated in **Gestalt theory.** It is the way that individual events are combined in total experience that is of interest. A gestaltist would argue, for example,

Some important contributors to modern psychology are pictured below. Top, left to right: Wilhelm Wundt; Karen Horney; Sigmund Freud. Bottom: Jean Piaget; William James; B. F. Skinner.

that you cannot understand the working of an automobile by studying the action of the carburetor, the spark plugs, and the pistons separately. Only when you know how these parts work together can you grasp what makes the automobile go. Gestalt theory is discussed more fully in Chapter 1.

Growing out of the Gestalt approach is **humanistic psychology,** which stresses self-understanding, creativity, and the development of one's potential. Humanistic psychologists argue for encounter groups, "letting go," and various forms of nonverbal communication as a way to approach the wholeness of experience.

5. *Psychologists should look below the surface of observable behavior.* In general, this is what is meant by **psychoanalytic theory.** Psychoanalysis deals with motives and forces buried within the mind. These are thought to influence behavior. Psychoanalytic theorists see the individual as being driven by powerful needs. These and our childhood experiences are thought to guide our actions.

People often believe that psychoanalysis *is* psychology instead of just one of many approaches to the study of behavior. Part of the reason for this is that psychoanalytical theorists were among the earliest and most influential contributors to modern psychology. These include the originator of this approach, Sigmund Freud, and other famous psychoanalysts, such as Anna Freud, Carl Jung, Karen Horney, and Alfred Adler. We will discuss their theories in many of the chapters to come.

As a practical matter, many psychologists use an **eclectic approach** to the study of behavior. That is, they combine various approaches in their work. In fact, in recent years, the sharp boundaries between theories have begun to break down. As you read this book, you may want to refer to the above description of the various approaches for studying behavior. It will give you a good framework for understanding much that follows. As we come to the many issues and questions raised by modern psychological research, we will often give the opinions of psychologists representing one or more of these approaches. We will say how behaviorists view such and such an issue, cognitive psychologists, Freudians, and so on. In other words, in this book, *we* will adopt an *eclectic* approach. We will present the theories to you and you can make your own judgments.

Section Review

1. Discuss: There are many answers to the questions raised by modern psychology.
2. Why are theories useful?
3. Describe major approaches for studying behavior. ৶

5. What's Ahead

Now you have a brief background for understanding what psychology is, and some idea about its difficulties, as well as its rewards and fascinations. As you study this text, keep in mind that you are not reading a fixed blueprint of behavior, good for everyone at all times. Rather you are being presented with a view of psychology as an ever-changing, ever-growing field.

Here's a preview of what's to come. This book is organized into units, each devoted to a general topic in the study of behavior. The units are further divided into chapters that deal with aspects of the unit topic. Below are summaries of the topics included in each unit. You might find it helpful to reread the unit summary for background as you begin each unit.

In **Unit 1, The Cycle of Life,** you look at what people are like as they move through the stages of development from before birth to death. You examine physical changes, intellectual growth, and social, emotional, and moral development. You think about how babies, preschool children, and school-age children grow and develop. You note the changes that turn children into adolescents, and you follow adults from young adulthood through middle age to the later years.

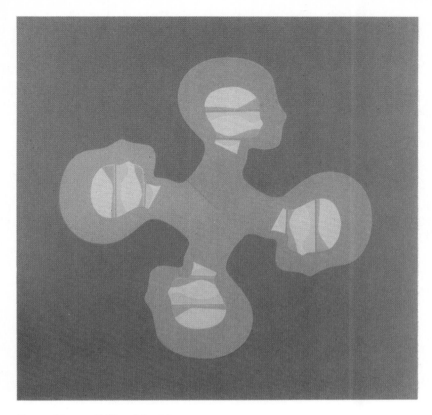

Ernest Trova, *Falling Man Manscapes*

In **Unit 2, Discovering the World,** you study the ways we discover the world around us. You learn that the first step in the discovery process is to *make sense* out of the information coming in through the senses. Then you consider how people use that information to think and learn. You also examine the world *inside* your head to see how learning and thinking work in the areas of memory and language, and you look at the nature of intelligence and creativity.

In **Unit 3, Roots of Behavior,** you begin by exploring the biological roots of behavior. First, you see how the brain operates as the body's command post. Then you'll look at the ways in which the brain's commands are translated into behavior by the body's electrical (nervous) and chemical (glandular) systems. You also see how the body responds to certain biological drives. You examine the ways certain so-cial and psychological needs—the need to seek approval, to explore and learn and achieve—pattern your behavior. Finally, you look at these patterns of behavior as they exist in various states of consciousness.

Unit 4, Who Are You? deals with the self—what psychologists believe goes into making each of us unique. You examine some theories that attempt to explain individual differences among people and what influences personality development. You also explore the concept of abnormality, as well as some common forms of mental disturbances. You look at some causes of mental disturbance and some strategies for staying mentally healthy.

In **Unit 5, You, Others, and Society,** you examine some theories psychologists have developed about how people interact with other individuals and with society as a whole. You look at what influences interpersonal attraction, and the nature of love. You consider how people are influenced by social groups and how groups affect their members. Finally, you think about the challenges facing you as an individual in our modern technological society.

Introduction Review

Section Summaries

1. Psychology Is . . .

Psychologists define psychology as the scientific study of the behavior of living things. Behavior includes physical characteristics, cognitive activity, emotional states, and social and environmental factors. Although psychologists are primarily interested in human behavior, they often use animals as subjects. Using animals lets psychologists conduct studies and experiments that would be difficult or unethical for human subjects.

2. Why Study Psychology?

Psychology has four goals: to acquire basic knowledge and to apply that basic knowledge to specific situations, clinical situations, and social problems. Studying psychology can help you unlearn incorrect notions about behavior and be both more scientific and sensitive in understanding other people. The study of psychology can help you in your career, as well as help you understand yourself.

3. Psychology Through History

Many ancient civilizations believed that "evil spirits" caused behavior disorders. Hippocrates thought that these disorders had physical causes, and Galen developed a theory of "humors" in the seventh century. During the Middle Ages, however, mentally disturbed people were imprisoned or killed. In the seventeenth century, the scientific revolution renewed the search for physical causes. In 1875 German professor William Wundt began to use introspection in the first psychology laboratory. In the United States, a Cornell University professor, Edward Bradford Titchener, developed an approach called structuralism, and William James at Harvard University developed functionalism.

4. Psychology: A Bunch of Theories?

Today there are five major approaches in psychology. Behaviorism stresses the role of the environment in shaping behavior. Cognitive psychologists feel that we use our ability to reason to control our environment. Some psychologists try to study individual bits of behavior. Others try to study the whole of behavior. Psychoanalysis deals with motives and forces buried within the mind. Many psychologists use an eclectic approach combining elements of each of these five theories.

5. What's Ahead

Unit 1, "The Cycle of Life," covers the stages of development from life to death. In Unit 2, "Discovering the World," you will study the ways we take in and process information from the world around us. Unit 3, "The Roots of Behavior," explores the biological roots of behavior. In Unit 4, "Who Are You?" you will study personality, as well as theories of abnormal behavior and modern forms of therapy. Unit 5, "You, Others, and Society," covers interpersonal attraction, as well as the ways that people are affected by social groups.

Psychology Skill Activities

1. Think of your own personal reasons for studying psychology. What do you hope to gain from this experience? What use can you make of it? Write out your thoughts. **easy**

2. Interview a psychologist or guidance counselor about the practical uses of psychology. Then report to your class. **challenging**

Testing for Understanding
Knowing Key Terms

Define these terms in your own words.

Section 1
psychology
behavior
cognitive

Section 2
clinical studies

Section 3
introspection
structuralism
functionalism

Section 4
behaviorism
cognitive psychology
Gestalt theory
humanistic psychology
psychoanalytic theory
eclectic approach

Reviewing Main Ideas

Section 1

1. What do psychologists mean when they define psychology as the *scientific* study of behavior?

2. Give an example of each of the four categories into which psychologists divide the study of behavior.

3. Explain why animals can be better subjects for psychology experiments than people.

Section 2

1. What are the general purposes of the science of psychology?

2. What are some benefits of studying psychology?

3. Where might a person who is trained in psychology work?

Section 3

1. What did Greek physicians contribute to the study of behavior?

2. What event launched psychology as a true science?

3. What contributions did Wilhelm Wundt, E. B. Titchener, and William James each make to psychology?

Section 4

1. Why do psychologists agree that there are no "right" or "wrong" answers about behavior?

2. How do psychologists use theories?

3. Which approach to psychology is associated with B. F. Skinner? With Jean Piaget? With Sigmund Freud?

Thinking Critically

1. *Drawing Inferences.* Which of the four categories do you think would be the easiest to study? Why?   **easy**

2. *Drawing Conclusions.* Tell which of the purposes of psychology you feel is the most important and why.   **challenging**

Demonstrating Psychology Skills

Use what you have learned in this introduction to complete this table:

Psychological Approach	Main Focus of Study
Behaviorism	
Cognitive psychology	
Gestalt theory	
Psychoanalytic theory	

Unit 1

The Cycle of Life

In this unit you will look at what people are like as they move through the states of development from birth to death—what physical changes occur, how intellectual growth takes place, and how we develop socially, emotionally, and morally.

Chapter 1

Starting Out: Infancy and Childhood

Sara Wilson is an active three-year-old. She plays well by herself and with her older sister Betty, who is almost five. But in the past two months her parents and neighbors have noticed a change in Sara. She has a tantrum if any little thing goes wrong. Also, she seems to have trouble sleeping.

Mrs. Wilson believes the unexpected death of Sara's grandmother, who was very close to Sara, is at the root of the problem. "Ever since my mother died," she says, "Sara's been behaving miserably." Betty's kindergarten teacher has another explanation. "It's common for a child to act up when an older brother or sister starts going to school," says the teacher. "Don't forget, Sara's never been without Betty before."

Mrs. Wilson wants to take Sara to a child psychologist, but Mr. Wilson will have none of it. "All children act like this at some point in their lives," he says, "so don't get excited. All she needs is a little more discipline when her father's not at home."

Problems like Sara's represent one of the concerns of developmental psychology. **Developmental psychology** is the study of behavior as it goes through stages of growth and change. Developmental psychologists study different aspects of human growth and development. Their studies include physical growth and emotional, social, and **cognitive** development, or development of thinking skills.

In this chapter we will look at development, or growing up, from several points of view. First, we will look at human development from before birth through the preschool years. Then we'll look at some stages of growth, and examine a few ideas of an important developmental psychologist, Jean Piaget. We will see how the physical characteristics of our parents combine to make each of us unique, and consider how and why psychologists study development. Finally, we'll look at some questions parents and others try to answer in relation to daycare for young children.

1. How Young Children Develop

A hundred years ago, many expectant mothers attended concerts and visited art museums because they thought the experience would help make their offspring lovers of music and art. Today we know that prenatal experiences won't have such effects. Yet what happens in the mother's womb can affect a baby's development in other important ways.

Prenatal Development

During the prenatal period, the fertilized egg grows and develops. The unborn **fetus** is a miniature and rapidly developing baby, who receives nourishment from the mother through the umbilical cord. The mother's health during pregnancy is important to the child's general health at birth. Malnutrition before birth can cause a slowdown of both

PREVIEW

In this section, read to find out:

1. how a fetus is affected by the mother's health.
2. why an infant's first year is important.
3. how toddlers and preschool children grow and change.

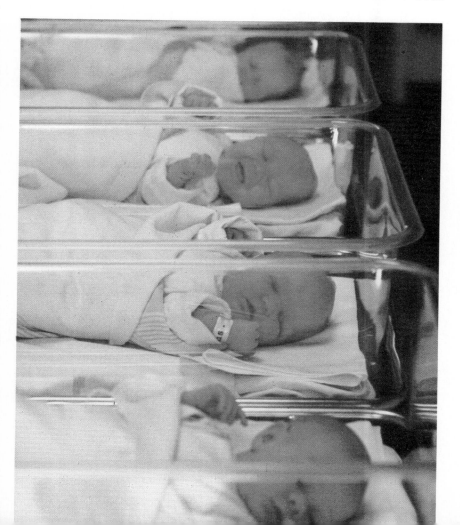

the physical and mental development of the fetus. Certain diseases in the mother can also cause damage. For example, if the mother has rubella (German measles) in the first three months of pregnancy, her baby may be born blind, deaf, or with brain or heart damage. Today doctors are very cautious in prescribing medications for pregnant women. In addition, they warn the mother to avoid cigarettes, alcohol, and other nonprescription drugs.

Less is understood about the effect of stress in the mother on the early emotional development of the infant. There are indications that excessive crying in some infants may be associated with the mother's stressful experiences during pregnancy.

Infants and Toddlers

At birth, a child leaves the controlled environment of the womb for the more unreliable outside environment. Yet a newborn child comes equipped with many ready-made responses to this environment. Newborn babies are able to follow slow-moving objects with their eyes.

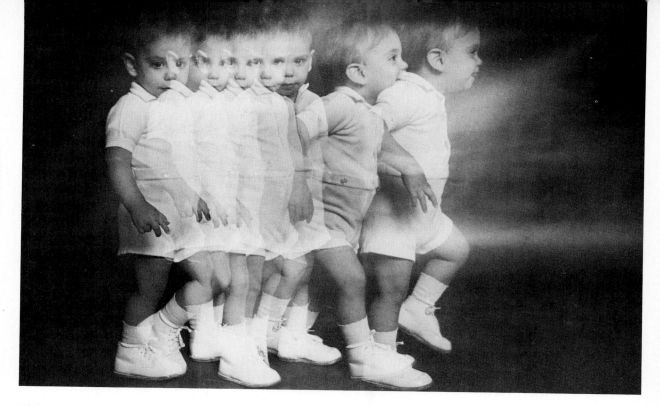

They perceive different types of sounds and are soothed by rhythmic sounds. They can distinguish a sweet taste from a bitter or salty taste. Newborn infants respond to strong, unpleasant odors, to temperature extremes, and to being touched. Their responses to the outside world increase rapidly.

We think of babies as helpless. It is true that they must be fed and protected. But the way they learn by themselves, even in the first six months, is anything but helpless. Babies naturally explore—at first by looking, reaching, and grasping, and later by creeping and crawling to the source of stimulation. Between a year and a year and a half, most children explore still more interesting things on their own wobbly legs. They learn to control both things and people. They play with toys—and smash them. They open and close books repeatedly to produce a delightful sound. At about a year, too, a child distinguishes between *me*—a body with feelings, needs and thoughts—and *not me*—other people and things.

Usually between the first and second years come two important physical changes, walking and toilet-training. Children begin walking when their coordination and muscular development make walking possible. Toilet-training involves learning to bring under control a

A child who feels loved and cared for during infancy is likely to achieve sound emotional development.

physical function that is already present. Those responsible for guiding a child through toilet-training are likely to use positive and negative reinforcement to achieve their goal. Developmental psychologists believe the atmosphere during toilet-training should be friendly, and the praise for each success should be immediate. Some of the differences of opinion about the best age for toilet-training may be explained in part by individual children's different rates of development.

Emotional Development During Infancy

Not all infants display the same feelings. You have heard a parent say "Patty is such a quiet baby" or "I can't understand why Peter cries so much." For years it has been known that the behavior of a child's caregivers influenced the child. A happy parent was likely to develop a happy child; a rejecting parent would probably develop a child who feels rejected, and so on.

But recent reports point up the ways a child influences the parent as well. A smiling child will probably get more affection and fondling. A difficult and demanding baby may get attention, but may also provoke the adult's temper and try his or her patience. The cycle of accepting or rejecting can continue throughout childhood. A baby and the baby's caregivers influence each other.

Trust or mistrust. Psychoanalyst Erik Erikson described the early period of a child's life as crucial for the development of what he calls **trust.** The infant's caregivers who fulfill the child's needs in a comforting way establish for the baby this sense of trust. A child who doesn't experience the environment as orderly and predictable in the first year of life develops, according to Erikson, an attitude of **mistrust** which can affect his or her whole emotional well-being.

During the second six months, a child forms a social attachment to the mother or other primary caregiver, added to the physical attachment that already exists. During this critical period, Erikson believes that mistrust can develop from a long separation from the primary caregiver. Such a separation may do great harm to a child's emotional development.

After nine months of age, mistrust can also come from long exposure to a new and unfamiliar environment. According to Erikson, during this later period of infancy the mother, or other primary caregiver, becomes the *protective figure* on whom the child depends for security. When this feeling of being loved and cared for is suddenly withdrawn, some babies become depressed.

The Harlows' monkey studies. For many years, psychologists Harry and Margaret Harlow of the University of Wisconsin have studied the effects of "mother love" during infancy—or the lack of it—on the emotional responses of a group of monkeys.

In one of their best known experiments, the Harlows substituted two artificial "mothers" for the real mother monkeys. One "mother" was a rounded wire grill with a nipple. The other was a padded terry-cloth "mother." The infants preferred the cuddly and soft cloth model to the wire "mother." Rubbing against and clinging to something soft seemed more important to the infant monkeys' development of a sense

The Harlows' infant monkeys preferred the soft cloth "mother" to the food-giving wire "mother."

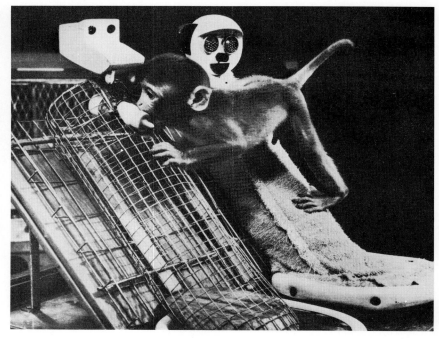

of security than ready access to food given by the wire "mother."

The Harlows also separated young monkeys from their cloth "mothers" several weeks after birth. At first, the youngsters rushed about trying to find "Mom." One by one, they gave up and huddled in corners, rocked, and clung to themselves. Normal monkey business in the group disappeared. Monkeys are playful. Like human babies, they examine new toys, push them around, then pick them up. But if the mother they are used to is absent, the infant withdraws and ignores these playthings. When the mother returns, the baby rushes to her, clings to her, and then plays with the toys. A strong attachment bond seems to be necessary for the development of confidence.

Human infants show much the same kind of behavior. When they are able to toddle into another room to explore toys, they tend to do it as long as the mother is seated nearby. If the mother leaves the area, however, or a stranger appears, exploring stops. Curiosity is strong but fear is stronger.

The Harlows' research findings, though done with animals, are consistent with Erikson's theories. Both stress the importance of the bond between a child and the primary caregiver, who is often the mother. These specialists agree that emotional development begins early and is important for a growing infant.

How institutions affect development. What happens when a human infant is deprived of a mother? To answer this question, British psychiatrist John Bowlby studied many children in orphanages during the 1960s. He discovered that depression was common among the children. Bowlby suggested that these infants showed the same symptoms of *grief reaction* that an adult shows when a loved one dies.

Other psychologists think that loss itself does not explain these reactions. They think the depression is caused by failure to replace the lost mother by another caring person and a normal environment. Whatever the reason, orphanage children are frequently slow to develop. Many investigators have noticed a hunger for attention and affection on the part of institutionalized children.

When conditions in an orphanage are good, social and cognitive development proceed at a normal rate. Many children who receive good care in institutions show little difference from children raised in their own families. The mother's absence does not seem to be the most important factor. Plenty of loving care, good nutrition, and stimulating sights and sounds in the environment together appear to make the major difference in children's development.

Preschool Development

By age four, a child is about half as tall as he or she will be as an adult. As children grow through the preschool years, they develop new physical skills. Throwing a ball, running, climbing, drawing, eating by themselves, and dressing themselves are a few of the skills they acquire. Preschool children need space to use large muscles, to run and shout, to try new skills and add new accomplishments. The preschool child also shows a new sense of independence. Unfortunately for parents, this can lead to tantrums aimed at getting a child's own way.

Play behavior. More of a social person than at earlier ages, the average four- or five-year-old wants to get out and play with other children. The *play* of preschool children often imitates the *work* of grown-ups. Developmentally, games of pretending seem to be a necessary link between the relative helplessness of infancy and the growing responsibilities of the middle years of childhood. Play activities that might seem useless to an adult are necessary to a child.

Psychologists L. Joseph Stone and Joseph Church have described a number of ways play behavior develops in a preschool child.

1. Almost everything a young child does becomes a game—eating, getting dressed, going to bed, taking a trip, even going to the bathroom. Ordinary activities become silly events that often annoy a parent but delight the child.

The average four-year-old is more of a social person than he or she was at earlier ages. Four-year-olds seek out other children for play. They also enjoy activities that allow them to exercise their newly developed physical skills.

2. Play becomes more purposeful and directed. Children become more serious.

3. Children recognize the world of make-believe as distinct from the real world where people exercise genuine power. Play lets a child invent a world he or she can control.

4. Play becomes more imaginative, as well as more social. New skills and knowledge make a child's play more creative.

5. Play becomes dramatic. Children assume roles from the real world of the family or society. They play "Mommy and Daddy," or "doctor and patient."

By age five, a child's make-believe world reflects more and more of what is seen in the adult world. Children seek out realistic toys—the doctor's bag complete with pills, lifelike dolls, kitchen ranges, dump trucks that really work, and other symbols of modern life.

Section Review

1. Name two ways a fetus is affected by what the mother does during pregnancy.
2. What two physical learnings are most important between the first and second years?
3. How do trust and mistrust develop in a young child?
4. Describe one of the Harlow monkey studies. Why do psychologists consider these studies important?

2. Intellectual Growth and the Developing Child

The person who contributed most to our knowledge of how thinking takes place in children was the Swiss psychologist Jean Piaget. For nearly fifty years he observed children, starting with his own. He noted how they explain what they can and cannot do at successive stages in their intellectual or cognitive development. He realized that to learn to think a child must be able to process information into new forms. This can be done only when the child is intellectually *ready.*

A child must be able to go beyond *perceiving* the environment to *constructing concepts* about it. For example, a young child who goes for a walk at night thinks the moon is following along. As the child gets older, he or she realizes that seeing is not necessarily believing.

For us, the disappearance of an object does not mean that it no longer exists. For an infant under one year, what cannot be seen, *isn't.* A toy that is out of sight does not exist, even if the toy is returned and taken away several times. In a game of peekaboo with a ten- or eleven-month-old, when your face keeps disappearing and appearing again, the child is amazed; to him or her you're not just hiding: you're nowhere. Only at about twelve months, Piaget told us, does a child have the understanding that an object has simply been moved to another place. This insight is an awareness of *object permanence.*

Experiences and Thinking

The sudden insights that occur throughout a child's growing years happen at fairly definite times, and each marks a sharp break from the earlier stage of cognitive development. Piaget explained that the new understanding of how things relate to each other grows as a child's capacity to respond develops. Children make progress in understanding through a combination of their experiences with the environment and their ability to interpret these experiences in new ways. Past experience and thought are both necessary; neither is enough by itself.

Piaget stressed three principles of child development. A child is not a miniature adult. A child needs to take an active part in learning. Intellectual development involves changes in ways of organizing information, not just acquiring knowledge.

Stages of Cognitive Development

Piaget divided cognitive development into four stages. The stages match age spans that run from infancy to early adolescence. A child progresses from one stage to the next in a given order, according to Piaget, and this sequence does not vary from child to child or from culture to culture.

PREVIEW

In this section, read to find out:

1. what Piaget's theory is.
2. the four stages of cognitive growth as observed by Piaget.
3. how some psychologists believe intellectual development can be stimulated.

Stage 1: Sensorimotor period (0–2 years)

Up to age two, an infant learns a great deal about the world by touching things. In this **sensorimotor period,** there is no thinking, in the abstract sense, but a great deal of sensing. During this period of feeling, a child learns that actions have effects. A ball bounces not only when he or she drops it, but when someone else does. This stage marks the beginning of causal thinking.

An infant is at the center of his or her world. In simple games of "What do *you* see?" and "What do *I* see?" infants under two consistently thought the other person saw what they themselves saw. Piaget called this experience of being unable to see that the environment looks different to someone else **egocentrism.**

Stage 2: Preoperational thought (2–7 years)

The main achievement of a child in the second period is being able to represent the outside world in his or her mind. An infant in the sensorimotor stage who is playing with blocks knows that two blocks and two other blocks make four blocks because he or she can see them. But in stage 2, the stage of **preoperational thought,** a child can add the blocks (or anything else) without looking at them. The number 4 becomes a symbol for a certain quantity of objects, any objects.

Words also come to stand for things, so a child does not have to be seeing a house to know what *house* means. With this use of symbols, children can represent not only events taking place in the present, but past and future events as well. But some phases of reality a child in stage 2 is not ready to grasp. One of them is the concept of **conservation.** This is knowing that the quantity of something may stay the same even though the shape changes.

Stage 3: Concrete operations (7–11 years)

The idea of *formal logic* plays an increasing role in cognitive growth at this stage of **concrete operations.** Children are able to make strides in learning measurement, class and set relationships, and concepts of space.

In stage 3, children also grasp the idea of conservation. The eleven-year-old boy above knows he is holding exactly one-half cup of butter. He checked the amount by dropping it into one cup of water; the combined total measured a cup and a half. Measuring displaced water when an object is immersed is a problem in conservation of *volume* solved correctly at about age 11.

Conservation of *number*, holding on to the knowledge of how many items there are after their position or arrangement is changed, is usually achieved at about age five or six. Conservation of *area* and *weight* are grasped between ages seven and ten.

Stage 4: Formal operations (11 years and above)

A person capable of **formal operations** can view a problem from several positions without making a move. While a child is still in stage 3, the ability to reason depends on the evidence of his or her senses. But as children approach and continue through adolescence, they can think more abstractly.

By associating things that have qualities in common, a pre-adolescent begins to form concepts. Symbols—words, numbers, or other signs—play a more important part in thinking. Adolescents have a concept of *space* apart from their own experience in it. They can organize facts and events in mature fashion. They can figure out possible moves and likely outcomes.

& & &

See **Exercise 4, Observational Studies,** on pages 481–482 of the *Psychology Skills Handbook*, for more information about this research method often used by Jean Piaget and other psychologists.

Evaluating Piaget's work. Piaget's theories have received some criticism. He has been criticized for generalizing from too small a sample. Also, his experiments have not always been well controlled. And, although Piaget's theory of cognitive development has revolutionized approaches to human learning, many psychologists disagree with his conclusions.

Harvard psychologist Jerome Bruner, for example, agrees with Piaget's view that cognitive development proceeds through stages. He doesn't believe, however, that thinking is strictly related to age. Bruner feels that children can be stimulated to think beyond their stage if they are exposed to the right educational settings and procedures.

Stimulating Intellectual Growth

Psychological research indicates that infants and toddlers can be stimulated to learn in informal ways that will benefit their intellectual development and help their school achievement later. Harvard psychologist Burton L. White studied hundreds of infants in their home environments over a ten-year period. White's research led him to conclude that no more than one child in ten receives the "education" he or she is capable of, especially between eighteen and thirty-six months.

What does White mean by "education"? For infants between five-

"Education" for the infant can be listening to nursery rhymes, which aid language development. *Pat-a-cake* improves motor skills as well.

and-a-half and eight months, this includes someone talking to them in simple, concrete words that refer to things the baby handles. Reading simple stories to the baby at bedtime is recommended. The infant should be allowed to roam about in a safe area and explore new objects. Playing games such as hide-and-seek and placing easy obstacles between the baby and a favorite toy are recommended. All these approaches stimulate the infant's inborn curiosity, and some of them aid the earliest sensorimotor skills. So do toys that require manipulation, such as fitting one object into another.

Between eight and fourteen months, a child's understanding and skills grow rapidly. Parents can use a more adult vocabulary. But they shouldn't force learning on the child, White believes. They should introduce new kinds of playthings that require more skill to operate, for example, but help out when help is needed.

During the next ten months a child will be able to understand simple cause-and-effect relationships and play more complicated games. Most of all, parents should build on the natural enthusiasm for learning that the one-and-a-half- to two-year-old shows. Sharing this enthusiasm and showing strong approval for this reaching out for new information are both easy and beneficial.

During the third year of life, parents can encourage young children to learn in many ways. Parents should use new words with children, help them to deal with abstract terms, draw children's attention to small details and cause-and-effect relationships, and encourage them to do things which are a little harder.

A factor that is often overlooked is the importance of good nutrition to the infant's cognitive development. In the first two years of life, the size of the brain increases rapidly. During this growth spurt the number of brain cells increases significantly in the normal infant. Lack of adequate nutrition slows this growth. Children who eat poorly have many problems in language ability and intellectual development.

Will television speed up intellectual development in young children? This is an area of controversy. Television seems to increase a child's vocabulary, but too much television at the expense of active pursuits may be damaging.

A child under six faces a problem of conservation. Piaget used lemonade to show conservation. He poured equal amounts into identical glasses. Five-, six-, and seven-year-olds all agreed that both the child and the experimenter had the same amount. Then the lemonade in the child's glass was poured into a taller, thinner glass. The experimenter kept his own lemonade in the original glass. Who had more now? The five-year-olds said they had more in their tall glasses. The children who were six weren't so certain, but thought they, too, had more. The seven-year-olds *knew* there was no difference.

Section Review

1. Describe Jean Piaget's way of studying early child development.
2. Through what stages does a child grow in cognitive development, according to Piaget?
3. How can parents stimulate a child's intellectual development, according to Burton White?

PREVIEW

**In this section,
read to find out:**

1. how ancestors affect what a person is like.
2. the opposite views of nativists and environmentalists.
3. some other views of development.

We are all born with certain physical characteristics. They combine, to some degree, the characteristics of our parents. Eye and hair color and facial resemblance may be most noticeable at first in an infant. Later, the baby begins to look like the parents in other ways. Curly hair, for instance, is an inherited tendency. So, for that matter, is baldness.

The characteristics passed on from generation to generation are said to be due to **heredity.** For example, we can say that heredity determines height. Whether a person grows up to be short, average height, or tall is determined by the physical structure of parents and grandparents.

Heirs of the Past

In spite of the importance of heredity, no child is a carbon of the parents. Brothers and sisters often do not have the same eye or hair color because they may inherit these characteristics from different sides of the family. Many ancestors contribute characteristics to each newborn baby, and these sometimes skip a generation or two before showing up in family resemblances. A tall youngster whose parents are short may be a "throwback" to a grandparent or great-grandparent who was tall.

A few of the many physical characteristics that are inherited are shown at right. You inherit either attached earlobes (shown) or free lobes and the ability to roll your tongue or not. The tendency to develop some diseases is also inherited. One such disease is sickle cell anemia, most common among black people. A normal red blood cell and a sickled blood cell are shown here. Early detection of sickle cell disease and proper care can keep the condition stable.

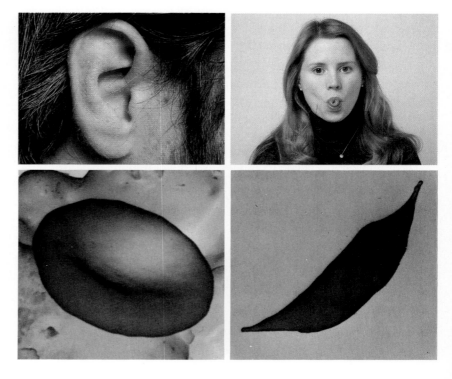

Genes and chromosomes. The tiny particles that carry the instructions from generation to generation are called **genes.** The genes are parts of larger particles known as **chromosomes,** which are present in every cell of the body. When the male sperm joins with the female ovum (egg) at conception, twenty-three chromosomes are supplied by the father. An equal number of them are furnished by the mother. This new combination of chromosomes, each containing thousands of genes, is what makes the offspring both similar to, and different from, each parent. The genes do the work of heredity.

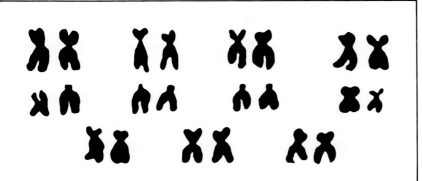

Greatly enlarged photo of chromosomes

Scientists do not agree about just how important heredity is in determining the way a person develops. Those scientists who emphasize the importance of heredity are called **nativists.** Those scientists who emphasize social and cultural factors in development are called **environmentalists.** For centuries, nativists and environmentalists have debated the importance of heredity. This debate was taking place even before psychology was recognized as a separate branch of science. Most of the controversy centers on intelligence as an inherited trait, as we will see in Chapter 7. There is also difference of opinion about the influence of heredity and environment on personality traits.

Personality Traits: Heredity or Environment?

A **personality trait** is a characteristic of a person's behavior in many situations. Traits reflect a person's feelings, attitudes, motivations, and values. We would say a person who likes other people and talks easily with them is sociable. A person who always looks on the bright side of things is said to be optimistic. But are these and other characteristics inborn, or are they due to experiences that have taken place in a person's environment?

For centuries scientists believed heredity was the key factor. Body fluids were thought to be especially important. Bile is a fluid, usually greenish, that comes from the liver. Early scientists thought a person who was usually angry simply had too much bile. People who were sad most of the time were thought to have a black bile. Today no psychologists accept this idea.

Body build and personality. Some psychologists believe inherited physical factors influence personality traits, however. For many years the findings of Harvard psychologist W. H. Sheldon were popular. He believed that body build went with certain personality traits. Sheldon rated two hundred college men according to how fat, muscular, or skinny they were. He said that the fat men were generally relaxed people who were deep sleepers. He found them very sociable. The muscular men were found to be competitive men who loved physical adventure. Sheldon found the skinny men tight in their physical movements, often tired, and not very sociable. Later studies did not find as close a relationship between physique and personality traits as Sheldon's studies had. But other studies reached the same conclusions Sheldon reached.

In a study of a group of college men, psychologist W. H. Sheldon sorted the information about their body build—whether they were fat or muscular or lean—and information about their personalities—whether they were relaxed or tense, liked being with other people or didn't, enjoyed competitive sports or not, and many other characteristics. His theory connecting personality with body build is widely quoted, although only accepted in part by many psychologists.

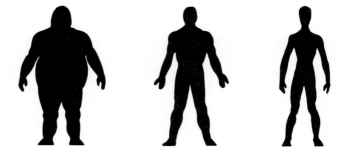

Sheldon's studies do not prove that physical features determine personality traits. It may well be, for example, that some fat people act jolly because other people expect them to do so. The precise ways that physical features—or other aspects of heredity—affect personality are not yet known.

Environmental influence. Psychologists who study learning methods believe changing an environment can cause changes in personality. Environmentalists see human nature as something that can be molded. They do not support the "once a sourpuss always a sourpuss" point of view. Still less do they believe that unsociable ancestry dooms the following generations to being unsociable, unless the environment promotes this trait.

Effects of the culture. Many anthropologists play down the importance of heredity in determining personality traits. Anthropologists study entire environments, rather than individuals. They use the term **culture** to describe the total way of life of a group of people. Anthropologists such as Margaret Mead and Ruth Benedict tried to show, years ago, that personality traits were due to the group's culture. Some anthropologists even argue that heredity plays no role at all in determining personality. They believe that a human being is like a blank slate at birth. How the baby is raised will determine the baby's personality traits.

The middle view. There is a middle position, and it is a popular one with psychologists. This is the view that heredity and environment work together to determine personality traits. A baby may be born with a tendency toward developing certain traits—smiling a lot, for example. But the baby's experiences will have just as much to do with the baby's personality traits. If people often smile at the baby, that trait will, in fact, develop.

Sometimes a person's experiences will change what the person's heredity would suggest. For example, a baby boy whose physical strength seems average for an infant may receive from his parents an excellent diet and outstanding care. Later he begins lifting weights and becomes an unusually strong person. Environment can play a vital part. The experiences we have determine what language we speak, our tastes in food and music, and many other characteristics.

Psychologist Albert Bandura offers the view that factors of environment are not alone in affecting the personality someone is born with. This **social learning theory** stresses that personal factors, choices, affect the environment. Our environment is somewhat of our own making. This view denies that people are either helplessly driven by inherited forces or helpless victims of their surroundings. Instead, they can make moves toward taking charge of their lives, influencing their own behavior.

Section Review

1. What is the difference between a nativist and an environmentalist?
2. Explain the views of W. H. Sheldon in the relation of physique and personality traits.
3. Why do the views of anthropologists and biologists on the heredity-environment question often differ?
4. Describe the view of social learning theory followers on heredity and environment.

It's Your Turn

As you have seen, there is a basic difference of opinion about influences on human development. Some psychologists are considered nativists—believers in the importance of heredity. Others are environmentalists—who emphasize the environment. Now *It's Your Turn*. Write your view in this debate. Use a specific example to support your opinion.

©1955, United Feature Syndicate, Inc.

35

Growing Up in Strange Places

NYT Pictures

Victor has his first encounter with fire in a scene from François Truffaut's film about Itard's work, entitled, "The Wild Child."

For years, psychologists and other scholars have been interested not only in children who develop normally, but in children who grow up in strange places and under unusual circumstances. Much about normal development can be learned by studying these children.

In 1800 three French hunters found a child about eleven or twelve years of age in the woods. The boy, who ran wildly about on all fours, was brought to Paris where he became known as the Wild Child of Aveyron. A young doctor, Jean Itard, tried to help the boy. Itard worked with Victor, as he called the boy, for several years.

Victor learned to understand many instructions and commands. He learned to keep himself clean, learned good manners, and even learned to sense injustice and take action against it. However, he was never able to fit in as an equal with young people his age. Although Victor learned to say a few words, he never learned to use speech for communicating. After five years, Itard found that Victor was making no new progress. There are many possible reasons for this. Perhaps the teaching began too late. Or maybe Victor's brain had been damaged in infancy, or even before birth, so that his progress would have been limited in any environment.

A young girl raised in India by wolves during her first eight years of life also made progress when cared for by humans. The girl, named Kamela, slept during the day and prowled about at night when brought to an orphanage in 1920. She howled like a wolf three times every night, and played more with the orphanage's animals than with the other children. Kamela too made slow progress but, like Victor, never really performed up to human expectations.

Children raised in isolation by humans have fared somewhat better. Every few years we read in the newspapers about a child raised in an attic or basement. Once discovered, these children usually begin developing very slowly. How much progress they make depends on the care they received before being discovered, the length of time spent in isolation, and the help they receive after discovery. The first two factors may be more important than the third. Poor nutrition is almost always present in these cases, as well as emotional neglect, making development after discovery extra hard. And the longer the child is isolated, the less chance there is for recovery.

4. How Psychologists Study Development

Human development is determined both by what we are born with and what happens to us after we are born. The subject of human development is the study of how people grow and change. The changes that take place in a person over a lifetime, and the differences in changes between individuals are both of interest to a student of human development. The period for which a psychologist studies change is not centuries, but the human life span. The changes that are studied are those in an individual's behavior, physical and mental. Learning how humans develop includes finding out how people learn, how they think, how they remember, and how they solve problems.

By describing how people behave in different situations, psychologists pile up information and set up norms. These help people to know, not what *should* be the way people behave, but what *is*.

The other thing psychologists do besides describing development is explain it. They set up studies and experiments to find out why people develop as they do, and why some differ from others in the ways they develop. Along the way, psychologists find ways people can make the most of development by changing environmental conditions, or by treatment.

PREVIEW

In this section, read to find out:

1. how psychologists look at human development.
2. what methods are commonly used to study development.
3. why psychologists have centered much study on infants and children.

Methods Used in Studying Development

Psychologists look at development in two ways. One is the **comparative method.** With this method, psychologists study a large number of three-year-olds, for example, at the same time. By studying this cross section, they are able to learn the skills and emotional traits these children have in common.

At age three, children have a vocabulary of over 1,000 words, but they are not able to read. They can ride tricycles but not bicycles. If we compare these children with a group of six-year-olds, we have a good idea of where the two groups are on the *developmental* schedule. The six-year-old is beginning to read and write, can dress alone, and handle other body needs—fortunately for parents weary of diaper changes.

The Comparative Method and Differences

Children don't all develop at the same rate, however. Some learn to walk, for instance, at one year, others not until eighteen months. Language ability varies, too. Still, the older child, if he or she is normal, will always be able to perform more tasks than the younger. Each child takes steps in order, from simpler to more complex functioning.

Although the comparative method tells us in general what to expect as a child moves up the developmental scale, it is not foolproof.

Children in some cultures are carried on their parents' backs at a time when infants in other societies are learning to walk. The child who converses with adults usually has a larger vocabulary by age five than the child who rarely talks with adults. A child's experiences may speed up or slow down the rate of development. When we say something is normal for a growth stage, we mean normal for a certain type of culture, for example, developing or industrialized. Within these limits, the comparative method gives a predictable timetable for development.

The Longitudinal Approach

By contrast, the **longitudinal approach** follows the development of the same child, or children, over a period of time, usually several years or decades. Because of the difficulty of keeping track of people as they move about, this type of research is less common.

The longitudinal approach has the advantage of studying children as individuals, not as representatives of developmental stages. Will a baby who is quiet and agreeable grow up to be easygoing and cheerful?

Case Study

Using Video Replay

Infant researcher Louis Sander's favorite home movie lasts just a few moments. In it, a young father is handed his crying eight-day-old baby. As the father continues to talk, he casually cradles the baby in his arm. Within a few seconds, the baby is asleep.

At first viewing, father and baby seem to ignore each other. A slow motion, frame-by-frame analysis tells a different story, though. Father and baby exchange several glances. At the same moment, they reach for each other. After grasping the father's little finger, the baby falls asleep.

Movies and videotapes like this are teaching researchers —and parents—more about the delicate sign language of infants. Researchers in one study found that as soon as an hour after birth, for example, most full-term newborns will return their mother's gaze. Such two-way communication helps mothers and fathers form emotional bonds with their infants.

Some hospitals also use videotaping to help parents form bonds with their premature infants. Because they spend their first weeks in an incubator, "preemies" often miss out on early opportunities for bonding. Furthermore, the premature infant and parent may be "out of sync." Because their brains and nervous systems are not mature, "preemies" may respond more slowly than normal, or the baby's responses may be so slight that the mother misses it. Over time, both parent and baby can feel rejected and mistrustful.

To prevent this, some hospitals videotape parent-baby play sessions. In other sessions, a psychologist plays with the baby while the parent watches. In both situations, the parent can be alerted to his or her baby's cues and responses. In addition, the baby has a chance to enjoy successful communication. The progress of bonding is also monitored through the parent's answers to questionnaires.

Most of the programs include follow-up counseling and home visits for as long as two years. In this way, psychologists hope to prevent emotional problems before they begin.

Do anxious babies turn into moody teen-agers, or alert infants into bright children? Psychologists now think that many such temperament traits may be inherited, or formed very early. By using longitudinal research, they can measure, to some extent, the influence of both early and later experiences.

Why Study Babies?

Much research on development deals with infancy and early childhood. Some psychologists believe a person's personality is pretty much set by age three. Others think that a person can change—sometimes a great deal—at any period in life. Yet almost all psychologists agree that infancy and early childhood should receive careful study.

Child-rearing practices and their effects. By observing babies and small children, psychologists try to identify child-rearing practices that produce healthy, well-adjusted adolescents and adults. Babies who receive much love and attention from their parents apparently are more likely to be warm and loving when they get older. By contrast, children who are punished constantly and severely tend to take on the role of punishers as adults, when they have children of their own. Psychologists have discovered that many of people's emotional problems can be traced back to experiences in early childhood.

Psychologists try to identify the experiences that are necessary for normal development. This can help parents tell when their children are

By studying children comparatively, psychologists are able to make up charts similar to the one below which gives the average age children learn certain skills.

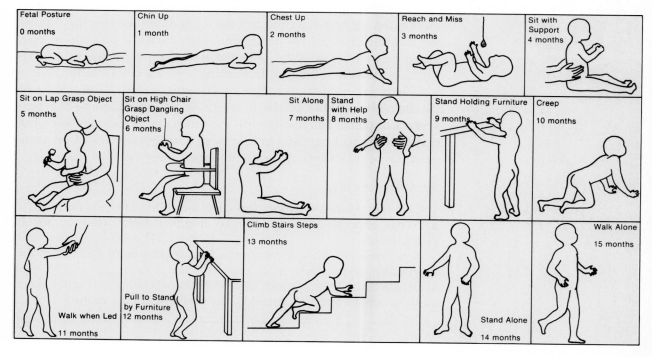

Fetal Posture	Chin Up	Chest Up	Reach and Miss	Sit with Support
0 months	1 month	2 months	3 months	4 months

Sit on Lap Grasp Object — 5 months
Sit on High Chair Grasp Dangling Object — 6 months
Sit Alone — 7 months
Stand with Help — 8 months
Stand Holding Furniture — 9 months
Creep — 10 months

Walk when Led — 11 months
Pull to Stand by Furniture — 12 months
Climb Stairs Steps — 13 months
Stand Alone — 14 months
Walk Alone — 15 months

It's Your Turn

You have been studying about babies and young children. Now *It's Your Turn*. Your friend, age fourteen, has been asked to assist in a childcare room while parents attend a civic meeting. Your friend has not been around young children much. From your study and what you already knew, list ten tips to help your friend do a good job and enjoy the session.

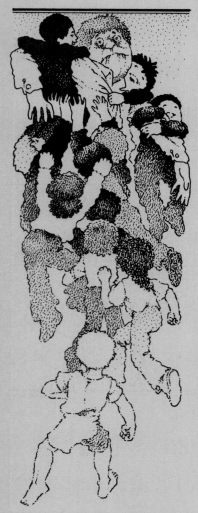

ready for these experiences. A baby's need for affection and attachment to another person must be satisfied, in large part, by the age of two. A child's basic ability to talk develops during the first six years. Between ages one and three a child should develop certain physical skills—such as walking. But a parent who expected a three-year-old to read would be making an unreasonable demand.

Knowing what to expect. A shouted "I just TOLD you," from an adult to a toddler in a supermarket may mean that the adult has unrealistic expectations about a small child's memory, judgment, attention, or need for positive reinforcement.

The studies of psychologists help us to know what to expect from other people and from ourselves. By having realistic expectations, parents and other guides of small children can avoid many disappointments. Accurately interpreting normal behavior makes it easy to accept normal behavior. For example, "Share the cookies with Billy," may be a reasonable encouragement to a seven-year-old. But a child under two, still in the egocentric stage, should not be expected to relate socially in the same way.

When help is needed. Psychologists point out ways people can be helped as they grow and change. Recognizing differences in behavior from what could be expected can lead to identifying a problem to be corrected, such as a visual or hearing problem or a learning disability problem.

Recognizing behavior that can be reinforced makes training in skills easier for both the child and the adult doing the training. Knowing how children behave at different ages makes it possible to plan group activities realistically, whether with the neighbors, in a baby-sitting or daycare setting, or celebrating a young child's birthday.

There is another advantage to knowing some of the results of psychologists' studies of the behavior of young children—the prevention of panic. Familiarity with growth patterns includes knowing that development happens in spurts, so a temporary lack of progress need not be over-alarming to the informed caregiver.

Section Review

1. Give two reasons why psychologists study human development.
2. What aspects of a child's life might interest developmental psychologists?
3. How does the comparative approach to development differ from the longitudinal approach?
4. Debate the following statement: "A child psychologist is more likely to know what's good for a child than even the child's mother."

5. The Daycare Question

As more and more families have either only one parent or two working parents, the number of children in daycare centers has grown enormously. This growth could have broad implications. Managing the physical, mental, and emotional development of great numbers of children is a responsibility calling for serious thought.

Types of Daycare

Five types of childcare arrangements have been identified by Donald Cohen, M.D., although variations are abundant.

1. Babysitting for either individuals or groups, where only the immediate needs of the child (health, safety, food) are considered, is called **custodial daycare.**

2. Nursery schools are educational half-day programs available from 2 to 5 days per week. Most nursery schools focus on cognitive development, although the child's social and emotional needs are also considered.

3. Many kinds of developmental opportunities for children are provided in **developmental daycare.** Trained caregivers, a planned curriculum, and consultants help assure that children's needs are met.

4. Comprehensive child development programs may provide daycare, but they also include family counseling, health and nutritional services, and other programs to meet families' needs.

5. Compensatory education is, by definition, a special program for children with special needs. Head Start programs, for example, provide cultural, language, and skills enrichment.

PREVIEW

**In this section,
read to find out:**

1. what kinds of child care there are for preschool children.
2. at what age daycare is approved by most psychologists.
3. what factors, other than age, are considered vital.

The Mission Head Start in San Francisco, California, is an example of a compensatory childcare center. Here children at Mission Head Start enjoy lunch with one of their teachers in the cheerful surroundings.

How Old Should a Child Be?

Most psychologists support good, quality daycare programs for children, though there is disagreement about how old a child should be before attending daycare. Psychologist Burton White feels either a parent or grandparent should stay home with a baby for the first six months. After that, White suggests that the parent or grandparent could do part-time work or other activities away from the child.

Other early childhood experts find White's views outdated and suggest that quality daycare can be an equally positive experience for young children. Psychologist Urie Bronfenbrenner said in an interview:

As far as I know—and I've reviewed the evidence on this question—there is no appreciable difference between day care and home care provided two conditions are met. First, it must be good quality care and much of ours isn't, since we are not willing to pay for it. Second, and equally important, the child should spend a substantial amount of time with somebody who's crazy about him.

Interviewer: "What do you mean exactly?"

Bronfenbrenner: "I mean there has to be at least one person who has an irrational involvement with that child, someone who thinks that kid is more important than other people's kids, someone who's in love with him and whom he loves in return."

Child education expert Bettye Caldwell also takes issue with White. She suggests, in fact, that a stay-at-home mother who is anxious to work won't do her child much good.

Caldwell and White do agree, however, on what parents should look for in quality daycare. For the first twelve months, the ideal daycare situation is to have an intelligent, nurturing person care for the baby in the baby's own home. However, Caldwell feels that, though this is ideal for babies, it may be boring for toddlers, who need more social interaction with other children. At the toddler stage, Caldwell recommends a small daycare facility. The facility should be carefully inspected by the parents to ensure that it follows these standards:

1. The center should be licensed and its staff trained in early childhood development.

2. The staff should follow appropriate health standards that, for example, minimize the spread of communicable childhood diseases.

3. There should be a small child to staff ratio—not more than five or six toddlers to one caregiver.

Here a child at Mission Head Start listens to a story while looking at the pictures in the storybook. This is an excellent activity for developing a child's readiness for reading.

Motor skills, visual skills, and a sense of starting and finishing a job are among the experiences that accompany preschool activity materials. Children of Mission Head Start are shown here working with materials that teach shapes.

Another option recommended by experts is a family situation, where a parent cares for his or her own children and a number of others. Here, too, parents searching for childcare should investigate to make sure that the atmosphere in the daycare home is warm and nurturant and follows appropriate health and legal standards.

Why Do Parents Use Daycare Services?

Parents who put their young children in daycare do so for a variety of reasons. In many cases, particularly single-parent homes, the reason is economic: while a parent works, someone has to care for the child. Even in two-parent homes, financially strapped parents feel they must both work to achieve the standard of living they want for their families.

Attitudes about daycare have changed dramatically in the United States in the last ten years. In the late 1980s, there were many companies that provided daycare facilities for their workers, as well as leave for parents to care for newborn or adopted children and more flexible work schedules and opportunities for part-time work. Even political conservatives, such as Utah's Republican Senator Orrin Hatch, supported federal aid to daycare centers in view of the fact that more than fifty percent of mothers of preschool children were now in the work force.

Section Review

1. What is the difference between custodial and developmental daycare?
2. Why do some psychologists criticize daycare programs for very young children?
3. Summarize the views that support daycare for young children.

Chapter 1 Review

Section Summaries

1. How Young Children Develop

Developmental psychology is the study of behavior during different stages of life. The unborn fetus can be damaged by the mother's malnourishment, rubella, smoking, and use of drugs. Although newborn babies must be fed and protected, they are able to respond to their environment and soon begin exploring and experimenting. Between the first and second years, infants begin walking and toilet-training. According to Erikson, children learn to trust or mistrust during their first year of life. Harlow's monkey studies demonstrated that "mother love" is important to normal emotional development. During preschool development, children develop play behavior.

2. Intellectual Growth and the Developing Child

Swiss psychologist Jean Piaget, from his observations of children, concluded that cognitive development proceeds in four stages that correspond to certain ages. In the first stage, the sensorimotor period, children learn that actions have effects, but they experience egocentrism. During the second stage, the preoperational thought period, children begin to use symbols. In the third stage, the concrete operations period, children begin to understand formal logic and concepts of measurement, space, conservation, and class and set relationships. By the fourth stage, the period of formal operations, children can use abstract thought and think in terms of symbols such as words, numbers, and signs. Other research has shown that a stimulating environment and good nutrition can stimulate intellectual growth.

3. Heredity and Environment

Characteristics are passed from generation to generation by heredity. Genes, which carry the instructions of heredity, make up the chromosomes found in every cell of the body. For centuries, nativists and environmentalists have debated the importance of heredity on intelligence and personality traits. Most psychologists believe that a baby is born with a tendency toward certain traits, but experience determines how those traits develop. Bandura's social learning theory stresses that personal choices affect the environment.

4. How Psychologists Study Development

Psychologists use comparative and longitudinal methods to study development. Studying babies identifies effective child-rearing practices and experiences necessary for normal development. This knowledge can help parents have realistic expectations of their children. Psychologists can also help parents identify and solve developmental problems.

5. The Daycare Question

Five types of daycare are custodial daycare, nursery schools, developmental daycare, comprehensive child development programs, and compensatory education. Most psychologists feel that daycare can be a positive experience in the right setting but are concerned that daycare should not be relied on to meet the child's total emotional needs. Parents need to carefully investigate daycare options to ensure that their child is in a safe and nurturant environment.

Psychology Skill Activities

1. Call a daycare center and ask if you and a friend may visit. Talk, if possible, with staff members, children, and parents. What goals are stressed? How could someone tell if the goals are being met? Ask about a typical day, what food is served, the costs, how parents and children interact, and whatever other questions seem useful. **easy**

2. Watch one television show and one commercial aimed at young children. Tell how each might affect young children's thinking and behavior. **challenging**

Testing for Understanding

Knowing Key Terms

Define these terms in your own words.

Section 1

developmental psychology

cognitive

fetus

trust

mistrust

Section 2

sensorimotor period

egocentrism

preoperational thought

concrete operations

conservation

formal operations

Section 3

heredity

genes

chromosomes

nativist

environmentalist

personality trait

culture

social learning theory

Section 4

comparative method

longitudinal approach

Section 5

custodial daycare

developmental daycare

Reviewing Main Ideas

Section 1

1. In what ways can a mother affect the health of her fetus?

2. What important physical and emotional changes occur in the first two years of life?

3. What changes occur during the preschool years?

Section 2

1. What is Jean Piaget's theory of cognitive development?

2. What are Piaget's four stages of cognitive development?

3. What are some ways that parents can encourage and stimulate their children's intellectual development?

Section 3

1. What do genes and chromosomes have to do with development?

2. In what ways do nativists and environmentalists disagree?

3. What is the middle position between the nativists and the environmentalists?

Section 4

1. What are two general goals of developmental psychology?

2. Describe the comparative and longitudinal methods.

3. How can developmental psychologists help parents?

Section 5

1. Describe the different types of daycare.

2. What do most psychologists feel about daycare?

3. What two factors does Urie Bronfenbrenner feel must be met for a child to have a positive experience in daycare?

Thinking Critically

1. *Drawing Conclusions.* What principles of parenting would developmental psychologists agree on? How might potential parents learn about these principles? **easy**

2. *Analysis.* What are reasons for and against trying to teach three-year-old children to read? **challenging**

Demonstrating Psychology Skills

Interpret the cartoon below in light of what you studied about cognitive development.

"Is this the way you plan to spend your peak learning years?"

Chapter 2

Middle Childhood and Adolescence

Psychologists see the years from six to twenty as a period of vast growth and change. At the start of the period, a child is only starting to lose his or her baby teeth. At the end of the period, the person should be on the verge of adulthood.

The development of each individual is, of course, different. Some young people grow up fast and assume adult responsibilities early. Others never become adults, in a psychological sense. But all persons go through tremendous changes during this time. The changes are physical, social, emotional, cognitive (thinking), and sexual in nature.

Most developmental psychologists consider the years from six to twelve, called **middle childhood,** to be a period of calm, whereas they call adolescence "the stormy decade." Emil Sinclair, the leading character in Herman Hesse's *Demian*, tells, below, of the change that takes place from those middle childhood years to the adolescent years.

If I wanted to, I could recall many delicate moments from my childhood: the sense of being protected that my parents gave me, my affectionate nature, simply living a playful, satisfied existence in gentle surroundings. But my interest centers on the steps that I took to reach myself. All the moments of calm, the islands of peace whose magic I felt, I leave behind in the enchanted distance. Nor do I ask to ever set foot there again.

That is why—as long as I dwell on my childhood—I will emphasize the things that entered it from outside, that were new, that impelled me forward or tore me away.

These impulses always came from the "other world" and were accompanied by fear, constraint, and a bad conscience. They . . . threatened the calm in which I would gladly have continued to live. ■

In this chapter we will examine sex role learning during the middle childhood years, moral development, and the identity crisis of adolescence. A section on adolescent issues concludes the chapter.

1. Middle Childhood: Six to Twelve

Middle childhood is generally a period of calm between two less calm periods—early childhood and adolescence. Yet middle childhood has important developmental tasks. Educator Robert Havighurst has listed nine, dealing with physical, cognitive, and social development:

a. Learning physical skills necessary for ordinary games.
b. Developing fundamental skills in reading, writing, and calculating.
c. Developing concepts necessary for everyday living.
d. Building wholesome attitudes toward yourself as a growing person.
e. Developing conscience, morality, and a scale of values.
f. Learning to get along with people your own age.
g. Learning an appropriate masculine or feminine social role.
h. Developing attitudes toward social groups and institutions.
i. Achieving personal independence.

Middle childhood is a time a child hears many rules but few reasons ("Shut the door when you leave." "Did you brush your teeth?" "You're not old enough yet . . ."). A special problem for this age group is to learn what adults really want—not just what they say they want, but what they really expect.

Playmates Are Important

The peer group relations that grow out of school and neighborhood contacts contribute greatly to a child's social development. In the

PREVIEW

In this section, read to find out:

1. some developmental tasks of middle childhood.
2. what boys and girls, ages six to twelve, are like.
3. how the sex roles children learn are changing.

The pictures below show the physical changes one person experienced during the periods of development covered in this chapter—middle childhood and early and late adolescence.

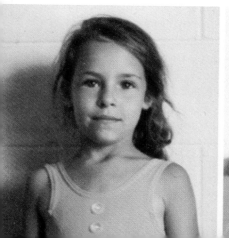

Best friends of the same sex are important during middle childhood.

society that children create—half real and half fantasy—the young people make their own rules and activities. Psychologists L. Joseph Stone and Joseph Church call this society "a proving ground where the child learns to live apart from adults . . ."

An intense desire to belong characterizes social relations during this period. Boys and girls form their own separate little groups of close friends. Members of these groups often build clubhouses and make up their own secret languages and passwords. The reverse of this intense desire to belong—the desire to exclude—is the cause of much unhappiness.

Male-female relationships during this period usually lack the intensity of adolescent and adult relationships. This is particularly true between ages 6 and 9. Fourth-grade children often say things such as "Boys are yucky" and "The only girl I like is my mother." Although boys and girls often talk about each other, few life-long romances begin during middle childhood.

Behavior during middle childhood varies with the environment. Middle-class urban children often have less freedom than small-town or rural children because of safety restrictions. Ghetto children are often "street-wise," displaying survival skills middle-class children don't need. Youngsters from small farms understand the family economy in a special way when they play a part in making it work. The roles of the children's society are shaped by the larger society.

Learning Sex Roles

Children start at an early age learning how to behave as males or as females. Yet it is during middle childhood that much learning of sex roles occurs. A **sex role** is the part a person plays in life, based on being male or being female. How are sex roles learned? There are many theories. Learning theorists stress the fact that a child models his or her behavior after adults. Adults of the same sex serve as models in sex-role learning. A boy learns how to act like a male from his father and other males. The mother and other females are important in a girl's sex role learning.

Brothers, sisters, aunts, uncles, teachers, and coaches are often powerful role models for the child—especially in the absence of a parent of the same sex. Television and movie stars, professional athletes, and musicians also have a powerful influence on sex role learning, judging by their fan mail.

In the view of some psychologists, sex role learning is also affected by the behavior of people of the opposite sex. For example, a mother who cooks may influence her son's interest in cooking. A father who loves sports may influence his daughter's interest in sports.

Some social scientists believe that the way sex roles are viewed in America is currently in the process of change. Women are rapidly entering occupations previously looked upon as men's jobs. The career housewife is becoming less common, although many women still

Learning to get along with others in a group is a developmental task of middle childhood. Children of this age also enjoy activities that test their developing physical skills.

Psychologists believe that sex role learning can come from sources other than parents. This young girl, for example, has modeled her behavior in part after that of a favorite aunt.

choose homemaking as their most rewarding career. The impact of sex role changes on males takes a number of forms. At work, men face an additional source of competitors for jobs and promotions. At home, fathers are becoming more involved in child-rearing. They are also doing more indoor household chores. This may be because of events other than sex role changes, however, as apartment and condominium living reduce outdoor chores.

Some people are happy with the **traditional sex roles**—the dominant male who goes out to work and the dependent female who stays at home. While society as a whole appears to be moving toward sex roles that are more nearly alike for males and females, called **joint sex roles,** the roles accepted by individuals during the transition period differ widely, and are largely a matter of individual choice. Some children, today, are learning traditional sex roles, some are learning joint sex roles, and most are learning something in between.

Section Review

1. Name three developmental tasks of middle childhood.
2. In what ways are peers important in the middle childhood years?
3. How are joint sex roles different from traditional sex roles in our culture?

2. Moral Development: Deciding What Is Right

In the middle childhood years a child adopts values, beliefs, and attitudes that are handed down by others. Essential to this aspect of social development are the **moral judgments** people make about their own behavior and that of others. Such judgments depend not so much on what we *can* do in a given situation as on what we believe we *ought* to do. For example, we don't push a small child down, even though we might not be caught or punished, because we believe that doing so would be morally wrong.

How does a child learn to make moral judgments? Is it simply a matter of learning to tell right from wrong? Harvard psychologist Lawrence Kohlberg has made an intensive study of the bases on which children and youth of various ages make moral decisions. He has found that moral growth also begins early and proceeds in stages.

Kohlberg based some of his findings on stories such as the following, which he showed to people of all ages.

A man named Heinz had a wife who was dying of an almost incurable disease. There was a drug that could save her. The drug, which cost $20,000 was owned only by a local druggist. Heinz didn't have the money to buy the drug and he was unable to raise the money. The druggist would not let him have any of the drug, so Heinz, desperate, broke in at night and took some. Should Heinz have done that?

Kohlberg was interested in the reasons people gave for Heinz' stealing or not stealing the drug. He noted that people of different ages answered the question quite differently. From the reactions he received to this and other stories containing moral dilemmas and questions, Kohlberg developed his theory of moral development.

Levels of Response

According to Kohlberg's research, for young children, self-interest and the avoidance of punishment form the bases on which a moral decision is made. A child might say, "He shouldn't steal the drug because he'll get caught and have to go to jail" or "If he lets his wife die, he'll feel bad afterwards."

At the next level, a child is primarily conscious of the effect his or her behavior is having on others. Behavior is designed to win approval or to maintain respect for authority. A level two response would be "People will think Heinz is a bad man if he lets his wife die" or "He shouldn't steal—it's against the law."

Finally, as the child reaches maturity, moral good is seen as residing in abstract principles rather than in individuals or even society. A

PREVIEW

In this section, read to find out:

1. what moral judgments are.
2. how age relates to moral judgments.

See **Exercise 5, Surveys,** pages 483–485 of the *Psychology Skills Handbook,* for a description of the use of surveys in psychological research.

A child is baptized in New York City (above), and Buddhist monks meditate in Sri Lanka (below). We learn much of our moral judgment from our religious heritage.

level three response might be "Human life is more important than someone's property rights. He should take the drug."

Kohlberg sees these three levels of moral development as consisting of distinct stages. See the table below.

These stages of moral development, like the other developmental levels we have discussed, are sequential stages, one following the other. Every child goes through them in the same order, although not necessarily at the same rate. In fact, according to Kohlberg, many people never reach level three, but remain all their lives at level two.

Kohlberg's Stages of Moral Development

Levels	Bases of Moral Judgment	Stages of Development
I	Moral value resides in a person's own needs and wants.	Stage 1. Obedience and punishment orientation. The child defers to superior power or prestige, or wants to stay out of trouble.
		Stage 2. The child realizes that right action satisfies his or her own needs and occasionally others'. Trade-offs are valued: "You scratch my back and I'll scratch yours." Intentions are valued.
II	Moral values reside in performing good or right roles, in maintaining the conventional order, and in pleasing others.	Stage 3. The "good boy-nice girl" orientation. The main thing is to get approval by pleasing and helping others.
		Stage 4. The support of *law* as the base of concern for the larger community directs Stage 4 judgments. Doing your duty, respect for authority, and maintaining the social order are seen as moral actions.
III	Moral values reside in principles, separate from those who hold and enforce them, and apart from a person's indentification with the enforcing group.	Stage 5. The rights of others as well as self are recognized. Rules agreed on by the whole society are accepted as binding, yet looked on as subject to change. Rights and duties are seen as derived from the social contract.
		Stage 6. The conscience or ethical principle viewpoint. Universally agreed-upon standards guide moral conduct, rather than rules alone. Justice and equality are examples of moral ideals.

Section Review

1. How is a moral judgment different from a cognitive one?
2. Which of the Kohlberg stages of moral development would most likely describe the moral reasoning of a child from six to twelve?
3. Write a one-page description of "How Growing Up Affects Moral Judgments."

PREVIEW

**In this section,
read to find out:**

1. some characteristics of the adolescent years.
2. how some psychologists classify adolescents by their style.

3.   The Adolescent Years

At about ages twelve to fourteen, a child moves from a society of children into a culture of youth. As the word *culture* implies, the customary behavior of this period is set as much by social forces as it is by physical changes. In fact, a person is called an adolescent only because society decided that he or she should be. The idea of **adolescence,** and even the word, has come into common use only in the last few generations.

In many parts of the world, a young person goes directly from childhood into adulthood. Western societies require longer periods of training and education for most young people. This happens in part because people must be more sophisticated to take part as adults in a technological society. Also, an extended adolescence keeps the competition of young people out of the work force a few extra years.

Physical Changes

A growth spurt precedes adolescence. For the so-called average child, this rapid growth takes place in the years from about age 10½ to 12½ in girls, and about age 12½ to 14½ in boys.

When this growth spurt ends, **puberty** begins—at about 12½ for girls and 14½ for boys. A boy of 12 suddenly shoots up to become, over the following two years, a tall youth with fuzz on his upper lip, a voice that sounds more and more like Dad's, and maturing sexual organs. Girls start to develop a woman's figure. The pelvic area enlarges, curves form, breasts emerge.

Physically speaking, puberty marks the beginning of sexual maturity. Why all this sudden fuss inside the body? Thank the **hormones,** secretions of the endocrine glands, sent out through the bloodstream from the pituitary gland at the base of the brain. This master gland regulates a number of other endocrine glands.

Among the glands regulated by the pituitary gland are the adrenals, the thyroid, and the gonads. The adrenals do their work primarily in stress situations. The thyroid governs metabolism—the body's temperature, use of oxygen, and general activity. The gonads produce sex changes in the body as well as the sperms and eggs used for reproduction. All these tiny organs work together in harmony. They signal one another when help is needed, or give each other the message to slow down. The hormones are easily activated. Because of this, we can respond quickly to danger or, for that matter, to an awareness of someone nearby who is physically attractive.

Although hormones are active throughout life, the sudden spurt in

Puberty is a time of rapid physical change. The sudden spurt in hormone activity during this period means that children of this age must suddenly deal with adult feelings and desires— often with responses that are quite childlike as the photo on the opposite page shows.

It's Your Turn

You have seen how Kohlberg explains the process of moral development. The stages and levels of response are one way of viewing moral development. One of Kohlberg's tools for investigation was stories with moral dilemmas, such as Heinz and his dying wife. Now *It's Your Turn*. Write what you think Heinz should have done. How would you answer this dilemma? What stage does your response indicate?

their activity beginning with puberty makes an impact on an adolescent. Suddenly, a boy or girl must cope with a newly adult body, even though thoughts and emotions may still be childlike. Physical urges collide with social taboos. Part of the turmoil of adolescence is biological and part is caused by the expectations in our culture.

Family influences. Many studies have sought to relate adolescent behavior to earlier experiences in the home. These experiences generally concern the way a child is brought up: strictly or leniently; with love or rejection; or with encouragement or indifference. It is agreed, for instance, that a trusting adolescent is likely to have been loved as a child, and that probably delinquent youth often suffered inconsistent and arbitrary punishment. Diana Baumrind of the University of California, Berkeley, studied adolescents and their families from several viewpoints. Her conclusions suggest strong links between parental styles and the development of competence by adolescents. Some of her propositions are described on the next page.

Case Study

Teenage Suicide

She is no stranger to success. In high school, she was active in sports, an honor student, editor of the school newspaper, and class valedictorian. In college, she joined a sorority and became a field hockey star. Now, as a young woman in her twenties, she works by day as an organic chemist and attends law school at night.

Yet, she is grateful that her successes include one major failure—her suicide attempt in March 1981. In a recent magazine article, she described the painful emotions and thinking that led to her suicide attempt.

By the time she was a junior in high school, she felt she was worthless and unlovable. Nothing she did impressed her father, and she could not get along with her stepmother. When her parents began to discuss divorce, she felt she was to blame. Ashamed to talk to her friends, she pushed away the help of concerned teachers. Convinced that her situation would never improve, she began to plan a "date with death." She took a handful of tranquilizers washed down with alcohol and fell unconscious on the way to a park.

She was rescued by a man walking his dog. Although she began seeing a psychologist and a social worker, she was still thinking about suicide when she began college. Slowly, however, life began to look up. New friends showed her she was lovable, and her confidence grew.

Now, looking back, she can see how she let her feelings build up until they overwhelmed her. By focusing on the negative, she robbed herself of hope. She would not let herself see solutions, such as changing the way she felt about her parents' behavior. Most importantly, she would not accept help, even when others reached out to her.

Today this young woman is a volunteer on a suicide hot line. It is her way of reaching out to other people who feel the same kind of pain and despair she once knew.

1. Socially competent adolescents come from homes where there is high social status and self-esteem. Youth tends to model itself on the family image.

2. Achieving and independent adolescents have parents who enforce high, but realistic, aspirations for their children. Enforcement includes criticism and hostility when the child displeases the parent, and warmth and support when the child pleases.

3. Adolescents who were able, as children, to talk out their problems with their parents are likely to have confidence that they can change what they believe needs changing "through self-assertive but nonviolent means." Parents who do not explain their demands tend to have dependent adolescent children.

Baumrind suggests a number of other relationships between family style and adolescent behavior. She believes that many troubled youths come from homes lacking firm discipline and strong emotional ties among family members. Girls are likely to grow up to be independent when parents make high demands on them and do not over-protect them. Middle-class mothers who are happily employed outside the home, Baumrind notes, often have admiring daughters who are ambitious for themselves. Perhaps some of these ideas apply to your family, or help explain the kind of adolescent you are.

The experiences that a child has within the family affects his or her adolescent behavior.

Styles of Adolescence

Adolescence comes in many styles. We cannot generalize much about this age group. Yet psychologists Stone and Church, working

It's Your Turn

Stone and Church classified adolescent personalities in four ways, as you have read. This is only one view of this difficult stage of human development. Now, *It's Your Turn*. Based on your observations and experiences with people your age, do you agree with these categories? What style do you fit into? Where do most of your friends or classmates fit? Write a brief description of your style.

largely from observation, classify adolescent personalities four ways. Do you or your friends fit into any of the following categories?

1. **Conventionalists** seldom rock the boat. Their aim is to fit into life and go along with society as it exists. They accept authority, have good manners, get along with others, make good volunteer workers, hold religious beliefs, and have strong family ties. Although they like fun, their participation in teen-age culture is largely a matter of doing what is acceptable and socially appropriate.

2. **Idealists** want to change society. They take up causes, and are keenly sensitive to what seems to them injustice. Some try to improve the world by starting careers in teaching or medicine or by becoming involved in community affairs.

3. **Hedonists** make fun their business in life. They live for the present without regard for future consequences. Theirs is a life of pleasure-seeking, of a search for kicks. Although they appear to enjoy life, hedonists are likely to be isolated—both from themselves and from the workaday world of other people.

4. **Psychopaths** are bullies without consciences. They have not developed a sense of moral concern for other people and seem to have no set of guiding principles to live by. They share the hedonists' self-centered search for pleasure, but do not feel guilt or shame as inhibiting emotions. Thus, they can act mindlessly, without caring about hurting someone or destroying something. They may be ruthless in business or in sexual conquests. Even unarmed, they can be dangerous.

Needless to say, labels such as these do not apply rigidly. Conventionalists can be idealistic about society, and idealists are frequently conventional at heart. The hedonist rises up, now and then, in most of us, and a trace of psychopathic behavior can be found in many of us, young and old, when our conscience fails us, when we don't feel guilty about hurting others, or when we can't share the feelings of another person.

The behaviors that mark adolescence do not suddenly stop at the age of twenty or twenty-one. Many are carried into adulthood. Conventionalists, for example, are inclined to stay conventional as they get older. They make up, by far, the largest group of adolescents, and psychopaths the smallest.

Section Review

1. Define adolescence. Is it found in all cultures? Explain.
2. Describe some physical changes that take place in males and females during adolescence.
3. Explain your own style of adolescence.

4. Erikson's Theory of Psychosocial Development

Psychoanalyst Erik Erikson thinks of human development as a series of **psychosocial stages.** In each stage, certain characteristics of a child's personality emerge. These characteristics remain with the person throughout life, unless changed by experiences in later stages.

As we read in Chapter 1, Erikson says an infant must develop trust in his or her primary caregiver, often the mother. If, instead, a sense of mistrust develops, the child is likely to have trouble developing trusting relationships with others in the future.

Each stage of life, according to Erikson, presents the individual with a developmental **crisis.** Erikson uses the word *crisis* to refer to a normal developmental task. We all experience a series of crises as we go through life. If we resolve them successfully, a positive aspect of our personality will develop. If not, a negative characteristic will result. People are usually not 100 percent successful nor 100 percent unsuccessful. Most people fall between the two extremes as they develop. There is evidence, too, Erikson notes, that a problem from an early stage may be resolved in a later stage, sometimes through psychotherapy.

Erikson's stages are shown below. Approximate ages are listed for each stage, though Erikson notes that different people experience different stages at somewhat different times.

PREVIEW

In this section, read to find out:

1. how Erik Erikson sees human development.
2. what crises arise at each stage of development.
3. what is meant by an "identity crisis."

Stage		Approximate Age	Result If Development Goes Well	Result If Development Goes Poorly
I	Infancy	0–1	Trust	Mistrust
II	Early Childhood	2–3	Autonomy	Shame and Doubt
III	Play Age	4–5	Initiative	Guilt
IV	School Age	6–11	Industry	Inferiority
V	Adolescence	12–20	Identity	Role Confusion
VI	Young Adulthood	21–35	Intimacy	Isolation
VII	Middle Age	35–65	Generativity	Self-absorption
VIII	Old Age	65+	Integrity	Despair

Erikson's view of a child's growth from early childhood through adolescence underlines a person's need for reassurance along the way. At ages two and three, a child's sense of *autonomy* should triumph over *doubt*. By exploring and handling the items in the immediate environment, a toddler discovers power to do such things as push and pull objects, and even balance them. Mastery over toilet training contributes toward a sense of autonomy.

At ages four and five, a child's attempts to think up and proceed with activities blossom, when encouraged. This stage of *initiative* triumphing over *guilt* sometimes challenges the patience of nearby adults, as a four- or five-year-old is an amateur at deciding which activities are desirable, and safe, to pursue.

At ages six to eleven, when *industry* must win out over *inferiority*, a child must learn basic skills in school and other social institutions (scouts, sandlot baseball teams, and so on). The influence of people outside the home becomes important. If a child is successful in these activities, a sense of industry will result. Otherwise he or she will develop feelings of inferiority.

The Identity Crisis

According to Erikson, forming a sense of who you are is probably the most important developmental task of late adolescence. During this period most young persons begin to question their own essence. Some aspects of what parents expect remains with an individual, but the search for identity can lead to a different, and often stronger, person.

Questioning values. Parental values are often questioned during adolescence. Parents who are religious may be dismayed to see their son or daughter turn away from the church or synagogue. Parents who believe economic security is important may cringe when their son or daughter says "Money doesn't mean much to me." A young person may want to move out of the home and neighborhood after graduating from high school, possibly disappointing one or both parents.

Sometimes career goals are questioned during this period. The girl whose mother wants her to become a nurse may suddenly decide she wants to go to medical school. Or she may decide to drop out of school, and move away to stay with friends for a while. Conflicts with parents about career goals occur frequently, with conversation such as the following quite common:

"It's my life. I'll do what I want."

"Don't be a fool. Your mother and I aren't going to stand by and watch you waste your life."

It may be some comfort to know that parents usually come around to accepting their children's career choices. Also, there is some comfort for parents in the fact that adolescents often change during young adulthood to a vocation more like the ones their parents wanted.

Looking inward. The **identity crisis,** as Erikson calls the development of a sense of who you are, deals with an individual's entire sense of self. This usually takes place during stage 5. Finding out that you are not the same person you thought you were often comes as a surprise during the adolescent years. A high-school football star may decide he doesn't like hard physical contact, as he discovers a sensitive and artistic side to himself he didn't know existed. A shy, nervous girl may bloom and become a self-confident, outgoing young woman. Changes are possible in many directions.

Along with identity formation, or soon after it, an adolescent may make a big move toward being independent, or toward starting to become intimate with another person. Independence is often thought of as starting when the adolescent moves out of the parents' home, but independence may start psychologically much sooner, or much later. Conflicts over an adolescent's independence are common in many families.

Late adolescence is often the time when a person first begins to experience **intimacy** with another person. This may occur in stage 6. Intimacy means sharing yourself with, and caring for, another person without losing yourself in the process. Erikson feels intimacy comes after identity, that you must know yourself before you can share with, and love, others. Some psychologists believe, however, that a close

Copyright © 1959 by Gerhard Hoffnung

61

Intimacy—the experience of sharing joys and sorrows with another person and of really caring for him or her—is usually first experienced during late adolescence.

relationship, a first steady boyfriend or girlfriend, for example, can be a vital part of identity formation.

Erikson suggests that in our culture the identity crisis is needed for a productive adult life. This wouldn't be true in some cultures, he acknowledges. In many cultures, a boy grows up, works in the fields or hunts, and takes his father's place in the community when his father dies. A girl cooks and weaves and lives a few yards from her mother, just as her daughters will grow up and live a few yards from her. Some American adolescents, particularly from small towns, also live a life structured by tradition.

Section Review

1. Describe briefly Erikson's view of human development.
2. Choose stage 2 or 3 or 4, and briefly describe it.
3. What are some concerns of an adolescent in the identity stage?

Sex Differences: Fact and Myth

Beliefs about sex differences are strong in our culture. Psychologists Eleanor Maccoby and Carol Nagy Jacklin examined more than 2,000 books and articles dealing with sex differences in social behavior, intellectual ability, and motivation, to see which beliefs about sex differences are backed up by evidence, which beliefs are not, and which still need to be tested.

From the beliefs below, check those you think are *fact* and those that are *myth*. Compare your answers with Maccoby and Jacklin's findings.

1. Girls are more "social" than boys.
2. Boys excel in mathematical ability.
3. Girls are more affected by heredity, boys by environment.
4. Boys excel in visual-spatial ability.
5. Girls have greater verbal ability than boys.
6. Girls are "auditory," boys "visual."
7. Girls are better at rote learning and simple tasks. Boys are better at high-level tasks.
8. Males are more aggressive than females.
9. Boys are more analytic than girls.
10. Girls are more suggestible than boys.
11. Girls have lower self-esteem than boys.
12. Girls lack motivation to achieve.

Notice that there are more myths (8) than facts (4). Some differences exist, nevertheless. From about age 12 or 13, boys do better at mathematics than girls do. Girls measure higher in verbal ability—spelling, fluency, comprehension of written material, and creative writing. We don't know whether such sex differences are inborn or are learned. Maybe girls learn that they are not *supposed* to be good at mathematics, and boys that they are not *supposed* to enjoy reading. Maccoby and Jacklin could not tell if one sex or the other is more active, competitive, dominant, sensitive to touch, passive, fearful, obedient, or good with children. More research is needed, the authors say, before stereotypes about these traits can be labeled myths or facts.

Answers to Sex Myth Quiz
1. Myth 2. Fact 3. Myth 4. Fact 5. Fact 6. Myth
7. Myth 8. Fact 9. Myth 10. Myth 11. Myth 12. Myth

PREVIEW

**In this section,
read to find out:**

1. some reasons
   adolescents and their
   parents come into
   conflict.
2. what contributions
   peers make during
   adolescence.
3. views on causes of
   juvenile crime.

5. Adolescent Issues

Adolescence is not an easy time. People in the twelve to twenty age group often face a variety of difficulties. While one person is straining to compete successfully for a scholarship, another is about to quit school in spite of opposition from parents, and a third may be depressed and thinking of suicide. Some problems center around the individual adolescent's psychological state, but most center around the adolescent's relations with peers, authority figures, and the larger society in general.

Parental Authority

Few adolescents have totally smooth relations with their parents. Conflicts seem to arise over the simplest matters. You may have said or heard some of the following statements:

"How I dress is my business."

"When I was your age . . . ."

"Why can't I use the car tonight?"

"You spend money like water."

"You must get good grades if you want to amount to something."

"He's my boyfriend, not yours."

"If you quit now, you'll be sorry all your life."

"Why don't you trust me?"

"I can't help you if you won't tell me what's bothering you."

Sometimes these problems have a common source, the difficulty of *letting go.* Parents know their son or daughter will soon be independent, so sometimes they need to say and sometimes to show "I'm still in charge." Sometimes parents go too far by exercising controls that are too rigid.

The difficulty of letting go affects young people as well. An adolescent sometimes expects full adult privileges without being willing to accept adult responsibilities. Other times, the young person is ready, but society refuses to grant adult responsibility. It is not an unusual situation for young people to want to be free of parental control, but still to want parental support. This sets up difficult expectations for parents to meet.

Peer Relations

Sociologist James Coleman maintained, as a result of his research, that adolescents have their own subculture. The *adolescent subculture,* he said, emphasizes different aspects of living from that of the adult culture. Coleman's argument was that parents, teachers, and other adults want adolescents to be good students, but adolescents are more concerned with other things. Males, he said, want to be good athletes while females want to be popular and attractive.

Psychologists and sociologists wrote articles defending and criticizing Coleman's view. Many social scientists believe that Coleman went too far in suggesting that there is a separate, distinct adolescent subculture. These scholars believe that most adolescents accept most standards of the adult culture, but are at odds with adult expectations on a few issues.

Importance of peers. Most social scientists agree with Coleman about the importance in your life of **peers,** the people your own age. More than once you may have heard someone say, "Joey's a good boy. He just got mixed in with the wrong crowd." People tend, especially during adolescence, to want to be like their friends—to dress the same way, like the same music, and have the same goals. For most people, being different is harder during adolescence than during adulthood.

Below: Adolescents tend to want to be like their friends—to dress the same way, like the same music, and have the same goals.

Juvenile Crime

Crime by adolescents has long been a problem in America. For years many social scientists used what might be called a socioeconomic explanation of juvenile crime. Most juvenile crime, they argued, was

Social scientists disagree on the cause of juvenile crime but poverty, absent-father families, and alienation have all been suggested as important factors.

committed by young city males from low-income families. To young black males, especially, they explained, crime was a means of survival and a way to both increase self-respect among peers and fight back against a racist society.

Later, the social scientists added a psychological twist to their theory. Crime by adolescents from fatherless homes was especially high, they noted.

Both the poverty theory and the absent-father theory have supporters. But the many males from low-income families where the father is absent who do *not* commit crimes indicate that the theories are incomplete.

In addition, there have been increases in the juvenile crime rate in wealthy communities. Stores have reported many cases of shoplifting by children of the well-to-do. Some psychologists extended the absent-father theory to many of these cases: "The father may live in the home," goes the argument, "but he's so busy making money he has little time for his children. Peer group influence becomes strong and you find rich adolescents stealing for social acceptance."

Explanations and more explanations. There are other ways to explain juvenile crime. One way is to describe those who shoplift as *alienated* from the society in which they live. **Alienation** means being cut off from society and not accepting society's **norms,** or standards of behavior. Some social scientists carry this argument further, saying that, at times, societies have unclear norms or even no norms at all.

Some social scientists see the main cause of crimes by adolescents as coming from within the individuals who commit these crimes. Others find the main cause in society. Most include both social and psychological factors in explaining juvenile crime. The explanations by social scientists of the causes of violent crime reflect their different views. Some offer psychological explanations: "Some people have violent personalities." Others give social explanations: "We live in a violent society."

It is clear that explaining adolescent crime is difficult. Preventing it is even more difficult.

Section Review

1. List three major issues in adolescence—not necessarily ones mentioned in this chapter.
2. Why are adolescents and their parents so often in conflict?
3. List three possible causes of juvenile crime; tell which you think is the main cause, and why.
4. Give an example of how a conflict might be resolved involving peer influence and adult guidance in the following cases: (a) choosing an elective in school, (b) deciding to get (or not get) a parttime job, (c) choosing between further education or going to work after graduation.

Chapter 2 Review

Section Summaries

1. Middle Childhood: Six to Twelve

Middle childhood is a period between six and twelve years of age. For this period, educator Robert Havighurst has listed nine important developmental tasks, which deal with physical, cognitive, and social development. Relations with peer groups, especially same-sex friends, contribute greatly to a child's social development. The freedom parents give to children depends, in part, on their environment. During middle childhood, children use role models as they learn about sex roles. Although some people are happy with traditional sex roles, others are more satisfied with joint sex roles.

2. Moral Development: Deciding What Is Right

Moral judgments are decisions about what people ought to do. Psychologist Lawrence Kohlberg has used stories to study the moral judgments children make at different ages. His research has identified three sequential levels of moral development. At the first level, the child makes judgments on the basis of self-interest and avoiding punishment. At the second level, the child's judgments are made to win approval or show respect for authority. At the third level, judgments are made on the basis of principles. Within each level, Kohlberg identified two specific stages. According to Kohlberg, children follow the same sequence of stages, but may do so at different rates.

3. The Adolescent Years

Adolescence follows a growth spurt. This rapid growth occurs between age 10½ and 12½ for average girls, and between 12½ and 14½ for average boys. This growth spurt is followed by puberty, caused when the endocrine glands begin to secrete hormones. Family influences play a large part in an individual's adjustment to the changes of adolescence. Stone and Church classify adolescent personalities as conventionalists, idealists, hedonists, and psychopaths.

4. Erikson's Theory of Psychosocial Development

Psychoanalyst Erik Erikson sees human development as a series of psychosocial stages. Each stage represents a developmental crisis, or developmental task. If the child resolves the crisis successfully, a positive aspect of personality emerges. If not, a negative aspect emerges. Erikson's view stresses the need for reassurance at each stage. During late adolescence, young people begin to question parental values, resolve the identity crisis, and begin to experience intimacy.

5. Adolescent Issues

Adolescents and their parents sometimes come into conflict over parental authority. Parents may want to grant greater freedom but may be concerned the adolescent is not ready for the responsibility. Adolescents may resist parental controls but still want parental support. Most psychologists agree that peers are very important to adolescents, who want to be like their friends. Early theories held that juvenile crime was caused by poverty and by absent fathers. Another explanation points to alienation from society's norms.

Psychology Skill Activities

1. Write an essay entitled, "What a Man or Woman Should Be." Compare your essay to those of your classmates. **easy**

2. Ask three adults and three people about your age the following questions: "What is the biggest problem facing adolescents in the United States today? Why is it a problem? What is one solution?" Write or record on tape the responses you receive. Compare the responses with those of your classmates. **challenging**

Testing for Understanding

Knowing Key Terms
Define these terms in your own words.

Section 1
middle childhood
sex role
traditional sex role
joint sex role

Section 2
moral judgment

Section 3
adolescence   idealist
puberty   hedonist
hormone   psychopath
conventionalist

Section 4
psychosocial stages   identity crisis
crisis   intimacy

Section 5
peers
alienation
norm

Reviewing Main Ideas

Section 1
1. What are some developmental tasks of middle childhood?
2. What are children generally like during middle childhood?
3. How do children learn sex roles and how are these sex roles changing?

Section 2
1. Deciding what people ought to do in specific situations is called what?
2. Describe Lawrence Kohlberg's theory of moral development.

Section 3
1. What physical changes are characteristic of adolescence?
2. What categories have Stone and Church used to classify styles of adolescence?

Section 4
1. What is Erik Erikson's view of human development?
2. What crisis is associated with each stage of psychosocial development between birth and adolescence?
3. Explain "identity crisis."

Section 5
1. Why is parental authority a source of conflict during adolescence?
2. How do peers influence adolescents?
3. What are some theories about the causes of juvenile crime?

Thinking Critically
1. *Analysis.* Which of Erikson's stages do you think is most important? Why?   **easy**
2. *Problem Solving.* Give two suggestions for improving the psychological well-being of the average adolescent. Let one suggestion be something over which the adolescent has control.   **challenging**

Demonstrating Psychology Skills
Use what you have learned in this chapter to decide whether the following changes belong to middle childhood or adolescence.

_____ 1. question parental authority
_____ 2. learn physical skills needed for games
_____ 3. learn sex roles
_____ 4. resolve the crisis of industry
_____ 5. begin puberty
_____ 6. form groups and close friendships with people of the same sex
_____ 7. become a conventionalist, idealist, hedonist, or psychopath
_____ 8. develop fundamental skills in reading, writing, and arithmetic
_____ 9. resolve the identity crisis
_____ 10. challenge parental values

Adult Living

Mark and Cindy Miller married the week after they graduated from college. Mark went to work as assistant manager in his father's restaurant. Cindy became a secretary but quit after a year to have their first child. At the time, Cindy was sure motherhood was the most beautiful career in the world.

Now it is ten years later. Mark knows he can soon become owner and manager of the restaurant, but he wants his life to include more than being just like Dad. He feels Cindy doesn't understand what's bothering him, so he now spends more and more time away from home, socializing with business associates and coworkers.

Cindy has concerns of her own. "David and Sara are wonderful children," she says, "but I've been a housewife for nine years, and I want to do something else. I graduated with honors from college, and I'd like to begin a career in law or business."

Mark used to kid Cindy about her support of "women's lib," but he doesn't kid her anymore. He wants her to have a career, but thinks she should wait at least three more years. Cindy and Mark are now seeing a marriage counselor. So are many other couples like the Millers.

It wasn't always like this. Years ago, decisions people made in their teens or early 20's determined the way most of them lived the rest of their lives. Now adult life often includes big changes—a new career for example, or a move to another part of the country. Psychologists now speak of the "30's crisis," a delayed resolution of the identity crisis until the person nears or passes age thirty. Also, psychologists have added the study of adult development to that of childhood and adolescence.

In this chapter, we will examine the stages of adult development and the stresses of adult life. We'll see how a mature person deals with

Adult life often includes important changes such as marriage.

basic social and psychological changes in living. These changes may result from forces in the person's environment or from physical changes brought about by the aging process.

Adult development is a relatively new branch of psychology, and much still needs to be learned. So far, it appears that development in adults, as in children, falls into fairly definite stages. Many researchers identify these stages in terms of age spans that, for social, physical, and psychological reasons, bring about behaviors typical of that stage. The major stages are **young adulthood,** middle age, and the later years—old age.

1. Young Adulthood

PREVIEW

**In this section,
read to find out:**

1. what psychosocial crisis often occurs in young adulthood.
2. how people set goals or tasks for themselves.
3. how growth applies to adult development.

It is not easy to tell when a person becomes an adult. A twenty-year-old may look twenty-four, show the emotional development of a sixteen-year-old, carry the social responsibility that goes with being thirty, and cope with a health problem that ordinarily comes at fifty. Becoming an adult is a highly individual matter.

Social psychologist Daniel Levinson thinks twenty-to-thirty-five-year-olds are typically motivated by a compelling vision, or dream. The major task of this period is to build your life around such a vision. You want your life to amount to something, which may mean a career—as a physician, a building contractor, or a teacher, for example. Or it may mean something else, such as getting an interesting job, raising a family, or being a good citizen. Your dream, whatever it is, becomes the basis for the choices you make.

Psychologist Bernice Neugarten, a pioneer in the study of adult life changes, notes that the change from adolescence to adulthood is marked by an increase in personal competence and independence. You are more sure of yourself, less reluctant to express your real feelings, more outgoing and, of course, less dependent on others. If everything goes well during your twenties and early thirties, you acquire a stable outlook on life and a sense of where you are headed. But what happens if everything doesn't go well?

Psychologist Erik Erikson believes that adult development depends in great part on a person's ability to form intimate relationships with others.

The Psychosocial Crisis: Intimacy, or Isolation

According to psychologist Erik Erikson, whether or not things go well depends in great part on the ability to form intimate, meaningful relationships with others. The preceding stage, adolescence, was marked by an identity crisis, or the "Who am I?" problem. To move beyond this stage, an adolescent must develop a clear sense of self.

A person shares himself or herself, in the **intimacy crisis,** by developing a supportive relationship with another person, often someone of the opposite sex. In Erikson's view, this sharing can happen only when you have no fear of losing your own identity in the process. Intimacy requires a new level of ego development. Sharing ourselves with another can be done only by satisfying the needs of that other, and this requires that we be *big* enough to stretch our concerns and feelings to include those of that other person.

If this ability to share identity is not achieved, according to Erikson, a person becomes too locked in with personal concerns. Establishing the tender relationships so crucial to adult development becomes difficult. Erikson saw the person who draws inside himself or herself ending in **isolation.** The individual *goes it alone,* sometimes quite successfully in a practical way, but many psychological needs remain unsatisfied. Loners are often more vulnerable to many of life's problems than are people who maintain social connections.

Physical and Psychological Changes

Physically, a person in good health is aware of few changes during young adulthood. There may be a slight decline in physical stamina but this can be prevented through exercise. Some of the physical awkwardness of adolescence smoothes out. The early adult years are good ones for athletes, as they perfect their abilities. Psychologically, young adults become more realistic about life than they were in their teens.

Social influences. A young adult settles into a job, with an interest in its long-range economic effects on his or her lifestyle. People's interests and attitudes jell somewhat during the period of young adulthood. Commitments are formed toward the second half of life. Some people set their goals on material rewards, and social status. Some put their energy into resisting conformity and emphasizing creativity. Others are motivated by different dreams.

Young adults are influenced—even pressured—by how others expect them to behave. Neugarten speaks of the norms society imposes for a particular time-span as a **social clock** by which we measure life stages. Interestingly, the social clock is set differently for different socioeconomic groups—at least among men. A number of men were asked when a man is "mature," "at the prime of life," and "most confident." People from the lowest economic group said age twenty-five. Working-class men picked age thirty. Lower-middle-class men chose thirty-five, and for those in the upper-middle class, the "mature" and "prime" period was age forty. But desirable masculine characteristics were regarded as peaking in early adulthood.

Developmental Tasks

Psychologist Raymond Kuhlen described early adulthood as a period of **growth-expansion.** Psychologically, young adults are oriented toward the future. They make new commitments, form new goals, and seek personal achievement. Self-confidence is high.

An outlet for the strivings of many young adults is marriage and family. Both partners surrender some independence to establish shared interests and responsibilities. Marriage becomes a test of each person's capacity for intimacy. Sexual adjustment is crucial. Yet the high divorce rate for this age group indicates that even if sexual relationships are good, the adjustments are difficult. An important bond of intimacy in marriage is often supplied by parenthood, as a couple shares the joys and problems of child rearing and new bonds of intimacy are established with the infant. The marriage may reach a critical point if the partners discover that they have been relating separately to the child rather than sharing a joint intimacy.

In their thirties, many people begin to ask, "Is this the way I want to spend the rest of my life?" Marriage counselors see about twice as many couples in this age group as in any other age group.

Many people give time and effort to projects that benefit others in the community during the young adult years. This blind skier, Chris Montgomery, volunteers her skill in instructing other blind skiers. This program is sponsored by the Chicago, Illinois Jaycees.

Building close family relationships is an important goal for many people during their young adult years.

Failure to progress at a chosen occupation can damage self-esteem. This, in turn, may affect a person's marriage and other personal relationships. By the same token, the pursuit of success may interfere with other aspects of development. For some workers the necessity of traveling or working long hours limits personal activities and family relationships. A wage earner may literally become a slave to the job and a stranger to the family.

Finding emotional satisfactions may make up for a boring work routine. These are satisfactions most constructively found in home and family life, in civic, cultural, and social activities, and in recreation. For both men and women, knowing when and how to play is an essential part of growth at this stage. It is also important that in becoming grown up, people stay in touch with the child within them—the curiosity and wonder at new discoveries, the delight in friends, and occasionally, the ability to put aside the practical side of nature and dream dreams.

Section Review

1. Tell briefly what happens in young adulthood psychosocially, physically, and psychologically.
2. What does Kuhlen mean by growth-expansion?
3. What do you think is the most difficult part of young adulthood for most people?

PREVIEW

**In this section,
read to find out:**

1. how middle-aged
   people see themselves.
2. what psychosocial,
   physical, and psycho-
   logical changes occur
   in middle age.
3. some tasks of the
   middle years.

2. Middle Age

When does the move from young adulthood to middle age take place? This varies in individuals, just as the stages of childhood and adolescence do. But even in general terms, psychologists do not agree about middle age. Some of them say young adulthood extends to age forty-five and middle age to seventy. Many others speak of ages thirty-five through fifty as early middle age, and fifty through sixty-five as later middle age. There is agreement, however, on many of the characteristics and tasks of middle age.

People in the middle years become more aware of time's passing than they were before.

In Neugarten's view, the middle aged see themselves as bridgers of generations. "Life is restructured in terms of time-left-to-live rather than time-since-birth." For people whose youthful dreams have not been realized, middle age becomes a time of regret and the "middle-age blues." A sense of humor rescues many in the middle adult years, and they accept the less-than-ideal circumstances of life philosophically. Efforts are directed toward family, job, and community. Giving and helping become necessary. The fantasies of fame and fortune need not necessarily give way to despair, but to making the most out of one's assets and planning future years sensibly.

Gradually, the developmental tasks shift from reaching goals to strengthening the position in life we have won for ourselves. People in the middle years become more conscious of biological change and sense, perhaps for the first time, their own mortality.

The Psychosocial Crisis: Generativity, or Self-Absorption

Erikson thinks the central conflict of this period involves **generativity** or, instead, **self-absorption.** By now the adult has shifted from being primarily a learning animal to a "doing" and teaching one. An important part of generativity centers on establishing and guiding the next generation. For many people, this involves their own family, but the truly generative person is also concerned with the world and helping to build a better society for all young people.

A generative individual is *productive* and, within personal limits, *creative*. The perfecting of earlier skills brings a new sense of accomplishment. There is more time for hobbies and leisure activities. Women whose children are grown may find a new career or return to a former one. Although we slow down biologically, there is no evidence of intellectual decline even in late middle age.

Failure to meet the challenge of generativity leads to *self-absorption*. In more ordinary words, we "get in a rut." Not only are we less open to new experiences, but we become absorbed in ourselves. Life becomes dull and uninteresting and we focus inward on our private worries and concerns. We just complain instead of trying to change things that irritate us. Unfortunately, the more self-absorbed we become, the more difficult it is to launch into new endeavors.

Physical Changes

Although there is a slight decline in physical vigor after age thirty-five, this is not an important developmental factor for most people in

Below: Middle age is a time when people's efforts are directed toward family, job, and community. By now the adult has shifted from being primarily a learning animal to a "doing" and teaching one.

The realization that physically youth is passing makes the middle years difficult for many—especially in a society like ours that values youth.

normal health. With professional athletes the decline usually marks a severe loss of skill and satisfaction. And women face the sex-related *change of life*, or **menopause,** in their late forties and early fifties. Physiological changes during this period include loss of fertility and the end of menstruation. Hormonal changes also occur, especially in the production of estrogen. It was long assumed that this change in body chemistry and function accounted for nervous symptoms associated with menopause, such as hot flashes and irritability.

But many women experience no unpleasantness at all. This has led some researchers to suspect that the most significant aspects of change of life are psychological. But other studies indicate that the amount of decrease in hormone production is crucial. This theory is supported by the fact that doctors have treated many women successfully with hormones, to ease menopausal symptoms.

A woman's attitude toward menopause as a life event is frequently more important than the physical symptoms. Menopause represents a transition into the middle age years when childbearing is no longer possible. Researchers have found that younger women tend to be somewhat fearful and negative toward menopause. Women who are experiencing it, or who have already been through it, view it as a release from family obligations and a chance to redirect energies.

At one time it was thought that men, too, went through a *male menopause* that was physical in nature. There is little evidence to support this view. It is now believed that the mid-life crisis in men is psychological only. Career and family pressures, along with approaching old age, cause anxieties in a society that values youth. The middle-aged man who has been a faithful husband sometimes seeks extramarital affairs, in part to prove his youth and vigor, and in part to recapture the romance of earlier years.

Psychological Changes

According to Kuhlen, middle age is usually a time of physical and social loss as opposed to growth-expansion. Hair turns gray and teeth fall out. Cosmetics fail to hide the wrinkles. The body sags in new places. The children grow up and frequently move away. There are more funerals to go to. The social clock ticks not only slower, but louder. Earlier dreams of great accomplishment are replaced by a less glowing view of what can be done.

Mid-life is seen as a turning point, a last chance to change directions and goals. This itself intensifies pressure to make good or to find happiness. Depression is a common mental disturbance of middle to late middle age. Among men, the suicide rate rises steadily over the succeeding decades. Among women, suicide declines in the later years. A number of factors seem to contribute to the psychological problems of middle age.

1. *Changes in subjective happiness.* Several studies suggest that the losses met in middle age lead to more general feelings of unhappiness. It becomes difficult to replace what has been lost. Possibly, too, in a world of violence and rapid change, middle-aged and older people find life less to their liking. For whatever reasons, a decline in happiness appears to be significant in the middle years.

2. *Change in self-concept.* The few studies that have been done in this area show a decline in self-concept as a person grows older. For example, a Draw-a-Person test was given in a study to a number of men and women of all ages. This test is believed to reflect a person's self-image. The men drew larger pictures up to about age thirty, and then smaller pictures. The women, however, drew larger pictures until age forty, after which they drew smaller figures.

In another study of self-concept, a younger and an older group of subjects were asked to rate themselves *(myself)* against the concept of the *ideal person.* Young men gave a surprisingly high rating to middle age (more than double the rating older men gave it). The rating given to middle age by women, both young and older, was low. Only about a third as many young women saw the *ideal person* as middle aged as did young men. But all groups viewed youth as preferable.

3. *Increase in anxiety symptoms.* The added responsibilities of middle age, along with social and physical losses of the period, seem to produce more anxiety in this group. While the younger person tends to worry about a specific problem, the middle-aged individual is not sure what is causing the worry—only that anxiety is more common.

A number of studies suggest that anxiety increases with age. To test this notion, the reaction time was measured in people of different age groups to words such as *worry, afraid, unhappy, restless,* and *anxious,* when these words were mixed in with other, neutral words. People usually take longer to respond to anxiety-producing words. In these tests the reaction time increased with age. Events that the words represent are apparently seen as more threatening as a person grows older.

Why do people become more fearful with the approach of old age? One reason is that we live in a society that glorifies youth. Although middle-aged people in our society may be respected, this respect can be threatened by an arbitrary retirement age. While other factors may be at work, the approach of old age adds to anxiety during middle life, and perhaps makes people feel old sooner.

Ten Warning Signs of Suicide

Suicide can strike at any age. In the last forty years, the suicide rate has tripled among young people aged fifteen to twenty-four. However, suicide is a far greater problem among older people. In fact, the highest suicide rate is among the elderly, those aged seventy-five to eighty-four. Here are ten warning signs that a person is contemplating ending their life and needs help.

1. dwelling on thoughts about pain, death, or suicide
2. veiled warnings of suicidal thoughts or plans
3. withdrawing from other people
4. neglecting personal appearance
5. losing interest in schoolwork or favorite activities
6. giving away prized possessions
7. erratic sleeping patterns and appetite loss
8. frequent irritability or unexplained crying
9. drug or alcohol abuse
10. impulsive or reckless behavior

Career progress in middle age can be important for reasons of economics and self-esteem, as well as for the intrinsic interest the work affords.

What can offset changes in happiness, self-concept, and anxiety? A person who, in Erikson's words, achieves generativity in life need not find middle age a time of trial. A generative person, in giving his or her best to the world, stops worrying and develops healthier attitudes. Old age does not seem as threatening.

Developmental Tasks

Perhaps the most difficult task of the middle years is accepting the fact that one is, in fact, middle aged. For the film star, the professional athlete, and the very attractive, this realization is particularly difficult. But even average people may feel that they have not lived up to the promise that was expected of them. So people try to find new sources of fulfillment. Possibly a person can become wiser than before, more needed by others, more independent, or better able to enjoy the small pleasures of life. People who can reframe their goals find it easier to overcome the crises of middle age. They are the ones who say, "I wouldn't be young again for anything!"

In a study of middle-aged men, four major developmental tasks of middle age were identified.

1. *Achieving occupational success.* Success in a career is a primary concern for economic reasons and for reasons of self-esteem.

It's Your Turn

In this chapter you've read about adult development. Now *It's Your Turn*. Apply the principles to your own life. Write three paragraphs about your life as you think it will be at ages 25, 40, and 55.

2. *Making marriage work.* The right marriage partner, a satisfying relationship, and children are seen as basic to a satisfying middle age.

3. *Adjusting to reality.* The often unrealistic expectations of earlier years are modified by the facts. With a more accurate view of limits on the power to control other people, the middle age period can bring a measure of calm. The job is knowing how and when to compromise. Ideas, goals, and social relationships are recognized as more complex than they looked in youth.

4. *Overcoming monotony and fear of change.* A major complaint of the men was monotony. Life is more routine and less exciting than it was in youth. But along with a desire for more variety is a reluctance to rock the boat. The conflict between boredom and fear of change leaves some men puzzled. The task is to find resources for change that do not threaten economic and emotional security.

Section Review

1. What does Erikson mean by generativity, as opposed to self-absorption?

2. List three changes people go through in middle age.

3. What do you think is the most difficult part of middle age for most people?

3. The Later Years

Getting old seems remote to most young people. Even people of sixty-five who are active and healthy tend to think of themselves as middle aged rather than old, and often insist that you are as young as you feel. But a person of fifty who is in poor health may feel very old. The machine runs down, and eventually wears out. Our attitudes and behavior reflect the gradual slowing of physical function.

We put off thinking about growing old. Yet reminders of old age are present from childhood. When young, we may have contact with an aging grandparent. Later we may be responsible for the physical and emotional needs of aging parents. Our experiences with aging friends and relatives will influence our own experiences in later years.

The study of old age, **gerontology,** is new to psychology. This is because old age itself is relatively new. In Roman times, the average life expectancy was twenty-two years. By the beginning of the twentieth century it was only about forty. Today it is around seventy. Within the next 100 years it could be pushed to ninety or more. This steadily advancing life span raises a troubling question. Do people live too long? Some people say yes, but often not about themselves.

What is old? Being old is an individual matter. Artist Georgia O'Keeffe and poet Marianne Moore continued to be productive in their eighties. Cellist Pablo Casals gave his last concert at the age of ninety-six. Anthropologist Margaret Mead, philosophers John Dewey and Bertrand Russell, and Supreme Court Justice Thurgood Marshall all were making significant contributions to American life and letters in their seventies.

What people make of old age is influenced by the health and the

Thurgood Marshall; Marianne Moore

© 1967 by Jill Krementz

viewpoint they bring to it. Cultural attitudes are important, too. Most cultures respect the aged. Yet, for many years, many Americans thought that a presidential candidate over sixty-five was "too old." This view changed with the 1980 election of Ronald Reagan, who took office at the age of seventy.

Physical Changes

In later life, the decline of most of the physical organs becomes evident. Lung capacity is reduced, and we can't climb hills without getting out of breath. The fatty deposits in blood vessels, that begin building up when people are young, may in old age reduce the flow of blood to the heart and brain. Blood pressure tends to rise. These and many other changes vary greatly in individuals. Although decline is inevitable, the rate of decline appears not to be. Experiments have shown that a vigorous program of exercise for one hour, three times a week, improves circulation and lowers blood pressure.

In an intensive study of elderly men, psychologist James E. Birren found that the body's metabolism and blood circulation in the brain showed little relationship to chronological age. Most of the men examined did not differ significantly from a group of normal men fifty years younger. In the cases where blood flow and consumption of oxygen were reduced, it was due to **arteriosclerosis** or hardening of the arteries.

Older people's brains put out less electrical energy, but this does not seem to affect mental flexibility and alertness. Reflexes also slow, although physicians in the National Institute of Health suggest that this may be because elderly people feel less confident about themselves and experience fewer challenges.

Pablo Casals; Georgia O'Keeffe

The Psychosocial Crisis: Integrity, or Despair

Erikson believes that the aging process results in feelings of either **integrity** or despair. Integrity means a person's ability to see his or her life as having been worthwhile. The past cannot be changed, but it is possible to combine it with the present and feel content with the outcome. The person with this kind of integrity can say, "I've lived the best life I could under the circumstances." According to Erikson, an individual who can do this faces death without great fear.

By contrast, *despair* sets in when life is seen as lacking in value. This may result from a person's feeling that he or she has not achieved worthy goals. It can also result from loss of physical and mental function or from social isolation and neglect. The man or woman who remains in good health, enjoys economic security, and feels wanted by others is unlikely to feel especially despairing about old age. Of course, this crisis, like all of Erikson's stages, is not usually an all-or-nothing adjustment. Most people fall somewhere between these extremes.

Other psychologists see developmental changes in old age as centering less on a person's attitude toward the past and more on restrictions imposed in the present. Three such age-related factors are:

1. *Loss of role.* With retirement—whether at seventy or sixty-five or sixty-two—people sometimes see themselves as no longer being productive members of society. They often feel they have been moved aside to make way for others. They miss the job satisfaction they had, and the economic security that went with it. Parents whose families are grown feel less needed than they once were. Because the nuclear family (parents and children) has largely replaced the extended family (three or more generations living together), many of the links between generations are broken. The views of grandparents are no longer sought in family management and, in some cases, are refused. The loss of role of director or adviser is especially hard for some older people.

2. *Loss of intellectual functioning.* Research on this subject has produced no final answers. Old people seem to think and act more slowly than younger people, but this may reflect more caution. Or, if they are no longer doing intellectual work, the aged may get out of the habit. Developmental psychologists K. F. Riegel and R. M. Riegel suggest that there is no real decline in intellectual functioning until shortly before death. Some psychologists point out that what appears to be a decline is a lack of stimulation. Old people are not challenged or do not challenge themselves to perform. Avoiding challenge may in itself reflect a loss of ability for some people. Style of thinking, however, may undergo change. In studying a number of elderly subjects, psychologist Nathan Kogan found them less abstract and conceptual in their

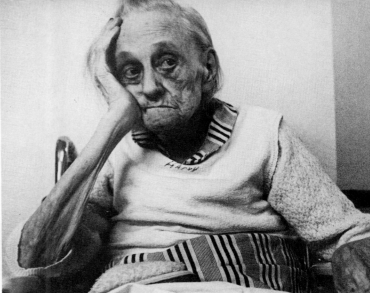

thinking than younger subjects. The aged were more likely to think in terms of concrete relationships and themes that had a specific, personal meaning for them.

3. *Loss of interest in others.* For a number of reasons, old people turn inward and attend increasingly to their personal needs. They no longer actively attempt to change their environment, but adopt a passive attitude toward it. Neugarten calls this "a movement of energy away from an outer-world to an inner-world orientation."

You may have noticed that some old people talk about the past a lot. The joys of their life are relived in memory. Enjoying life through what others do also becomes important. This is called **vicarious living.** Did you ever notice a grandparent at a wedding or graduation?

Sociologist Elaine Cumming and developmental psychologist William E. Henry call the shift from an active to a relatively passive type of life the process of **disengagement.** Cumming and Henry argue that withdrawing from other people is a natural way to adapt to old age. They believe that old people who successfully disengage experience higher morale than those who attempt to remain involved.

The idea of disengagement has been criticized by other social scientists for several reasons.

1. Many old people never become highly engaged and therefore do not disengage.
2. For other old people, physical problems and loss of mobility are the causes of withdrawal.
3. Disengagement may be a decision of society, not the individual.

Declining physical functioning is a source of depression for many older people.

The last criticism of Cumming and Henry's theory of disengagement may be the best criticism. As we have seen, people tend to be displaced as they grow older. It is society that disengages from the elderly. At best, perhaps, the process is mutual. Older people don't want all the responsibilities and involvements of a younger person, and society offers few substitutes. What appears to be adaptation is, in reality, making the best of things. Think of some elderly people you know and ask yourself how disengaged they are. It's surprising the number of eighty- and ninety-year-olds who, given the opportunity, remain active, keen-minded participants in the life around them.

Developmental Tasks of the Later Years

Whatever the degree to which the elderly disengage, maintaining *integrity*, or self-esteem, remains a central task. This must be done in the face of increasing physical losses, loss of job and social roles, and quite possibly loss of income. Finally, for the married there is the loss of a spouse, typically the lifetime friend and closest companion. Each change can be traumatic, and all require difficult adjustment.

Psychologists Barbara M. Newman and Phillip R. Newman suggest three ways older people meet the losses that come with time:

1. *Redirecting energy to new roles and activities.* Retirement need not mean being thrown on the scrap heap. Leisure activities, hobbies, study groups, and volunteer work provide opportunities for a later life that can be as rewarding, in its own way, as the preceding period of work and family management. For some people, retirement communities are an answer. Many retired people travel to new places. Some elderly people find in old age the opportunity to do things they missed out on in youth or middle age.

For people who redirect their energies to new roles and activities, old age can be as rewarding as any earlier stage of development.

Members of the American Association for Retired Persons are active in lobbying and other educational and political efforts to improve the life of older Americans.

2. *Accepting life.* In large part this involves being philosophical about failures and disappointments. Many people become more objective in their later years, and can weigh their gains and losses in the perspective of time. Someone who had been indifferently successful in business takes comfort in the knowledge that the children have done well, or that civic contributions have made him respected, or that success in business looks less vital than it once looked. Others brood over past failures and become embittered cranks. Their inability to integrate past experience with present circumstances leads to despair.

3. *Developing a point of view about death.* In a sense, this means the ability to confront death directly, something few of us are willing to do at any age. Among the very old especially, the realization that not much time is left often leads to last-minute reversals, the completion of unfinished business, and a new serenity of spirit. Several studies have shown that, although elderly people do not welcome the idea of dying, neither do they shy away from discussing death, nor are they especially fearful of it.

Section Review

1. What does Erikson mean by integrity, as opposed to despair?
2. List three changes people go through in old age.
3. What do you think is the hardest part of old age for most people?

The Greening of the Aged

A visit to many homes for the aged can be depressing. Many of the men and women we see there seem listless, unresponsive, and incapable of performing simple tasks. Two researchers from Yale University, Ellen Langer and Judith Rodin, decided to see whether they could reverse the condition of residents in an old-age home. Their sample was made up of ninety-one residents, ages sixty-five to ninety, all well enough to be walking about. The investigators reasoned that the crucial psychological process a person missed in such institutions was taking responsibility for decisions. To be an actor in life's drama, we must act, decide, and be responsible for the consequences.

About half of the participants in the study received instructions that emphasized responsibility for caring for themselves and improving the quality of life in the home. They were then asked to choose a plant from among a box of them as a present, with the understanding that they had to care for it. In contrast, a second group of patients was given instructions that stressed the responsibility of the *staff* to provide good services for the residents. They were handed a plant as a present and told that the nurses would water it for them.

The results were dramatic. The experimental "I'll do it myself" groups showed significant improvement over the "We'll do it for you" group on alertness, active participation, and sense of well-being.

Eighteen months later, these positive results had not changed, as indicated by nurses' higher ratings of the happiness, sociability, and vigor of the personally responsible group. But most startling of all, inducing the residents to be responsible for themselves and their plants made them live longer! Following the experiment, only 15 percent of the personally responsible residents died, compared to twice as many in the no-responsibility group.

4. Death and Dying

Until a quarter-century ago, *death* was a taboo word in most Western countries, and little attention was paid to the psychological needs of the dying. This attitude has changed dramatically in recent years and a new discipline, **thanatology,** has come into being. Thanatology means the study of death. As the expected life span has grown to seventy-seven years for women and sixty-nine for men, more people are dealing with parents and other older relatives who contract lingering illnesses. Caring for elders, not only physically but emotionally, has brought many people face to face with an inevitable reality of life—death.

PREVIEW

**In this section,
read to find out:**

1. which people live a long time.
2. what stages of adjustment a dying person goes through.

Life Expectancy

At the Duke University Center for the Study of Aging and Human Development, medical sociologist Erdman Palmore and his colleagues devised a **longevity index** to predict how many years of life were left to people once they reached old age. Palmore's subjects were 268 normally healthy community volunteers ranging from sixty to ninety-four years of age. They were studied for thirteen years. By the end of that time, 121 subjects had died. Palmore measured certain characteristics of both the deceased and the survivors. He found that physical condition had a great deal less influence on life expectancy than did psychological and social factors. His *longevity index* proved far more accurate than the tables used by life insurance companies, which are based largely on physical health.

As expected, general good health at the time of the initial interview was one reliable sign. For people between sixty and sixty-nine, use of tobacco made a significant difference in shortening life. For men, little could be predicted on the basis of physical activity. For women up to age sixty-nine, this was the single most important indicator of how long they would live. Active women lived longer than those who led a more passive existence.

A person's income made almost no difference in life expectancy. More important were the nonmaterial rewards of a job, what Palmore calls work satisfaction. The ability to do things well was another good predictor. This ability, along with leisure activities, work satisfaction, and overall happiness proved to be a more reliable guide to long life than physical health, exercise, or the use of tobacco. In short, a useful role and a cheerful view of life provide the best way to outlive the insurance companies' predictions.

Psychologist Morton A. Lieberman found that entering an institution for the aged shortens life. Lieberman compared people between the ages of seventy and ninety-five in institutions with those of similar background who remained in the community. Of 1,000 patients who entered a home, 24 percent died within six months, two and a half times as many as those who remained outside. Lieberman concluded that the cause of their deaths was essentially psychological. For many of these people, the crisis of going into an institution, perhaps not by choice, weakened their will to live.

The Process of Dying

Deaths from illness or accident occur to people of every age and stage of life, even the prenatal. In the elderly, however, studies have been made that point to some characteristics of the process of their dying. When old people die, developments take place that determine whether there is a disintegration of personality or a final, more positive, restructuring. This crisis is framed by three events: social death, psychological death, and, at the very end, biological death.

Social death takes place when the dying person is shunned by others. This may occur if the individual is in the hospital, and possibly hooked up to various life-support systems so that the care the dying person receives is from machines—not humans. Under such conditions, the person is isolated from family and friends.

Gradually, *psychological death* sets in. This may happen if a person's faculties become clouded. The memory fails. Close relatives may not be recognized. But it may also come through isolation and false hope that is translated as deceit. ("You're all right; you'll live to be a hundred!") Dying people who are turned over to hospitals sometimes lose their autonomy. Much of their psychological decline can be traced to this feeling of helplessness and of being cut off from loved ones.

Biological death occurs when the vital organs stop working. But there is a problem of *which* organs. Is a person alive because the heart is beating, or dead because the brain has stopped working? With the increased use of life-support equipment, deciding just when a person is dead has become more difficult.

Psychiatrist Elisabeth Kübler-Ross identified five distinct stages, or moods, through which dying people pass as they approach their death. Her book, *On Death and Dying,* has become the bible of the new thanatology movement. Kübler-Ross believes a dying person follows a well-defined script by which he or she symbolically communicates with others. The stages of adjustment to death are these five:

1. *Denial.* The person refuses to believe he or she is dying. People say, "It can't be me," and seek other reasons for their condition.

2. *Anger.* The protest becomes a question: "Why does it have to be me?" A sense of unfairness and injustice is present. It is often directed at doctors and nurses.

3. *Bargaining.* No longer in doubt as to the severity of the illness, an individual now bargains for time. There is unfinished business to be taken care of. In this stage many people offer their lives to some worthy cause in return for a few more years on earth.

4. *Depression.* Kübler-Ross sees this period as a person's attempt to express sorrow and grief about himself or herself.

5. *Acceptance.* At the very end, a patient who has worked through the preceding stages may achieve an acceptance of death. It is no longer feared, and the person dies peacefully.

In Kübler-Ross' view, these stages constitute a hidden language by which the dying ask for help. Those who care for such people can make the task easier if they recognize what the person is trying to tell them.

Survivors often experience guilt feelings after the death of a loved one or anger at being left alone in the world.

Anger, for instance, should be understood and even encouraged. Grief should be shared, not opposed by false cheerfulness. Let the dying person know that others share this time of sorrow.

How to help. By recognizing the feelings a patient clings to, both family and medical staff can help dying people through their struggle and, in a sense, teach them how to die. At the same time, family and professionals also learn to manage their own reactions. They may also learn to face their own deaths with courage and dignity.

When someone is dying, members of the family often have feelings of guilt. These feelings may come from conflicts with the dying person that have not been settled. Often, family members feel it is wrong for the dying person to die while they survive. This attitude can lead to guilt feelings, which may need to be resolved in therapy.

If you have ever had a death in your own family, you know how upsetting it is to everyone. This is not only because you have lost someone dear to you, but also because the survivors are frequently confused about the role they should play in the dying process. If we share the concerns of the dying, as well as tend to their physical needs, death is easier for all.

Section Review

1. List some factors that influence how long a person is likely to live.
2. Why might many middle-aged adults not appreciate the research findings that indicate old people who live in institutions for the aged die sooner than other old people?
3. In what ways could Kübler-Ross' research on dying help people who work with the aged?

5. The Stress of Life

Stress can occur at any age. When psychologists and physicians speak of **stress,** they usually mean something negative. But stress can also have positive excitement value, as in sports, chess, or work. In this section, however, we are concerned with harmful effects of stress. This is the stress we often try to avoid. A traffic jam is an example of a stress situation. Having to make a tough decision, worrying about bills, and having a nightmare are stress situations.

Sources of Stress

Many things we do every day are stressful to some degree. Most of these stresses are not serious, and we readily adjust to them. The water is too hot in the shower, so we turn up the cold water. The boss pressures us to do more work, but we go along, hoping to get a raise.

PREVIEW

**In this section,
read to find out:**

1. how stress can be either good or bad.
2. some common causes of stress.
3. how psychosomatic illnesses relate to stress.
4. some ways of handling stress.

Family tensions are a common source of stress.

The ordinary stress of life is useful because it nudges us to work out new approaches to different situations. Stress keeps us adapting to an everchanging environment. But when we must cope with too many changes at one time, or adapt to radical changes we are not ready for, stress becomes serious. Boredom and monotony are also stressful. Loneliness can cause serious stress. Anything that requires a major adjustment in our way of life can turn stress into *distress*.

Stress and life events. Think back over some situations in your life that really shook you up. The death of a best friend or a parent certainly would be one. Perhaps you left home and the security of your family, and you were seriously homesick. This would be a stress reaction.

For more than twenty years, psychologists Thomas H. Holmes and Richard H. Rahe studied the effect stresses have on individuals over the course of time. Based on ratings by many people, Holmes devised a scale. Starting with 100 units for the death of a spouse, he scaled the units down through 11 for a parking ticket. He called the scores Life Change Units. To measure their impact he weighed them against the health of his subjects. Too high a score, he believes—over 200 in a single year—is more than the average American can take without a risk of getting sick in the near future.

High on the list of stress situations is the need to stand in the unemployment line. Some days, occasions for stress seem to rise up on all sides as the photo on the opposite page illustrates.

Events	Scale of Impact
Death of spouse	100
Divorce	73
Marital separation	65
Jail term	63
Death of close family member	63
Personal injury or illness	53
Marriage	50
Fired at work	47
Marital reconciliation	45
Retirement	45
Change in health of family member	44
Pregnancy	40
Sex difficulties	39
Gain of new family member	39
Business readjustment	39
Change in financial state	38
Death of close friend	37
Change to different line of work	36
Change in number of arguments with spouse	35
Mortgage over $10,000	31
Foreclosure of mortgage or loan	30
Change in responsibilities at work	29
Son or daughter leaving home	29
Trouble with in-laws	29
Outstanding personal achievement	28
Spouse begins or stops work	26
Begin or end school	26
Change in living conditions	25
Revision of personal habits	24
Trouble with boss	23
Change in work hours or conditions	20
Change in residence	20
Change in schools	20
Change in recreation	19
Change in church activities	19
Change in social activities	18
Mortgage or loan less than $10,000	17
Change in sleeping habits	16
Change in number of family get-togethers	15
Change in eating habits	15
Vacation	13
Christmas	12
Minor violations of the law	11

Holmes & Holmes, 1970

The table on this page shows Holmes' **scale of life changes.** The scores are based on average ratings. For you, changing personal habits or social activities may not be stressful. On the other hand, getting married might have much more impact than the 50 points shown on the scale. Finally, your physical condition and the kind of help you get in a crisis change your response to the stress. You might score yourself and see if you have gone over the 200 mark in the past year.

What your score means. Critics of the scale point out that it does not take into account the broader social context in which changes take place, your ability to deal with them, and the support you might get at the time. A low score could spell as much trouble as high score. For example, "No change" in your financial state when you need more money may be stressful. Your score should be interpreted in the light of the way you usually handle stressful events.

It's Your Turn

Many events in the Holmes scale of life changes apply to adult living. Some categories are probably not appropriate for someone your age. Now *It's Your Turn*. List five events that would be appropriate in a scale of life changes for people your age. Compile a list with other class members. Which events are most stressful? Which are least?

Psychosomatic Disorders

Sometimes we experience stress physically, in the form of physical illness. The illness reactions usually involve the nervous system, whose functions we have little conscious control over. Illnesses that stem from psychological sources are called **psychosomatic.** What's hard about tracing their source is that they can, instead, be brought on by purely physical or environmental causes. A person might get a rash from too much exposure to the sun or, instead, from an emotional problem.

How does this work? An executive, for example, plans a trip which she knows will force her to carry out an unpleasant decision—having to fire a manager who is a good person but an unsuccessful manager. Two days before the executive is to leave, she breaks out with a severe case of hives and must cancel the trip. Her mind has displaced its stress on the body, although the woman may not be aware of this.

It's not imaginary. Many psychosomatic disorders can be serious. High blood pressure is thought to result when a person feels continually threatened or holds back rage. Tense people and those who are uncertain how to express their anger, often suffer from **colitis**—an inflammation of the lower bowel. Peptic ulcers occur in people who do not deal satisfactorily with their frustrations. Such individuals are frequently ambitious and striving. In **migraine,** or tension, headaches, the cranial arteries are dilated. This painful response can come from worry or from a sustained effort to solve some personal problem.

Stress from decision conflict. Psychologists Neal Miller and John Dollard experimented with animals to measure decision-making conflict. They trained rats to go to a specific spot for food. Then they surprised the animals (once only) with an electric shock at the place where the food was expected. After that, the rats showed confusion, not knowing if they should *approach* the place for food or *avoid* it to stay away from what might be another shock. The psychologists discovered, after many trials, that the desire to *approach* increases as the goal gets near, but the desire to *avoid increases even faster*. When the rats started their approach to the goal *from far off*, the desire to avoid the shock mounted higher than the desire to approach the food, so the rats turned back.

How does this *approach-avoidance* conflict affect people? You may know of cases of a person whose wedding date is set but who gets "cold feet" and has the date postponed. If the fear (whatever its cause) has enough time to mount higher than the desire, fear takes over, and avoidance by postponement follows.

Two other related conflicts are the choice between two desired goals and the choice between two events to avoid. The first might occur when you expect money a week from now that will buy you either a jacket or shoes. You want both but can get only one. As the time grows near, and you *approach* the moment of owning the jacket or *approach* the moment of owning the shoes, your desire for one grows while your desire for the other recedes. *Approach-approach* conflict is often mild.

An example of an *avoidance-avoidance* conflict might be a choice between two places you should be next Saturday evening, neither of which is where you'd like to be. As the time to avoid one or the other grows near, your desire to avoid one becomes stronger, and your view of the other dissolves into, "It might not be so bad."

Coping with Stress

As we cannot avoid some degree of stress, it pays to know how to cope with it effectively. Physician Hans Selye gives three coping strategies: (1) learn how to behave in various situations so as to minimize stress, (2) recognize the source of your stress, and (3) find the level of stress at which you are most comfortable.

Note that in his first point Selye emphasizes *learning.* You can learn to adapt to stressful situations on the basis of similar experiences in the past. Selye believes that it is not usually stress as such that bothers us, but rather how we deal with it.

We can seldom deal with stress successfully if we don't recognize its source. Does the migraine headache just start up, or can you relate it to worry over some social or financial problem? Is it not being able to see a movie tonight that is frustrating you, or was it your failure to get an "A" on your term paper yesterday? People frequently take out their frustrations on the *wrong object.* Once we identify the stressor accurately, whether it is physical or emotional, we have a chance of bringing our response under control.

Happy stresses. Selye's third suggestion for effective coping—finding the level of stress at which you are most comfortable—lets you discover the positive values that some kinds of stress may give you. He thinks people who enjoy their work, no matter how demanding it is, are less stress-ridden than people who are bored. If you are doing something you like, you are more likely to handle either frustration or conflict effectively.

Section Review

1. What are some of the stresses of adult life?
2. Describe briefly the three types of conflict.
3. What is a psychosomatic disorder?
4. What are some ways to cope with stress?

The Coddington Life Events Scale for Adolescence (abridged)

Events	Weight
Death of a parent	108
Death of brother or sister	88
Divorce of your parents	70
Marital separation of your parents	62
Death of a grandparent	52
Hospitalization of a parent	52
Remarriage of a parent to a step-parent	51
Birth of a brother or sister	50
Hospitalization of a brother or sister	49
Loss of a job by a parent	46
Major increase in parents' income	41
Major decrease in parents' income	43
Start of a new problem between your parents	41
End of a problem between your parents	30
Being told you are very attractive by a friend	26
Going on the first date of your life	42
Finding a new dating partner	34
Breaking up with a boy/girl friend	39
Being told to break up with a boy/girl friend	35
Start of a new problem between you and your parents	43
End of a problem between you and your parents	35
Beginning the first year of high school	19
Moving to a new school district	41
Failing a grade in school	47
Suspension from school	34
Graduating from high school	33
Being accepted at the college of your choice	39
Recognition for excelling in a sport or other activity	24
Getting your first driver's license	32
Being responsible for an automobile accident	36
Appearance in a juvenile court	31
Failing to achieve something you really wanted	32
Getting a summer job	35
Getting your first permanent job	40
Deciding to leave home	41
Being hospitalized for illness or injury	50
Death of a close friend	63

Coddington, 1983

Chapter 3 Review

Section Summaries

1. Young Adulthood

Adult development covers young adulthood, middle age, and old age. Social psychologist Daniel Levinson thinks the major task of young adulthood is to build a life around a compelling vision or dream. Another task is what psychologist Erik Erikson calls the intimacy crisis, in which a person must learn to develop a sharing and supportive relationship with another person or face isolation. Young adults in good health are aware of few physical changes. As young adults settle into jobs and plan for the future, they begin to make lasting commitments. Psychologist Bernice Neugarten thinks many young adults are pressured by a social clock of norms and timespans.

2. Middle Age

Psychologists do not agree on the ages included in middle age. According to Erikson, the central conflict of this period is generativity versus self-absorption. Physical vigor declines slightly after thirty-five, and menopause signals the end of fertility in women. Gray hair, wrinkles, and sagging bodies are reminders of age. Changes in subjective happiness, changes in self-concept, and increase in anxiety symptoms seem to contribute to the psychological problems of middle age. A study of middle-aged men identified four developmental tasks: achieving occupational success, making marriage work, adjusting to reality, and overcoming monotony and fear of change.

3. The Later Years

Gerontology is the study of aging. What people make of old age depends on their health, their viewpoint, and cultural attitudes. In later life, physical decline usually becomes evident. Erikson feels that the psychosocial crisis of this stage is integrity versus despair. Some psychologists trace the developmental changes of old age to loss of role, loss of intellectual function- ing, and loss of interest in others. To maintain integrity, psychologists suggest that older people direct their energy to new roles and activities, accept life, and develop a point of view about death.

4. Death and Dying

Thanatology is the study of death. Medical sociologist Erdman Palmore has found that psychological and social factors are more important than physical condition in predicting life expectancy. The process of dying is framed by social death, psychological death, and biological death. Psychiatrist Elisabeth Kübler-Ross identified five stages of adjusting to death: denial, anger, bargaining, depression, and acceptance.

5. The Stress of Life

Stress can be both positive and negative. Holmes' scale of life changes ranks several common sources of stress. People who experience too much stress stand the risk of becoming sick in the near future. Critics point out that the scale does not reflect the broader social context of changes, personal abilities to deal with stress, and the role of social support. Psychosomatic illnesses, which result from psychological sources, include colitis, ulcers, and migraine headaches. Approach-avoidance conflicts can be a major source of stress. Physician Hans Selye identified three coping strategies: learn to deal with stress; recognize the sources of stress; find the level and type of stress that is most comfortable for you.

Psychology Skill Activities

1. Interview a young adult, a middle-aged person, and a senior citizen about the greatest joys and difficulties of their lives. Present your findings in an oral or written report.　　**easy**

2. Use the Psychology Skills Handbook exercise on surveys to help you create a survey on sources of stress for people in your age group. Include questions that will allow people to rank sources of stress from most to least serious, as well as questions about the way people typically cope with stress. Present a summary of the information.　　**challenging**

Testing for Understanding

Knowing Key Terms
Define these terms in your own words.

Section 1
young adulthood
intimacy crisis
isolation
social clock
growth-expansion

Section 2
generativity
self-absorption
menopause

Section 3
gerontology
arteriosclerosis
integrity
vicarious living
disengagement

Section 4
thanatology
longevity index

Section 5
stress
scale of life changes
psychosomatic
colitis
migraine

Reviewing Main Ideas

Section 1
1. What psychosocial crisis do most people resolve during young adulthood?
2. What kinds of goals do young adults set and what pressures affect their decisions?
3. What physical changes are associated with young adulthood?

Section 2
1. Explain psychologist Bernice Neugarten's ideas of how middle-aged people see themselves.

2. Describe the psychosocial, physical, and psychological changes that occur during middle age.
3. What are some developmental tasks of middle age?

Section 3
1. Describe the physical and psychosocial changes of old age.
2. What are some of the criticisms made of the idea of disengagement?
3. How can older people deal with the losses of old age?

Section 4
1. Which factors are most useful in predicting longevity?
2. What stages do people often follow in adjusting to death?

Section 5
1. Is stress a positive or negative force in life?
2. What are some of the more serious sources of stress on the Holmes and Rahe scale of life change units?
3. What role does stress play in psychosomatic illnesses?
4. What strategies did Hans Selye recommend for coping with stress?

Thinking Critically
1. *Drawing Conclusions.* How can you tell whether strategies for coping with stress are effective or ineffective?   **easy**
2. *Drawing Conclusions.* Why does the Holmes scale of life changes include some happy events?   **challenging**

Demonstrating Psychology Skills
Interview two young adults. Ask them to describe three important choices they made in their late teens or their early twenties. Then ask them to analyze how each choice might affect or has affected (1) the person's own middle and later years and (2) the lives of other people.

Experimenting with Psychology

Children's Views of Morality

As people grow and develop they change in many ways. They develop physically, emotionally, psychologically, and intellectually. A child's view of life is often different from an adult's. In addition, children go through stages in development. As we have seen, some of these stages involve intellectual growth. A child's way of thinking progresses and changes gradually into that of an adult.

The following experiment investigates one specific area of intellectual development—people's views of right and wrong. The experiment is based on Kohlberg's stages of moral development.

To do this experiment, you will need several children from ages four to eight. (You may want to combine your results with those of your classmates, to get a large enough sample of children.) Try to interview five children, with at least one of each age from four to eight.

Each child should be interviewed separately, and your results recorded in a chart similar to the one below. Tell each child the following story, using boy-character names if you are interviewing a boy and girls' names if you are interviewing a girl.

"This story is about two people. Johnny (or Janey) was playing in a friend's room. He/she *accidentally* bumped into a shelf and broke *ten* of the friend's record albums. The other child Billy (or Susy) went into a friend's room and broke *one* of the friend's record albums *on purpose.* Which person do you think did something worse? *Why?*"

RECORD OF RESULTS

Name of subject	Age	Picked as worse (check one) #1	#2	Reason given

Do you see a pattern to your results? (or the combined results of the class?)

Does the age of the child make a difference in the answer?

Is there a "critical age" when the opinion changes from person #1 to person #2?

CONCLUSIONS: What conclusions do you reach about moral development? Do they support Kohlberg's theories? How would *you* answer the question you asked your subjects?

Unit 1 Test

Matching (20 points)

Match each topic to a researcher below.
1. cognitive development
2. body build and personality
3. adulthood
4. moral development
5. thanatology
6. sex differences in development
7. psychosocial development
8. mother-child relations in monkeys
9. educational development of children
10. stress

a. Kübler-Ross
b. Piaget
c. Kohlberg
d. Erikson
e. Neugarten; Levinson

f. Harlows
g. White
h. Maccoby and Jacklin
i. Sheldon
j. Holmes and Rahe; Selye

Multiple Choice (20 points)

Circle the choice that best completes the statement or answers the question.
1. Which word does not refer to development as discussed in this unit? (a) growth (b) change (c) urban renewal (d) maturity
2. Most three-year-old children can do all the following, except (a) walking (b) talking (c) reading (d) climbing.
3. A person with no conscience is called a (a) psychopath (b) hedonist (c) conventionalist (d) idealist.
4. "Finding yourself" in late adolescence or early adulthood is called (a) generativity (b) identity crisis (c) autonomy (d) initiative.
5. The term Piaget used to describe the first stage of cognitive development is (a) sensorimotor (b) concrete operations (c) preoperational thought (d) formal operations.
6. The type of daycare that is generally called babysitting is (a) developmental (b) compensatory (c) nursery school (d) custodial.
7. According to Maccoby and Jacklin, which statement is a myth? (a) Boys excel in mathematical ability. (b) Girls are more "social." (c) Girls have greater verbal ability. (d) Males are more aggressive.
8. According to Erikson, the key developmental task of middle age is (a) independence (b) intimacy (c) generativity (d) integrity.
9. Kübler-Ross is known for her work with (a) infants (b) the dying (c) young adults (d) middle-aged women.
10. The study of aging is called (a) thanatology (b) cognitive psychology (c) gerontology (d) morphology.

True-False (20 points)

Decide whether each statement is true or false. Correct any false statements.
1. Middle childhood is ages three to eight.
2. Psychologists agree that heredity and environment affect development equally.
3. Adulthood as a stage of development was not studied by psychologists fifty years ago.
4. Adolescence exists in all cultures.
5. Peers are very important in adolescence.
6. Developing a sense of trust is the major developmental task of middle age.
7. Nativists are scientists who emphasize the importance of heredity in development.
8. The longitudinal approach compares large groups of persons at one particular time.
9. Middle age is the happiest time of life for most Americans.
10. Among the aged, income is not a reliable indicator of life expectancy.

Critical Thinking Essays (40 points)

Complete any two of the items below.
1. List five stages of development. Tell what you think is the most important developmental task at each stage, and explain your reasons.
2. Compare Erikson's ideas with those of Piaget or Kohlberg.
3. Explain, with examples, how heredity and environment, together, influence development.

Unit 2

Discovering the World

In this unit you will study the ways we discover the world around us—how we make sense of the information we receive, how we learn and think, and how we define and measure intelligence and creativity.

Taking It All In

Glance quickly at the illustration at the bottom of this page, then look away. What did you see? How would you describe what you saw? Now take a longer second look. What do you see in the illustration this time?

What you see depends on your **perception** of the illustration. What do we mean by perception? Perception is a two-stage process. It begins with **sensation.** Sensation means that our senses have picked up a message from the environment. We see, hear, taste, feel, or smell something. When we look at the illustration, we sense the figures and shapes. Then we interpret what we have sensed. We try to figure out

M. C. Escher, *Symmetry drawing B*

what the figures and shapes mean. This process of giving meaning to sensation is the important second stage of perception. Perception can be defined as the psychological interpretation of physical events. Even more simply, perception is making sense out of sensation.

In this chapter, we will look at the basic senses by which we discover our world, and the many ways we interpret sensations—how we "take it all in."

1. Sensation: How It Works

Practically speaking, most of what you know about the world comes through five of your senses—sight, sound, touch, taste, and smell. Of these, vision and hearing are the senses about which most is known.

Vision: The Eyes Have It

The human eye works much like a camera—a motion-picture camera, at that. For most people, the visual system is made up of not one camera but two, both of which send images to the "darkroom" where they are made into one image. Within its range, the human eye is capable of more accurate and sensitive performance than most cameras. However, it has more working parts that can break down and these parts are not easy to replace or repair.

Study the detailed drawing of the eye on page 107. First, notice the cornea. This protective window covers the exposed surface of the eyeball. A thin film of fluid bathes the cornea and keeps it clean. Besides protecting the eye, the cornea bends incoming light rays toward the lens. The lens focuses the light rays on the retina.

How much light does the eye need in order to see something? The amount depends on several things, such as whether the day is cloudy or bright, or whether we are doing close work or just looking out the window. The iris, the colored part of the eye just in front of the lens, regulates the amount of light entering the eye at any one time. The iris contracts and expands the pupil, the round opening in the center of the eye. In bright light, the pupil gets smaller. In darkness, it gets larger. Only the amount of light needed reaches the lens.

The lens of the eye focuses light on the retina. The retina has layers of tissue that pick up signals through sensory cells, called rods and cones.

The rods and cones make vision possible. These cells change light energy into nerve energy, ready to be sent to the brain. The **cones,** in the center portion of the retina, work best in bright light. They handle

PREVIEW

In this section, read to find out:

1. what senses bring in the most knowledge about the world.
2. what the basic principles of vision are.
3. how people see colors.
4. how hearing works.

color vision. The **rods,** located near the edges of the retina, provide both night vision and side vision.

The signals from cones and rods come together in one main cable, the optic nerve. The optic nerve sends the nerve impulses on to the part of the brain that handles seeing. When no light energy can get through to the brain because of diseased or damaged eyes, the individual is blind.

This photograph illustrates the idea that we actually "see" upside down. The brain turns the image right-side up.

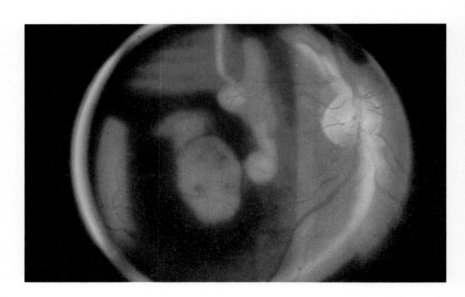

Vision and the Brain

The most important part of the visual process takes place in the brain. The brain takes the scrambled impressions the eye has received and decodes them. For example, the pattern of light that falls on the retina makes an image that is upside down. But in the brain, the pattern is somehow perceived in its real position. Still, what we see would not mean much if the brain didn't compare the picture with what is already in its data bank of past images. The image we see has meaning only because we've experienced similar images before. To a new baby, the world is something of a blur of shapes, forms, and colors. The infant organizes these into meaningful patterns as he or she grows older.

Finally, the part of the brain that handles sight passes along the information it receives to the parts of the brain that direct action. These messages tell us to duck when an object is thrown at us, or to walk around a pile of rubble that is in our path.

Human eye structure

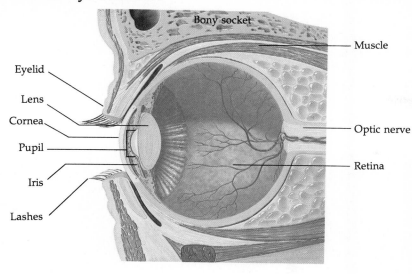

Bony socket

Muscle

Eyelid

Lens

Cornea

Pupil

Iris

Lashes

Optic nerve

Retina

Color Vision

Color vision is handled by the cones in the retina. Each of about eight million cones picks out wavelengths of light that make up only one primary color—red or blue or yellow. These primary colors are thought to be mixed to form the hundreds of colors of the spectrum.

In each color that we see, three aspects can be perceived. The first is the **hue.** This is the family of color. The hue is the color's quality of being red, or blue-green, or some other color. The second aspect is the color's **brightness.** This refers to the lightness or darkness of the color. The third aspect of a color is its **saturation**—the purity of the hue. This has to do with the amount of gray we see mixed with the pure color.

Suppose, for example, you were looking at something painted a pure, bright, orange color. Its *hue* would be halfway between red and yellow, because that's what orange is. Its *brightness* would show it as neither light orange nor dark orange. Its high color *saturation* would show no gray.

Lighter, darker, or grayer mixtures of any combination of hues make many colors possible. The many aspects of color affect people in different ways. People often associate different perceptions and even moods with variations of the same color. Spending hours in rooms that are bright red may have a different psychological effect on a person from the effect of being in rooms that are pale pink, although both colors have the same hue.

It's Your Turn

If you ever walked into a movie theater after the show started, you probably had a hard time, at first, seeing which seats were occupied and which were not. In fact, not much around you was visible as you felt your way down the aisle. The reason: you had just come from a well-lighted lobby or street, and the pupils of your eyes were set for the greater amount of light. But in a short time, as your pupils opened wider to let in the dim light inside the theater, you began to see things quite clearly. Your eyes adapted to the darkness. This dark adaptation, or night vision, is an example of how our senses adapt to changing conditions in the environment. Now *It's Your Turn.* Give another example of sensory adaptation.

Certain people can't see differences among colors. These people are color-blind. Being color-blind is caused by damage to the cones in the retina. Some people have red-green color-blindness, and others have blue-yellow color-blindness. Some people are totally color-blind; they see everything in shades of gray. People with red-green color-blindness see only blue and yellow hues along with grays. Those with the blue-yellow type see green and red and shades of gray.

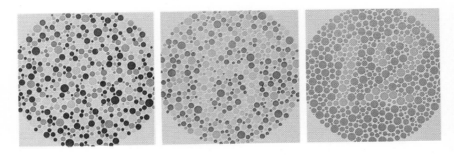

The charts at right are used to test for color-blindness. If you have normal color vision, you will be able to see in the circles from left to right, a 26, a 6, and a 12.

Hearing: The Full-Circle Sense

Unlike the eyes, which focus on one thing at a time, the ears give us a full circle of contact with the world. Sensations come to the ears in waves of dense and thin air. These waves come from pressure differences made by a sound from a source such as the human voice, a bell, or a musical instrument.

If a boulder plunges into the Grand Canyon, and no human or animal life is present, does the boulder make a sound? Yes, it does, but there is no hearing. Hearing takes place when the sound waves are perceived through a sensory receiver. Sound waves send their message through the ear and through a nerve to the brain. How does this come about?

The sound waves enter the outer part of the ear. They are funneled to the eardrum, a membrane at the entrance to the middle ear. The eardrum vibrates. Its vibrations are carried through three middle-ear bones and through another membrane to the inner ear. At the inner

Below, this page: A sound spectogram, showing the pattern of sound waves from a human voice; opposite page, the sound waves made by a bell.

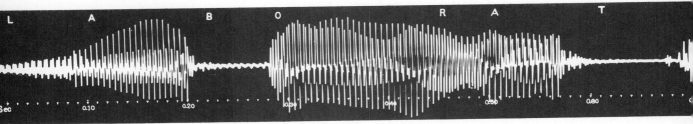

108

Human ear structure

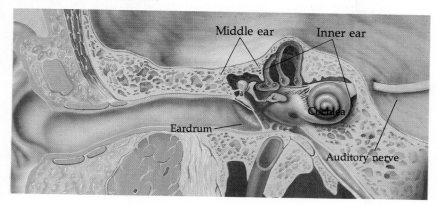

ear, in the cochlea, the real work begins. Fluid in the cochlea moves in the rhythm of the sound waves. Vibrations bend tiny hair cells inside the cochlea, and they activate nerve impulses in the auditory nerve. These nerve impulses travel along the auditory nerve to the hearing portion of the brain.

How Sounds Differ

But sounds aren't all alike. When someone plucks the D-string on a guitar, the sound is different from what is heard when the E-string is plucked. And the sound of D on a guitar is easy to tell from the D on a flute, or a person singing D on a musical scale. Sounds sent to the brain are sorted out. They are identified as having qualities of pitch, loudness, and timbre.

Pitch. The **pitch** of a sound is how high or low it is. The faster sound waves vibrate, the higher the pitch. Pitch can be determined by measuring the *frequency* with which waves follow one another. Frequency can be seen on such things as sound spectograms, which show sound energy as visible lines. One is pictured below.

Loudness. The volume of a sound is its **loudness.** Loudness reflects the sound's intensity. On a spectogram, the height of a wave reflects the amount of energy it has. The more *height* the wave has, the

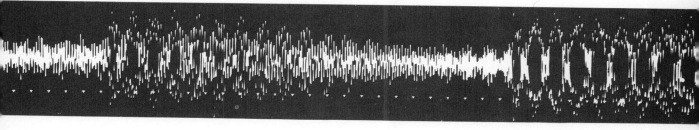

louder the sound. Loudness is measured in **decibels.** Leaves rustle at 12 decibels. Ordinary conversation is carried on at 50 to 60 decibels. Jet planes take off at 115 or more decibels. Long exposure to loud sound is believed to cause permanent damage to hearing.

Timbre. A guitar string vibrates not only as a whole, but also in quarters, thirds, and other parts, all at the same time. We hear *overtones* of the sound. The pattern of overtones gives the sound its special timbre. **Timbre** is the complexity or unique pattern of each sound wave.

The pitch, loudness, and timbre of sound waves make it possible to tell one sound from another.

Other Senses

Because the seeing and hearing senses are used so much, we may tend to forget how important the other senses are. Without the cutaneous, or skin, sense, however, people would not feel pain, cold, or warmth. We pay even less attention to the balancing sense and the kinesthetic sense because they seem to be so automatic. The balancing sense gives us the directional ability that tells us whether or not we are right side up, and warns us if we are about to fall. The kinesthetic, or muscle sense, makes us aware of pressure and movements inside us, and lets us know the position of our arms and legs. Much of the time these senses carry messages that cause us not merely to *feel* the stimulus, but to perceive its meaning, and to respond in some way.

The eye—it cannot choose but see;
We cannot bid the ear be still;
Our bodies feel, where'er they be,
Against or with our will.

These lines from a poem by William Wordsworth and the illustration on the opposite page suggest how our senses are constantly being bombarded by messages from the environment. Sometimes, the vast quantity of messages coming in through our senses makes it difficult for our brain to keep up with its function of sorting out sensations. Psychologists call this situation *sensory overload.* The result of sensory overload is physical fatigue and mental stress.

Opposite page: A rock concert is designed to appeal to not only our hearing sense but our visual sense as well.

Taste

Smell

Olfactory nerve fibers

Bulb of Olfactory nerves

To Olfactory center of the brain

Taste and smell are sometimes called the chemical senses because they respond to chemical sensations rather than to sensations produced by light or sound energy. Research indicates that there are only four basic taste sensations—sweet, sour, salty, and bitter. These are centered in different areas of the tongue, as the illustration on page 111 shows. The many different tastes we perceive are combinations of these four basic tastes.

Other research shows that there are six basic odors—flowery, putrid or rotten, fruity, spicy, burned, and resinous. These odors enter your nose as gases. These gases are picked up by olfactory nerve fibers (shown in the illustration on page 111) which signal the olfactory nerves to send impulses to the olfactory center of the brain.

Section Review

1. Describe the process of vision from the cornea to the brain.
2. What are the three aspects of color?
3. Describe the process of hearing.
4. What are three qualities of a sound?

PREVIEW

In this section, read to find out:

1. what influences our perceptions.
2. how we locate sounds and objects in space.
3. how we judge distances.

2. Perception: Interpreting What We Sense

Sensation of the world around us is the first step toward "taking it all in." The second step is perception—interpreting what we sense. When we perceive anything, many influences can affect our interpretation. In this section, we will consider first some general factors that affect the way we perceive and then some techniques we all use as we perceive.

General Influences on Perception

Imagine you live in a medium-sized city and friends from New York visit you for the first time. You proudly show them the local skyscraper—a 15-story building called the Tower. Your friends, however, are not impressed. "Where we come from," they say, "that would be a small building."

Experience and perception. Perception of height, as of many other things, is relative. Your friends' perception of skyscrapers has been formed by seeing 100-story buildings. People respond to events by relating them to previous experiences of a similar nature.

Past experience influences perception in a number of ways. What we expect is one way. It is called a **perceptual set.** We get ready to perceive an event. For example, when you hear the words *star spangled*, you are ready for the word *banner*. You expect a red traffic light to change to green. Your response may even affect your timing, and you jump the light. Just before a race begins, the racers have an auditory set as the starter's pistol is raised.

Early experiences work in another way. They teach us how to see. Previous experience in a certain environment affects the way we learn to perceive even common forms or shapes—horizontals, circles, angles. Among the Zulu people, there is no word for (and no real concept of) *square* and *rectangle*. The Zulu world is one of round huts with round doors and windows. Villages are laid out in circles. Zulus and certain other groups of people do not perceive angles in the same way that people raised in the "carpentered world" do. Their experience has not taught them to see the world in this way.

Zulu houses and villages

Perception and needs. A second general influence on perception is personal need. The more you need or want something, the more strongly you perceive the things that promise to satisfy that need. A hungry person perceives cues relating to food. A desert traveler suffering from thirst may see water where there is none. Needs do not have to be physical to influence perception.

An object that is important to a person for emotional reasons is likely to be perceived differently from one that is not. An example of this is the "Santa Claus effect." In a study of children's drawings made at different times of the year, researchers found that, as we might expect, with Christmas approaching Santa appeared more frequently. After the holidays, he began to disappear. What we might not expect, however, is that the figure of Santa got bigger as Christmas got nearer and smaller when Christmas was over. Other figures in these drawings did not change size. What do you think these perceptual changes reveal about the children's needs or wants?

Moods, attitudes, values, and perception. Another important influence on perception is a person's mood, attitude, or values. Did you ever get out of bed in the morning "on the wrong side"? For a few hours everything displeases you. Your family's "good morning" sounds insincere. Your egg is overcooked. At school, your teacher seems to frown at you all the time. Then, as the morning passes, you begin to feel better. It occurs to you that you were in a bad mood because you had an argument with a friend the night before. Come to think of it, your family really did mean to wish you a good morning. The egg was as good as ever. Your perception of these events—in this case, your misperception—was influenced by your own mood. It was colored by the way you felt. When your feelings changed, so did your perception. (See the Close-Up, *How Do You Know They're Happy?* on page 119 for a description of an experiment about moods and perception.)

Deeply held beliefs and attitudes affect even more permanently the way people look at the world. In general, we respond to the kind of

Your experiences influence your perceptions. How would the perception of "neighborhood gathering" differ for the people pictured here and on page 115? Why?

environment that agrees with our value system. Our values, in turn, influence the way we perceive the environment, and may even help to change it.

Collective perception. Finally, people's perceptions can be influenced by what others say *they* perceive. Several people may witness the same event. Many of them will not be certain just what they actually saw. If a number of them seem to be quite certain, however, the others are likely to believe that they saw it that way, too. The **collective perception** is trusted more than the person's own individual perception.

Learning to Perceive: Some Tricks of the Trade

Besides these general influences on perception there are some specific techniques, or tricks, we all begin to use at an early age. These techniques influence our interpretation of the sensations coming into us from our environment. They help us locate sounds and objects in space.

Locating sounds. How loud a sound is helps us decide how far away its source is. Because sound energy fades as it travels through the air, we perceive a soft, faint sound as coming from farther away than a loud sound. Because we know that a factory whistle is usually loud, we decide that it is far off if we can barely hear it.

A more important clue to locating sound is the fact that our two ears don't hear most sounds at exactly the same split second. Depending on where we are in relation to the source of the sound, one ear usually receives the sound before the other ear. This difference in time, although very slight, is enough to tell the brain what it needs to know to judge a sound's direction. The ear that is nearer to the sound hears it a bit sooner. The second ear waits for the sound waves to travel past the head. This slight difference signals the direction the sound is coming from. Timing and loudness both help us fix the approximate point where a sound originates.

Locating objects in space. In locating objects in space we use what we know of depth, as we experience the three dimensions of the world around us. You know in a number of ways that the world is three-dimensional. You know it because you move around in it, up and down, forward, back, and to the side. You know it because your balancing sense keeps you right side up in space, and because the sounds you hear come from various distances and directions. Besides all these cues, the brain, in some way that is not fully understood, changes the flat two-dimensional image projected onto the retina into a three-dimensional image. Although perception of space is an inborn capacity, it improves as you grow older, and it can be changed through learning and experience.

A baby's fear of being dropped is one sign of our inborn sense of space. The photos below show a device used to measure the ability to perceive depth visually. A glass floor is over the visual "cliff." An infant can't really crawl over the edge, but the cliff looks so real that it

A newborn goat introduced to the visual cliff walks on the "shallow" end of the glass, but won't venture out onto the "deep" end. An infant won't crawl out on the glass over the cliff, even though he tests it and knows it's solid.

exposes him or her to an apparent fall. Babies as young as ten months stop at the danger line. Visually, they perceive the depth, although they have no earlier experience with falling off cliffs.

Depth perception cues. What we perceive in space are certain objects that relate to each other, to ourselves, and to the total visual field. Psychologists call these relationships *cues.* Six major cues that help us perceive depth are listed below. The photograph on page 116 shows some of the ways these cues work.

1. *Overlay or interposition.* An object that blocks part of another object appears to be closer to the observer. One object is obviously in front of another.

2. *Relative size.* The larger of two like objects tends to be seen as nearer. The one that fills more space seems closer to us.

3. *Relative position.* Near objects usually appear at the bottom of the field of vision and distant objects at the top.

4. *Relative clearness.* Because of dust and other particles in the air, objects far away are less clear. Shadows also create a sense of depth on flat objects.

5. *Linear perspective.* As two parallel lines move farther away from us, they appear to come together. Railroad tracks, for example, seem to come together at the horizon. We know that the tracks are just as far apart a long way off as they are nearby. But in our perception of them, they come together as distance increases.

6. *Known standards.* What we already know about the size or shape of an object guides us in measuring other objects. Because we can guess at the size of a person, we can compare the size of nearby objects.

All of these depth cues are *monocular.* They work well with each eye alone. In everyday experience we ordinarily use two eyes. This *binocular* vision helps depth perception greatly. As you focus on an object, an image falls on each retina. Each image is seen from a slightly different angle by each eye. This difference between what the left eye sees and what the right eye sees is called **retinal disparity.** The brain compares and combines the two images, allowing inspection of objects around and a bit beyond the edges seen by each eye alone.

Section Review

1. Explain three of the general influences on perception. Give an example of each.
2. Discuss the two clues used to locate a sound in space.
3. List and explain four of the perceptual cues used to locate objects in space and to perceive depth.

It's Your Turn

We have seen how many subjective factors influence our perceptions. For example, do you like rock music? If you do, you may not perceive it as being as loud as someone who does not like it (perhaps your parents?). Now *It's Your Turn.* Write an example of a situation in which your perception of an event or object might be influenced by one or more of the general factors that affect the way we perceive.

Visual cues tell us about distance, helping our depth perception. *Size* is a cue, for example. People who look tiny in the picture are farther away. Someone on the left, bent over, seems to be missing a head, because of the *interposition* of a nearer person's shoulder. The *linear perspective* of the aisle, seeming to change from wide at the bottom to narrow farther up, tells us the narrower part is farther away. The *clear outlines* of several hanging bouquets tell us these are closer than the bouquets that appear hazy. Can you find other cues to distance?

3. Organizing Perceptions

As we have seen, many perceptions depend on context. How, when, where, or with whom an event is experienced, or even the mood of the observer, influences the way the event is perceived. However, our senses must agree about certain aspects of the physical world no matter who we are or under what conditions we perceive them. If this were not the case, perception would not give people a reliable way of getting to know the environment. In this section we will look at some ways our senses organize this world consistently and predictably.

Seeing the World As It Is: Perceptual Constancies

One way our senses organize the world is through things that seem the same, time after time. These are **perceptual constancies.** The shape, size, color, and movement of an object, within limits, always appear the same to a viewer, no matter what change there is in other

How Do You Know They're Happy?

The perception of an object or event is often influenced by the surrounding environment. Some years ago at Brandeis University, psychologists Abraham Maslow and N. L. Mintz conducted an experiment using three very different rooms. One room was luxuriously furnished and brightly painted. Indirect lighting cast a mellow glow over the wall-to-wall carpeting. Comfortable lounge chairs invited visitors to make themselves at home. Maslow and Mintz called this the "beautiful room."

Room two was plainly furnished with an ordinary wooden desk, straight-back chairs, a worn rug, some bookcases, and filing cabinets. It was not an unattractive room, but there was nothing special about it, either. This was the "average room."

Room three was a janitor's storeroom. Pails and mops stood in one corner. Wooden crates were used as seats. Light came from a single, dim light bulb that hung from the ceiling. It was small and cramped. This was called the "ugly room."

Groups of students were taken into one of the rooms and shown a set of photographs of people's faces. They were asked to study these faces and then rate them on a scale that ranged from "zestful" and "content" to "weary" and "irritable." The same photographs were shown in all three rooms. Maslow and Mintz had predicted that what a person sees would be greatly influenced by the surroundings in which the act of perception takes place.

Their experiment indicated that this was the case. Students in the "average room" saw the faces pretty much as they were in the photographs. But those in the "beautiful room" found them "zestful" and "content," while students in the "ugly room" rated the faces "weary" and "irritable." Do you think your perceptions are affected by your surroundings? Imagine, for example, that you ride out to your favorite spot overlooking the ocean, and you reach it just about sunset. How might your perceptions be influenced by your surroundings?

conditions, such as distance and angle of viewing. Two important constancies are *size* and *shape*.

Because of size constancy, you perceive a known object to be the same size even when you look at it from different distances. For instance, suppose you see a man standing fifty yards away from you. Is he smaller than a man of the same height who is a few feet away from you? The retinal image cast by the nearby man is much larger. But your eye and brain work together to tell you that the two men are the same height. In perceiving the size of the farther person, you include the distance. In this way you correct for the size difference of the two images on the retina.

You can check this for yourself. Close one eye and hold up a quarter about a foot in front of your other eye. Now turn so the quarter is between your eye and an ordinary lampshade about twelve feet away. The shade has been covered by the quarter!

Why doesn't this tell you that the quarter is bigger than the lampshade? You have corrected the image you perceived to allow for distance. You have also corrected to fit what you already know. You know that lampshades are bigger than quarters, so your perception is not fooled by the apparent similarity in size. However, prior knowledge is not necessary for the perception of size constancy. Tests with babies indicate that this ability is either inborn or learned very early. The shape of an object is also perceived as constant, no matter what angle it is viewed from.

Gestalt Psychology and Perception

At one time, it was believed that we perceive the objects in our environment separately, and then add them together, like pieces of a jigsaw puzzle, to make a whole. This view is no longer widely held.

The principles of **Gestalt** psychology reflect a different approach. Gestalt is a German word that means, loosely, "form" or "configuration." Followers of this school say that we perceive the whole, or the

Similarity **Proximity** **Closure**

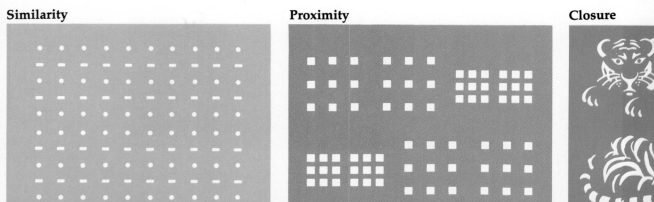

big picture first, and then fit the parts into it. Gestalt psychologists believe that we have built into our minds a natural way of perceiving forms and patterns. Our brain adds a kind of order, in a predictable way, to what we perceive. This happens, according to Gestalt psychology, whether we've had experience in the same field or not. In short, we don't *learn* to see things in those orderly ways. We are born knowing how. Some of the Gestalt principles of organization are similarity, proximity, closure, continuation, and common fate. The illustrations below show examples of these principles.

Similarity. Things that are like each other in color, size, weight, or shape are grouped by the eye because of their **similarity,** even though they are separated by other objects. Your eye picks out the similar objects and perceives them as forming a pattern.

Proximity. Objects that are close together tend to form a pattern by their **proximity,** even though they are not alike. The brain groups things into perceptual units by their closeness to one another.

Closure. The brain fills in gaps to make an unfinished form complete. The brain perceives the parts needed to complete a shape or pattern, even though they are not in sight.

Continuation. The brain *continues* a line or a curve just as it *closes* an incomplete circle. You expect a straight line to continue being straight, not to suddenly become crooked or irregular. Your brain completes the missing parts by relating them to the direction that the senses perceive.

Common fate. Things that move in the same direction are seen as belonging to each other. When alternate dancers in a ballet line step forward and perform the same movement, they are perceived as a unit.

The Gestalt theory of perception says that our environment is organized psychologically, rather than physically. We take random or disorganized items and put them in order. In the Gestalt view, the total that is perceived is always greater than the sum of its parts.

Continuation

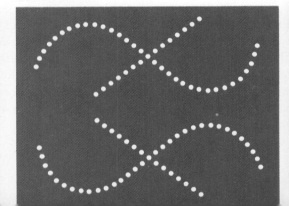

Common Fate

Do you see one white vase or two black faces in profile? Can you see both at once? Read on to find out about this phenomenon.

Perceptual Illusions

Much of what we know about visual space perception has been learned from experiments in which the environment is seen in an abnormal way. The normal process in visual perception can be better understood if we study the kinds of errors and compensations caused by optical **illusion.**

Before the start of the century, a psychologist invented a pair of eyeglasses with lenses that seemed to turn the world upside down. When he first wore the glasses, he had trouble orienting himself to his environment. The world looked strange, and he felt dizzy. After a while, however, he became used to this different ordering of things and was able to move about quite easily. Visual space now agreed with his new expectations. People who have worn lenses of this kind find that they can even ride a bicycle. They become unaware that their visual world is, in fact, upside down.

Experiments have shown that the eye and brain in human beings are remarkably flexible. People can adjust the *normal* way they see the world. Such adjusting occurs to us in more ordinary ways. We see it when we adapt to strange environments. In fact, if you have ever been fitted with new eyeglasses, you know that it takes a few days, or even weeks, to get used to them. In time, however, your brain adjusts to the different environment and makes the corrections that are needed.

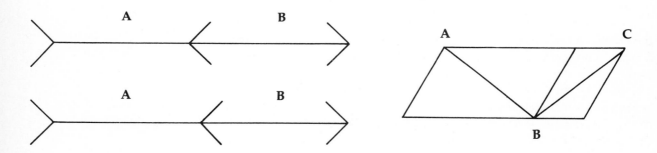

On the other hand, the ease with which the eye can be fooled is seen in the illustrations above. Two commonly used illusions show that the apparent length of a line can depend upon related cues. In the Muller-Lyer illusion (left) parts A and B of the upper horizontal line look about equal in length, but they are not. On the lower line A and B look different, but they're the same. Measure them and see. In the parallelogram (right) the diagonal line that goes from A to B looks longer than the one from B to C, but they are equal.

Illusions give us perceptual cues that conflict with one another. In the distorted room shown above, we see a person grow tall by walking from one side of the room to another. The conflict is resolved in favor of our past experience with rooms, which are normally rectangular. It is simply easier to see a "wrong" size person than the actual, distorted shape of the room. Other illusions, or misperceptions of reality, are shown on pages 124 and 125.

Perception of Field

In everyday perception, we don't usually see objects in isolation. They are generally part of a much larger picture or field. The brain does not perceive all parts of the field as having equal significance. It must pick out a pattern. To do this, the brain depends on the visual cues described earlier and other perceptual cues. It sets off some things in the field, for example, for easier study.

The figure-ground relationship. A common example of how we set off certain objects before us for easier viewing is called *figure-ground relationship*. It means that any time we look about us, certain things stand out more than others simply by where they are located within the field of vision. In perceiving what is around us, we tend to separate a figure from the background that is behind it. The eye searches for these clues to understanding.

Sometimes, figure and ground are not easy to tell apart. This is what happens when something is camouflaged. The foreground object seems to disappear because it has taken on the colors and design of the

Can people grow taller simply by crossing a room? See the diagram below for an explanation of how your eyes are fooled by this illusion.

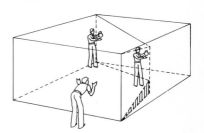

background. In other cases, the eye changes *figure* into *ground* and back again. This is because the visual cues can be read either way. Look closely at the illustration on page 122. Do you see a white vase or two black faces in profile? Can you make it change? Note that only one image or the other stands out at any one instant of viewing. What you perceive as background one minute is changed by your eye into the central figure the next.

Selective attention. One reason we are able to separate figure and ground, and see two objects in each of these examples, is because of what our senses are able to do. They can decide which parts are important and which are not, tuning out the messages that don't count in favor of the ones that do. In short, we perceive what we need to perceive. This is called **selective attention.** Your brain can divide its attention to some extent. For example, you might be able to read a book while the radio is on. Your brain tunes down the music and devotes most of its attention to the book. In this way you are able to concentrate on a task in spite of background static.

To perceive efficiently, the senses constantly help each other out. In a pitch-dark room, you *feel* your way to the light switch. If you look at imitation brick wallpaper, you may have to *touch* the paper to discover that it is really smooth. Sometimes if a sense organ isn't working at all, another organ will take over part of its work. When a blind person taps

At first, what's going on in the pictures on these pages appears unremarkable—until you notice that there is a Martian peeking out of the can the sanitation worker is carrying (below), that there are ''burglars'' sliding down from the roof of the store (opposite page, top), and that the tunnel is really on the back of a building (opposite page, bottom). These illusions were all created by artists.

124

a cane along the street, he or she is not only feeling the way but, more importantly, hearing it. The quality of the echo from the tapping cane tells whether objects are nearby or how far away an intersection is. Often, if one sense is lost, the others can become stronger.

Section Review

1. What is meant by size and shape constancy?
2. Describe three of the Gestalt principles of organization.
3. What are optical illusions?
4. What is meant by selective attention?

4. Extrasensory Perception

PREVIEW

In this section, read to find out:

1. what ESP is.
2. the types of ESP.
3. how we can study ESP scientifically.

Up to now, we have been considering ideas about *normal* perception. Some things that happen, however, seem to involve perception outside the field of what we think of as normal. For example, a university student claimed that he could *visit* different places with his consciousness while his body remained where it was.

To parapsychologists—who study perceptions that appear to occur outside the normal sensory channels—this action, if it really exists, is known as an *out-of-body* experience. It is one of several types of extrasensory perception **(ESP).** ESP is perception that cannot be explained by ordinary sensory means.

Types of extrasensory perception. There are several types of ESP, including: telepathy, clairvoyance, premonition, and psychokinesis.

1. *Telepathy* is mind-to-mind communication. Sometimes it is called mind reading. It involves one person sending a message directly to another person's mind without the use of any of the normal five senses.

2. *Clairvoyance*, or second sight, involves knowing something about an object or event a person could not know about through any normal channels. For example, knowing that a friend was in an accident hundreds of miles away while it was happening might be described as clairvoyance.

3. *Premonition* is knowledge of the future. It is being able to predict things before they happen.

4. *Psychokinesis*, or *levitation*, is control of objects by an act of thought or will. It may involve moving objects with the power of the mind alone. These experiences are sometimes collectively referred to as *psi* phenomena.

Most psychologists are skeptical of claims made for ESP. To believe that people can bypass the sense organs and send or receive messages, even from the dead, contradicts everything we know about the physical nature of perception and communication. To investigate the possibility of this power on the part of certain individuals or "psychics," scientists have set up stiff laboratory tests.

Experiments with ESP. In the case of the university student who said he could visit somewhere else without taking his body along, several "detection labs" were set up about a half mile from his "launch site" on the university campus. Assistants who monitored these experiments were not told when the out-of-body experiences were to take place or which lab his free-floating self would visit. The student was given instructions only a few minutes before the launch. Then he was told what he was to do during his *visit*. The results of several extended trials were intriguing, if inconclusive. Human detectors felt the student's "presence" more often than would be accounted for by chance, although not by a wide margin. However, a kitten that he had handled earlier stopped crying and became contented when the student was "present" in an out-of-body experience.

Remarkable deeds of "psychic power" are claimed by Uri Geller, the young Israeli who appears to be able to mend broken watches, bend spoons, and perform other psychokinetic acts simply by concentrating on the object. Tested by a group of researchers at Stanford University,

Israeli entertainer, Uri Geller, appears to possess amazing powers of psychokinesis. Below he holds a key he has bent with his "thoughts."

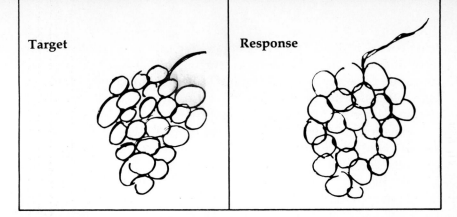

Target | **Response**

Target

Response

At the Stanford (California) Research Institute, researchers asked Uri Geller to use his powers to reproduce drawings they had hidden from his view. Above are their target (original) drawings and Geller's responses.

Geller was found to have "paranormal," or extra-normal, powers. Other psychologists, however, said the tests lacked tight controls. Magicians who have watched Geller perform as a professional entertainer say his acts are really sleight-of-hand tricks.

Another person investigated by the same group of psychologists tested high in clairvoyance. This retired policeman described events taking place while they were happening hundreds of miles away.

During the 1930s and 1940s thousands of experiments in telepathy were carried out. In a typical experiment, 5 cards were used, each with a different geometric shape on it. The tests were run by having a sender look at one of the cards while a receiver "guessed" which symbol was being looked at on each of 200 trials. The receiver could not see either the sender or the cards. If the guesses were completely random, a correct guess or *hit* would occur in an average of 1 out of every 5 trials. In 200 trials, then, chance alone would account for forty hits. Most of the people tested did no better. But a few people scored higher, time after time. Some people's power to perceive objects concealed from them seems far greater than can be explained by pure chance.

Research into the paranormal, no matter how well controlled, doesn't really *prove* things. Mainly, it allows us to reject other explanations of what is being studied, while encouraging our confidence in a particular explanation. Often, a study is affected by unconscious attitudes and biases on the part of the researchers. A major criticism of parapsychology research is that the people conducting it are too eager to prove the existence of ESP. As scientists, they are said to be less skeptical than they should be.

Judging Research

Evidence to support claims for ESP must pass the test of four basic research methods.

1. All other possible explanations for ESP must be ruled out. In the

card experiments, you would have to know that the sender did not consciously or unconsciously select the cards that the receiver seemed to "guess" most often, as this would raise the score.

2. High-scoring subjects must do about as well when tested in different laboratories by independent investigators.

3. The particular research method must be able to get similar results when used with the same subject at different times or by different investigators.

4. It should be possible to create research procedures that do more than expect us to infer that ESP is being used, because of the laws of probability. If ESP exists, it must have other measurable characteristics. For instance, if psychokinesis can be used to bend spoons and fix watches, its effects should also be measurable by scientific instruments. So far, no such tests have been performed. Until this is done, the evidence is incomplete.

Although there are some fairly well-documented examples of ESP, most of what we hear about it comes to us second-hand. And what we witness in person often depends as much on our own state of mind as it does on the mind of the "psychic." Many people have a strong desire to believe that the impossible is possible. The will to believe can greatly influence our perception of an event. Also, if we take part in an ESP experiment, maybe we are too involved personally to be objective. When someone "reads" our thoughts, sometimes we are so impressed with the few correct answers that we tend to ignore the misses.

The power of suggestion is another important factor in our willingness to believe. Seances are especially good at creating a mood that overrides the familiar perceptual processes. Dim lighting and haunting music help convince the sitter that the table is, indeed, moving, or that "voices" from the dead are coming through. A person's desire to communicate with a departed loved one also contributes to belief. And if the individual is part of a group, group consensus may play a part.

Until all types of ESP are more thoroughly investigated by neutral scientists, evidence for psychic power must be regarded as open to question. It may be that our "sixth sense" is really our other five senses playing tricks on us.

Section Review

1. Define ESP.
2. List three types of ESP.
3. Describe four tests ESP research should pass in order to be acceptable.

Chapter 4 Review

Section Summaries

1. Sensation: How It Works

Most of what we know about the world comes through the five senses—sight, sound, touch, taste, and smell. The sensation of sight begins when the eye's cornea, iris, and lens gather and focus light upon the retina. Within the retina, cones handle color vision and rods provide night and side vision. Signals from the rods and cones come together in the optic nerve, which sends nerve impulses to the brain, where they are decoded. In people who are not color-blind, the cones are able to distinguish hue, brightness, and saturation.

The sensation of hearing begins when sound waves in the air enter the outer ear and cause the ear drum to vibrate. The ear drum carries the vibrations to the three bones of the middle ear, which send the vibrations to the fluid-filled cochlea of the inner ear. There the vibrations move tiny hair cells, which then create nerve impulses in the auditory nerve, which sends them to the brain. Sounds differ in pitch, loudness, and timbre.

2. Perception: Interpreting What We Sense

Perception is the interpretation of sensation. General influences on perception include perceptual set, personal needs, moods, attitudes, and values, as well as collective perceptions. In addition, specific clues help us locate sounds and objects in space.

3. Organizing Perceptions

The perceptual constancies of size and shape help people organize their sensations. Some of the Gestalt principles of organization are similarity, proximity, closure, continuation, and common fate. Studying optical illusions has helped psychologists identify visual and perceptual cues that aid visual space perception. Perceptual cues include figure-ground relationships and selective attention.

4. Extrasensory Perception

Parapsychologists study extrasensory perception. ESP includes telepathy, clairvoyance, premonition, and psychokinesis, or levitation. Most experiments in ESP have been inconclusive, and the researchers have been doubted because they were not skeptical enough. To be accepted, ESP research results should pass four basic tests. Witnesses are not trusted because their perceptions may be fooled by the situation or by the power of suggestion.

Psychology Skill Activities

1. Blindfold your eyes for one hour. What sensory experiences do you notice that you would not usually notice? Report to your class. **easy**

2. Choose several paintings from a museum or from an art book. Analyze them from the standpoint of visual cues mentioned in this chapter. **challenging**

Testing for Understanding

Knowing Key Terms

Define these terms in your own words.

Section 1
perception
sensation
cones
rods
hue
brightness
saturation
pitch
loudness
timbre

Section 2
perceptual set
collective perception
retinal disparity

Section 3
perceptual constancies
Gestalt
similarity
proximity
illusion
selective attention

Section 4
ESP

Reviewing Main Ideas

Section 1
1. Name the senses that are usually called the "five senses."
2. Explain how the eye works.
3. Describe color vision and the three aspects of color people can perceive.
4. Describe the process of hearing.

Section 2
1. List some general influences on perception and give an example of each.
2. Describe some of the ways we locate sounds and objects in space.
3. Explain some depth perception cues.

Section 3
1. What are two important perceptual constancies and how are they used?
2. What are some Gestalt principles of organization?
3. Why are illusions useful to psychologists?

Section 4
1. How is ESP different from ordinary human perception?
2. The general term "ESP" includes which categories of experiences?
3. Explain the tests that are used to judge support for claims about ESP.

Thinking Critically
1. *Drawing Conclusions.* People who visit a "psychic" in hopes of making contact with a dead but loved person often come away satisfied. Why do you think this is so?   **easy**
2. *Problem Solving.* What problems could color-blindness cause for an individual? How could a color-blind person overcome these problems?   **challenging**

Demonstrating Psychology Skills
Look at this enlarged sample from a computer printout. Which Gestalt principles let you see words instead of random dots?

Paris in the the spring.

Look again at this sample. Did you catch the mistake? If not, what perceptual influences or cues might have been at work?

It's Monday, 10:00 A.M., and you are sitting at your desk in English class. The teacher is discussing the next day's assignment. Some students are asking questions. Some are listening quietly. Others stare into space, occupied with their own thoughts. You try to follow the discussion, but your mind keeps drifting away. You think about your friends, the past weekend, the book you're reading. Suddenly, a sharp piercing sound interrupts your thoughts. You gather up your things, and you are out of your seat and on the way to your next class before you realize what you're doing!

Everyone has probably experienced this reaction at one time or another. The class dismissal bell rings, and without thinking, you're on your way. Is jumping up at the sound of a bell an inborn human response? No, it's *learned* behavior. Years of schooling have taught us that there is a connection between these two events—the bell sounding and the dismissal of class. Such a strong association has been formed between these events, in fact, that when we hear the bell, we automatically *assume* that class is dismissed. (Teachers who try to continue long after the bell *know* the strength of this association. They find themselves addressing an empty classroom!)

Not only do we learn the association between the bell ringing and the dismissal of class, we also learn the effect these events have on us: "Class is dismissed; now I move on to the next class." We learn to make the response that is appropriate to this event and necessary to get us to the next class on time. This is a second kind of association we learn— the association between our behavior and its consequences: "If I do not get to my next class on time, there may be unpleasant consequences."

The study of learning processes is basic to any understanding of human behavior. For the most part, we *learn* to be human beings, to live with others, to attend, to perceive, to reason, to relate, and to act. The following chapter focuses primarily on two patterns of learning—classical conditioning, or learning by association, and operant conditioning, learning by consequences. Studying these learning processes can help you to understand more about how you have learned in the past and what you will learn in the future.

1. Learning: What It Is and Isn't

Learning appears to be a simple idea. You wouldn't think it would be difficult to recognize. Look at the two pictures below. Do they show learning?

PREVIEW

**In this section,
read to find out:**

1. what learning is.
2. what stimulus-response relationships are.

A

B

If you said that picture "A" doesn't show learning, that's one correct answer for you. You don't have to *learn* to pull your hand away from something hot as the child in the picture is doing. This is a **reflex,** an automatic inborn response. The child might be learning to be cautious around stoves in the future, because they might be hot. But the picture doesn't show this.

Learning *might* be taking place in picture "B," but we can't know for certain. The only way we can tell that learning has occurred is by observing the behavior of the learner. The woman in picture "B" might be learning something, but she isn't exhibiting any *behavior we can see* that shows learning has taken place.

By the same token, you might say you *learned* the material you were assigned in history class this week. But, a psychologist would say that it is impossible to know whether you learned your history or not until you demonstrated you learned it by your behavior—such as passing a test on the material.

Psychologists have developed complicated definitions of learning. Most of the definitions include the following ideas.

a. Learning is a change in mental state. It goes on *inside* the learner.
b. Learning can't be seen directly. You can tell that it has taken place only by observing the behavior of the learner.
c. Learning involves a change in behavior.
d. Learning results from experience.
e. Learning is relatively permanent.
f. Learning can be applied from one situation to another. Because of this, learners can adapt to new conditions.
g. Learning need not involve direct experience. It can come from watching and listening to others or from reading about ideas and concepts.

A short definition of **learning** as psychologists mean it is a relatively permanent change in behavior that results from experience.

Stimulus-Response Relationships

Most theories of learning are based on the concept of making associations between what psychologists call stimuli and responses. A **stimulus** is anything in the environment that brings about a reaction in an animal or human. A **response** is the activity of the human or animal that occurs because of a stimulus. Stimulus-response relationships generally follow one of two basic patterns.

1. A stimulus can precede a *response*. For example, the *stimulus* of hunger pangs can cause an infant to *respond* by crying. The class dis-

missal bell is the *stimulus* that causes your *response* of leaving the classroom. A psychologist could say that, in this case, a stimulus *elicits* or *evokes* a response. This means that a stimulus causes or produces a response. This process is often expressed this way [S→R].

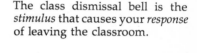
The class dismissal bell is the *stimulus* that causes your *response* of leaving the classroom.

2. Sometimes a response occurs in anticipation of a stimulus. For example, the baby whose hunger stimulated him or her to respond by crying soon learns that crying is followed by the appearance of a concerned adult. So baby learns to *use* the response of crying to get the stimulus of adult attention—to be picked up, held, cuddled. Baby has learned that association between the response he or she makes and the consequences it has on the environment. An association in which a response evokes a following stimulus is expressed this way [R→S].

These kinds of stimulus-response relationships form the basis of much of the discussion that follows in this chapter.

Section Review

1. Give a definition of learning as psychologists mean the term.
2. Describe two behavior changes that are not considered "learned." Explain why not.
3. Explain the meaning of this statement: "A stimulus elicits a response."
4. Describe the basic kinds of stimulus-response relationships.

PREVIEW

**In this section,
read to find out:**

1. what Pavlov did.
2. how Pavlov's most
famous experiment
was carried out.
3. what classical
conditioning is.

2. Pavlov: The Case of the Drooling Dogs

Probably the most famous study of learning based on the association of stimuli was conducted, not by a psychologist, but by a Russian biologist named Ivan Pavlov. Pavlov began experimenting with animal behavior shortly before 1900. His discoveries about learning are even more remarkable when we consider that he was really studying something else—how dogs digest their food.

Old Responses to New Signals: When the Bell Tolls

In his laboratory studies of digestion, Pavlov wanted to measure the amount of saliva that was produced when meat powder was offered to dogs. To do this, he ran tubes from the dogs' mouths into containers designed to catch their saliva. Food, such as meat, stimulated the flow of saliva. After a time, Pavlov observed that saliva began to flow even before the meat was put into the dogs' mouths. (When you salivate at the sight of a sizzling pizza, you say your "mouth waters." Just the sight of food is enough to stimulate the saliva glands.) It became clear to Pavlov that even the sight of the food dish or the sound of an assistant's approaching footsteps caused the dogs' mouths to water. The dogs acted as if they knew food was on the way! Two different kinds of stimuli had become associated in the animals' minds. New stimuli, the footsteps, the food dish, had become associated with the old stimulus—food.

Pavlov and his staff demonstrating his conditioned learning experiment

But what happened if Pavlov took away the old stimulus and the food didn't arrive after the footsteps? As he expected, the dogs drooled anyway—at least for a while. Next, Pavlov started giving the meat after sounding a bell. Soon the dinner bell alone produced salivation because the dogs expected it to be followed by food. The dogs were responding to a learned association (the bell and food). In short, the dogs had been conditioned. They had transferred their normal response of salivation from an appropriate stimulus—food—to a previously inappropriate stimulus—a bell. This observation became the core of Pavlov's theory.

Basic Principles of Classical Conditioning

Pavlov's experiments have become the model for what is called **classical conditioning** ("classical" because those experiments set the standard for later research along the same lines), or learning by association. Classical conditioning involves associating different kinds of stimuli: unconditioned and conditioned.

An unconditioned stimulus (abbreviated UCS) is one that causes an unconditioned response (UCR)—a natural response—without learning. The food causing salivation was the unconditioned stimulus causing the natural, or unconditioned, response.

A conditioned stimulus (CS) elicits a response that has been learned. It is the result of experience. In Pavlov's experiment, the bell was the conditioned (learned) stimulus, learned only because it became associated with the unconditioned stimulus of food. This association is the key to classical conditioning. Dogs have no inborn desire to listen to bells or to respond to them by salivating. This association had to be learned. As the dogs' natural reaction to the food (UCS) was called the unconditioned response (UCR), Pavlov called the dogs' reaction to the bell alone (CS) a conditioned response (CR). Now, the unconditioned stimulus was no longer necessary to produce the response. As a result of experience and association, the conditioned stimulus comes to take the place of the unconditioned stimulus. See the illustration below.

It's Your Turn

Now that you are aware of the basic principles of classical conditioning, learning by association, you can probably think of many things in your own life that you or those you know have learned through this process. For example, if you own a dog, this may sound familiar to you—"Whenever anyone in our family uses the electric can opener, our dog comes running into the kitchen. He has learned to associate the sound of the can opener (CS) with his canned dog food (UCS). He even comes running when it's not his food being opened—and is often disappointed!" Now *It's Your Turn*. Write an example of classical conditioning in your life. Label the UCS, UCR, CS and CR.

Unconditioned Stimulus **(UCS)**
(food) ➡ Unconditioned Response **(UCR)**
(salivation)

{ Conditioned Stimulus **(CS)**
(bell)
+
Unconditioned Stimulus **(UCS)** }
(food) ➡ Unconditioned Response **(UCR)**
(salivation)

Conditioned Stimulus **(CS)**
(bell) ➡ Conditioned Response **(CR)**
(salivation)

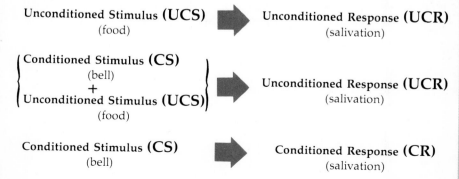

Our Experience with Paired Stimuli

Pavlov's scientific approach to conditioning explains a great deal about our own everyday experience with paired stimuli. When you go to the movies and the lights are suddenly lowered, you stop talking to your friends and wait for the film to begin. When driving, if you hear a siren, you pull to the side of the road because you know that an emergency vehicle is approaching. A person who has never seen a movie or heard a siren would not have these responses.

We all learn to associate a variety of signals. We make learned associations every day. Some are natural, some human-made. But they all have two things in common: (1) the signal (stimulus) and the thing signaled (response) have been experienced close enough together in space and time that we see them as related; and (2) they occur together frequently enough to provide a consistent and reliable pattern. Learning these associations helps us make sense of the sights and sounds that confront us from morning to night.

Expanding Pavlov's Research

Pavlov's work encouraged psychologists to carry out conditioning experiments of their own. These experiments led to more discoveries about conditioned learning. Four of the most important discoveries follow.

Generalization. Psychologists have found that when two or more stimuli are similar, animals respond to all of them in the same way. This is called **generalization.** For example, when Pavlov's dogs had been conditioned to a particular bell, they would also produce the conditioned salivary response when hearing any similar bell tone. In humans, a baby who is frightened by a man with a beard may thereafter be frightened of all men with beards.

Generalization is useful because it allows us to apply what we've learned in one situation to other similar situations. Once we learn that a siren means an approaching emergency vehicle, we have little trouble adjusting to the different siren sounds of different vehicles. We can even generalize from one person to a group of people. If someone we dislike has red hair, we may carry this dislike over to all people with red hair—no matter how unfair this is. Thus, generalization is not always a good thing. It can lead us to wrong as well as correct judgments of people and events.

Discrimination. In some cases, we do not generalize. For example, we do not usually confuse an emergency siren with a lunch whistle or school bell. We soon learn to make distinctions between two related sounds or recognize the difference between two somewhat similar

DOES THE NAME PAVLOV RING A BELL WITH YOU?

stimuli. We learn to discriminate, or tell the differences among the many different objects in our environment. **Discrimination** is the opposite of generalization.

Discrimination has great value for people. If we had to respond to all stimuli in the same way, regardless of their meaning for us, much of our time and energy would be wasted. We would lack flexibility in coping with the changed environment. Instead, human beings can change their behavior as events change. We respond to the new stimuli and stop responding—or pay less attention—to the old. This ability to discriminate is another example of our flexibility.

Extinction. The processes of generalization and discrimination are not the only variations of classical conditioning. For example, what would happen if dogs were conditioned to drool in response to a bell, and then the psychologist decided not to feed the animals at all after they heard the bell? In other words, the CS would be presented without the associated UCS. Pavlov tried this. The salivation response weakened and eventually disappeared. The dogs stopped responding to the useless bell signal altogether. With people, the process is somewhat complicated by certain factors like memory, desire, and fantasy. Nevertheless, the "out-of-sight, out-of-mind" principle generally tends to prevail for us too. Psychologists call this weakening or fading process **extinction.**

A child who is frightened by a man with a beard, and thereafter is frightened by *all* men with beards, is demonstrating the psychological process of *generalization*.

Spontaneous recovery. Does extinction mean that a response is lost forever? Not at all. The response is suppressed, or hidden, but not gone, Pavlov discovered. After extinction had occurred, Pavlov rang the bell with the food, and then without. Salivation appeared right away, at nearly full strength. The response had not been lost completely. This revival of an extinguished response after a period of non-responding is called **spontaneous recovery.** It is often seen in people who have had a threatening or harmful experience early in life. Many years later, stimuli associated with the danger bring back the original response of fear, even though the new situation does not itself carry a threat. See the Close-Up, *How the Body Remembers When the Mind Forgets,* on page 143 for an example of spontaneous recovery.

Section Review

1. Describe Pavlov's famous experiment with dogs. What was its original purpose? What was Pavlov's important discovery?
2. Give an example of classical conditioning. Label each part of the learning process.
3. Explain how generalization and discrimination could be present in the conditioning situation you gave as an example.

3. Watson: The Case of Anxious Albert

Pavlov showed that simple responses could be called forth by new stimuli as a result of conditioning. But what about more complex human behaviors? Can they be changed by conditioning too? John B. Watson, an American psychologist, thought so. Shortly before World War I, Watson brought Pavlov's ideas to the United States and, in the years that followed, extended their range. He set out to demonstrate that people could be made more loving, more courageous, more fearful—or less so—by planned stimulation from the environment.

Watson and Behaviorism

Watson's belief in the influence of the environment on human behavior was a radical idea in the 1920s. Most psychologists believed then that "instincts" determined much of human behavior. They thought that people's lives were set at birth. Watson disagreed. He saw people as being like putty. He believed that we are all molded by our environment. "Give me a dozen healthy infants," he once wrote, "and my own specified world to bring them up in and I'll guarantee to take any one at random and train him [or her] to become any type of spe-

PREVIEW

In this section, read to find out:

1. how little Albert was conditioned to fear rats.
2. how Peter was conditioned *not* to fear rabbits.

cialist I might select—doctor, lawyer, artist, merchant-chief, and yes, even beggar-man and thief, regardless of his [or her] talents, penchants, tendencies, vocations and race of his [or her] ancestors."

Today we know more about the psychology of learning than Watson did. However, his idea of behaviorism is still important. It means looking at behavior in terms of the environmental conditions that seem to cause it and the consequences of behavior on the environment.

John B. Watson

Learning to Be Afraid

Watson was never given his dozen healthy infants—only one, and just for a brief time. He did demonstrate that a fearless small child could be made very fearful by the way stimuli were presented to him. Little Albert was not quite one year old when Watson and his associates began their experiment. First, they let Albert play with a white rat, a rabbit, a dog, a monkey, a ball of cotton, and some masks. All of these objects were soft and cuddly. Albert had no fear of them. He reached for them all without hesitation.

Then one day, as he presented the rat, Watson made a loud noise behind Albert's head. The loud noise so startled the child that he started to cry. Each day for the next seven days, this act was repeated. By the end of the week, Albert cried and crawled away from the rat as soon as it appeared. He had been conditioned to fear an object (CS) that

Psychologist Mary Cover Jones demonstrated that it was possible to neutralize a child's fear of an animal.

he had not feared before, because it had become associated with a stimulus that naturally caused fear (the loud noise, UCS).

For a week after that no training occurred. At the end of the second week, Albert still showed fear of the rat. This shouldn't surprise us. More interesting, when the rabbit and other furry objects were presented, Albert now feared them too, even though they had never been directly associated with the unpleasant noise. Watson clearly demonstrated one of the principles of learning theory. Albert's reaction (fear) had generalized to similar types of stimuli (the furry objects). Discrimination had taken place too, as shown by the fact that quite different objects, blocks and nonfurry things, brought no such response.

Unfortunately, the boy's parents removed him from the experiment before Watson could carry out his plan to deprogram Albert. Nevertheless, Watson had made his point. Adult fears (and other traits, he believed) must have been learned in this way.

Learning Not to Be Afraid

Another psychologist, Mary Cover Jones, continued Watson's experiment with a three-year-old boy named Peter, who was afraid of rabbits. First, she played with a rabbit herself in the boy's presence, showing him that it did not harm her. This did not reduce his fear.

Mary Cover Jones

She then decided to neutralize Peter's fear of rabbits by introducing a pleasurable stimulus whenever the rabbit was present. One day while Peter was enjoying his food (UCS), the rabbit (CS) was brought just inside the door at the far end of the room. Peter eyed the animal warily but went on eating. Over a period of several days the rabbit was gradually brought closer and closer. Finally, the boy could eat happily with the rabbit beside him—or even in his lap (CR).

The cases of Albert and Peter are simple examples of how behavior is modified through learning. Peter's case also illustrates the method of desensitization used today in some types of therapy. Things that arouse anxiety are associated with an experience that is pleasant, and the anxiety is lessened. Removing the feared object is not enough. Something pleasant must be paired or associated with it.

Watson's ideas are no longer totally accepted. However, his application of classical conditioning to humans is valuable in our study of learning.

Section Review

1. Explain the concept of behaviorism.
2. Describe the process of conditioning used to make Albert afraid of the rat. (Label the stimulus and response.)
3. Describe the process used to eliminate Peter's fear of rabbits.

How the Body Remembers When the Mind Forgets

A person being chased by a dog feels his or her heart pound and pulse race. The unconditioned stimulus signals *danger* and elicits an unconditioned response. (Extra adrenalin is pumped through the person's system, helping him or her to get away.) Later, the person's heart still beats wildly at the sight of a dog—even though it's quite friendly and shows no sign of giving chase. The danger has disappeared, but the adrenalin goes to work anyway.

Why does this rush of adrenalin take place? Apparently, this type of unconditioned response can remain with us in the form of a conditioned response. The conditioned response continues to operate even though it may not be necessary. The conditioned organ has learned too well, and there is little or no extinction.

This process is called *schizokinesis. Schizo* means divided or split. *Kinesis* means action. Schizokinesis is a body response that goes off in two directions. When schizokinesis occurs, a

given stimulus (seeing a dog) no longer causes a coordinated response between the organs that sense danger and those that are mobilized to take action. The original response was so useful that the action organs still get alarmed, even when the threat of danger is no longer real.

How stubbornly our bodies hang on to inappropriate responses was shown in an experiment with hospitalized Army and Navy veterans of World War II. These veterans were exposed to a repetitive gong, sounding at the rate of about 100 percussions a minute. This signal had been used as a call to battle stations aboard U.S. Navy ships during the war. When the Navy veterans heard the gong, their nervous systems—the part that warns us of danger—quickly went into action. They became jumpy and nervous and charged up—even though 15 years had passed since this stimulus had signaled danger. The Army veterans, however, showed little response. They had never been called to battle stations this way.

Battle stations, during a raid on the *U.S.S. Hornet,* February 1945. U.S. Navy photograph

Harvard psychologist B. F. Skinner is well known for his theory of **operant conditioning,** or learning by consequences. This is the second kind of learning included in our study. For many years Skinner's ideas dominated psychological research in the United States. Articles about his ideas still appear in popular magazines and newspapers. Much of Skinner's experimental work has been done with animals. But, like Watson, his primary interest is in the behavior of human beings. Skinner believes that control and modification of behavior through conditioning can be made a precise science.

"Laws" of Conditioned Learning

Whether they are followers of Pavlov, Watson, or Skinner—or influenced by all three—psychologists agree on the following theories, or "laws" of conditioned learning.

a. The basis of conditioning is the law of association. Things that happen together are associated with each other. Whether it is bells and food (in Pavlov's case), frightening noises and furry objects (in Watson's case), school and schedules, or rock music and good times, we learn to associate those stimuli that occur at the same time.

b. Repetition is a part of conditioning. It is true that "one-time learning" takes place. You probably wouldn't need to touch a hot stove more than once to associate that action with a burn. However, it is also true that you will form a stronger association if stimuli are paired several times than if they are paired only once.

c. The third important point about conditioned learning can be put in the words of an old saying: "You can catch more flies with honey than with vinegar." It seems to be true that animals tend to do what feels good and to avoid what feels bad.

The Theory of Operant Conditioning

Operant conditioning theory is based on the fundamental principle that we tend to repeat behaviors that are associated with reward and avoid those that are associated with punishment. This is what we mean by "learning by consequences." The consequences, or results, of what you do will generally determine if you repeat the behavior again. This is true whether your behavior results in reward or punishment.

Classical conditioning and operant conditioning—how they differ. Operant conditioning differs from classical conditioning in two basic ways. The first difference is in the way the psychologists view the learners. Pavlov and his followers looked on their animal subjects primarily as passive, reacting only when a stimulus was given. Classical

"Boy, do we have this guy conditioned. Every time I press the bar down he drops a pellet in." (Adapted by permission from *Jester*, Columbia College.)

conditioning is thus based on a stimulus + stimulus pattern. Through repetition, the animal learns to associate stimulus events. For Skinner and his followers, however, animals are active, repeating those responses that have been followed by a particular stimulus. Thus, operant conditioning follows a response→stimulus pattern. What is learned is the association between behavior (a response) and its consequences (a stimulus).

The second difference lies in the concept of reinforcement, a central idea in Skinner's theory. One way to understand reinforcement is to think of it as a reward. A stimulus that makes the response paired with it more likely to occur again is called a reinforcing stimulus. For example, a rat pressing a lever is rewarded by a bit of food. When the rat presses the lever again to get more food, we infer that the food is satisfying to the animal and is thus a reinforcing stimulus, or reward.

Positive and negative reinforcement. Reinforcing stimuli that seem to give pleasure to the subject are called **positive reinforcements.** On the other hand, the animal will learn to avoid a stimulus that is painful or unpleasant, such as a mild electric shock. The stopping of a painful or unpleasant stimulus is known as **negative reinforcement,** such as shutting off an electric shocking device. This is really a reverse form of reward. In operant conditioning, desired behaviors (responses) are reinforced. Soon the animal (or person) learns to make the response required to receive reinforcement.

A pigeon pecking at a disk in a Skinner box

Skinner observed these behaviors when he experimented with white rats. He put them into "Skinner boxes"—small, bare cages with levers that the rats could press to get food or water. In exploring the box, the rats stumbled on the lever. When pressed, it brought them something to eat or drink. They discovered that they could eat or drink if they pressed the lever. More pressing brought more food or water. The response of lever pressing was reinforced and became more likely to be repeated. Later, Skinner switched to pigeons as subjects. He adapted his box, adding disks that the pigeons could peck at to get their food. Skinner boxes are in use in psychology laboratories all over the country today.

How Operant Conditioning Works

With his boxed-in pigeons, Skinner advanced his theory of operant conditioning in two ways. First, he learned a great deal from the pigeons by observing the way they behaved under various conditions of reinforcement. Second, and just as important, the pigeons learned a great deal from Skinner. They learned, for instance, that food arrived

& & &

See **Exercise 1, Experiments,** on pages 473–475 of the *Psychology Skills Handbook,* for a descrip– tion of how psychologists set up experiments.

Worn and faded jeans might be secondary reinforcers to the peo- ple pictured below. Secondary reinforcers have little value in themselves. They only acquire value when associated with something that *is* important— such as feelings of belonging.

when they pecked at a disk in the box. Pecking at the floor or walls brought no reward.

Skinner decided to take his experiments one step further. He rein- forced disk-pecking only when a green light was on in the box. Could the pigeons learn to associate the green light with food as they had already done with the disk? In other words, could they discriminate? Skinner furnished food only when the animals pecked while the green light was on. Soon the birds pecked only in the presence of the light. In this case, Skinner was teaching the pigeons *when* to respond. The green light was the discriminative stimulus that set the stage for pecking (re- sponse), to be followed by reinforcement (food). [R→Reinforce- ment.]

Primary and secondary reinforcers. For the pigeons, food pellets were satisfying in themselves: they had primary value. The presence of food, therefore, became a **primary reinforcer.** To get the food, the ani- mals had to peck disks and watch green lights, stimuli that in them- selves have no real value for pigeons. It was only after they learned the connection between these objects and food that the pigeons took an interest in them. They became a means to an end. Such stimuli are called **secondary reinforcers.**

Food, sex, avoidance of pain, and a feeling of belonging are exam-

ples of primary reinforcers—"primary" because we do not have to learn to like or dislike them. But suppose you wear blue jeans, not because they keep you warm, but because they are popular with your classmates. They give you a feeling that you "belong," especially if they are worn and faded. In this case, jeans are a secondary reinforcer. Secondary reinforcers have little or no "real value" in themselves. They acquire value only when they are associated with something that already has value. For most of us, money is the most common secondary reinforcer. It is a secondary reinforcer because it buys access to so many different primary reinforcers.

Section Review

1. What is operant conditioning?
2. Explain the difference between classical and operant conditioning.
3. Define positive and negative reinforcement. Give an example of each.
4. Name two primary and two secondary reinforcers.

5. Operant Conditioning: Variations of the Idea

Like classical conditioning, operant conditioning is not simple. There are many important and useful variations of the idea.

Schedules of Reinforcement

Skinner found that once a response is learned, it can be maintained without being reinforced every time. Skinner claims to have discovered this one weekend when his grain supply ran low and he tried to stretch it over more trials with his pigeons than he could reinforce. Skinner was surprised to find that his animals performed as well on partial reinforcement, say one pellet for every other correct response, as they had on continuous reinforcement. In one way, their performance was actually better. The animals that were on partial reinforcement continued to respond longer than those who had reinforcement after every response. This discovery started a whole new line of research on how different schedules of reinforcement would change the rate of responding.

Basically, there are two different types of reinforcement schedules. **Ratio schedules** involve the number of responses that must be made to gain a reward. The other type, the **interval schedule,** has to do with the time that elapses between reinforcements. Each type can be in either a fixed or variable pattern.

PREVIEW

**In this section,
read to find out:**

1. how schedules of reinforcement are used in conditioning experiments.
2. what shaping and chaining are.

It's Your Turn

You have now been introduced to the basic ideas of operant conditioning, learning by consequences. There are many things in your life which you have learned in this manner. For example, as a child your parents may have taught you to eat all your vegetables at dinner by rewarding you with dessert. Now *It's Your Turn*. Give an everyday example of operant conditioning. Label the response and the reinforcement involved.

Ratio schedules

1. *Fixed ratio schedules*. A reward can be offered for a given number of acceptable responses. If every peck by a pigeon is reinforced with a food pellet, that is a one-to-one reinforcement schedule. If food is delivered only on every fourth peck, that is a one-to-four schedule. Factory workers who are paid by the number of items they produce are on a fixed ratio schedule—so much money for each piece of work they turn out.

Response rates on a fixed ratio schedule tend to be steady and high. If a reward is offered consistently, the subject responds consistently. But, of course, pigeons will not remain hungry forever. They eat until they are full and then slow down their response rate. People on piece work will work for additional money only so long. Eventually, they tend to find rest and relaxation stronger reinforcers, and they lower their response rates.

2. *Variable ratio schedules*. The number of responses required before a subject is rewarded can be varied, or changed. For example, a pigeon may be rewarded after the first, the third, and the fifteenth responses. Or the amount of the animal's reward can be varied. It may be one pellet or two or six or seven. The animal has no indication of when the reward is coming or how much it will be.

This schedule is a powerful one. With an unpredictable reward pattern, learners never know when the *big payoff* might come, so they keep responding. Many forms of gambling are examples of variable ratio scheduling. Because there is occasionally a big payoff, the gambling response is reinforced.

Interval schedules

1. *Fixed interval schedules*. If you have a dog or a cat that you feed at regular times, you have probably noticed that it is more active and may start pestering you when mealtime is approaching. It is responding to fixed interval reinforcement—a pattern that follows the clock. Responses during the intervals between rewards are not reinforced, so your pet has learned that only those responses that occur at certain times get rewards.

Children sometimes become "little angels" just before their birthdays or other holidays associated with receiving gifts. You may have found yourself driving a little faster as you near the end of a long trip, or getting hungry as mealtime approaches, even though you have had a substantial snack. All of these responses can be explained as results of fixed interval reinforcement schedules.

When Skinner's pigeons were placed on a fixed interval schedule, they learned to stop responding during periods of no reinforcement.

(Have you ever found that you tend to study more just before an exam and less—or not at all—when you know no exam is due?)

2. *Variable interval schedule.* When the time between rewards is varied, the pigeon or the person doesn't know when, or if, a reward can be expected. Response rates tend to be low with this pattern of reinforcement, but they tend to be persistent.

People who fish know about variable interval schedules. You might catch two beauties in rapid succession and then have to wait hours for the next nibble. With this schedule, any moment could be your lucky one. You keep at it as long as you are occasionally rewarded.

People who fish are responding to a variable interval schedule of reinforcement. On this type of schedule, responses are persistent because people don't know *when* or *if* a reward will come. Diane Nyad, who successfully swam from the Bahamas to Florida in 1979 after two other unsuccessful attempts, was also responding to this type of schedule.

Shaping and Chaining

Everything we have talked about so far has dealt with fairly simple "one-to-one" behaviors (response-reinforcement) relationships. Let's go back now and see how Skinner is getting along with his pigeons. By this time, the pigeons have been conditioned to discriminate between different stimulus conditions and to peck at disks without getting reinforcement every time. But they are not yet using their responses in

STANLEY   By MURRAY BALL

Copyright 1977, Universal Press Syndicate

complex behavior sequences. Now it is time for them to shape up.

Skinner decided to teach pigeons how to bowl. He did this by rewarding their "bowling behavior" with food. Since pigeons are not born bowlers, the trick was to condition this behavior by reinforcing it a step at a time. And this is precisely what Skinner did. The object of the experiment was to get the pigeons to push a miniature ball into the tenpins. Skinner had to link the behaviors the pigeons already knew with this end goal. He did it by means of a whole series of intermediate responses, all moving in the right direction, one step at a time.

With this method, the pigeons learned to roll the ball in the right direction in about two hours. First, they were rewarded for just being near the ball as they waddled about their boxes. This initial response was made through trial and error. Once it was made, however, the pigeons were ready for the next step. Now the reinforcer was given only when the pigeons got very close to the ball, and later when they touched the ball.

Skinner was trying to narrow down the birds' behavior to even more precise responses. The pigeons were no longer rewarded just for coming close to the ball. They had to touch the ball with their beaks. Once the pigeons mastered this, they were rewarded only if they moved the ball and finally only if they moved it in the direction of the pins. By the end of the training, only the whole bowling sequence was followed by a reward. According to Skinner, all complex behavior patterns are built out of simple responses by a process of **shaping.**

Animal trainers have been able to get their subjects to put together elaborate sequences of shaped actions. This is called **chaining.** The polar bear you see riding a bicycle in the circus is a good example of shaping and chaining. The bear had been taught a whole chain of separate behaviors until it eventually learned that it would get a fish only by putting the entire package of responses together.

Behavior patterns like these are involved when we learn a complex series of new responses like driving a car, playing the piano, or dancing. Individual segments are performed, sometimes in rough form. Then they are perfected by selective reinforcement and put together into the final form.

Section Review

1. Your little sister spends hours of her time during the summer collecting bottles to return for deposit. What type of reinforcement schedule would you say she is responding to?
2. Give everyday examples of the other schedules of reinforcement.
3. Describe the process of shaping and chaining.

6. Conditioning: Issues and Applications

One important issue in operant conditioning is the use of punishment instead of reward. **Punishment** is the presentation of an unpleasant stimulus after a response. It makes the response less likely to occur in the future. For example, children reach for an open flame, and we slap their hands away. The dog snatches a steak off the table, and we catch it by the scruff of the neck and scold it. Punishment is often an effective way of stopping a specific behavior, like shouting during class. It is less effective in stopping a general type of behavior, like "being uncooperative." Being uncooperative can mean anything from reading an English book in math class to interrupting the teacher.

To stop a behavior, punishment should be given right away and given every time. It should be severe enough to be worth avoiding but not so severe or prolonged that it causes other undesirable behavior.

The Effects of Punishment

The problem is that punishment may do more harm than good. Research has shown that punishment has certain effects.

1. In the learning of a new response, punishment for errors may slow down learning instead of speeding it up. The learner needs to identify the differences between right and wrong answers, but giving punishment for this purpose may just create anxiety.

2. In getting rid of "bad" behavior, punishment may suppress not only "bad" behavior but "good" behavior too. The young school child who is repeatedly humiliated for clowning in class, for example, may lose all desire to please the teacher or do well in school. He or she may end up with the attitude, "Why should I try at all?"

3. The punished behavior may disappear, only to surface later when the punisher is not around. You have probably known a child who was a "little angel" at home but a bully outside. Parents who punish are often surprised to learn that their child is a troublemaker at school.

4. When human beings, especially children, are punished there is a danger that they will come to think they—rather than their behaviors—are bad, stupid, or clumsy. With such an attitude, they expect to fail. Children who are humiliated often become more concerned with protecting themselves against anxiety than with taking positive action. Such children may become withdrawn. Or they may strike out in retaliation, thereby inviting a new round of punishment. In either case, the punishment becomes self-defeating.

5. If punishment is routinely used as the way to enforce good behavior, children learn no other training method. They see punish-

PREVIEW

In this section, read to find out:

1. what the effects of punishment are.
2. how operant conditioning is used in everyday life.

ment as the appropriate way for those in power to behave. So when they grow up, they treat their own children the same way. Studies have shown that the parents of battered children were usually abused themselves as children.

6. Punishment has an unfortunate effect on the punisher. Giving vent to frustration feels good. Thus, punishing is reinforced, especially if the bad behavior stops. The punisher is more likely to use punishment the next time. This starts a vicious circle in which more punishment is used. The person punished may lose all motivation to do anything but avoid punishment—or get even with the punisher.

If punishment is used, it should be clear that certain behavior will also be rewarded. Research has shown that if children get attention for good behavior, they are less likely to try to get it by bad behavior.

Methods of Behavior Modification

Skinner's work showed that behavior can be influenced by a system of rewards and punishments. It was later proven that many of the principles of conditioned learning that apply to animals also work with human beings. Learning theorists have developed methods for increas-

Case Study

The Premack Principle

Nursery-school children love running and shouting—much more than sitting still and listening in class. The resulting chaos can mean real headaches for their teachers. After pleas, punishment, and a bit of screaming failed, a frustrated teacher turned to a psychologist for help.

What would happen, the psychologist wondered, if sitting still was rewarded by a chance to run and shout? Would there be an increase in sitting-still behavior? This is exactly what happened.

The psychologist created a new set of rules for the children. As before, they were told to sit qui-

etly in their chairs and look at the blackboard. If they did this, the psychologist said, a bell would sound at certain intervals, followed by the order, "Run and scream." At the sound of the bell, the children could then leap to their feet and run around screaming.

Another signal meant the children had to return to their chairs and look at the blackboard. Within a few days, the teacher had almost perfect control of the class.

Psychologist David Premack later used experiments to show that almost any preferred activity can be used as a positive reinforcer. The Premack principle en-

courages parents and teachers to look for reinforcers that will be valued by an individual child.

The Premack principle can also be a powerful tool for self-management. For example, like many people, you may find it hard to study when you would rather visit friends (a preferred activity). The next time this happens, promise yourself a chance to visit—*after* you have studied for a certain length of time. If you do this on a regular basis, you may even learn to associate studying with the pleasure of seeing friends. A Premack maxim: Pleasure before study makes study a pain; pleasure after study makes study a gain.

ing the frequency of desirable behavior and decreasing behavioral problems. These techniques are called **behavior modification.**

Some nursery and elementary schools, for example, use a reward system called a "token economy" approach, which is based on Skinner's ideas. Pupils earn tokens by giving correct answers to questions and by making contributions to classroom activities. Later, these tokens can be exchanged for a number of different prizes or privileges.

Another example of an application of Skinner's ideas is the teaching machine. In human learning, the rewards are less tangible than those given to animals in a Skinner box. The satisfaction of knowing that he or she has given the correct answer is often a powerful reward for a human learner. This is the principle of the teaching machine. Information is divided into small pieces, thus increasing the probability that the learner will be able to answer questions correctly. A bit of information is presented by the machine, and a question is asked about it. If the learner answers correctly, the next bit of information appears, followed by a question about it. If not, the learner tries a different answer and, if necessary, still another. The learner receives immediate positive reinforcement when he or she makes a correct response, and doesn't suffer any embarrassment for making an incorrect response.

Conditioning is also used to change undesirable behaviors into more acceptable ones. Behaviors, from alcoholism to nail biting, have been changed through this approach, often in a fairly short time. An example of this type of conditioning is the use of a tasteless drug called Antabuse in treating alcoholics. Drinking alcohol after taking Antabuse makes the drinker vomit. The unpleasant stimulus (nausea) is paired with a "pleasant" stimulus (alcohol) and the alcoholic learns to avoid drinking.

In one form or another, operant techniques are used in health care institutions and in prisons, as well as in daycare centers, reading clinics, and other educational institutions. In the business world, employers use "behavioral technology" to try to make employees more efficient and happier in their jobs. Rewards come to those who work and who know when to work to gain positive outcomes.

Section Review

1. Discuss the effects of punishment on a learner.
2. "It hurts me more than it does you," has an element of truth in it. How can punishing hurt the punisher?
3. Describe two practical applications of operant conditioning.

Chapter 5 Review

Section Summaries

1. Learning: What It Is and Isn't

Psychologists define learning as a relatively permanent change in behavior that results from experience. Automatic inborn responses, called reflexes, are not learned. Most theories of learning are based on the concept of making associations between stimuli and responses.

2. Pavlov: The Case of the Drooling Dogs

Ivan Pavlov's experiments with dogs shortly before 1900 have become the model for classical conditioning. During classical conditioning, animals and people learn to give the same response to both unconditioned and conditioned stimuli. Later studies showed that animals could both generalize and discriminate between similar stimuli. After a conditioned response has been extinguished, it can be revived. This revival is called spontaneous recovery.

3. Watson: The Case of Anxious Albert

Shortly before World War I, American psychologist John B. Watson tried to prove that classical conditioning could change human behavior. In the 1920s Watson conditioned Little Albert to fear rats and other furry objects. His plan to deprogram Albert was thwarted, however, when Albert's parents took him home. Another psychologist, Mary Cover Jones, later used conditioning to overcome a boy's fear of rabbits. Jones' work is an example of desensitization, which is used in some types of modern therapy.

4. Skinner: The Case of the Pecking Pigeons

B. F. Skinner's theory of operant conditioning holds that we tend to repeat behaviors that are associated with positive reinforcement and to avoid behaviors that are associated with negative reinforcement. Skinner taught pigeons to discriminate and to respond to secondary reinforcers, such as green lights, to obtain primary reinforcers, such as food.

5. Operant Conditioning: Variations of the Idea

Skinner found that conditioned responses could be maintained on two basic types of reinforcement schedules. Ratio schedules involve the number of responses that must be made to gain reinforcement. Interval schedules involve the amount of time that elapses between reinforcements. Each type can be in a fixed or variable pattern. Shaping is used to teach specific behaviors, and chaining is used to teach more complex behavior patterns.

6. Conditioning: Issues and Applications

Although punishment can stop a specific behavior, it is less effective in stopping general types of behaviors. In addition, research has shown that punishment may do more harm than good. Behavior modification uses operant conditioning techniques to increase desirable behaviors and decrease behavior problems. Another application of Skinner's work is the teaching machine.

Psychology Skill Activities

1. List five stimuli that caused you to respond in the last two days. Be as specific as, "I waited for the light to turn green before crossing Elm Street." For each stimulus, explain how you think conditioning affected your behavior. **easy**

2. Make a list of some of your short-term and long-term goals. Then make a list of some classical or operant conditioning techniques you might use to help yourself achieve these goals. For example, you might reward studying with a pleasant activity, such as going to a movie. Try using one or two of these techniques for two weeks. Then report to your class. **challenging**

Testing for Understanding

Knowing Key Terms

Define these terms in your own words.

154

Reviewing Main Ideas

Section 1
1. Describe the characteristics of learning, as psychologists use the term.
2. Explain the two basic patterns of stimulus-response relationships.

Section 2
1. Why do psychologists remember Ivan Pavlov, a biologist?
2. Describe Pavlov's most famous experiment.
3. What is classical conditioning and how does it use generalization, discrimination, extinction, and spontaneous recovery?

Section 3
1. Explain how John B. Watson demonstrated his idea of behaviorism.
2. How did Mary Cover Jones use behaviorism to end a little boy's fear of rabbits?

Section 4
1. Describe the basic process of operant conditioning.

2. Explain how classical and operant conditioning are the same and how they differ.
3. How is positive reinforcement different from negative reinforcement?

Section 5
1. Describe the four schedules of reinforcement and explain how each is used.
2. How and when are shaping and chaining used?

Section 6
1. Which is more effective in learning, reward or punishment? Explain.
2. Describe some applications of operant conditioning.

Thinking Critically
1. *Drawing Inferences.* Describe how a student who mows lawns during the summer for spending money might be paid on each of the following schedules: fixed ratio; variable ratio; fixed interval; variable interval.   **easy**
2. *Problem Solving.* Using the techniques described in the chapter, describe how you would teach a friend a new dance step.   **challenging**

Demonstrating Psychology Skills
Read this description of a learning experiment and then label the UCS, UCR, CS, and CR below.

A small electric shock is delivered to the hand of a subject; the subject immediately removes the hand from the shock plate. Next, a light flashes, followed by another shock; the subject again removes the hand from the shock plate. Finally, the light flashes and the subject removes the hand immediately.

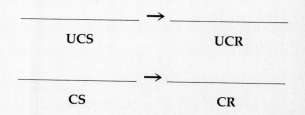

Chapter 6

Thinking About Thinking

Imagine you are imprisoned in a tower. A friend smuggles a rope to you with a note that says: "Divide this rope in half. Tie the two halves together and you can reach the ground." How would you go about doing this? (Think about it and time yourself. How long does it take you to come up with an answer?)

Now a second problem. Take the letters GANRE and rearrange them to make a word. See how long it takes you. Try to make another word out of the same letters (and time yourself). Now do the same thing with the letters TARIL, again looking for two solutions.

The first problem asks you to "unthink" your normal tendency to cut the rope across the middle. You have to search for another solution—like dividing the rope lengthwise! This answer probably came to you "in a flash," although the flash might have taken a bit of time in arriving.

The second problem involves word games called anagrams. The object is to make words out of non-words by rearranging the letters. If your first answer to GANRE was RANGE, and it took you in the neighborhood of 8 seconds to arrive at it, you're on a par with college students! It took one group of college students an average of 114 seconds to come up with a second solution—ANGER. (How long did it take you?) And it took them an average of 7 seconds to rearrange TARIL into TRAIL and 240 seconds to come up with a second solution—TRIAL.

The two tasks you have just finished illustrate problem-solving situations. Some psychologists believe you cannot "learn" the answers to such problems through any kind of classical or operant conditioning. You must use your powers of reasoning.

This reasoning ability is part of what we call thinking, or **cognition.** Thinking includes all the forms of mental activity you are aware of and have some conscious control over. Thinking is working problems, remembering, daydreaming, selecting words, understanding the words others use, making decisions, and sometimes making mistakes. It is controlling your actions and making deliberate choices. In this chapter, we will discuss such important thinking processes as using language for communication and thought, reasoning, and remembering the past.

1. Learning About Language

Humans have the ability to think *abstractly*, to use symbols or labels to stand for things in the real world and our ideas about them. Most of these symbols are part of what we call language. (See the Close-Up, *Planet of the ''Talking'' Apes*, on page 163 for a description of language research with animals.)

Communicating by language seems so natural that it is difficult to remember that we had to learn to do it. Yet without this ability, the human race would have no record of its past, no idea of its future. Life as we know it simply would not exist. Of all our skills, language is one of the most useful. To understand this complex skill, we should start with the simplest units.

PREVIEW

In this section, read to find out:

1. how language affects thinking.
2. how humans learn language.

Children learn to say words and understand the meaning of language by listening to adults.

Phonemes, Morphemes, and *Jabberwocky*

Press your tongue against your upper front teeth and blow out gently. The sound "th" is formed. Now close your lips and "pop" them open. You get "p." If you "explode" at the back of your palate, "k" (as in kick) results. There are forty-five such sounds in the English language called **phonemes.** Phonemes are the smallest units that can be recognized as separate speech sounds.

Phonemes have no meaning by themselves. They are simply the units out of which we create sounds that do have meaning. By combining the phonemes f + e (eh) + ch, we get the word *fetch.* This is a **morpheme.** A morpheme is the smallest unit of language that has meaning. Morphemes, however, need not be words. The prefix *tele,* meaning far, is a morpheme that is combined with other morphemes such as *phone* or *pathy* to form words. Out of morphemes we construct the 20,000 words that most of us use in everyday speech and the more than 500,000 English words found in unabridged dictionaries.

How do we come to understand the many combinations of phonemes and morphemes that make up our thoughts? Probably the best way to begin to understand how the outer speech of language and the "inner speech" of thought works is to look at an unusual example—a page from a children's book by Dr. Seuss, reprinted on the opposite page. It shows how the structure of normal language can give meaning to what at first glance looks like nonsense.

Even though Dr. Seuss's verses include made-up, whimsical words like Zumble-Zay, they are strictly grammatical. Dr. Seuss suggests the meaning he wants to convey by fitting such made-up words into familiar sentence patterns that include some real words. The real words provide clues for understanding the overall meaning.

Grammar—the rules of language—plays an important role in communication. Only by having the rules can we break them from time to time and still convey our meaning. This is what we do when we use some slang expressions.

Rules also allow us to produce new messages. A parrot, for instance, can "speak" with perfect diction, but it can't use the rules of grammar. It can't say anything it hasn't heard before, or combine sentences into new statements.

How Language Is Learned: Some Theories

Children learn to say words and to understand the meaning of language by listening to adults. Gradually, often by the time they are a year old, babies acquire a small vocabulary of useful morphemes. By the age of eighteen months, most are combining morphemes into two-word sentences. By the age of two, most children have a vocabulary of

Get on your way!
Please, Marvin K.!
You might like going
In a Zumble-Zay.

A mother reads a Dr. Seuss book to her daughter. Dr. Seuss, the pen name of Theodore Geisel, has written many books for young children. His stories frequently include whimsical, made-up words like "Zumble-Zay," which have meaning only in their grammatical context.

about 50 words and are beginning to form sentences of three or four words. By the time they are three years old, their vocabulary has grown to over 1,000 words. By the age of five, the average child has mastered most of the complex rules of language—all without any formal instruction.

How do children learn language? B. F. Skinner and other behaviorists think that imitation and conditioning account for most language learning. A baby tries to imitate adult speech and adults reward him or her for correct speech production.

Imitation and reinforcement, however, don't seem to be the whole story. Children brought up in institutions often receive little individual attention and few rewards for "doing right." Yet they also learn to speak, although at a slower rate. Imitation and reinforcement explain even less when it comes to the construction of sentences. Children often say things they don't hear adults say. Sentences like "All gone Daddy" or "Her curl my hair" are common. Children aren't copying adult speech in these cases. They are putting words together on their own. A child who says, "Me go car Mommy" or "Me Mommy go car" is using a shortened, but meaningful, word order. And if the sense of the child's sentence is correct, an adult will probably reward the child with approval no matter what grammar he or she uses.

In fact, research has shown that children develop a simple grammar of their own from the time they begin to use two-word sentences. Several studies have shown that the speech of children between the ages of two and three is highly structured, even though it has little

&&&
See **Exercise 2, Sample Populations,** on pages 476–477 of the *Psychology Skills Handbook,* for a description of how psychologists choose sample populations to use in their research.

Children learn language as they hear it spoken. Consequently, children who are deaf from birth have trouble learning speech. At the John Tracy Clinic in California, children learn to form words by first feeling the vibrations as a therapist speaks.

resemblance to adult speech. This structure, moreover, varies little from child to child. This and other evidence indicate that children grasp the basic, deep structure of language long before they learn all the formal rules of grammar.

A "Blueprint" for Language

Some psychologists theorize that language ability is built in at birth. This does not mean that children automatically know (or learn) a particular language, such as French or English. Rather they believe all of us are born with thought patterns that carry basic language structures.

The best-known advocate of this theory of language is Noam Chomsky. Chomsky says, in effect, that we have in our heads the blueprint for the forms that human languages can take. This blueprint helps us to learn the specific rules of our own particular language rather easily. If this is the case, then all children should be able to develop similar rule systems regardless of the language they speak. This does, in fact, seem to be true. A comparison of children in different parts of the world shows that they learn their native language at approximately the same age, and that they use similar rule systems.

How Language Is Understood

Other things, besides structure, are involved in how we understand language. The interests and values of the listener or reader influence his or her understanding. The **context** of the word or sentence also is important. Words are interpreted according to the situation in which they occur. For example, some unabridged dictionaries give the word *state* nineteen definitions as a noun, four as an adverb, and three as a transitive verb. Only if we know the context in which the word is used—the meanings of the other words and sentences around it—can we grasp the author's or speaker's meaning. Below is a description of other ways the brain uses context to understand written and spoken information.

1. You seldom store the exact wording of a sentence that you hear or read. Instead you remember the overall meaning. If you were asked to repeat a sentence or paragraph you have read, you probably could not say every word of it. However, you would probably recall its general meaning and important points. When words are strung together, the brain seems to seize on a few cues, or key phrases, and to build meaning out of these.

2. The brain often creates an exact meaning from an inexact one. From past experience with meanings, the brain fills in the missing

It's Your Turn

We have discussed the ways in which the context of a word or sentence can be very important in understanding its meaning. Sometimes people in public life say they are "misquoted" by having their words "taken out of context." For example, if a theater critic were to say that an actor's performance in a new play was "incredible—if you enjoy incredible bores," and a newspaper only reprinted the first half of this statement, the review would not be understood accurately. Now *It's Your Turn*. Write an example of a statement you've said that could be misunderstood if the context were not considered.

"Pinit, putahtraletungay" [Translation] Finish potato salad hungry. For a while [Ginny and Gracie Kennedy, shown at right] were thought to be retarded. But at the same time they seemed to be speaking an original language. At the very least their exchanges were thought to represent the most developed form of idioglossia ever recorded in medical history. Idioglossia is a phenomenon, badly documented at best, in which two individuals, often twins, develop a unique and private language with highly original vocabulary and syntax . . . Twins usually give it up at age three. But Gracie and Ginny were discovered at six, still unable to speak English . . . Gracie and Ginny now attend separate severe language disorder classes . . . Put in different schools so they will not fall back to their private communication, they speak jerky, passable English . . . Clinic Chairman Chris Hagen [of San Diego Children's Hospital where the twins' language was studied] says: "They were in a somewhat sensory–deprived environment . . . To me, their private language represents strong evidence that [people have] a basic drive to communicate beyond minimal needs."

parts. If you are told that a woman building a birdhouse pounded a nail into some boards, you would probably assume that she used a hammer to pound the nail. You infer an additional bit of information here because nails are usually driven with hammers. You might be wrong. She might have used a brick or a block of wood. Misunderstanding may occur if we make too many assumptions about statements on the basis of "normal" relationships among objects and ideas.

3. A third way we get meaning from a sentence is to assign particular meanings to particular words in a manner suggested by the context. For example, if someone tells you, "The container held flowers," you think of the container as a vase. But if someone says, "The container held matches," you probably interpret container as a box. Flowers and matches are cue words. They bring to mind appropriate kinds of containers, although in fact no such meaning appears in either sentence. Likewise, to say, "He batted the ball," "He putted the ball," and "He kicked the ball," tells you that a different ball is used in each case. The speaker does not have to specify just what kind of ball is being used.

Section Review

1. Define the terms phoneme and morpheme.
2. Explain some of the psychological theories about how humans learn language.
3. Describe some ways context affects our understanding of language.

C L O S E———U P

Planet of the "Talking" Apes

Washoe signing "hat"

Animals can't talk. Or can they? Using the techniques of operant conditioning, a chimpanzee named Viki was taught to pronounce "Mama," "Papa," "cup," and "up," though only with great effort. The vocal cords of chimps can't easily produce the vowels required for human speech. Chimps carry on their most impressive conversations with hand gestures.

This has led some researchers to attempt to teach chimps to talk using sign language. Psychologists Allen and Beatrice Gardner of the University of Nevada have taught a chimp they named Washoe the American Sign Language, widely used by deaf people in North America. In little more than a year, Washoe learned to use 14 signs reliably, and by the age of five knew over 160.

An impressive thing about Washoe's performance so far has been her ability to combine words into simple phrases. Her longer phrases, such as "Please tickle more" or "Hurry gimme tooth brush" are perfectly grammatical constructions in sign language, comparable to the language young children use when they first begin to form sentences.

The possibility that chimps might use sign language to communicate with *each other* has also intrigued Roger Fouts, of the Institute for Primate Studies at Norman, Oklahoma. Fouts, who now works with Washoe and several other chimps, has had encouraging results. Washoe and her friends signal each other to "Come, hug," or "Come, hurry" and to play various tickling games. On one occasion, Washoe and several other chimps were on an island when a snake approached them. Most of the chimps ran screeching for safety. Washoe signed "Come, come, hurry, hurry" to the others. It is important that at a time of stress Washoe "talked" instead of screeching.

PREVIEW

**In this section,
read to find out:**

1. what the basic building blocks of thought are and how we use them to think.
2. how we use language to think.
3. how we use reasoning to solve problems.

So far we've discussed the fact that we cannot learn all the answers to all the possible questions in life just by acting and observing others. We must *think*. We must process ideas, determine meanings, and see relationships. We do this, as we've seen, largely by using language.

What we haven't seen is *how* our minds process information to solve problems and create new meanings and *how* we use language to think. In this section, we'll begin by considering the basic building blocks of thought—images, concepts, and symbols (primarily words). Next, we'll see how language influences our thinking. Then we'll go on to look at another form our thinking can take—the reasoning process.

How We Think with Images and Concepts

Images are the simplest of the building blocks of thought. They're mental representations, or pictures, of real people, places, or things. Suppose, for example, someone asked you to describe your best friend. As you prepared to do this, a mental picture of your friend would probably flash into your mind, like a slide projected on a movie screen. This mental picture is an **image.**

For most people, the use of images is limited and plays a small part in the overall thinking process. But, for some, images play a powerful—almost overwhelming—role in thought. Call up the image of your friend again on your mental movie screen. You probably picture your friend as he or she looked when you last met. Can you answer these questions based on your mental picture? What was your friend wearing when you last met? (A plaid shirt and jeans, you say?) What kind of plaid was the shirt? Can you duplicate it in the correct colors? What style and color shoes was your friend wearing? What color socks? Was he or she wearing a ring or watch? Can you describe it exactly? Did the watch, for example, have Roman or Arabic numerals on the face? Can you describe exactly what your friend was carrying?

Most of us couldn't answer detailed questions like these based on our images. When most people "image" things, they take in only aspects or highlights of the real things. But a person with very strong visual imagery, called **eidetic imagery,** would probably be able to recall all the details of a friend's attire at their last meeting—down to the label on his or her jeans! People with eidetic imagery frequently can tell the exact position of a formula or fact on the printed page of a textbook. They can glance at an object, such as a comb, and give a complete description, down to the number of teeth. Individuals with eidetic imagery are often said to have "photographic memories."

One of the most remarkable examples of eidetic imagery was illustrated by psychologist A.R. Luria. After examining the table of numbers below for three minutes, a Russian man was able to reproduce the table perfectly, calling off each number in succession in less than 40 seconds.

6	6	8	0
5	4	3	2
1	6	8	4
7	9	3	5
4	2	3	7
3	8	9	1
1	0	0	2
3	4	5	1
2	7	6	8
1	9	2	6
2	9	6	7
5	5	2	0
x	0	1	x

More than that, he could recite the numbers in either the columns or the horizontal rows, in both forward or reverse order. All this was done from the picture in his head! Yet Luria's subject was unable to understand even the simplest abstract thoughts, because he could not "see" them as concrete visual images.

To be able to perform feats such as these might seem to be the answer to your studying problems. Just trip the mental flashbulb, snap the picture, and print it out at exam time! In fact, it seldom works this way. Eidetic imagery often obstructs thinking rather than helps it. Because material is stored in the brain as a unit, it isn't easily broken down and reassembled into new patterns. This lessens flexibility in thought. See the example of how eidetic imagery lessens flexibility in thought in the margin on page 164.

Concepts. Most of us quickly move beyond images in our thinking. We combine images that are similar in appearance or represent objects that have similar functions into a single category, or **concept.** It is with concepts that we do much of our thinking.

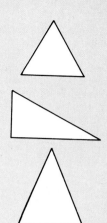

The word concept can refer to objects, ideas, people, or events. Knowing that some person or object or idea belongs to a larger group of people or objects or ideas gives us a greater understanding of the sort of thing it is. This in turn helps us to know its purpose and meaning. If we had to consider every idea, person, or object one at a time, making sense of the world would be very difficult and time consuming. For example, look at each of the three forms in the column on this page. Each form can be converted into a mental image of a three-sided drawing. They have the quality of three-sidedness in common, although the length of each side differs from one to another. The images themselves are replaced in our thinking by a concept that we call "triangle." When someone says this word, you know what is meant.

Symbols. Most words are **symbols** that stand for concepts. The word *vehicle*, for example, stands for a family of objects that move and transport things. This concept could include automobiles, buggies, sleds, and bicycles. The concept itself is general. The details can be filled in later.

We can easily understand a concept like vehicle because we can *see* examples of it. But many concepts are quite arbitrary. For example, sometime in the distant past this symbol —6—came to stand for "six of something." It might just as easily have been decided that this symbol —G—meant "six of something." Likewise, this arrangement of letters—*garm*— could have come to stand for the objects shown here. As it is, this symbol—*shoes*—stands for the objects. The arbitrary meanings assigned to number and word concepts must be learned.

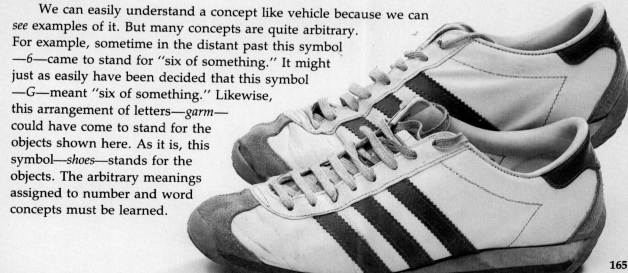

The many bird motifs in Hopi art indicate its importance in Hopi culture and language. Some examples of Hopi art appear on these pages. Below: "Bird" *kachina* (ceremonial figure); wicker basketry plaque. Opposite page: Bird motifs in modern Hopi pottery designs.

How Words Enter into Thinking

Using concepts in our thinking keeps us from having to use the original objects, or even to "image" them. A formula in chemistry, for instance, might represent materials we can't even see, such as oxygen, carbon dioxide, and nitrogen. We can use symbols in place of objects. Symbols, usually words, are the *tools* of thinking.

To what extent do words actually shape our thoughts? Do we use words to think, or do words use us? Some linguists believe that the way we think is determined by the words, symbols, and images we learn. One of the major proponents of this theory of language was Benjamin Whorf. Whorf believed that because thought and perceptions are filtered through language, language determines what we see and think about. Whorf's ideas were based on his observations of many different cultures around the world.

For example, Eskimos have seven different words for different kinds of snow, while English-speaking people have just the single term. The Hopi Indians have one word for birds and another for all other things that fly (from airplane to bee). Further, the Hopi language lacks tenses. It makes no distinction between past, present, and future. Whorf would argue that these characteristics of language cause the Eskimos and Hopis to think differently about their experiences than other people who use other languages.

There is some reason to believe that the particular language we grow up with does prepare us to think along certain lines. (As we saw in Chapter 4, Zulus "think round" because they have no word for "square" or "rectangle" and their buildings and settlements are all round in shape.) However, in such cases we can never be sure what is cause and what is effect. Perhaps the Eskimo language has seven different words for snow because snow is important in Eskimos' lives. An Eskimo born and raised in Houston might not make these distinctions. We probably image our world first, and then find labels to describe the images with which we do our thinking.

Being Reasonable

Reasoning is thinking, or cognition, with a purpose. Reasoning is thinking directed toward a specific goal or task. Here's how reasoning seems to work.

Information is apparently processed in a series of steps. Our mind tries out various combinations of data, throwing out things that do not fit together or that do not contribute to the ideas we are exploring. Gradually (or with the speed of lightning!) these associations form a pattern in our minds. Three of the patterns reasoning can take are discussed below.

First, we will consider **deductive reasoning.** Basically, deduction is reasoning from the general to the specific. You have a general concept in mind and proceed to arrange the facts so that they make sense and fit into your logical assumptions. Here's an example of deductive reasoning.

Two people are driving past a farm. One of them says, "I see that the sheep in the field have just been sheared." But her friend replies, "No, the only thing we know is that they have been sheared on one side." To the second person, all the evidence is not in. The first person used deductive reasoning. She feels her conclusion is justified because she knows that farmers usually shear both sides of a sheep. We can put this reasoning the following way: Farmers usually shear an entire sheep. These sheep have been sheared on the side I can see. Therefore,

the side I cannot see must be shorn too.

A second common reasoning pattern is **inductive reasoning.** In the process of induction, the thinker builds from the specific to the general. The observation of some specific events leads the thinker to make a general assumption that explains them. For example, remember the description of Pavlov's work in Chapter 5. Pavlov noticed that laboratory dogs salivated not only at the sight of their food, but also at the approach of their feeders and at the sound of the food being placed in their dishes. Based on his observations of these specific events, Pavlov made the general assumption that the dogs probably had learned to associate the approach of the feeders and the sound of the food being placed in their dishes with the food itself. Pavlov tested his assumption by ringing a bell just before feeding the dogs. As he expected, the dogs soon came to associate the sound of the dinner bell with their food, and the sound of the bell alone produced salivation.

In inductive reasoning, the thinker often does what Pavlov did. He or she tests a general assumption by finding other evidence that supports or rejects it. Inductive reasoning forms the basis of much scientific thinking.

The third type is **evaluative reasoning.** Many times we are not concerned with abstract or theoretical problems. Instead, we are faced with real-life situations in which we must choose among several possible solutions. One of these solutions will seem more practical, attainable, or desirable than the others. This type of thinking involves judging the suitability, goodness, or effectiveness of an idea, as opposed to trying to create or add to it.

Here's an example of how evaluative reasoning works. Suppose you are shopping for a pocket calculator. You consider several factors before you buy—the cost, quality, and functions you want it to perform. The standards here are reality (how much can I afford to pay?) and appropriateness (what kinds of problems must the calculator be able to handle?). On the basis of your answers to these questions, you make a choice. In evaluative thinking, there is seldom a single "right" or "wrong" answer, merely answers that are "better" or "worse" as they apply to you.

Section Review

1. Define image, concept, and symbol and give an example of each.
2. Do we use words to think, or do words use us? Discuss both arguments of this question.
3. Describe the differences among deductive, inductive, and evaluative reasoning.

3. The Mysteries of Memory

We ask you to begin this section by taking a memory test. Below is an imaginary telephone number. Read it a few times and try to remember it.

368-0691

Now cover up the number and read the following few paragraphs.

This section of our chapter is called the "mysteries of memory" because there is much about the topic that is unexplained. For instance, it is not clear just what part, or parts, of the brain are used to store information, or how much information the brain can store. Estimates range from 200 million units of information in a lifetime to several billion. We do know that memory takes in about ten "frames" of visual data a second during every waking hour.

We know a great deal more about how memory works than what memory is. That's because we can't see memory at work. We have to infer its operations from people's performances on memory tasks. In fact, you are performing a memory task right now.

Can you remember the telephone number you memorized a few moments ago? Chances are you've forgotten it already! But can you recall your telephone number at home? Almost certainly you can. Now try to remember as many of your old phone numbers as you can. Try to remember old addresses or zip codes. Why can you remember so many old numbers when you have already forgotten the new number given at the beginning of this section? This is one of the mysteries of memory we will be dealing with in the next several pages.

How We Remember

Psychologists separate the memory system into three parts: sensory, short-term, and long-term. Sensory memory lasts a very brief time—less than a second, in fact! Information comes in through the senses and is held by **sensory memory** long enough to be used in perceiving, comparing, judging, and so on. In that same split second, the brain also decides whether or not it needs the incoming information for present or future use. If it seems useful, it is passed on to short-term memory. If not, it is discarded. Sensory memory uses a "file or forget" approach to its job.

Short-term memory performs a second screening job on the information passed on to it by sensory memory. You can think of it as a sort of "desk-top" memory. Data arriving in the "in" box is looked over,

PREVIEW

In this section, read to find out:

1. what memory is.
2. how memory works.
3. how memory can be distorted.

Some people are able to remember visual images more clearly than information that comes in through other senses. How is your visual memory? Study the photo above for five seconds. Later, you'll see how accurate your memory is.

sorted out, and acted on. Like most desk tops, however, short-term memory often gets cluttered up with many different items. Generally speaking, short-term memory can deal with no more than seven or eight items at any one time. (There are strategies, however, for expanding its capacity.) Every few minutes the "desk top" is cleaned off to make room for more information. The "junk" mail is thrown into the wastebasket and ideas are sorted into meaningful groups. What remains will be filed in the "out" box to be sent on to long-term memory.

Long-term Memory

Long-term memory used to be thought of only as a mental filing system. Information was stored away in long-term memory, and there it sat until it was retrieved at some later date. Now psychologists know that **long-term memory** is actually very active. It is continually interacting with short-term memory to provide us with the information we need to make decisions. In this process, long-term memories are reactivated, combined with short-term memories, and then filed away again, along with any new material that seems worth saving.

How does long-term memory file, or organize, information? First, images are "tagged," or categorized. A round object will be perceived as such and filed under the general heading of "roundness." If it is also red, it will also be remembered for its "redness." Next, long-term memory puts the memory impressions into groups. Useful associations tie the groups together. Locating one memory sometimes reminds us of another. It is a "search and match" operation. Events that occur in close relationship to one another, but are separated by other qualities, are "cross-indexed" in the brain. Although we are not certain how this takes place, it plays a significant role in learning and thinking.

Long-term memory seems to have its own instant index to the information it has on file. For example, have you ever been asked a question that you *knew* you knew the answer to but couldn't come up with right away? You might say, "It's right on the tip of my tongue. Give me a minute to think about it." Or you might immediately reply, "No, I wouldn't know that in a million years!" In the latter case, your brain has told you right off that it doesn't have the information you've been asked for. In the first case, your brain goes right to work without further instructions. It *knows* the material is there someplace and starts looking for it. Apparently the brain can scan its "memory index" in an instant and know whether the information you've been asked for is on file. This automatic process of knowing what you know is truly one of the mysteries of memory.

Productive Memory

So far we've been discussing memory's ability to reproduce exactly information it has stored away. This is called **reproductive memory.** Learning vocabulary lists of foreign words, mathematical formulas, telephone numbers, important dates in American history—all are examples of reproductive memory at work. There are many kinds of thoughts and memories, however, for which this kind of recall is neither possible nor necessary. As you study for your next test in this course, you will certainly not try to recall exact sentences, word for

It's Your Turn

As we have said, there are some things we remember and some we don't. Try to quickly answer these questions: What is the color of your father's eyes? What is the color of your dentist's eyes? What did you have for dinner last night? Chances are some of these answers are easier to remember than others. Your attitude and interest in the topics may affect your memory. Now *It's Your Turn.* Like the fellow below you've probably forgotten things from time to time. Write down some examples of things you've forgotten. Explain how your feelings or attitudes might have affected your memory.

word, as written in this textbook or spoken by your teacher. You will try to remember the most important ideas and vocabulary. When you *produce* this kind of generalized or "processed" information from your memory systems, you are engaging in a process called **productive memory.**

Productive memory enables you to pick out a few key events or images and build your recall on them. You make your own inferences from what you remember and say, "It must have happened this way." This ability is important in dealing with complex loads of information, especially if they've been stored in long-term memory for a long time. Productive memory helps you recall the meaningful gist of an event rather than its exact details. It gets rid of the excess baggage to better remember what is important.

The active production of memories does have its problems, however. For many of us, memory becomes so active that we tend to "remember" things that didn't happen, to create memories which aren't always accurate reproductions of the past.

How Memory Is Distorted

One of the first persons to study productive memory was the English psychologist F. C. Bartlett. He believed that the same event might be recalled differently at different times. If the information were passed on to another person, and he or she passed it on to someone else, the original information would be even further distorted. In fact, this often happens when people spread gossip.

Bartlett called this technique successive reproduction. He showed that a memory event can be altered as it is recalled under different circumstances or is passed on to other people. For example, one person might be shown a picture and asked to remember it. After some time, this person would be asked to reproduce the picture from memory. A second person would be given the first person's drawing as the picture to be memorized and reproduced, and so on. The drawings at the top of page 173 show a typical result. In this series of drawings the original picture of an owl was gradually transformed into one of a cat.

Distortions of memory also occur because of the way you are asked to recall events. It is known that police officers who ask victims, "How tall was your attacker?" will get a bigger estimate than if they ask, "How short was your attacker?"

Bartlett thought that memory retention was closely related to other forms of behavior. One's attitude toward an event, interest in it, and even temperament affect memory. If you follow baseball, you probably remember all kinds of batting averages and other odd facts about your

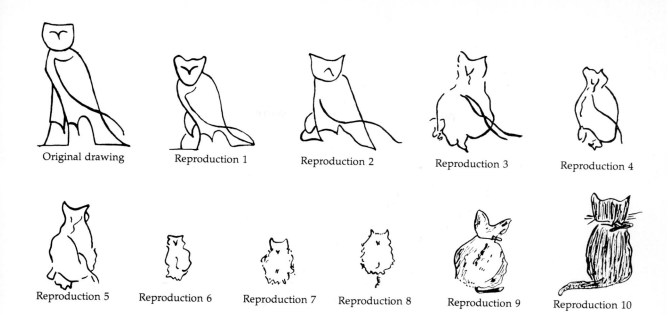

Original drawing   Reproduction 1   Reproduction 2   Reproduction 3   Reproduction 4

Reproduction 5   Reproduction 6   Reproduction 7   Reproduction 8   Reproduction 9   Reproduction 10

favorite players. Remembering things is possible if a person has a strong interest in the subject at the time it was learned. In school, too, things that are exciting and adventurous are recalled more easily and vividly than tiresome and boring experiences. The reason is that they are strong stimuli. They stand out from the general background of things that are not worth remembering.

How Psychologists Study Memory

Psychologists have developed several techniques for studying memory. The four most common measures of memory are serial anticipation, recognition, relearning, and recall.

A typical experiment involving **serial anticipation** uses numbers, words, or nonsense syllables. The experimenter shows the subjects a list of these items. Then the subject is shown each item individually. As each item appears, the experimenter asks the subject to "anticipate" the item or items which follow on the list.

Recognition is usually tested by presenting a picture of an object, face, or symbol, and then asking the subject whether it is something he or she has seen or learned before. Another method is to present several items and ask the subject whether he or she recognizes any as something learned before. In these tests, a *reaction-time meter* is often used to measure the exact length of time it takes for the subject to make a decision that the item is recognized or not recognized.

In a typical **recall** experiment, the researcher asks the subject to memorize a list of items. Then, instead of asking the subject to recall them in the correct order as in serial anticipation tests, the researcher asks the subject to recall all the items that he or she can remember in whatever order. Typically, the subject remembers the first and last items on the list the best. Items in the middle are the hardest to remember.

In **relearning** experiments, subjects study new material until they can reproduce it perfectly on a test. Then, after a specific time period, subjects study the same material again until they can pass the same test equally well. Researchers have found that even though material may be forgotten from the first learning, relearning is usually faster, indicating that some of the original learning is still present in memory.

Most of these techniques are already familiar to you. You've already met them in taking tests. Multiple choice tests are, for the most part, measures of recognition. Fill-in-the-blanks and essay questions test your recall of material you've learned. And you've probably had experience relearning material for mid-term or final exams.

Remember the photo you studied earlier? This is a silhouette of the people in it. Try testing your memory. Describe as much about each person as you can remember. Include details about their clothing and objects they were holding. Now check back to page 170. How well did you do?

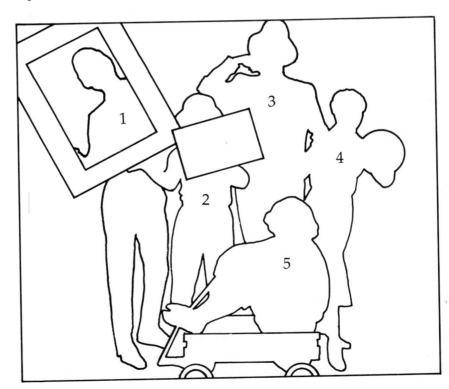

Section Review

1. Describe the three parts of the memory system.
2. Explain what productive memory is.
3. List some things that cause memory distortions.
4. Describe some ways psychologists measure memory.

4. Why We Forget

PREVIEW

**In this section,
read to find out:**

1. why we forget.
2. how memory cues help us remember.

If there is one fact about memory that all of us know, it is that we do not remember everything. In fact, there are times when it seems we can't remember anything. People's names, appointments, material crammed for an exam, telephone numbers—all escape us just when we need them most. At the same time, we often remember other things that don't strike us as being very important. Much research has been done on this problem and psychologists have several theories to explain how and why we seem to forget material we have learned.

Some Theories About Forgetting

One explanation of why we forget is the **interference** theory. We have all had the embarrassing experience of being interrupted in the middle of a conversation and not being able to pick up where we left off. We completely forget what we were talking about. Often, the people we were talking with will help out by giving us a cue. "You were saying something about John Smith." Our companions haven't forgotten because they were not interrupted.

The "Where was I?" phenomenon illustrates the role of interference. It refers to the fact that new material gets in the way of old material. This type of interference is called *retroactive* (retroactive means "backward-working"). Because of retroactive interference, we remember the new information but forget the old information. Conversely, if an older memory stops the remembering of new material, the process is called *proactive* ("forward-looking") *interference.* When we say, "Where was I?" we are demonstrating retroactive interference. We have been interrupted and the new experience interfered with our memory of the earlier discussion. If, however, we became so involved in our earlier discussion that we continued to think about it and did not pay much attention to the interruption, we might have forgotten the new information—or never have learned it at all. This is an example of proactive interference.

What explains the interference process? One theory suggests two explanations. The first explanation is that new material overpowers the

People's names, telephone numbers, appointments, material crammed for an exam—these aren't the only things that require memory. Dance and many sports require participants to remember whole series of complicated movements.

older learned material and becomes stronger and more dominant in our memory. Another idea that has received more experimental support is that the interfering material causes the other knowledge to be unlearned—we forget old material so that we may learn new material more readily. This view suggests that there is a limit to the amount stored in memory at any one time. As new information arrives, it pushes out things that are already in readily available locations. If no additional material comes in, then no forgetting will occur.

Another explanation of forgetting is referred to as **dead storage**—forgetting as loss of access to material. If you put something in the attic, or in a cabinet that is seldom used, you often forget what you did with it. You know it's in the house, but where? You look in the obvious places without success. You have to think back, to search for clues that associate the object with something you do remember. Then, because one thing leads to another, you discover that the object is not lost after all. You simply had to get on the trail of it.

Memory Cues

By the same token, some psychologists think that we never forget anything. For one reason or another, the information merely becomes temporarily inaccessible "in the back of our mind." If only we can find the right cue, it will come to us. These cues are the key to unlocking long-term memory. Three types of cues have been widely studied.

One cue involves the associations we make between one word and another, or one person and another. Suppose you meet a boy on the street and are unable to remember his name. Suddenly his girlfriend Alice, whom you know very well, appears and the name Fred springs to mind. Alice is the cue word that retrieves the less frequently remembered name of her boyfriend.

Another cue is the use of **mnemonic devices.** Mnemonics are tricks, jingles, poems or any type of association which help us remember something more easily. For example, if you play a musical instrument, you may have learned to read the notes on the scale by memorizing phrases such as *Every Good Boy Does Fine*, or *All Cows Eat Grass*. These tricks can be very helpful. What other mnemonics can you think of?

A third type of cue is the context in which material is learned and remembered. You can see how this works if you try to "re-create" a particular event. A general memory will lead you to increasingly precise details. The third cue may be the person's internal mood or body posture. Some psychologists tested this notion by having subjects either stand up straight or lie down while they learned a test word and while they later tried to remember it. Subjects who were in the same position for both learning and recall had a better memory for the test than those who changed their posture. This could explain why studying in bed might not be as effective as studying at a desk—unless you can persuade your teacher to let you take the test lying down!

Memory and Motivation

A final explanation for forgetting involves wanting to forget, or *motivational* theories. Psychoanalyst Sigmund Freud argued that we forget because we *want* to forget. Some things are so painful or disturbing to us that they get pushed into the unconscious mind. Freud called this **repression.** Although the material is "forgotten," it is certainly not gone, for it may stay at an unconscious level even though we are unaware of it.

Is a repressed, or "lost" memory gone forever? There is some evidence that this is not the case. Wilder Penfield, a Canadian neurosurgeon, discovered that when he stimulated certain portions of the brain with electrodes, his patient exhibited total recall of past events. People who are hypnotized are also able to recall long-lost events of their past in exact detail. In everyday life, of course, we neither get stuck with

Some mnemonic devices appear below.
"i" before "e" except after "c"

Phrases like <u>Every</u> <u>Good</u> <u>Boy</u> <u>Does</u> <u>Fine</u> and <u>FACE</u> help people remember the notes of the scale.

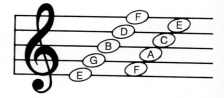

Thirty days hath September,
April, June, and November;
February has twenty-eight
  alone,
All the rest have thirty-one,
Excepting leap-year, that's the
  time
When February's days are
  twenty-nine.

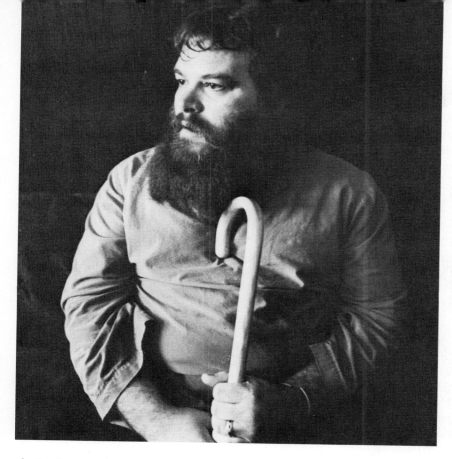

Forgetting can be involuntary; the mind pushes disturbing things into its unconscious. Remembering can also be involuntary. People who have undergone traumatic experiences are sometimes plagued by recurring memories of the event. Victims of air crashes or other disasters sometimes unexpectedly relive the horror even years later. Memories of wartime experiences can be painful and recurring too—as they are for Viet Nam veteran, Vernon Wike. Medical corpsman Wike was trying to save a wounded Marine when the dramatic photos on the opposite page were shot by Catherine Leroy of Associated Press. "He had a T and T wound," Wike recalls, "through and through both lungs. He had a heartbeat when I got to him, and I found the entry wound and had it dressed. Then all of a sudden he was gone." Today, Wike, shown at left, is still haunted by his memories. "I can be assured of having flashbacks. They hit me anytime. I was at a party once, and I remember standing with my back against the wall for more than an hour. Everybody in the room became Vietnamese."

electrodes nor hypnotized when we want to recall something. Most recall is voluntary on our part—we make an effort to remember certain events. We want these memories back so that decisions about incoming information can be made.

Freud emphasized the negative influence of motivation on memory. But isn't it possible that we also want to remember some things more than others? When you cram for a test, you are highly motivated to remember the information, at least until the test is over. This works surprisingly well for many people. But then you discover that the learned material is very quickly forgotten afterwards, when there is less reason or motivation to remember it.

Section Review

1. Discuss some theories about why we forget.
2. Describe some memory cues that help us remember.
3. Explain the influence of motivation on memory.

Chapter 6 Review

Section Summaries

1. Learning About Language

"Cognition" is a term that takes in all forms of thinking. The human ability to think abstractly is part of language. Phonemes, the smallest units of speech, are combined to form morphemes, the smallest units that have meaning. Grammar—the rules for language—lets us understand language and communicate with others. Behaviorists think children learn language through imitation and conditioning, but research has supported the view that humans are born knowing basic language structures. Another important aspect to understanding language is context.

2. Using the Old Noodle

Images are the simplest units of thought. However, eidetic imagery often interferes with thinking because the images are stored as fixed patterns. Similar images about objects, ideas, people, or events can be combined into a single category, or concept. Most words are symbols that stand for concepts. Benjamin Whorf believed that language determines what we see and think about.

Reasoning, or thinking with a purpose, can follow several patterns. Deductive reasoning moves from the general to the specific. Inductive reasoning moves from the specific to the general. Evaluative reasoning is used to choose among several options.

3. The Mysteries of Memory

Psychologists separate the memory system into sensory memory, short-term memory, and long-term memory. Reproductive memory, the ability to reproduce information exactly, is needed less often than productive memory, the ability to recall generalized information. However, productive memory sometimes distorts information. Psychologists study memory through serial anticipation, recognition, recall, and relearning.

4. Why We Forget

Interference theory states that we forget because of retroactive and proactive interference. Another explanation for forgetting is that information is "filed" in dead storage. Some psychologists think that memory cues can help us remember any information. Memory cues include word associations, mnemonic devices, and context. Another explanation for forgetting came from Freud, who thought that repression lets people forget what they want to forget.

Psychology Skill Activities

1. Test the memory span of some friends with the following test. Have each person repeat these numbers aloud after you. See how long a string each person can do. (Seven is average.)
3-4-6; 4-2-1-7; 5-2-4-3-8; 6-7-2-4-8-1; 8-7-3-1-2-5-6; 9-7-2-5-6-7-1-8; 9-4-3-7-2-8-4-6-5. **easy**

2. After you read each of the following words, write down the first word that comes to your mind. Then analyze your list to find some clues to long-term storage.
apple, chair, grape, bottle, comb, boy, peach, light, dog, lemon, jar, paper, tape, orange, golf, cup **challenging**

Testing for Understanding

Knowing Key Terms

Define these terms in your own words.

Section 1

cognition	morpheme
phoneme	context

Section 2

image
eidetic imagery
concept
symbol
reasoning
deductive reasoning
inductive reasoning
evaluative reasoning

Section 3

sensory memory
short-term memory
long-term memory
reproductive memory
productive memory
serial anticipation
recognition
recall
relearning

Section 4

interference
dead storage
mnemonic devices
repression

Reviewing Main Ideas

Section 1

1. Describe the basic connection between language and thinking.

2. Explain the major theories about how humans learn language.

Section 2

1. Describe how people use each of the basic building blocks of thought.

2. Explain Benjamin Whorf's theory about thought and language.

3. What are some of the types of reasoning people use to solve problems?

Section 3

1. What are the names psychologists have given to the three parts of the memory system?

2. How does each part of this memory system work?

3. Explain how productive memory can distort memory.

Section 4

1. Describe some theories of forgetting.

2. What are some memory cues that can improve memory?

Thinking Critically

1. *Analysis.* Analyze your study habits and then explain how some of the memory strategies described in this chapter could improve your studying. **easy**

2. *Forming Hypotheses.* Does language determine the way we see our world or does language change to reflect changes in our world? Give some examples to support your answer. **challenging**

Demonstrating Psychology Skills

Read the following description of a psychological experiment and decide whether the experimenter's conclusion was based on inductive, deductive, or evaluative reasoning.

An experimenter invited a number of college women to give a mild electric shock to a target subject whenever a green light went on. Another group received similar instructions, but these women wore hoods. As a result, they were anonymous and could not be identified by their "victim." The results of the experiment showed that the hooded subjects were more willing to shock and give stronger shocks than the subjects without hoods. The results indicate that, all things being equal, anonymity encourages aggression.

Intelligence and Creativity

A ten-year-old boy growing up in a city slum was asked the question, "How many uses can you think of for a newspaper?" Here is his reply:

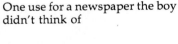 You can read it, write on it, lay it down and paint a picture on it. If you didn't have covers, you could put it around you. You can burn it, put it in the garage and drive the car over it when you wash the car, lay it down and put your baby on it, put it on a busted window, put it in your door for decoration, put it in the garbage can, put it on a chair if the chair is messy. If you have a puppy, you put newspapers in its box or put it in your back yard for the dog to play with. When you build something and you don't want anyone to see it, put newspaper around it. Put newspaper on the floor if you have no mattress, use it to pick up

One use for a newspaper the boy didn't think of

something hot, use it to stop bleeding, or catch the drips from drying clothes. You can use newspaper for curtains, put it in your shoe to cover what is hurting your foot, make a kite out of it, shade a light that is too bright. You can wrap fish in it, wipe windows, or wrap money in it and tape it (so it doesn't make noise). You put washed shoes on newspaper, wipe eyeglasses with it, put it under a dripping sink, put a plant on it, make a paper bowl out of it, use it for a hat if it is raining, tie it on your feet for slippers. You can put it on sand if you had no towel, use it for bases in baseball, make paper airplanes with it, use it as a dustpan when you sweep, ball it up for the cat to play with, wrap your hands in it when it is cold. ▮▮

Could you have thought of as many uses for a newspaper as this ten-year-old boy? Think of some ten-year-olds you know. Do you think they would have given the replies this boy did?

The ten-year-old quoted above ranks only "average" on standardized tests of intelligence. Yet, to some, his response would seem highly "intelligent" and "creative." On the other hand, the boy's replies might not seem unusual to his friends and neighbors. The boy's experiences might have shaped his reply, and his responses might not seem unusually intelligent or creative to those with similar experiences.

Psychologists ask many questions about the whole subject of intelligence and creativity—many more questions than they can answer. In this chapter, we'll look at some of the answers psychologists *do* have for some of these questions. We'll examine the meaning of intelligence and creativity. We'll see how intelligence and creativity are measured and we'll look at some criticisms of such measures. Finally we will discuss the range of intelligence possessed by human beings from those with superior ability to those with capabilities significantly below the average—the mentally retarded.

1. Intelligence and Intelligence Tests

Ask five different psychologists their definitions of intelligence, and you'll probably get five different answers.

"Intelligence is the ability to think and learn."

"Intelligence is the ability to profit from experience and to reason from the known to the unknown."

"Intelligence is the ability to see and understand relationships."

"Intelligence is the ability to adapt to new and changing conditions in the environment."

"Intelligence is the ability to understand problems and to develop solutions."

PREVIEW

In this section, read to find out:

1. what intelligence is.
2. what IQ is.

Our hypothetical psychologists emphasize different aspects of intelligence. Probably the broadest definition of **intelligence**—the one most psychologists could agree with—is the ability to profit from experience and to adapt to new conditions in the environment.

Part of the problem with defining intelligence is that it's an abstract idea. Intelligence isn't something we can see or touch. It doesn't exist in one specific part of the brain. Like so much in psychology, it can only be inferred from the behavior, or performance, of the individual. Many psychologists, therefore, have attempted to develop accurate measures of intellectual performance. Some psychologists argue that the only reliable definition of intelligence is "whatever intelligence tests test!"

What Intelligence Tests Test

What *do* intelligence tests test? Most intelligence tests are made up of tasks that have been developed based on common-sense ideas about what makes up "intelligent behavior." Most of these tasks test such things as the ability to understand relationships among words, numbers and spatial patterns, memory skills, general information about the world, and problem-solving skills.

Some researchers have attempted to analyze intelligence test results to bring us closer to an understanding of what intelligence is. One of the first to do research in this field was psychologist Charles Spearman. His results suggested a *two-factor* theory of intelligence. He believed intelligence test items measured both a *general factor* of intelligence and a *specific factor*, different for each test. Spearman considered the general factor a kind of "mental energy" which guided thought. The specific factors helped to express this general energy and were related to it. Later researchers found that these two factors were not detailed enough to explain all the types of intelligence. Multiple-factor theories—such as the one advanced by psychologists L. L. and Thelma Thurstone—are now widely accepted. The Thurstones classified intelligence into seven specific factors or abilities. They are:

(1) number factor—the ability to do arithmetic problems,

(2) space factor—the ability to visualize things in three dimensions and to see the relationships between various objects,

(3) verbal fluency—the ability to communicate and use words to make oneself understood,

(4) verbal comprehension—the ability to understand words,

(5) memory factor—ability to recall past experiences,

(6) reasoning factor—the ability to solve problems logically,

(7) perceptual factor—the ability to see details and quickly notice differences in stimuli.

Each individual can have different amounts of each ability. Some people are better at one factor than another.

Later, psychologist J. P. Guilford identified 120 different intelligence factors. Guilford broadened the scope of the intelligence concept by adding creativity and imagination as factors. (Tasks testing creativity developed by Guilford are included on page 207.)

Originally, specific intelligence factors were thought to be independent of one another. Each factor was considered distinct and unrelated. More recent research, however, has shown that the factors seem to have some relationship to one another, and are not entirely independent. There may be some general intelligence factor present, in addition to the specific factors.

The Origin of Intelligence Tests

The intelligence tests used most often today are based on the work of a Frenchman, Alfred Binet. In 1905, Binet was asked by the French Ministry of Education to develop a way to identify those children in French schools who were too "mentally deficient" to benefit from ordinary schooling and who needed special education. The tests had to distinguish those who were merely behind in school from those who were actually mentally deficient, or retarded.

Alfred Binet

The items that Binet and his colleague Theophile Simon included on the test were chosen on the basis of their ideas about intelligence. Binet and Simon believed intelligence includes such abilities as understanding the meaning of words, solving problems, and making common-sense judgments. Two other important assumptions also shaped Binet's and Simon's work: (1) that children with more intelligence will do better in school and (2) that older children have a greater ability than younger children.

Binet's first test consisted of thirty tasks. They were simple things most children learn as a result of their everyday experiences. The tasks were arranged in groups according to age. Binet decided which tasks were appropriate for a given age group by giving them first to a large number of children of different ages. If more than half of the children of a given age passed a test, it was considered appropriate for that age group.

Determining IQ

Binet compared the number of tasks an individual child completed correctly with the average performance of children of the same age. This gave him what he called the child's mental age (MA). Binet then compared this figure with the child's chronological (actual) age (CA) to arrive at his or her **intelligence quotient** (IQ). This was done by dividing MA by CA and multiplying by 100 to eliminate fractions or decimals.

$$\frac{MA}{CA} \times 100 = IQ$$

If a child's mental and chronological age were the same, his or her IQ would be 100.

$$\frac{6\ (MA)}{6\ (CA)} \times 100 = 100$$

If a child completed fewer tasks successfully than the average person of his or her age, then his or her IQ would be less than 100. For example, if a six-year-old child took the test and earned an MA of 4, his or her IQ score would be 67 (IQ = $\frac{4}{6} \times 100 = 67$). By the same token, if a child did more on the test than the average person his or her age, the IQ would be greater than 100. For example, a six-year-old child who earned an MA of 9 years would have an IQ of 150 (IQ = $\frac{9}{6} \times 100 = 150$).

The formula does not work well for adults. In adulthood, an increase in chronological age does not necessarily mean an increase in mental age. So, for adults, IQ is calculated by comparing a person's score with those of others in his or her age group. Thus, if a person scores in the middle of the group, his or her IQ is average (100). This **deviation IQ** tells how far above or below the group average an individual stands.

"You did very well on your IQ test. You're a man of 49 with the intelligence of a man of 53."

A normal curve. The test scores of people in a large test group tend to be distributed in a **normal curve.** (See the graph below.) This means that the great majority of people will have scores in the middle of the distribution, ranging from 84–116. These scores are regarded as "average." Those below 84 are considered "below average." Those above 116 are "superior." As we move away from the center of the distribution, or the average score, there are fewer and fewer people. People with very high or very low scores are rare. For example, in the IQ range between 84–116 we find about 68 percent of the population; between 116–130 about 14 percent; between 130–145 about 2 percent; and above 145 only 1 percent.

&r &r &r

See **Exercise 3, Summarizing Data in Tables and Graphs,** on pages 478–480 of the *Psychology Skills Handbook,* for more information about how psychologists use these methods of data analysis in their research.

Normal Curve

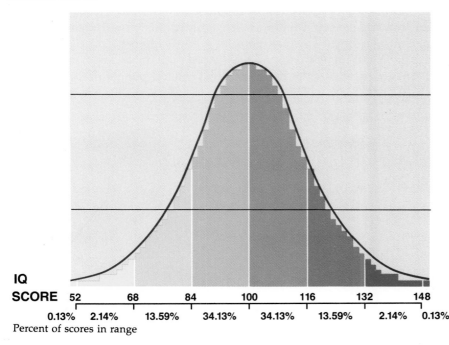

IQ SCORE

| 52 | 68 | 84 | 100 | 116 | 132 | 148 |

| 0.13% | 2.14% | 13.59% | 34.13% | 34.13% | 13.59% | 2.14% | 0.13% |

Percent of scores in range

If the distribution of IQ scores for a group of randomly selected people was plotted, the graph would look much like the **normal curve** shown here. The range of IQ scores is shown on the top line of the horizontal axis (across the bottom of the graph). The percentage of people who scored within each range is shown on the bottom line of the horizontal axis. You can see that the greatest (highest) percentage of scores are at the average IQ of 100. As the scores get farther away from the center, fewer people are shown at each score. What percentage of people scored below 68? What percentage scored above 148?

IQ Testing in the United States

Binet's test has been revised and adapted many times since it was first introduced. In the United States, psychologist Lewis Terman of Stanford University modified it to produce the Stanford-Binet Intelligence Test in 1916. The Stanford-Binet provided for different tasks for different age groups as Binet's original test did. But Terman made his task assignments on the basis of tests of thousands of children. A psychologist is shown giving a typical task from the Standard-Binet on page 189.

One criticism of the Binet tests is that most of the items test verbal ability and abstract reasoning. In the 1950s, psychologist David Wechsler introduced tests which stress both the verbal and the non-verbal, or performance, aspects of intelligence. These tests are WPPSI (Wechsler Preschool and Primary Scale of Intelligence), the WAIS (Wechsler Adult Intelligence Scale), and the WISC (Wechsler Intelligence Scale for Children). These tests are divided into two parts. One part is devoted to verbal tasks, testing such things as general knowledge, comprehension, arithmetic abilities, memory skills, and vocabulary. Sample items from this part of the WISC test appear on page 189. The performance section contains tests of picture completion, block design, picture arrangement, and object assembly. Some of the performance tasks are shown below.

Group intelligence tests. All of the tests we have discussed so far are individual tests. A trained test examiner must give these tests to one person at a time. This can be a long and expensive process. During World War I, the Army found itself faced with the problem of having to evaluate the abilities of the nearly two million people pouring into its

Some materials from a Wechsler test

At left, a psychologist administers a Stanford-Binet to a four-year-old. The task pictured here involves tracing the shortest path to the end of a maze within a specified time period. Some other tasks are duplicating a pattern of blocks made by the test examiner and drawing a picture of a person.

ranks. In order to accomplish this enormous task quickly, group intelligence tests were developed. These are paper-and-pencil tests that can be given to many people at a time. Group tests are widely used in schools and other institutions today. One widely used group test is the Otis Mental Ability Test. Some sample questions appear on page 190.

The Uses of Intelligence Tests

Intelligence tests are widely used in schools and other institutions in the United States. You have probably taken at least one yourself. In the schools, IQ scores can be useful in helping to identify slower students who might need remedial help and superior students who also might benefit from special attention. IQ tests can also be used to help diagnose conditions such as severe confusion or possible brain damage. And IQ scores *do* seem to be useful for predicting future school success especially at the elementary level. At the high school and college levels, prediction is less accurate.

Predictions cannot be based on the results of one test, however, and especially not on one of the group tests, which are less accurate than the individual tests as bases for prediction. Also, although IQ scores may predict success in school work, they are not necessarily a good indication of future achievement in life. By focusing on cognitive

Test items such as the following are used in the WISC test:

General Information
How many wings does a bird have?
General Comprehension
What should you do if you see someone forget his book when he leaves his seat in a restaurant?
Arithmetic
Three women divided eighteen golf balls equally among themselves. How many golf balls did each woman receive?
Similarities
In what way are an hour and a week alike?
Vocabulary
This test consists simply of asking, *"What is a _____?"* or *"What does _____ mean?"* The words cover a wide range of difficulty or familiarity.

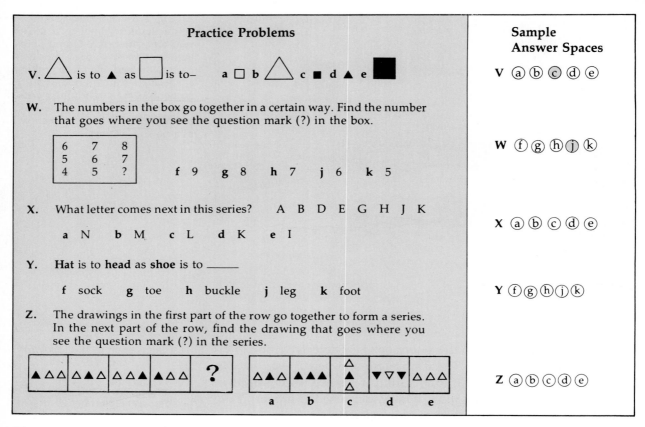

Practice Problems

Sample Answer Spaces

V. △ is to ▲ as ☐ is to— a ☐ b △ c ■ d ▲ e ■

V ⓐ ⓑ ©️ ⓓ ⓔ

W. The numbers in the box go together in a certain way. Find the number that goes where you see the question mark (?) in the box.

6	7	8
5	6	7
4	5	?

f 9   g 8   h 7   j 6   k 5

W ⓕ ⓖ ⓗ ⓙ ⓚ

X. What letter comes next in this series?   A B D E G H J K

a N   b M   c L   d K   e I

X ⓐ ⓑ © ⓓ ⓔ

Y. **Hat** is to **head** as **shoe** is to _____

f sock   g toe   h buckle   j leg   k foot

Y ⓕ ⓖ ⓗ ⓙ ⓚ

Z. The drawings in the first part of the row go together to form a series. In the next part of the row, find the drawing that goes where you see the question mark (?) in the series.

Z ⓐ ⓑ © ⓓ ⓔ

These are practice problems from a popular group test of intelligence, the Otis Quick-Scoring Mental Ability Test.

measures, many psychologists define intelligence too narrowly. A person with a moderate IQ, who is well motivated toward worthwhile goals and makes the most of his or her intellect, may be far more successful in life than a person with a high IQ who isn't so motivated.

Some psychologists have questioned the usefulness of IQ scores altogether. They point out that research has shown that IQ tests measure many different abilities. Two people with the same IQ might have totally different abilities. One might score high on the verbal and general knowledge sections of an IQ test. Another might do well on memory and arithmetic tests. For this reason, some psychologists argue that it's much more useful to know an individual's scores on tests which measure specific areas of *achievement* rather than a general IQ score.

Section Review

1. What is intelligence? What is IQ?
2. How is IQ calculated?
3. Describe an individual test of intelligence.
4. List some of the uses of IQ scores.

2. Criticisms of IQ Tests

One of the most basic criticisms of intelligence tests is not of the tests themselves, but of how test scores often are interpreted. Most psychologists agree that intelligence tests give an accurate measure of a person's *performance* on certain types of problem-solving tasks. This kind of problem-solving ability is necessary for success in school and many types of jobs. That is why IQ test scores are good predictors of school success.

But many psychologists argue that an IQ score does not give an accurate representation of a person's intellectual *capacity*. Intelligence tests do not measure such things as a person's ability to develop new ideas or to question the assumptions underlying old ones. Yet, IQ scores often mistakenly are interpreted as indicating the *limits* of a person's intellectual capacity.

Factors That Affect IQ

Many factors besides intelligence can affect an IQ score. This is another reason why many psychologists believe IQ scores should be viewed with caution as indicators of intellectual ability. Studies show, for example, that the values of a child's family, ethnic group, or social class can affect his or her performance on a test. Children who are brought up to compete, for example, generally do better on tests than those who are brought up not to be very competitive. Anxiety levels can influence test performance. Some children become very anxious in test situations and do not perform up to their ability. The expectations of a child's parents and teachers can also influence test results. Children who are made to feel confident that they will succeed often fulfill adults' expectations of them.

Other things beside cultural and personality factors can affect a child's performance on a test. The child's health and mood during a test can have a big influence on test results. Children with past experience in test taking generally do better than those with no previous experience with tests.

Finally, there are serious criticisms of the tests themselves. Questions have been raised about the reliability of standardized group intelligence tests. **Reliability** means that a person taking the same test twice should ideally score the same each time. If this is not the case, then the test is not reliable.

IQ Tests and Cultural Bias

The main criticism of standardized IQ tests, however, is that they are *culturally biased*. The questions on IQ tests are said to reflect the

PREVIEW

In this section read to find out:

1. what factors influence IQ scores.
2. why IQ tests are criticized.

Case Study

Culture-Adjusted IQ

No teacher can be sure that a poor child's IQ predicts intellectual capacity. In fact, many teachers would suspect that the test score actually measured the child's poverty and disadvantaged background. How can a teacher be sure? This is the dilemma that faced teachers for a nine-year-old black girl named Bernice. On a standardized intelligence test, Bernice scored 68, or mildly retarded. Should Bernice be assigned to a regular class or to a class for the retarded?

In a regular class, Bernice might be frustrated and teased by other children. In a class for the retarded, however, she might never have a chance to develop her fullest potential. Also, the label "retarded" would probably follow her the rest of her life.

Before they made their decision, school officials asked Bernice and her family to take the SOMPA Assessment. The SOMPA Assessment is designed to broaden the traditional measure of intelligence. Unlike culture-free tests, the SOMPA tries to adjust an IQ score to reflect the influence of economic and cultural factors. The SOMPA does this by gathering information from four different sources.

The first source is a standardized intelligence test, like the one Bernice had already taken. The second source was an hour-long interview with Bernice's parents. During this interview, a psychologist asked the parents about their social and economic background and about Bernice's medical history.

Bernice's parents also completed an adaptive behavior inventory. This survey including questions such as "How many pupils in his or her class does your child know?" and "Does your child prepare his or her own lunch?" This survey measured the child's social adjustment.

The final source of information is a thorough medical exam. This exam can identify physical problems, such as poor vision or hearing, that might hinder learning.

The interview with Bernice's parents revealed a very impoverished background. Bernice scored high on social adjustment, however, and showed a high degree of self-reliance. Using the SOMPA raised Bernice's IQ from 68 to 89, which is in the average range. As a result, Bernice was placed in a regular class.

language and experience of white, urban, middle-class children. Minority group children, those from poverty backgrounds, and those from rural areas are put at a disadvantage by many IQ tests, according to critics. For example, most IQ tests place strong emphasis on verbal ability and reading skills. But test instructions and questions are written in *standard* English and test *standard* concepts. Children from homes where a variation of standard English or a language other than English is spoken are handicapped when taking a test heavily weighted toward reading standard English and using standard language skills.

Some psychologists suggest the use of **culture-fair** tests designed to help lessen the language and experience bias against some minority group children. They would eliminate questions such as the following from standardized tests:

Symphony is to composer as book is to:

1) paper 2) sculptor 3) musician 4) author 5) man

This is a reasoning task which the testmakers estimate children over twelve should be able to complete. But what about a child who has not had any experience with symphonies and composers? Such a child may be able to understand the *reasoning* in the question but be unfamiliar with the *situation* or the *vocabulary*. A study has shown that when this question was included on a test, 81 percent of upper- and middle-income children got it right, while only 51 percent of lower-income children did so. (See the Close-up, *Can You Pass the Chitling Test?* on page 200 for more discussion of cultural bias in IQ tests.)

The Controversy over IQ Differences

As we have seen, IQ tests—whether they measure intelligence or not—do a good job of helping to predict which children will succeed in school. This fact makes both psychologists and sociologists interested in which groups of children do well on IQ tests, which groups do not, and, especially, why there is a difference.

When IQ tests are given to the general population, scores fall into the distribution we call the normal curve. But this distribution doesn't occur when certain groups are separated from the random population and matched against the normal curve. Studies of three-to-five-year-old children from poverty backgrounds, for example, show that they rank below the average IQ of 100. In this country, non-white groups generally score lower than whites on IQ tests, and the scores of children in isolated rural areas lag behind children in city slums.

For many years psychologists considered these differences in IQ scores to be due totally to environmental factors—poverty, social inequalities, and so on. In recent years, however, debate has arisen over the question of whether these differences are caused *only* by environmental factors or by **genetic** (inborn) differences among groups of people. Most theories of intelligence now consider both biological and environmental factors as important in determining level of intellectual performance as measured by IQ tests. But disagreements arise as to which element is more important.

In the 1970s, psychologist Arthur Jensen of the University of California at Berkeley fueled this controversy by indicating that studies he conducted showed that 80 percent of the differences between the IQ scores of black children and white children were due to genetic differences between the two races. Since then, other psychologists have pointed out problems with Jensen's research methods. Others have said that while hereditary factors may influence scores, they may also be strongly influenced by environmental factors. Many psychologists also criticized the IQ tests on which Jensen's research was based saying they were culturally biased.

In fact, support for much of the criticism of Jensen has come from the findings of a study Jensen conducted himself. Jensen compared the IQ scores of a racially mixed sample of 1,479 children from a poor town in Georgia with the IQ scores of a sample of black children and white children from Berkeley, California. In Berkeley, black children's IQs remained relatively unchanged as the children grew older. In rural Georgia, however, the black children lost an average of *one IQ point per year* between the ages of five and eighteen. The IQs of generally more affluent rural white children did not significantly decrease with age.

Can IQs Be Raised?

The question of what causes the differences in average IQ scores between different groups of people is an important practical problem which may affect our educational system in the United States. If children from limited environments do tend to score lower on tests, then it stands to reason that improving the children's environments at an early age should also improve their scores. Many studies have been made to see if this is what happens. The results suggest that experience does indeed have an influence on IQ scores.

Enriching the environment of children living in slum conditions can increase their IQ scores by as much as thirty points over those of a control group, according to a study made in Milwaukee. The subjects were 40 newborn children of mothers living in a Milwaukee slum whose own IQ scores were below 75. Children in one group received daily mental stimulation and, from the age of two, attended special classes at an Infant Education Center. At the age of three and a half, the IQs of these children averaged thirty-three points higher than those of the group who did not get extra enrichment.

Edward Zigler, a child psychologist at Yale University, thinks that "good" environments don't improve IQs. Rather, "poor" environments hinder children's abilities to realize their natural potential. Better conditions don't make children smarter, but they do make it possible for children to learn more easily. Learning habits, character, and self-concept are also improved—which is more important, in Zigler's view, than sheer "intelligence." "It's the whole child that is being educated," he says, "not just the brain."

Section Review

1. List three factors, besides intelligence, which may influence an individual's IQ test score.
2. Why do critics say IQ tests are *culturally biased?*
3. Explain the controversy over the reasons for IQ differences.

3. The Range of Human Intelligence

The vast majority of people, as we saw earlier, fall into the middle, or average, IQ range. In this section, we'll look at the special characteristics and problems of those who fall at both extremes of this range.

Mental Retardation

Mental retardation is a term generally used to describe an individual with an IQ below 70 as measured by intelligence tests. Many psychologists, however, object to describing mental retardation in terms of IQ alone because many factors besides intelligence can influence the outcome of an IQ test. For example, fatigue, malnutrition, or emotional problems are just some of the factors that can negatively affect how an individual does on an IQ test.

The term **mental retardation** might be better defined as referring to people who since childhood are unable to do and understand things most people their age can do and understand. A retarded child has trouble keeping up with others in such things as learning to walk, talk, tie his or her shoes, play games with other children, do school work, and so on.

Levels of Retardation

Four levels of mental retardation have been identified. Retarded people are described as either being profoundly, severely, moderately, or mildly retarded. Most retarded people are in the mildly retarded group.

The lowest level of functioning is described as **profoundly retarded.** If you think of abilities of the average three-month-old child, you will realize the extremely limited capabilities of people in this group. Profoundly retarded people are not able to understand or to use spoken language. They cannot take care of themselves and must be fed, dressed, and kept clean by someone else. They require twenty-four-hour supervision. In some cases, profoundly retarded people can learn to walk, but even in adult years they remain virtually helpless.

The **severely retarded** function at the level of a child just learning to talk. Like the average three-year-old child, they have trouble using language, because it is abstract and symbolic. (See Chapter 3 for a description of how we use language to think.) Severely retarded people need constant care and supervision, because they do not understand the ordinary dangers of life.

Moderately retarded people have a better ability to learn than those in the lower groups. There also are many more individuals in this group than in the severely or profoundly retarded groups, but they still

PREVIEW

In this section, read to find out:

1. what mental retardation is.
2. what the different levels of retardation are.
3. what people of superior intelligence are like.

represent only a small portion of all the mentally retarded. The moderately retarded can learn to feed and dress themselves, to keep themselves clean, and to avoid the basic dangers of life. Moderately retarded individuals can advance academically to the intellectual level of about six years, especially with the benefit of specialized instruction. In some cases, vocational training can provide them with the basic skills to perform simple jobs in a sheltered workshop. Moderately retarded individuals can live comfortably in the community, provided they live in a residential home with careful supervision.

Most retarded people are what is known as **mildly retarded.** Mildly retarded youngsters can attend school and can reach an intellectual level of eight to twelve years. They can learn such basic skills as handling money, doing simple arithmetic, reading and writing, and also some job skills. Schooling goals for mildly retarded youngsters involve mainstreaming them as much as possible into a normal school setting. Sometimes this means that the retarded student might be in a separate classroom or have special teachers for certain subjects but would, at other times, attend regular school classes and activities.

For most retarded individuals, especially those who are mildly retarded, the outlook is much brighter today than it was twenty years

In surroundings where their contributions are accepted, moderately retarded children and adults can live fairly normal lives.

ago. As late as the 1960s, many mentally retarded people spent their lives in often overcrowded mental institutions. That has now changed. We now know that most mentally retarded people are capable of doing much more than was previously thought, but they need stimulation and challenges to do so. For the majority of retarded people, the focus is on helping them function as much as possible within the community. Rather than being institutionalized, retarded individuals today live either at home or in supervised group homes with other retarded people. Mildly and moderately retarded children who are unable to live at home may live in private homes with specially trained foster parents who work with them on perfecting the skills that will help them lead more independent and productive lives. Some mildly retarded adults can live on their own with only periodic supervision from health care of social service personnel. If the community and people around them are kind and supportive, the mentally retarded individual will develop to his or her potential. Many can qualify for many different jobs and can become productive members of their communities.

A mentally handicapped child accepts the award she has won in the Special Olympics, held for the mentally and physically handicapped.

It's Your Turn

As we have said these extremes of human intelligence are rare. However, it is not uncommon for us to come in contact directly or indirectly with people in these groups. Have you ever had any experience with either retardation or superior intelligence? Have you had experience with a friend or family member? Perhaps you have read a book, such as the one pictured below, or seen a movie on this subject. Now *It's Your Turn*. Describe your experience in this area. Now that you know more about this subject would your reaction be different?

Causes of Retardation

One of the most difficult questions to answer about mental retardation is "what causes it?" There are many possible answers to this question. Only about one-fourth of the retarded people have something physically wrong with their brains. Some types of retardation, such as Down's syndrome, are caused by genetic factors. Other causes include exposure of a child to poisonous substances, infections contracted by the mother during pregnancy, brain injuries, and malnutrition.

Is there a cure for retardation? Depending on the suspected cause, drugs, surgery, or vitamin therapy have been of some use in helping the retarded to live more normal lives. But, in order to live more normal lives, retarded people need special attention, affection, and understanding, not criticism, rejection, and ridicule. The majority of mildly retarded people have not learned to use the intellectual ability they have. Many have been brought up in lonely and dull environments which have added to their problems. If given a chance to interact with other people in their environment, they might blossom and be able to lead fairly normal lives.

Superior Intelligence

What is superior intelligence? IQ scores are used as one measure of superior intelligence. People with IQs of 140 or above are considered **gifted.** The term **genius** is sometimes applied to people with IQs of 150 or above. What sort of people are the intellectually gifted? What are they like and what do they do?

Gifted children may learn to read, write, and do arithmetic problems sooner than average children their age. Studies show that gifted children are usually leaders in school. They tend to be aware of society's problems at an earlier age than most children. Gifted people generally have a wide range of interests, and are better adjusted than average people. Lower rates of suicide and divorce are found in this group.

One important study of gifted people was started in 1922 by psychologist Lewis M. Terman and his colleagues at Stanford University. They studied over 1500 individuals from school years through adulthood. On the average, the study found that the superior children stood out from the crowd in many respects. They were, on the average, taller, healthier, stronger, and weighed more at birth. They walked earlier, talked earlier, and had fewer physical and emotional problems. Their social interests were normal, and they read on a wide range of topics. As adults, many of them achieved advanced degrees and became professionals, scientists, and writers.

One kind of gifted person is the child prodigy, who performs like an adult while still a young child. Mathematical and musical prodigies have appeared from time to time.

These musical prodigies, shown at left, were professionals in the 1930s and 1940s: Ruggiero Ricci, Loren Maazel (conducting), and Ruth Slenczynska, shown with her father.

Dr. Ruth Slenczynska, shown above, played her first piano recital at age four. She now is artist-in-residence at Southern Illinois University, where her husband is also a faculty member. In her memoirs she described the terrible pressures put on a child performer forced to match adult standards. This dampened public enthusiasm for concert performances by children.

These findings corrected some common myths about gifted people. They were previously believed to be physically inferior, to have narrow, academic interests, and to be a bit peculiar. It also must be noted that the people followed in Terman's study were not without their problems. One of five in the group had an above average number of personal and emotional problems. Some of them even flunked out of college! Evidently, superior intelligence is not all that is needed to succeed fully in life.

Section Review

1. Define mental retardation.
2. List and briefly describe the four levels of retardation.
3. Describe some characteristics of people with superior intelligence.

C L O S E——U P

Can You Pass the Chitling Test?

Robert L. Williams

Intelligence tests have been criticized because test instructions and questions written in standard English and testing standard concepts may not make sense to children who use a different language to deal with nonstandard concepts. Sociologist Adrian Dove set out to illustrate just how big the gap is between standard and black English. In 1968, Dove developed the Dove Counterbalance General Intelligence test, a set of thirty multiple-choice questions. This test, also known as the "Chitling test," uses black English to test knowledge of black cultural concepts. For example, could you pick the place where the "Hully Gully" started on a multiple choice test?[1] Do you know what a "blood" is?[2] How long should you cook chitlings?[3]

Psychologist Robert L. Williams feels that the difference in language can be much more subtle than the black English used on the Chitling test. He and psychologist L. Wendell Rivers designed a study to measure the actual effect on IQ scores of this difference in language. They translated the instructions of a standard IQ test into familiar English. This IQ test asked children to mark a picture that matches a concept of time, space, or quantity. Their subjects were 890 black children attending kindergarten, first, or second grade. The children were divided into two groups. One half was given the standard version of the test and one half was given the familiar or "nonstandard" version. The results? The children who took the nonstandard version scored significantly higher than those who took the test with the standard instructions. And the nonstandard instructions differed very little from the standard! For example, the instructions on the standard version read "behind the sofa," while the nonstandard version asked the child to mark a picture of something "in back of the couch." On the standard version, a child was to mark the picture of a boy "beginning to climb the tree." On the nonstandard version, this was changed to "starting to climb the tree." Even if small, these differences are important.

Answers to Chitling test: 1) Watts 2) a black person 3) 24 hours.

4. Creativity

Psychologists disagree about the relationship between creativity and intelligence. Studies of people who have achieved success in fields where creativity is important show that these individuals were more intelligent than average people. Intelligence, however, is only part of the story. A very intelligent person might or might not score high on tests of creativity. Intelligence seems to be necessary for achieving success in creative fields, but it is not enough by itself.

Creativity: What Is It?

Much research has gone into defining **creativity** and into determining what makes a creative person. Most people think of creativity as the special quality associated with people like Marie Curie, Ludwig van Beethoven, Albert Einstein, Georgia O'Keeffe, or Pablo Picasso. In fact, whether we realize it or not, all of us are creative at one time or another, in some way. The difference between us and Curie or Picasso is that the things most of us are creative about do not have world-wide impact.

Left: "Jack-in-the-Pulpit, iv," by Georgia O'Keeffe
Right: "The Red Armchair," by Pablo Picasso

Pablo Picasso, *The Red Armchair.*
Collection of The Art Institute of Chicago

Left: This three-tiered tree-house, equipped with lookout, grew out of the imagination and hard work of the Empire Tree-House Club during the summer of 1972. Right: Organic know-how and a little inventiveness turned what might have been scrap material into a frame for a botanical garden.

This may make us less newsworthy than famous people, but it does not mean that we are uncreative. When psychologists study creativity they look at four main aspects: the *process* of creating, the *product* that is created, the *factors* that influence creativity, and the *nature* of the creative person.

Something new is added. The process of being creative involves expressing one's thoughts or feelings in a new way. Familiar materials—words, paint, musical tones, mathematical data—are rearranged to produce a unique product that expresses the capabilities of a unique individual.

The creative process involves being unconventional—striking out on your own and doing something differently. If you copy another person's painting, not adding anything to the other person's idea, your work is not creative, no matter how skillful you are. But even a poor

Top: Cave homes are the invention of Andy Davis. The idea came to him as he ventured inside an abandoned mine—an environment, he realized, that is cool in the summer and warm in the winter. Liking the cave home that he built for himself so much, he now builds and markets them for anyone interested in this lifestyle option.

Bottom: "If somebody had told me years ago that I'd be a sculptor, I'd have called 'em crazy," said Fred Smith, creator of what he calls his "children." His children are the over 300 figures made of concrete decorated with broken bottle glass that surround his home in Wisconsin. It all started in 1950. The idea came to him as he was helping a neighbor with some construction. Soon he was creating huge life-size shapes by pouring concrete into holes he had dug. Then before they were dry, he'd haul them up, add arms, legs, and give them coats of colored glass. How did the idea occur to him? "I don't know how to explain it. It's just in a person. Can't teach it."

painting or a badly worded sentence can be creative, if it brings new insight and freshness to the topic. Novelty, unconventionality, and freshness are essential ingredients of the creative process.

The new thing has value. Originality in itself, however, does not guarantee the creative spark. What you create must have value for either yourself or others. You can work at a problem in many new ways, but if your answers are consistently wrong, your originality means nothing. Creativity is always appropriate to the problem or situation. You can talk in gibberish, but if no one understands what you're saying, your originality is without value. Value and appropriateness both characterize the creative product.

Factors That Influence Creativity

Many talented people grew up in families that were headed by talented parents. Johann Sebastian Bach, for instance, did not simply discover his musical ability; his father was a court musician and probably taught his son to think in musical terms from an early age. This *situational* factor is thought to be important in developing creativity. Also, some freedom to experiment, to develop one's own approach to problems, seems more likely to result in creative and meaningful solu-

Although it's possible to buy almost anything already made these days, people still have the urge to put their creativity to work in designing their own clothes.

tions. In school, for example, if students are always given the answers by the teacher, they do not need to find answers for themselves.

Another important factor in creativity is thought to be *motivation*. To be creative, you need an incentive, or reason to create. In experimental situations, it has been shown that incentives can come from either some outside reward or from a desire for self-expression and doing something that is personally satisfying. It seems that positive reinforcement, which we discussed in Chapter 5, brings out certain creative abilities in people, under certain conditions.

Erez Klein and John Wickham were given three weeks vacation from school to complete the project—setting up 135,215 dominoes. What happened next? The first domino knocked down flattened the entire rink-full.

It took Sam Rodia of Los Angeles 33 years, but he single-handedly constructed the Watts Towers, mainly from refuse. When asked why he built the garden of spires (two of them are nearly 100 feet tall), he just replies, "I had it in my mind to do something big and I did."

But many psychologists believe that a truly creative person doesn't wait to be told or rewarded. According to these psychologists, the creative person starts the creative act herself or himself. This inner, self-determined creativity is said to be spontaneous. The act of creation is its own reward. If the resulting product is valued by others, so much the better.

The Creative Person

What are the characteristics of creative people? Researchers have found that creative people have a great deal of curiosity. They also think flexibly, are aware of subtleties, and are more than usually energetic. But since these qualities are often found in people who are not especially creative, what else is involved? Psychologist D. W. MacKinnon added these characteristics. The creative person is (1) open to experience, (2) free from crippling restraints, or inhibitions, and (3) independent in thought and action. Other researchers in creativity have emphasized the trait of noncomformity—a willingness to go against the crowd and to take calculated risks. Finally, there is considerable evidence that creative people are less authoritarian than noncreators, meaning they believe in letting other people go their way and they expect to go theirs. Creative people are playful, enjoy exploring for the sake of exploration, and are relatively indifferent to other people's opinions of their work.

All of this suggests that for most people creativity is not something we are born with. It grows out of personality traits that can be enhanced to some degree. With a little imagination nearly everyone can bring some originality to a valued task. Learning to act in this manner is itself a way of being creative.

As we have said everyone has some creative ability. This is a difficult thing to measure accurately, but here are some problems, developed by psychologist J. P. Guilford, which may give you some ideas about the factors involved in creativity. Give them a try.

1. Two men played chess. They played five games, and each won three. How do you explain this? (A tie is not a win.)

2. Explain the following true statement. "In my bedroom the nearest lamp that I keep turned on is 12 feet from my bed. Alone in the room without using wires, strings, timers, or any other aids or contraptions I can turn out the light on that lamp and get into bed before the room is dark."

3. List ten uses for each of these: brick, potato, horse, spoon.

4. On a separate paper, place nine dots positioned as below. Connect all nine dots by drawing four straight lines, without taking your pencil off the paper or retracing a line.

Section Review

1. Define creativity.

2. Describe the situational and motivation factors that influence creativity.

3. Describe some characteristics of a creative person.

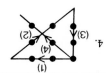

Answers to creativity problems:
1. They did not play each other.
2. It is done in the daytime.
3. varies

Chapter 7 Review

Section Summaries

1. Intelligence and Intelligence Tests

Most psychologists would agree that intelligence is the ability to profit from experience and to adapt to new conditions in the environment. Most intelligence tests include tasks that test general knowledge about the world, the ability to understand relationships among words, numbers and spatial patterns, as well as memory and problem-solving skills. In 1905, the Frenchman Alfred Binet developed an intelligence test for children. Each child's score was expressed as an intelligence quotient. In large groups, scores tend to be distributed in a normal curve. In the United States, Binet's test was modified in 1916 to produce the Stanford-Binet Intelligence Test. In the 1950s, David Wechsler developed intelligence tests that covered both verbal and non-verbal abilities.

2. Criticisms of IQ Tests

Most psychologists argue that these tests measure current performance, not the limits of performance. IQ scores can also be affected by such factors as cultural values, anxiety, and mood. Critics have also questioned the reliability of IQ tests. The main criticism, however, is that the tests are culturally biased. Thus, many psychologists suggest the use of culture-fair tests.

3. The Range of Human Intelligence

The term "mental retardation" refers to people who since childhood are unable to do and understand as much as most people their age. The four levels of retardation are profoundly retarded, severely retarded, moderately retarded, and mildly retarded. Moderately retarded people can reach an intellectual level of about 6 years, and the mildly retarded can achieve an intellectual level of between 8-12 years. People with IQs of 140 or above are called gifted. People with IQs higher than 150 are considered geniuses.

4. Creativity

In studying creativity, psychologists study the process of creating, the product that is created, the factors that influence creativity, and the nature of the creative person. The process of being creative involves expressing one's thoughts or feelings in a new and valuable way. Creativity is influenced by situational factors and by motivation. Researchers have found that creative people are curious, think flexibly, are aware of subtleties, and are more than usually energetic. In addition, they seem to be free from inhibitions and high in nonconformity.

Psychology Skill Activities

1. Read a biography of a creative person. Report to the class about what factors seem to contribute to the person's creativity. **easy**

2. Try to create some questions for an intelligence test. Write some questions that would be biased toward the culture of your school, and then try to write some questions that would be culture-fair. Identify the factors that make each of your questions culture-biased or culture-fair. **challenging**

Testing for Understanding

Knowing Key Terms

Define these terms in your own words.

Section 1
intelligence
intelligence quotient
deviation IQ
normal curve

Section 2
reliability
culture-fair
genetic

Section 3
mental retardation
profoundly retarded
severely retarded
moderately retarded
mildly retarded
gifted
genius

Section 4
creativity

Reviewing Main Ideas

Section 1
1. How do psychologists define the term "intelligence"?

2. What do MA, CA, and IQ stand for in this formula?

$$\frac{MA}{CA} \times 100 = IQ$$

Section 2
1. Describe some of the factors that can influence scores on intelligence tests.

2. What are come criticisms that are made of intelligence tests?

Section 3
1. Is it better to define mental retardation in terms of IQ or in terms of an individual's general inability to keep up with people of the same age? Why?

2. What are the characteristics of the different levels of mental retardation?

3. Explain what Terman's study revealed about gifted people.

Section 4
1. What standards do psychologists use to determine that an act has been creative?

2. What are some characteristics of creative people?

3. How do psychologists test creativity?

Thinking Critically
1. *Problem Solving.* Calculate the IQ of a six-year-old child with a mental age of eight years. **easy**

2. *Making Applications.* Use the standards described in this chapter to identify something creative that you or someone you know has done. **challenging**

Demonstrating Psychology Skills
Below is a "normal curve" showing a distribution of IQ scores in a randomly selected group. Answer the questions following the graph.

Normal Curve

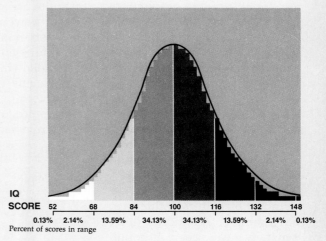

1. What percentage of people have IQs between 85 and 115?

2. What percentage scored below 50?

3. What percentage scored above 150?

4. Which group is larger (a) those between 85-115 or (b) those below 85?

5. What is the most common IQ according to this graph?

Experimenting With Psychology

Conditioned Perception of Taste

According to a recent national survey, eating is one of America's top ten leisure activities. Eating not only keeps us alive and healthy, but it is an important part of our social and emotional lives as well. Much of the way we feel about food, and the effect it has on us, is learned behavior. As we grow up, we are conditioned to respond to food in certain ways.

We all have different tastes in food, of course. Sometimes we even say we have a favorite food. Your favorite, for example, might be different from your sister's or from the person's next door. But, generally your "favorite" will come from the range of foods offered to you by your family. Family preferences are, in turn, largely determined by cultural influences. For example, Americans don't generally eat eel, although it's considered a delicacy in the Netherlands, northern Germany, and Scandinavia. And, most Americans would also probably pass up octopus, a favorite in Greece and Italy. Similarly, the Japanese eat raw fish in much larger quantities than Americans do. Japanese visitors to the United States, on the other hand, are often dismayed by the steady diet of beef and starches offered by America's most popular chain and fast-food restaurants.

Another factor affecting food preference is appearance. Though seemingly unrelated to taste, the appearance of a food can sometimes have a strong effect on our opinions of it. These feelings illustrate the effects of previously conditioned learning. The following experiment will show you the powerful influence of this conditioning on perception. To do this demonstration, you will need two volunteers and at least four of the following: (1) two glasses of milk, one colored blue with food coloring; (2) two glasses of orange juice, one dyed black; (3) two scrambled eggs, one colored bright green; (4) two servings of mashed potatoes, one colored purple; (5) two servings of rice, one colored green; or (6) two pieces of toast, one with patches of food coloring to make it look moldy. (You can substitute your own examples for these, of course.)

Once the items have been assembled, blindfold the two volunteers, so they don't see the foods before they eat them. Ask them to taste the foods. Then record their reactions on a chart similar to the one below. Then remove their blindfolds and ask them to finish eating. Record the volunteers' reactions to the various foods now that they can see them.

Reaction Sheet: Conditioned Perception of Taste Experiment

Food	with blindfold	without blindfold
1. regular		
odd color		
2. regular		
odd color		
3. regular		
odd color		
4. regular		
odd color		

Summary of Results:
1. How did volunteers react to the odd-colored food?
2. Was one food rejected more than others?
3. Did both volunteers react in the same way?
4. What conclusions about food preferences can you draw based on the results?

Unit 2 Test

Matching (20 points)

Match each definition with a term below.
1. linking a sequence of behaviors
2. change in behavior as a result of experience
3. interpreting what is sensed
4. as parallel lines get farther away they appear closer together
5. reasoning from specific to general
6. thinking, problem-solving
7. reasoning from general to specific
8. trick to aid memory
9. sudden realization of answer to problem
10. activity that occurs because of a stimulus

a. learning
b. linear perspective
c. response
d. deductive
e. cognition
f. mnemonic device
g. perception
h. insight
i. inductive
j. chaining

Multiple Choice (20 points)

Circle the choice that best completes the statement or answers the question.
1. The four basic tastes are (a) sweet, salt, bitter, spicy; (b) salt, sweet, sour, bitter; (c) fruity, spicy, salt, bitter; (d) salt, sweet, fruity, spicy.
2. Which of the following is *not* a type of ESP? (a) telepathy, (b) psychokinesis, (c) vestibular, (d) premonition
3. The part of the environment that brings about a reaction in an animal or human is called (a) response, (b) association, (c) stimulus, (d) none of these.
4. In classical conditioning, an association is made between the (a) CR and CS, (b) CR and UCR, (c) CS and UCS, (d) none of the above.
5. Which of these is *not* an application of operant conditioning? (a) getting hungry at mealtime, (b) token economies, (c) teaching machine, (d) behavior modification therapy
6. Because many images are similar, we combine them in our thinking into a single, (a) context, (b) concept, (c) symbol, (d) image.

7. Which of the following is *not* true about creativity? (a) Originality is involved. (b) Situational factors influence creativity. (c) Intelligence is usually involved. (d) The product does not have to have value.
8. The order of the three steps in the human memory process is (a) long-term, short-term, sensory; (b) short-term, long-term, sensory; (c) sensory, short-term, long-term; (d) none of these.
9. The ability to adapt to situations in the environment is called (a) reasoning, (b) creativity, (c) intelligence, (d) perception.
10. IQ test scores are most commonly used by (a) business, (b) industry, (c) schools, (d) none of these.

Fill in the Blanks (20 points)

Choose the word that best completes each statement.
1. The part of the eye sensitive to color is called _____.
2. Using two eyes to see is called _____.
3. A _____ makes behavior less likely to occur.
4. Money is an example of a _____ _____.
5. Technically, in conditioning giving a reward is called _____.
6. If intelligence is the result of inherited factors, it is _____.
7. A _____ has an IQ greater than 150.
8. Learning theorists believe that most language learning is the result of _____.
9. The kind of memory that allows you to reproduce exactly information that has been stored away is called _____.
10. A _____ is the smallest unit of speech with meaning.

Critical Thinking Essay (40 points)

Discuss how processes of the senses and learning are related in human behavior. Give examples of the types of sensations (and perceptions) we have and the types of learning and thinking we are capable of. How do these perceptions affect learning? How does intelligence affect learning? Be specific.

Unit 3

Roots of Behavior

In this unit you will explore the biological roots of behavior—how our brain operates, how emotion and motivation influence our behavior, and what changes occur in our consciousness when we are awake, asleep, or under the influence of hypnosis, medication, or drugs.

Biology and Behavior

In the following passage from *The Terminal Man* by Michael Crichton, the author describes attempts to alter the behavior of Harry Benson, a man suffering from epilepsy as a result of an automobile accident. Benson is subject to violent seizures and has twice tried to kill people. Surgeons have attached forty wires to his brain in an attempt to control or modify his behavior by means of electrical stimulation. Other characters of the novel are Dr. Ross, a psychiatrist, and two computer experts, Gerhard and Richards.

"What are we doing today?" Benson asked.

"We're going to stimulate your electrodes to see what happens."

He nodded. He seemed to take this calmly, but Ross had learned not to trust his calm. After a moment he said, "Will it hurt?"

"No."

"Okay," he said. "Go ahead."

Gerhard watched through the one-way glass as Ross and Benson began to talk. Alongside him, Richards picked up the taperecorder microphone and said quietly, "Stimulation series one, patient Harold Benson, March 11, 1971."

In the next room, Ross was saying, "You'll feel a variety of sensations. We want you to tell us what you feel."

Richards said, "Electrode one, five millivolts, for five seconds." Gerhard pressed the buttons. The computer screen showed the current snaking its way through the intricate electronic maze. They watched Benson through the one-way glass.

Benson said, "That's interesting."

"What's interesting?" Ross asked.

"Well, it's like eating a ham sandwich."

"Do you feel hungry?"

"Not particularly."

"Do you feel anything else?"

"No. Just the taste of a ham sandwich." He smiled. "On rye."

Gerhard, sitting at the control panel, nodded. The first electrode had stimulated a memory.

Richards: "Electrode two, five millivolts, five seconds."

Benson said, "I have to go to the bathroom."

Ross said, "It will pass."

Electrode three produced no effect on Benson.

"Electrode four," Richards said into the recorder. "Five millivolts, five seconds." The shock was delivered.

And Benson, in an oddly childlike voice, said, "Could I have some milk and cookies, please?"

Richards, watching the reaction, said, "How old would you say?"

"About five or six, at most."

Benson was talking about cookies, talking about his tricycle, to Ross. Slowly, over the next few minutes, he seemed to emerge like a time-traveler advancing through the years. Finally he became fully adult again, thinking back to his youth, instead of actually being there. "I always wanted the cookies, and she said they were bad for me."

"We can go on," Gerhard said.

Richards: "Electrode five, five millivolts, five seconds."

In the next room, Ben-

son shifted uncomfortably in his wheelchair. Ross asked him if something was wrong. Benson said, "It feels funny."

"How do you mean?"

"I can't describe it. It's like sandpaper. Irritating."

Gerhard nodded, and wrote in his notes, "#5—potential attack electrode." This happened sometimes. Occasionally an electrode would be found to simulate a seizure.

"Electrode six, five millivolts, five seconds," Richards intoned, and the stimulation series continued. ▄

The situation described in *The Terminal Man* is fictitious. But real-life experiments have been carried out with similar results. Electric shocks to particular parts of the brain *do* conjure up memories of past experiences, even the behaviors of childhood. This has led some researchers to theorize that, for the most part, behavior results from electrical impulses in the brain. This means that those emotions you feel—the occasional anger at a friend, the love for a family member, the fear of the unknown—are mostly the result of an electrical system—although a chemical system is also at work coloring your behavior.

Your electrical and chemical systems are the genesis for all thinking, feeling, and acting. Your ability to visualize different hues of blue, to remember the scent of a rose, to express sadness or happiness, to respond in an emergency, or to make plans for the future all begin with a biological process. More than anyone ever thought possible, mind and body are one.

In this chapter, we will look at what recent research has taught us about the mechanisms of the brain and the body that make feeling and action possible, that make human beings human.

PREVIEW

In this section, read to find out:

1. some historical examples of brain research.
2. some of the advanced techniques for studying the brain.

1. How the Brain Is Studied

A lobotomy is a surgical procedure in which the brain's frontal lobes are disconnected from the rest of the brain. It is in the frontal lobes where emotional processes interact with high-level thinking and decision-making.

The first lobotomy was performed on human beings in 1935 by a Portuguese doctor named Egas Moniz. Moniz was so impressed with a report on how violent chimpanzees became passive and quiet after frontal lobe surgery that he decided to try it on several of his very agitated, emotionally disturbed patients.

The results were dramatic. Violent patients became quiet and manageable. Moniz won worldwide renown and eventually was awarded a Nobel Prize for his discovery.

Soon lobotomies were being performed in the United States. Thousands of emotionally battered soldiers returning from World War II were overcrowding psychiatric wards. Tranquilizers, which are now used to control violent behavior, had not yet been discovered. Believing that certain defective brain cells were the root of patients' behavioral problems, doctors disconnected these tissues in as many as fifty brains a day. Thousands of veterans, once violent, were now quiet. But the "cure" in many cases proved only temporary. Some lobotomized patients suffered bizarre personality changes. (One of Dr. Moniz' "cures" went berserk and shot the doctor.) Many were unable to make plans for the future or do anything but the simplest of tasks.

Finally, by the early '50s, the medical world began to regard the lobotomy "cure" as almost worse than the "disease." At about the same time, tranquilizers made their debut. But it was not before lobotomies had been performed on some 50,000 people, many of whom had slid into vegetablelike states.

This reflection back to the days of lobotomies illustrates how science learns from its experiments and from its mistakes. Today, the medical world knows that trying to surgically disconnect a "diseased" point in the brain is like trying to pluck out one thread in a closely spun spider web without tearing the rest of the fabric.

The techniques for studying the brain that you will read about in this section are being performed today. Medical science has come a long way since the days of primitive lobotomies, and yet lobotomies were performed in our very recent past. In thirty years, the techniques of today may look as primitive as lobotomies do to us now.

Techniques Used Today

Advanced techniques for studying the brain and the nervous system have added greatly to our understanding of the relationship between biology and behavior. Today there are five main approaches for studying the brain.

1. Electron microscopes are used to analyze brain and other nerve cells after the organisms have died. They can magnify nerve cells many thousands of times. *Microscopic analysis* has identified not only the physical structure of these cells, but their chemical makeup as well.

2. *Injection of drugs* into the brains of laboratory animals allows the study of behavior changes in the living organism. This is done by implanting tiny tubes in different areas of the brain and then applying very small amounts of drugs in various strengths directly to brain sites.

On the left above is an EEG recording of normal brain wave activity. On the right is a recording of a severe convulsive seizure.

By using the brains of living animals, scientists can more precisely study the chemical and biological processes that are at work.

3. *Lesioning* of brain tissue is done in live animals by severing a nerve area or removing a section of brain, and then observing the performance of the animals. Karl Lashley was one of the pioneers in this technique. Removing different regions of rats' brains, he found, affected the rats' ability to remember their way around a maze. However, it was not the specific *section* that was cut out, but rather, the *amount*. Even with the removal of much brain tissue, the rats were still able to perform, although at a much simpler level. Memory storage thus appears to be widely distributed in the brain.

4. The brain, as the body's control center, functions electrically. As brain cells work, they give off tiny amounts of electrical energy. The *general electrical activity* of the brain can be measured by an *electroencephalograph* or EEG machine. Wires from the EEG machine are taped to several points on the head. Electrical energy from the brain activates a pen on moving graph paper. Certain brain cells release electrical energy in rhythms; these rhythms, or brain-wave patterns, are recorded on paper. As the brain performs different functions, from sleeping to intense thought, the patterns change. In effect, the brain is "writing" out its messages, leaving scientists to determine what type of mental activity is taking place.

Because every person has different brain-wave patterns, the expression "being on a different wave length" is not just a figure of speech. A young child has a wave pattern quite distinct from an older person, while identical twins have very similar EEGs. Yet, like fingerprints, the brain waves of no two persons are exactly the same. Unlike fingerprints, brain waves change constantly, reflecting the unique electrical activity taking place at a given moment. When the EEG is "flat"—when no activity is present in the brain—the brain is dead.

5. In the 1930s, Dr. Wilder Penfield of the Montreal Neurological Institute pioneered a promising new technique for treating patients who suffered from epileptic seizures—a technique that makes *The Terminal Man* look outdated 40 years later. He *stimulated different parts of the brain with a mild electric current.*

Although Penfield's purpose was to relieve the patient's disorder, in the process he learned how the brain functions in more precise ways than had ever been known before. Patients were fully conscious during treatment. (The brain, although it is largely made up of nerves, does not "feel" anything itself.) So they were able to report just exactly how they felt. "There's a tingling in my left thumb . . . now it's on the left side of my tongue . . . now my tongue is moving . . ." People "saw" scenes from their childhood that had been long forgotten. As a result of sessions like this, Penfield was able to "map" a large part of the brain. He also concluded that nothing the brain takes in is ever really lost.

Another result of this technique was the discovery of pleasure sites in the brain. James Olds taught rats to press a lever that delivered electrical stimulation to the pleasure sites in their own brains. So rewarding was the experience that some rats pressed the lever 7,000 times an hour, passing up food even though they were hungry.

Many believe experiments with animals are cruel and unnecessary. And some question the use of electrical stimulation to *control human* behavior. Recently, the medical profession has begun to set up guidelines to protect people from over-enthusiastic brain tinkerers. The question of animal experimentation is as yet unanswered. The ultimate issue is the use of power: who should have the power to push *your* button?

Section Review

1. Tell how it is known that parts of the brain perform certain functions? Why is this information important?
2. Describe the techniques used to study the brain.
3. How does Penfield's work illustrate the fact that the brain operates electrically?

José Delgado is a pioneer in the brain implantation of radio-activated electrodes. His ability to find an exact point in an animal's brain is so precise that he can trust his life to it. Here, even after the bull has started to charge, Delgado can stop it by a radio message to electrodes planted in its brain. After repeated experiences such as this, the animal becomes permanently less aggressive.

2. How the Brain Works

Soon after completing the world's first heart transplant, Christian Barnard declared that a brain transplant was unlikely in the near future, for the nature of tissue in the central nervous system (which includes the brain) made the operation virtually impossible. The renowned surgeon then added that one cannot really talk of transplanting a human brain, even if techniques were available, because the transfer of the organ could only be looked upon as providing it with a new body. The operation would therefore be a body transplant, not a brain transplant. The recipient would be certain to see himself as the donor fitted out with a new body.

This excerpt from Leonard Stevens' book, *Explorers of the Brain*, emphasizes something few of us can easily accept—that the colorless, characterless piece of biological material we call the brain is the command center for literally billions of personalities and behaviors, both past and present. It is the wizard that discovered fire and put human beings on the moon. It is one and the same with our conscious selves. It is both mind and body.

The Development of the Human Brain

The brain is not a single organ, but rather a collection of organs. Some of the organs of the human brain are grouped into what is called the "old brain" or **subcortex.** It is called the old brain, because it is thought to have been the first part of the human brain to develop. The

Without the smooth functioning of all the parts of the human brain, juggling atop a galloping horse would not be possible. Neither would a thousand other activities, far less complicated.

subcortex rests *under* the other organs of the human brain which are classified as the "new brain" or **neocortex.** The neocortex is the thinking brain, the part of the brain that is unique to human beings alone.

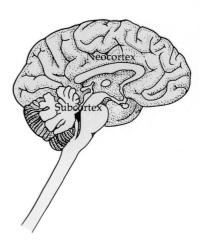

The Old Brain: The Subcortex

The subcortex, found in the brains of most animals, is responsible for basic survival functions such as breathing, eating, drinking, sleeping, and mating. Appetite, thirst, and arousal are triggered here, as well as basic instinctual emotions such as aggression and fear.

The subcortex has several parts, each of which has a specific assignment in keeping the body working efficiently. For our purposes in thinking about behavior, the most important parts of the subcortex are the following.

The thalamus. The **thalamus** is in almost the exact center of the brain. Like a post office, it receives incoming sensory messages, sorts them, and passes them on to the appropriate parts of the subcortex and neocortex.

The hypothalamus. The **hypothalamus** is your body's thermostat. It also regulates food and water levels and, to some extent, controls emotional behavior. When you are cold, the nerves that monitor temperature send messages to the brain. ("Hey, it's getting cold down here.") The hypothalamus acts immediately, sending a return message to the nerves in the muscles. What happens? Your muscles, answering the call, begin to shiver in an attempt to raise your body temperature back up to normal.

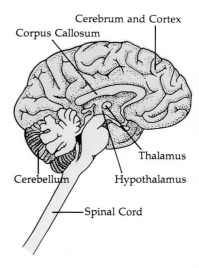

A similar thing happens when you are confronted by danger. The hypothalamus signals the adrenal glands to release adrenaline into the blood stream. This speeds up the heart rate and blood pressure to help you respond in an emergency.

The cerebellum. The word **cerebellum** means "lesser brain." The cerebellum acts as a helper to the neocortex in coordinating motor functions. It does not initiate muscle action. But if you are about to pour a glass of milk, the cerebellum makes sure you hit the glass and not the tabletop beside it. Acting as a fine tuner, the cerebellum helps the body maintain balance, posture, and eye-hand coordination.

The New Brain: The Neocortex

The neocortex is the thinking brain, the part that distinguishes human beings from all other forms of life. It is here that the highest, most creative and complex level of brain activity takes place. Without a functioning neocortex, the body works, but we are classified as "brain dead."

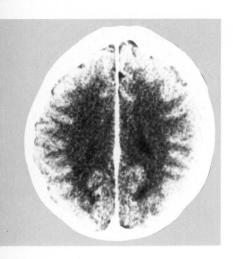

The left and right hemispheres of the brain (above) are each divided into four lobes (below). Each lobe represents different areas of brain function.

Lobes of the Right Hemisphere

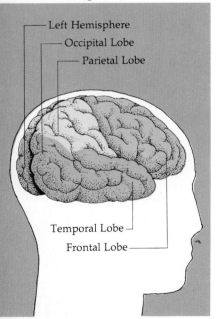

Left Hemisphere
Occipital Lobe
Parietal Lobe

Temporal Lobe
Frontal Lobe

The cortex and the cerebrum. The cortex and the cerebrum make up the neocortex. The word **cortex** means bark. It is the thin outer layer that covers the cerebrum. The cortex is wrinkled into thousands of tiny folds which evolved to help pack the maximum number of brain cells into the limited space available. (The brains of lower animals are smooth or have far fewer folds.) The cortex and the cerebrum are generally thought of as a single working unit.

The **cerebrum** makes up 80 percent of the brain's mass. Together with the cortex that covers it, it is responsible for all the active thought and planning that goes on in the brain. The cerebrum and cortex make possible thoughts like these. "That project I did in art class today needs something, but I can't figure out what." "I like that song playing right now." "I've got to convince the teacher that paper was worth a higher grade. Wonder what I should say."

Hemispheres. The cerebrum is divided into left and right **hemispheres** which are separated by a deep split. Generally speaking, the left hemisphere manages the right side of the body; the right hemisphere manages the left side. A person who suffers a stroke in the left hemisphere may become paralyzed on the right side. Speech may also be affected because the motor nerves that control the vocal cords, lips, and tongue are also located in the left hemisphere.

Lobes. Each hemisphere is divided into four regions called **lobes.** As nearly as we can tell, each lobe has a specific function.

1. Traveling from the optic nerve, visual information is processed in the *occipital lobes* at the rear of the cortex. It is here that you "recognize" what you are seeing. It is here that you visualize that art project you're working on.

2. Sounds that you hear are deciphered in the *temporal lobes* along the sides of the cortex. Your ability to hum a melody inside your head without making any sound is the work of the temporal lobes. In fact, Ludwig Van Beethoven was deaf the last years of his life, yet he continued to compose. Symphonies must have boomed from the loudspeakers in his temporal lobes.

3. Your ability to concentrate, to pay attention, to think through problems, and to think creatively is thought to take place in the *frontal lobes* just behind the forehead. It is here also that your personality takes shape. You not only plan your behavior in your frontal lobes but initiate body movement in order to carry out your plans.

4. Sensory data from all parts of the body are coordinated in the *parietal lobes* located in the middle of the brain. Without the use of your parietal lobes, you could not distinguish between an apple and a banana by touch.

Hemispheres: Which Side Does What?

Since both hemispheres of the brain carry on many of the same functions, why don't they work at cross purposes? Competition between them is usually avoided because the cortex divides the work so that each is responsible for specific functions. Generally, the left hemisphere is responsible for logical, analytical thinking while the right hemisphere controls emotional, artistic, and creative functions.

EEG readings taken from both sides of the brain while various activities are being performed have shown which hemisphere is more active during specific tasks. When subjects were drawing a picture or humming a tune, the right hemisphere was more active. The same was true for remembering and recognizing visual images, colors, and spatial forms—the right hemisphere was more active. When subjects were writing, speaking, thinking analytically, or processing information in a logical sequence, the left hemisphere was the active side. The normal brain seems to function best when one side is temporarily idling while the other operates at full throttle.

Which side's in charge? In most people, one hemisphere is *dominant*. This means that one hemisphere has the tendency to "take charge" more often than the other. In most people, the left hemisphere is dominant, and the right hemisphere is the silent partner much of the time. In people with left-hemisphere dominance, the right hemisphere usually only speaks up for the most artistic and emotional sides of their nature. When a left-hemisphere person suddenly gets a hunch about something out of the blue, it may be that his or her right hemisphere has snapped to attention for the moment.

Since the left side of the brain manages the right side of the body, left-hemisphere people write, throw, eat, and dial their telephones with their right hands. (And, since *most* people are right-handed, this is a nice way to remember the fact that the majority of people have dominant left hemispheres.) You would think that in left-handed people the right hemisphere would be dominant. However, more than half of all left-handed people have dominant left hemispheres. Psychologists cannot explain this phenomenon. This is just one of countless unsolved mysteries of the brain.

Corpus Callosum: The Bridge Between the Hemispheres

The ability to describe a sunset (speech is a function of the left hemisphere) as you visualize it (an activity of the right hemisphere) is the work of the **corpus callosum,** a pathway of nerves that bridges the hemispheres. In general, the corpus callosum lets the right-hand side of the body know what the left-hand side is up to, and vice versa.

When this bridge of nerves is damaged or surgically severed (as is done in some cases of severe epilepsy), the result is a person with a *split brain*. Both sides of the brain then operate more or less on their own. Each half seems to have its own sensations, perceptions, memories, and feelings. That sunset you visualized? You could probably still "see" it, but would be unable to describe it. The message would not be communicated to the next-door hemisphere. Although it is not easy, split-brain patients can learn to compensate.

The brain's emergency repair service. In the brain, various regions have the capacity to take over some of the work of damaged areas. Functions of damaged areas must be *relearned* in other parts of the brain. For example, the speech of a stroke victim gradually improves as other brain areas relearn the skill. Although the other regions may not act as effectively as the original structure, they will continue to perform its vital functions. In other words, the brain has more than one structure that can perform any function. This feature of the brain is called **redundancy.**

Section Review

1. Discuss the differences between the subcortex and the neocortex in terms of evolution, in terms of separating human beings from lower animals, and in terms of function.
2. Name the four lobes in each hemisphere and describe the main function(s) of each.
3. Since both hemispheres carry on many of the same functions, why don't they work at cross purposes?
4. How might you behave if your corpus callosum were severed?

PREVIEW

In this section, read to find out:

1. how a single nerve cell conveys messages.
2. the relationship between behavior and the body's nervous systems.

3.   It Takes a Lot of Nerve

You're fishing, and your finger gets stuck on a fishhook. What do you *hope* happens next? What do you direct your body to do? You wouldn't want your nervous system to respond by causing you to lift your foot. It is your *finger* that must be disengaged. But how does your brain get the message that your finger is stuck? How do the muscles in your arm and hand get the message to disconnect that finger from the fishhook? The answer: the electrical part of your body's communication system, the nervous system, goes to work.

Think of the body's nervous system as a vast network of electrical circuits. These circuits relay messages to and from the brain to and from all parts of the body. The nervous system is divided into two parts which perform different functions—the **central nervous system** and the **peripheral nervous system.** The brain, the body's command post for this elaborate network, and the spinal cord, the main cable from the brain to the rest of the body, together make up the central nervous system.

The peripheral nervous system is another network of circuits that connects the central nervous system with muscles, glands, and other bodily parts. Together, these two systems make up the complex power network that transmits messages throughout the body. The basic building block of this communications system is the single tiny nerve cell.

Anatomy of a Nerve

Your entire nervous system is made up of billions of nerve cells called **neurons.** Neurons come in all shapes and sizes; some are minute, some are as long as three feet. Neurons form systems of "one-way streets." Messages can travel only one direction along these one-way streets. They can't back up or turn around. When a neuron is activated, we say it is firing. Its receiving antennae (*dendrites*) receive an electrical signal at one end, send the signal along the length of the neuron (*axon*), and, with a tiny release of chemicals, transmit the signal (via the *terminal buttons*) across a gap called a **synapse** to the next neuron. The process is repeated until the message reaches its destination.

Neurons are specialized by function. There are three kinds of neurons. *Sensory neurons* gather information, from inside and outside the body. (Inside the body, they monitor such things as warmth, pain, sugar or water levels; outside the body they receive information from the five senses—sight, hearing, smell, taste, and touch.) *Interneurons* pass the signals along, routing them toward their appropriate destinations. They are not connected to muscles or organs, but instead communicate only with other neurons. They serve as connectors between the sensory neurons and the third kind of neuron—the motor neuron. *Motor neurons* carry return messages from the brain and spinal cord (the

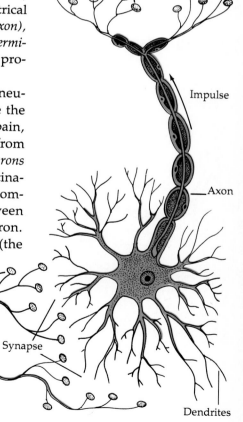

Anatomy of a Nerve

Terminal Buttons

Impulse

Axon

Terminal Buttons

Dendrites

Impulse

Axon

Synapse

Dendrites

225

Brain
Interneurons

Motor Neurons

Sensory Neurons

Spinal Cord Interneurons

central nervous system) to the muscles, glands, and organs. Some sensory messages do not require the brain's attention. When you are walking, for instance, you do not have to remind yourself to move your legs. This motor activity is handled at a lower level in the central nervous system, by the spinal cord. If you should stumble, however, the new message would be switched to the brain for instructions.

There are times when it is neither necessary nor convenient for information to be sent to the brain for decisions. In such cases the spinal cord "short circuits" the incoming messages and handles the problem itself. Reflex actions happen this way. You experience a reflex action when the doctor taps your knee with a rubber mallet. The knee "jerks" before you have had time to think about it. If, for some reason your head was missing, the knee would still jerk.

Other motor actions are also carried out by reflex action. In an emergency incoming information might reach the brain too late to protect you. Then the interneurons in your spinal cord switch the signals from the sensory to the motor nerves for immediate action. This is what happens if you put your hand on a hot stove. Your hand jerks away and the action registers in your brain an instant later.

So, where are we in the fishhook problem? The message traveled to the brain via sensory neurons. Following instructions from the brain, interneurons passed the "ouch" message from the sensory neurons to the motor neurons. The motor neurons rushed an order to the muscles in your arm and hand to disengage your finger from the fishhook. How long did that take? Nerve signals or impulses have been estimated to travel at approximately 250 miles an hour. That means your brain can receive information from the tip of your toe, process it, and send a return signal to your toe in a few hundred milliseconds.

The Peripheral Nervous System

When you studied the brain in the previous section, you were studying the central nervous system. All traffic along nerve highways is coordinated in the central nervous system—some of it in the brain itself, some of it only in the spinal cord.

Under the command of and acting alongside the central nervous system is the peripheral nervous system. It conducts information from the central nervous system to the outer parts (organs, glands, muscles) of the body and relays information back again. The peripheral nervous system is composed of two parts: the **autonomic nervous system** which generally controls involuntary processes like digestion and breathing and the **somatic nervous system** which controls voluntary functions like walking or throwing.

The autonomic nervous system. The President of the country is probably too busy to do his own housekeeping. He hires others to perform those chores. So like the President's staff, the autonomic system in your body relieves the brain of thinking about the body's housekeeping functions and normally performs them on its own. Unlike the President's staff, the autonomic system works 'round the clock. Functions like digestion, breathing, heartbeat, and glandular secretions are regulated by the autonomic system and go on working whether we are awake or asleep.

There are two sets of nerves in the autonomic system which function in two separate ways. Think of one set as the accelerator in a car, the other as the brake system. When our lives are threatened or when we experience strong emotions or anxiety such as fear, rage, or worry, the accelerator part of the autonomic system must step up its work. During those times, your heart races, your palms sweat, your adrenal glands signal to release additional hormones to provide "quick energy." Some blood vessels are constricted, as in the digestive tract, in order to provide more blood to the heart and the muscles where it is needed. This part of the autonomic system is called the **sympathetic system.**

But once your body is "keyed up," what brings it back down to normal? Does your car stop racing just because you take your foot off the accelerator? No, you must apply the brakes. This is where the **parasympathetic system** comes in. It slows breathing, reduces your heart rate, returns blood vessels back to normal, and generally helps your body recover from its taxing situation. The sympathetic and parasympathetic systems oppose and consequently balance each other.

The somatic nervous system. The somatic part of the peripheral nervous system works when it is called upon to do so. It is primarily a voluntary system. When you catch a ball, open a window, take a walk, or write a letter, you are using the somatic part of your peripheral system, the part that coordinates the vast array of skeletal movements. When you are asleep, the somatic system is for all practical purposes "shut down."

Section Review

1. Tell the difference between the central nervous system and the peripheral nervous system.
2. Explain the functions of sensory, motor, and interneurons.
3. What roles do the autonomic and somatic systems play when you are jogging?
4. Why does your body need the parasympathetic system?

The Human Nervous System

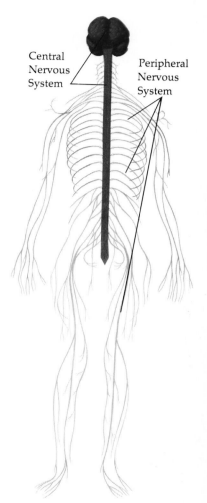

Central Nervous System

Peripheral Nervous System

The central nervous system, represented by red highlighting, is composed of the brain and the spinal cord. Acting as command post, it directs traffic along appropriate nerve highways. The peripheral nervous system, represented by black lines, is composed of all the nerve highways that connect the central nervous system with the rest of the body.

PREVIEW

**In this section,
read to find out:**

1. about the functions of specific glands.
2. how hormones affect behavior.
3. how the nervous system and endocrine system work together.

4. Chemicals That Shape the Mind and Body

He used to be fairly quiet and shy. He was not very good in competitive sports. "Not enough drive," "lets people push him around," were frequent comments about him. He always seemed sluggish and slightly remote, though his girlfriend said she liked his gentle manner.

It was at the first fall football practice of his senior year when the changes in Keith were first noticed. On an end sweep coming his way, Keith smashed through a guard and nailed the halfback who had to be carried off on a stretcher. Later, a fight broke out between Keith and a fellow teammate; it ended when Keith knocked him out. "What's gotten into Keith?" everyone was wondering.

His recent twenty-pound weight gain and his steadily increasing height were just explained by his greater appetite. His girlfriend noticed a change in the way he related to her: now he was aggressive and demanding. He participated in weekly weekend brawls.

Upon returning home from his father's funeral, Keith finally realized something was wrong inside himself. He had loved his father very much, but didn't grieve at his loss. His emotions were cold, lacking any real feeling. Adding further misery to Keith's worries, the headaches he was having kept coming more often, and each seemed worse than the last. Despite it all, Keith kept on growing.

When a doctor examined Keith, he readily diagnosed why Keith had become such a different person in the past four years. Keith was suffering from a tumor at the base of the brain, or more precisely on his pituitary gland. The pressure on the gland stimulated it to release more hormones. One of these was the hormone that controls body growth. Keith was on his way to becoming a giant.

The tumor also triggered the release of other hormones from other glands—those that are involved in stress reactions and emotions. Biologically, Keith was at a peak in emotional stress all the time! Eventually he might have died from an enlarged heart or circulatory problems caused by his constant state of stress.

Everything changed abruptly after the tumor was removed. His headaches vanished. He grew weaker; his appetite diminished. He was no longer a tough guy and stopped picking fights.

By the sweep of the surgeon's wand, the twenty-one-year-old superman was literally transformed back to his mild-mannered "Clark Kent" personality.

What had been happening to Keith? His behavior had been chemically programmed in an abnormal way. Abnormal, because much of your behavior is chemically programmed, programmed by the glands

Biofeedback and Relaxation

You'll remember that we said the autonomic system was responsible for carrying out the body's involuntary functions such as heartbeat, blood pressure, and digestion. That would suggest that these functions are not subject to voluntary control. Apparently, this is not the case. In the laboratory, both animal and human subjects have learned to speed up or slow down their heart rate, raise or lower their blood pressure, and produce particular brain-wave patterns.

The individual learns to control certain "involuntary" processes by watching an instrument that records such things as brain waves, blood pressure, and heartbeat. By seeing the changes recorded as they occur, the individual is able to influence both the rate and direction of change. Exactly how this is done is not fully understood. Apparently, one's ability to concentrate on the particular bodily function is an important factor. Using this method, people have been able to change skin temperature as much as nine degrees Fahrenheit, reduce blood pressure 15 percent, relax tense muscles, and alter brain waves on command.

Much the same result is claimed by various meditation techniques. There is some indication that training in simple relaxation can also lower blood pressure and thus reduce symptoms of stress. People who are hospitalized with dangerously high blood pressure have been able to lower the pressure when it rises by thinking relaxing thoughts or making their muscles go limp. Feedback from the machine— knowing their efforts are successful— seems to help.

Despite the promise of biofeedback, much remains to be discovered before it becomes a cure-all for stress. But who knows? In a few years, people may be preventing their own heart attacks.

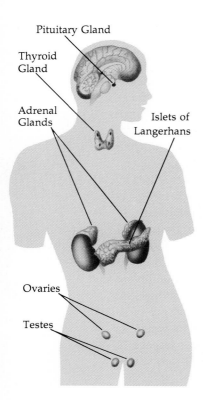

The Endocrine System

in your body. Your complex nervous system is an electrical system, just one of the communication systems that affect your behavior. Working alongside it and in close cooperation with it is a chemical communication system—the system of **endocrine glands.**

The Endocrine System

You'll remember that in the section before, we said that sensory neurons inside the body monitor such things as sugar levels in individual cells. And that if the sugar level is found to be abnormal, the message is relayed to the hypothalamus which then, via the neurons in the peripheral nervous system, signals the imbalance to be corrected. What does it signal and how is the imbalance corrected? The glands are signaled; the glands release chemical messengers called hormones into the bloodstream which greatly affect behavior, the functioning of the body, and the course of its development. The word **hormone** means activator and comes from the Greek word for "I excite." In fact, an excitable person *might* be this way because one of the glands is producing an oversupply of hormones. A tired person may be receiving too few.

Releasing or *secreting* their chemical messengers, glands direct the growth and development of the body and coordinate various bodily processes. Hormones, traveling in the bloodstream, can deliver messages to just one or two organs, or they can signal the whole body generally. They can slow it down or speed it up as needed.

Located almost in the center of the brain, the **pituitary gland** secretes a number of different hormones. One is a growth hormone which is responsible for the development of the body during the early years. People who receive too little of this hormone grow up to be abnormally small (dwarfs), while people who receive too much, as Keith did, become abnormally large (giants). The other hormones that the pituitary secretes find their way to the other glands in the body. These glands release their hormones upon chemical command from the pituitary, which is why it is often called the "master gland" of the endocrine system. The pituitary receives its orders from the hypothalamus.

The **thyroid gland** consists of two lobes located on either side and in front of the windpipe. It regulates the body's *metabolism*—the rate at which the body's cells manufacture energy from food or produce new cells. A thyroid that produces too much of its hormone causes a person to become nervous, lose weight (despite an increased appetite), and feel "keyed up." An underactive thyroid causes loss of hair, increased sensitivity to cold, and a tired feeling. The body does not produce enough energy for its requirements.

The **islets of Langerhans** are part of the pancreas, a gland in the abdomen. They secrete the hormone *insulin,* which regulates the level of sugar in the blood. When the level rises, insulin checks the increase and the glucose (sugar) is removed from the blood and is absorbed harmlessly into other tissues. When something goes wrong with the pancreas and not enough insulin is secreted, diabetes can result. The person loses weight and energy, and may contract such diseases as cataracts and hardening of the arteries.

Two **adrenal glands** are located at the upper end of the kidneys. When you are threatened or under stress or confronted by an emergency, the sympathetic system of nerves signals the adrenal glands to release their hormones. These hormones act on the nervous system to increase the blood pressure and the heart rate. They also raise the blood sugar level to give the body the needed additional energy. These glands also produce *steroids,* some of which convert proteins into sugar and maintain a proper balance of salt in the system.

In the male, the testes produce the sperm cells necessary for reproduction as well as the hormone *testosterone.* This hormone causes male sex characteristics, such as the growth of facial and body hair and change of voice. Testosterone also stimulates the growth of the skeleton, the muscles, and some of the internal organs in men. In part, this accounts for the fact that men are usually larger than women.

In the female, the ovaries are located within the pelvis. In addition to producing the egg cells, they secrete two female hormones, *estrogen* and *progesterone.* Estrogen stimulates the development of female sex organs. Progesterone affects the uterus so that pregnancy can be maintained. It also controls the menstrual process. When the estrogen supply stops, a woman goes through menopause, or change of life. Painful symptoms caused by menopause can be relieved with artificial doses of estrogen. After menopause, the woman is not able to bear children.

You have just read extensively about the body's two communication systems. Now you know that behavior is not just a response to the external world. All behavior—thinking, feeling, acting—begins in these electrical, chemical communication systems.

Section Review

1. Why is the pituitary called the "master gland"?
2. How do hormones act as chemical messengers? How are they like and unlike neurons as messengers?
3. You have just been told to make a speech in front of the whole school. You are not given any time to prepare. How do you react? Specifically, how did your nervous system and endocrine system interact to result in the behavior you experienced?

Chapter 8 Review

Section Summaries

1. How the Brain Is Studied

Today there are five main approaches to studying the brain: microscopic analysis, injection with drugs, lesioning, the use of EEG machines, and electrical stimulation of the brain. By stimulating different parts of the brain, neurosurgeon Wilder Penfield was able to "map" a large part of the brain. Because patients often relived childhood memories, Penfield concluded that nothing the brain takes in is ever lost. Penfield also discovered pleasure centers. Some people question the use of electrical stimulation to control human behavior. As a result, the medical profession is working to establish guidelines to protect patients.

2. How the Brain Works

The subcortex controls basic survival functions such as breathing. Within the subcortex, the thalamus receives sensory messages, sorts them, and passes them to other parts of the brain. The hypothalamus regulates body temperature, food and water levels and, to some extent, controls emotional behavior. The cerebellum helps the neocortex coordinate motor functions. Thinking and other complex brain activity take place in the neocortex. The neocortex is made up of the cortex and the cerebrum. The cerebrum is divided into left and right hemispheres, and each hemisphere is divided into four lobes. Generally, the left hemisphere handles analytical tasks. The right hemisphere controls emotional and creative functions. In most people, one hemisphere is dominant. The corpus callosum acts as a bridge between the hemispheres. Redundancy allows the brain to compensate for some types of brain damage.

3. It Takes a Lot of Nerve

The nervous system is divided into two parts. The central nervous system is made up of the brain and the spinal cord. The peripheral nervous system connects the central nervous system with muscles, glands, and other bodily parts. Neurons receive electrical signals at their dendrites and pass them on to the axons, where chemicals are released that bridge the synapse. Sensory neurons gather information, interneurons communicate with other neurons, and motor neurons carry signals from the brain to the muscles, glands, and organs. The peripheral nervous system is made of the autonomic and somatic nervous systems. Within the autonomic nervous system, the sympathetic nervous system speeds up basic functions. The parasympathetic nervous system slows down the same basic functions.

4. Chemicals That Shape the Mind and Body

The endocrine glands work with the brain to affect behavior. By secreting hormones, the endocrine glands direct growth and development and coordinate various bodily processes. The pituitary gland is often called the master gland because it controls other glands. The thyroid gland regulates the body's metabolism. The islets of Langerhans, a part of the pancreas, secrete insulin. The adrenal glands control the body's reaction to stress. In the male, the testes produce testosterone and sperm cells. In the female, the ovaries produce egg cells, plus the hormones estrogen and progesterone.

Psychology Skill Activities

1. Reproduce the diagram of the brain on page 221. Then "map" its functions. Show where sight, hearing, thought, and other brain functions take place.   **easy**

2. Devise an IQ test for people whose right hemispheres are dominant.   **challenging**

Testing for Understanding

Knowing Key Terms
Define these terms in your own words.

Section 2
subcortex
neocortex
thalamus
hypothalamus
cerebellum
cortex
cerebrum
hemisphere
lobe
corpus callosum

Section 3
central nervous system
peripheral nervous system
neuron
synapse
autonomic nervous system
somatic nervous system
sympathetic system
parasympathetic system

Section 4
endocrine glands
hormone
pituitary gland
thyroid gland
islets of Langerhans
adrenal glands

Reviewing Main Ideas

Section 1
1. How were mental and emotional disorders treated for a brief period in the years following World War II?
2. How do scientists study the brain today?

Section 2
1. What are the two major parts of the brain?
2. How are the functions of the subcortex different from the functions of the neocortex?
3. How does the neocortex coordinate the similar functions of each hemisphere?

Section 3
1. Explain how a neuron transmits electrical signals.
2. How does each part of the nervous system work to control the body?

Section 4
1. What is the function of the endocrine glands?
2. Explain how each of the body's hormones affects behavior.
3. What controls the endocrine glands?

Thinking Critically
1. *Making Inferences.* How might you be affected if your interneurons failed to fire? **easy**
2. *Drawing Conclusions.* How might our society be different if most people had dominant right hemispheres? **challenging**

Demonstrating Psychology Skills
Copy the chart below. Then classify the parts of the central nervous system that are most active in certain activities by marking the appropriate boxes. Tell what parts of the peripheral nervous system are also in use.

	Spinal Cord	Central Nervous System						
		Brain						
		Subcortex			Neocortex			
		Thalamus	Hypo-thalamus	Cerebellum	Occipital Lobes	Temporal Lobes	Frontal Lobes	Parietal Lobes
sleeping								
eating								
outlining a term paper								
playing with a pet								
pulling hand away from hot stove								
having just hit another car in an intersection								

Emotion and Motivation

Jenny is a high-school senior. She is standing in line at a supermarket checkout counter when a classmate steps ahead of her. Jenny's first response is anger. Her temper flares, and she says some harsh words to the line crasher. When this doesn't work she physically forces him aside and resumes her place in line. Other people in line can see plainly that Jenny is mad. One of them says, "You did just the right thing. It's time we all stood up for our rights."

But suppose it had happened this way. The person who steps in ahead of Jenny is an elderly woman. Jenny's response is anger, all right, but this time she keeps it under control. The people in line know that she is annoyed when she mutters something under her breath and gives the woman an angry look. But there are no harsh words and no pushing. Jenny is polite when it comes to elderly women and suffers her anger in silence.

In each version of the story above, the circumstances are the same. The *emotions* Jenny felt are the same. But the *actions* she took in each case are very different.

What makes the difference? Jenny's motivation. **Motivations** are the needs, desires, and thought processes that cause our behavior. **Emotions** are the feelings connected with behavior. In the first version of the story, Jenny was *motivated* to assert her rights strongly, because the young male line crasher was an acceptable target for her anger. But she knew that giving the elderly line crasher a shove *wasn't* socially acceptable, so she wasn't motivated to act on her anger.

Emotion and motivation are strongly linked. Emotions in themselves are not necessarily motivations. (Without her anger, however, Jenny wouldn't have been motivated to action in either case.) In this chapter we will see how emotions and motivation act on each other and how they color and direct behavior.

1. Emotions

Your heart pounds. Your pulse races. Your hands are damp and clammy. You experience a mild sensation of nausea. The blood drains from your stomach and rushes toward your brain, heart, and muscles. What are you feeling? You could be feeling any number of emotions—fear, anger, dread, worry—even love or excitement. This points up one of the reasons why emotions are so difficult to study. The same physical responses occur for many different emotions.

A similar problem occurs when researchers attempt to use facial expressions as measures of emotion. You can experiment with this yourself. Look at the photographs on page 236. Can you identify the emotion each person is experiencing? Now look at the photos of the same people on page 238. Did you interpret their emotions correctly?

If someone showed you photographs of your own face, taken under different conditions, would you be able to name an appropriate feeling for each expression? In 1924, psychologist Carney Landis asked subjects to undergo different emotional situations in his laboratory. The stimuli, each designed to evoke a specific reaction, ranged from mild and pleasant (listening to music) to drastic and unpleasant (mul-

PREVIEW

**In this section,
read to find out:**

1. how emotions are studied.
2. two different theories of how emotions occur.
3. how emotions affect behavior.

Can you tell from these people's facial expressions what they are feeling? Check yourself on page 238.

tiplying numbers while receiving severe electric shocks). Photographs were taken of each subject while the experiment was in progress.

A week later the participants were called back to the laboratory and asked to assume the facial expressions appropriate to the previous experimental situations. These new expressions were photographed and compared with the original ones. Landis wanted to find out how closely the assumed emotions (second set of pictures) matched the "real" expressions. He discovered that they *didn't* match at all!

From the first set of photographs, it was difficult to tell what the people were feeling. In examining the second set, however, there was no doubt about the emotions being expressed. Although the subjects were receiving *no stimulation* at all, most of their expressions were what one would expect the various test situations to produce. Landis believed that these people were expressing not what they had actually felt, but rather what they believed they *ought* to feel.

If Landis was right, expressions may not be responses to emotional situations, but a means of social communication. This suggests that emotions and facial expressions are learned.

However, in 1872, Charles Darwin theorized that emotional expressions are evolutionary remnants from our prehuman ancestors. For example, the facial expression of anger might have evolved from the snarling behavior of animals about to attack.

One group of researchers reasoned that if Darwin were right, that if emotional expressions are **inborn** or biologically programmed, then certain facial expressions should be common and recognizable to all peoples of the world, regardless of culture. They chose photographs of faces depicting happiness, sadness, anger, fear, surprise, and disgust. These were shown to people of many cultures. In all the cultures studied, the expressions were identified in the same way.

Two experiments: both seem valid but arrive at opposite conclusions. Which is right? Probably both. Probably some emotional expressions are genetically "prewired" and identifiable to all peoples. Probably many are learned as means of cultural communication.

Emotions: Before or After Behavior?

If you asked a person with good common sense which comes first, emotions or behavior, she or he would probably say: "Bodily changes (a faster heartrate, a quickening of pulse, a tensing of muscles, etc.) are caused by and follow or accompany emotions (fear, anger, etc.)." But that view is only one of several theories.

The James-Lange theory. William James (1884) believed that bodily changes come *before* emotion. People do not tremble because they are afraid, but are afraid because they are trembling. James used the example of a man walking through the woods who comes across a bear. Such a person would not be frightened and then run away. Instead, he would run away and *then* he would experience fright. Fear was seen as a consequence of fleeing and not as the perception of a threat. James believed that the physical reaction—running away, crying, laughing—always came first and the emotion followed. A Danish scientist, Carl Lange, came to very similar conclusions at about the same time. The viewpoint is now termed the James-Lange theory.

The Cannon-Bard theory. An American physiologist, Walter Cannon (1929), criticized the James-Lange theory. He showed that different emotions accompanied the *same* physical state; for example, how can trembling *cause* fear when it accompanies other emotions like excitement or anger that don't involve fear? Cannon reasoned that bodily changes are too slight and come about too slowly to account for rapid changes in feeling.

Cannon also pointed out that we continue to feel our emotions even *after* our bodily changes have slowed down or stopped entirely. You can go on feeling angry about something long after the signs of anger—the red face and shaking hands—have disappeared. If physical factors cause emotion, then the emotion should stop when the physical reaction has ended.

Can you see any basis for Darwin's claim that the human expression of anger evolved from the snarling of animals?

Cannon proposed that emotions begin in the brain and not in the body, as James had suggested. He saw the cortex or "thinking" brain as an umpire that governs the thalamus, which, as you will remember, is the part of the "old" brain that receives, sorts, and passes along sensory messages to other parts of the brain.

Cannon's theory was extended by Philip Bard, and it is now known as the Cannon-Bard theory. Essentially, this theory holds that the cortex keeps the thalamus in check. When an emotion-producing situation occurs, the cortex can decide not to let the thalamus act or it "gives" the thalamus a "go" signal. If the latter happens, the thalamus then sends the feeling message in two directions—up to the cortex, when the emotion becomes conscious, and down to other organs where an emotional *behavior* is produced. When a very strong stimulus is received, the thalamus acts without instruction from the cortex, "notifying" it later that action has been taken.

Recent research called the Cannon-Bard theory into question. Our emotional functioning seems to be more complicated than first thought. The general view today is that emotions are controlled by many different interacting parts of the brain, rather than by any single emotion "center."

Now that you know the situation, do you have a different judgment of the emotion being expressed by the people pictured on page 236?

How Emotions Affect Behavior

Emotions can have positive or negative effects on behavior. Positively, emotions help us organize our behavior. When you enjoy doing something and feel good about doing it, you take care to do it well. Fear can mean survival when it helps a person avoid or deal with danger.

But emotions can also be disorganizing. Someone who is in a "blind rage" will strike out wildly, making the situation worse or hurting others in the process. Fear may be so strong that it paralyzes us and we "freeze." Students who fear taking an exam often become upset and are unable to deal with the questions rationally.

Emotions do affect behavior, though it is a mistake to say they cause behavior. Sometimes, however, an emotion is a motivation in itself ("I felt embarrassed, so I ended our conversation abruptly"). Sometimes emotions *energize* motivation; that is, they make it more likely that you will act, but the form the action takes depends on other factors. Jenny, in the supermarket, is a perfect example of this: she was mad and acted on her anger the first time. In the second instance, she was mad, and yet something *motivated her* to hold her behavior in check. She did *not act* on her anger. Emotions are the feelings associated with behavior; motives are the reasons we behave as we do.

Section Review

1. Explain the James-Lange and the Cannon-Bard theories of emotion. Discuss the differences between them.
2. What are the differences between emotions and motivations?
3. How can emotions have a disorganizing effect on behavior?

2. What's the Motive: Biological Motivation

"The first thing we look for in cases like this," said Inspector Crawford, "is the motive. Why would anyone want to break open the safe—*especially since it wasn't locked?*"

"Perhaps he didn't know that," remarked the woman houseguest, one of several people interviewed at the scene of the crime.

"Not likely," the Inspector replied. "And you're assuming the safecracker was a man. The only thing missing is a diamond ring."

"There's your motive—"

"Perhaps. But was there *motivation* —the thing that makes an individual try to attain a goal," Inspector Crawford said. "That might or might not have been the ring itself. There was a curious motivation here, because the door of the safe wasn't locked. If all our thief had wanted was the ring, it could have been taken without using a sledgehammer and damaging the safe."

"Perhaps he or she didn't want to leave any fingerprints."

"You don't need a sledgehammer to conceal fingerprints. You wear gloves. No, this was done the hard way and that may have been more important than stealing the ring."

"You're making this very complicated."

"No, the thief made it complicated. Whoever it was wanted to throw us off the track by making us think that only a man would use a sledgehammer to smash a safe. Generally speaking, women don't do such things. But in this case, I'm satisfied it was a woman. She wanted to tell us something—perhaps that was the real challenge—the satisfaction of proving that she could do it. The motive was to show us that a woman jewel thief could be as daring as a man."

"So we look for a woman who wants to prove that she is the equal of a man, at least when it comes to stealing jewels."

"You're on the right track," Inspector Crawford said. "We don't search for the ring; we search for the woman who is bold enough to think she had succeeded. And that's where she made her mistake."

The houseguest turned white.

"Motivation is not a simple thing," the Inspector went on. "Finding out why people do the things they do is the reason we have detectives—and psychologists. You've made your point, my dear lady. Now will you please hand over the ring?"

As Inspector Crawford pointed out, understanding motivation is understanding the reasons people behave as they do. All behavior is motivated in some way. Some motivations are obvious. Or you may not

PREVIEW

**In this section,
read to find out:**

1. that motivations can be grouped into two categories.
2. how the body regulates its internal environment.
3. some of the social and psychological influences on hunger.

Peanuts

© 1978 United Feature Syndicate, Inc.

even know why you do some things. For example, why do you make friends? Why do you play a certain sport?

Generally motivations fall into two groups. First, there are the motivations necessary for your survival, such as hunger, thirst, and the need to sleep. You did not have to *learn* that you wanted to eat, drink, and sleep. These **biological motivations** are inborn. All other motivations fall into the second category. These are the **social and psychological motivations** that affect your behavior. Most of these are learned. However, you should realize that it is nearly impossible to completely separate learned motivation from inborn motivations.

Biological Motivations

Every living thing needs food, water, and sleep to stay alive. Every organism also has to have some way to maintain a constant body temperature, a way to supply itself with oxygen, and a way to avoid bodily damage (pain serves as the body's signaling system). These are biological **drives**, forces that arise from needs and push the organism to fulfill its needs. Drives motivate living things to regulate their own internal environments. They eat when they are hungry, drink when they are thirsty, and sleep when they are tired. This drive to keep body conditions stable is called **homeostasis.**

But fulfilling biological needs is only temporary. After you eat, you are no longer hungry. Your drive is reduced for the time being until you are hungry again. In this way, biological motivation is cyclical.

Organisms go to great lengths to respond to the cyclical problems of homeostasis. Squirrels, early in the fall season, begin to hoard food for the winter. Bears gorge themselves in the fall to develop thick layers of fat that serve as energy supplies during the long winter months of hibernation. And human beings are the most ingenious species of all! Not only have we learned to eat before hunger pangs hit, but we have developed agricultural systems and food storage and preservation techniques that insure constant food supplies.

Hunger. What makes you hungry? Is it your growling stomach? Is it the image of a juicy hamburger that keeps reappearing in your mind's eye? Or is it because the clock says it's time?

The biological reason we eat. Although hunger has been studied more thoroughly than any other drive, we still do not know exactly how it works. It used to be thought that hunger pangs caused by contractions of the stomach signaled the need for food. Then it was found that hunger occurs without stomach contractions—and even without a stomach! Dogs and rats whose stomachs have been removed still eat about the same amounts of food at about the same times.

Then it was assumed that sensory neurons monitored the amounts of sugar in cells, and that when the amount was low, the message was relayed to the hypothalamus which, in turn, instructed the organism to eat. Further research showed that this assumption was wrong. We stop eating while food is still in our stomachs, long before it has had time to be absorbed into the cells, long before it could ever be measured by sensory neurons. Somehow, the message that food was on the way was relayed to the brain and eating stopped.

Today it is thought that the hypothalamus serves as a general "drive" center. It does not create hunger directly, but instead is assumed to bring about certain conditions in the nervous system that lead to the physical process of eating. For example, when the "hunger center" of a rat's brain is electrically stimulated but no food is present, the animal will gnaw on wood.

What meaning does that discovery have for you? We're not sure. Certainly if you were deprived of food for a number of days, your body would tell you in vivid biological signals. But we hope that won't ever happen to you. Under normal circumstances, you respond to the cyclical, biological motivation in social, psychological ways.

The social and psychological reasons we eat. Do you ever eat when you're not hungry? Would you rather eat your least favorite meal with a favorite person than eat your favorite meal alone? Does the environment in which you eat affect how much you eat? If you answer any of these affirmatively, then your biological drives are being modified by other needs.

Let's take overeating as an example. According to the theory of homeostasis, the body should regulate its own weight. Yet many people eat when they are not hungry. To begin with, many people respond to external cues—the attractive restaurant, good company. They are responding to eating as a social event. Perhaps they are being driven by their need for social companionship.

What motivates people to eat too much or to snack monotonously between meals when they are alone? We cannot be sure. But some believe that these people overeat because food is a substitute for what they lack emotionally, a response to emotional deprivation. In cases like this, emotions may be the motives that actually channel behavior.

Then there are people who clean up their plates whether they are hungry or not. Perhaps these are the people who were told as children, "Clean up your plate!" and they still feel guilty if they don't. What is the motivation? Perhaps a leftover drive to please a parent in response to the need to feel loved and accepted.

It's Your Turn

A biological drive is often modified by social and psychological needs. This is the case with hunger. Drinking is also affected in this way. Now *It's Your Turn*. Write a description of what you observe about people's drinking or eating patterns. Include biological, social, and psychological factors.

All these behavior patterns represent the way a biological drive is modified by other needs—social and psychological. Drinking and sleeping, the other biological needs, are affected in similar ways.

Section Review

1. How does biological motivation differ from social and psychological motivation?
2. Describe the body's efforts to maintain homeostasis.
3. Why do people eat when they are not hungry?

3.   Social and Psychological Motivation

People do not live merely to satisfy their bodily needs. They spend a lot of time and energy doing such things as working puzzles, reading, going to church, visiting friends, and a host of other activities that serve no immediate biological purpose. Unlike biological drives, which are similar for all members of the species, psychological and social motives are much more variable and dependent on cultural learning. For example, our culture encourages individual competition; being a "winner" enhances our self-esteem. In other cultures, such as those of mainland China and some American Indian tribes, competition is frowned upon. Needs for self-esteem are met, not by excelling individually, but by being a contributing member of the group.

What we will look at here are those motivations that pattern our lives. Some may be characteristic of our culture alone. Some may span cultures. Sometimes you are self-motivated; you climb a tree for the fun of it. Sometimes you are motivated by forces in your environment. Often the reasons why you did something may be interpreted in a number of ways. In these instances, psychology is guesswork. Only you know what makes you tick.

Curiosity and Exploration: The Need to Know

Young children seem to be naturally curious about their world. Adults are perhaps less so, because, having already been children, they have had more opportunities to explore. Yet few of us can resist knowing what is on "the other side of the hill." Curiosity is a strong motive in human behavior.

Numerous experiments have shown that infants will toddle into a strange room in order to examine new toys. Such behavior is believed to be important to later development. Animal studies indicate that the desire to explore may be inborn.

When rats are put into a maze and allowed to explore it freely, they

PREVIEW

In this section, read to find out:

1. how behavior is affected by the need to explore, to seek approval, and to achieve.

2. some views concerning aggression.

What motivates Christo? A self-supported master of "packaging," he erected his 24-mile long "Running Fence" through the hills of northern California (photo on opposite page). It lasted only a fortnight. Before that, he gift-wrapped a mile and a half of Australian coastline and hung "Valley Curtain" between two mountains in Rifle Gap, Colorado.

venture into the least familiar areas. Even rats who are hungry or thirsty will explore a novel environment rather than stop to eat or drink. Only after they get a feel for the environment do they settle down for a good meal.

In one of the Harlow experiments, monkeys were placed in a cage with a metal hook-and-eye contraption fastened to the wall. Although their efforts went unrewarded every time, they learned to disassemble the "puzzle" by removing the hook from its ring and then pulling the hinged metal plate away from the wall.

People, too, have the urge to manipulate objects, as anyone familiar with small children knows all too well. The less familiar a thing is, or the more complex its design and shape, the more it is likely to be handled. *Extreme* newness, however, may be frightening. Fear and caution tend to suppress exploration. Why do some people display more curiosity than others? Have you ever seen a child who was told not to touch any objects except for a few toys? That child may be less curious than the child who is given the freedom to explore. Some teachers promote curiosity more than others. We may be born curious, but curiosity is influenced by our environmental opportunities.

Curiosity seems to be a good example of self-motivation. Is there a need involved? Perhaps all curiosity-satisfying activities fulfill our need to learn. Learning is obviously necessary for adaptation and survival. We may be simply responding to an inborn survival mechanism.

The Need for Social Approval

In the following excerpt from *Manchild in the Promised Land*, Claude Brown describes how social approval is won in the Harlem ghetto.

"As I saw it in my childhood, most of the cats I swung with were more afraid of not fighting than they were of fighting. . . . They lived by the concept that a man was supposed to fight. When two little boys got into a fight, [people] would egg them on. They'd never think about stopping the fight. . . . You had to fight, and everybody respected people for fighting. . . ."

Why do some people conform to their groups even when it means doing something they fear? Why does the class clown perform even though it annoys the teacher? Why do some people "go along with the crowd" even if it means surrendering their own values or integrity? The need for social approval is a powerful motive. At an early age, children learn that behaving in certain ways brings them smiles, hugs, or other forms of approval from their parents. They also learn at an early age those times that cause approval to be withheld.

Getting approval means we are accepted for what we are or for what we have done. Many of the things we do are not done for their own sake, but to get other people to notice, appreciate, help, or love us.

Often, many of the needs we experience are all rolled up into our need for social approval: the need for self-esteem, the need for security, the need to compare ourselves with others, the need to conform or not to conform, the need to belong, the need for human contact. The list goes on and on. How is each of these needs satisfied? How do you exercise your need for approval? How do you feel when you are deprived of approval? What is your response then?

The Need for Achievement

No student in the United States needs to be told that there is great emphasis in this country on achievement. The hard-driving corporation executive, the student who strives to graduate with honors, the runner who tries to break the four-minute mile, the artist who takes pride in his or her work—all are motivated to achieve. Although this motive is closely linked to the need for social approval, many psychologists believe the need to do one's best is an important motivating factor in its own right.

Research has shown that the goals you set down to achieve are strongly related to the chance for success and the difficulty involved in achieving them. For example, if you were given an opportunity to throw a ring around a peg at any distance between one and fifteen feet, where would you stand? Think about it a minute before you read on.

Chances are, you would throw the ring from somewhere between nine and twelve feet away. This is what happened in several experiments with both young children and college students. To stand very close almost guarantees success—in fact, it makes it too easy. The distant line, though, makes success very difficult. Most people choose a middle distance because it makes achievement more probable and more worthwhile.

In some cases, people strive for very high or very low goals, not because they are motivated toward success, but because they want to avoid failure. Many students who are anxious about a test will often try

Putting a man on the moon was one of humankind's greatest achievements. You may live to see the curiosity drive take human beings beyond our solar system.

to answer only the easiest questions. This way they avoid the possibility of failing the more difficult ones. On the other hand, some students attempt to answer the hardest questions. Failure to answer those is not as disappointing because the expectation for success is not as high. Failure is not really seen as failure, but as "trying hard."

Aggression

Aggression has been defined as an act intended to injure or harm others. Whether aggression is inborn or learned is open to question. Some believe we are born with aggressive urges. In all cultures people behave with hostility now and then. War is an example of large-scale aggression that has erupted throughout history. Social scientists point to aggression in animals as further evidence of inborn aggressive tendencies in all species. Fighting in lower animals, they say, is commonplace. Animals by nature establish a pecking order in their groups, based on the ability of the stronger to subdue the weaker.

Other social scientists argue that aggressive behavior is a consequence of learned experience. They point out that some people are never aggressive, even when angry. Not all nations go to war, and in many cultures aggressive behavior is virtually unknown. Neuropsychologist James Prescott found that in peaceful societies a high degree of physical affection was given infants. Similarly, in societies where sensory contact was low, violent behavior occurred more often. The Harlows' monkey experiments discussed in Chapter 1 support this. The Harlows' monkeys, deprived of physical contact with other monkeys from birth, became aggressive, fearful, and sexually abnormal when they grew up. Many psychologists think that lack of affectionate contact in human infants produces violence-prone adults.

Other studies suggest that aggression is learned from parents or as a result of experiencing painful stimuli. Later, you will see how young children in experiments conducted by Albert Bandura learned to kick and punch a balloon doll by watching others perform the same acts. It is believed that child abuse is learned from parents and consequently is passed from one generation to the next. Other researchers have found that children who experience painful stimuli, such as difficulty in teething, are more prone to aggressive behavior than others.

Aggression may be viewed as the consequence of not fulfilling other kinds of drives. It may be the result of feeling frustrated. Have you ever put money into a vending machine and discovered that nothing came out, not even your money? You undoubtedly felt frustrated. Some of you might have responded with verbal or even physical assaults against the machine. The same thing can happen when social

It's Your Turn

The quote from *Manchild in the Promised Land* which you have read gives you a good example of the process of winning social approval. We all experience this need, but it can be satisfied in many different ways. Now *It's Your Turn*. Think about your own situation and your own need for approval. Write a description of how social approval is won in your circles. How does this affect your own behavior?

Violence and Sports

Some writers maintain that organized athletics, especially body contact sports, "ritualize" violent behavior in both player and spectator. According to this notion, people work off their aggressive impulses by taking part in or watching violence.

Writer James Kunen notes that not only do basketball, hockey, and football players play rougher than ever, but that the fans who watch them are often excited into a frenzy of violence themselves. Following a recent overtime game between the Celtics and the Phoenix Suns, the *New York Times* reported, "Buoyed by 3 hours and 8 minutes of beer drinking, debris throwing, and mudslinging, many in the capacity crowd of 15,320 were hauled away by police for fighting with the referees, players, coaches, and each other."

The Stanford Research Institute reports that in 1974 National Football League players sustained 1,169 injuries. One hundred nineteen of these injuries required surgery. Hockey is notoriously violent, and a game without at least one good brawl is considered tame by many.

Why have sports become so violent? Psychologists think that the competition to win at any price in a business that has grown to billion-dollar proportions has lessened the ideal of sportsmanship. In his book, *The Madness in Sports*, psychiatrist Arnold Beisser relates spectator violence to a breakdown of community ties. The local team remains one of the few institutions people feel strongly about.

Kunen writes, "The fan thinks of himself as part of the team. This intensifies his emotional reaction to what goes on in the game." At the same time, this feeling is not reciprocated by the players, who look upon their fans as an anonymous crowd. The fans' "love for their heroes is [denied,] their desire to identify is frustrated. All that [is left] to cling to is victory—if not victory for the home team, then some small personal victory over the faceless tormentor masquerading as the fellow in the next row."

needs are not met. The person feels frustrated or perhaps even inferior and reacts aggressively in order to "feel better." When aggressive behavior like this is reinforced, it can become a general pattern of behavior. These people have found out that aggression pays—needs in some form are fulfilled.

Section Review

1. Why do some drives differ from culture to culture?
2. Why do some people display more curiosity than others?
3. How can the need for social approval affect behavior?
4. How do you learn the need for achievement?
5. How is aggression learned?

4. Theories of Motivation

You have just studied *some* of the biological, social, and psychological motivations that pattern behavior. Because it is nearly impossible to study each and every one individually, psychologists have tried to develop underlying principles of human behavior to account for people's drives and needs. In spite of their efforts, however, no single unifying theory encompasses all of the sometimes conflicting reasons for behavior. Here we will look at some of the major theories that have had a wide influence on psychology.

Drive Theory

Many psychologists believe that motivation follows cycles that occur as the organism experiences and fulfills its needs. According to drive theory, there are consequences that cause a need to arise. For example, your hypothalamus informs you that you *need* to eat. Second, this creates in you a *drive,* a desire to act. Your hunger tells you you want to eat. Third, after the need has created a desire to act, you act or respond. Your *response* is your behavior, the action you take to reach your goal. You go *get* something to eat. After you eat, you are no longer hungry. The need has been satisfied. Time passes; this interval is called **deprivation.** You are depriving yourself of food. You go from a point of being satisfied, having just eaten, to the endpoint of the interval, hunger, and the cycle repeats itself.

Drives which stimulate the organism to fulfill its biological needs are called **primary drives.** These are inborn—the drive to eat, sleep, and drink. Social and psychological drives are categorized as **secondary drives.** These, generally, are learned. Some psychologists believe, however, that the desire to reduce secondary drives can be as powerful as the desire to reduce primary drives.

PREVIEW

In this section, read to find out:

1. some of the theories of motivation.
2. that no one theory answers all the questions of human behavior.

Behavior Theory

Based on Skinner's theory of operant conditioning, **behavior theory** holds that the actions of human beings are governed by rewards and punishments. Motives for behavior are to seek pleasure (food, sex, companionship) and avoid pain (social rejection, physical harm, lack of food). Behavior theory assumes that the *consequences* of an action determine behavior. We seek out those experiences that have been rewarding to us in the past and avoid those that have not been rewarding.

Behaviorists also have identified another important aspect of motivation. Most research has been concerned with what drives people *toward* goals. There is, however, a reverse kind of motivation—that which drives you *away* from goals. Failure, physical pain, and inadequate reward are all examples of negative incentives.

Psychodynamic Theory

Developed by Sigmund Freud, **psychodynamic theory** is a more complex approach to motivation. For Freud, some of our most power-

Case Study

When Dieting Goes Beserk

In 1983, pop singer Karen Carpenter's strong and vibrant voice was stilled. She was dead of a heart attack, brought on by an eating disorder called anorexia nervosa.

People with anorexia nervosa are driven to diet, even when they are seriously underweight. Anorexia usually begins sometime between puberty and the age of twenty-five. Although anorexia does occur in males, it is far more common in females.

Unlike normal dieters, these anorexic young women show fierce determination. Often they will set punishing exercise schedules for themselves. If they are not stopped, many will lose much of their body weight. At sixty and seventy pounds, many will still insist they are too fat. Over time, their weight loss can cause severe heart and stomach problems.

What throws the normal motivation to eat so out of balance? No one is sure, but there are several theories.

Some psychologists have noted that victims of anorexia are often high-achievers who never disappoint their parents. Beneath the surface, however, these "perfect" teens may resent the pressure to achieve and conform. Dieting may be one way they can rebel.

Another view is that anorexia begins with a poor self-image. These adolescents may feel their successes are undeserved or too hard to maintain. This stress may become unbearable when they are faced with a major life change, such as puberty. Dieting may be their way of trying to control the stress.

Our culture may be partially to blame, too. Many psychologists feel that fashion designers and models put too much emphasis on thinness. Some young women, they fear, will die trying to meet these unrealistic standards.

Most researchers agree on one fact—anorexics cannot control their dieting without help. Yet they may be unwilling or unable to seek help by themselves. You can help if you notice when a friend loses a great deal of weight in a short time. Express your concern. Urge them to seek professional help.

ful motives are unconscious. The individual is not aware of his or her own motivations or repressed urges. These reside in the hidden part of the mind, and thus, cannot be controlled by reason. We behave by instinct, but unconsciously concoct socially acceptable "reasons" for our behavior.

Cognitive Theories

Various **cognitive theories** of motivation have been developed that explain behavior as the result of rational choice. Neither the unconscious nor inborn drives are seen as important sources of motivation. A person is not simply driven toward a goal, but rather evaluates options and chooses goals which fit with his or her desires and needs and which are appropriate to a given time and place. It is this ability to choose, to evaluate different options, and to select from a broad range of goals that distinguishes human beings from lower animals.

Abraham Maslow

Humanistic Theory

Psychologist Abraham Maslow theorized that motivations fall into a natural hierarchy. First, people try to fulfill their most basic biological needs, those at the bottom level of the hierarchy—hunger and thirst. Only after they have met these needs can they think of fulfilling what Maslow terms *stimulation needs*—sex, sensory contact, exploration. When these are met, people are then capable of fulfilling still higher needs like safety, love, self-esteem, and self-understanding.

As a humanistic psychologist, Maslow believed that everyone was born with the ability to fulfill the highest need, but this is possible only after the lower needs are satisfied. People who have not achieved security in their lives, for instance, will not be fully motivated toward love and belonging. **Humanistic theory** stresses the importance of personal growth and self-fulfillment, but does not deny the existence of innate drives.

Probably no one theory answers all the questions of why we do the things we do. There is no one theory that explains our needs to survive and at the same time fully explains our desire to seek the company of other people, to create, to achieve, and to explore.

Maslow's Hierarchy of Needs

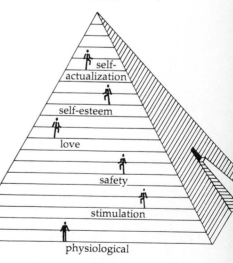

Maslow believed that everyone has the potential to reach the highest level, but this is possible only after the lower levels have been surmounted.

Section Review

1. Describe the steps in the motivational cycle of drive theory and relate them to biological and social/psychological motivation.
2. Discuss Maslow's theory of motivation.
3. How do behaviorists explain motivation?
4. How is fear of failure a motivation?

Chapter 9 Review

Section Summaries

1. Emotions

Motivations are the needs, desires, and thought processes that cause behavior. Emotions are the feelings connected with behavior. Emotions are difficult to study because the same physical changes and facial expressions may signal different emotions. Landis showed that people may learn to use facial expressions to communicate certain emotions. Other research supported Darwin's idea that facial expressions are inborn and common to people of different cultures. Both the James-Lange and the Cannon-Bard theories of behavior have been questioned by current research. The general view today is that emotion is controlled by many different interacting parts of the brain.

2. What's the Motive: Biological Motivation

Motivations are divided into two classes: (a) biological motivations and (b) social and psychological motivations. Drives push living things to maintain homeostasis by eating, drinking, and sleeping. Today it is thought that the hypothalamus directs behavior, such as eating, that will satisfy drives. In many cases, the biological drive of hunger is modified by social and psychological motivations.

3. Social and Psychological Motivation

Unlike biological drives, social and psychological drives vary and may depend on cultural learning. Curiosity and the need to explore, strong motives in human behavior, are also found in animals. The need for social approval, another strong motive, appears at an early age. Another powerful motive in the United States is the need for achievement. Whether aggression is inborn or learned is open to question.

4. Theories of Motivation

Drive theory holds that motivation follows a cycle. An interval of deprivation creates a drive, which motivates behavior that ends the deprivation. Primary drives are inborn. Secondary drives are generally learned. Behavior theory holds that people are motivated to seek pleasure and avoid pain. According to Freud's psychodynamic theory, some of our most powerful motives are unconscious. Various cognitive theories hold that our rational choices motivate our behavior. As a humanistic psychologist, Abraham Maslow theorized that motivations are ranked in a natural hierarchy. Once basic biological needs are met, people can seek to satisfy higher needs.

Psychology Skill Activities

1. What did you do yesterday? List each action. What biological, social, and psychological factors influenced each action? Now think back to your childhood or interview your family members. Can you explain how you acquired these motivations?   **easy**

2. Conduct your own experiment to see if facial expressions are good indicators of emotion. One small group of students should serve as a control group that is responsible for collecting photographs of faces. These photographs should express a range of emotions, which should be known to the control group. Display the photos. The rest of the class should decide what emotions are being expressed. Check the results and report to the class.   **challenging**

Testing for Understanding

Knowing Key Terms
Define these terms in your own words.

Section 1
motivation
emotion
inborn

Section 2
biological motivation
social and psychological motivation
drive
homeostasis

Section 3
social approval
achievement

Section 4
drive theory
deprivation
primary drive
secondary drive
behavior theory
psychodynamic theory
cognitive theory
humanistic theory

Reviewing Main Ideas

Section 1
1. Why is it difficult to study emotions?
2. How is the James-Lange theory of emotion different from the Cannon-Bard theory?
3. How do emotions affect behavior?

Section 2
1. What are two basic categories of human motivations?
2. What is the function of homeostasis?
3. How do biological motivations interact with social and psychological motivations in eating?

Section 3
1. How does learning seem to affect social and psychological motivations?

2. Why do some psychologists believe aggression is inborn but others believe it is learned?

Section 4
1. Describe some major psychological theories of motivation.
2. Why are none of the theories accepted without questions?

Thinking Critically
1. *Drawing Conclusions.* How might curiosity have been necessary to survival in prehistoric times? In the last two hundred years?   **easy**
2. *Making Applications.* How might psychodynamic theory explain the jewel thief's motivation in the story at the beginning of Section 2? How might behaviorist theory? Humanistic theory?   **challenging**

Demonstrating Psychology Skills
Read the following list. Tell what motives and emotions might occur in each situation. What role does each motive or emotion play in each situation?

_____ climbing a mountain

_____ swimming across a very deep lake on a dare

_____ skipping class because others did it

_____ working to make the best grade in class

_____ storming away from a friend who accuses you of not being a good friend

_____ panicking on a test and not being able to think

_____ cleaning the house without being asked

_____ kicking a post because you missed a bus

States of Consciousness

Helen underwent exploratory surgery. She had been given a deep general anesthesia because her surgery involved painful probing of the mouth area.

During surgery, the physician exclaimed, "Good gracious. . . . It may not be a cyst at all. It may be cancer!" Fortunately, though, the biopsy proved the cyst to be benign and the physician's reaction was a false alarm. There was no need for Helen to worry.

But in the days following surgery, Helen was worried and depressed. She cried uncontrollably for no apparent reason. Attempts to relax her and restore her usual good spirits were unsuccessful. Under hypnosis, a therapist asked Helen to lift her hand if something was disturbing her. Helen's hand shot up suddenly.

"Good gracious," she exclaimed. "The cyst may be cancerous!" After being able to express her fear openly and being reassured, Helen's depression lifted. Was it possible that in her unconscious anesthetized state, some part of Helen's mind was still conscious of its surroundings, still registering information?

To investigate this possibility, studies were conducted to see if anesthetized patients were responsive to information presented during operations. Afterwards, none remembered their operations. Yet under hypnosis, half of them remembered crucial statements made by the surgeon or anesthetist during the operations.

These examples force us to recognize the powers of the human mind to perceive. Even when deeply anesthetized, we may still remain conscious of significant events taking place in our environment. And, even if we have no memory of the events in our normal waking state, they may still influence our moods and behavior.

Consciousness is the degree to which you take in information

about yourself and your environment. Consciousness changes. In this chapter, we are going to explore changes in consciousness that occur naturally—that are common to every living human being—from alert, attentive wakefulness, to sleep and its variety of dream worlds. We will also look at those altered states of consciousness which do not occur naturally, such as hypnosis, drug-induced changes, and self-induced changes brought about by meditation.

1.   Waking Consciousness

Since you were born, you have been traveling through regular cycles of consciousness. Now, you travel through one cycle about every twenty-four hours. You sleep, you dream much of that sleep, then you wake into an alert consciousness that lasts about sixteen hours. Then you sleep and dream again. When you were a baby, the cycles were shorter, more frequent. You spent much more time sleeping and dreaming. The reason babies seem to need more sleep than adults is a mystery. A healthy, **waking consciousness** depends a lot on a healthy sleeping consciousness, though again, we're not sure why. Consciousness is a mystery. It is also very personal. Your sleeping habits are highly personalized. Your dreams are your own private worlds. And your waking consciousness is colored by your personality, your emotions, your motivations, and your physical well-being. There are, however, some general statements that can be made about the natural states of consciousness through which you travel every day.

PREVIEW

**In this section,
read to find out:**

1. that consciousness is personal.
2. some of the characteristics of waking consciousness.

Consciousness and Perception

Think about your impressions of what happened in the last session of this class. Describe what happened. Compare this with some classmates. Are your impressions the same? Is there any disagreement? Do you remember the events in the same way? Chances are, your impressions varied considerably. And yet you were all awake, you were all consciously paying attention. You were all bombarded by the same stimuli. And yet the impressions you walked away with were as varied as your personalities. What, then, is waking consciousness?

Waking consciousness is determined by much more than what merely "is." Your perceptions shape your consciousness. So do your motivations, your emotions, and your past experience. You probably pay more attention to the aromas coming from restaurants when you're hungry, smells that at other times your consciousness might ignore. You may be able to study with the radio on. You can "tune out" that background sound. Even though you have "tuned out," however, your ears might "perk up" when you hear that one song you particularly like. Other people need the radio turned completely off before they can study or concentrate. And some people's concentration can be broken by the noise from the street far below or the gurgling of the radiator.

Waking consciousness is a highly personal state. No two people perceive things in exactly the same way. No two people are aware of themselves and their environment in the same way. Consequently, the concept of consciousness is fuzzy and subjective and difficult to define. Psychologist Caryl Marsh, however, has identified four basic features of waking consciousness.

Focus. When you are awake, alert, and conscious, you are focusing on something. You can be focusing on something outside yourself, in the external environment (something the teacher is saying, the song that is currently playing, or the traffic around you as you drive). Or you can be focusing on something within yourself, a thought or a feeling ("I was embarrassed when . . ." or "If I had only known that Stan was going, I would have . . .").

Structure. Your consciousness is divided into a background, foreground, and an aerial view. First of all, in the background of your consciousness, you always seem to know where you are, what you're doing, what the posture of your body is. You're aware of the time, place, and space that you're in even if it has nothing to do with what you're focusing on at the moment. Then, the foreground of your mind is occupied with other things, the thoughts and impressions that sail in and out of your immediate attention. It is in the foreground of your

Bridge Over a Pool of Pond Lilies. Claude Monet. The Metropolitan Museum of Art, Bequest of Mrs. H. O. Havemeyer, 1929. The H. O. Havemeyer Collection.

consciousness that you focus on things. Then, you can sometimes step outside yourself and look at yourself as others might see you. You observe yourself from some outside point, as though from an aerial view. These divisions of consciousness seem to work together as you keep your consciousness steady and on course. They shift as your state of consciousness shifts.

The categorizing mechanism. You mentally categorize or describe what passes through your consciousness. Images that you see, for example, you might register as distorted or realistic, blurred or clear. Situations you might classify as significant or meaningless, controlling or controllable, familiar or unfamiliar.

Flow. One characteristic of consciousness that is always certain is that it is always changing. You are constantly shifting your focus. Fleeting thoughts, memories, impressions, wishes, and associations dart in and out of your awareness. Some certainly are more pronounced than others; some are indeed faint. But rarely is your consciousness pinned to one idea for long. Other thoughts and perceptions constantly bubble to the surface of your awareness.

The photo at left above shows a bridge in Giverny, France. At right is the same bridge as perceived by artist Claude Monet. Revolting against the academic painting of his era, which was largely done in the studio, Monet and other painters of the Impressionist movement took their easels outdoors to paint real objects in natural light. Their perceptions of how sunlight seemed to "dissolve" objects were unique at the time and helped pave the way for a whole generation of modern painters. Monet painted the same scene many times; each time he brought something different to the canvas.

Section Review

1. What are four characteristics of waking consciousness according to Marsh?
2. How do the divisions of consciousness work?
3. How do perceptions affect waking consciousness?

PREVIEW

**In this section,
read to find out:**

1. the stages of sleep.
2. some of the theories
   about why we dream.

2. Sleeping and Dreaming

All of us know what sleep is. We drop off, toss and turn from time to time, have a few dreams (of which, we remember only fleeting fragments), and then wake up. Sleep would seem to be a fairly simple matter. Yet, research over the last twenty-five years has shown that sleep is a complicated phenomenon. It is no longer believed that the brain merely goes to sleep during sleep. Electroencephalograph (EEG) measurements of brain wave activity reveal the brain to be a hubbub of activity during sleep.

The Stages of Sleep

"Our subjects get ready for bed. They are each assigned a small sleeping cubicle which is 'bugged' for sound. In turn, they each submit to the ritual of getting hooked up. By the time they are ready, they will be living transmitters. Eight electrodes are being attached to each volunteer's head. The wires are color coded for placement—two to the outside edge of each eye, two behind the ears, two on the scalp, two on the forehead. Now these circuits are checked. The tester sends through a tingle of electric current if contact is being made with the right tissues. 'Lights out!' Plugged in, the four immediately begin sending EEG waves. Sleep sounds come through the loudspeakers as our students thrash around and snore gently. Tension builds as we wait for the first erratic waves of REM. . . . "

Using techniques like the one just described, scientists have learned much about the physical and mental activity of the sleeper. There are variations in eye movement, in the rhythm of breathing, and in the electrical activity of the brain. Predictable stages of sleep have been discovered. These stages show changes in brain wave activity. They recur in regular cycles throughout the night.

One sleep researcher, psychologist Barry Leichtling, has compared the sleep stages to a ladder that you begin climbing down when you fall asleep. Once at the bottom (after about two hours), you start climbing back up the ladder, passing through the same stages that were experienced on the way down. Each trip up and down the ladder includes alternate periods of light sleep and deep sleep.

Sleep onset. This is the period between complete wakefulness and unconscious sleep. You still have some control over your thoughts, but they are beginning to float around in a twilight zone of their own and you make little effort to hold onto them. Your body is "winding down" its physical activities. This is the time when your temperature begins to drop, breathing becomes lighter and more regular, and the pulse rate slows. The brain, meanwhile, is relaxing. A regular pattern of rhythms is recorded by the EEG.

Although your eyes may be partly open during this presleep period, you see nothing. The channel for vision has been cut off in the cortex of the brain. You might, however, have a short dream, probably about events that took place earlier in the day.

Stage I sleep. This stage lasts about ten minutes and is marked by a sharp shift in brain waves on the EEG record. Breathing becomes irregular, body muscles relax, and the heartbeat continues to slow down. The brain also loses its sense of time. If awakened, a person often cannot tell whether sleep has lasted a few minutes or several hours.

Stage II sleep. This stage is characterized by alternating bursts of very high-voltage and very low-voltage brain waves. It lasts about thirty minutes. Eye movement also begins during Stage II, as the eyes roll slowly from side to side.

Stage III sleep. During this stage, the irregular EEG pattern of the previous stage continues but is changed somewhat by the appearance of large, slow waves that occur about once a second. Dreaming can take place during Stage III, but the content of the dream is not likely to be remembered.

Stage IV sleep. This is "deep sleep." Some scientists believe it is during this stage that the brain restores its supplies of chemicals that were used up during the day. If we are unable to get into deep sleep for

Case Study

The Body Clock

Mammoth Cave is dark year round. Deep inside, blind fish swim in frigid streams that flow among fantastic rock formations. In 1938, researchers Nathaniel Kleitman and Bruce Richardson set up camp in this eerie world. Isolated from natural sunlight, they relied upon lamps to tell night from day. Their mission: to find out if they could reset the body's natural clock.

With uncanny accuracy, this clock regulates the body temperature and brain waves that accompany sleep and waking. Normally, our body's clock operates on a circadian cycle of about twenty-four hours. Kleitman and Richardson wanted to see if they could adjust to a 28-hour day. For 19 hours, the lights were on, for 9 hours they were off.

The results? After 32 days, Richardson had adjusted, but Kleitman had not. His sleep remained fitful and disturbed. Since then, other research has shown that the body's clock can be reset, but not easily.

Today this knowledge is being used to help adjust work sched-ules to human needs. Within factories and hospitals, for example, workers are typically assigned to shifts that rotate over a period of days or weeks. When schedules ignore the body's clock, workers tend to make mistakes.

For airline pilots, this can become a matter of life or death—for themselves and for their passengers. After flying from coast to coast or overseas, pilots are now allowed time off to adjust to "jet lag," the tiredness and mental confusion that can result from crossing too many time zones too quickly.

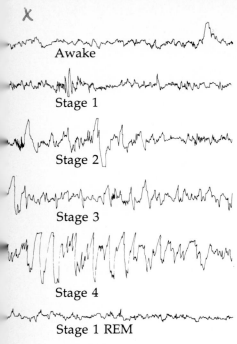

Alert wakefulness and the different stages of sleep are marked by different EEG patterns. After going through stages I through IV, the sleeper begins the cycle again, with one difference. This time in stage I, rapid eye movement begins. It is in this stage that most dreams occur.

any length of time, we feel unrested the next day. During this part of the cycle, which lasts from an hour to an hour and a half in most adults, we are "dead to the world." People sometimes walk or talk in their sleep at this time but have no recollection of doing so.

The second descent. Having "touched bottom," the sleeper now begins to climb back up the ladder to the first level, after which the entire process will be repeated. However, marked differences occur during the second descent.

At this second Stage I, a period of rapid eye movement, **REM sleep,** takes place. The eyes move wildly from side to side. Brain waves resume their low-voltage "waking" pattern. Blood pressure fluctuates as though the sleeper were emotionally excited or physically active. Breathing becomes irregular. Although the brain appears to be aroused and alert, the body is essentially paralyzed and voluntary movements are not possible. At the same time, involuntary movements increase. Muscles twitch. There are changes in the eyes' pupil size.

Time spent in REM sleep increases as the sleeper goes up and down the ladder. By contrast, nonrapid eye movement, **NREM sleep,** periods grow shorter. By early morning, REM periods are as long as thirty minutes. This is when we have our most memorable dreams.

To Sleep; Perchance to Dream

Despite much research concerning sleep, scientists still aren't sure what it does for us physically or mentally. What seems to be important is not just the amount of sleep that an individual gets each night, but the pattern of sleep and wakefulness that the person becomes accustomed to—the hours you usually go to bed and get up in the morning, for example. When this cycle is changed, even if it means you get more sleep than usual, your performance usually suffers the next day.

But as researchers are discovering, sleep, in itself, may not be the key to good health. Instead, the secret may lie in our dreams. Why do we dream? And why do we dream what we do?

Theories of dreams. Sigmund Freud believed that dreams act as an emotional release, that they free us from the inhibitions of waking life. He analyzed dreams to try to identify the fantasies and impulses that his patients were repressing—things they would not ordinarily do or even discuss. Most of these impulses, he thought, had to do with sex and hostility. Thus, dreaming, he believed, functions as a "safety valve," and furnishes clues to a person's motivational state.

Psychotherapist Ann Faraday believes that dreams often reflect the more immediate experiences of everyday life. Whether they are rooted in past conflicts or in yesterday's quarrels, they often symbolize aspects

Cycles of Sleep Through the Night

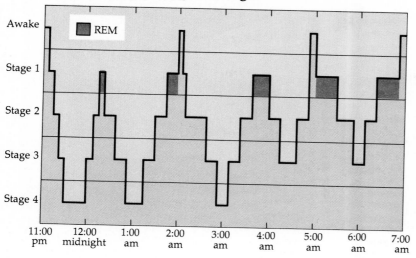

The sleeper climbs up and down the "ladder" through the different stages of sleep, completing as many as five cycles a night.

of our personality that might not otherwise be apparent to us. They help us find solutions to our wakeful problems. This is especially the case when a series of dreams have a recurring theme.

Faraday suggests that if something is troubling you, it is often helpful to tell yourself to dream about the problem just before retiring. Review it in your mind as you fall asleep. There is a likelihood that your troubles will symbolically rearrange themselves in a dream and that you will be better able to interpret their meaning when you wake up.

But the content of dreams is not always this meaningful, believes neurobiologist Steven Rose. Dreams may simply be the results of brain cells firing at random. For example, every day the brain takes in and stores billions of pieces of sensory information. During waking hours, these irrelevant and random bits of information are filtered out of your consciousness. The brain is taking care of relevant matters. But during dreaming, there is no censoring or control mechanism at work. Brain cells fire at random and out of sequence. The result—dreams, bizarre combinations of images that don't seem to make sense.

The need for REM sleep. Researchers have found that sleepers dream during both REM and NREM sleep stages. However, REM dreams seem to have greater significance to our mental and physical well-being. When a person is deprived of his or her REM dream-time over several nights, the behavioral effects are quite noticeable.

This was shown in an experiment in which one group of volunteers was awakened each time they began REM sleep. Subjects in a control group were awakened the same number of times in NREM

Surrealism, a style of art that developed in the late 1800s, tries to show what takes place in dreams and in the subconscious mind. In his painting, *Mystery and Melancholy of a Street*, 1914, Surrealist Giorgio DeChirico explores the eerie night side of the human psyche. With its unnaturally long shadows, the painting has a strange unreal sense of foreboding about it. DeChirico even found words to express the dream-like eeriness of his work:

"Life, life, vast mysterious dream,
how many are the enigmas
You propound: joys and sudden gleams!
Porticos in sunlight. Slumbering statues . . .
Forever the unknown: the waking
in the morning and the dream
One's had: dark presage, cryptic oracle."

sleep. REM-deprived sleepers tried to make up for their lack of dreams by starting more REM periods each night. When finally permitted to sleep undisturbed, they REM-dreamed about 60 percent more than they normally did. Moreover, the longer these people were deprived of their dreams, the more irritable, anxious, and tense they became. They had difficulty concentrating and reported memory lapses. Control subjects disturbed during NREM periods were not affected.

Further investigation reveals that REM dreams take place in the old brain, the subcortex. It has also been found that the lower mammals that were studied spend much of the night in REM sleep. If these findings are indeed true, it would seem to suggest that REM dreaming existed in our prehuman ancestors, that it was so vital to survival that it survived millions of generations over literally millions of years.

The "dreams" of infants. Michel Jouvet, a researcher in Lyon, France, uncovered still other mysteries about REM sleep. Conducting

Total Number of Hours of Sleep in a Day

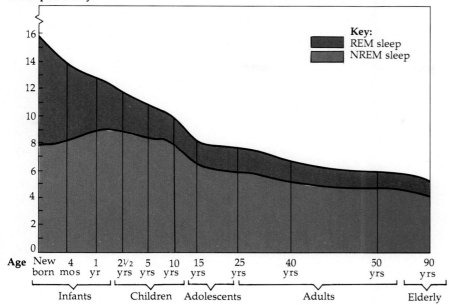

Newborn babies, who sleep 16 hours a day, spend 50 percent of their sleep time in REM sleep. By the time children reach 10 years of age, they are devoting only about 20 percent, or 2 hours out of 10, to REM sleep. This percentage stays roughly the same throughout adolescence and adult life. Note: Because of the difficulty of graphing sleep over an entire life span, the intervals between years are not necessarily represented equally.

dream research on newborn human babies, Jouvet discovered that they devote as much as 50 to 80 percent of their sleep time to REM dreaming. From the time of birth on, the REM rate declines sharply, dropping to about 20 percent where it remains throughout young adulthood and middle age. In old age, REM time shortens even more. And the pattern is the same in animals at various ages.

Mammals, including human beings, develop slowly. During infancy, the young are sheltered and protected by their parents. But the brain needs exercise, excitement, and stimulation in order to develop properly—to build the circuits and neural networks of the central nervous system. Where can the developing offspring find such vigorous stimulation at a time when it is still leading a very sheltered life? Jouvet concludes that REM sleep provides the answer. Dreams are a substitute for real life experiences. REM sleep plunges the developing brain into the furious activity that is needed for growth.

&&&
See **Exercise 6, Figuring Averages,** on pages 486–487 of the *Psychology Skills Handbook,* for more information about this method of data analysis.

Section Review

1. Describe the stages of sleep.
2. How do Freud, Faraday, and Rose explain the need to dream?
3. What is REM sleep? Why is it important? What conclusions did Jouvet reach about REM sleep?

PREVIEW

**In this section,
read to find out:**

1. some beliefs about what hypnosis is.
2. how memory and perception can be altered under hypnosis.
3. how hypnosis is used clinically and in police investigations.

3. Hypnosis

Participating in a contest of endurance are two subjects: Steve, a 235-pound varsity football player and his classmate, Cynthia, a compact 5'3", 120-pounder. Steve and Cynthia roll up their sleeves, and on the count of three, plunge their right arms deep into an ice chest. The contest of willpower begins. The contestant who keeps the arm submerged in the ice pack longer is the winner.

They call out numerical reports of the pain they are experiencing. First, they are at the "0"; then "1" and "2" levels. Pain mounts rapidly in response to the intense cold. After a few minutes, Steve moves to "3," then "5," then up to "7." "It's freezing in here!" he shouts. Cynthia just smiles and repeats her "2" report. Steve is now struggling in his seat. "It's 8, no 9," says Steve, and listens with disbelief as his opponent says, "Yes, it's getting colder; I'd say 3."

"Ten!" shouts Steve, ripping his blue arm up through the ice. "I give up." Cynthia does not gloat over her victory. In fact, she seems coolly detached. When the instructor gives the signal, she lifts her blue arm out of the ice and with a faint smile says, "Maybe it's 4."

"It's rigged somehow," declares Steve who is positive he can endure a lot more pain than most people. And, of course, he's right. The contest was rigged. Cynthia had been hypnotized. She was given an hypnotic suggestion that *she* would feel little pain even though *her arm* might get cold.

What We Know (and Don't Know) About Hypnosis

No one is sure exactly how or why hypnosis works. Several theories have been developed to explain the phenomenon, though none seems completely satisfactory. We do know that **hypnosis** is not sleep. Some believe it is a radical alteration of waking consciousness. Others, however, believe hypnosis is not an alteration of consciousness, but is simply a mind-over-matter response to a suggestion. The nearest thing it can be compared to in waking consciousness is losing yourself in a thought. For example, have you ever been reading when you suddenly realize you have been completely unaware of your surroundings? You haven't heard your mother asking you a question. You haven't heard your dog barking to be let in. Driving for a long time on a straight highway can produce the same kind of trance effect, an effect called **highway hypnosis.**

Under hypnosis, people become deeply relaxed, both physically and mentally. There is a lessening of tension, anxiety, fear, and a strong tendency to block out distractions. Under hypnosis, the subject's ability to respond to stimuli is changed. Hypnosis can block out physical sensations that otherwise would be responded to. Consciousness is reduced to a narrow ribbon of attention. Somehow the censoring or screening ability of the mind is turned off and the subject becomes very vulnerable to suggestions made by the hypnotist. A hypnotized person can accept an imaginary situation as real or a real situation as imaginary. These suggestions can carry over to acts performed after the subject is awakened, in which case they are called **posthypnotic suggestions.**

Inhibitions that would normally govern one's waking actions, however, are not surrendered. A person who would not ordinarily attack someone will not follow an order given under hypnosis to do so. Hypnosis does not alter one's normal moral behavior any more than any other unusual circumstances might.

The hypnotized subject. Not everyone responds the same way to hypnotic suggestions. Some people cannot be hypnotized. Children seem to be the most receptive subjects. Some believe it is because they are able to lose themselves in a make-believe world. Imaginative adults are also more responsive to hypnosis than are, say, highly analytical adults. Some think the ability to be hypnotized may be an inherited tendency. For example, identical twins are more similar in their hypnotizability than are brothers and sisters who are not twins.

Though vulnerable to the hypnotist's suggestions, most subjects remain in touch with their surroundings. They are able to walk and talk and maneuver around obstacles. Unless instructed to forget the session, subjects can usually recall what happened.

The Powers of Hypnosis

Whether it be mind over matter or a radical alteration of waking consciousness, people are able to accomplish feats under hypnosis they would normally be unable to do. As more is learned about hypnosis, researchers are realizing more uses for its powers. Habits are kicked with the use of hypnosis. Pain is killed. Anxiety is relieved. And sometimes criminals are found because witnesses have, under hypnosis, remembered clues crucial to cases.

Memory enhancement. Under hypnosis, people may recall things that they are unable to remember otherwise. Some police departments employ hypnotists to probe for information that crime victims or witnesses to crimes do not realize they have. In 1976, twenty-six young children were kidnaped from a school bus near Chowchilla, California. The driver of the bus caught a quick glimpse of the license plate of the van that he and the children were driven away in. However, he remem-

For years, hypnosis was valued mainly for its "show business" qualities.

Through hypnosis, school-bus driver Frank Ray was able to recall information about the men who kidnaped him and 26 school children.

bered only the first two digits. Under hypnosis, he recalled the other numbers and the van was traced to its owners.

In another instance, a woman was an eyewitness to a murder. But because she had been drinking and taking drugs, she could remember little of the incident. Investigators were skeptical of using hypnosis because her perceptions were cloudy, at best. But because they had little else to work with, they tried hypnosis anyway. Like watching a slow-motion replay, the woman related every detail. She had no trouble describing the killer, down to the dots on his tie. From her description, police artists drew a sketch, and later, the suspect was identified in a line-up. Said Martin Reiser, psychologist for the Los Angeles Police Department, "If you liken conscious perception to a camera, her lenses were all fogged up with booze and pills, and she wasn't aware of any auditory or visual input. But down at the subconscious level she was recording this stuff, and we got it back through hypnosis."

Instances like these suggest that at one level of consciousness the brain never forgets anything it takes in. Penfield's work, described in Chapter 8, illustrated the same idea. Electrical shocks to particular points in the brain elicited memories that had been completely forgotten in the subject's conscious mind. If we do operate on different levels of consciousness, hypnosis may be the gateway to a level of consciousness that perceives separately from our waking consciousness.

Distortion of memory and perception. Hypnotized people can not only be made to remember things they have forgotten, but to "forget" things they know or believe. Some subjects, especially children, can be made to forget particular names, numbers, or events. In one experiment, when subjects were told that the number 3 would disappear from their minds, they were unable to use it in counting. They reported, "1, 2, 4, 5 . . ." or "11, 12, 14, 15 . . . ." Forgetting under hypnosis is called **hypnotic amnesia.**

When people are hypnotized they can be told to experience events that are not occurring or to change actual perceptions into imaginary ones. These are types of **hallucinations.** In one experiment, a hypnotist demonstrated sensory hallucinations. The hypnotist held an open bottle of ammonia under the noses of hypnotized subjects and told them it was perfume. Instead of coughing and gagging at the smell, they sniffed it eagerly. Similarly, telling the subjects that the room was overheated made them flushed and red, even though the room was cool. A hot room was perceived under suggestion as cold and the subjects shivered as they put on coats or sweaters.

Variations of this approach—using hypnosis to distort memory or perceptions—have been used as treatments in hospitals, clinics, and doctors' offices. Hypnotism is used increasingly in ridding people of habits and phobias. Physicians report a high degree of success in helping smokers kick their habits; a third of the people treated stopped after just one session. People who are terrified of flying are taken through an imaginary situation where they pack their bags, go to the airport (so they think), and board the plane. They run through this kind of scenario until they have desensitized their fears. In their waking memories, they have conquered their fears. In the event that their fears should recur in actual situations, hypnotists train their subjects to induce their own imaginary hypnotic states where again their fears become conquerable.

Hypnosis is also used to overcome pain. Often, pain-killing drugs, though effective, bring complications and undesirable side effects. Hypnosis has helped cancer victims deal with the pain of their disease, and those crippled by migraine headaches have felt relief after years of agony. Hypnosis has also been used as an anesthetic during operations. Using mind-control in surgery is often safer than using anesthesia, and it speeds up the patient's recovery time after the operation.

People who have been taught to hypnotize themselves can lower their own blood pressure, lessen their own anxiety, and cope with or cure their own insomnia. As in biofeedback, people can bring functions of the autonomic nervous system under conscious control.

Age regression. This represents a special case of memory alteration. The subject relives, rather than remembers, an earlier experience. Under hypnosis, people have actually returned to infancy; a nineteen-year-old, told he was six months old, hungrily sucked his imaginary bottle, wet his pants, and fell asleep. In this state, subjects experience the environment the way it seemed at that time. Everything around them seems extraordinarily large, especially the huge faces looking down at them.

Psychotherapists sometimes use age regression to draw on material that has been repressed or forgotten from an earlier time of life. Sometimes simply recalling an initial trauma helps alleviate the effects that are suffered from it in later life. Freud, in fact, began his analytic treatment using hypnosis in this way. He later discarded it in favor of free association—letting the patient recall events spontaneously.

Section Review

1. Tell how hypnosis is different from waking consciousness.
2. What changes in memory can take place under hypnosis?
3. In what ways is hypnosis used?

MAKE VOCAB. page

✓

PREVIEW

In this section, read to find out:

1. how meditation affects consciousness.
2. some of the physical changes brought about by meditation.

Mandalas, like this one from Tibet, are symbols of the universe. Used as an aid to meditation, they direct the eye of the meditator to the center of the form.

4. Meditation

Focus your attention on a nearby object, say a globe, a vase, or a book end. Now concentrate on the side of the object that is closest to you. Look at it in detail. Look at the form of it, its surface, its texture. You see it as separate from yourself; it is very much a thing out there. Now try to center your attention on the far side of the object, the part you can't see. Think of this as mere looking. Gradually, you should become aware of the volume and weight of the object rather than its surface and distance from you. The longer you do this, the more the object will seem to merge into your physical self. You are no longer aware of its distance from you, but rather of its being a part of you. You are not operating on the object, but letting the object operate on you. Your consciousness has changed.

The ability to switch consciousness like this was illustrated in a study conducted by psychologist Arthur Deikman. He asked a number of students to concentrate on a blue vase—to meditate on it. After they had done this for a time, they were asked to describe their perceptual experiences. Here are some of the results.

"The vase became more vivid and luminous."

"It seemed to move, to have a life of its own."

"I began to feel almost as though the blue and I were merging."

"When the vase changed shape, I could feel it in my body . . . I could experience it happening."

Did you feel any similar perceptions? Interestingly, while you were concentrating on the object, you might have experienced measurable body changes. Your muscles might have relaxed, and although you may not have realized it, your heartbeat might have slowed a little. What you might have experienced was a change in consciousness through meditation.

What Is Meditation?

How does meditation work? How does it alter consciousness? It works much the same way hypnosis does. You reduce your awareness to a single ribbon of attention. In **meditation,** the meditator concentrates on a single, unvarying source of stimulation for a certain period of time. This can be an imaginary image or a real object. Some meditation instructors tell students to concentrate on their breathing or to repeat over and over again a single word or sound. The purpose of concentrating is not to study the object of concentration, but rather to relieve the mind of distractions and all active thinking. Once freed from these distractions, consciousness changes.

People who meditate regularly report profound changes in the way they think and what they think about.

1. *Passive alertness.* Meditators report that as the mind is relieved of active thought and distraction, it becomes relaxed and passive. It remains, however, fully alert. Thoughts and feelings are experienced with vivid clarity.

2. *Enhanced sensations.* Perception is heightened. Sensory input becomes richer as it did in the blue vase experiment. The blue became "more vivid and luminous."

3. *Harmony.* The meditator feels at one with the surrounding world, rather than set apart from it. Many express a feeling of great harmony with nature and life, a sense of calm and peace.

4. *Ineffability.* The experience of meditation cannot be described fully in words but can only be felt.

5. *Transcendence.* Knowledge gained through meditation is different from and transcends or goes beyond that attained by the five senses. The feeling of oneness is achieved directly, seemingly without the use of the senses.

Experimenting with meditation. Psychologists have performed laboratory experiments that have produced states of mind similar to that of meditation. In one particular experiment, psychologists D. Lehmann, G. W. Beeler, and D. H. Fender had their subjects view a **stabilized image** on a screen. (A stabilized image is one that moves as the eye moves so that it is always focused at the same point on the retina.) After the subjects had concentrated on the image for several minutes, it disappeared. A sudden noise returned the image to the subjects' consciousness.

This experiment suggests that it is the monotony of the stimulus that tends to blank out the perception of the stimulus causing a state of relaxation. Sensory input is narrowed until there is a loss of contact with the external world. Meditation works, then, because the mind is able to bypass unwanted sensory channels and transcend the normal selecting process of the brain.

Can Meditation Affect Health?

When awareness is limited to a single source of stimulation and consciousness tunes out the surrounding world, a marked change in certain brain waves occurs. These brain waves indicate that the mind and body are relaxed, a fact meditators can attest to. A number of autonomic body functions also change significantly during and after the meditative state. Blood pressure lowers, and the heart and respiratory rates decrease. Muscle tension lessens and the metabolic rate also

It's Your Turn

In this section you've read about some of the physical and psychological benefits of meditation. Now *It's Your Turn.* Learn by doing. Follow these simple steps and see if meditation helps you relax or brings you greater inner peace. (1) Sit quietly in a comfortable position. (2) Close your eyes. (3) Relax all your muscles, beginning at your feet and progressing up to your face. (4) Breathe through your nose. Become aware of your breathing. As you breathe, say the word, "ONE," silently to yourself: in, out, "ONE"; in, out, "ONE"; etc. (5) Continue for 10 or 20 minutes. When you finish, sit quietly with your eyes closed. (6) Stay passive. Permit relaxation to occur at its own pace. When distracting thoughts occur, try to ignore them by not dwelling on them and return to repeating "ONE." Do not worry about whether you achieve a deep level of relaxation.

This is a story told by holy men in the East. A seeker after Truth sought out a yoga master and begged him to help him achieve the enlightenment of perfect union with his true self. The Master told him to go into a room and meditate on God for as long as he could. After just two hours the seeker emerged distraught, saying that he could not concentrate, since his mind kept thinking about his much beloved bull he had left at home. The Master then told him to return to the room and meditate on his bull. This time the would-be yoga entered the room and after two days had still not emerged. Finally the Master called him to come out. From within the seeker replied, "I cannot; my horns are too wide to fit through the door." The seeker had reached such a state of concentration that he had lost all sense of separation from his object of concentration.

decreases, indicating a drop in oxygen consumption. For these reasons, it is believed that meditation is beneficial to health.

To test this idea, thirty patients with high blood pressure underwent nine weeks of twice-daily meditation. At the end of this period, their pressure had dropped to a normal range. Those who stopped meditating after the nine-week trial, however, experienced a return to their previous levels. Other experiments have been conducted with similar results. In general, the deep relaxation that results from meditating seems to free the autonomic nervous system to act in the face of physical and emotional stress.

Psychological effects. Meditation is a self-induced form of mind control. People who stick with it probably have a genuine desire to achieve more self-understanding and more power over their own lives. Studies have shown that people who meditate regularly can do more than relax on command. In one investigation involving 1,862 subjects, the number of nonusers of alcohol increased from 40 percent to 75 percent after twenty-one months of meditation. Marijuana users, who made up 80 percent of the sample dropped to 12 percent. Cigarette smoking was also curbed, falling from 48 percent to about 6 percent.

One psychiatric hospital taught 150 patients to meditate. The most positive effect appeared to be that the patients realized that they had some influence over their own conditions and felt responsibility for their improvement. Many patients required less medication and reported an improvement in their sleep disorders.

Meditation doesn't work for everybody. Like all forms of self-discipline, interest tends to lessen after the initial enthusiasm—and perhaps after a failure to achieve results. The dropout rate is fairly high. For this reason, the research data on the effects of meditation should be regarded with some skepticism. People who stay with meditation tend to be strongly committed to "self-improvement" and might have achieved the same results (less smoking and drinking, a more relaxed attitude, etc.) in other ways. Meditation affords a channel for the development of these improved behaviors, but it may be the individual's determination that matters most. Meditation surveys, therefore, do not represent a typical sample of the general population, but rather a self-selected group highly motivated to make changes in their lives.

Section Review

1. How is a change in consciousness achieved through meditation?
2. What happens physically during meditation?
3. How is meditation similar to highway hypnosis?

A Trip to the Hereafter

More than eighty years ago, a Swiss geology professor, Albert von St. Gallen Heim, took a mind-altering "trip" without using any drugs whatsoever. Like many of his countrymen, Heim was an ardent mountain climber. On one occasion, he plunged several hundred feet from a precipice with nothing below him to break the fall. Heim thought he was headed for certain death and during his descent experienced a dramatic shift in consciousness.

"Everything glowed with a heavenly light. Everything was beautiful—without grief, without anxiety, and without pain," Heim reported later. "I felt no conflict or strife; conflict had been transformed into love . . . like magnificent music a divine calm swept through my soul. . . . Then I heard a dull thud and my fall was over."

Over the next twenty-five years, Heim sought out and interviewed many others who had survived falls, asking them to describe their experiences in the "last" seconds of life. Later, he included people who had been rescued from drowning and victims of railway disasters. All reported experiences very similar to Heim's own. Once the initial reaction to struggle against dying had been given up, the "trip" was glorious.

The person felt "a sense of oneness with other human beings and the entire universe. No grief was felt, nor was there paralyzing fright. . . . There was no anxiety, no trace of despair, no pain. . . . The person experienced a flood of thoughts and often heard beautiful music and fell in a superbly blue heaven containing roseate cloudlets . . ."

Psychologically, such an experience might be explained by sensory distortions that occur from falling rapidly through space. Free-fall parachutists often report similar sensations before the chute opens, and astronauts speak of having "oceanic" feelings while floating through space. Whatever the true explanation for this phenomenon, it is clear that the mind is quite capable of having a psychedelic "trip" on its own. All it needs is a push in the right direction.

PREVIEW

**In this section,
read to find out**

1. the effects of various drugs on consciousness.
2. some assumed characteristics of drug users.

5. Drug-Induced Consciousness

Different kinds of drugs change perception in different ways—from mood alteration to sensory perceptions to the way the body experiences pain. When our perception of the world is altered, so too is our consciousness. We will look at drugs that fall into one of six categories, depending upon their effects on the mind and body: depressants, narcotics, tranquilizers, stimulants, marijuana, and hallucinogens.

It is important to note that all the drugs discussed below—except alcohol and caffeine—are either illegal or available only through a doctor's prescription. The effects of some of these drugs can cause **addiction,** usually defined as a physical dependence on a drug. Addicts have no control over their bodies' need for the drug, feel compelled to seek it, and can suffer severe physical pain if they don't get it. In addition, users can develop a psychological dependence on drugs.

Depressants

Two widely used **depressants,** or sedatives, are alcohol in its various forms and barbiturates, or "sleeping pills." Both are known to depress the central nervous system. Beyond that, their exact chemical action on the body is unclear.

Alcohol is sometimes viewed as a social stimulant because its early effects make people relaxed and friendly. This relaxation, however, signals the depressant's dulling of sensation and perception. As drinking continues, the ability to think, feel, and act deteriorates. Reaction time slows, and coordination and judgment are impaired. Some drinkers become aggressive and violent. Alcohol abuse and alcoholism, or addiction to alcohol, is a major problem in the United States. Alcohol is now the nation's third leading cause of death and is involved in more than half the automobile accidents that involve death or serious injuries. Over time, the effects of alcohol abuse are great: hypertension, liver damage, and even brain damage are just some of the physical affects. The psychological toll is great, too, with alcoholism being cited as a factor in many divorces and lost jobs.

Barbiturates, in light doses, are used to sedate, or produce a calming effect. They are dangerous prescription drugs, however; large doses depress both mental and physical functioning, quickly inducing sleep. Taken in excess, they can lead to coma and even death.

Narcotics

Narcotic drugs, which include opium, morphine, and heroin, act on the nervous system and can be used medically to ease pain. They also alter the psychological response to pain. The user becomes emotionally detached from pain, and a sense of general well-being occurs.

Although medically of great value, these drugs are powerfully addictive. The body becomes dependent upon them for its normal functioning, and larger and larger doses are required to produce the same effect. Heroin users who take the drug for its mood-altering properties are easily "hooked." Withdrawal symptoms are acute, and death from overdose occurs frequently. For these reasons, the medical use of heroin is not allowed in the United States.

Tranquilizers

Like barbiturates, **tranquilizers** are prescription drugs that calm anxieties and tension. Unlike barbiturates, tranquilizers seem to lower anxiety without depressing consciousness or alertness, in some way blocking emotional messages to the brain while letting the informational messages through. Users perceive anxiety-producing events but remain emotionally detached from them. For this reason, tranquilizers can be destructive to psychological health if used for a prolonged length of time. They tend to alter reality in our minds instead of allowing us to use our minds to alter the unpleasant reality in our lives.

Stimulants

Stimulants stimulate the central nervous system, increasing arousal and alertness. Caffeine, a common stimulant, is found in coffee, tea, chocolate, and in some soft drinks and nonprescription medicines. Stronger, more dangerous stimulants include amphetamines and cocaine. Initially, amphetamines, also called "uppers" or "speed," make users feel invincible and energetic. Greater doses, however, cause irritability, anxiety, paranoid fears, and auditory hallucinations. Over time, users develop *tolerance*, meaning they must take larger doses to produce the same effect. Cocaine initially causes euphoria and increases confidence, but continued use produces frightening hallucinations. A relatively new form of cocaine is called "crack" or "rock." Some people call it the most dangerous drug, because its immediate, intense high can cause heart failure and death. Although cocaine and amphetamines do not cause physical addiction, users easily become psychologically addicted. Cocaine is illegal; amphetamines must be prescribed by a doctor.

Marijuana

Marijuana is taken from the plant *cannabis sativa*. Though widely used, marijuana is illegal in the United States. Its effects vary from person to person and seem to depend upon the mood of the smoker prior to smoking and the environment in which it is smoked. For example, if the user is unhappy or is in unfamiliar surroundings, marijuana smoking may invite fright, depression, or panic.

Regular web (top). Twelve hours after this spider was given "speed," its web was irregular and disjointed. (center). Twenty-four hours later, its web was still not perfect (bottom).

stretches out and seems to last much longer.

There are several negative effects of marijuana which you, the student, should be aware of. Recent studies indicate, for example, that the active ingredient in marijuana, THC, accumulates in the tissues of the body. High levels of THC impair concentration and interfere with short–term memory processes. Marijuana also "demotivates" the user for a time after it is smoked, and some users experience flashbacks and feelings of panic and paranoia. Prolonged psychological effects can include psychotic reactions, personality changes, and changes in life style.

Hallucinogens

These are the psychedelics—mescaline, psilocybin, and the powerful and dangerously unpredictable phencyclidine (PCP) and lysergic acid diethylamide (LSD). **Hallucinogens** are illegal drugs and can be distinguished from the other categories of drugs by the fact that not only do they alter mood and perception, but in many instances, for the user, they alter reality. Physiological changes occur. Blood pressure increases. The pupils dilate. Body temperature rises and the hair stands on end. The user experiences little or no fatigue and can go for long periods without sleep.

Mescaline and psilocybin come from certain cactus and mushroom plants. It is believed that they act on the central nervous system and somehow unleash the brain's censoring mechanism. Hallucinations are common while using these psychedelics.

The effects of PCP are totally unpredictable. Though its only legal use is as an animal sedative, PCP, or "angel dust," has become popular among drug users. Users can experience a "good trip" one time and hallucinations and extreme aggression the next.

LSD is synthetic, or man-made, and is much like a natural chemical in the brain that has to do with the firing of nerves. It is thought that LSD interferes with this function, producing a range of behavior changes from intense excitement and heightened sensations to depression, fear, and in some instances, psychotic reactions.

During an LSD trip, the user experiences a loss of conscious control over his or her own thoughts and perceptions. Emotional sensitivity increases. Acute changes occur in the user's ability to interpret stimuli and perceptions. Sounds might be *seen* as waves. An image of one's own face in a mirror might suddenly dissolve into ashes. Crucial and frightening meanings might be applied to such perceptual phenomena. They might be viewed as "deeper" reality. It becomes increasingly difficult to distinguish among past, present, and future. Self melts into the environment. The user sometimes needs other people to help monitor what is inside and what is outside "self." Efforts must sometimes be made to hold the personality intact. Depending on dosage, acute effects can last from four to eight hours.

Not much is known about the long-term effects of hallucinogens. Although psychotic reactions are not common under the influence of psychedelics, some users do "freak out" or have flashbacks of the experience long after use.

Characteristics of Drug Users

What kind of person is most likely to use drugs and for what reasons? To answer this question, psychologist Jerome Singer and his colleagues studied 1,000 subjects consisting of college students and young military recruits. They divided these people into four groups: (1) those who used alcohol only; (2) those who used marijuana only; (3) those who used neither drugs nor alcohol; and (4) those who used several different drugs, such as heroin, cocaine, and LSD. This last group represented a small proportion of the total subject population.

A common characteristic of all young drug and alcohol users was the lack of both spontaneous daydreaming and a satisfying fantasy life. These people are restless and impulsive. They seek outside stimulation and lifestyles, and drugs offer change. Hard drug users, as well as those who used depressants and stimulants, sought an escape from normal reality. They were "less likely than soft-drug users to have rich daydreams or to use their fantasies to solve problems."

By contrast, nonusers "appear to be more orderly, more conformist, and more interested in achievements and in the future. Their daydreams reflect these characteristics."

Section Review

1. How is consciousness affected by stimulants, depressants, narcotics, and tranquilizers?
2. Think about the four characteristics of waking consciousness discussed in the first section of this chapter. How is consciousness affected by marijuana?
3. Describe how consciousness is changed under the influence of LSD.

Chapter 10 Review

Section Summaries

1. Waking Consciousness

Consciousness is the degree to which people take in information about themselves and their environment. Waking consciousness is an alert state that follows sleep in a regular cycle. Waking consciousness has four basic features: focus, structure, a categorizing mechanism, and flow.

2. Sleeping and Dreaming

EEG recordings have shown that four sleep stages recur in regular cycles throughout the night. After the first cycle, rapid eye movement (REM) sleep occurs during Stage I. Freud thought that dreams act as an emotional release. Another view is that dreams reflect more immediate concerns and can be used for problem solving. Dreams occur during both REM and NREM sleep stages, but REM dreams seem to be more important for mental and physical well-being. Because REM dreams take place in the subcortex, researchers think prehuman ancestors also dreamed. Newborns spend 50 to 80 percent of their sleep in REM sleep, but this figure declines with age.

3. Hypnosis

No one is sure how or why hypnosis works. Hypnosis causes deep relaxation, intense concentration, and vulnerability to posthypnotic suggestions. Children and imaginative adults are more responsive than people who are highly analytical. Hypnosis can be used to enhance or distort memory and perception. Age regression, which allows subjects to remember past events, is sometimes used by psychotherapists.

4. Meditation

In meditation, meditators clear their minds by concentrating on a single source of stimulation for a certain period of time. Meditation results in passive alertness, enhanced sensations, and feelings of harmony, ineffability, and transcendence. Because the mind and body relax, meditation is thought to be beneficial to physical health. Continued use can increase feelings of self-control and confidence in one's abilities at self-discipline.

5. Drug-Induced Consciousness

Some drugs cause physical or psychological addiction. Depressants, such as alcohol and barbiturates, depress the central nervous system. The narcotics, opium, morphine, and heroin, can be used to relieve the perception of pain. Narcotics quickly cause powerful addictions and painful withdrawal symptoms. Tranquilizers calm anxieties and tension without reducing alertness. The resulting emotional detachment can be dangerous to psychological health. Stimulants act on the central nervous system to increase arousal and alertness. Both amphetamines and cocaine can cause psychological addiction, and "crack" can cause heart failure. The effects of marijuana vary from person to person. Over time, accumulations of THC impair concentration, short term memory, motivation, and personality. Hallucinogens, such as LSD, alter mood, perception, and the experience of reality. Young drug users, who often lack spontaneous daydreaming and satisfying fantasies, use drugs for stimulation or for escape.

Psychology Skill Activities

1. Try analyzing your own waking consciousness. For one minute (time yourself), write down every thought that crosses your mind. Write the more pronounced thoughts in large letters, the fainter ones in degrees of smallness. What conclusions can you make?   **easy**

2. Assign four people to assume the roles of Freud, Faraday, Rose, and Jouvet. Then debate these questions: *Why do we dream and why do we dream what we do?* After they have made opening statements and debated their positions, invite the class to ask questions.   **challenging**

Testing for Understanding

Knowing Key Terms

Define these terms in your own words.

Section 1
consciousness
waking consciousness

Section 2
REM sleep   NREM sleep

Section 3
hypnosis
highway hypnosis
posthypnotic suggestion
hypnotic amnesia
hallucinations

Section 4
meditation   stabilized image

Section 5
addiction   stimulant
depressant   marijuana
narcotic   hallucinogen
tranquilizer

Reviewing Main Ideas

Section 1
1. Why is consciousness personal?
2. Describe the four characteristics of waking consciousness.

Section 2
1. What are the physical changes that occur in each sleep stage?
2. Explain some of the theories about why we dream.

Section 3
1. How do researchers explain hypnosis?
2. How can hypnosis alter a person's memory and perception?
3. How do the police and some therapists use hypnosis?

Section 4
1. In what ways does meditation affect consciousness?

2. Why is meditation thought to benefit health?

Section 5
1. How does each of the six major types of drugs affect consciousness?
2. What characteristics are common to most young drug users?

Thinking Critically

1. *Drawing Conclusions.* After reading the following facts, what generalizations can you make about the possible existence of *levels* of consciousness? (a) Under hypnosis, people can remember things they had forgotten. (b) While anesthetized, the brain can take in information. (c) Freud found that psychological problems can stem from traumas that took place years earlier and had apparently been forgotten. **easy**

2. *Making Inferences.* What might be some of the social and psychological reasons that drug use and drug abuse have become so widespread and troublesome? **challenging**

Demonstrating Psychology Skills

Complete the chart below to illustrate how the characteristics of waking consciousness change when consciousness changes.

	focus	structure	categorizing mechanism	flow
Sleep				
Hypnosis				
Meditation				
Depressants				
Hallucinogens				

Experimenting with Psychology

Keeping a Dream/Sleep Record

Why do we dream what we dream? Why do we dream at all? For years researchers have collected mounds of data in sleep clinics and laboratories all across the country. New facts have been uncovered; more theories have been concocted, and yet the mysteries remain. Now you have an opportunity to contribute to the research.

The purpose of this activity is to gather information on your own personal patterns of sleeping and dreaming. After the results are in, you may want to compare them with the others in your class.

This is the procedure you should follow: keep a record of your sleep time and dreams for at least one week. Use a chart similar to the one below (your teacher may want you to modify it). To be of maximum use, the record must be as accurate as possible. Try not to skip a day. If you have trouble remembering your dreams, try these hints: before you go to sleep each night, remind yourself to remember your dreams. Keep a pad and a pencil next to your bed. Record the night's activity on your chart as soon as you wake up each morning.

Dream/Sleep Record	Day 1	Day 2	Day 3	Day 4	Day 5	Day 6	Day 7
1. # of hours of sleep							
2. # of dreams you can remember							
3. how many dreams were you in?							
4. were they color (c), black & white (b/w), mixed (m), or don't remember (d/r)							
5. was there sound in your dreams?							
6. —smell?							
7. —taste?							
8. —touch?							
9. brief description of each dream	dream 1 _____ dream 2 _____ dream 3						
10. important events of the day before							
11. your interpretation of each dream	dream 1 _____ dream 2 _____ dream 3						
12. general feeling the following day (alert, sluggish, etc.)							

Conclusions:

On the average, how many dreams do you have (remember) each night?

Do you see any patterns to your sleeping? To your dreaming?

Is there any relationship between items 9 and 10?

Do you see many symbols or hidden meanings in your dreams?

Do you see any correlation between item 12 and any of the other items?

Unit 3 Test

Matching (20 points)

Match each phrase with a term or name below.
1. old brain
2. hormone that regulates blood sugar
3. psychodynamic theory of motivation
4. measures the brain's electrical activity
5. severing a nerve area in the brain to study the effects on behavior
6. where auditory signals are decoded
7. result when the corpus callosum is severed
8. refers to a type of sleep
9. changing consciousness without drugs
10. where highest, most complex brain activity takes place.

a. Freud
b. neocortex
c. meditation
d. split brain
e. insulin
f. REM
g. lesioning
h. temporal lobes
i. EEG
j. subcortex

Multiple Choice (20 points)

Circle the choice that best completes the statement or answers the question.
1. The part of the brain where most of the basic survival functions take place is called the (a) neocortex (b) hemisphere (c) corpus callosum (d) subcortex.
2. The psychological theory of emotion that says that bodily changes come first and emotion follows is (a) Cannon-Bard (b) Skinnerian (c) James-Lange (d) Freudian.
3. The connector cells between sensory and motor nerves are called (a) steroids (b) hormones (c) synapses (d) interneurons.
4. The psychologist identified with the humanistic theory of motivation is (a) Maslow (b) Freud (c) James (d) Skinner.
5. The theory of motivation that holds that our most powerful motives are unconscious is the (a) humanistic (b) behavioral (c) psychodynamic (d) cognitive.
6. The hypnotic technique in which an earlier experience is relived rather than remembered is (a) memory (b) age regression (c) posthypnotic suggestion (d) transference.
7. The gland that secretes a growth hormone is the (a) thyroid (b) pituitary (c) hypothalamus (d) thalamus.
8. Your nervous system is made up of billions of nerve cells called (a) synapses (b) glands (c) neurons (d) reflexes.
9. The word meaning lesser brain is (a) neocortex (b) cerebrum (c) cerebellum (d) cortex.
10. Drugs that block emotional messages to the brain area are called (a) amphetamines (b) hallucinogens (c) depressants (d) tranquilizers.

Fill in the Blanks (20 points)

Write the word or phrase that best completes each sentence.
1. The parts of the neuron that receive impulses are called _____.
2. The area of the brain where visual signals are decoded is the _____.
3. The rate at which the body produces energy is called _____.
4. Other regions of the brain taking over for an injured part is called _____.
5. Together, the brain and the spinal cord make up the _____.
6. After you have just eaten, you enter a period of _____.
7. The characteristic of waking consciousness that describes its constant changing is called _____.
8. Drugs that lower the functioning of the central nervous system are called _____.
9. It is believed that REM sleep survived over millions of years because it takes place in the _____.
10. Sleep occurs in a series of predictable _____.

Critical Thinking Essay (40 points)

Pick five behaviors you have performed today and tell (a) what motivated them or (b) what physiological processes accompanied them.

Unit 4

Who Are You?

In this unit you will study the "self"—how we differ in our personalities, what mental disorders may befall us and how they occur, and some strategies we can follow for staying mentally healthy.

Self and Personality

How would you describe yourself? Write a brief description. Or describe someone you know—a close friend, perhaps. Sometimes it's easier to describe someone else; you can usually be more objective.

When you wrote your description, chances are you listed a number of traits you feel you or your friend possesses. A trait is a relatively stable characteristic that can be measured. When a person's behavior seems to fall consistently around certain traits, we often use those traits to refer to the person as, for example, sociable, optimistic, shy, or generous. The sum total of what characterizes someone as an individual is called **personality.**

The study of personality deals with what is unique about each person—what makes each of us different from others. Personality study also deals with what is consistent about us—how we know we are the same person throughout life. Many things make up your personality—your feelings and how you express them, your values and prejudices, and what gets you into motion. These qualities make up the person that others recognize as you.

Yet by themselves, these characteristics tell only part of the story. Personality consists of the way typical behavior patterns are tied together. It includes the consistency with which a person deals with other people and the environment. Everyone is irritable at times, and many of us are greedy when we want something very badly. But some people are irritable even when things go well. Some are greedy even when they have no special need for something. Then, we suspect that these qualities of irritability or greed are central to the individual's personality. In identifying personality, we look for the consistent traits that are organized into a pattern of behavior. The search for how this pattern can best be described, so people can understand and predict each other's behavior, is the study of personality.

Our personality or *self* affects everything we do. In this chapter we will look at how psychologists measure this self, and what they believe goes into making this self. Psychologists are a long way from agreeing with each other about personality. We will explore three views—psychodynamic, social learning, and humanistic.

The puzzle of human personality has been the subject of many psychological theories.

1. Measuring the *Self*

When we describe ourselves or our personalities we may need several types of descriptions. We are not just one person, but several. Taken together, these images of ourselves make up a picture—the picture you carry around in your head about yourself. This composite image is your **self-concept.** It is how you see your own personality.

How Self-Concepts Are Formed

Many aspects of your self-concept come from the way you feel about the self you were born with—for example, your sex, physical appearance, and race. Although you can do little to change these *inborn* physical features, how you look at them and how others respond to them determine, in part, your self-concept. How you look at your abilities and typical responses, at all the *behaviors* you've acquired, also determines your self-concept—probably to an even greater degree.

At an early age you were rewarded or punished for certain behaviors. From the various cues in your social environment, you learned to be *you*. These cues may have been picked up from teachers, friends, or family. In time, how other people see you becomes, in many ways, how you see yourself.

Your looking-glass self. Sociologist Charles Horton Cooley called this aspect of identity the *looking-glass self*. To some extent, our behavior reflects what others expect us to be. We carry around as many social selves as there are people who know us. To a parent, you are a child. Your teacher sees you as a student. Your best friend may see you as amusing and fun to be with. In general, we show different sides of our personality to different people, depending upon our relationship to them.

Social philosopher George Herbert Mead extended Cooley's idea by including as part of the *self* the values and attitudes that we get from others. A parent is imitated for his or her admired qualities. These become part of a child's self-concept. But we know now that there is another side to this coin. If children feel that they cannot live up to these qualities, the result can be a negative self-image. This self we see when we look at ourselves through the eyes of others is called the **me.**

Your inner self. Is the mirror image we read in other people's eyes all we know about ourselves? No. Each of us has a private, deeper self we keep somewhat hidden. G. H. Mead called this self the **I.** This is the self experienced from inside. Usually, we think of this inner self as our *true* self. It is a kind of safe-deposit box where we keep our beliefs, standards, dreams, and fantasies. It is this part of our personalities that

The photo at left illustrates G. H. Mead's theory that personality is the composite image of a person's *body self*, *social self*, and *private self*.

we show only to our closest friends or relatives.

Our identities are composite images built on many self-concepts. Our self-concepts form around the qualities we are born with (the *body* self), our interactions with others (the *social* self), and the inner world of our feelings and values (the *private* self).

How Personality Is Evaluated

Discovering more about the identity, or personality, of an individual is a goal of psychologists. Many methods are used to measure or evaluate personality. Beginning with your first days in school, the teacher probably started making notes about your personal qualities. For the most part, these impressions were formed by watching you and other pupils in the class. Later, you may have been given IQ tests to attempt to measure your intelligence. Still later, you may have taken aptitude tests that reveal in some measure what kinds of skills you are good at. Employers sometimes use personality assessment as one way of predicting how well we will do our jobs. The results from the tests and interviews are compared with the job requirements.

To evaluate personality, psychologists try to measure a person's feelings and attitudes. Two basic approaches are used. The **objective test**, or direct method, looks at your personality from the outside. You answer questions or tell an interviewer about yourself. The indirect or **projective test** attempts to probe more deeply into your personality. By having you interpret ambiguous pictures or inkblots, complete unfinished sentences, or make up stories, the tester tries to bring out aspects of your personality that you may not be aware of. The results of projective tests must be interpreted by psychologists who are trained for this kind of work.

Objective Tests

Objective tests are often used in evaluating applicants for schools, training programs, and jobs. Generally they are given in one of two ways—an interview or a self-inventory.

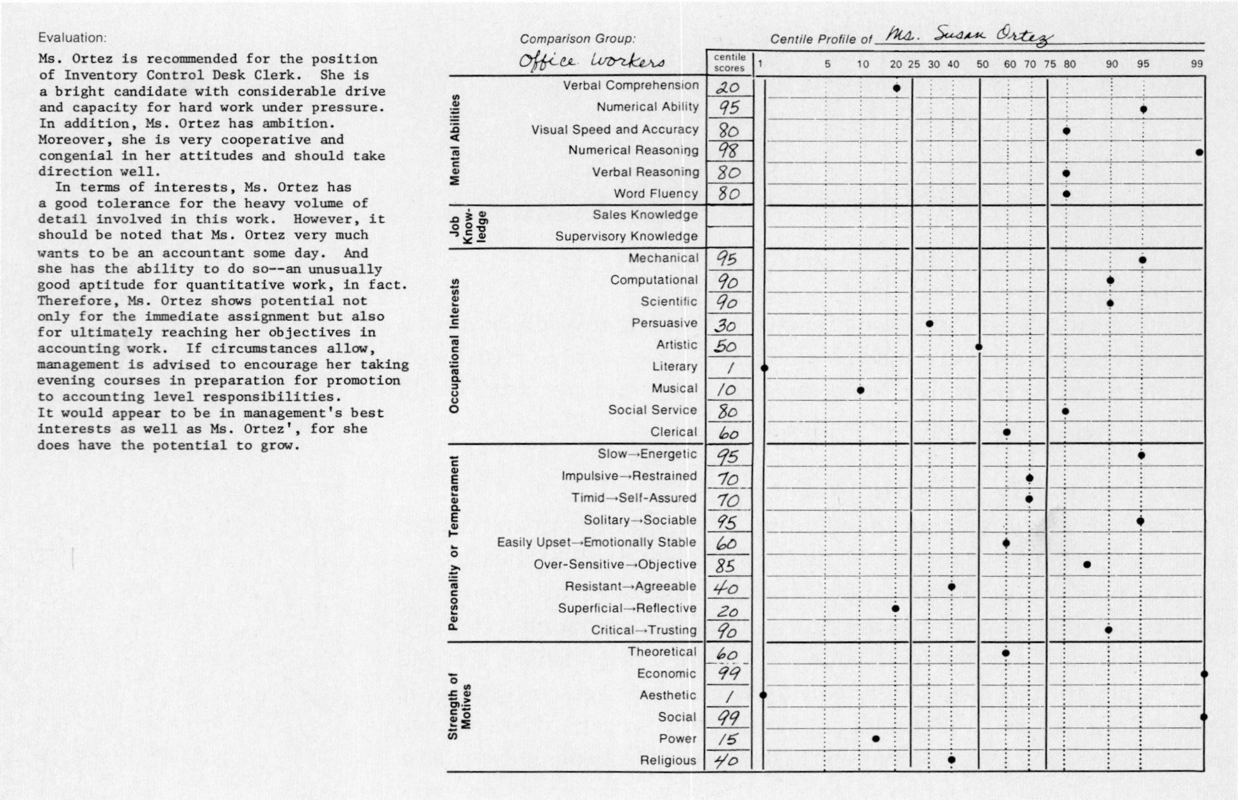

Data from a person's objective tests are often measured against standardized scores for a given group of people. This gives the tester an idea of how a person performs in relation to others in his or her group. In the profile that appears below, the scores of applicant Ortez are compared with those of other office workers. The psychologist's interpretation of Ms. Ortez' scores appears at right below.

Evaluation:

Ms. Ortez is recommended for the position of Inventory Control Desk Clerk. She is a bright candidate with considerable drive and capacity for hard work under pressure. In addition, Ms. Ortez has ambition. Moreover, she is very cooperative and congenial in her attitudes and should take direction well.

In terms of interests, Ms. Ortez has a good tolerance for the heavy volume of detail involved in this work. However, it should be noted that Ms. Ortez very much wants to be an accountant some day. And she has the ability to do so--an unusually good aptitude for quantitative work, in fact. Therefore, Ms. Ortez shows potential not only for the immediate assignment but also for ultimately reaching her objectives in accounting work. If circumstances allow, management is advised to encourage her taking evening courses in preparation for promotion to accounting level responsibilities. It would appear to be in management's best interests as well as Ms. Ortez', for she does have the potential to grow.

Comparison Group: Office Workers

Centile Profile of *Ms. Susan Ortez*

		centile scores	1	5	10	20 25 30 40	50	60 70 75 80	90	95	99
Mental Abilities	Verbal Comprehension	20				●					
	Numerical Ability	95								●	
	Visual Speed and Accuracy	80						●			
	Numerical Reasoning	98									●
	Verbal Reasoning	80						●			
	Word Fluency	80						●			
Job Knowledge	Sales Knowledge										
	Supervisory Knowledge										
Occupational Interests	Mechanical	95							●		
	Computational	90							●		
	Scientific	90							●		
	Persuasive	30				●					
	Artistic	50					●				
	Literary	1	●								
	Musical	10			●						
	Social Service	80						●			
	Clerical	60					●				
Personality or Temperament	Slow→Energetic	95								●	
	Impulsive→Restrained	70						●			
	Timid→Self-Assured	70						●			
	Solitary→Sociable	95								●	
	Easily Upset→Emotionally Stable	60					●				
	Over-Sensitive→Objective	85							●		
	Resistant→Agreeable	40				●					
	Superficial→Reflective	20			●						
	Critical→Trusting	90							●		
Strength of Motives	Theoretical	60					●				
	Economic	99									●
	Aesthetic	1	●								
	Social	99									●
	Power	15		●							
	Religious	40				●					

284

The interview. If you apply for a job in a large corporation, you may be interviewed by someone in a personnel department. The person may have had some training in psychology. The interviewer may sit back and let you do most of the talking. This is known as free interviewing. It is hoped that you will stress things that are important to you. The interviewer listens for clues to your interests and ambitions, and forms an opinion about hiring you. Or the personnel department person may ask you specific questions. This is called directed interviewing. The questions may be about your hobbies, why you think you could handle the job, whether you like to travel, or perhaps something about your background.

The self-inventory. A number of different types of questionnaires are used to attempt to measure basic personality traits. One true-false questionnaire has items like this:

Circle *true* if the statement below is true about you; circle *false* if it is untrue; and circle the *question mark* if you do not know or cannot make up your mind.

| True | False | ? | (1) Most people are out for all they can get. |
| True | False | ? | (2) I have a hard time making decisions. |

Another kind of self-inventory is known as the Agreement Scale. The instructions read more or less as follows:

Make a check on the scale after each statement to indicate the degree to which the statement is true of you.

(1) Most people are out to get all that they can get.

| Strongly Agree | Agree | Agree and Disagree Equally | Disagree | Strongly Disagree |

(2) I have difficulty making decisions.

| Never | Rarely | Sometimes | Often | Always |

A third self-inventory method is the adjective checklist. On this forced-choice scale, you are asked to choose the adjective in each group that *most* closely applies to you and the one that *least* applies to you.

| (1) Temperamental | Placid | Worried | Sentimental |
| (2) Artistic | Athletic | Sociable | Studious |

Sometimes you are asked on self-inventory tests to rate aspects of your personality on a scale from one to ten. For example:

				HONESTY					
1	2	3	4	5	6	7	8	9	10
Least honest				Average honest					Most honest

It's Your Turn

In each person there are really many different people. Your *self* is affected by people around you. To your parent you are a child, but to your child you will be a parent. We tend to act differently in different situations. Now *It's Your Turn*. Write a list of the different *selves* you have in you. Think about how this affects your behavior in different situations. What happens when two conflicting situations come together? Can you give an example?

The data from objective tests are often measured against standardized scores that have been developed for certain groups of people—students, soldiers, or business people, for example. The tests are used to screen out individuals whose scores are either extremely low or extremely high on particular traits.

Limitations of Objective Tests

Two major criticisms are made of interviews, questionnaires, and rating scales. One is that they usually deal only with superficial aspects of personality—things we are aware of and can talk and write about. Objective tests would not help much, for instance, in predicting difference in performance under stressful conditions.

A more common objection is that objective tests may not actually measure what they are supposed to measure. True-false and forced-choice questions may force the test-taker to make arbitrary and quick decisions that do not reflect his or her real thoughts. Another problem is that it is natural for most people to want to give answers that present them in the best light. Psychologists are aware of this tendency and allow for it when scoring the results. People with the opposite tendency, who strain to avoid bragging, are harder to recognize in the test results. Supporters of these tests emphasize that individual answers do not matter so much as the pattern or distribution of answers.

Projective Tests

The *projective* approach to personality measurement is designed to get beneath the surface and tap a person's deeper feelings and needs, to get at the *I* beneath the surface. In these tests, the person being tested is expected to *project* his or her feelings into unstructured, ambiguous situations. Projective tests try to draw out a person's inner, dynamic qualities, rather than sort out surface traits and attitudes, as the objective tests do.

Projective tests encourage freedom and diversity of response. There are no *right* or *wrong* answers. Three tests are commonly used: the Word Association Test, the Thematic Apperception Test, and the Rorschach Test.

The Word Association Test. This relatively simple test presents *stimulus* words, one by one, and asks you to respond as quickly as possible with the first word that comes to mind. The purpose of the test is to uncover *abnormal* or long-delayed responses that may show mental or emotional upset. A few unusual answers are not significant, but a consistent pattern of strange answers is considered a good clue to mixed-up thinking. On the other hand, unusual or remote associations

A picture from the TAT test

are also a clue to more original and creative thinking. What group of *different* answers means mixed-up and what group means creative? This decision has to be made by a trained psychologist.

The Thematic Apperception Test (TAT). This test assumes that people reveal their deeper feelings and needs by fantasy. If you were to take a TAT, you would look at a series of pictures and tell a story about each of them. Your stories would be interpreted by a psychologist, who would look for indications of trust, anxiety, fear, or the need for achievement. You might not be aware of these feelings, and they probably would not be revealed on objective tests.

The Rorschach Test. Originated by the Swiss psychiatrist Hermann Rorschach in 1911, this test uses a standard collection of inkblots, one on each of a series of cards. The inkblots are totally ambiguous. They are not supposed to represent any particular object. You describe what you see in them, and a trained examiner interprets your responses. This test is thought to give information about the core, or *I*, level of your personality that might not be brought out by interviews. For example, the way you react to color in the blots may throw light on your emotional responses to the world.

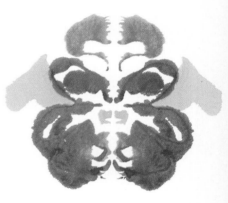

Limitations of Projective Tests

The data gathered from projective tests are usually checked against other sources of information about a person. Taken alone, critics of this method point out, the tests often give unreliable results. Another objection to the projective method is that it does not necessarily tap only hidden processes. A subject's *mood at the time of the test* may also change the responses to either inkblots or photographs.

And finally, the test conditions can influence responses. The personality of the examiner is one example. The sex, appearance, or manner of the examiner may affect a person's answers.

In general, tests help point up personality differences that are more than mere impressions. In this way they add to our overall knowledge of behavior. Like most of the psychologist's equipment, tests provide clues and suggestions rather than definite answers. However, psychological tests are only as good as the theories on which they are based. Let's look at some of those theories.

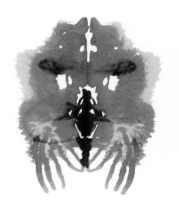

In the Rorschach test, the subject is asked to describe what he or she sees in a series of inkblots.

Section Review

1. What is self-concept?
2. Describe the difference between the **me** and the **I**.
3. Give an example of an objective personality test.
4. Describe a projective personality test.

PREVIEW

**In this section,
read to find out:**

1. what is meant by the unconscious mind.
2. what the id, ego, and superego are.
3. how Freud saw personality as developing in stages in childhood.

A number of theories about personality have grown out of the psychodynamic, or psychoanalytic, approach to personality development. These theories are based on what psychoanalysts observed in working with patients. The theories focus on the part of personality that lies *beneath* observed behaviors, rather than the surface acts themselves. In locating the sources of personality traits, psychoanalytic theory stresses the importance of early childhood experiences.

The person who first investigated these deep inner feelings systematically was psychoanalyst Sigmund Freud. Freud's theory of the unconscious revolutionized the study of personality. Freud believed our personalities are built around elements that cannot be directly observed. He felt that our daily lives are influenced by past experiences we can't readily recall. According to Freud, we are aware of only a small part of our feelings and thoughts. The part of the mind that deals with things we are aware of, Freud called the **conscious** mind.

Yet another part of the human mind, made up of motives, needs, and feelings we are unaware of, is much larger. Freud called this the **unconscious.** Freud compared the mind to an iceberg, nine-tenths of which is under water. The submerged part represents the unconscious self. According to Freud, the unconscious controls the deeper, irrational forces that lie below the level of mental awareness.

Id, Ego, and Superego

Freud described three elements as working within the human mind. He called them the **id,** the **ego,** and the **superego.** These elements are not *parts* of the mind in a physical sense. They are elements in a dynamic process of thinking and feeling that Freud believed was behind all human activity.

The id. In Freud's view, the *id* represents the primitive part of our personality. It is unconscious, and is the powerhouse of our selfish, natural urges. The id drives us to satisfy the libido, our sexual energy or desire, and all other physical pleasure drives. It speaks for our biological self. The id is said to operate on the **pleasure principle.**

The id insists on what it wants, immediately. It knows no restrictions. But not every id impulse can be gratified. You might be hungry when no food is available. Urges that cannot be satisfied directly are said to be partially satisfied by creating a mental image of the thing desired. You might imagine yourself eating a good meal. More often, this kind of *wish fulfillment* is expressed in dreams, which Freud saw as revealing our innermost needs and anxieties.

The ego. Some id instincts can't be satisfied either directly or by wish fulfillment. Some must be dealt with consciously. Satisfying the biological drives may involve learning to be patient, seeking alternative solutions, or directing such instincts into other channels. Conscious management of needs and drives is a task performed by the *ego*, the visible part of the iceberg. The ego represents the purposeful mind. As the id is said to operate on the pleasure principle, the ego works on the **reality principle**. For instance, the ego might put you to work obtaining food rather than imagining it.

Part of the ego's job is to choose actions that fulfill id impulses without bad results. Suppose you have the urge to spend a school morning at home in bed. Your ego tells you to get up and get going if you don't want to fail a class. Or the ego might substitute an acceptable urge for a dangerous one. If your id comes up with a wild impulse to fly by leaping from a cliff, your ego suggests skydiving or a ride on a roller coaster, instead. An important part of the ego's function is to settle disputes between the blind desires of the id and the real world—whatever makes sense in a given culture at a given time. The ego comes between the id and the superego.

The superego. The ego works in a person's self-interest. But behavior in our own interest often conflicts with the self-interest of others. Freud saw that a third dimension of consciousness was needed to hold the id and ego in check. He called this the *superego*. Unlike the id and the ego, the superego is not present at birth. It develops as a child learns which actions are socially acceptable and which are not. The superego holds society's values and moral attitudes.

The superego includes what we mean by conscience. It tells us right from wrong. A growing child internalizes rules made by parents and other adults. Gradually, this right-wrong response enters a child's own system of behavior, independent of its original source.

The superego, as Freud saw it, does more than distinguish right from wrong. It also compares the ego's view of itself with an ego ideal of perfection. This ego ideal is our view of the sort of person we feel we should strive to become. We base it on our own hopes and on the kind of person others think we should be.

The superego combines conscience, that tells us right from wrong, with the ego ideal, that inspires us to make things better for all. In the Freudian view, conflict between the id and the superego is inevitable. A person can deal with the conflict either by directly suppressing unacceptable urges, saying *no* to them, or by hiding them deep inside. Hiding unacceptable urges means repressing full awareness of them by keeping them in the unconscious.

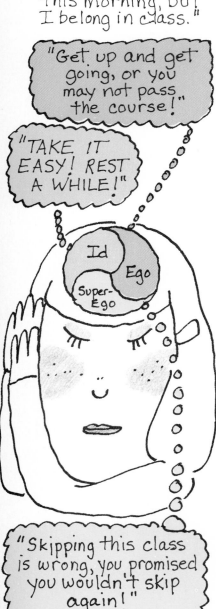

Childhood Experiences and Adult Behavior

Freud's theory emphasizes the experiences of childhood. Freud believed childhood events determine in large measure the type of people we become as adults. He saw infants as pleasure-seeking creatures, whose existence centers on satisfying the biological urges and drives he called the id.

Because of the id, Freud believed that all of us, as children, pass through a series of psychosexual stages. During these stages we get sensual satisfactions through stimulation of various zones of the body—first the mouth, then the anus, and finally the genitals. The many ways an individual gets gratification from body stimulation are called *libido*. The libido, or sexual energy, changes as the child matures. When the libido receives too little or too much gratification, conflicts take place which stall the psychological development of the child in a fixation at that stage. The term *fixation*, important to Freud's theory, means that a person who did not receive enough gratification at a particular stage of development, or who received too much, will attempt to make up for the imbalance throughout life. The person will not be able to proceed to the next level of functioning. There are four stages during which a fixation can occur: oral, anal, phallic, and genital.

The **oral stage** begins at birth and continues for about one year. During this period the mouth is the main source of pleasure and contact with the environment. Infants and young children get great pleasure out of sucking. They should outgrow this stage. Failure to do so results in oral fixation which may show up later in excessive enjoyment of food, gum chewing, smoking, or sucking the ends of pencils.

The **anal stage**, according to Freud, occurs during the second and third years of life. It centers on bowel movements, first the eliminating of waste, then not letting it go. A child gets pleasure from the process of going to the bathroom, and at the same time does not want to give up the interesting thing produced. How toilet training is handled is crucial. Too early, or too rigid, training may result in a person with a life-long anal fixation, according to Freud. This may include stinginess, extreme neatness, or rigid, compulsive behavior.

The third period of erotic satisfaction is the **phallic stage**. Beginning at about age three, children learn that they can derive pleasure from exploring and stimulating their own bodies. But such pleasure is usually forbidden by adults. Freud believed suppression of the phallic urge could lead to unnecessary guilt feelings in later life.

During the phallic stage, says Freud, a boy feels jealous of his father. He wants his mother to himself, and may even say he wants to

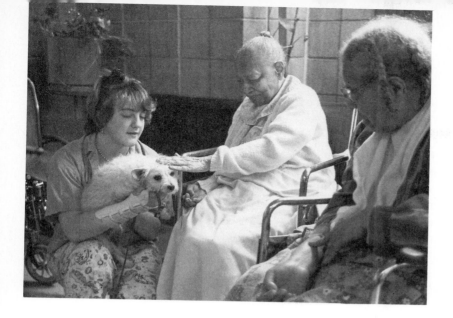

A teenage volunteer brings a pet to share at a nursing home. According to Freud, as adolescence progresses, self-love is replaced by unselfish love.

marry her. Girls go through a similar attachment to the father and rejection of the mother. The situation is resolved, says Freud, by an identification with the parent of the same sex.

Following the phallic stage, there is a period of *latency*, when sexuality *goes underground* for a few years. The final, **genital stage** begins at puberty. Sensual pleasure then begins to be associated with the opposite sex. As adolescence progresses, pleasure focuses less on a person's own body (self-love) and more on others (unselfish, romantic love).

Each of these four stages, in Freudian theory, plays a distinct role in the development of personality. A person's adjustment to others, feelings about himself or herself, and individual behavior patterns all depend, to some extent, on the outcome of these earlier conflicts.

This sketch provides a brief outline of Freud's theory of personality development. Freudians believe that an individual's ability to adjust in later life is determined by early childhood experiences. When painful childhood conflicts are repressed, hidden but not resolved, they do not just go away. They continue in adulthood—through the unconscious—to influence an individual's thoughts, feelings, and behavior.

Section Review

1. Discuss differences between the conscious and unconscious minds.
2. Describe the interaction of the id, ego, and superego.
3. Explain briefly these stages of development: oral, anal, phallic.
4. Describe what a fixation is.

PREVIEW

**In this section,
read to find out:**

1. what defense
   mechanisms are.
2. what is meant by an
   inferiority complex.
3. the meaning of the
   collective unconscious.
4. the difference between
   introverts and
   extroverts.

3. Psychodynamic Theory and Personality

Freud's **psychodynamic theory** is based upon the idea that personality is the outcome of conflict. Conflict exists between the id, with its primitive impulses, and the superego, with its conscience and ideals. To handle this conflict the ego builds **defense mechanisms.** It *defends* itself against feeling anxiety about unacceptable urges. A number of these unconscious mechanisms were identified by Anna Freud, British psychoanalyst and daughter of Sigmund Freud. To some extent defense mechanisms are helpful. They enable us to handle anxiety and to cope with emotional crises. Overuse of them, however, can prevent people from facing up to their problems. Here are some common defense mechanisms.

Displacement. Sometimes we take out our feelings on another person or object. This is displacement. A child who is angry at a parent sometimes strikes a younger brother or sister. An adult who has forgotten the car keys kicks a tire.

Reaction formation. If we know that being hostile toward someone may have results that will make us anxious, we might become overly polite and formal. Reaction formation involves containing our anxious feelings by behaving in an opposite way.

Denial. This means that we adopt a reassuring, contrary belief

This man might be exhibiting the psychological defense mechanism of *denial*, as he sits peacefully and seemingly unconcerned on his storefront porch during the height of the crisis over the Three Mile Island nuclear power plant located near Harrisburg, Pennsylvania. A series of breakdowns in the plant's cooling system in early 1979 caused the release of radioactive gases and raised the possibility of a catastrophic "meltdown" of the reactor's core. Children and pregnant women were evacuated from communities within a five-mile radius of the plant and plans were being made to evacuate those living within 10 to 20 miles downwind of the plant when the crisis was resolved.

about whatever reality we want to avoid. Denial protects the individual by shutting off anxiety-producing information.

Projection. This involves seeing your own thoughts or motives in others. A student said, "The reason I failed the course is because the teacher didn't like me." In fact, the student didn't like the teacher, and projected the feelings of dislike onto the teacher.

Rationalization. Rationalization means finding reasons to justify our behavior. These reasons are usually thought up "after the action," and provide an acceptable explanation for what might be considered an undesirable behavior. A student said, "I left school early because I remembered that this was my mother's birthday." The student left for other reasons, but rationalized the act by finding a *good* reason that is not the *real* reason.

Repression. Repression is preventing thoughts from entering consciousness. It is the most basic of the defense mechanisms. Repression is involuntary. The event is blocked from consciousness, or forgotten. A boy may feel hostile toward his father, but because he would find it unacceptable to admit this feeling, he remains unaware of it.

Regression. Regression means going backward to an earlier stage of development, to cope with a problem. If an individual feels too much anxiety to deal with a situation as an adult he or she may revert to childish ways such as crying, throwing a tantrum, or pouting.

Compensation. When we use compensation we try to make up for a lack in one area by trying to do well in another area. People may do this consciously or unconsciously. A person who is not good at sports may work hard to excel in other school work. Often, this reaction can be desirable. The problem comes when people go too far—overcompensating—to cover up or balance their feelings of inadequacy.

Procrastination. This is a common method of dealing with anxiety or ego conflict. We put off making a decision. We delay to escape what we don't want to face.

Adler: Personality as the Drive for Power

Freud's theory is not the only one that falls into the category called psychodynamic. Other theories recognize the importance of the unconscious. One is the theory of psychoanalyst Alfred Adler.

Adler was a student of Freud's who later broke with him. Adler believed, as Freud did, that early childhood experiences shaped the human personality. He emphasized the social nature of a child's urges, and believed that the urges could, for the most part, be brought under rational control. Adler rejected the sexual content of Freud's theory. He substituted the "will to power" for Freud's idea of libido.

Anna Freud, Alfred Adler

The power of positive thinking that Adler advocated was turned into a fortune by insurance executive W. Clement Stone. Stone believed, and trained his sales people to believe, that with a positive attitude you can accomplish just about anything you set out to do.

Adler said that people are basically striving for superiority as a result of having felt inferior to others when they were small and helpless. This **inferiority complex** was said to be the foundation for most human motivations. Adler believed that all people feel inferior at one time or other, and try to overcome these feelings by compensation.

In a sense, Adler was the first to advocate the power of positive thinking. He believed that every individual had three potential qualities that made for growth and normal adjustment. These were courage, common sense, and social interest. Social interest was the desire to love, to participate with others, and to share in society's goals. Adler believed that if any of these potentials were neglected during childhood, the individual developed a mistaken style of life. The person then had problems in dealing with others.

Were you pampered? Adler tried to trace most adult psychological problems to early parent-child relationships. He saw adults with serious problems as having been either pampered or rejected by their parents. Adler found that first-born children were more likely to be pampered and later-born children (in large families) more likely to be

Adler believed that a person's birth order and the competition he or she might experience with brothers and sisters for parental attention are crucial factors in personality development. At right are Karen and Eric Anderson with their quintuplets.

Photograph by Ron Green courtesy of Redbook Magazine

rejected. These attitudes, he believed, had profound effects in later life. The competition among brothers and sisters for their parents' attention is another crucial factor in Adler's idea of personality development. Anna Freud, a pioneer in the use of psychoanalysis with children and adolescents, developed therapy techniques for use with the young.

Carl Jung's Theory of Personality

Carl Jung is another psychoanalyst who broke with Freud to form his own school of thought. Although he agreed with Freud that unconscious feelings shape behavior, he believed Freud placed too much emphasis on psychosexual urges and personal experiences.

Carl Jung

Jung expanded on Freud's idea of the unconscious mind. He described the unconscious as divided into two parts. The **personal unconscious** is similar to Freud's concept. It is made up of each individual's personal experiences that were once conscious but have since been forgotten. But a more influential part, according to Jung, is the **collective unconscious**. This contains the memories from our ancestors. It is universal—the same for everyone. Jung called these universal ideas **archetypes.** They reflect common experiences and beliefs of humanity.

Jung found common archetypes in the myths and stories of many cultures. For example, most societies have somewhat similar stories of the creation of the world. Most cultures also have a story of a small weak person conquering a large evil person, such as David and Goliath.

Jung says in many of these stories there is a conflict between opposite types. He concluded that human personality also centers around two opposite types: **introversion** and **extroversion.** According to Jung, most people are either primarily introverted or primarily extroverted. An introvert is a person who tends to look inward. Introverts are oriented toward themselves. They are generally shy and quiet. Extroverts are the opposite. They tend to look outward and be outgoing and friendly. They are at ease with people and are often the "life of the party." Jung believed that one aim of life was to bring these two tendencies together, but that most people remain one or the other.

Section Review

1. Give an example of the following defense mechanisms: displacement, rationalization, procrastination.
2. Describe what Adler meant by an inferiority complex.
3. What is the collective unconscious?
4. Define introversion and extroversion.

C L O S E ———— U P

Extroverts Take Their Coffee Strong

Carl Jung first used the terms *extrovert* and *introvert* to explain contrasting types of personality. An extrovert, an outer-directed individual who likes people, takes part in many activities, and seems to need a high level of outside stimulation. Introverts tend to keep to themselves, to seek tranquil surroundings, and to be less confident in dealing with people. According to Jung, either introversion or extroversion predominates to some degree in everyone.

Experiments suggest that these personality differences can be measured by the way an individual responds to stimulation. Psychologist William Revelle and his colleagues sorted 101 graduate students along an extroversion-introversion scale. They then gave them a standard sixty-question test. Students took the test under three sets of conditions: (1) a ten-minute time limit and 200 milligrams of caffeine (about two cups of coffee); (2) a ten-minute time limit but no caffeine; and (3) unlimited time and no caffeine.

The results showed that introverts did better when relaxed than they did either under the stress of the deadline or when stimulated by caffeine. Extroverts did better with the caffeine, and poorly without it, no matter how much time they had. Revelle concluded that one difference between extroverts and introverts is in the way they respond to situations that stimulate the brain. To function well, extroverts seek more outside stimulation and introverts less. Revelle suspects that this effect of stimulation applies to most intellectual activities.

4. Personality: Is It Learned?

The *learning* approach to personality development is in marked contrast to the *psychodynamic* theory. Psychologists who support the learning view believe human personality can be molded, not that it is *fixed* at some point early in life. All we know about a person's behavior, according to learning theory, is what we see from the outside or what the person tells us. What we see are behaviors a person has acquired through either experience or observation. Inner thoughts and instincts are ruled out. Psychologists differ, however, in the emphasis they place on how learning takes place.

PREVIEW

**In this section,
read to find out:**

1. what the behaviorist view is.
2. what the cognitive view is.
3. some criticisms of learning theories.

The Behaviorist View

As you saw in Chapter 5, behavioral psychologists like B. F. Skinner stress the role of reinforcement in personality development. Behaviors that are rewarded by approval—from the family, for example—are strengthened and repeated. Behaviors that are punished are less likely to occur. Skinnerians argue that it is similarity of present and past experience that makes people behave consistently, rather than internal traits or drives. For example, the salesperson at your door may be assertive because assertiveness in similar situations has been rewarded with sales. What appears to be a personality trait in the salesperson is really a learned response to similar rewards. In fact, the same individual may be less assertive in situations where such behavior is not rewarded, as in social situations outside of work.

The Cognitive View

For other theorists, previous reinforcement is only part of the story. Instead, these *cognitive theorists* think that personality results from the cognitive, or thought, processes people use to organize and interpret events around them. These thought processes then become the basis for a person's characteristic ways of reacting to the world. A leading proponent of this theory is Albert Bandura, who has created a theory of **social learning,** or **second-hand learning.**

According to Bandura's studies, people learn not only by doing but by watching others do things. This evidence indicates that you do not have to experience reward or punishment yourself, in order to learn a new behavior. You can see others being rewarded and punished and then figure out the probable results of your own behavior.

In a study, children watched someone hit, kick, and punch a big balloon doll. The children were then put through a mildly frustrating experience. After that, they were given a chance to play with several

Albert Bandura

It's Your Turn

As we have seen, Carl Jung felt most people are either introverted or extroverted. But most people have some qualities of both types. Also, we may change somewhat as we get older. Now *It's Your Turn*. Which group do you think you belong to? Describe on paper some of your own characteristics that you think identify you as an introvert or an extrovert.

objects, including the same balloon doll. They showed, with enthusiasm, that they had learned the appropriateness of the hitting, kicking, and punching by doing them very well. The same learning took place whether children watched a *live* model of the doll-kicking episode, the same model on film, or a filmed cartoon-character model. This kind of learning is called *modeling*. The subjects learn from what someone else does without having to do it themselves first.

Bandura calls this approach a theory of *social learning*. He points out that we don't even have to *see* models performing the actions. We can read or hear about their actions. Vicarious learning lets us multiply our experiences as we read, or see dramatized, events in the lives of other people. Both fiction and nonfiction offer this type of learning, as do daily contacts with the media.

Personality Formation

As our personalities are formed, we learn some behaviors by observing how others close to us act in given situations. People frequently say that children take after one or the other of their parents. Boys often adopt the habits and attitudes of their fathers and girls often follow the model of their mothers. The similarities between parent and child may include such behaviors as speech mannerisms, gestures, and body carriage. We imitate behaviors early in life as we identify with a parent. Small children sometimes model television heroes in their play, as well.

Models and rewards. Bandura offered several principles about the modeling process. He found that it is the consequences of the model's actions that most influence the learning observer. Seeing a model rewarded for an action increases the likelihood that the act will be learned. Attitudes as well as actions can be learned by watching models. Unselfishness as a general pattern of behavior, for example, might be imitated if we see a person benefiting from unselfish acts. Finally, learning from models can be aided by instruction. If the model not only

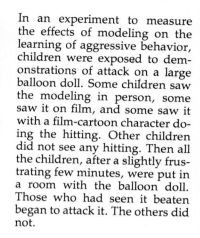

In an experiment to measure the effects of modeling on the learning of aggressive behavior, children were exposed to demonstrations of attack on a large balloon doll. Some children saw the modeling in person, some saw it on film, and some saw it with a film-cartoon character doing the hitting. Other children did not see any hitting. Then all the children, after a slightly frustrating few minutes, were put in a room with the balloon doll. Those who had seen it beaten began to attack it. The others did not.

performs the act but calls attention to it verbally, it helps focus the learner's attention on details that might otherwise be missed.

Modeled behaviors include parental values and strategies. Studies have shown that families that settle disputes by engaging in loud arguments are likely to have children who become argumentative adults. Children tend to develop characteristics of both parents, favoring the more active parent.

Criticisms of Learning Theories

One criticism is that the behaviorists take a too-simple view of human personality. If personality is merely the result of repeated rewards and punishments, critics ask, how can we explain new, creative behaviors? What process of shaping or chaining explains the capacity to love or hate? Although reinforcement may explain isolated behaviors, how can it explain the interacting parts of an overall personality? Furthermore, the behaviorist view seems to ignore the importance of freedom of choice.

This last criticism cannot be made of the cognitive theories. One of their basic ideas is that individuals are free to choose the way they interpret their world. Yet, some critics charge that cognitive theories put too much stress on thought and not enough on emotions and unconscious motivations. Another criticism is that internal thoughts and perceptions are hard to measure. Despite these criticisms, cognitive therapists have helped many people deal with emotional problems by rethinking the way they view the world.

Section Review

1. Describe Skinner's view of personality development.
2. How does Bandura's view differ from Skinner's?
3. What is the major criticism of learning theory?
4. How is learning theory different from psychodynamic theory in explaining personality?

PREVIEW

**In this section,
read to find out:**

1. the meaning of self-actualization.
2. Rogers' ideas of self-concept and regard.
3. humanism's strengths and weaknesses.

Humanists see personal growth as something that develops from inner needs and desires rather than from outside events. A person is shaped in part by past experience, as in both the psychodynamic and the learning theories. But the person is also oriented toward future accomplishments and states of being. Humanists emphasize the rational side of human development, the sense of wholeness and inter-relatedness in life, and the long-term advancement of human welfare. They believe a developing personality can best be understood as an open-ended system. It is constantly striving to grow and change in the process of becoming. Humanists take an optimistic view of human nature. They believe that each individual is uniquely creative in his or her own way.

Humanistic psychologists do not deny the darker forces of the *id*. However, they believe that a person's deep-seated urges are also directed at such acceptable behaviors as affection and control of the environment. Such forces are seen as being secondary to those behaviors that the individual can freely control. Humanistic psychology stresses the importance of self-criticism, the ability to make choices, imagination, and hopes for the future. Everyone has the potential for these qualities. By and large, they make us what we are, in the view of the humanists.

Personality as Self-Actualization

The concept that unites many humanistic ideas is often called **self-actualization.** Self-actualization means going beyond meeting biological needs and learning to get along socially, to a striving toward independence and autonomy. The person who is self-actualized is said to be fully functioning. A carpenter who is happy with his or her work, competent, and highly regarded as a person would be considered self-actualized. So would a famous singer who is paid thousands of dollars for each performance and who has grown as a person. Both have fulfilled the potential of their lives in satisfying ways.

Psychotherapist Carl Rogers used many ideas of self-actualization. He believed that every normal child *could* become fully functioning. At the same time, he saw many people whose potential had been blocked. The important thing in Rogers' viewpoint is the way a person sees these obstacles to his or her own self-actualization. How obstacles look to a person depends largely on that person's self-concept, or self-understanding.

Self-concept develops early in life. In Rogers' view, this comes in

Carl Rogers

Terry Bradshaw was the Pittsburgh Steelers' No. 1 draft choice in 1970, and everyone expected great things of him. Instead, Bradshaw's rookie year was a nightmare, of incompleted passes and interceptions. Teammate Andy Russell explains: "Here he was, a rookie from the country faced with a bunch of cynical veterans. You can imagine the scrutiny he was put under." Bradshaw says: "The pressure kept building . . . I wasn't used to booing. The first time I heard it my knees shook." As the season wore on, Bradshaw often froze from panic, and couldn't call plays; he developed a stutter and often cried after poor performances. He eventually overcame the obstacles that confronted him—a frequently hostile coach, teammates, and public, and his own fear—to lead his team to four Super Bowl victories. Humanistic psychologists would call Bradshaw's effort to conquer the obstacles that prevented him from performing to his highest potential an example of the human desire for self-actualization.

part from the *regard*—whether positive or negative—that others have for our actions. The individual also builds *self-regard* from actions and accomplishments that are personally satisfying. Both the regard of others and the self-regard from our own actions build our attitudes about whether rewards or punishments will result from an action on our part. The two kinds of regard, together, form a person's self-concept. Your self-concept acts as a filter for new experiences. Your self-concept lets in those experiences that fit your self-image, and keeps out those that don't. New experiences and opportunities may be rejected unless they are consistent with your self-concept.

People with good self-images are more open to experiences that are rich and varied. They are better able to tolerate different points of view. Those with a narrow or negative self-image tend to be less open to experiences. To them, many experiences will be seen as threatening to their view of themselves.

Personality as Striving Toward an Ideal

Abraham Maslow contributed to people's knowledge about personality, from his work as a humanist psychologist. You may recall Maslow's hierarchy of needs from Chapter 9. Unlike Rogers, Maslow was not primarily a therapist. His interests centered optimistically on what makes up a normal personality. For Maslow, the psychologically

Shy, reserved, and lacking in self-confidence as a teen-ager, Eleanor Roosevelt soon developed into a person quite different. She fought to improve social conditions in her country and around the world, she worked actively in political campaigns, and, as shown in the photo at right, she served as U.S. Ambassador to the United Nations.

healthy person was not just one who was free of abnormality. A healthy person would show the positive, self-fulfilling, and admired traits that make life worth living.

In describing such an individual, Maslow looked at the lives of people in history, such as Beethoven and Lincoln, and persons alive at the time of his study, including Einstein and Eleanor Roosevelt. Maslow made a list of fifteen characteristics he felt were typical of self-actualized persons. The major qualities he chose can be summarized as follows:

A self-actualized person. To be self-actualized is to accept yourself for what you are and other people for what they are. Self-actualized people are spontaneous, natural, and concerned with ethical and human values. They dislike falseness and often have a mission, or a cause in life. An important quality of self-actualization is autonomy, or independence. Maslow saw this strength as stemming from plenty of love and respect in the past, so that the person "is free to act relatively independently of these needs in the present." At the same time, the relationships self-actualizers develop may be more profound than those of other people. They identify strongly with humanity, and work to stop unjust and dehumanizing conditions. For these people life is meaningful.

Among other qualities that stand out in a self-actualized person are creativity, originality, and a positive attitude toward important tasks. A self-actualized individual often has moments of supremely intense and pleasurable awareness. Maslow described this almost mystical *peak experience* as any experience where self-actualizers lose or overcome their sense of self. At this time, they are said to feel at the peak of their powers, and using all capabilities to the fullest.

Goals of humanism. Humanism's strength lies in its inspirational appeal and its concern for social problems. It assumes an ideal toward which individuals can strive. It asks people to discover what they are really like, and to aim at what they can best become. Few of us ever reach this goal. Even Maslow freely admitted that even these ideal type people went off the track from time to time, lost their temper, and acted out of character. Nevertheless, the striving persists, and in Maslow's view, you are constantly creating yourself.

In sum, humanism holds out the promise of an ideal to which we can strive. Humanism has no fixation on the past. It is not limited to the current situation. The present is shaped by the past, influenced by its own conditions, and given purpose by the future. In this respect, humanism stands in sharp contrast to the theories discussed earlier.

© 1959, United Feature Syndicate, Inc.

Criticisms of Humanistic Theory

Psychologists who regard themselves as more fact-minded than the humanists find considerable fault with Maslow and Rogers. They say that humanism tends to ignore the negative side of personality. In the view of many critics, humanism tells too little of what behavior is really like and too much about what it should be like. Moreover, the ideal of self-actualization is hard to define. It is criticized as a subjective concept that can mean different things to different people.

Some of the self-actualizing traits would also seem to be contradictory. Many highly creative people, instead of having well-rounded personalities, are often hard to live with. The traits of sympathy, warmth, and lovingness, say some of the critics, are often in short supply in people with the independent, detached characteristics that Maslow also saw as typical.

Section Review

1. Try to define self-actualization.
2. What does Rogers mean by regard and self-regard? How are they related to self-concept?
3. How does Maslow describe a self-actualized person?

6. Comparing Personality Theories

Some personality theories you have been considering may seem to contradict each other. If we are driven by unconscious forces, how can we freely control our development? Here Freud clashes with humanist and cognitive views. In many cases the theorists are looking at personality from various perspectives, differing in their emphasis on what should be studied. Each individual has his or her own view of human behavior. These views may influence the personality theory the individual supports. It is important for students of this subject to be open to all perspectives.

Conflict Below the Surface

Freud, you recall, compared the human personality to an iceberg. Only a small part of it extends above the water. The part that we can't see is where most of the iceberg is. It was this submerged area that Freud explored most fully. Thus Freudians look at personality from within. They tunnel into the self and search for the instinctive urges and long-buried desires and fears that have been repressed. Sooner or later, they say, these repressed elements will open up cracks in the top part of the iceberg, and when this happens the whole mass is in danger of breaking up.

Adler believed our struggle for personality was against an inferiority complex. Jung believed the collective unconscious supplied us all with archetypes, ideas deep in humans everywhere. Jung also said that, individually, we are either extroverts or introverts.

Few personality theorists would deny that what goes on beneath the surface is important in accounting for behavior. But some of them stress that other parts of the iceberg may be as important or more important. See the illustration at left.

Making the Most of What Can Be Seen

Learning theorists believe in studying what people do, and what events in their environment can be used to help people to improve their performance.

Both the behaviorists and the social learning theorists are concerned with the iceberg's outward features. Their interest is in the constantly shifting nature of these features.

As the personality iceberg is shaped by storms, moved around by ocean currents, hit by other icebergs, and occasionally rammed by an ocean liner, its shape and movement change and will change again as other conditions prevail. According to the learning theorists, for all

PREVIEW

In this section, read to find out:

1. why psychologists disagree about personality theories.
2. why many theories may be correct.

Freudians exploring submerged areas of personality

practical purposes the bottom part of the iceberg can't be penetrated and may not even exist. We can only know the visible part that responds to external conditions.

View from the Top

As you might suspect, the humanists stand at the tip, or peak, of the iceberg. They are the lookouts among personality theorists. They scan the waters for clear channels and chart their position by the stars in the heavens. For the humanists, the submerged portion of the iceberg is a necessary anchor, but only from the top can the whole be accounted for. What lies ahead, not behind, is what matters to the humanist.

This highly simplified illustration should not be taken too literally. It may serve to remind us, however, that the investigation of personality can be approached from several viewpoints. The interests and background of the psychologist often determine which particular behaviors will be studied. Sometimes this variety in approaches leads to interpretations that overlap. More often, the contrasting approaches open up a number of avenues for measuring specific personality characteristics.

Which Theory Is Right?

Describing human personality is a difficult task. It can probably never be complete to everyone's satisfaction. None of the theories you have been reading about can be considered altogether *right* or *wrong*. They are different approaches. It is possible that you do not agree with any one theory as it exists. Many people do not. Instead, they take an eclectic view—combining elements of different theories. This may be the course you prefer.

On the other hand, you may agree strongly with one particular theory. If so, you will still do well to avoid dismissing the other theories entirely. It is important to understand what each theory says. Then if you disagree, you will have an *educated* point of disagreement. Perhaps you will come up with your own theory! You may feel it describes personality more fully than any of the others. And it may.

Section Review

1. Why do theorists disagree about personality development?
2. Explain why Freudians are said to explore the submerged part of the iceberg.
3. Why are humanists located at the top of the iceberg?

It's Your Turn

You have read about many different personality theories. You may agree with some of them, none of them, or all of them. Now *It's Your Turn.* Describe your own view of human personality. It may be similar to one or more discussed in the book, or it may be brand new.

Chapter 11 Review

Section Summaries

1. Measuring the *Self*

Personality is the sum total of a person's characteristics. The self-concept is made up of our feelings toward our inborn physical features (the body self), the looking-glass self (the "me" or social self) and the inner self (the "I" or private self). Personality can be evaluated by objective or projective tests.

2. Freud: Personality and Conflict

Freud compared the mind to an iceberg. Only one-tenth is above water (the conscious mind); nine-tenths is below water (the unconscious mind). The id, ego, and superego are dynamic forces within the mind. The id operates on the pleasure principle, and the ego works on the reality principle. The superego holds society's values. During the psychosexual stages of childhood, the id's libido is focused on different zones of the body. Too little or too much gratification at any one stage can cause fixation.

3. Psychodynamic Theory and Personality

Freud's psychodynamic theory is that personality is the outcome of conflicts between the id, ego, and superego. Adler's theory is that the "will to power" leads people to compensate for inferiority complexes. Jung divided the unconscious into personal unconscious and collective unconscious, which includes archetypes.

4. Personality: Is It Learned?

Learning approaches hold that personality can be molded by experience. Behaviorists think that personality results from rewards and punishments. The cognitive view is that personality results from the thought processes people use to interpret events around them. Bandura's studies in social learning showed that children model the behavior of others. Personality is shaped by the models the child imitates and by the rewards or punishments those models receive. The behaviorist view is criticized for over-simplifying personality and denying individual freedom. The cognitive view is criticized for ignoring emotions.

5. Humanistic Theories: Personality as Growth

The concept of self-actualization unites many humanistic theories. Carl Rogers tried to help people overcome obstacles to self-actualization. Abraham Maslow used his study of famous people to create a list of characteristics of self-actualized people. Humanism's strength lies in its inspirational approach and concern for social problems. Critics charge that humanism ignores negative aspects of personality, and that self-actualization is hard to define.

6. Comparing Personality Theories

Psychodynamic theorists stress submerged areas of personality, but behaviorists and social learning theorists study outward features. None of the theories is right or wrong, and many researchers take an eclectic view.

Psychology Skill Activities

1. Watch a Saturday morning television show with some little children. Do they model any of the characters they see? **easy**

2. Write a brief autobiography. Include any events in your life that you feel have greatly shaped your personality. **challenging**

Testing for Understanding

Knowing Key Terms

Define these terms in your own words.

Section 1

personality	I
self-concept	objective test
me	projective test

Section 2

conscious	reality principle
unconscious	oral stage
id	anal stage
ego	phallic stage
superego	genital stage
pleasure principle	

Section 3

Section 4

Section 5

Reviewing Main Ideas

Section 1

1. What are the three aspects of the self-concept?

2. Explain how self-concept is related to personality.

3. What are the two basic approaches used to evaluate personality?

Section 2

1. How did Freud use the image of an iceberg to explain the human mind?

2. Explain what Freud meant by the id, ego, and superego.

3. What role do psychosexual stages play in Freud's theory of personality?

Section 3

1. Explain what Freud meant by a defense mechanism.

2. According to Adler, how do inferiority complexes affect behavior?

3. What did Jung mean by the "collective unconscious"?

4. What is the difference between extroverts and introverts?

Section 4

1. What is the behaviorist view of personality development?

2. How is the cognitive view different from the learning view?

3. What are some of the criticisms that have been made of learning theories of personality?

Section 5

1. Explain the concept of self-actualization.

2. In Rogers' view, what role do regard and self-regard play in the development of self-concept?

3. Describe the main strengths and weaknesses of humanism.

Section 6

1. What is a basic difference between the psychodynamic theories and other theories of personality?

2. Why do many psychologists adopt an eclectic view of personality?

Thinking Critically

1. *Drawing Conclusions.* Does the process of self-actualization ever end? Explain.   **easy**

2. *Making Applications.* List some personality traits you feel you share with your parents. How would you explain the similarities? How would you explain differences?   **challenging**

Demonstrating Psychology Skills

Decide whether each of the following statements would be made by Sigmund Freud, Albert Bandura, or Carl Rogers.

1. Little girls learn sex roles by watching their mothers.

2. My patient's potential for self-actualization was blocked by lack of self-regard.

3. My patient's behavior is a clear case of reaction formation.

4. Personality is an open-ended system that is constantly striving to grow and change.

5. This woman's overeating shows she is fixated at the oral stage.

6. People are more likely to model behaviors that they see are rewarded.

7. People may have negative feelings, but the urge toward positive growth is more powerful.

8. The pleasure principle often comes into conflict with the reality principle.

9. Watching violent television shows will probably affect a child's personality.

10. Nine-tenths of our minds are subconscious.

Abnormal Behavior

WHAT DOES Psych. DISTURBED mean TO YOU?
Let me read

At some time in our lives, many of us will have an encounter with what is sometimes called "mental illness." Your own life, or the life of someone close to you, may be touched by it. Below, Mark Vonnegut, son of novelist Kurt Vonnegut, Jr., describes his own encounter with mental illness. He was in his early twenties and living with friends on a farm in British Columbia when the first signs of illness occurred.

read

It started with pruning the fruit trees. One saw cut would take forever. I was completely absorbed in the sawdust floating gently to the ground, the feel of the saw in my hand, the incredible patterns in the bark, the muscles in my arm pulling back and then rushing forward. . . . Suddenly it seemed as if everything was slowing down and I would never finish sawing the limb. Then by some miracle that branch would be done and I'd have to rest. . . . The same thing kept happening over and over. Then I found myself being unable to stick with any one tree. I'd take a branch here, a couple there. It seemed I had been working for hours and hours but the sun hadn't moved at all.

I began to wonder if I was hurting the trees and found myself apologizing. Each tree began to take on personality. I began to wonder if any of them liked me. I became completely absorbed in looking at each tree and began to notice that they were ever so slightly shining with a soft inner light that played around the branches. . . . (Then) from out of nowhere came an incredibly wrinkled, iridescent face. Starting as a small point infinitely distant, it rushed forward, becoming infinitely huge. I could see nothing else. My heart had stopped. The moment stretched forever. I tried to make the face go away but it mocked me . . . I was holding my life in my hands and was powerless to stop it from dripping through my fingers. I tried to look the face in the eyes and realized I had left all familiar ground. ■

During the next weeks, Vonnegut's symptoms increased. He cried a great deal. Periods of terror were followed by moments of ecstasy. "There were times I was scared, shaking, convulsing in excruciating pain and bottomless despair." He went for twelve days without food or sleep. Once, while visiting friends in a nearby town, Vonnegut stripped and ran down the street naked. He considered suicide.

Mark Vonnegut eventually recovered from his breakdown after two brief periods of hospitalization. Officially, his illness was diagnosed as "schizophrenia."

Mark Vonnegut describes behavior that is not what most people would consider "normal." Rather they would say Vonnegut's behavior was abnormal. They might say his actions are a sign of extreme mental *or psychological* disorder, or insanity.

Abnormal behavior and **mental disorder** are terms psychologists and other mental health professionals use to describe behavior that is not normal. **Insanity** is a purely *legal* term. It is used in our court system to describe a person who is not able to manage his or her affairs or understand the consequences of his or her actions. This term would not be used by a psychologist unless he or she used it in a legal context.

would you want to be around someone who is or has been? How do we treat them? Sometimes we discrimate against them, however, it is the same as any other illness & could affect any of us at anytime. More about that later

In this chapter we will consider what is normal and what is abnormal behavior. We will also look at different types of mental disorders and what causes them.

1. What's Normal? What Isn't?

In previous chapters of this book, we have talked about the anxiety and stress that affect all of us in everyday life. We have seen how people sometimes have difficulty dealing with these conditions. Most people are upset occasionally. They fly off the handle now and then. Sometimes they even lash out at someone else in anger. Although these responses might not be the most desirable solutions to a given problem, they are part of most normal people's reactions to stress. To be continually in a rage, however, to lie constantly, to become hostile to every person who frustrates a goal—these are not normal responses to stress. They are likely to be signs of psychological problems. Most people are unable to resolve these problems without professional help.

Defining Normal Behavior

To say that something is "abnormal" means that it differs from the norm, or standard, in some significant way. But what determines the norm? Until fairly recently, normal behavior was defined as "what most people do." It was a definition based on numbers. The difficulty with such a definition is that people are not numbers. Today, our own society increasingly accepts behavior that once would have been considered deviant. In short, the norm itself has been redefined to include a wider variety of personal behaviors.

Many psychologists are now moving away from the statistical norm definition of normality. They are moving toward a more person-centered one. They view the normal individual as one who is "psychologically healthy." This is a person who functions effectively within a

PREVIEW

In this section, read to find out:

1. what abnormal behavior is.
2. how abnormal behavior is recognized.
3. how abnormal behavior is classified.

"Bedlam," an eighteenth-century mental hospital in England was widely known for its sorry conditions. Patients were ordinarily chained to the walls of dark, unlighted cells. It was customary to allow the public to view the bizarre behavior of the "lunatics," as the two "ladies of fashion" are doing here.

chosen life-style. This is not necessarily a person whose behavior conforms to traditional guidelines. As long as a person's behavior is not harmful to himself or herself or to others, almost any behavior can be considered normal.

But what does being "psychologically healthy" mean? Most psychologists would agree that an individual is healthy if he or she has the following characteristics.

1. A healthy person is one who can *function in everyday life.* Healthy people can cope with the necessary routines of life. They deal with the demands placed on their time. These might include getting up on time, getting dressed, and going to school or work.

2. A healthy person is one who can *get along with others.* He or she can function reasonably well in the real world. He or she understands reality and can deal with it. Healthy people can form relationships with others—family, friends, classmates, co-workers, and employers. They can hold down jobs and cope with most other demands of society.

3. Healthy people are *comfortable with themselves* and do not intentionally cause pain to themselves or others. They feel at ease with themselves and their identity. They do not do harmful things to themselves such as engage in accident-prone behavior or abuse of drugs.

Typically, healthy people are able to cope with disappointments and problems. They share their feelings and enthusiasms with those around them and are open to new experiences. They make friends and take a useful role in the larger worlds of family and community. By these standards, most of us—whatever our hang-ups and differences—lead fairly normal lives. It's also important to remember that even though we are normal, we all occasionally show some signs of abnormal behavior. These occasional, temporary signs are nothing to worry about. It is normal to "act a little crazy" once in a while.

Recognizing Abnormal Behavior

It is not always easy to determine when someone is acting abnormally. All too often abnormal behavior is what some other person does, and normal is what we do. The fact that psychologists use several criteria to distinguish between abnormal and normal behavior indicates that no simple definition is possible.

Probably the most important of these criteria has to do with the consequences of behavior. First, what is the effect of the person's behavior on others? Is it harmful or destructive? Second, what is the effect on the person who is doing the behaving? Is it potentially harmful to him or her? A third criterion is to judge behavior by its motive, or reason. The reasons for behavior can affect the way we judge it.

Similarly, the definition of abnormal behavior also depends on the *context* in which the act occurs. A person who enters a church or synagogue, then prays aloud, is thought to be religious. But in Western societies someone who prays aloud on a busy street will almost certainly be regarded as acting strangely. In Japan, suicide has traditionally been seen as a courageous (and normal) act. In most Western countries, it is seen as an act of despair (and abnormal). What is considered acceptable in a foreign culture is often objectionable in our own. Sometimes it is the other way around.

Yet there is little disagreement that some kinds of behavior are indeed abnormal. Confusion, hallucinations, distorted emotional reactions, and uncontrolled violence are usually taken as signs that a person should be watched closely, given help, and perhaps hospitalized. Most people would agree that these types of behavior are not only different, but seriously abnormal. In other words, they interfere with daily life.

Normal or Abnormal: Who Decides?

To decide whether behavior is abnormal, someone has to evaluate the behavior and judge it. In our society today we generally consider individuals to be in need of treatment on the basis of some combination of the following evidence.

1. *Society says so.* The individual's behavior is so "disturbed" that it draws the attention of others.

2. *The person who is disturbed says so.* An individual may not behave abnormally but may feel he needs help. Feelings of severe anxiety and depression, for example, may prevent normal functioning.

Is "abnormality" in the eye of the beholder? It is all too easy to regard one's own ways as "normal"—also moral, rational, and superior—and to see different values and customs as inferior and "abnormal." But what seems strange is in large part a matter of what you happen to be used to. Your ways can seem as strange to others as their ways do to you.

Participant in political convention, USA

Ceremonial costume, Bali

Woman at cosmetics counter, USA

Tribal dance, Bali

Bagpipers, Canada

Veiled women, Morocco

Frog-jumping contest, USA

Asaro mudmen, New Guinea

Cheerleaders, USA

3. *The experts say so.* A psychiatrist or clinical psychologist makes a diagnosis of mental disturbance. The principal function of the "expert" is to determine what specific type of disorder the person is suffering from. He or she also decides the likely course of the disturbance if it is not treated. Also decided is what kind of treatment is most suitable.

Unfortunately, none of these judging agents is perfect. It is important to keep all factors in mind when arriving at a diagnosis of mental disorder.

Types of Abnormal Behavior

There are many kinds of abnormal behavior. The American Psychiatric Association (APA) has an elaborate classification system for mental disorders. A list of some of the major disorders included in the most recent revision of the APA system appears on page 315.

In this chapter, we will explore only disorders of *psychological* origin—commonly known as neuroses, psychoses, and personality disorders. (The APA is trying to discourage the use of the terms neurosis and psychosis. These terms are believed to be too broad and general to be useful in diagnosing and treating mental disorders. But most mental health professionals, as well as the general public, continue to use them.) Other types of mental disorders included in the APA list, such as those caused by physical damage to the brain or developmental dis-

Estimated Number of People Suffering from Various Mental Disorders*

30 million Americans (19–24 percent of the population) suffer some form of recent diagnosed mental disorder

14 million (8–15 percent) suffer anxiety/somatoform disorders, including phobias, panic, and obsessive disorders

10 million (6 percent) suffer substance abuse or dependence, most from alcohol-related problems

10 million (5–7 percent) suffer affective disorders

1.5 million (1 percent) suffer schizophrenic disorders

1.5 million (1 percent) suffer antisocial personality disorders

2 million   (1–3 percent) suffer severe cognitive impairment

*Figures based on a recent, long-term survey of the National Institutes of Mental Health, reported in the *Archives of General Psychiatry*, Shapiro et al., 1984.

*Shapiro, S., et al. (1984) Utilization of health and mental health services. *Archives of General Psychiatry, 41,* 971–978.

orders, are beyond the scope of this chapter.

As additional helps in diagnosing and treating mental disorders, the APA added two new dimensions to its classification system in its latest revision. One is a scale for rating the severity of stress a person is experiencing. (See the table on page 316.) Another addition is a scale for rating a person's level of functioning in social, job, or school situations. Before the development of these scales, what one psychologist might describe as "severe stress" might have been viewed as "moderate stress" by another. Now the stress as well as the function scales enhance more uniform diagnoses.

Limits of classification. Classifying mental disorders gives us an easier and more systematic way of discussing abnormal behavior. But there are limitations to any classification system. Most categories in the APA system are *descriptions* of behavior, not *explanations*. Just because we have given a name to a disorder doesn't mean it can be fully explained. Also, some people criticize the system because only

The list of major mental disorders is only a partial one. The American Psychiatric Association has categorized and subcategorized many other disorders. For a complete listing, as well as additional examples of disorders within each major category, you may wish to refer to the manual cited beneath the chart.

Major Mental Disorders
(former categories in parentheses)

Categories	Disorder Example	Behavioral Description
Personality Disorders	Compulsive Personality Disorder	task-oriented perfectionism; excessive devotion to work to the exclusion of pleasure
Anxiety Disorders (neuroses)	Phobic Disorder	persistent and irrational fear of some specific object, activity, or situation
Somatoform Disorders (neuroses)	Hypochondriasis	preoccupation, despite medical assurance, with bodily sensations as possible signs of serious disease
Dissociative Disorders (neuroses)	Psychogenic Amnesia	sudden, extensive inability to recall important personal material (not caused by physical disorders)
Sleep Disorders	Primary Insomnia	excessive daytime worrying about not being able to fall and stay asleep
Mood Disorders (neuroses and psychoses)	Depressive Disorder	loss of interest or pleasure coupled with feelings of sadness, discouragement, and dissatisfaction
Delusional Disorders (psychoses)	Persecutory Delusion	feeling that one is constantly being spied on and plotted against
Schizophrenic Disorders (psychoses)	Catatonic Schizophrenia	marked psychomotor activity that may involve stupor, negativism, rigidity, excitement, or posturing

Based on the American Psychiatric Association, *Diagnostic and Statistical Manual of Mental Disorders, 3rd Edition-Revised (DSM-III-R)*, 1987.

Severity of Psychosocial Stressors Scale: Children and Adolescents

Code	Term	Examples of stressors	
		Acute events	Enduring circumstances
1	None	No acute events that may be relevant to the disorder	No enduring circumstances that may be relevant to the disorder
2	Mild	Broke up with boyfriend or girlfriend; change of school	Overcrowded living quarters; family arguments
3	Moderate	Expelled from school; birth of sibling	Chronic disabling illness in parent; chronic parental discord
4	Severe	Divorce of parents; unwanted pregnancy; arrest	Harsh or rejecting parents; chronic life-threatening illness in parent; multiple foster home placements
5	Extreme	Sexual or physical abuse; death of a parent	Recurrent sexual or physical abuse
6	Catastrophic	Death of both parents	Chronic life-threatening illness
0	Inadequate information, or no change in condition		

Based on the American Psychiatric Association, *Diagnostic and Statistical Manual of Mental Disorders, 3rd Edition-Revised* (DSM-111-R), 1987.

The above scale provides clinicians with a method for coding the overall severity of a stressor or stressors on a child or adolescent. Over a period of time, stressors may contribute to the development, recurrence, or worsening of a mental disorder. A similar scale has been developed for typical adult stressors.

individual behaviors are covered. The behavior of groups—families, cults, and societies—is not directly dealt with.

However, the system does have its strong points. It does provide a good idea of the range of behavior considered abnormal. Also, it helps to make sure that everyone is talking about the same thing when referring to mental disorders.

A final "warning." Finally, as you read the description of the mental disorders that follow it is important to keep in mind the fact that it is common for normal people to show some type of abnormal behavior occasionally. This does not mean that the person is abnormal or has a mental disorder. When people study mental disorders for the first time, they often see themselves, members of their family, or friends as having the symptoms of every mental disorder under discussion. Try to avoid the "amateur psychologist" trap. Remember it takes years of training to make a mental health professional, and only a professional can really evaluate abnormal behavior.

Section Review

1. List three characteristics of a psychologically healthy person.
2. What is meant by "abnormal behavior"?
3. Give an example that shows that context is important in determining abnormal behavior.
4. Describe the types of mental disorders that will be discussed in this chapter.

2. Neurotic Disorders

Most people in therapy today are being treated for some type of neurosis. It has been estimated that at least 20 million people in the United States suffer from neurotic disorders. Neuroses are rarely severe enough to require hospitalization, but they can have devastating effects on people's lives.

There is no clear-cut dividing line between the normal and the neurotic. The difference is one of degree. Most of us have *neurotic tendencies.* Maybe you worry needlessly about unimportant things. Or maybe you are so concerned about your health that you crawl into bed at the first sign of a sniffle. These are examples of typical behavior that borders on the neurotic. But, if doctors can't convince you that your sniffles only indicate a simple head cold, and you persist in believing you are dying of pneumonia, or if you worry so much about everything that you feel like a "nervous wreck" all the time, then you are probably displaying neurotic behavior. Neurotic individuals spend a great deal of time trying to defend themselves against, or trying to avoid, imagined dangers. A **neurosis,** then, is an emotional disturbance characterized by excessive anxiety and the overuse of defense mechanisms. Defense mechanisms are those unconscious strategies for coping with stress you studied in Chapter 11.

Anxiety: The Basis of Neurosis

Most psychologists believe that anxiety is the basis for all neuroses. Does this mean that anyone who feels anxious is neurotic? No. Everyone is anxious at times. Recall how you felt on your first day of high school. Perhaps even today you get "butterflies" when you begin a final exam, play a big game, or take off in an airplane. All these experiences represent unknowns that signal possible discomfort or danger. In such cases, anxiety is normal and even useful. It can make you prepare especially hard for your final exam. It can cause you to be especially alert during the big game.

The neurotic individual, however, feels greater than normal anxiety in facing the ordinary problems of living. He or she finds that ordinary ways of dealing with anxiety are not enough. The neurotic individual comes to rely more and more on defense mechanisms, and the defenses he or she uses become more and more extreme. We will look at some of these extreme defenses later in this section.

Characteristics of neurotic anxiety. In general, then, neurotic people live an unhealthy life-style aimed at avoiding and lessening anxiety. Neurotic anxiety has the following characteristics.

PREVIEW

In this section, read to find out:

1. what a neurosis is.
2. the symptoms of neurosis.
3. what the different types of neurosis are.

Everyone experiences anxiety at one time or another—those troubled, uneasy feelings that occur in the face of a discomfort or an unknown. Stage fright—fear of speaking before a group—is just one example of normal anxiety.

1. The ordinary functioning of the person is disrupted in some way. The desire to avoid anxiety takes over day-to-day behavior. This prevents the person from living a normal life.

2. The individual displays a seemingly illogical pattern of behavior. He or she does something that doesn't make sense. This might take the form of repeating an action over and over again or developing an unreasonable fear of something as ordinary as riding in an elevator. These neurotic defenses are aimed at relieving anxiety, but they generally aren't successful.

3. It should be pointed out, however, that even though their anxiety is often overwhelming, neurotic people stay in touch with reality. They are able to function in the real world. They don't live in the fantasy worlds that people with more severe mental disorders often retreat to. And, the neurotic individual is usually upset by his or her abnormal behavior. This is often called the **neurotic paradox.** Neurotic people usually *know* there is something wrong with their behavior, but they can't seem to change it. However, the fact that the neurotic person recognizes that his or her behavior is abnormal may eventually make treatment easier.

Other Characteristics of Neurotic Disorders.

Anxiety forms the underlying basis for most neurotic behavior. But neurotic individuals display other typical behavior as well. Pioneer psychoanalyst Karen Horney identified the following characteristics of neurotic individuals.

1. *Excessive need for affection, and dependence on others.* The neurotic individual seeks attention and demands reassurance for virtually every action. At the same time, such a person finds it difficult to be genuinely affectionate toward others.

2. *Feelings of inferiority and inadequacy.* The neurotic individual is insecure, is generally uncomfortable in the presence of strangers, is ill at ease in social situations, and is often very shy and inhibited. Such people fear a negative evaluation of their conduct and thus avoid situations where they will be judged by others.

3. *Incapacity to plan.* Neurotic people are often extremely poor organizers. They may be very neat, but they are unable to plan ahead and are always absorbed with the problems of the moment.

4. *Aggressive and hostile behavior.* In contrast with the neurotic person who is shy and inhibited, some neurotics are overbearing and bossy. They may have a strong need to feel powerful and important. Actually, such people are usually compensating for their own feelings of hostility and fault-finding. In Horney's words, they feel "easily cheated . . . imposed on or humiliated . . ." and believe the whole world is against them.

5. *Abnormal sexual functioning.* The truly neurotic person often has a compulsive need for sex, or an unconscious fear of it. This often keeps the neurotic person from forming healthy relationships.

Neurotic behavior can sometimes take the form of unprovoked and unnecessary aggression and hostility in response to what others might consider a normal situation.

Types of Neuroses

In the APA's latest classification of mental disorders, the neuroses are broken down into four general categories: (1) anxiety disorders; (2) somatoform disorders; (3) dissociative disorders; and (4) mood disorders.

Anxiety Disorders

As we have seen, anxiety and the individual's efforts to control it are the key factors in neurotic behavior. In the category known as **anxiety disorders,** the anxiety itself or the coping efforts are the central symptoms.

Anxiety states. Although anxiety is a central feature of all neuroses, all the other types use avoidance mechanisms to reduce the feelings of threat. Some neurotic individuals, however, live in a constant state of tension and anxiety. This inner turbulence sometimes erupts into a full-blown *anxiety attack.* During an attack, feelings of panic overwhelm the person, although there is no apparent reason for the person's extreme anxiety. An anxiety attack is sometimes accompanied by heart palpitations, sweating, diarrhea, and difficulty in breathing.

Obsessive-compulsive disorders. Anxiety also can be expressed through an obvious behavior. Sometimes, neurotics protect themselves against unconscious feelings of threat by performing a particular act, or concentrating on certain thoughts. The anxiety is focused on the behavior itself and thus becomes more manageable.

One of the most famous examples of obsessive compulsive behavior in literature is found in Shakespeare's play, *Macbeth.* Plotting with her husband, the King of Scotland, Lady Macbeth (left) murders one who she believes is a threat to her husband's crown. She experiences no remorse for her deed, but sees her hands as stained with the blood of her victim. She continually walks in her sleep, and performs a handwashing ritual, after which she says in a famous line from the play, ''Here's the smell of blood still; all the perfumes of Arabia will not sweeten this little hand.'' Hetty Green (right) might have been labeled compulsive. Living in the early 1900s, she could be seen daily going into the vault at the Chemical National Bank in New York City. There she would pull out the trunks and bags that were stored under a staircase and would sit cross-legged on the floor rummaging through the masses of papers and documents that represented her fortune. Going by a number of assumed names, Hetty Green often spent each night in a different cheap boardinghouse in order to save money and escape the tax assessor. When her son injured his knee, Hetty Green nursed him herself rather than pay for a doctor. Three years later his leg had to be amputated. Hetty Green died in 1916 at the age of 81, leaving her son and daughter an estate worth over $100 million dollars.

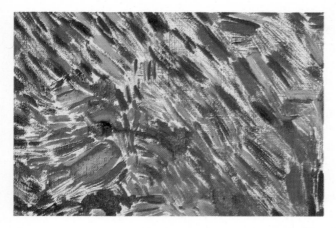

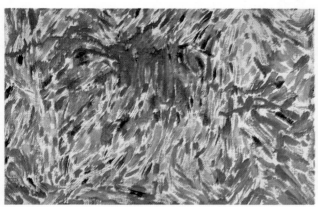

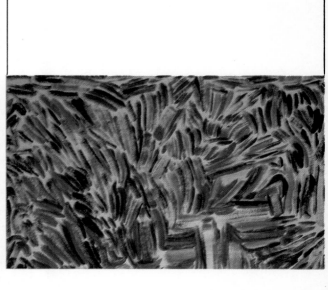

An **obsession** is a thought or mental image that won't go away. If a familiar tune runs endlessly through your head or if you keep asking yourself "Did I really lock the door?" you are experiencing a mild (and harmless) type of obsession. True neurotic obsessions are much more insistent. They are so disturbing that they come to interfere with all facets of the individual's life. Extreme obsessive reactions make it impossible for the individual to concentrate on any other thought.

Compulsive behavior consists of repetitive, ritualistic actions that serve no rational purpose. Almost everyone has superstitious mannerisms that are compulsive in nature. Truly compulsive people, however, are driven far beyond the relief of nervous tension. These people usually realize that their behavior does not make sense, but they cannot seem to control it. Such people may wash their hands every time they touch a doorknob. They may insist that every object in their room be kept exactly in the same position. Often they save a great many things

These paintings, all different in kinds of paints and brushes used, were done by a neurotic patient with obsessive-compulsive tendencies. These tendencies are illustrated by rigid brush strokes that are all alike. In an effort to break the patient from his rigid mold, the therapist gave him a piece of paper twice as large as the ones on which the previous paintings had been done. The patient, however, folded the paper to the same size as the previous paintings and did the same kind of painting (above).

It's Your Turn

Phobias are some of the most interesting of neurotic disorders. Much research has been done on their causes and treatment. Many methods of treatment now prove successful. A list of some common phobias appears in the table on page 323. Now *It's Your Turn.* Do you have any phobias? Perhaps they are just extreme fears? Write them out for yourself and try to think of their possible causes.

© King Features Syndicate, Inc. 1977

they have no use for. Their daily routine seldom varies. They may do things a fixed number of times or in a fixed series. Below is a case study of a typical pattern of compulsive behavior.

A middle-aged, married woman had the compulsion to shake every article of her own clothes and those of her children. The shaking ritual—which occupied over an hour of her time each morning—required that each piece of clothing be shaken three times in each of three different directions and at each of three different levels. In addition, most of the clothes had to be brushed inside and out; whenever anything was washed, it had to be washed three times. The woman also found it difficult to stop washing her hands once she had started and repeatedly felt a compulsion to rub her hands together in each of three different ways. ■

Interviews with the woman during treatment revealed that she had fears about germs and disease. Treatment involved helping her to distinguish realistic fears about disease from unrealistic ones. Behavior modification techniques were used in which noncompulsive behavior was positively reinforced. Within six months after treatment began the woman's compulsive behavior disappeared. This type of treatment has proved to be very successful with obsessive-compulsive disorders.

Phobic disorders. A **phobia** is an unreasonable fear or dread of something that most people find tolerable. The fear persists even if there is no actual danger. If we see a snarling dog, we are naturally afraid of it. We are not being phobic, however, since there is a good reason for our fear. But if we fear all animals, even friendly puppies (zoophobia), if we consistently avoid elevators and other confined areas (claustrophobia), or if we fear all heights (acrophobia), we must look beyond the immediate situations for the cause of our dread.

A phobia becomes a major problem when the feared object is not easily avoided. It thus interferes with a person's ongoing behavior. For example, when a person must work or live in a high-rise building and has a phobia of elevators, his or her phobia would become a major problem. Whatever the reason for the phobic disorder, it, like obsessive compulsive disorders, also can usually be treated quite successfully with behavior modification techniques. For a list of some commonly occurring phobias, see the table on page 323.

Somatoform Disorders

The second category of neurotic behavior is the **somatoform disorder.** "Soma" means body. This group of disorders involves individ-

**Some Common Phobias
and the Feared Object**

Acrophobia
   (high places)
Agoraphobia
   (open places)
Ailurophobia
   (cats)
Algophobia
   (pain)
Astraphobia
   (thunderstorms, lightning)
Claustrophobia
   (closed places)
Hematophobia
   (blood)
Mysophobia
   (germs or contamination)
Nyctophobia
   (darkness)
Ocholophobia
   (crowds)
Pathophobia
   (disease)
Pyrophobia
   (fire)
Syphilophobia
   (syphilis)
Xenophobia
   (strangers)
Zoophobia
   (animals or some particular
      animal)

uals who complain of physical symptoms for which no physical causes can be found. In other words, there is really nothing physically wrong with them.

Hypochondriasis. One of the most common of these disorders is **hypochondriasis.** Hypochondriacs worry excessively about their physical health, even when there is little or no evidence that anything is wrong with them. When one symptom goes away, another takes its place. The individual may have pains in the chest one day, stomach cramps the next, and headaches the third. These complaints do not usually follow any logical pattern.

If matters stopped here there would be no great problem. Many of us experience the symptoms of hypochondriasis at one time or another. But the true hypochondriac usually sees these symptoms as evidence of deadly illnesses. They are preoccupied with health matters and have unrealistic fear of disease. A clean bill of health from various doctors may provide little reassurance. The hypochondriac either continues to believe that the illness is present or acquires another to take its place.

Conversion disorder. The conversion disorder is one of the most interesting, yet confusing disorders. It involves some physical problem of loss of function without any physical reason. For example, if your

Uptight, Not All Right

In the movie, *The Caine Mutiny*, Humphrey Bogart played the disturbed Captain Queeg, who compulsively rubbed two ball bearings together in his hands.

The stress of ordinary living can make any of us uptight from time to time, and we should learn to recognize our obsessive-compulsive tendencies when they occur. Psychologist Leonard Cammer has developed a test for this purpose—the Obsessive-Compulsive Personality Inventory.

Rate yourself on each statement below with a **1** if it applies to you **none of the time**; a **2** if it applies to you **some of the time**; a **3** for **a good part of the time**; and a **4** for **most or all of the time**. Then add up your score to find out how compulsive you are.

1. I prefer things to be done my way.
2. I am critical of people who don't live up to my standards or expectations.
3. I stick to my principles, no matter what.
4. I am upset by changes in the environment or the behavior of people.
5. I am meticulous and fussy about my possessions.
6. I get upset if I don't finish a task.
7. I insist on full value for everything I purchase.
8. I like everything I do to be perfect.
9. I follow an exact routine for everyday tasks.
10. I do things precisely to the last detail.
11. I get tense when my day's schedule is upset.
12. I plan my time so that I won't be late.
13. It bothers me when my surroundings are not clean and tidy.
14. I make lists for my activities.
15. I think that I worry about minor aches and pains.
16. I like to be prepared for any emergency.
17. I am strict about fulfilling every one of my obligations.
18. I think that I expect worthy moral standards in others.
19. I am badly shaken when someone takes advantage of me.
20. I get upset when people do not replace things exactly as I left them.
21. I keep used or old things because they might still be useful.
22. I think that I am sexually inhibited.
23. I find myself working rather than relaxing.
24. I prefer being a private person.
25. I like to budget myself carefully and live on a cash and carry basis.

Scoring

25–45. Not compulsive or uptight.

46–55. Mildly O-C. Your compulsiveness is working for you, and you are successfully adaptive.

56–70. Moderately O-C. You are adaptive, but uptightness has crept into your personality function, and you experience uncomfortable days of high tension.

71–100. Severely O-C. You are quite uptight and driving hard. You have many days of high tension. The closer you are to the rating of 100 the nearer you come to the exhaustion of your adaptive reserve and to a slump into depression.

How did you score? "Mildly O-C"? "Moderately O-C"? Even if you scored "Severely O-C," don't be too alarmed. Remember that the function of this type of test is not to provide a professional diagnosis. Use this, and all tests of this type, as a way to identify areas of your life where you may be too uptight. Then see if there isn't some way to ease your tensions.

right arm becomes paralyzed every time you see "Bill Jones" you would certainly go to a doctor. Tests show no physical basis for the paralysis, and you are sent to a therapist. After a number of interviews, the therapist discovers that you have always deeply resented Bill. He suggests that, unconsciously, and without any organic reason, your arm has become paralyzed to keep you from striking him. Freudians term this kind of reaction **conversion hysteria.** It is called this because the energy you might expend in striking Bill is *converted* into paralysis to keep you from doing so. Your mental problem is converted into a physical symptom.

The conversion can take different forms. A person may become hysterically blind, or a would-be singer may develop paralyzed vocal cords just before the big audition. The symptoms, however, do not fit with medical fact. Patterns of paralysis, for example, may not correspond to actual nerve pathways. The hysterical symptoms may disappear when the person is asleep or under hypnosis. Individuals who develop conversion reactions tend to be immature, emotional, and demanding.

Dissociative Disorders

In a dissociative disorder the person avoids stress or anxiety by "escaping"—or dissociating—from his or her core personality. Parts of the individual's consciousness may literally split from one another. This is a relatively rare, but fascinating, phenomenon.

Amnesia and fugue. Amnesia is partial or total loss of memory. It is likely to occur when a person's inner conflicts are so intolerable that the memory simply "shuts down." This permits the individual to escape into a new identity. The individual cuts off an unhappy past and is able to start all over again, constructing the present on its own terms. In unusual cases—called **fugue episodes**—a person literally escapes by combining amnesia with travel to another place. A person might begin a new career, marry, and raise a family, only to discover, when memory returns years later, that he or she already has a family in another city. Such a person has unknowingly dropped the past in order to create a new, more acceptable self. In the neurotic type of amnesia, however, the forgotten material is really not lost. It is still there beneath the surface of consciousness, and may return at some future date.

Multiple personality. The most extreme form of dissociation is **multiple personality.** In this type of reaction which is very rare, the individual may develop two or more distinct, even radically different, personalities. Each takes over conscious control of the person for varying periods of time. Usually, although not always, each personality

In the winter of 1926, Agatha Christie (shown below) disappeared from her home near London. After her car was found abandoned in an isolated area, she became the subject of a nationwide police hunt. Then, eleven days after her disappearance, she was found, unharmed, in the seaside town of Harrowgate, registered under the name of her husband's secretary. She gave no explanation of her behavior at the time—or many years later in her autobiography. At the time, however, her husband, Colonel Archie Christie, suggested she had amnesia. Within two years after the episode, the Christies were divorced, and Archie Christie married his secretary.

does not know of the others.

Students frequently make the error of confusing such cases of multiple personality with so-called "split personality," known technically as schizophrenia. This is a psychotic disorder in which the individual is "split off from reality." In multiple personality, the conscious part of the personality remains in contact with reality, though reacting to it neurotically.

Although cases of multiple personality are very rare, they have received much publicity in the media. The story of Chris Sizemore, a woman who showed seven sets of three different personalities over twenty years, was made into a book and a movie—*The Three Faces of Eve*. More recently the book and television movie, *Sybil*, was based on a case of a woman with 16 different personalities.

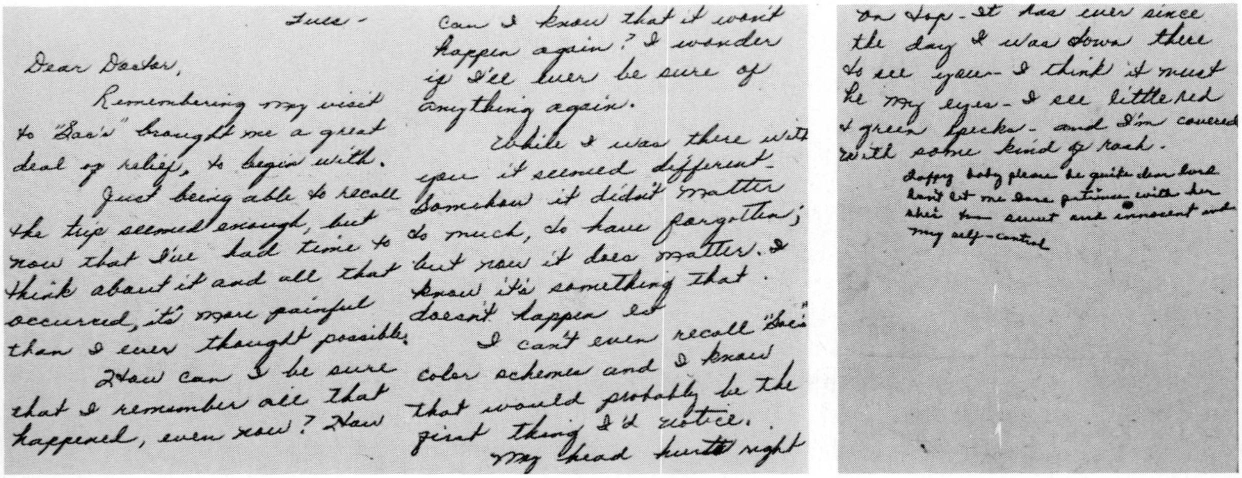

Shown here is a letter written by Chris Sizemore, the subject of *The Three Faces of Eve*, to her doctor. The different handwriting at the end of the letter indicates that a personality dissociation took place at that point.

Mood Disorders

A final type of neurosis centers around mood, or emotional, problems. The most common mood disorder is depression. Nearly everyone feels "down" or depressed at some time or other, and usually for good reason. However, when an individual doesn't "bounce back" afterwards, or can't find a reason for recurring or persisting bouts of depression, the condition is thought to be neurotic. For example, if you lose a parent or grandparent, you normally grieve until you

Chris Sizemore, the subject of *The Three Faces of Eve,* had three distinct personalities: one was nervous, moralistic, inhibited, unhappy, and full of hatred; another was outgoing, fun-loving, and had an active interest in men; the third represented a balance between the other two. Today Ms. Sizemore reports that her behavior has stabilized into one well-adjusted personality. At left, she displays four of her own paintings, produced during various changes in her behavior.

adjust to the loss, which may be a matter of months. But if you lose all interest in life, if you turn on yourself, experience feelings of guilt and unworthiness, and become despondent about the future, your depression is much more serious. In severe cases, the person may be unable to work or go to school. He or she may sit alone hopelessly staring into space, able to see only the dark side of life.

Sometimes the depressed person becomes alternately agitated and withdrawn, refuses to eat, does not sleep well at night, and may attempt suicide. In this case the person may require hospitalization for his or her own protection. Any severe emotional crisis might cause such a reaction. Whatever the reason, depression is probably the most prevalent mental illness in the United States.

& & &
See **Exercise 7, Case Studies,** on pages 488–489 of the *Psychology Skills Handbook,* for a description of case studies as a research method.

Section Review

1. Define neurosis.
2. Describe the relationship of anxiety to neurosis.
3. What are the general characteristics of neurotic behavior?
4. Give one example of each of the four categories of neuroses.

PREVIEW

**In this section,
read to find out:**

1. what the symptoms of psychoses are.
2. how the various types of schizophrenia differ.
3. what a delusional disorder is.
4. what a bipolar disorder is.

The murals that cover the walls of the room shown at right are part of artist Walter Anderson's tribute to "Creation" and the rich flora and fauna of the Mississippi Gulf Coast. In 1947, following his hospitalization for a mental illness diagnosed as schizophrenia, Walter Anderson retreated to this family-owned cottage in Ocean Springs, Mississippi. From that time until his death, Anderson remained a recluse, celebrating the relationship between a lone human being—himself—and Nature. As Nature's loving witness, Anderson painted hundreds of watercolors and kept a diary of his impressions of the plants and wild creatures around his home and on nearby Horn Island. During the last four years of his life, Nature engulfed Anderson's indoor world too as he painted these murals on the walls of his cottage. The murals were discovered after his death in 1965.

3. Psychoses: "Going Mad"

To a person suffering from a **psychosis,** the world is strangely different from the one the rest of us know. A psychotic individual may hear voices, see images, and smell odors that don't exist. He or she may be deeply withdrawn or "raving mad." A bit of sad news may bring laughter. Sometimes close family members are not recognized. There are many different types of psychoses, but they all have one thing in common. They all involve a loss of contact with reality. Also, psychotic behavior is clearly abnormal, but unlike neurotics, psychotics rarely realize that what they are experiencing is out of the ordinary or a problem. This often makes treatment difficult.

Psychotic Symptoms

Besides this first and most basic characteristic of psychosis—disorientation, or loss of contact with reality—there are other symptoms. One is the presence of **delusions,** or false beliefs. These delusions are firmly held by the individual in the face of all evidence to the contrary. There is a definite breakdown in the thought process that can lead the patient to believe he or she is some famous person or to hold some other illogical belief.

A third important symptom of psychosis is perceptual distortions or **hallucinations.** Many psychotics see or hear or feel things around them that are in fact not there at all. These may include voices telling them to do bizarre or dangerous things.

Emotional disturbance is another common mark of psychosis. Many psychotics experience wild swings in mood and feeling. Their

emotions are up and down. And they are sometimes inappropriate to the situation and often are impossible to control. A psychotic's emotional outbursts are very often unrelated to things happening around him or her.

Another characteristic of psychotic disorders is the presence of disturbances of verbal communication. The individual may not be able to speak normally or to communicate his or her thoughts logically. Often this takes the form of echoing everything other people say, using nonsense words, or reciting long unconnected strings of words.

Motor disturbances also are often associated with psychoses. Many psychotics seem unable to control their body movements. They adopt certain characteristic mannerisms, such as ritualistic hand gestures, facial grimaces, and rigid posturings.

Finally, the psychotic person's sense of self is disturbed. Psychotics often are confused about their identities and the boundaries that separate them from the rest of the world. They often report feelings of being "one with" or "melting into" the universe.

Kinds of Psychoses

There are many different kinds of psychoses. The three major groups are: (1) the schizophrenias, (2) delusional disorders, and (3) severe mood disorders.

The Many Faces of Schizophrenia

The most common psychosis is **schizophrenia.** The two most basic characteristics of schizophrenia are a withdrawal from reality and a pattern of nonlogical thinking. More specifically, the schizophrenias are a group of psychotic disorders characterized by gross distortions of reality, little social contact, and disorganization of perception, thought, and emotion.

Despite its usual severity, however, not all schizophrenics are hospitalized. For the majority of schizophrenics, the condition lasts only a short time. It may, however, recur throughout a person's life. When we hear about someone having a "mental breakdown," an acute form of schizophrenia is usually involved. The disorder is *acute* in the sense that it comes on rather suddenly, without previous symptoms. While it lasts it may result in severe loss of self-control and strange behavior.

Schizophrenia expresses itself in different forms. When one or more of these forms is clear the person is diagnosed as having a specific type of schizophrenia. Treatment is generally based on these classifications.

Undifferentiated schizophrenia. This is a "catch-all" category. It's

Dr.: What's your name?
Pt.: Who are you?
Dr.: I'm a doctor. Who are you?
Pt.: I can't tell you who I am.
Dr.: Why can't you tell me?
Pt.: You wouldn't believe me.
Dr.: What are you doing here?
Pt.: Well, I've been sent here to thwart the Russians. I'm the only one in the world who knows how to deal with them. They got their spies all around here though to get me, but I'm smarter than any of them.
Dr.: What are you going to do to thwart the Russians?
Pt.: I'm organizing.
Dr.: Whom are you going to organize?
Pt.: Everybody. I'm the only man in the world who can do that, but I'm going to use my atomic bomb media to blow them up.
Dr.: You must be a terribly important person then.
Pt.: Well, of course.
Dr.: What do you call yourself?
Pt.: You used to know me as Franklin D. Roosevelt.
Dr.: Isn't he dead?
Pt.: Sure he's dead, but I'm alive.
Dr.: But you're Franklin D. Roosevelt?
Pt.: His spirit. He, God, and I figured this out. And now I'm going to make a race of healthy people. My agents are lining them up. Say, who are you?
Dr.: I'm a doctor here.
Pt.: You don't look like a doctor. You look like a Russian to me. . . .

a term used to apply to individuals who display all the symptoms of psychosis—disorientation, delusions, hallucinations, and other types of abnormal behavior. But they haven't developed the distinctive symptoms of one of the other types of schizophrenia. Individuals in the acute, early stages of a schizophrenic breakdown usually fall into this category. Mark Vonnegut, whose breakdown was described at the beginning of this chapter, was diagnosed as suffering from this type of schizophrenia.

Paranoid schizophrenia. Delusions of grandeur or persecution are obvious in this type of schizophrenia. Individuals with paranoid delusions may think they are some exalted being, such as the President of the United States, Napoleon, or even God (delusions of grandeur). They may believe just as strongly that people are out to "get them," are spying on them, or are plotting against them (delusions of persecution). The person often becomes hostile, suspicious, and aggressive. Violent behavior is common. To overcome deep feelings of inferiority and failure, paranoid schizophrenics often build up fictions about themselves and others. The conversation between a paranoid schizophrenic and his psychiatrist reprinted in the column at left shows delusions typical of this kind of schizophrenia.

Catatonia. This type is marked by vivid hallucinations and delusions. The person also experiences periods of stupor and excitement. In the catatonic stupor, or trance, the individual may remain rigid and unresponsive like a statue for extended periods. At other times, the patient becomes violent and unpredictable.

Disorganized type. This patient shows the most severe disorganization of personality. Behavior becomes childish. Thought, speech, and actions become bizarre. Hallucinations may occur, and body movements are poorly coordinated. Patients often giggle uncontrollably, sing meaningless songs, or pull their hair out. Violent behavior, however, is rare in this type of schizophrenia.

Delusional Disorders

Unlike the other psychoses, **delusional disorders** have one major symptom—persistent delusions. The American Psychiatric Association currently recognizes six types of delusional disorders. These are erotomanic, grandiose, jealous, persecutory, somatic, and unspecified. Each of the first five delusions is based on a single delusional theme. The last type, unspecified, may include several themes in which none of them are predominant.

The main theme of the erotomanic type of delusion is that a person, usually of higher status, is in love with the subject. People with this type of delusion often go to great lengths to contact the object of the delusion, a person who often times is a complete stranger.

The grandiose type of delusional disorder is one in which the person has a false sense of worth. Often the person is convinced that she or he possesses some great talent or insight.

The main theme of the jealous type of delusion is that one's spouse or sexual partner is unfaithful. The person with a jealous type of delusional disorder often confronts the spouse or partner and presents him or her with "evidence" to justify the delusion.

People who have persecutory types of delusions are convinced that they are being treated malevolently in some way, such as being conspired against, cheated, spied upon, or obstructed in the pursuit of goals.

Somatic types of delusional disorders are those in which a person strongly believes that he or she has some physical defect, disorder, or disease. Such people often consult physicians for "treatment."

Severe Mood Disorders

A far different type of psychotic disorder is seen in the severe mood disorders. Like the neurotic mood disorders, these disorders are centered around emotional disturbances. They are most likely to involve the person's moods. These disorders should not be confused with the ordinary depression that most of us experience at some time in our lives and for which there is usually a good explanation. The psychotic individual doesn't know what causes the exaggerated moods, and therapists often aren't certain either.

Bipolar disorders. The mood of a person suffering from a **bipolar disorder,** or **manic depression,** may alternate between extreme "highs" (mania) and extreme "lows" (depressions). The extreme moods may alternate with periods of normal moods. During the manic swing, the individual feels continually elated or "high." He or she develops elaborate ideas about past accomplishments and future prospects. The person may display great energy, talk a mile a minute, flit from subject to subject, and get involved in elaborate but poorly conceived money-making schemes. In his or her own mind, the manic is a superstar for whom nothing can go wrong. Many such people are bright, witty, and fun to be around—until they fall off the brink.

The depressive phase of the disorder is the complete opposite of the manic behavior. The person is now dejected and self-accusing—indeed, nothing can go right. Personal appearance is neglected, energy fades, and sleep disturbance is common. There is a loss of appetite and interest in ordinary living. The individual may become agitated, and

In catatonic schizophrenia, individuals may alternate between relatively normal motor behavior and catatonic stupors in which they appear completely frozen and unaware of people or activity around them.

331

attempts at suicide are not uncommon. This stage may last for several months.

In most bipolar disorders, the disturbed patient experiences only one of these intensified moods at a time, with depression being the more common.

Section Review

1. Describe the general symptoms of psychoses.
2. Choose two types of schizophrenia. Describe their symptoms and their differences and similarities.
3. Explain the difference between grandiose and persecutory types of delusionary disorders.
4. Describe a manic-depressive reaction.

PREVIEW

In this section, read to find out:

1. what a personality disorder is.
2. what is the range of personality disorders.
3. how psychologists view drug and alcohol abuse.
4. what sexual disorders are.

4. Personality, Substance-Use, and Sexual Disorders

People with these kinds of disorders may include adult criminals, drug abusers and addicts, problem drinkers, habitual delinquents, and sexual deviates. These people do not suffer from the neurotic's anxiety, nor are they out of touch with reality, as is the psychotic. Instead, they display behavioral patterns that violate the basic moral and social values of the community. Thus, they are more likely to be viewed as "real bad" than as "quite mad."

In the APA classification system, these disorders fall into three categories: (1) personality disorders, (2) **psychoactive substance-use disorders** (drug and alcohol dependence and abuse), and (3) sexual disorders. In recent years the APA has made several changes in the way these disorders are classified. For example, the pschoactive substance-use category has been broadened to include nicotine dependence. We will discuss each of these categories in turn.

Personality Disorders

A **personality disorder** is a fixed and rigid pattern of behaviors that results from faulty personality development. People with personality disorders often have trouble adjusting to society and relating to other people. Their problem lies in a failure to grow up, to become mature, socialized, civilized adults. They are self-centered, impulsive, and irresponsible. Because they act their selfish desires, many people with personality disorders pose a threat to society. Unfortunately, the treatment they receive is not always therapy for their psychological disorder. Instead, they may be imprisoned for breaking the law.

The Range of Personality Disorders

The category of personality disorders is a broad one, with behavior problems that differ greatly in form and severity. On the mildest end of the spectrum we find people who generally function well but who would be described by their relatives or friends as troublesome or eccentric. They have characteristic ways of approaching situations and other people that make them difficult to get along with. Yet they are often quite capable or even gifted in the work world. At the other end of the spectrum are individuals whose more extreme "acting out" against society makes them less able to function in a normal setting. Many are in prisons or maximum security hospitals.

Inspired to commit "the perfect crime," Nathan Leopold (left) and Richard Loeb (right) murdered fourteen-year-old Bobby Franks in 1934. Defended by Clarence Darrow (center), the two were convicted of kidnaping and murder. Neither displayed any remorse for the cold, premeditated slaying.

There are many sub-types within this broad group. One is of particular interest. This is the **antisocial personality disorder,** also known as the psychopath. An extreme example of the psychopathic personality is the "cold-blooded" murderer (such as Charles Manson, leader of the "family" that brutally killed actress Sharon Tate and her houseguests). Such an individual has little compassion for others, shows no remorse for a criminal action, is capable of bizarre forms of cruelty, and displays a twisted sense of moral values. However, not all psychopaths are murderers. Chronically delinquent youths and hardened criminals who may never use violence often have psychopathic traits. They can be quite intelligent and charming, but they seemingly have very few real feelings for others. For better or worse, they operate "outside the system" or manipulate the system for their own ends.

It is generally assumed that psychopathic behavior develops in early childhood. Often psychopaths come from families where all must look out for themselves. There are few if any consistent standards of moral conduct and little emotional warmth. Rules are arbitrary and often unjust. Physical punishment is common, and the child learns early that manipulating others pays off. Psychopaths often come from families in which the parents themselves also have psychopathic tendencies.

Psychoactive Substance-Use Disorders

For a relatively small but increasing number of people in our society, dependence on drugs, such as "cocaine," "speed" and heroin, represents a form of abnormal behavior. For many more, alcohol and barbiturates provide "relief" from the daily cares and stresses of living. Alcohol, for example, is so widely used—and abused—that it is the nation's number one drug problem.

The misuse of drugs may take the form of dependence or abuse. In traditional usage, *dependence* meant psychological reliance on a particular drug, while *addiction* was reserved for physical need, as indicated by withdrawal symptoms if the drug were to be discontinued. Recently, however, drug dependence has come to mean both psychological and physical dependence. The term drug abuse is used to indicate the excessive use of a drug, whether or not an individual is truly dependent on it. Of course, drug abuse often leads to drug dependence.

Currently, drug abuse is recognized as one of our most serious problems. The most commonly used problem drugs are alcohol, barbiturates, amphetamines, cocaine, heroin, and marijuana. More substances have the potential for abuse. These include drugs that adults can purchase legally: tobacco, caffeine, and prescription drugs.

Many researchers argue that drug dependence is caused by an underlying emotional disorder. Others see it as a learned behavior, and still others believe that individual body chemistry plays a part. Whatever the cause, reactions to long-term use of certain drugs can be severe.

Attempts to treat addicts and alcoholics by conventional therapy have not been particularly successful. Other more social approaches, such as Alcoholics Anonymous, have had somewhat better results. These approaches demand rather extreme changes in the addict's lifestyle. The fairly high relapse rate of addicts suggests that some people have an "addictive" personality. Addicts cannot meet and solve emotional problems in a mature fashion.

Sexual Disorders

Sensitive, caring, and responsible sexual experiences are an important part of maturing and learning to make a commitment to others. Sexual experiences can also be a great source of conflict, as sexual taboos war with sexual temptations. For some people, this conflict leads to **sexual disorders.** Psychologists usually divide sexual disorders into three categories.

The first category deals with sexual dysfunctions, such as lack of sexual desire, impotence, or frigidity. These are troubling experiences that often lead people to seek help.

Homosexuality is another type of behavior that can lead people to seek help. In 1973, the American Psychiatric Association officially *declassified* homosexuality as a mental disorder. Homosexuals did not need "treatment," the APA ruled, unless they wanted it. Yet homosexuality remains a difficult and controversial subject. Some homosexuals form lasting, monogamous relationships. Others engage in wildly promiscuous behavior. This kind of behavior has been associated with the rapid spread of acquired immune deficiency syndrome, or AIDS. The widespread fear of this fatal disease has reawakened concern over the issue of homosexuality.

The second category of sexual disorders deals with sexual paraphilias. Paraphilia refers to a deviation (para) to which a person is attracted (philia). Generally speaking, paraphilias refer to behavior that violates social morals and norms. Most people can be sexually aroused by a wide variety of harmless experiences. In contrast, the person with a sexual paraphilia is aroused only by certain bizarre or harmful situations, such as sexual activity with children, masochism, and sadism. Over time, the paraphilia may become a compulsion that endangers innocent, unwilling victims.

The third category, other sexual disorders, exists for disorders that cannot be classified in the other two. An example would be persistent and marked distress about one's sexual orientation.

Section Review

1. Describe the antisocial personality disorder.
2. Discuss the difference between addiction and dependence. Be specific.
3. What does a paraphilia refer to? Why are paraphilias considered sexual disorders?

PREVIEW

In this section,
read to find out:

1. what physical factors
   may lead to disorders.
2. some of the psy-
   chodynamic factors
   that may lead to
   disorders.
3. why child rearing
   practices can lead to
   disorders.
4. how social and envi-
   ronmental factors
   contribute to distur-
   bance.

5. Mental Disturbance: The Search for Causes

Of all the mysteries of human behavior, none has proven more complex and baffling than understanding why people develop mental disorders. Discovering the solution to this perplexing problem will help us to better understand the nature of human behavior. It is also a practical need. Tens of thousands of people are seriously affected by mental and emotional disturbances. We will now look at some of the factors that seem to contribute to the development of mental and emotional disturbances in general. We will also look at the causes of some of the specific disorders that we have discussed in previous sections.

Because every deviant behavior is in a sense unique, we can reasonably say that there is no single cause of abnormal functioning. Psychologists approach this aspect of abnormal behavior from several points of view. Some look for physical causes, others for mental causes. Some also look to social forces. All of these models have proved useful in treating mental and emotional disorders, as well as other types of abnormal behavior. However, they are not to be thought of as watertight compartments. Psychologists studying behavior disorders, and the therapists who treat them, frequently take an eclectic approach. They use what seems best from one or more of these models according to the situation they are involved in. For example, the same behavior may be due to different causes in different individuals. Psychiatrist James C. Coleman writes ". . . one case of homicidal behavior may be closely associated with drug intoxication, another with pent-up frustration and hostility, and still another with the learning of criminal values in a faulty environment."

Genetic Influences

A common observation is that mental disturbance often "runs in families." However, this in itself is no proof that the disorder is inherited. People can learn to be "crazy," or neurotic, from prolonged and close contact with other family members. To separate environmental from possible genetic factors is usually very difficult. Nevertheless, some evidence exists that a predisposition to schizophrenia, the tendency toward it, can be inherited.

For example, the chances of a person developing schizophrenia increase with the degree of genetic relationship to another schizophrenic. Early studies showed that the full sibling of a person with schizophrenia was twice as likely to have the illness as a half sibling—although both shared the same environment. If both parents were schizophrenic there was a marked increase in risk. It was greatest of all among identical twins reared together—more than a 90 percent chance. More recent studies have questioned these findings.

Obviously, more work needs to be done before we can either confirm or rule out faulty genes. At best, genes may contribute to the development of schizophrenia only in combination with psychologically stressful situations. High-risk individuals, if forewarned, can often avoid these situations or learn to adjust to them.

Biological Factors

Some biochemists suggest psychotic disturbances are caused by biological malfunctioning brought on by an imbalance of certain body chemicals. For example, drugs like amphetamines and mescaline produce a wide range of psychotic reactions, such as hallucinations that look like the behavior of the schizophrenic. These drug-induced psychotic states suggest that chemical agents play a role in schizophrenia. Evidence that this might be so has been found. When large amounts of certain naturally occurring brain substances are injected into animals, the results look like psychotic reactions. It is thought that an imbalance of certain of these chemicals may account for some forms of human schizophrenia.

For example, chemical substances such as serotonin have been found in abnormally high quantities in the blood of psychotic patients.

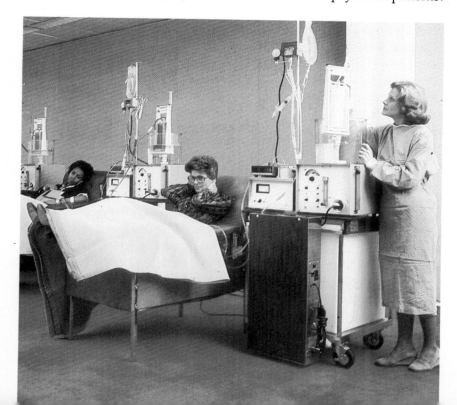

A new—and as yet experimental—treatment for schizophrenia involves the use of dialysis, which has been used for many years to treat patients with kidney disease, like those shown here.

A relationship between these substances and psychosis has not been established. Many investigators believe that the emotional stress of psychosis itself accounts for the presence of the chemicals, just as stress in normal individuals produces high levels of adrenalin. Recent claims that megavitamin therapy has been used successfully with some schizophrenics suggest that a severe vitamin deficiency accounts for certain aspects of the disorder. The evidence for this, however, is disputed and awaits additional research.

Psychodynamic Factors

Many clinical psychologists, and all psychoanalysts, look for the causes of mental disturbance "within the mind." This is especially the case with the neuroses. Freud found that under hypnosis many of his patients could be made to reexperience the repressed incidents that gave rise to their neuroses and thus free themselves of them.

If Freud had stopped there, he would be a minor figure in the history of psychiatry. However, he found that the effects of hypnosis were often temporary and sought a more lasting method of treating nervous disorders. Freud then developed the methods of psychoanalysis which will be discussed more fully in Chapter 13. By uncovering repression with his "talking cure," he hoped to find the source of the individual's neurotic behavior and thus get rid of it.

As we have seen in Chapter 11, Freud's theory of the mind involves three parts. The *id* is a concept standing for a person's inborn biological needs. The *ego* acts as a mediator between these needs and the demands of the outside world. And the rules and customs of this outside world become part of a person's conscience in the form of the *superego*. However, there are inevitable conflicts between the "instinctual" demands of the id and the restraining forces of the ego and superego. Freud believed that an unresolved conflict in a child produced great anxiety and that this, in turn, laid the foundations for a neurotic adulthood.

Child Rearing Factors

Many of Freud's followers agreed that mental disorders had their roots in the experience of early childhood. They disagreed on the *types* of experiences that caused later mental disturbances. Alfred Adler stressed that the feelings of helplessness and inferiority that children acquire in early life were the major sources of neurosis. He also studied the relationships among brothers and sisters as the source of a child's feelings of inferiority. Psychotherapists now recognize that many factors in a child's early life can lay the foundations for later emotional instability, depression, neurotic behavior, and schizophrenia.

The double-bind. Children who receive no real affection from their parents, yet are expected to show affection for them, find themselves in what is called a "double-bind." They are forced to behave in a manner that contradicts their own feelings and perceptions.

If they try to be affectionate, they are met with stiffness and hostility. When they remain distant, they are criticized for not being more loving. Such children receive contradictory messages, and there is no way out of the bind. To respond positively to one message is to deny the other. This may lead to severe disturbances.

Unrealistic parental attitudes. Parents sometimes try to "mold" their children to their own ideal. Through parental attitudes, children can acquire unrealistic expectations about themselves. Perhaps a father who had always wanted to be a successful engineer was forced to settle for a more ordinary kind of job. His ambitions are transferred to a son, who strives to fulfill the ideal his father has of him. If this does not prove possible, the gap between the idealized self and reality may cause intolerable feelings of guilt and failure. The now-grown man becomes self-accusing and depressed. Many of the people who seek professional help today do so because they feel that they have not lived

Case Study

Winter Depression

For Nell Krabacher, the depression began in the fall. As the Alaskan days grew shorter and shorter, her spirits plummeted. She would burst into tears or stare into space. Unable to control her cravings, she binged on carbohydrates. Before she fled the Alaska winter, she had gained twenty pounds.

Today Krabacher is back in Alaska year-round. However, every winter day, she flips the switch on her "sun box," a bank of special fluorescent lights beside her office desk. Thanks to this unique light fixture, she is able to ward off seasonal affective

disorder or SAD. Researchers have been studying this form of depression since the early 1980s, and in 1987, the disorder was added to the APA classification system.

Winter depression, like Krabacher's, is the most common type of SAD. These people may feel fine the rest of the year. Yet when the gray days of winter arrive, they begin to feel listless, irritable, and deeply depressed. Like a hibernating animal, they crave sleep and carbohydrates. Some people with SAD gain as much as forty pounds every winter and then lose the weight in the spring. SAD usually makes its first appearance in the early

twenties, but it has been found in children as young as nine.

No one is sure what causes SAD or why the sun box helps lift the depression. Latitude is clearly an important factor. Cases of SAD increase and are more severe the further one moves away from the Equator. One explanation is that, in some people, the limited winter sunlight throws off the body's natural clock and disrupts the production of certain brain chemicals. The sun box, which imitates natural sunlight, seems to reset this natural clock. Genetics may also be a factor, since more than two-thirds of SAD victims share the disease with close relatives.

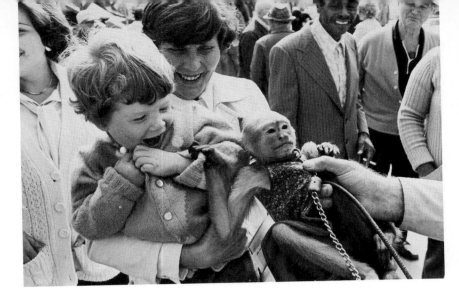

Social learning can teach healthy and unhealthy responses. Here, the encouragement and enjoyment of adults help prompt a positive response from an unsure child.

up to all that was expected of them.

Many psychologists feel that neurosis never occurs in isolation. It exists as part of a family pattern. From this perspective the roles that the family members play are pathogenic (disease-causing) factors. For example, in some families, children are taught to avoid pleasurable activities and to renounce their drives for self-satisfaction. They grow up to feel guilty about "enjoying life" which, indeed, they find they cannot do. As adults, these people are likely to be self-punishing, or masochistic.

Faulty learning. A somewhat narrower view of mental disorders is expressed by the various learning theorists. You will recall how John B. Watson made a loud noise every time little Albert reached for a white rat. In time, the boy came to fear the rat even without the frightening noise. This conditioned response (fear) was later generalized to other furry objects. This is a simple example of how faulty learning can lead to neurotic behavior in many people.

Parents don't, as a rule, make loud noises to frighten their children. However, they may unintentionally provide other kinds of frightening and long-lasting experiences that bring about feelings of insecurity and anxiety. For example, parents may imply that "We won't love you if you don't clean your plate." Or a mother may threaten a child, "Just wait until your father gets home. Are you going to get it!" As we will see, the behaviorists believe that behaviors learned in childhood can be "unlearned" through several specific techniques.

Going a step further, social learning theorists, such as Bandura, point out that because children imitate other behavior, they can develop neurotic traits simply by seeing their parents' neurotic behavior.

By identifying with their parents as general models, children may acquire neurotic patterns which may serve no purpose for them.

Social and Environmental Factors

Few people become mentally ill without a "good reason." Often the reason can be found in forces that are beyond the individual's control. Some theorists, such as psychiatrist R. D. Laing, argue that the pressures of modern society are a strong influence on mental illness. Automation, bureaucracy, the breakdown of customs and norms, the loss of spiritual values—all these have put us out of touch with our own humanity and left us rootless and alienated. Other writers, such as Margaret Mead and Alvin Toffler, say that it is not change itself, but the rate of change, that matters. People simply cannot adapt quickly enough. They endure severe strain, and escapist activity, whether neurotic or psychotic, results.

Specifically, poverty seems to contribute to emotional and mental disorders. Slums, poor schooling, malnutrition, disease, job problems, and discrimination create hostility, distrust, and an eventual distortion of reality. For many poor people life is just "too much." They feel guilty about their situation yet are unable to change it.

Quite a different problem exists for the middle class. It is the compulsion to be productive. The fear of failure and loss of economic status result in neurotic insecurity. The result is anxiety and its symptoms.

An extreme example of the social stress theory is found in the writings of the "radical" psychiatrists Thomas Szasz and R. D. Laing. Laing suggests that it is the schizophrenic who is sane and society that is crazy. Psychosis, he believes, is a kind of special insight into what reality ought to be, a radical revolt against questionable assumptions about the purpose of life. The schizophrenic adopts a subjective reality because that is the only reality that makes sense in a world of distorted values. His or her actions are a sane response to an insane world.

Intriguing as this argument may be, it lacks solid evidence. In one way or another, the world has always been in a mess. Adapting to it is the price of survival.

Section Review

1. Describe two possible explanations for schizophrenia.
2. How does Freud see the cause of neuroses?
3. Give an example of the effect the family situation can have on the development of disorders.
4. Tell how social and environmental factors contribute to mental disturbance.

Chapter 12 Review

Section Summaries

1. What's Normal? What Isn't?

Abnormal behavior and mental disorder are terms psychologists use. "Insanity" is a legal term. Normal people can function in everyday life, get along with others, and are comfortable with themselves. Behavior is judged to be abnormal when it draws the attention of others, when a person seeks help, or when an expert makes a diagnosis. The American Psychiatric Association's classification system is used in diagnosis. All classifications are descriptions and not explanations of abnormal behaviors.

2. Neurotic Disorders

A neurosis is an emotional disturbance characterized by excessive anxiety and the overuse of defense mechanisms. Neurotic anxiety disrupts ordinary functioning and causes illogical behavior and the neurotic paradox. Karen Horney observed that neurotics have an excessive need for affection and dependence, feelings of inferiority and inadequacy, incapacity to plan, aggressive and hostile behavior, and abnormal sexual functioning. The APA classifies neuroses as anxiety disorders, somatoform disorders, dissociative disorders, and mood disorders.

3. Psychoses: "Going Mad"

In a psychosis, the person loses touch with reality and acts in ways that are clearly abnormal. Psychotic symptoms also include delusions, hallucinations, and disturbances in emotions, speech, movement, and sense of self. Schizophrenia is characterized by a withdrawal from reality and by nonlogical thinking. The major symptoms of delusional disorders are persistent delusions. Bipolar disorder, a type of severe mood disorder, involves wide mood swings between mania and depression.

4. Personality, Substance-Use, and Sexual Disorders

A personality disorder is a fixed and rigid pattern of behaviors that results from faulty personality development. People with antisocial personality disorder display a twisted sense of morals. **Psychoactive** substance-use disorders involve dependence and addiction on drugs. Most researchers agree that dependence is caused by an underlying emotional disorder. The fairly high relapse rate of addicts suggests that some people have "addictive" personalities. Sexual disorders are divided into three categories: sexual dysfunctions, paraphilias, and other sexual disorders.

5. Mental Disturbance: The Search for Causes

Psychologists frequently take an eclectic approach because the same behavior may have different causes in different people. Explanations for abnormal behavior focus on genetic influences, biological factors, psychodynamic factors, child rearing factors, and social and environmental factors.

Psychology Skill Activities

1. Do some research on the extent of substance-use disorders in the United States. Be sure to include all the substances that are abused. Which is the most abused? Present your results in a chart or bar graph.   **easy**

2. Use the "Psychology Skills Handbook" to help you conduct a survey on the things people fear. Give the survey to as many people as possible. What are the ten most common fears? Present your results in a chart or bar graph.   **challenging**

Testing for Understanding

Knowing Key Terms

Define these terms in your own words.

Section 1
abnormal behavior
mental disorder
insanity

Section 2

neurosis
neurotic paradox
anxiety disorder
obsession
compulsive behavior
phobia
somatoform disorder
hypochondriasis
conversion hysteria
amnesia
fugue episode
multiple personality

Section 3

psychosis
delusion
hallucination

schizophrenia
delusional disorder
bipolar disorder
manic depression

Section 4

personality disorder
antisocial personality disorder
substance-use disorder
psychoactive substance-use disorder
sexual disorder

Reviewing Main Ideas

Section 1

1. What are the characteristics of a person who is in good psychological health?
2. What criteria are used to identify abnormal behavior?
3. What is the main function of the APA classification system?

Section 2

1. How is neurotic behavior different from normal behavior?
2. What are the symptoms of neurosis?
3. What are the main types of neuroses?

Section 3

1. Describe the symptoms of a psychosis.
2. Describe the types of schizophrenia.
3. What are the major symptoms of delusional disorders?
4. What characterizes a bipolar disorder?

Section 4

1. How is a personality disorder different from a neurosis or psychosis?
2. Why are antisocial personalities of special interest to psychologists?
3. How are sexual disorders classified?

Section 5

1. What role might genetics and biological factors play in abnormal behavior?
2. How has Freud's work contributed to our understanding of abnormal behavior?
3. What are some child rearing practices that might cause mental disorders?
4. What are some social and environmental factors that contribute to mental disorders?

Thinking Critically

1. *Making Inferences.* Explain the advantages and disadvantages of classifying and labeling mental disorders.   **easy**
2. *Making Inferences.* How would you decide whether an individual is in touch with reality?   **challenging**

Demonstrating Psychology Skills

Describe the type of disorder the person in the following case study is probably suffering from. Give specific reasons for your answer.

"The patient was a 49-year-old man whose main problem was a preoccupation with the number 13. If he heard the word, he felt a shock and experienced a period of acute anxiety. His everyday life was a continuous effort to avoid any reference to 13, so much that his activities were seriously handicapped. In some way or another, it seems as if everyone was always saying 13 to him. If they met him in the morning they would say, 'Oh, good morning,' or later in the day it would be 'Good afternoon' (13 letters in each). He stayed in bed on the thirteenth day of each month, skipped the thirteenth tread in a stairway, and found it necessary to count letters and phrases, his steps and streets to avoid the number 13."

Chapter 13

Achieving Mental Health

Multiple personality is a rare, although highly publicized, form of neurosis. How is it treated? Can a person suffering in this way be helped? The following true account illustrates several therapy techniques used in such a case.

In 1975, psychiatrist Ralph Allison began treating a man named Dana Hawksworth. Hawksworth requested treatment with the drug lithium carbonate, having previously been diagnosed as a manic depressive. He would get depressed and go on periodic drinking sprees.

The lithium chemotherapy helped, but when Hawksworth suddenly went off on another drinking binge, Dr. Allison tried hypnotherapy. Under hypnosis, Dana reported that he felt it was not he, but another person—"Johnnie"—who had been drunk. Dana identified Johnnie as an imaginary childhood playmate.

Dr. Allison then used the therapeutic technique of automatic writing under hypnosis. This revealed that Johnnie was indeed the excessive drinker, and that at least three other personalities, "Phil," "Peter," and "Jerry," were present in Hawksworth's mind.

During therapy, Dr. Allison identified age periods in Hawksworth's life that seemed to be related to Johnnie's troubles. The psychiatrist then regressed Hawksworth hypnotically to each of these stages starting at age four. Dr. Allison suggested that Dana symbolically expel Johnnie into a jar and hold him there. This action temporarily suppressed the personality of Johnnie.

At one dramatic point, Dr. Allison helped Hawksworth fuse Phil and Peter into Dana. The three personalities became one, and the patient thought he had recovered completely. Then a setback occurred. Johnnie took over and caused an accident. The next day, Dana, now back in charge, sought hospital care for serious suicidal urges.

A teacher advises a student in an art therapy class.

In the hospital Dana was asked to write down all his thoughts. At this point, he decided that he was only an "alter personality," that "Henry" was the real person. The patient's full name was Henry Dana Hawksworth.

During more age regression hypnotherapy, Dr. Allison asked Dana to find Henry and lead him out. Dana said goodbye to Dr. Allison and the next voice that spoke was that of a three-year-old child—Henry. Though he was forty-three years old, he had no memory of the past forty years. Henry rapidly absorbed the memories, talents, and attitudes of his other personalities. Two weeks later he returned to work, and soon became a top salesman.

As this case study indicates, there are many techniques for treating mental disorders—from drug therapy to hypnotherapy. In this chapter, we will examine several of these methods of psychotherapy. We will also discuss some strategies for preventing mental disorders before they happen.

PREVIEW

In this section, read to find out:

1. who treats mental disorders.
2. what physical treatments are used.
3. what psychoanalysis is.
4. how group therapy works.

1.   Who Treats Mental Disorders and How

Therapists disagree about the causes of mental disorders, and so their methods of treatment differ. However, regardless of the approach used, the general goal of psychotherapy is to help people become more self-accepting and to develop a fuller sense of personal satisfaction and competence.

The Therapist

Many types of psychotherapists practice in the United States. They help people deal with emotional and mental problems on various levels of professional expertise. Often, the first group that comes to mind is **psychiatrists.** These are physicians who have completed medical school and an internship or residency in a mental hospital. They have a specialty in the field of mental, emotional, and neurological illness. As physicians, psychiatrists are permitted by law to use drugs and other physical means of treatment for mental problems.

Psychotherapists who are not physicians treat disturbed patients whose problems do not require the use of physical treatment or drugs. **Psychoanalysts** are specialists in the particular form of therapy developed by Freud and his followers, a treatment Freud called his "talking cure." Most psychoanalysts have medical training and, in addition, have completed postgraduate studies in a psychoanalytic institute.

Clinical psychologists are therapists who have a Ph.D. in clinical psychology, followed by an internship in a hospital or clinic. They cannot prescribe any form of medication but rely on verbal and behavioral forms of therapy.

There are a number of other professionals and paraprofessionals who are qualified to give psychotherapy. See the table on page 348 for a more complete listing of these mental health care professionals and their qualifications.

Physical Treatments

Many physical approaches to healing are available to a modern psychiatrist. The most commonly used is drug therapy. Until just after World War II, barbiturates were used to calm patients and make them more manageable. With the discovery of tranquilizing and antidepressant drugs, a new era of treatment opened up. With these more effective drugs, patients were often able to stay out of the hospital. Although drugs usually treat the symptoms of an illness and not necessarily the cause, their value is still great. Drugs not only make patients feel better, but also make them more responsive to other forms

of therapy. For most patients, if drugs are used at all, they are supposed to be only the beginning of treatment.

Unfortunately, in many overcrowded hospitals drugs have often been used only to keep patients quiet and *manageable*. This type of drug abuse can lead to neglect of an individual's underlying disturbance.

In some psychotic conditions, medication alone seems to be the most effective treatment. Many people who were formerly made helpless by recurrent cycles of mania and depression—euphoric highs and despairing lows—now lead fairly normal lives on lithium therapy. The salt lithium (used in the treatment of Dana Hawksworth) controls long-standing manic-depressive reactions in many patients.

In other forms of psychotic depression, electroshock therapy is sometimes used. A mild electric current is passed through the patient's brain. This causes a brief period of convulsion, followed by sleep and a temporary loss of memory. A series of treatments sometimes results in dramatic improvement in the patient's condition. Shock treatments can also result in permanent, damaging changes in an individual's personality and mental functioning, however. For this reason, electroshock therapy is highly controversial and is generally regarded as a last resort, used when traditional procedures bring no improvement. Exactly how electroshock therapy works has never been fully understood. Some therapists feel the shock serves as a punishment that relieves extreme feelings of guilt.

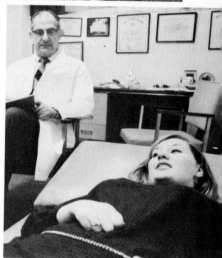

Many psychoanalysts still conduct therapy sessions in the way Freud did—with patients reclining on a couch. The top photo shows Freud's office as it looked in his time.

Personnel in Psychotherapy

Professional
Clinical psychologist (Ph.D. in psychology with both research and clinical skill specialization; one-year internship)

Counseling psychologist (Ph.D. in psychology; internship)

Psychiatrist (M.D.; internship; residency in psychiatric hospital or mental health facility)

Psychoanalyst (M.D. or Ph.D.; intensive training in theory and practice of psychoanalysis)

Psychiatric social worker (B.A., M.S.W., or Ph.D. with specialized training in mental health settings)

Psychiatric nurse (R.N.; specialized training)

Occupational therapist (B.S. in occupational therapy; internship with physical and/or psychological handicap specialty)

Paraprofessional
Community mental health worker (works under professional direction)

Alcohol or drug-abuse counselor (trained in evaluation and management of alcohol and drug problems)

Pastoral counselor (training in psychology; internship in mental health facility as a chaplain)

In both mental health clinics and hospitals, psychiatrists, clinical psychologists, social workers, psychiatric nurses, and occupational therapists may work together as a treatment team.

Psychoanalytic Therapy

Psychoanalytic therapy is based primarily on the theories of Sigmund Freud. This approach assumes that in the unconscious, beneath the surface of awareness, a conflict takes place between biological strivings and social realities. The major goal of Freudian therapy is to bring the conflict into awareness, where it can be dealt with successfully.

Psychoanalysis consists of interview sessions between patient and analyst. The two meet for about fifty minutes from one to five times a week. These sessions may continue for years, until the patient is significantly improved. The purpose of these interviews is to uncover the unconscious motivations behind the patient's troubling behavior. The analyst then tries to bring insight into the conditions that caused it. The analyst uses several methods to do this.

Methods of analysis. In **free association,** the psychoanalyst encourages the patient to relax, let his or her mind wander freely, and give a running account of thoughts, physical sensations, and memories as they occur. The analyst works to probe the patient's unconscious and bring repressed thoughts and feelings to the surface of conscious awareness.

An analyst also looks for clues to this repressed material in a patient's dreams. **Dream analysis** explores the symbolic meaning of the content of a dream, the expression of which might be unacceptable in waking life. You read about dreams in Chapter 10. Hypnosis, also considered in Chapter 10, can be used in psychoanalysis as well. It is used as a means of reaching the unconscious thoughts of the patient.

During the course of therapy, patients often come to identify the analyst with someone important in their lives—for example, a parent or a spouse. This process is called **transference** because the patient's attitudes and feelings about another person are transferred to the analyst. Transference may be either positive or negative, depending on the nature of the relationship that is being relived. The therapist helps the patient to interpret the transferred feelings, and to understand their source in earlier experiences and attitudes.

Psychoanalytic therapy attempts to bring about a radical change in an individual's basic personality structure. It is time consuming, costly, and not always successful. However, Freudian analysts believe it is the only approach that fully uncovers the buried childhood repressions that cause mental disorders. People who do best under this method are usually fairly well educated, verbal people, capable of achieving insight into their lives and their problems.

Varied views. Many analysts depart from Freud in placing more emphasis on the current social environment and less on childhood

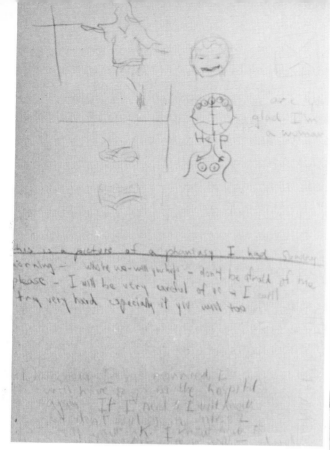

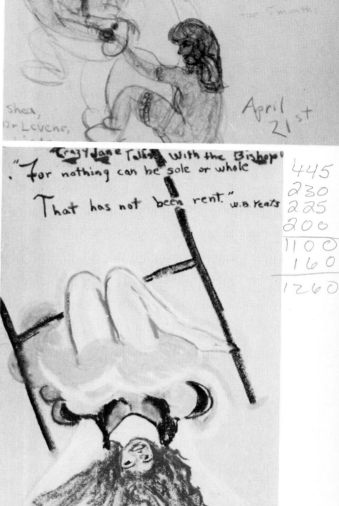

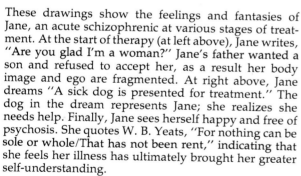

These drawings show the feelings and fantasies of Jane, an acute schizophrenic at various stages of treatment. At the start of therapy (at left above), Jane writes, "Are you glad I'm a woman?" Jane's father wanted a son and refused to accept her, as a result her body image and ego are fragmented. At right above, Jane dreams "A sick dog is presented for treatment." The dog in the dream represents Jane; she realizes she needs help. Finally, Jane sees herself happy and free of psychosis. She quotes W. B. Yeats, "For nothing can be sole or whole/That has not been rent," indicating that she feels her illness has ultimately brought her greater self-understanding.

experience. Generally speaking, they agree with many of Freud's teachings but adapt them to more flexible treatment procedures.

Karen Horney, for instance, sees one cause of emotional disturbance in the conflict between our competitive, *get ahead* philosophy and our professed standards of cooperation and kindness. Faced with this dilemma, some people *opt out* of the system. Others come to hate themselves for staying in it. In either case, they feel powerless to change their own lives or the system, and their emotional disturbance results.

With psychoanalytic therapy, improvement often takes place before any real insight is achieved into the basic cause of the problem. For whatever reason, just working on the problem seems to make a difference.

Group Therapy: Talking It Out with Others

For many people with emotional problems, being with others who have similar types of problems seems to provide insight into their own feelings and behavior. This treatment is called **group therapy.** Under the leadership of a group therapist, patients are encouraged to express their real feelings, to be angry or affectionate. They analyze the motives

Case Study

Team Therapy

Eugene Davis first "hit bottom" when he was 24. After struggling against lethargy and lack of interest all through college, he quit his job. As he withdrew more and more, he realized he wanted to die. He turned to his church, enlisting as a Mormon missionary. Still, he brooded about suicide.

Mercifully, the despair seemed to lift over the next six months. Davis earned a master's degree, got married, and began a family. Then, around Christmas of 1982, the depression settled back on his shoulders.

After five weeks of uncontrollable crying spells, Davis sought the help of two psychotherapists. Through them, he came to see his problem as a disease, like flu or diabetes. He accepted a doctor's prescription for a widely used antidepressant. Within weeks, he began to recover.

Eugene Davis's case is just one of many that are providing new answers to an old question. For years, psychiatrists and psychotherapists have debated which is most effective, drug therapy or "talking therapy." Today these specialists agree that teamwork may produce the most effective results of all.

According to Dr. Jonathan Cole, "An antidepressant may not help you find out where you're going in the world, or whether you need a divorce, but it will help you think rationally so that you're not frozen in a life crisis, wringing your hands in a corner."

Today a one-two punch of drugs and therapy is being used to combat such life-threatening disorders as bipolar disorder, schizophrenia, cocaine dependence, and bulimia. In bulimia, for example, victims alternate between frenzied eating attacks and self-induced vomiting. Left untreated, the disorder can be fatal. Treatment begins with drugs that break the self-destructive cycle, followed by psychotherapy for underlying emotional problems.

Why does this help? One explanation compares the mind to a computer. In serious disorders, both the hardware—the brain—and the software—our thoughts and emotions—may need fixing. Drugs, it seems, can "fix" the hardware, while psychotherapy helps rewrite the software.

behind their behavior, and try to be completely honest with other members of the group. Participants are also encouraged to feel free to criticize one another. By extending the discussion of a problem to everyone, the leader tries to develop in the group a more mature outlook on this particular problem.

Group therapy has proved especially successful with those people who find it hard to form good social relationships. For them, the group setting itself may provide positive reinforcement. Undesirable characteristics are not reinforced by the group. More positive qualities are. Participants can thus learn to modify problem behaviors.

Human Potential Movement

The growth of the human potential movement in recent years has led to the formation of several other kinds of groups. Their work is often directed not toward people suffering from emotional problems but toward normal individuals who want to deal more effectively with others. Sensitivity training groups, or T-groups, for example, have become popular with people who simply want to get more out of life. People seem to be seeking the human relationship skills that can make this possible.

An important thing about these groups is that they focus on the immediate situation and what people are feeling at that time. What happened in the past or may happen in the future are both ignored, as participants try to analyze the forces influencing their personal relationships within the group.

Encounter groups use intensive give-and-take sessions, which may last a weekend or several days. During this time, participants give each other feedback on what they think, believe, and feel. Under the

MY ENCOUNTER GROUP DOESN'T UNDERSTAND ME.

Washington Star Syndicate

In the dance therapy class shown at left, children with mental disorders learn to express their feelings and to release their frustrations.

Sensitivity group sessions provide opportunities for participants to interact with other group members.

guidance of a trained leader who sincerely cares, and who understands how people can achieve self-change, strong positive outcomes have been reported. With incompetent or too aggressive leadership, on the other hand, participants may be in danger of developing problems requiring psychiatric treatment. But when the leadership is skillful and responsible, these groups can be a safe place to try out new behaviors.

Section Review

1. What is a basic difference between a psychiatrist and a psychologist?
2. List two possible physical treatments for mental disorders.
3. Describe two techniques used in psychoanalysis.
4. Explain one advantage of group therapy over individual therapy.

2. Humanistic and Behavioral Therapy

An outgrowth of humanistic psychology, discussed in Chapter 11, is **humanistic therapy.** This approach was pioneered by Carl Rogers. It emphasizes the role of the patient rather than the analyst. For his own work, Rogers replaced that term *patient* with *client,* describing his therapy as client-centered. He believed a person's own perception of a problem should be the guide in providing insight for solving it. Under the guidance of a therapist, people in client-centered therapy assume a good part of the responsibility for treating themselves.

Humanistic Therapy and the Self

For Rogers, a major source of a person's anxiety is the gap between the individual's *real self*—the way you see yourself, and the *ideal self*— the way you would like to be. Resolving this difference becomes an important goal of therapy. By demonstrating a positive regard for the client, the analyst serves as a sympathetic bystander. He or she offers neither praise nor blame but accepts whatever is said. Clients are helped to clarify their own reactions. Thus client-centered therapy is *nondirective.* No specific advice is given. No judgments are expressed. By talking about their problems to a sympathetic listener, clients are able to bring into their awareness attitudes and experiences they didn't even know they had.

In working with his clients, Rogers tried to create conditions that

PREVIEW

In this section, read to find out:

1. what humanistic therapy is.
2. what behavior therapy is.
3. how rewards and punishments are used in treatment.

allowed them to express their real feelings without any sense of being threatened. He tried to encourage greater self-acceptance. Rogers' "self" theory is widely used as a therapeutic technique in group therapy sessions, encounter groups, sensitivity training groups, and in various clinical situations. Feedback from therapists and other patients can help a person to better self-understanding. When everyone in a group is open, and freely expresses his or her emotions, individuals in the group find it easier to release bottled-up feelings.

Behavior Modification Therapy

Many people with emotional and behavioral disorders now receive treatment called **behavior modification therapy** from professionals called behavior therapists. These therapists apply theories of conditioning, discussed in Chapter 2, to abnormal behavior. Their approach uses principles of learning to change undesirable behaviors such as addictions, fears, or compulsions. The change is brought about, not by insight, but by substituting new patterns of reinforcement.

Therapists who use behavior modification techniques see unhealthy behaviors as responses to be extinguished. They work to replace the undesirable actions with more effective social and personal responses. The therapists attempt to change unwanted behavior by adding or withholding reinforcement. They also *pair* stimuli that ordinarily cause anxiety with those that are pleasant or relaxing. They may also punish the unwanted response in some way. Several specific techniques are used in behavior therapy.

Desensitization: thinking the unthinkable by relaxing. Assume you get extremely anxious about taking tests. When you start a test you "freeze" and are unable to answer many of the questions. For such a condition, a desensitizing procedure may be used to prevent the anxiety. Through **desensitization,** you are made insensitive to the thought of sitting down to a test, through a step-by-step process. By meeting and overcoming each of your fears in advance, you are able to face the actual test without too much anxiety.

How does this work? Desensitization is based on Pavlov's observation that when two emotional responses are opposite, the stronger response blocks the weaker response. In dealing with anxiety, the key to the problem is finding its opposite. A moment's thought will tell you that the opposite of being anxious is being relaxed. For the anxious student, relaxation, a pleasurable response, is substituted for fear of the test, an unpleasurable response.

The first move is training the patient in methods of deep relaxation. Following this, the steps in the anxiety-producing stimuli are

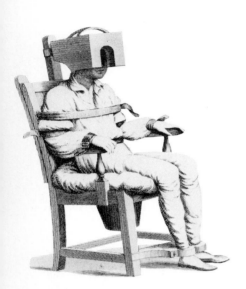

An early form of "therapy," the "tranquilizing chair," was used in mental institutions during the 19th century to calm violent patients.

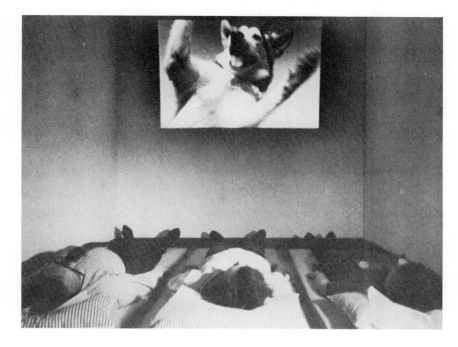

In the desensitization session shown at left, patients are treated for their phobia by being exposed to the thing they fear in a safe and relaxed atmosphere.

arranged in a logical order. The steps might look like this:

1. Thinking about taking tests while at home during the summer.
2. Sitting in a classroom on a day when there is no test.
3. Studying for the test a week before.
4. Studying for the test three nights before.
5. Studying for the test the night before.
6. Walking to the test classroom.
7. Sitting in the classroom starting to take the test.

The object now, if you are the patient, is to picture yourself experiencing the weakest stimulus—meanwhile remaining completely relaxed, with no anxiety. If you can do this, you go on to concentrate on the next stronger stimulus, step 2, and try to combine it with total relaxation. You continue the process until the strongest stimulus is reached. If at any point anxiety reactions occur, you stop and concentrate on relaxation again.

Implosion therapy: facing the music. Quite the opposite approach is used in implosion therapy. It is called this because the client who is troubled by an intensely frightening event is made to experience the event again and again in a friendly environment, until the anxiety "explodes" inwardly (implodes). With **implosion therapy,** instead of first imagining mildly frightening stimuli and gradually working up to the

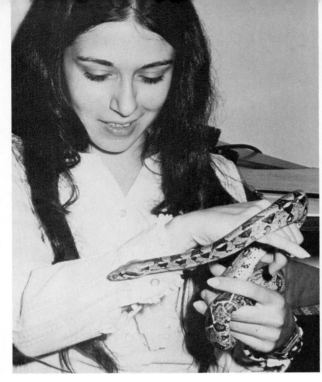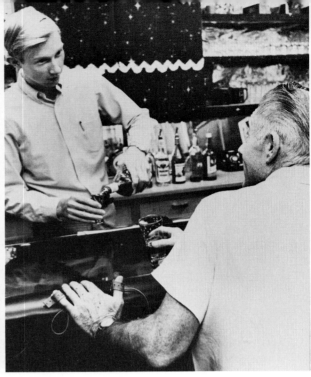

Two examples of behavior modification therapy are shown above. Implosion therapy enables a patient to conquer her fear of snakes, and, as part of his aversion therapy for alcoholism, the man at right receives a shock every time he takes a drink from the therapist.

really terrifying ones, the client is plunged right into imagining the most terrifying scene that can be imagined. Rather than reducing anxiety, the therapist intensifies it. This is an effort to produce a short-order confrontation from which the patient cannot run away. As this happens again and again in the safety of the therapist's office and no harm occurs, the event loses its power to cause anxiety. In a sense, the client has been inoculated against fear.

In one study, ten subjects who were afraid of snakes were asked to imagine the following terrible scenes with snakes, as vividly as possible, using all their senses. They were to imagine being attacked by a huge snake, having a snake slowly crawl over their bodies, having a snake coil tighter and tighter around their necks. Subjects were periodically reminded, however, that nothing was actually happening to them. After this forty-five minute session, seven of the ten were able to pick up a snake.

Aversion therapy: punishing "bad" behavior. An unwanted response is eliminated in **aversion therapy** by pairing it with an even more unpleasant stimulus. This approach is just the opposite of desensitization. In desensitization therapy, a desired response such as freedom from anxiety is paired with a pleasant stimulus such as relaxation. In aversion therapy, an aversive or painful stimulus that increases anxiety is associated with the act that is undesirable.

In one case, a 19-year-old girl had a severe compulsion to wash her hands every time she touched herself. In treatment, she was instructed to touch herself. Then she was given an electric shock if she began to wash her hands. After seven months her compulsion disappeared and no other abnormal behaviors developed. Note that in aversion therapy, as in other types of behavior therapy, the therapists are not especially interested in *why* the individual is performing an undesirable or anti-social act. They are simply trying to change the behavior.

Critics of aversion therapy have charged that, when practiced in institutional settings, it is little more than a form of legalized torture. To be most effective, this kind of treatment should provide an alternative response that is positively reinforced. It is not enough to punish and thereby suppress the unwanted behavior. For example, you should be able to substitute an activity that is both satisfying and constructive. Without this, when punishment is stopped the old behavior may start again.

Positive reinforcement: rewarding "good" behavior. Positive reinforcement uses some of the same principles as does desensitization. Instead of punishing a harmful or unwanted act, the therapist rewards a desirable act. In Chapter 2, you saw how positive reinforcement is used in some classrooms in the form of "token economies."

Here's an example of how positive reinforcement is used in therapy. In one case, a five-year-old girl scratched herself so badly that her body was covered with sores. Spanking the child did not help. The mother was instructed to ignore the scratching since any attention was a form of reinforcement. Instead, she was to show approval whenever her daughter played with toys or looked at a book. In six weeks, all the sores had healed and the extra reinforcers were gradually withdrawn.

Positive reinforcement is really a program of operant conditioning. The desired response must be one that the person comes to value more than the old harmful behavior. This change is accomplished by ignoring irrational behavior, rather than rewarding it with attention. Acts that are more normal and acceptable are rewarded.

Observation: imitating "good" behavior. Albert Bandura's studies have revealed how children can overcome their fear of dogs or snakes by watching other children their own age approach these animals and handle them. For example, severely withdrawn preschool-age children can learn new behaviors when they see on film other children being rewarded for the same behaviors. Similarly, mute schizophrenic children learned a limited vocabulary by being rewarded for imitating "model" sounds made by the therapist.

It's Your Turn

Behavior therapy has many variations. We have introduced several here. Now *It's Your Turn*. Think of a problem that you or someone you know may have. Describe a program of treatment that might be helpful in dealing with this problem. Include one or more kinds of behavior therapy.

357

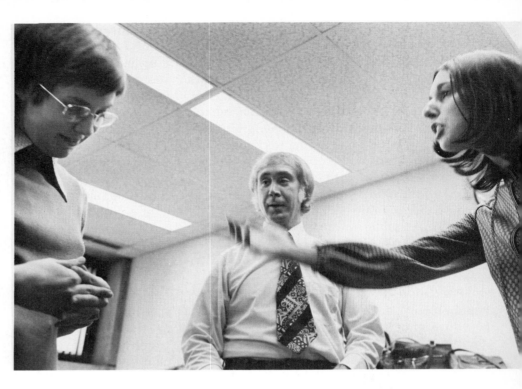

An assertiveness training session.

The **modeling** technique has been adapted for people with certain mild but distressing personality problems. In assertiveness training, a shy, withdrawn, or emotionally inhibited person may watch other people act out situations that the client would normally feel unable to cope with. The client is then asked to act out a prepared assertive script based on what the model has just done.

Researchers report that the technique has proved effective. Individuals can learn to reevaluate situations and to control their environment, rather than letting themselves be controlled by it. To the extent that they develop a sense of mastery and effectiveness, they change for the better. This is a central element in successful psychotherapy. The person feels more in control, and less at the mercy of inner or outer forces.

Section Review

1. How does humanistic therapy differ from other types of psychotherapy?
2. What is the goal of behavior therapy?
3. Compare aversion therapy to positive reinforcement treatment.

3. The Role of Institutions

Most people who get treatment for a mental or emotional disorder do so outside of hospitals. But when the behavior becomes too disorganized, too dangerous to others or to self, or even too upsetting for others to cope with, the person is committed to an institution. Patients either commit themselves voluntarily or are committed by their families. The hospital stay may be short, although hospitalization for mental disorders is usually longer than for any type of physical illness. In the hospital, a diagnosis is made and short-term therapy is provided. For many patients, this is enough.

Advantages. Stubborn disorders are not handled so easily. For these cases, a long-term stay in the hospital may be required. There are certain advantages to being in the hospital. The patient is removed from the home situation which may be contributing to the problem. The institution can supply a complete, twenty-four-hours-a-day, therapeutic environment—in contrast to the brief time spent in a therapist's private office. Various types of therapy can be used in combinations that would be impractical on the outside. And, finally, accepting the fact that they have to be in the hospital helps some patients to be realistic about really needing treatment. In this sense, entering a hospital may be a commitment to change.

Disadvantages. However, being in the hospital has its drawbacks. Sometimes a patient adopts the role of being sick as a way of life, and begins to depend on the staff and the institutional environment for meeting everyday needs. Then regression can result, rather than improvement, and some patients spend the rest of their lives in the institution.

Public Institutions

Of the million or more patients admitted each year to mental hospitals in the United States, the vast majority are in public institutions. The major criticism made of these hospitals is that they are severely overcrowded and provide little more than custodial care.

In many public institutions with limited staff and resources, only the patients considered "promising" receive treatment. The rest are given drugs to keep them manageable and shunted off to back wards, TV lounges, and the making of pot holders. Patients are allowed to make few, if any, decisions. For some, this is a welcome relief from the frustrations and stresses of life outside the institution. They apparently use this period, free of responsibility, to get back on their feet.

Others are not so fortunate. About two-thirds of the people in

PREVIEW

In this section, read to find out:

1. which people need to enter institutions.
2. what public institutions are like.
3. what approaches are used in private institutions.

mental hospitals are suffering from chronic schizophrenia. There is good evidence that their condition actually worsens with long hospitalization. Freedom of action, self-determination, and independence are surrendered to the institutional managers. Under these conditions, the patient is gradually cut off from the real world, and recovery becomes more difficult.

Findings from some studies suggest that those patients who are liked by the staff stand a much better chance of receiving more and better care than those who are seen as "unattractive." Disliked patients were more likely to be given larger amounts of tranquilizers and to be transferred to maximum security wards. Patients who were cooperative and didn't make trouble received more of the staff's time and were considered to have a better chance of improvement.

Halfway houses. In trying to do away with the bad effects of long hospital stays, some institutions have set up halfway houses. These homes are for patients who are sufficiently improved to leave the institution but not ready to resume a normal life. The smaller settings of the halfway house provide a somewhat protected transitional environment in which an individual can function with greater freedom and responsibility. Some large institutions also use behavior therapy with chronic patients. The most successful technique is a reward system.

Private Institutions

Many newer methods are found largely in private hospitals. These facilities are usually much smaller than public hospitals. They often

Some examples of art done in an art therapy class are shown below.

have a higher staff-to-patient ratio, and attract more skillful and dedicated professional personnel. They are also expensive. Typically, two basic approaches are used, depending upon the hospital.

A Structured Approach

Institutions that follow a highly structured approach provide their patients with a stable, predictable, nonstressful, and somewhat disciplined social environment. Treatment procedures include drugs and both individual and group psychotherapy. Patients are closely supervised. These hospitals are often set apart, possibly in the country or in a parklike setting, and may be called an institute or a retreat. Except for being locked in, the patients might think they are staying at an expensive resort.

A neurotic patient may benefit from this structured treatment. The hospital gives a pattern to life, which may formerly have been disorganized and frightening. Regular visits with a psychiatrist help the patients to know themselves better. In a carefully supervised setting, using step-by-step procedures, the hospital helps the patients to develop their potential.

Therapeutic Communities

A recent trend in institutional treatment is the **therapeutic community.** It may look like a small residential hotel. To a degree, patients make their own rules. The staff has authority, but carries it out in a

One of the oldest examples of a therapeutic community is Gheel in Belgium shown in the photo at left below. Since the 13th century, pilgrims have visited a shrine at Gheel as a place where the mentally ill can be miraculously cured. Over the centuries, many of the pilgrims remained at Gheel, and the inhabitants of the community took them into their homes. In the mid-1970s, more than 2,000 certified mental patients suffering from various types of psychoses, personality disorders, and mental retardation, lived in the homes of townspeople and worked beside them. Patients have few restrictions, and often choose to remain in Gheel even after the supervising therapist judges them recovered.

A patient and some townspeople, Gheel, Belgium

non-authoritarian manner. When someone breaks a rule, a meeting is held and everyone decides what the punishment should be. Therapy, rap sessions, and social interaction are frequent.

This environmental treatment doesn't work for everyone. It is most successful with patients whose illness is not chronic, and who have fair-to-good contact with reality. At the same time, it prevents patients from sinking into the pattern of monotony associated with long-term care. In many therapeutic communities the average stay is six weeks to two months. Patients in a therapeutic community are not passively accepting treatment for an illness. Instead, they are learning to take responsibility for their own actions, within the framework of the hospital setting.

Whether traditional or experimental in their approach, mental health specialists are learning that a hospital cannot dehumanize patients and cure them at the same time.

Section Review

1. Why are some people put in institutions?
2. What are some criticisms of public institutions?
3. Describe some differences between the structured approach and a therapeutic community.

4. Staying Mentally Healthy

Your best health insurance, physical and mental, is a set of good living habits. This can help prevent trouble before it starts.

Preventing Trouble

Staying strong physically, through exercise, sleep, and good nutrition, does not guarantee freedom from mental problems, but it gives the nervous system, along with the rest of the body, strength to resist trouble. You are least likely to fall victim to emotional disorders during periods when you feel strong and full of vigor, and are busy with your friends. Author John Steinbeck referred to the absence of this kind of resistance when he wrote ". . . the line between hunger and anger is a thin line."

Outlets. People need outlets such as active participation in creative or other recreational activities. Carl Rogers compared creativity to the ". . . curative force in psychotherapy—man's tendency to actualize himself, to become his potentialities." So if you go beyond spectator activity, to making, fixing, doing, playing, and other active participation, you do your mental health a favor.

Laughter. Wisely referred to as the tranquilizer with no side effects, laughter has many champions. In the 1960s, magazine editor

PREVIEW

In this section, read to find out:

1. how to help yourself stay mentally healthy.
2. how to deal with crisis situations.
3. how to motivate yourself to deal with problems.

Laughter — "the tranquilizer without side effects"

On Being Sane in Insane Places

Could a normal, "sane" person who has never suffered from serious psychiatric symptoms be admitted to a mental hospital and not be detected as sane once inside? According to a study by psychologist David Rosenhan, this fear is partially justified. Once a person is labeled as insane and admitted to a hospital, nothing that the person does is likely to be considered normal.

Rosenhan and seven other normal people had themselves committed to twelve different mental hospitals in five states on the East and West coasts. Each of these pseudopatients complained of hearing "unclean" voices that said things like "empty," "hollow," and "thud." Except for this falsehood, and altering their names, vocations, and employments, everything else they said was truthful. In almost every case they were diagnosed as "schizophrenic"; the exception being at the only private hospital in the sample where "manic depressive" was the diagnosis.

Once on the psychiatric ward, the pseudopatients stopped hearing voices and behaved as "normally" as possible. Despite this, they were never detected by the staff. To get out required the intervention of wives, friends, or lawyers. Length of hospitalization ranged from seven to fifty-two days, with an average committment of nineteen days. Each was discharged with a diagnosis of schizophrenia "in remission," (meaning there were no visible symptoms) and then only through the intervention of spouses or colleagues.

Rosenhan's study has several implications. For example, real patients were quick to spot the imposters, even though the doctors didn't. Normal activities, such as making notes, was seen by the nurses as "writing behavior," and noted as abnormal. The label "schizophrenic" just wouldn't come off.

Norman Cousins became a special one. Suffering from a serious blood disease, Cousins was given one chance in 500 to live. With the cooperation of his doctor, he directed his own recovery. For his success he gave major credit to laughter and his unshaken conviction that he was going to live. Cousins learned ". . . never to underestimate the capacity of the human mind and body to regenerate."

Other people. Social activity is a major contributor to mental health. Psychologist James Lynch pointed out with statistics, in his book *The Broken Heart,* that many illnesses occur at a greater rate among the isolated. For example, heart disease, strokes, and cancer occur twice as often among the divorced as among the married. Get yourself a few friends, and take good care of them.

Luckily, most of us do not suffer from serious mental problems. We do, however, go through occasional periods when we have trouble coping with life's everyday problems. We need to find ways to deal with these situations.

Coping with Crisis

At some time, your mental health may seem to be at stake. How can you deal with this type of problem? Perhaps it is too simple to say that we can learn *rules* for good mental health. However, we can develop attitudes and strategies that will help us stay well or handle a serious crisis if it occurs. Because mental illness often stems from psychological causes, preventing trouble means using psychology on ourselves. These guidelines can help you maintain your psychological well-being.

1. *Know your own weaknesses.* What kinds of situations throw you for a loss or make you feel threatened? Should you avoid them? Not necessarily. In fact, sometimes you can't avoid trouble. But identifying the problem is a giant step toward solving it. You can analyze the situation, consider all your choices, and develop a program to solve the problem. Go at this a step at a time until you feel that the situation is under control. And start with an easy problem, first.

2. *Use ordinary stress,* the sort you have learned to handle, *to develop* socially acceptable, reality-based *problem-solving techniques for the future.* When a serious problem threatens to overwhelm you, ask yourself how you dealt with similar threats in the past. Some people find that time pressure is their biggest source of stress. By better advance planning they can learn to avoid being overwhelmed at the last minute.

3. *Know what led up to the crisis.* Can you relate it to external events—a death in the family, striking out on your own for the first time, getting involved in something that is over your head? Knowing

One method of dealing with serious crises is to develop yourself as a person. Take stock of your strengths and weaknesses and grow in the direction your individual abilities and interests lead.

It's Your Turn

You have read some suggestions for ways to cope with a crisis. These are only some possibilities. You may be using some already. Others may be good ideas for you to add to your behavior. Now *It's Your Turn*. Think of a crisis or problem you have, or have had in the past. List the ways you used to meet the crisis or solve the problem. What ways might you have used that would have been better?

the reason for a crisis helps you choose a course of action. Just doing something about the problem is itself helpful.

4. *Substitute positive for negative thoughts.* Sometimes our problems are not rooted in actual fact, but in our interpretation of events. One therapist suggests the following. Instead of letting worry or criticism get you down, use an alternative way of thinking. Stress the positive aspects of the situation. Decide that the criticism isn't going to worry you.

5. *Learn relaxation techniques.* One method recommends a quiet environment, closed eyes, a comfortable position, and a repetitive mental device. Most traditional, and most religious, meditation techniques meet these requirements. Another method teaches people to alternately tense and relax specific muscles. Daily practice in this control has produced relaxation.

6. *Develop your potential as a person.* Not many of us can be concert pianists, professional athletes, or accomplished painters. But we can all grow in the directions our individual talents and interests lead. Take inventory occasionally. Add up your strengths and weaknesses. Build on your strengths. They provide the building blocks of self-esteem so necessary to good mental health. Faced with a crisis, we can draw on these resources to help us get through it.

7. *Give yourself instructions.* Train yourself to deal with stress situations. Do it in steps. Prepare yourself; confront the situation; cope with the fear; and reinforce yourself. Tell yourself such things as "I can make a plan for handling this situation." "This anxiety is normal." "I will do what I must do right now." "I'm making progress; good for me!"

8. *Develop and maintain social contacts.* Loneliness and isolation from other human beings are both a cause and a result of nearly all forms of mental illness. We are social beings. We need others for support, recognition, praise, and corrective feedback. The responses of others help us to evaluate our own actions, and to give and receive love. By turning toward others we can put our own problems in a better perspective, and feel better as a result.

9. *Know when to go for help.* Some problems probably cannot be solved alone. They should not be allowed to get out of hand. Go for help when you begin to feel that the problem is controlling you, instead of you controlling it. Most of us have taken our trouble to an outsider at one time or another. Don't bottle up your despair or feelings of agitation. And don't be too proud to ask for help.

10. *Know where to go for help.* Sometimes family and friends can give all the help we need. In grief situations, we usually turn to the people

closest to us for comfort. But problems we feel are too personal may be best discussed with someone who can be objective. Someone not involved, such as a member of the clergy or a school psychologist, may be best. If you get acquainted with sources of help before you have problems that create stress, going for help will be easier when you need it.

If a crisis is acute and threatening, calling your local *hot line* can put you in touch with a qualified mental health professional. Doing this doesn't mean you are really sick. Most therapy is short-term, and it can be effective.

Many communities have "drop-in centers" where young people can go for advice and help with problems.

Section Review

1. Describe two ways you can help yourself to avoid mental health problems.
2. List three ways to cope with a crisis situation.
3. When should you probably seek help for a problem?

Chapter 13 Review

Section Summaries

1. Who Treats Mental Disorders and How

Psychiatrists are physicians who are specialists in mental, emotional, and neurological illnesses. Psychoanalysts are specialists in the therapies developed by Freud and his followers. Clinical psychologists are therapists who have a Ph.D. in clinical psychology, followed by an internship in a hospital or clinic. Physical treatments include drug therapy and electroshock therapy. The methods of psychoanalysis include free association, dream therapy, and analysis of transference. In group therapy, the therapist leads patients in group discussions of individual problems. In the human potential movement, sensitivity training and encounter groups are used to help people focus on feelings and develop human relationship skills.

2. Humanistic and Behavioral Therapy

Humanistic therapy was pioneered by Carl Rogers, who thought a major source of anxiety was the gap between the client's real self and the ideal self. The humanistic therapist offers positive regard but is nondirective, in the hope of encouraging self-acceptance. Behavior modification therapy uses theories of conditioning to change undesirable behavior. Techniques include desensitization, implosion therapy, aversion therapy, positive reinforcement, and modeling desirable behaviors.

3. The Role of Institutions

One advantage of institutions is that they substitute a potentially troubling home environment for the therapeutic environment of the institution, where various combinations of therapy can be used. Another advantage is that entering the hospital can signal the patient's commitment to change. The disadvantage is that the patient sometimes adopts the role of being sick. Public institutions are criticized because they are overcrowded and provide little more than custodial care. Halfway houses provide a transition between the institution and normal life. Although private institutions are smaller and more expensive than public institutions, they have larger and more skillful professional staffs. The structured approach of some institutions helps relieve the anxiety of neurotic patients. In a therapeutic community, the staff allows the patients to make and enforce rules for themselves.

4. Staying Mentally Healthy

One way to stay mentally healthy is to prevent trouble by seeking outlets, laughing, and maintaining contact with other people. Another way is to learn to cope with crises. This involves knowing personal weaknesses, learning problem-solving techniques, analyzing events that led up to the crisis, substituting positive for negative thoughts, learning relaxation techniques, developing your potential as a person, giving yourself instructions, developing and maintaining social contacts, knowing when to go for help, and knowing where to go for help.

Psychology Skill Activities

1. For three days, keep a two-part log. In one part, describe situations that seem to follow the chapter's guidelines for achieving mental health. In the second part, describe situations in which the guidelines do *not* seem to be followed. Names are not needed, but do explain why you feel the situation does or does not follow the guidelines. **easy**

2. Design several possible treatment programs for either a phobia or for compulsive smoking. Use a variety of methods in your design. **challenging**

Testing for Understanding

Knowing Key Terms
Define these terms in your own words.

Section 1
psychiatrist
psychoanalyst
clinical psychologist
psychoanalysis
free association
dream analysis
transference
group therapy

Section 2
humanistic therapy
behavior modification therapy
desensitization
implosion therapy
aversion therapy
positive reinforcement
modeling

Section 3
therapeutic community

Reviewing Main Ideas
Section 1
1. Explain how a psychiatrist, a psychoanalyst, and a clinical psychologist differ in their training and approach.
2. What do therapists mean by the expression "physical treatments"?
3. Describe the process of psychoanalysis.
4. How is group therapy used?

Section 2
1. How are the ideas of humanistic psychology used in therapy?
2. What are some successful techniques of behavior modification?
3. How does desensitization reduce anxiety?

Section 3
1. How is the decision made to treat someone inside an institution?

2. Describe the typical public institution.
3. How are private institutions different from public institutions?

Section 4
1. Describe some ways to maintain good mental health.
2. What are some healthy techniques for coping with crisis?
3. How can you know that you need to seek the help of others?

Thinking Critically
1. *Drawing Conclusions.* Which ways of staying mentally healthy do you think are the most effective. Why? **easy**
2. *Making Inferences.* A psychotherapist once said that many people who seek therapy are actually looking for friendship. Do you agree or disagree? **challenging**

Demonstrating Psychology Skills
Suppose a good friend of yours is suffering from unusually deep depression. What advice would you give? If your friend decides on treatment, what possibilities are there? Consider all the alternatives.

Experimenting with Psychology

Observing Abnormal Behavior

Dealing with abnormal behavior or mental disorders is a difficult task for most of us. We often don't know how to react to a person whose behavior is deviant, or different from the ordinary. Because most of us are "normal," we find it difficult to understand and sympathize with abnormal behavior, however harmless.

The following activity is designed to give you some experience with observing abnormal behavior. Observation is a research method used by psychologists that involves watching and recording how living things behave in their natural surroundings. (Refer to **Exercise 4, Observational Studies,** on pages 481–482 of the *Psychology Skills Handbook,* for more information on this method of gathering data.) By abnormal behavior, we mean anything that is different from the ordinary behavior society expects of us. Some examples are people acting confused, disoriented, or needlessly aggressive, talking to themselves, and so on.

When you are in a public place such as a park, shopping center, center of a big city, or a subway or at some public event like a fair, carnival, parade, or sporting event, look for examples of abnormal behavior. As you are observing the abnormal behavior, take note of your reactions. How do you feel about this behavior? Do you think it's embarrassing or amusing? Do you feel compassion for the person? Annoyance? Next, observe how other people react to the behavior. Do they ignore it? Laugh about it? Become afraid?

Record your results on a chart similar to the one below, and draw some conclusions from your data.

Record of Results

	Description of Behavior	Your Reactions	Other People's Reactions
What? Where?			

Conclusions:

Explain why you think you reacted as you did.

Tell what you think motivated other people's reactions.

Unit 4 Test

Matching (25 points)

Match each phrase with a term below.
1. learning from experience of others
2. Maslow's view of Abraham Lincoln
3. not introverted
4. objective and projective
5. fear of closed places
6. Carl Rogers' view of those he helped
7. undue fear of something ordinary
8. basis of all neuroses
9. excessive worry about your health
10. physical treatments of mental illness

a. extroverted
b. claustrophobia
c. self-actualized
d. vicarious
e. phobia
f. hypochondriasis
g. drugs and electroshock
h. clients, not patients
i. kinds of tests
j. anxiety

Multiple Choice (25 points)

Circle the choice that best completes each answer.
1. A psychodynamic approach could be called (a) modeling, (b) psychoanalytic, (c) self-actualizing, (d) humanistic.
2. Unconscious methods of coping with anxiety are called (a) personalities, (b) drives, (c) departments, (d) defense mechanisms.
3. Learning by watching others is part of the theory of (a) the unconscious, (b) social learning, (c) psychoanalysis, (d) inferiority.
4. The disorders known as neuroses do not include (a) hallucinations, (b) hypochondriasis, (c) anxiety, (d) amnesia.
5. Paralysis caused by a problem that is mental, not physical, is called (a) fugue, (b) schizophrenia, (c) conversion hysteria, (d) accident-prone.
6. A person judged in court to be unable to understand the consequences of his or her ac-tions is called (a) psychotic, (b) neurotic, (c) mental, (d) insane.
7. Disorders such as multiple personality and fugue episodes are (a) depressions, (b) deliberate, (c) dissociative, (d) psychoses.
8. Positive reinforcement is (a) diagnosing, (b) punishing, (c) imitating, (d) rewarding.
9. A psychologist would not give physical treatment as therapy labeled (a) nondirective, (b) group, (c) drug, (d) relaxation.
10. Loss of contact with reality is a characteristic of (a) neuroses, (b) personality disorders, (c) multiple personalities, (d) psychoses.

Fill in the Blanks (25 points)

Write the word or phrase that best completes each sentence.
1. A person who thinks he is Napoleon or God is said to have delusions of _____.
2. Excessive dependence or need for affection is a sign of being _____.
3. A child forced to behave the opposite of the way he or she feels is in a _____ bind.
4. Some people grow up feeling guilty about enjoyment and become masochistic or self-_____.
5. Neuroses are usually easier to treat than _____.
6. Psychiatrists are physicians who specialize in treating _____.
7. Free association, finding clues in dreams, and transference are methods of _____.
8. Sessions with a therapist for several patients together are called _____.
9. Implosion therapy is facing a frightening event in a friendly _____.
10. A community helping former patients is known as a _____ _____.

Critical Thinking Essay (25 points)

Think of ways a non-professional acquaintance, relative, or friend might help someone who shows signs of severe emotional stress, while taking care to avoid doing harm. List Dos and Don'ts (two or more of each) and explain.

Unit 5

You, Others, and Society

In this unit you will examine how people interact with others and with society as a whole—what influences our attraction for other people and the nature of love, how we are influenced by social groups, and what challenges we face as individuals in our modern technological society.

Person to Person

The room was stark white except for the machines. As the volunteers entered, their eyes scanned the array of electrical equipment. They were met by an experimenter who told them that, in the interests of medical science, they were to be subjects in an experiment using electric shocks.

Bear in mind that no shock was ever given. The experiment was designed to induce a state of fearfulness and to study its effects on social behavior.

The experimenter, psychologist Philip Zimbardo, gave one group of volunteers the choice of waiting alone or with others who were to undergo the same shock experiment. The second group was given the choice of waiting alone or with people who had already *completed* the shock experiment. In the first group, the majority of the subjects chose to be with others who were in a like situation—those who were waiting for the experiment to begin. In the second group, most of the subjects chose to wait alone instead of with those who supposedly had completed the shock experiment. The people who had "completed" the experiment could have told the others a lot of information. They could have told them the number of shocks given and could have described the severity of the shocks. Their information could even have helped lessen the volunteers' anxiety. Yet, that information apparently was unimportant to the participants. Instead they preferred to be with people who shared their anxiety, who were in the same emotional state as they were.

Have you ever needed the company of people who were "in the same boat" as you were? Have you ever wondered why people choose to be with certain people? Why do people choose to be with other people at all? Why do people choose to be alone? These are some of the subjects that will be discussed in this chapter.

He affectionately painted aspects of American life that seemingly never change—a boy's first haircut, a Thanksgiving dinner, the comfort of an ordinary conversation. Norman Rockwell is probably best known for his paintings which appeared on more than 200 covers of the weekly magazine, *The Saturday Evening Post*. The one at left was painted for the *Post* cover, November 24, 1945.

1. Contact with Others

Isabella's parents kept her isolated in a dark room from the time she was born. When a social worker discovered her at the age of five, Isabella could not walk or talk. In the presence of strangers Isabella acted like a wild animal. Yet, with the help of a team of psychologists and speech therapists, Isabella eventually became a normal adolescent and adult.

This case is not rare. It is one of several that happen every year. Children like Isabella are not necessarily the victims of physical abuse. They are the victims of neglect. Parents or other caretakers ignore them; they fail to provide their children with love and attention, and the children do not grow and develop. In Chapter 5, you saw that children in some institutional environments respond in this way too. Lack of attention and stimulation causes a decline, not only in physical growth, but in mental development as well. Doctors and psychologists have labeled this response to neglect the *failure to thrive syndrome*. When placed in environments where they are given care and attention round the clock, these children, if it is not too late, respond as though making up for lost time. They gain weight rapidly and grow in leaps and bounds.

PREVIEW

**In this section,
read to find out:**

1. that people need human contact as well as privacy.
2. how human beings use space.

The Need for Contact

Cases like these indicate the great need we human beings have for human contact. A lack of nurturing from the first day of life can leave children, at worst, suffering malnutrition and facing death at a very premature age. At best, these children are left emotionally scarred for life, often facing adulthoods of loneliness, depression, paranoia, violence, or even suicide. Yet too much protection and nurturing can cause problems too.

Human beings seem to go through life responding to conflicting needs—the need for human contact and the need for independence. These needs seem to pull us in different directions at almost every stage of life. In mother's presence, two-year-olds will explore unknown surroundings readily without requiring her involvement. But if she should leave the room, exploring ceases and anxiety sets in. The same kind of thing is true of adults in relationships. Each partner needs the love, protection, and security provided by the other, but he or she also needs independence, self-fulfillment, and self-esteem. In Zimbardo's electric shock experiment, subjects "in the same boat" needed to be together even though it meant not finding out what the experiment would hold for them.

Good mental health, stability, and the ability to adjust in later life depend a great deal upon the degree to which the need for contact and the need for independence are fulfilled during childhood. If a balance is not struck between these two drives, maladjustment and personality disorders can often follow.

Relationships that are established during a lifetime either between friends or between lovers all are influenced by this primary bond between parent and child. The child of a loving, supportive family usually learns to trust others, to share with them, and to enjoy their companionship. Such a child also develops a strong regard for self and approaches life with a strong sense of security. He or she needs human contact but also needs and is comfortable with privacy.

Children sharing the things of childhood. Young adults venturing into the vulnerability of give and take. Relationships of a lifetime are born of the first bond between baby and parent.

Educators found that open classrooms were too open when the students began to erect their own makeshift cubbyholes. Teachers who use this method now try to provide private areas for youngsters who need some time and place to be alone.

The Need for Privacy

How would you feel if you discovered someone had been eavesdropping on your telephone conversations? Or if someone had been opening your mail? Or giving out confidential information about you? Privacy is much more than physical isolation. You probably have more privacy in a crowded bus than you do eating dinner with your family. On a bus you are not expected to reveal your thoughts and feelings to others. **Privacy** is a psychological state. You can experience it alone or in a crowd. According to psychologist A. F. Westin, privacy is your freedom to determine "when, how and to what extent information about [yourself] is communicated to others."

Westin believes that there are many reasons why people seek privacy. One is the need for *personal autonomy*. Privacy provides a sense of individuality and independence. You are your own person making your own conscious choices.

Another reason is the need for *emotional release*. "Getting away from it all" is often useful in reducing stress especially if the stress is related to overcrowding or to the tension and conflict that arise in certain social situations. Privacy not only distances us from the source of the stress, but lets us see the problem from another perspective.

The opportunity for *self-evaluation* is a third reason for privacy. For most of us, self-evaluation usually means closing the door on the world in order to think things out. Privacy enables us to process all the information that has been going through our minds, to make decisions, and to plan for the future. One study found that subjects who were anxious but were unaware of the source of their anxiety preferred privacy to being with others. Those who were fearful of a specific event wanted to be with others; they had no specific need to sort things out.

Fourth, privacy serves the function of *limited* and *protected communication*. This is best illustrated by the sign on your door that reads: "Please do not disturb." For whatever reason, you want control over who has access to you and when.

The Need for Space

Just as people need psychological space, so they also need to surround themselves with a certain amount of physical space. For example, when you ride on a bus and have a choice of seats, are you more likely to sit next to someone, or do you look for a pair of unoccupied seats and pick one of them? How close do you stand when you are talking with a good friend? With your instructor? With a stranger? According to anthropologist Edward Hall, each of us wears an invisible protective bubble of space to ensure that others keep their distance. This bubble, which differs from culture to culture, inflates and deflates when we are in different situations. Hall broke down our uses of space into four zones. First, there is **intimate distance** which we reserve for intimate relationships either between close friends or family members. Intimate distance ranges from actual contact to eighteen inches. However, if closeness is forced, as in an elevator or a crowd, people create private space by tuning the others out, keeping their bodies rigid, and avoiding eye contact.

A conversation at a party, a confidence shared while taking a stroll—these take place in **personal distance,** which ranges from eighteen inches to about four feet. While this distance implies familiarity, it does not necessarily invite an invasion into intimate space. **Social distance,** generally from four to seven feet, is the distance in which we conduct impersonal or personal business, such as asking a librarian for a book or confronting an employer about a raise. When you choose a seat in the last row of a classroom, you are establishing, according to Hall, **public distance** between yourself and the teacher. The distance from a politician to his or her audience is also public distance.

Professional roles, age differences, social status, and ethnic background all seem to affect the amount of space we put between ourselves and others. However, regardless of the size of the bubbles we put around us, if anyone invades them, we feel uncomfortable and find ourselves backing away.

Protecting your turf. Not only do people carry their protective bubbles with them wherever they go, they sometimes claim and defend parts of the environment as their own. It might be a particular seat in the library, a certain parking space, or a particular place at the dinner table they claim for their own.

Author Robert Ardrey believes that these examples are evidence of a *territorial instinct* in humans. **Territoriality** doesn't necessarily mean ownership—but the right to exclusive use. Ardrey believes that humans carve out territory of their own in the way animals stake out and defend territory to gain control over food, to provide a security zone against attack, and to enforce dominance over other animals. While Ardrey's views are supported by very little hard evidence, there does seem to be some truth to his theory. What seems to be important is how people react when their territory is threatened.

Julius Fast, author of *Body Language,* demonstrated how people defend their space. "At supper the other evening, my wife and I shared a table in an Italian restaurant with another couple. Experimentally I moved the wine bottle into my friend's 'zone.' Then slowly, still talking [I began] rearranging the wine glass and napkin in his zone. Uneasily he shifted in his chair, moved aside, rearranged his plate, his napkin, and finally in a sudden, almost compulsive lunge, moved the wine bottle back. He had reacted by defending his zone."

Often people use a specific space to express their unique tastes and attitudes. The space becomes an extension of self. Often you can learn something about a person by seeing his or her study, bedroom, or office. When thrown together in a single large setting, people look for ways to separate themselves from others. A good example of this happens in the "bullpen" office arrangement. By piling their desks with books and papers, people manage to carve out enough personal space to give themselves the psychological illusion of private territory.

Privacy and social interaction. On the surface, it might seem that privacy is primarily a form of social withdrawal. However, it often works the other way. When deprived of privacy, people retreat. The more privacy available, the better the chances for social interaction. A study conducted in a psychiatric ward of a general hospital revealed that when patients occupied small, private rooms of their own, they tended to spend a great deal of their time interacting with each other.

When they were assigned to large multi-bed rooms, the patients tended to keep to themselves. They were more guarded and more self-involved. The lack of privacy seemed to restrict their social activity.

The general picture of privacy, then, is not only that it gives us a place of retreat, however important this may be; it also encourages social behavior because it enables us to control the terms of the interaction. We are free to make that human contact when we want to.

When faced with crowded uniformity, individuals often carve out personal territory using color schemes and ornamental woodworking.

Section Review

1. How might a person be affected if human contact were deprived during childhood?
2. List four reasons people need privacy.
3. According to Hall, how do we use zones of space?
4. How does privacy affect social interaction?

The following is a description of a videotaped interview between an inexperienced counselor who was learning counseling technique and a troubled fourteen-year-old girl in need of counseling.

The girl sat at a table with her head down, her face hidden from the counselor, her left hand covering her eyes and her right hand stretched across the table top.

As the interview progressed, the girl's posture remained the same—her shielded eyes seemed to say, "I am ashamed. I cannot face you! I am afraid." But her outstretched hand almost invited, "Touch me! Take my hand and force me to look at you!"

The counselor, inexperienced and thoroughly frightened by the situation, sat upright with her legs crossed and her arms folded across her chest. She moved only to tap the ash of her cigarette, then her hand came back defensively across her chest. Her posture said, "I am frightened and I cannot touch you. I don't know how to handle the situation, [and] I must protect myself."

After viewing the videotape of herself and analyzing her own fears, the counselor was able to make physical contact with the girl. She put her arm around her, hugged her, and gave her some of the mothering she needed. The physical contact was the first step toward verbal communication. The nonverbal messages had to be read and understood before the two women could talk verbally and give and receive help. ▪

Nonverbal Communication

The spoken word is only one of the languages we use to communicate with others. Another form of human communication is our **body language.** If you have ever shrugged your shoulders or raised an eyebrow, then you are probably a master at a language you weren't even aware of knowing.

Each part of the body conveys messages; it can speak even without moving. An erect posture—shoulders back, head up—conveys confidence and self-assurance. A slumped posture suggests insecurity. Shoulder shrugging might say, "I don't care," and finger or foot tapping spells out nervousness or impatience. The eyes are the most expressive of all. A mere suggestion of a look can reveal truths that words would never divulge. Many linguists believe that human beings communicated with gestures long before languages were ever formed. It is estimated that we can produce, through facial and body movement, close to 700,000 different gestures—an astounding number

When feeling vulnerable or threatened, individuals often protect themselves with crossed-arm barriers.

when compared to the eight or ten thousand words in our everyday vocabulary.

Keeping others out. If it is true that we in this culture do surround ourselves with a bubble of privacy, then how do we do it? It's probably not through any verbal communication. At least you've probably never said or heard anyone say, "Hey, you're invading my bubble—back off!" Chances are, the message was conveyed through body language.

The way you maintain privacy is by manipulating space. Where do you sit on a park bench? If you sit squarely in the middle, you're asserting your dominance. You're saying to the world, "I want this bench to myself—sit down on it and you're an intruder." Or if you sit way over at one end, you're saying "Sit down at the other end if you must, but leave me alone."

The boss whose desk separates him or her from others uses the desk as a barrier. This barrier may indicate power to others—they may not approach the boss in his or her own territory behind the desk, but the boss may come around to them at will.

Police officers know that barriers give people a sense of safety. When questioning suspects, they often leave no furniture between themselves and the suspect. As questioning proceeds, the officer will move in closer and closer. It has been found that physical invasion of a person's territory can sometimes break a suspect's resistance and defenses. People without physical barriers often put on emotionless stone faces as protective devices. We all are aware of the protective masks we wear when we are trying to keep out intruders.

Inviting others in. When avoiding contact with others, people's bodies close up and their eyes become guarded. Conversely, when people want to make contact with others, the opposite happens. Arms are open, free from barricade positions. Posture is relaxed. Eye contact is made easily. Glances are held longer, but not so long that they become rude or embarrassing. Smiling invites human interaction.

Whether or not they are aware of doing so, people read others' body language and respond to it accordingly. For example, suppose two friends are at a dance. They choose a table on one side of the room. One of the friends is not particularly beautiful by Hollywood standards, but has a winning smile and likes meeting new people. That person faces the dance floor; one arm rests on the table, the other drapes the back of another chair. The other friend is handsome by any standard, but is shy and fearful of meeting new people. That person too faces the crowded room, but without a smiling face. The arms are braced across the body, and when someone approaches, the head

It's Your Turn

Look around at the other students in your class. Observe the body language they are currently displaying. Now *It's Your Turn* to draw conclusions. Based on what you know about their personalities, what meanings can you attribute to their body language messages?

When friends meet face-to-face, they often assume almost identical body language.

drops and eye contact is not made. The not-so-beautiful friend is asked to dance repeatedly. The beautiful one is not approached, but desperately wants to be. What is the difference?

When approaching the two friends, one can easily recognize that the smiling face and corresponding open posture welcome newcomers. Persons who approach are assured of acceptance or at least a warm reception. The beautiful friend's posture says to the world, "I'm afraid. I will feel self-conscious if you approach me. I will be tongue-tied and will sound stupid if you try to talk to me." People recognize these danger signals and know if they approach, they will surely face the embarrassment of rejection, so they steer clear.

When two people have established a close bond and like and trust each other, body language changes. Postures seem to mirror each other's. This phenomenon is called **congruence.** Over lunch, when one friend leans forward with elbows on the table, the other one echoes the movement. When one leans back, the other does the same.

In a study done over a period of time, films were taken of people talking together. When shown in slow motion, it was found that the speakers moved in rhythms as they spoke. It was also found that the listeners imitated these movements. The better the friends, the more in unison they were.

Verbal and Nonverbal Communication Work Together

No one can say for sure that crossed arms are barriers that signal "No Admittance!" Or that slumped shoulders always signify insecurity. Body language is not precise by any means. Gestures must be judged in the context of spoken language and behavior.

Body language and spoken language are dependent upon each other. As psychologist Julius Fast noted, "If we listen only to the words when someone is talking, we may get as much distortion as we would if we listened only to body language." You know this to be only too true if you have hurt another's feelings, and after you apologized, the friend said, "That's all right," but you could plainly see by the eyes that the hurt was still there. When body language messages conflict with spoken messages, we often tend to believe the message the body relays.

Sometimes this disagreement between body language and spoken language can spell trouble for a child. For example, a parent who behaves one way but verbally communicates a different attitude can cause great confusion in a child. **Double messages,** or contradictions between verbal and nonverbal messages, can leave children anxious and, in extreme cases, mentally ill in their adult years.

Verbal Communication

Body language changes as people get to know each other better—from nervous barricading at first to mimicking movement as friendship deepens. According to one theory, verbal communication follows a similar progression.

First, comes an initial **awareness** of the other. Something about the other person sparks our interest. Something makes us know we'd like to know more. Then conversation takes root. After stops and starts of inconsequential chitchat, names are exchanged.

Finally, as the friendship begins to unfold, conversation becomes more longwinded, though masks are still very much intact. This is the stage of **surface contact.** Real feelings and attitudes are disguised under a lot of smiling and politeness. Subjects discussed are generally limited to current topics or to those of mutual interest such as the class the two people are in together.

For the relationship to continue, masks must be dropped. Usually this begins with an exchange of personal information. Telling others pieces from our pasts serves as a substitute for experiences the almost-friends have not yet shared. Finally real feelings and opinions are ventured. If feelings and opinions and frankness are met with understanding and a return of honesty, then trust builds. The stage of **mutuality** begins. You talk about yourself, your feelings, your worries, your

Levels of a Relationship

0. Zero Contact (two unrelated persons)

1. Awareness (impressions of the other, but no interaction)

2. Surface Contact (some interaction)

3. Mutuality (a continuation of stages, from some self-disclosure, to sharing some joint attitudes and behavior, to total disclosure and complete interdependence, which is an extreme case)

Adapted from G. Levinger and J.D. Snoek. *Attraction in relationship: A new look at interpersonal attraction.* 1972. Copyright to the authors, 1978.

385

goals. Each person's actions and attitudes are strongly influenced by the other. You talk from your innermost self, and you listen as your friend does the same. There is great interdependence.

These stages of communication are the same in loving relationships as well as in friendships. And yet there is never a guarantee that one stage of communication will grow into the next. If that were always true, we would fall in love with anyone who sparked our interest and everyone we'd meet would become a friend. As it is, most relationships burn out before unmasking takes place.

Section Review

1. Describe some of the symbolic barriers people use and tell why they use them.
2. What are the three stages of verbal communication?
3. What can happen when body language and spoken messages disagree?
4. At what stage of communication do you think most relationships burn out? Why?

PREVIEW

In this section, read to find out:

1. some of the factors involved in choosing companions.
2. some of the obstacles that stand in the way of making contact with others.

3. Interpersonal Attraction

Even though we may enjoy and need to be alone now and then, human beings are basically social animals who need the company and cooperation of other human beings. We need to make friends, to like and be liked, and to form loving relationships with at least a few people who are in some way special to us. To like or love someone means that you enjoy that particular individual for certain unique qualities that fit with your own interests and needs. It means too that you have, not just an opinion, but a feeling about that person. In studying the relationships that people form, it is important to realize that we are not studying individual behavior. Instead, we are studying behavior between pairs of human beings and the reasons people like and love those they do.

Physical Appearance

Psychologists have found that physical attractiveness is a factor in our initial decision to like another person. To find out what college freshmen looked for in choosing dates, Elaine Walster and her colleagues led students to believe they were involved in computer dating. Personality, attitudinal, and intellectual data were obtained from the students, and their physical attractiveness was assessed by showing their photographs to a panel of college sophomores. Students were *not* matched according to personal preference as they believed, but were instead randomly assigned blind dates for the "computer" dance. During intermission, students were asked how much they liked their dates, how satisfied they were with the pairing, and if they anticipated pursuing future dates with the same partner.

Interview data indicated that the physical attractiveness of the date was the only factor significantly related to liking and to anticipating future dates with the other. Neither personality nor intelligence proved to be an influential factor in determining who was attracted to whom.

But are we willing to admit that beauty and good looks are what we look for most in judging the attractiveness of another person? Is there a difference between what people say they look for and what they actually do look for? When asked to list characteristics they consider important in determining whether they will like another person, male and female college students generally rank good looks as a relatively unimportant quality. Sincerity, honesty, stability, intelligence, and a variety of personality and character traits are given high ranks.

Sample Computer Dating Questionnaire

A. All of the following information in this section will be held in strictest confidence. Check all that apply or that you are in agreement with.

1. My education is:
   ____ grade school
   ____ some high school
   ____ high school graduate
   ____ some college
   ____ college graduate
2. My date's education should be:
   ____ about my own
   ____ doesn't matter
3. My personal appearance is:
   ____ attractive
   ____ somewhat attractive
   ____ plain
4. To me, physical appearance is:
   ____ very important
   ____ somewhat important
   ____ unimportant
5. I participate in sports:
   ____ actively
   ____ somewhat actively
   ____ occasionally
   ____ never

B. Check the one word from each pair that MORE NEARLY describes you personally.

____ jealous	____ trusting
____ read often	____ read seldom
____ pessimist	____ optimist
____ participant	____ observer
____ prone to habit	____ changeable
____ ambitious	____ contented
____ romantic	____ realistic
____ thrifty	____ generous
____ adventurous	____ cautious
____ humorous	____ serious
____ impulsive	____ level-headed
____ talkative	____ quiet
____ punctual	____ often late
____ well-informed	____ uninterested
____ diplomatic	____ direct
____ outgoing	____ reserved
____ imaginative	____ unimaginative
____ affectionate	____ unaffectionate
____ joiner	____ loner

Competence Counts

Physical attractiveness is not the only factor affecting liking and likability. Researchers have discovered that competent persons are considered more likable than less competent persons. Subjects of a study were asked to listen to tapes of college students "trying out" for the television show, *College Quiz Bowl*. One group listened to a student, who was described as highly competent, answer almost all the difficult questions posed. The second group listened to a student who was described as average. He answered only 30 percent of the questions successfully. After hearing the tapes, the two students were rated in terms of likability. The highly competent person was liked significantly more than was the average person.

The same study was conducted again; this time both students were highly competent, but one blundered while the other didn't. It was found that competent people who occasionally made mistakes were considered even more likable than competent people who never blundered. People may respect competence, but it helps if the competent person seems as human as the rest of us.

In choosing a date, college students were found to look for physical attractiveness and competence, but they also ranked as important such qualities as sincerity, honesty, stability, and intelligence.

CATHY

Like Attracts Like

Although there is a significant relationship between competence, physical attractiveness, and liking, there is also evidence that "like attracts like." There is a tendency for people to like, befriend, date and ultimately marry individuals whom they consider their equals. This tendency is called the **matching phenomenon.**

Social psychologist B. I. Murstein used a five-point scale to obtain physical attractiveness ratings for each partner in ninety-nine couples who were either dating steadily or engaged. Raters did not know who was paired with whom. The researcher also obtained attractiveness ratings upon a control group of ninety-nine couples who had been randomly paired. Prematched couples were rated as being significantly more alike in attractiveness than the randomly assigned pairs. There is also much evidence to suggest that persons who like each other and ultimately establish long-term relationships tend to share similar backgrounds, socioeconomic status, religion, education, attitudes, values, and beliefs. For example, a man who likes to travel is unlikely to have much in common with a woman who likes to stay at home. A woman who values prestige may not be happy with a man who has a low-paying job. A feminist probably will not get along with a man who believes "a woman's place is in the home."

But Opposites Attract Too

Like almost all rules, the rule that "like attracts like" has a rather important exception. This exception is labeled **need complementarity,** which is, simply, a fulfilling of each other's needs: if you have something I need, and I have something you need, we will probably get

It's Your Turn

Is there a difference in what males and females look for in the people they choose to date? *It's Your Turn* to speculate. Men, write two paragraphs, one entitled, "What Males Look for in Female Companions" and "What I Think Females Look for in Male Companions." Women, your paragraphs are entitled, "What Females Look for in Male Companions" and "What I Think Males Look for in Female Companions." Compare the paragraphs. What differences do you notice?

along quite well. For example, if I have a need to be protected and you have a need to be protective, we have the basis for a liking relationship. Both parties to the interaction will derive some satisfaction from the experience.

To the extent that complementary needs remain unchanged, interpersonal attraction should remain relatively constant and may even increase. However, if the needs of one individual change and the needs of the other do not, their needs would no longer be complementary or mutually satisfying. If I no longer need to be protected and you continue to need to be protective, the liking relationship will probably suffer.

Nearness Counts

It has been found that **proximity** or nearness promotes liking. The idea is that the more people see each other, the more they will like each other.

In 1973, three psychologists did a study in which they tested the proximity principle using unacquainted female subjects who were shifted from one booth to another under the pretense of tasting various kinds of liquids. The shifting of subjects resulted in each being exposed a different number of times to five other women. Following the tasting session, each subject was asked to tell how much she liked each of the five women with whom she had been in contact. Results indicated increased liking came with increased contact.

But suppose you were thrown into repeated contact with someone whose values and attitudes were quite different from yours. Wouldn't proximity promote disliking or neutrality rather than liking? In one study, college students who held widely dissimilar beliefs, attitudes, and values were paired as roommates. In almost all cases, regardless of dissimilarity, proximity proved to be the overpowering factor in determining interpersonal attraction. Though they were free to make friends with anyone in the dormitory, roommates liked each other the most.

Through repeated contact, we are exposed to a wide range of personality factors. As we get to know each other better, communication progresses. Perhaps this contact is what is more influential than beliefs, attitudes, or values. Many of us make good friends in school or at work simply because we are with these colleagues every day, even though our background and interests may be quite dissimilar. Likewise, friends who are separated for extended periods of time gradually become less attached or attracted to each other.

Obstacles to Interpersonal Contact

None of the factors we have discussed mean very much without a look at the personal qualities of the individual. Is he or she outgoing, friendly, trusting, and approachable? Or withdrawn, fearful, and shy?

For a number of reasons some people keep others at a distance. Proximity makes them uneasy or self-conscious. Shyness is often a barrier to having good relationships with other people. Typically, the shy person is someone who wants to join in, to share personal intimacies, to feel comfortable about being with others, but somehow is inhibited from doing so. Often this is because he or she has low self-esteem. Such individuals frequently become tongue-tied when they try to speak. They blush if others become friendly or intimate with them. The social exchange is seen as an emotional threat—not an opportunity. The shy person backs away from the encounter for self-protection.

Of course, there are positive aspects to shyness. Some people simply might prefer their own company to that of others. But the person who likes to be alone can pay a high price for such privacy. When he or she does need contact with others, it may not be there. It takes two to relate.

Although we tend to assume most people have the appropriate social skills necessary for relating to others, there are many who do not. A large number of people have not learned the "nuts and bolts" of social interaction. They must be taught basic social skills essential for starting conversations, keeping them going, and ending them. They need to learn how to make eye contact and to be attentive listeners; these are skills that can be acquired. Without these skills, the person with the motivation to relate ends up either ignoring others or being ignored.

There are a handful of clinics that help people overcome these problems. Clients are taught how to think more positively about themselves. Assertiveness training is offered. Clients role play real-life situations that create high anxiety for them. Experience shows that confronting situations openly helps build confidence, and rehearsing one's own role in advance makes this easier.

Section Review

1. How does physical appearance affect one's choice of companions?
2. Describe the college roommate experiment testing proximity's effect on liking.
3. How does shyness affect a person's need for human contact?

C L O S E ———— U P

Are You Shy?

Below are twenty-eight items from the Social Avoidance and Distress (SAD) scale. By answering true or false to each statement, you can tell whether you have a tendency to be at ease or shy in various social situations.

1. I feel relaxed even in unfamiliar social situations.
2. I try to avoid situations which force me to be very sociable.
3. It is easy for me to relax when I am with strangers.
4. I have no particular desire to avoid people.
5. I often find social occasions upsetting.
6. I usually feel calm and comfortable at social occasions.
7. I am usually at ease when talking to someone of the opposite sex.
8. I try to avoid talking to people unless I know them well.
9. If the chance comes to meet new people, I often take it.

10. I often feel nervous or tense in casual get-togethers in which both sexes are present.
11. I am usually nervous with people unless I know them well.
12. I usually feel relaxed when I am with a group of people.
13. I often want to get away from people.
14. I usually feel uncomfortable when I am in a group of people I don't know.
15. I usually feel relaxed when I meet someone for the first time.
16. Being introduced to people makes me tense and nervous.
17. Even though a room is full of strangers, I may enter it anyway.
18. I would avoid walking up and joining a large group of people.
19. When my superiors want to talk with me, I talk willingly.
20. I often feel on edge when I am with a group of people.
21. I tend to withdraw from people.
22. I don't mind talking to people at parties or social gatherings.
23. I am seldom at ease in a large group of people.
24. I often think up excuses in order to avoid social engagements.
25. I sometimes take the responsibility for introducing people to each other.
26. I try to avoid formal social occasions.
27. I usually go to whatever social engagements I have.
28. I find it easy to relax with other people.

A shy person would probably answer "false" to items 1,3,4,6,7,9,12,15,17,22,25,27, and 28 and "true" to items 2,5,8,10,11,13,14,16,18,19,20,21,23,24, and 26.

4. This Thing Called Love

It would be nice to begin our discussion of love with an accepted definition. Unfortunately, we can't; no such definition exists. Because it is an extremely general concept encompassing many kinds of interpersonal relationships, love is very difficult to define. The love that a parent feels for a child is not the love felt by brothers and sisters for each other or for their parents; nor is it the same as that experienced by husband and wife. In quite another way, we love ourselves. In still another sense, we "fall in love" with someone with whom we have had no previous relationship, perhaps "at first sight." We speak of "spiritual love" and "sexual love." We "love" certain kinds of food. The term is used so often and in so many contexts that it has almost ceased to have meaning.

In the past, researchers focused little attention upon love as a psychological phenomenon. One reason for this lack of research may be that love traditionally has been thought of as synonymous with sex, which until recently, was considered taboo as a research topic. Another reason may be that people prefer to think of love as being impossible to explain. They are comfortable that its mysteries reside outside the science of psychology. However, psychologists have begun to investigate love.

In his book *Liking and Loving,* social psychologist Zick Rubin cites the following definitions of love: "Love is the active concern for the life and growth of that which we love," and "When the satisfaction or the security of another person becomes as significant to one as is one's own satisfaction or security then the state of love exists."

Learning to Love

Whatever the definition, most psychologists agree that the ability to love, to care for others, and to engage in mature sexual behavior is a product of learning that begins during infancy. As you saw in the first section, we need to be loved and are born with the capacity to love, but love has to be learned.

You will recall from the Harlows' experiments, monkeys that were deprived of affection during infancy showed acutely disturbed behavior as adults and frequently lacked the inclination or ability to mate. Females proved to be rejecting and unsuitable mothers.

Cases of child abuse and neglect illustrate this point. Research has shown that abusive and unloving parents are more than likely the products of loveless and abused childhoods themselves. Prison studies reveal that a high percentage of criminals were physically abused or neglected as children. Being deprived of loving experiences at critical points in childhood can produce unhealthy behavior in later life. People learn to love. Love doesn't just happen. It does not appear to be an innate or inborn characteristic. The ability to love must be taught and is acquired within a social context. It is a skill upon which other relationships build.

The Characteristics of Loving

Assuming that love has been learned at an early age, mature love later in life is composed of four components, according to psychologist D. A. Prescott.

1. A person who loves has *empathy* for the loved one. That person understands and even feels the feelings the other experiences. Experiences are shared intimately.

2. A person who loves is *deeply concerned for the welfare* and happiness of the loved one. This concern is so deep that it enters into the way a person patterns his or her daily existence. It affects how that person makes decisions and plans for the future.

3. A person who loves is not merely concerned about the loved one's welfare, but does something about it. The person who loves *finds pleasure in actively working for the other's welfare.* Time and money are given freely toward this end.

4. A person who loves *allows the loved one the freedom and independence* to chart his or her own course in life. A person who loves is not possessive, but fully accepts the other's unique individuality. The loved one is free to act and become whatever he or she wants to become.

These characteristics of love apply equally well to parent-child relationships, to friendships between old friends, and to long-term partnerships between lovers.

Falling in Love

The phrase "falling in love" seems to be reserved for the romantic, passionate kind of love that occurs between lovers. For example, you do not fall in love with your mother or with a brother or sister though you may love them. According to psychologists E. Walster and G. K. Walster, passionate love is being completely obsessed by another person. It happens suddenly. When passionate love strikes, it is generally accompanied by sexual excitement and physical arousal.

Initially, the love-struck person is ruled more by the heart rather than the head. Images and fantasies about the other will not leave the mind of the love-struck as much as he or she may try to push them aside. There is an addictive quality about being passionately in love, and sometimes even a sense of feeling physically ill.

In fact, passionate love seems curiously composed of conflicting emotions. For example, if we are truly in love, why do we inflict on ourselves the pain and agony of jealousy? Why do some people invariably fall in love with those who are unattainable or who repeatedly reject them? Why do we torture ourselves inventing and living in fantasies that probably will never come true? Researchers have found that pleasure and pain seem strangely interwoven in the falling in love process. For example, it was discovered that any experience that evokes fear or apprehension tends to draw people closer together, and in doing so, arouses feelings that can be interpreted as love. The thrill and gripping excitement of a roller coaster ride at an amusement park might be just the physical arousal needed to spark passionate feelings. Studies also have shown that when a love-struck person encounters opposition to his or her chosen romantic partner from family or friends this often tends to heighten arousal.

Given the right companion, the arousal we feel on a roller coaster can be perceived as fear—or it can be interpreted as a completely different emotion.

Falling in love seems to be a magical experience. Certainly poets and writers have proclaimed it for centuries. And yet it lasts only a short time. Often it burns out, leaving the once love-struck person wondering how and why it all happened. Or if the relationship prospers, love changes from a passionate love to a compassionate love and takes on the characteristics described by Prescott. Communication matures beyond mutuality. Loved ones can become so attuned to each other that communication can take place often without words at all.

The Joy of Intimacy

Liking, loving, and sexual relationships form the human connection that expands the boundaries of self. The person who does not reach out for the hand of another, or whose extended hand is not grasped by another, is cut adrift. The isolated individual may become lonely or depressed. But the person whose life includes love and intimacy is a person whose life is enriched.

What form does our sexuality take? Sociologist J. H. Gagnon believes ". . . people become sexual in the same way they become everything else. Without much reflection, they pick up directions from their social environment. They acquire and assemble meanings, skills, and values from the people around them. Their critical choices are often made by going along and drifting. People learn when they are quite young a few of the things that they are expected to be, and continue slowly [to define] who they are and ought to be throughout childhood, adolescence, and adulthood."

Sexuality has been the subject of much controversy over the years. It was not too long ago that marriage manuals described sexual behavior as "a dangerous evil which, unfortunately, is necessary for the perpetuation of the species." It is not difficult to imagine the psychological impact—the guilt, shame, and fear—of such repression.

However, things have changed somewhat since then. In marriage today, sex is seen as a vital, fulfilling part of the loving bond formed by two people. There is less emphasis now on defining what is normal, socially acceptable, sexual behavior than on focusing on the positive aspects of a mutually satisfying sexual relationship between consenting, caring adults.

To promote a positive outlook on our own sexuality, we need to remember that sex is more than just a set of learned techniques, of pleasurable sensations. We need to accept our own body and the responsibility for someone else's. We must be willing to give and receive. But it is not enough to know what to do physically. For many, the most satisfactory sexual relationship takes place within a loving, caring relationship. If we want sex to reach its potential as a fulfilling human experience, we need to develop attitudes of trust and sharing. Sex strips us of our protective masks. It opens up our vulnerability. That is why it can be so frightening if misused and so glorious if filled with assurances of love and respect.

Section Review

1. How is love learned?
2. According to psychologist J. W. Prescott, what are the components of love?
3. Describe how passionate love changes into compassionate love.
4. Describe Gagnon's view of the form our sexuality takes.

Chapter 14 Review

Section Summaries

1. Contact with Others

Human beings have conflicting needs for human contact and for independence. Relationships with others are influenced by the primary bond between parent and child. Privacy provides a sense of personal autonomy, emotional release, opportunities for self-evaluation, and limited and protected communication. Our use of space can be divided into intimate distance, personal distance, social distance, and public distance. People use territoriality to defend their personal space. Ironically, privacy increases the chance that people will seek social interaction.

2. The Languages of Communication

Body language can be used to maintain privacy or encourage social interaction. When two people have established a close bond, their body language will be in congruence. In double messages, we tend to believe the body language, although such messages can confuse children and cause lasting anxiety. Verbal communication between friends is thought to follow a progression of awareness, surface contact, and mutuality.

3. Interpersonal Attraction

Physical appearance is a factor in our initial decision to like another person. We also like highly competent people who make occasional mistakes. The matching phenomenon refers to the fact that people tend to marry people whom they consider their equals. Needs complementarity refers to that fact that we tend to choose mates who fulfill our needs. Proximity also promotes liking, but shyness can be an obstacle to interpersonal contact.

4. This Thing Called Love

Rubin defines love as "the active concern for life and growth of that which we love." Most psychologists agree that the ability to love is learned, beginning in infancy. Mature love is made up of empathy, deep concern for the loved one's welfare, pleasure in actively working for the other's welfare, and an attitude that allows the loved one freedom and independence. Falling in love is generally accompanied by sexual excitement and physical arousal. In marriage today, sex is seen as a vital part of the loving bond between two people.

Psychology Skill Activities

1. For the next week, keep a diary of your need for privacy. Assess *when* you need privacy, *why* you need it, *how* you seek it, and *what* your reactions are when you are denied it.   **easy**

2. Create a body language dictionary. Form small groups, each of which is responsible for describing and defining as many gestures as possible about one area of the body. Pool your groups' results into an alphabetical dictionary.   **challenging**

Testing for Understanding

Knowing Key Terms

Define these terms in your own words.

Section 1

privacy
intimate distance
personal distance
social distance
public distance
territoriality

Section 2

body language
congruence
double message
awareness
surface contact
mutuality

Section 3

matching phenomenon
need complementarity
proximity

Reviewing Main Ideas

Section 1

1. How is the need for human contact related to the need for privacy?

2. Describe the four types of distances people use in relating to others.

Section 2

1. What are some uses of body language?

2. How are body language and spoken language related?

3. What are the stages of verbal communication that people go through in forming friendships?

Section 3

1. What are some of the factors we weigh in choosing companions?

2. What factors act as obstacles to making social contact?

Section 4

1. Where does the ability to love come from?

2. What are some of the characteristics of loving?

3. How do frightening experiences affect the chance that people will fall in love?

Thinking Critically

1. *Drawing Conclusions.* How does the way you see yourself affect body language?   **easy**

2. *Making Inferences.* How would you explain the fact that in our country billions of dollars are spent each year on cosmetics and clothing?   **challenging**

Demonstrating Psychology Skills

Write a two-page guide for people your age called "How to Be Liked." The guide should be based on both the research mentioned in this chapter and your own experiences.

Social Behavior

Psychologists often ask difficult questions about people's social behavior. For example, would you give an electric shock to a stranger? Would you give someone a shock so intense that it could cause harm to the person? Would you do this under any circumstances? Suppose someone important asked you to do it. Would you?

Or—would you say something you didn't believe? Would you change your opinion about a situation, if asked to? Would you change your views if they were different from those of everyone else in a group? Would you give an opinion even if you were not sure of it?

Consider these questions: Would you tell a stranger something that was not true? Would you change your opinion about something if paid to do so? Would you lie to a stranger if you were paid to do it? How uncomfortable would this make you feel?

These difficult, but fascinating, questions have been asked by social psychologists. Many interesting answers have been discovered through research and experimentation.

Social psychology is the study of how people influence each other. How individuals affect groups and how groups affect individuals are both matters of concern in social psychology. First, social psychologists look at the behavior of people in groups. They study how people's attitudes and actions are shaped by face-to-face contact with others. Secondly, they look at the more remote influences in society. These include books and magazines, movies and television, social customs, and other media events that try to persuade us to change our minds about something. Finally, they pay special attention to the psychological bases of social conflict. Such things such as aggression, war, crime, and racism are studied in an effort to develop better relationships among people. In this chapter we will be concerned with the relatively less personal relationships that people have in the social community.

We all know that social influence can take many forms. Advertisers use psychology, by flattering or frightening us, to persuade us to buy their products. Public speakers play on our emotions to convince us that what they are saying is important. We observe many customs and roles because it is the approved thing to do. We adopt certain attitudes because the mass media are powerful forces in manipulating opinion. Authority, attitude formation, group affiliation, conformity, persuasion, and conflict are some of the topics that make up the field of social psychology. Social psychologists work to understand the more complex systems of the larger, less controllable world where things appear to happen naturally.

People join groups for various reasons. For most of the members of the Apollo Chorus, a nonprofessional commmunity-chorus in Chicago, the reason they joined their group is because they love music and singing. The Apollo Chorus, shown here performing Handel's *Messiah*, has been entertaining Chicago-area audiences since 1872.

1. Behavior of Groups

There are many reasons why people affiliate, or join, with others in groups. We are members of a family group by birth or adoption. We join clubs because we like to sing, ski, hike, or participate in some other activity a group offers. If you go to a crowded football game, you have a kind of fun you could not have by yourself. People tend to join groups when danger threatens, because in associating with others they feel more secure. Also, it is only by joining with others and working together that people can achieve certain goals, such as persuading their senator to support a certain bill or raising money for their senior class.

Reasons for group formation generally fall into three categories—*influence, achievement,* and *affiliation.* People generally want to be able to influence others. They also want some control over the things that happen to them. People need a sense of achievement. Having others to compare themselves with gives validity to the standards by which they measure themselves. Being accepted helps people to feel successful and have a sense of accomplishment. Finally, people need friends. They need to affiliate with others. In many cases, belonging to a group is an efficient way of achieving some basic human goals.

Groups are not random collections of people. Groups function as distinct entities, each with its own personality, objectives, and ways of acting. When you join a group, your individual behavior can be affected in four ways:

1. *The group's goal* can become important. You are influenced to share the objective of the group. Even though holding this objective may have been the principal reason you joined, your reason will be strengthened when you take part in the group's activities designed to achieve that goal.

2. *Group pressure* works on you. You are influenced to be a team player—and possibly to go along with collective actions that you might not go along with if you were alone.

3. *The group identity* becomes an influence. You tend to behave as the people do in the group. In your actions and appearance you tend to resemble the others in your group.

4. *Group perceptions* affect your thinking. You may come to believe something that you might otherwise disagree with, because the majority of the group sees it this way. You often trust the group's judgment more than your own.

Group Dynamics

Because groups are not simply collections of people, we know that they exist for a purpose. To achieve this purpose, each member contributes something to the functioning of the group. This is true whether the group is a family, a class in psychology, an athletic team, or a hiking club. You know how this works from your own experience in organizations. The various members usually offer ideas, discuss alternatives, and divide up the tasks. Members are expected to participate in carrying out the group's purpose. This process has been called **group dynamics**, because a new, collective behavior comes from a series of individual interactions.

The purpose for which a group is organized, its type of leadership, the composition of its membership, the social situation, and the methods used to exchange information all affect the *dynamics* of a particular group.

Reasoned evaluation. When a group exists to solve a specific problem or to determine what action to take in a situation, suggestions from the various members become valuable in arriving at a final decision. Everyone's ideas are discussed and evaluated, more or less on their merits. By combining the strengths of the individual members, the group as a whole has a better idea of what its options are. Essentially, this is what happens, or is supposed to happen, in committee meetings. Although the chairperson may guide the discussion, the process of decision making is a collective one. If two heads are better than one, then four heads should be better than two.

Group problem solving seems to be most effective when there is a correct solution, or when a variety of skills can be brought to bear on a single problem. However, if creative thinking is called for instead of analytical thinking, individuals often do better than the group. Apparently, group unity tends to stifle creative thinking and stops some individuals from expressing their best judgment.

Case Study

Group Responses to AIDS

Dateline Florida: After being kept out of school for a year, three young brothers with AIDS win a court order allowing them to return to school. The first day of school, more than half their classmates are kept at home. The school receives bomb threats. Hundreds attend a "Citizens against AIDS" rally. While the family is away, a fire bomb guts their house.

Dateline Illinois: Parents meet with their child's principal and teacher to find out if AIDS will bar the child from school. The answer is no. Without releasing the child's name, school officials mail a package of pamphlets and articles about AIDS to every household. A hot line is set up and counseling is offered to staff members. The results: almost total community support for the school.

Dateline Massachusetts: A popular eighth-grader discovers he has AIDS. After talking to the boy's doctor, the superintendent decides to let the boy attend school. When the news reaches the local media, one family starts a petition, and others boycott the school. Only thirty-four people sign the petition, however, and the parents eventually give up the boycott. By the time the boy dies, mothers have held a raffle that raises $10,000. The boy's father credits the children with teaching the parents not to fear.

The same problem, three different reactions. How can these differences be explained? No one can be sure, but psychological research can provide some clues.

One clue can be found in research into the effects of anonymity. Researchers have shown that people are more likely to be aggressive when they or their victims are anonymous. This might have been the case for the boys in Florida, who had been away from school for a year. In contrast, the boy in Massachusetts was very well-known.

A second clue might come from research that shows that cognitive (thinking) processes can reduce fear. In Illinois, for example, school officials organized an intensive information campaign.

A third clue might come from leadership studies. In Illinois, school officials took the lead in support of the child with AIDS. In Massachusetts, classmates filled the same role.

It's Your Turn

As we have seen, people are social creatures. They interact in groups of all types. Now *It's Your Turn*. List the groups you belong to. For each, answer: Why do you belong? What role do you play? What type of leadership pattern is evident?

Risk taking. You would think that group decisions would be more moderate than individual decisions, extreme positions having been thrown out in favor of group agreement. Curiously, this is not always what happens. In many instances, people are willing to take greater risks when acting with a group than they would by themselves. This is called the *risky shift*. The degree of risk taking for the group as a whole is increased when others share the consequences, and when responsibility for the act is spread out among the entire group. We see this in committees that take a strong stand on an issue when individual members would be reluctant to take that stand alone.

Social psychologist Irving L. Janis labeled this tendency "groupthink," and expressed the belief that it was responsible for such historical occurrences as the lack of preparedness of the United States at Pearl Harbor, the Bay of Pigs Cuban invasion, and the involvement in Vietnam. By shifting responsibility to the group, the individuals making the decisions lessened their personal responsibility for the consequences. Being a "good" team player became more important than being a "smart" one.

Can the dangers of "groupthink" be lessened? Janis recommends procedures that force individuals to evaluate their own and others' ideas. He advocates feedback from *outside* the group, and counsels group members to analyze and role play the opposition's reactions and strategies.

Do groups always take bigger risks than the individuals in the group would take? For example, would a group of bettors, pooling their money, play longer odds than any one of them might individually? The risky shift hypothesis would predict so. But in fact, it seems to depend upon how much risk is involved for each individual, personally. If the tangible, potential loss is relatively high per member, there is a tendency for groups to take a more cautious position. The individual who is tempted to "go for broke" is held back by the others in the interest of reducing risk for the group.

Social status. Our jury system is based on the idea that if two heads are better than one then twelve heads will be better yet. Each jury member is assumed to be qualified to weigh evidence and speak up for his or her interpretation of it. Each argues in favor of a particular verdict, which then must be unanimous.

In actual practice, jury behavior is not this simple. Jurors do not treat each other as equals. Some members of a jury may be more persuasive than others, and some may have a better developed sense of justice. Apart from this, a member may be more impressed by *who* the other juror is than by *what* he or she says. In a study based on forty-nine mock jury trials, it was found that the social status of the juror was a strong factor in influencing other jurors, and in being influenced by them. Rightly or wrongly, people tend to attribute expertise to the more economically successful in our society.

Leading and Following

If twelve heads are better than two, are a hundred or two hundred heads better than twelve? There is a practical limit to the number of people who can take an active part in making a decision. As groups increase in size, the potential for group interaction decreases, and the role of the leader becomes more important. In effect, the group agrees with the decisions of those who have leadership in the group. What qualities does a group look for in its leaders?

Leaders are usually popular with the group. They know how to get along with people and make friends. They usually demonstrate an ability to take charge, show signs of good judgment, and are reasonably intelligent. Ambition is also present. Good leaders generally want to lead, and often excel at it. They take the first step in achieving the group's goals.

Studies show that a juror's social status is a strong factor in influencing the opinions of other members of the jury.

Chairman Mao Tse-tung, leader of the People's Republic of China from its beginnings in 1949 until his death in 1976, had an *autocratic* style of leadership.

In the People's Republic of China, the government encourages artists who support the government's goals. In Tsao Yu-tung's painting entitled *Night Battle*, shown at right, enthusiastic workers labor late into the night to repair a dam. Everyone is smiling and energetic, despite the lateness of the hour and difficulty of the work. Banners supporting the workers and the revolution appear in the background. The message of the painting is clear: Obey your leaders; work long and cheerfully for the revolution and you will have the happiness and peace of mind these workers enjoy.

Many social psychologists believe that leadership power in a group grows out of one or more of five other sources of power. The five are: **expert power**—being seen as knowledgeable in an area of group concern; **referent power**—being liked by the group; **legitimate power**—holding an official position that carries power; **reward power**—being able to give others in the group what they want; and **coercive power**—being able to punish others in the group. A school principal, for example, sometimes has power from all of these sources. The principal may be an expert in education, and be liked and respected by teachers and students. At the same time, the principal has power that is officially granted, as well as the ability to give rewards, such as recommendations and awards, and punishments, such as suspension.

Leadership Styles and Group Behavior

Another question social psychologists have asked is how a particular leader's style influences the followers' general effectiveness and behavior. There are basically three leadership styles. The **autocratic** leader acts generally as a dictator. Everything the group does is decided by the leader. The **democratic** leaders allow everyone to exert some influence on the group. They encourage group decision making, under their guidance. The **laissez-faire** leaders allow members of the group to do as they please. Little influence is exerted by this type of leader.

An *authoritarian* style usually encourages members to depend on the leader. It does not encourage individuality among the followers. The people in these groups are usually submissive. They do what the leader says. Yet, at the same time, they are less happy than members of other types of groups. They are more hostile toward the leader, each other, and outsiders.

A *democratic* style promotes personal satisfaction and efficiency. Motivation and interest are generally stronger in democratic groups than in other style groups, and originality is greater. In addition, more group-mindedness and friendliness are often found.

A *laissez-faire* atmosphere provides more "freedom" than the other two styles, but little direction. Initiative may be low in undertaking new activities. Less work, and poorer work, is often done by members of laissez-faire groups. Democracy, despite some drawbacks, appears to offer the best leadership system for combining efficient group work and individual happiness.

An important source of the Rev. Dr. Martin Luther King, Jr.'s power as a leader (left) was *referent power*. He was popular with the group he was leading, Americans who believed in a nonviolent solution to the nation's racial problems. Most democratically elected leaders, like President Franklin Roosevelt (right), owe their rise to leadership positions in part to referent power. Once in office, elected leaders exercise *legitimate power*, because they hold a powerful official position. Soviet leader Joseph Stalin (middle) had legitimate power as head of the Soviet communist party, but he also held *reward power* and *coercive power*.

Section Review

1. Discuss three reasons why people join groups.
2. Give an example of group dynamics—collective behavior of individuals in a group.
3. Define the five sources of power for the leader of a group.

In considering leadership and group dynamics, you have seen how individuals affect the behavior of groups. It is also true that groups affect individual behavior. Let's take a look at why all of us find it useful, at times, to conform to what others do, and to believe what others say.

The Power of Social Norms

The most powerful forces that influence conformity are the laws, rules, standards, and customs built into our particular society. These expected standards of conduct are called **social norms**. But norms are more than a means of narrowing behavior to a set of prescribed rules. They also allow us to expand behavior within a general framework. Norms allow each person in society to anticipate how others will enter a social situation, for example, what they will wear. Social norms give us a range of behaviors others are likely to accept from us without ridicule or rejection. Norms suggest possibilities for action, as well as limits.

Norms influence us from early childhood. They are part of the *socialization* process. We learn to wait our turn in line, to obey the law, to speak quietly in the library, to offer our seats to elderly people on the bus, and to listen while the teacher speaks. A person who travels to many countries becomes keenly aware that certain norms are limited to particular cultures. Male friends in France frequently greet each other with a kiss on the cheek; American men shake hands. In Turkey, a dinner guest compliments the host by belching after the meal; in most other countries belching publicly is considered rude.

Power of Persuasion

One of the questions that you were asked at the beginning of this chapter is, "Would you give a harmful electric shock to a stranger?" People's answers to this question can often be affected by social persuasion, and by the influence of authority.

In 1965, social psychologist Stanley Milgram, then at Yale University, conducted an experiment to get an answer to this question. The experiment was part of a study on obedience to authority. Milgram wanted to know just how far a person would go in punishing another person with electric shocks, if ordered to keep on giving the punishment. His subjects, all volunteer adult males, included both Yale students and a wide cross section of other men, including unskilled workers, white-collar workers, and professional workers. Each subject was paid to take part in the hour-long experiment.

The subjects were told that the purpose of the study was to investigate the effect of punishment on memory. Each volunteer was to be a "teacher" whose task would be to give punishment, in the form of an electric shock, to a "learner" whenever the learner made a mistake on a memory test. The learner, "Mr. Wallace," was a pleasant, mild-mannered man about fifty years old—not the kind of person you'd go out of your way to punish. Before "Mr. Wallace" was strapped into an "electric chair" in an adjoining room, each subject-teacher was given a sample shock of 45 volts, enough to make it clear that the shocks really hurt. The volunteer, who had thirty marked switches in front of him, was then directed to start testing the learner. If a wrong answer was given, the teacher gave the learner a "Slight Shock" (15 volts). The subject was commanded to increase the shock to the next level each time the learner made an error or failed to respond, up to a maximum level, labeled "Danger: Severe Shock" (450 volts). Since the learner made many errors, the level of punishment rose quickly.

Stop a moment and decide how far you might go. Where do you think Milgram's average subject stopped?

Before we go on to the answer, let's see how the experiment was actually designed. You've probably guessed that the study was set up so that no one was actually hurt. "Mr. Wallace" was a partner in the experiment. He didn't receive any shock, in spite of the reading on the shock generator. However, the "teacher" heard, over an intercom, a tape recording in which the learner was reacting dramatically. At 75 volts he began to moan and grunt. At 150 volts he demanded to be released from the experiment. At 180 volts he beat on the wall and cried that he could not stand the pain. At 300 volts he insisted that he would no longer take part in the experiment and must be freed. Over the last series of trials he failed to respond at all. Could he have passed out or had a heart attack?

Ironically, if the "learner" was not really suffering, the "teachers" certainly were. Most of them complained loudly and protested that they could not go on with their job. When this happened, the experimenter replied, "Teacher, you have no other choice; you must go on." Some subjects urged the learner to get the answers right so they would not have to continue shocking him. Some insisted that the experimenter accept responsibility for any harm to the "learner." In spite of their conflicts, however, they went on. The majority protested, *but they did not disobey*. Nearly two-thirds of them (62 percent) went all the way, obeying orders and delivering the maximum 450 volts. The average voltage administered by everyone who took part was nearly 370 volts. Was this close to your prediction? Probably not.

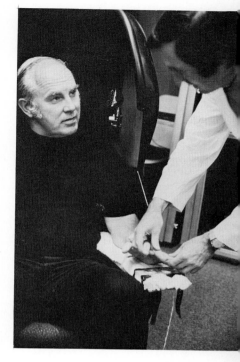

Psychologist Stanley Milgram prepares the "victim" in his experiment on obedience to authority.

See **Exercise 8, Determining Variability and Relatedness,** pages 490-492 of the *Psychology Skills Handbook,* for more information about how to interpret data obtained in Stanley Milgram's experiment.

Meaning of Milgram's Work

Do Milgram's findings imply that the majority of these subjects were mean or sadistic? On the contrary, personality tests given to the subjects did not reveal any traits that were different in those who obeyed and those who refused. The research demonstrates that social forces in the environment in which we live, work, and play have power to overwhelm individual personality, and even morality.

Three basic reasons can be cited for the subjects' behavior. First, many of the subjects *projected* the blame for their actions onto others. They blamed the authority figure, saying it was the experimenter's fault for making them continue. They also said it was the "learner's" fault for answering the questions incorrectly. Secondly, many subjects *dehumanized* the learner. They forgot he was a real person, and began to see him as an object in the next room. Finally, many subjects became so *absorbed* in the experiment that they virtually lost touch with reality. They were so caught up in the process, they no longer realized what they were actually doing. Such situational control of behavior has been shown in other studies, as well.

The level of obedience was shown to vary with certain features of the situation. It went down when authority—the experimenter—was farther away from the "teacher/shocker." Compliance was also reduced when a subject observed another person refusing to follow the destructive commands.

Real Life Tests of People's Responses

How do these somewhat artificial experiments relate to events in real life? During the Vietnam War, over four hundred civilians were shot by Lieutenant William Calley and his company in the village of My Lai. Investigation later revealed that in the conditions at the time, this atrocity didn't seem to the soldiers much different from standard procedure. The humans seemed like objects, not people, to the soldiers. Cruelties performed by Nazi officers during World War II also suggest that, given the right setting, such as a war or an ideological crusade, and given sufficient authority, some people will gladly "pull the switch" on others. And at a distance, many more people will support such action.

From Milgram's study and others, we may conclude that evil deeds resulting from blind obedience to the commands of authority are not necessarily the product of weak egos or a certain character type. Our responses are shaped by subtle forms of social programming. We are trained to be obedient children, to respect authority, and to oblige a request for a favor. We should make no trouble, complete tasks we

begin, stay where we're told. In Milgram's experiment it was society, not the researcher, who trained the subjects to blindly obey authority. The researcher merely created the setting that would reveal the extreme consequences of earlier social programming.

Where is the dividing line between reasoned compliance and blind obedience? Not all social forces have a destructive or harmful effect on individual behavior. Let's look at more social forces.

What is the dividing line between reasoned compliance and blind obedience to authority? This is a question many Germans must have considered during the Nazi era.

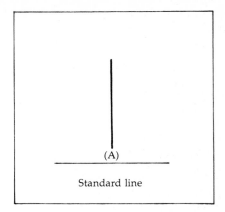

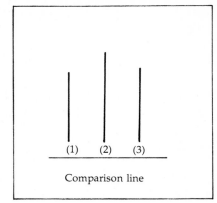

Standard line   Comparison line

The Power of a Majority

Just about everyone develops acceptance of social norms over a period of time. In groups particularly, *if everyone else is doing it*, or sees it a particular way, others tend to agree that there must be something to it. Psychologist Solomon Asch demonstrated this tendency to agree with the majority view in a deceptively simple laboratory experiment. First look at the standard line in the illustration above. Then look at the three comparison lines 1, 2, and 3. Which of the comparison lines is the same length as the standard line?

There's probably no doubt in your mind that line 2 is the same length as the standard line. But would you say this if, before you were asked for your opinion, three other students were asked, and all three declared that line 1 was the same length as the standard line? When Asch performed this experiment with many groups of male college students, he used a number of confederates. These people were all told to give the same wrong answer. A subject who was not told anything answered last. This subject yielded to the consensus of the group, agreeing with the wrong answer, 35 percent of the time.

Why were the subjects unwilling to stick with what their own eyes told them? They were not being rewarded in any direct sense for agreeing, nor punished for disagreeing, with the majority. What seems to have happened is this. The need to be accepted by their peers overcame the subjects' willingness to express their private judgments. In later studies, when subjects were asked to make the comparison in private, rather than in the presence of others, they made few if any errors. Group pressure, apparently, is a powerful force, but only when we are in the presence of the group. Moreover, the group is most likely to cause conforming behavior when it is unanimous. In situations similar

Acceptance has an important influence on conformity. A person who feels part of a group that others are excluded from will tend to accept the opinions of the group in which he or she has won acceptance.

to the Asch experiment, when at least one other confederate rebels from the group view and sees the lines correctly, the subject's tendency to conform is sharply reduced.

Variables Affecting Group Conformity

In the real world, *right* or *wrong* is seldom as clear-cut as the length of a line. Whether we conform or not depends to some extent on a number of factors that make us more, or less, persuasible. For example, if we have made a prior commitment to an opinion or judgment we are less likely to be swayed by the opinion of the group.

Psychologists also look at the kind of person who is being subjected to pressure, and the character of the group. Research shows that individuals with low self-esteem are more easily pressured and more ready to defer to authority than individuals with high self-esteem. And if an individual has little self-confidence for a specific task he or she is more likely to conform to the majority opinion than the individual who, from prior experience, knows better. The makeup of the group also makes a difference. If you're working with experts in a particular field, the chances are you will accept their judgment, as a group, even when it does not agree with your individual judgment.

Group attractiveness also influences conformity. The more desirable the group, the harder you work to gain admittance and the more likely it is that you will comply with its standards. "Members only" is a powerful force for conformity. Acceptance means not only that you belong, but that others are kept out.

Practical Applications

The studies on persuasion and conformity have many important applications in everyday situations. Most people are strongly influenced by authority figures. Many of us are easily persuaded. We often face situations where we conform, or go along with a group.

Situations in which we conform may be ones that an individual faces daily. For example, we have all probably been in a position of going along with a group. Perhaps a group of people whose friendship you value is going on a hiking trip. Even if you are not particularly fond of hiking, you may go along in order to be part of the group. You may even take an active role in planning the trip, or speak enthusiastically about it, to strengthen your position in the group.

Other situations of persuasion and conformity have a broader, societal impact. The recent spread of cult groups and the possible use of brainwashing techniques are examples. Many feel that the increase in cult activities reflects some individuals' increased need to feel a sense of belonging. A cult is a tightly knit group with many norms and values of its own. These values are often in conflict with those of society as a whole. Individuals with low self-esteem may feel more secure in this type of group. People with low self-esteem are also especially susceptible to the methods of persuasion and conformity.

Section Review

1. Explain why Milgram got such "shocking" results to his experiment on obedience to authority.
2. Define "norms."
3. Describe two factors that affect group conformity.

Members of a cult group

3. Being Consistent: Dissonance Theory

Moving on from studying about how groups and individuals influence each other, let's look at what goes on inside us as we change our thinking. What goes on in the mind of an individual who is being influenced? A central factor in determining whether or not people will be influenced is the need for consistency. What they think and how they act must seem to agree, or they are uncomfortable. To explain this tendency to change your thinking so it doesn't seem contradictory, psychologists offer a theory called inconsistency, or **cognitive dissonance.**

Since dissonance theory was first formulated by Leon Festinger in 1957, it has become an important part of social psychology. Hundreds of experiments have been carried out to test its validity. The essence of the theory is easily stated. If you have two conflicting beliefs, you will want to resolve the conflict between them. You will be motivated to take some action.

Because conflicting attitudes make us uncomfortable, we have a strong desire to do a little changing and bring them into line. The term used to describe this adjustment of the conflict is **dissonance reduction.** It is a reframing of your views to cut down the discomfort of having conflicting attitudes about something. Dissonance reduction can be thought of as a kind of self-justification.

Students often use the following line of thinking, for example, when they cheat in schoolwork. Suppose you were to cheat on an exam. You feel guilty about this because you are opposed to cheating on principle. You now hold two conflicting or dissonant beliefs: You have cheated, and you don't like cheating.

Then you learn, with some relief, that others in the class have also cheated. Furthermore, you argue with yourself, no one was injured by your action and, under the circumstances, it was more important to pass the course than to be honest. You can't quite swallow that, so you remind yourself that you are honest most of the time, and that exceptions are permissible now and then. Gradually, you reduce the dissonance and your feelings of guilt.

To resolve dissonance, you must change one of the two things in your mind that conflict—the fact that you've cheated, and your dislike for cheating. Since the cheating itself has already been done and cannot be changed, the belief against cheating must be changed, if only temporarily, if the conflict is to be resolved.

Depending on the situation, the ways people resolve conflict may be classed as either external or internal.

PREVIEW

In this section, read to find out:

1. what cognitive dissonance is.
2. how dissonance is resolved.

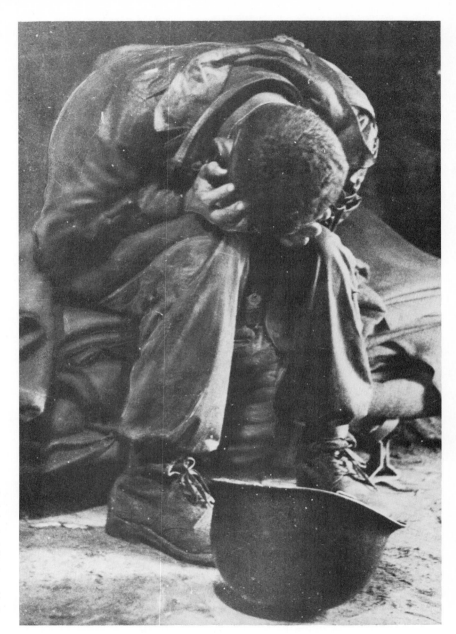

In wartime, soldiers often experience cognitive dissonance because they have to violate firmly held beliefs that it is wrong to take human lives. This dissonance is reduced by the belief that such action is necessary to protect their country, way of life, or loved ones. But the conflict between these important values takes its toll.

External Justification: The Situation Calls for It

Most soldiers in battle can bring themselves to take human life because that is part of their job. They have been ordered to kill, and their discomfort is lessened because the act has been approved by outside authority. Perhaps this is also what happened, at first, to the kidnapped heiress, Patty Hearst. Her captors ordered her to denounce the "establishment." After this, she seemingly came to hold this attitude willingly as she participated in the program of her captors. Resolving a serious conflict is easier when an individual can see no choice offered by the situation. The dissonant act then seems necessary, or at least justifiable. We can assume that the same process was at work in Milgram's obedience experiment. The reluctance of the majority of the "teachers" to deliver severe shocks was overcome, and their dissonance reduced, by three external factors: (1) they had agreed to take part in the experiment; (2) they were paid to do so; and (3) they were ordered to do so. In their minds, the responsibility for the act was shifted to an outside authority.

We find **external justifications** to explain things we say or do that are out of character. "I had too much to drink." "I didn't want to hurt their feelings." "I cheated because everybody else was doing it." By externalizing the causes of a given behavior, we say it's not our fault. But suppose no external reasons are available. How do we resolve the conflict then?

Internal Justification: Doing Is Believing

Suppose you usually do not like to go to dances. But you decide to go to one, and you have problems. People step on your toes, the music is deafening, and you get stuck with the worst dancer on the floor. How do you justify your misery in a situation like this?

After a while you may tell yourself that you *are* having a good time in spite of everything. Or else why would you be there? If you were truly consistent, you would walk out. Instead, you make the best of the situation. Convincing yourself that you're having fun helps reduce the dissonance.

Experiments in changing your mind. Many experiments have shown people's tendency to bring attitudes into line with behavior. One of these experiments answers a question asked at the beginning of this chapter: Would you lie if paid to do so? And if you did, how would you feel?

In the experiment, college men were asked to perform an exceedingly boring task—sorting out small objects, turning screws, and so on. Each student was then asked to lie about the task to another student who was waiting a turn at the experiment. They were asked to say the experiment was fun and enjoyable. Some of them were paid twenty dollars for telling the lie. Others got only one dollar. When the experiment was over, the experimenter asked the men how much they had *really* enjoyed the task. Their answers might surprise you.

Some people found guilty of activities related to the illegal break-in at Democratic campaign headquarters in the Watergate complex during the 1972 presidential campaign gave as a justification for their actions that they hadn't done anything worse than other politicians do, they had just been caught. This is an example of internal justification. At right is the Senate committee set up to investigate the Watergate affair.

Shouldn't those who received a larger reward for telling a fib be more pleased with the task than their underpaid companions? Not at all! After having told the lie, the twenty-dollar subjects readily admitted that the work was dull, which it was. But the one-dollar subjects had changed their minds about the task. After lying about its enjoyability, they rated the work as enjoyable. Because they had little external justification for their lie, in receiving such a small amount of money, the one-dollar subjects had to *reduce* the *dissonance* between their lie and their feeling about the task by **internal justification,** by assuming the attitude, "If I said such a crazy thing for only one dollar, I must have liked the job after all." To resolve the dissonance, they either had to change what they were paid to say—and refuse to cooperate with the experimenter—or they had to change their attitudes. The twenty-dollar group had an external justification for their behavior, so they could say, "I only did it for the money." They did not need to change their real attitude.

Where dissonance is aroused, the less external justification there is, the more the *private* attitude shifts in the direction of the *public* statement or action.

Saying and believing. If doing is believing, so is saying. For example, ordinarily decent people sometimes find themselves performing an act of cruelty. How do they justify it? One method—used widely by

It's Your Turn

Cognitive dissonance is a common experience for people. Perhaps you have been in a situation such as this: You have a close friend that you are fond of. This friend wears clothes that you do not like at all. This creates dissonance or conflict for you. Perhaps you change your opinion of the friend—or your opinion of the clothes. Now *It's Your Turn*. Write an example of a situation of cognitive dissonance that you have experienced. How did you resolve it?

parents who spank their children—is to tell themselves, "This hurts me more than it does you." In other words, if the parent suffers mentally, punishing the child physically is justified. In this way, the dissonance is resolved painlessly—for the parent.

Another method of resolving dissonance is to put down the victim. Once we have performed a cruel deed, we tell ourselves that the hapless individual was an unworthy person who got what he or she deserved. This method of reducing dissonance was used by some of Milgram's subjects.

Cognitive dissonance is an exciting theory of social interaction, but it is not without its critics. Some point out that too much of the theory relies on too difficult-to-measure, internal events such as "cognitions" and "psychological discomfort." How do we know that people are really thinking what they claim to be thinking? Although the objections have some validity, most psychologists accept the general idea of dissonance as an important addition to psychological theory.

"His mother wants to know if you'll give him a haircut after you remove his tonsils."

Section Review

1. What is cognitive dissonance?
2. Give an example of external justification.
3. Give an example of internal justification.

Virtually every day we are bombarded by attempts to influence the way we think, feel, and act. Advertisers try to persuade us to buy their products and services. Politicians try to influence our votes; teachers, our intellect; and religious leaders, our moral behavior. Friends influence our style of dress, vocabulary, and taste in music. Our parents often shape many of our attitudes about right and wrong behavior. We often accept ideas and attitudes without realizing how much we are influenced by the persuasiveness of others. How do people change our attitudes? What is it about human behavior that makes us either susceptible to persuasion or resistant to it?

What Attitudes Are

An attitude differs from an opinion, a belief, or simply a point of view. An **attitude** implies a feeling about something as well as knowledge of it. Attitudes have a dynamic, motivational impact that the other concepts lack. When beliefs or opinions are emotionally tinged, when they involve existing situations, and when they cause us to respond in a consistent way toward people or events, they become attitudes. Thus attitudes have three parts: (1) beliefs, ideas, or knowledge about the way things are, or ought to be; (2) emotions or feelings associated with the beliefs; and (3) action—a readiness to respond in specific ways. An attitude is a learned tendency to respond in a certain way because of beliefs, feelings, and readiness to act.

People learn attitudes, like patriotism, in formal and informal ways as the photos on these pages show.

How Do We Get Attitudes?

We get our attitudes from many sources. From reading a book on social conditions in Cambodia, you might feel compassion for the people of this region and support a movement to help them. If you visit Cambodia you might have an even stronger response. In one case, your attitude is based on what you read. In the other, it is based on what you saw.

Attitudes can also come from observing models—seeing how other people do things. Attitudes can come from being rewarded or punished for conforming or not conforming to standards our family or peers consider important.

When we are influenced to form an attitude, there are three levels at which we can hold this attitude. The first is **compliance.** This is the weakest level. When you comply you only seem to form the attitude, in order to avoid rejection or win approval. For example, if people in your school generally have a much more liberal attitude in politics than you entered with, you may also act in a more liberal way. By doing this, you gain friends. However, this may not be a true attitude change.

The second level of attitude formation is **identification.** You adopt an attitude as a result of an emotional attachment to a person or group. For example, you may like disco music. If you go to a school, however, where almost everyone prefers rock music, you may begin to change your attitude in order to feel part of a group you value. While the identification process is strong, it can also be temporary. If you should

change your feelings toward the group, or change schools, you may also change your feelings about the type of music.

While identification is a stronger kind of attitude formation than compliance, the strongest level is **internalization.** Internalization means you take the new attitude into your own belief system. You believe it for your own reasons, not just because of others. The attitude becomes part of you. If your attitude is internalized, you are not just *saying* you like rock music, which would be compliance. You are not just liking it because others do, which would be identification. You like it for your *own* reasons.

What Changes Attitudes?

Most social psychologists view individuals as thinking creatures whose attitudes can be changed by persuasion. Under what circumstances can you be persuaded to "buy" a given product or political idea? Whether you need and can afford the product are two important factors. But three other variables will have a profound influence on your decision: (1) the source of the message—who says it; (2) the message itself—what is said; and (3) yourself, or the nature of the audience—who listens.

Source characteristics. Someone you like and trust will be able to persuade you more easily than a stranger or someone you have found unreliable in the past. An attractive source is important. As you'll recall from Chapter 14, attractiveness may derive from the person's sex, previous acquaintance, physical appearance, personality features, and other factors. You perceive the message in terms of who is trying to put it across. An expert is more likely to be believed than someone who knows little about the subject. A key to whether or not people accept persuasive appeals is *communicator credibility*. This is the listener's opinion of how knowledgeable and trustworthy the source is. Many television and magazine ads use famous people to sell products because the people seem to have the qualities that will make others believe what they say.

The source need not be an individual. We develop a liking for newspapers, magazines, political parties, labor unions, companies, and many other institutions in our society. If we like the group or institution we very often come to like what it stands for.

Message characteristics. Attitudes are not easy to change. For example, no matter how attractive the source that tells you, you are not likely to be convinced that the moon is made of green cheese, or that the earth is flat. The message must be *believable*. It has to fit in with your previously acquired knowledge and evaluation of an event.

Second, the message needs to be *understandable*. You should be able to comprehend it, and weigh and interpret the information without too much difficulty. For example, because the principles of nuclear energy are hard for most people to grasp, arguments about it that are based on technical considerations are frequently lost on the reader or listener. People are likely to evaluate the source of the statement or its emotional appeal rather than the message itself.

Finally, you will be influenced by the *style* in which the message is presented. If it is given in person, how effective is the speaker? Are both sides of the issue presented, or only one side? Does the message include solid evidence as well as opinions? In the case of print media, you might be influenced by clever illustrations, a smooth style, and impressive statistics. Generally, a combination of facts and an emotional appeal is the most effective. Whether written or spoken, the way a message is put forth is often more influential than what is being said.

This advertisement tells about *Reader's Digest*'s campaign to mobilize young people to develop community programs to stop drunk driving. The nationwide, anti-drunk driving campaign was launched with an award-winning poster of Stevie Wonder that said, "Before I'll ride with a drunk, I'll drive myself." Why would such an appeal be effective in persuading young people to "buy" this idea? How does this campaign ultimately help the magazine?

Audience characteristics. Would an American Legion group be more receptive or less receptive to a talk on the dangers of communism than a Soviet-American Friendship Society? Are women or men more easily persuaded on the value of women's liberation? Your answers tell you something about the importance of audience receptivity. The communicator will probably try to discover the common denominator of the group—the interests, biases, and personality attributes that a majority of the audience shares—and appeal to it. Politicians often do this, and so do salespeople. The same product may be advertised in two different ways to two different groups. For example, in selling a toy, if the audience is adults, the educational and safety features may be stressed. If the audience is children, the fun aspects may be stressed.

Act First, Think Later

Recently, investigators have begun a new kind of attack on attitude change. As you read, in considering cognitive dissonance we often adopt attitudes that conform with our behavior rather than behave according to our attitudes. When behavior comes first, the attitudes tend to fall in line with the behavior.

A communicator often will tailor his or her remarks to appeal to the interests and attitudes the majority of the group shares. Here, presidential candidate Rev. Jesse Jackson shakes hands with supporters. Opposite page: Colorado Congresswoman Patricia Schroeder talks to a group of constituents.

Let's recall the example of the person who dislikes social dancing, but suppose a few details are different. You expect to get your toes stepped on by people you have never met before, to feel uncomfortable making small talk, to find the music too loud, and to get stuck with someone unattractive. But your best friend drags you to a dance one night and almost forces you to learn a few steps. You enjoy the music, dance with some attractive partners, and find yourself having a ball. You are now aware of the positive aspects of dancing, and your private attitude changes to fit that new public experience.

Getting people to comply with a small request has also been shown to increase their tendency to go along with a larger request. This is known as the *foot-in-the-door* technique. Perhaps something like this happened to Patty Hearst. After her kidnapping, she apparently repudiated the establishment to become—temporarily—Tania, an urban guerrilla. Although other factors are involved, it seems that once Patty began to act as a member of the Symbionese Liberation Army, her previous attitudes underwent a dramatic change. From all we know, she changed her beliefs at that time, and changed them back again when she returned to her parents and fit into the public role of an innocent victim of brainwashing.

Section Review

1. What is an attitude?
2. Describe the three levels of holding an attitude.
3. Discuss some characteristics of a persuasive source.

The Invasion from Mars

On the night of October 30, 1938, long before the time of flying saucers and UFO's, the United States was "invaded" by men from Mars—or so it was believed by several million radio listeners who tuned in to Orson Welles' *Mercury Theatre*. Presented as a news documentary, this wholly imaginary event was so realistically performed that, for many who heard it, fiction turned into fact. Some rushed from their homes in panic. Some, like the man above, "took to the barricade." Others assembled in prayer. Police switchboards around the country lit up like Christmas trees as people sought help. Not until the next morning was it clear to these listeners that the "invasion" was only a drama, and was not to be taken seriously.

For social psychologist Hadley Cantril of Princeton University this event was a ready-made experiment in mass persuasion. Later, a study of the program was made. Cantril's team interviewed 135 individuals to find out why they had believed the unbelievable.

One important factor was that many who reacted strongly to the broadcast had tuned in late, missing the announcement that it was entertainment. For these, and others too, the documentary form of the broadcast overcame any doubts they might otherwise have had about its truthfulness. Interviews with "public officials" sounded real. "I believed the broadcast as soon as I heard the professor from Princeton and the officials in Washington," one listener said. A major influence was the *trustworthiness of the source.*

Why didn't every listener who tuned in late believe the broadcast? Cantril said the significant variable was conditioned suggestibility. Those most likely to believe were receptive to the idea that such an occurrence was possible. Many were highly religious people who saw the invasion as an act of God. For those with a strong belief in the wonders of science, the invasion was a realistic possibility.

Listeners who felt emotionally insecure were open to suggestion when confronted with apparent danger. Critical judgment weakens when a person already feels threatened from within. Though no *actual* danger existed, the *perceived* danger became a powerful force for irrational behavior by otherwise normal people.

5. Understanding Prejudice

How can psychologists—and all of us—influence attitudes, improve people's perceptions of one another, and help to modify behavior toward actions and values that are more just and humane? Can social structures themselves be changed for the better? In this section of the chapter, we will look at a social problem that is especially related to psychology—prejudice and racism. Prejudice gives root to discrimination. The unfortunate consequences affect most of us—those discriminated against, those who discriminate, and those who stand by, silently, and let discrimination continue.

PREVIEW

**In this section,
read to find out:**

1. what prejudice is.
2. some causes and effects of prejudice.
3. methods of reducing prejudice.

The Nature of Prejudice

The tendency to categorize people (or places or things) on the basis of generalized attitudes is one reason we are all prejudiced against something. Some of us are against certain foods we have never tasted, countries we have never visited, people we have never met, or political systems that we have only heard about. However, psychologists are concerned mainly with how stereotyped attitudes are applied to people. A **prejudice** is an attitude with a blind spot. More formally, prejudice is an attitude that is unsupported by reasonable evidence, that persists over time, and is based on an emotional feeling about the person or group being judged. Prejudice usually implies that the other person or group is in some way inferior to your own group.

Many experiments have shown the power of generalized attitudes to override concrete judgments. In one study, 150 student subjects were shown on a screen photographs of college girls. The students were asked to rate the girls on a scale of one to five for beauty, intelligence, character, ambition, and general likability. Two months later, the same photographs were shown to the students. This time the girls in the photographs were arbitrarily given family names. Five became Italian, five Irish, and five Jewish. The rest of the names, selected from the signers of the Declaration of Independence and from listings in the social register, formed the WASP subgroup (White, Anglo-Saxon Protestant).

Following this second screening and rating, the students' judgments were compared with their original ratings. Did names make a difference? Having an Irish, Jewish, or Italian name lowered the viewers' opinions. The WASP names caused no significant change in rating. As the student judges responded to the photographs the second time around, their previously acquired attitudes about ethnic groups evidently overpowered their original judgments.

Handicapped people, like Bill Rush shown on the opposite page, have in the past been denied equal employment and educational opportunities. In recent years, however, laws have been passed to prevent discrimination against the handicapped. Bill Rush, for example, aggressively pursues a college degree at the University of Nebraska despite a disorder which prevents him from walking, talking, or using his hands. He communicates with a "headstick," a foot-long piece of copper tubing worn on his forehead with which he points to letters and words on a board across the arms of his wheelchair. A talented student, Bill's sense of humor makes him popular with his classmates. The T-shirt he's wearing is one of a big collection including, "Jogger," "And, I'm Smart, Too," and "Guess Which Part of Me Is Not Bionic?"

In the past, black people in the United States have been forced to use separate educational facilities and separate areas in restaurants, buses, trains, and waiting rooms. Today, under the impact of federal laws, such blatant examples of discrimination as that pictured at right, have all but disappeared.

Effects of Prejudice

One harmful effect of prejudice is that it results, at times, in discrimination, such as avoiding or demeaning people, or refusing them employment or housing accommodations. Perhaps even more damaging, prejudice sometimes persuades members of the group treated as inferior that they really *are* inferior in some way. Then they tend to "act the part," lowering their self-esteem to fit the stereotype. For example, many women have been taught to believe that they are intellectually inferior to men. Although this view is changing, thanks largely to the women's movement, as recently as 1968 the attitude of women toward the intellectual abilities of women remained negative. A number of female college students were asked, in an experiment, to evaluate several scholarly articles as to content, style, and other factors. They gave much higher marks to the articles they believed had been written by men than to those by women. Along with many other sex differences, the students had "learned" from childhood that men are supposed to be superior to women. Thus they were set, in their minds, to interpret male performance as better. This acceptance of a rating of inferiority has been shown to operate among most minority groups.

The psychologist who has probably done more than any other to increase our understanding of prejudice is Gordon Allport. Allport's book, *The Nature of Prejudice* (published by Addison-Wesley, 1979), is still the classic study of this topic. It is recommended to anyone who wants to explore this subject further.

©Look Magazine

It's Your Turn

Advertisements are common sources of persuasion. You have read, here and elsewhere, about techniques that are used in advertising. Now *It's Your Turn*. Choose an ad from a magazine, and analyze it according to these techniques of persuasion. Is the ad an effective one? Why or why not?

"I hate the way these commercials exploit us kids and subtly implant desires in us for nonessential material goods."

Social Factors in Prejudice

Clearly, there is no single cause of prejudice. A major influence on someone like the television character Archie Bunker is physical appearance. To Archie, people's color is the main thing about them. *Visible difference* is a powerful force in prejudice. We have been conditioned to accept the appearance of our own group as normal and the appearance of other groups as abnormal. In a society in which Caucasians are in the majority, many people in such racial minorities as Hispanic, Black, Asian, or American Indian are susceptible to prejudice on the part of the majority because of skin color or other visible differences. Severely handicapped people often suffer a similar kind of rejection because of visible difference. As we observe the difference, dissonance reduction goes to work. We need a better reason for our hostility than just physical appearance, so we tend to think of the other group as inferior. We look for negative qualities rather than positive qualities.

Another powerful factor in prejudice is *differences in beliefs and lifestyles.* As a member of one group, you may be prejudiced against those not in your group—those who think or act differently. Allport points out that it is easier to hate a group than it is an individual. In fact, we can hate a group without ever meeting an individual from that group.

A third force that contributes to prejudice is *conformity to social norms.* If the majority of people in your community hold that a certain group is not to be trusted, it is easy to accept this view. People tend to conform publicly to majority opinion, even when they privately disagree with it.

A final, and perhaps the most important, source of prejudice is *early learning.* In the words of a song from the musical *South Pacific,* "you got to be taught to hate." If parents feel strongly about any group of people, children usually adopt the same attitudes. Our most deeply embedded prejudices often stem from identifying with parents and childhood friends. Without any reason being given, we learn that one group is "bad" and another is "good."

Fortunately, prejudice does not have to last forever. If, for example, you are a gentile raised in a small town where antisemitism has taken root, and you later move to a cosmopolitan area where you become acquainted with more people, you usually discover that Jews are much like everyone else. "They are members of the human race," Mark Twain wrote, "Worse than that I cannot say of them." As you come to know Jews—or members of some other group—on an equal basis and make friends with them, your prejudice fades. Prejudice can be reduced as people become more dependent on each other, although it may never disappear entirely.

Personality and Prejudice

It might appear, at first, that prejudice results entirely from a combination of family, group, and cultural factors. Why, then, isn't everyone who is exposed to these pressures prejudiced to an equal degree? The fact that some people are relatively tolerant of conditions that create prejudice in others suggests that differences in personality and temperament also play a part.

When groups become frustrated and fearful, they often use another group—usually a minority group—as the scapegoat for their anger and fears. After the Japanese attack on Pearl Harbor in 1941, some 110,000 Japanese Americans—70,000 of whom were American-born citizens—were forced to "relocate" from their homes on the West coast to distant states. Italians and German Americans, however, did not receive such treatment although the United States was also at war with Germany and Italy. Historians believe that Japanese Americans became scapegoats for Americans' fears about being attacked by Japan.

One such difference is a person's ability to tolerate frustration. There is some evidence that people who are easily frustrated are, in general, more likely to react in a prejudiced way than are people who are not easily frustrated.

This observation has led to the *scapegoat theory* of prejudice. In Chapter 9, you examined the idea that when a goal is blocked, people attempt to overcome frustration by lashing out at whatever stands in their way. When the cause of the frustration cannot be dealt with directly, aggression is displaced on any innocent object available, preferably one that cannot strike back. In many cases this turns out to be a powerless group that the larger social group holds in low esteem. The scapegoats, or target group members, get the brunt of frustrated and pent-up feelings they had no part in creating.

When Germany was left in an economic shambles after World War I, many Germans were frustrated by the wild inflation that ravaged their country, and at their inability to make a living. Hitler was able to focus their inner feelings of frustration against a minority, the Jews. This group was assigned the blame for almost everything that had gone wrong. Devastating physical aggression against the Jews resulted. Where violence against a target group is prevented, as it is in most countries, more subtle outlets for frustration occur, such as housing and job discrimination. People who dislike a certain group will, when frustrated, use the group as a scapegoat.

Jews became scapegoats for German frustrations during the post-World War I era.

Low tolerance for frustration is only one of the personality variables that sometimes accompany prejudice. People with low self-esteem are more likely to be prejudiced than people who have high respect for themselves. Individuals who lack self-esteem look for others who can be seen as more unworthy than they themselves are. Guilt feelings about behavior are also projected onto people whose own behavior is what the prejudiced people see as bad about themselves, but cannot admit.

Allport lists some characteristics of a prejudiced personality that have to do with style of thinking. A central trait is the tendency to cling to past solutions. Prejudiced people lack flexibility in their thinking and seem afraid to say "I don't know." They have a strong need for definiteness. They are intolerant of uncertainty and tend to "choose up sides." Their thinking tends to be restricted to a few easily perceived alternatives, so that they are, quite literally, "narrow-minded."

Many psychologists believe that these personality traits are the result of child-rearing practices. Many deeply prejudiced people have been brought up in a harsh and punitive family environment. They have little feeling of security, and experience a great deal of threat.

Overcoming Prejudice

To eliminate prejudice entirely is probably an unrealistic hope. To reduce it is not. Social psychologists have studied several strategies to reduce prejudice.

Change attitudes first. This is probably the least effective method of countering prejudice. For most people, hostile attitudes are too deeply rooted in their own beliefs and way of life to be changed by persuasion alone. Showing people educational films and explaining or preaching the immorality of prejudice has not proven effective with large numbers of people. The attitudes that underlie prejudice can be hard to change because they often reflect unconscious needs. Feelings of prejudice against others are often a feeling of personal insecurity or self-hatred. Until this is corrected, the prejudices may remain intact.

Interdependence and opportunities for person-to-person contacts help break down prejudice.

Change behavior first. Engaging in a particular act first often brings about a change in thinking afterward. Social psychologists were a long time realizing the implications of this process for combatting racial prejudice. Changing attitudes by changing behavior is easy enough when individuals give it a try. However, when the object of the prejudice is to avoid the other group, the interchange that can reduce prejudice is prevented.

Change the law. Although prejudice itself cannot be outlawed, one of its consequences—**discrimination**—can be. Laws reduce a victim's vulnerability to prejudice by changing behavior that is based on prejudice. Laws provide an official norm in human relations, even when they are not always obeyed. In 1942, 70 percent of the white people in this country approved of segregated schools. By 1957, three years after the Supreme Court's decision outlawing segregation, the figure had dropped to 51 percent. And by 1970, with integrated schools operating in most communities, 75 percent of the white population *favored* desegregation.

Most people want to be thought of as law abiding. To this extent the court's decision helped change racial attitudes. But more importantly, the majority of integrated schools worked out in routine fash-

ion. Few of the terrible predictions of the racists came true. Many positive features resulted. Educators, parents, and students found that integration was not so bad after all.

Change social contacts. One benefit of integration is that it allows students to change their social contacts. Among your fellow students are probably some whose racial background differs from your own. In the classroom you are all on the same footing. You have interests in

In groups like this, people from many different backgrounds come together on an equal footing and share common goals.

common, and share a set of goals—getting through the course.

In bringing about a change in attitude, contact by itself means little. Common interests, shared goals, and relatively equal status draw people together as individuals. Interdependence and opportunity for person-to-person relationships tend to break down prejudice. Equal status contact provides exceptions to existing stereotypes, and thus weakens the stereotypes.

M. Deutsch and B. E. Collins studied interracial attitudes in a large housing project. One section was integrated, the other segregated. In the integrated section white and black families were scattered throughout the buildings. In the segregated section the two races were in separate buildings.

The contrast between the attitudes of the residents of the two types of housing was striking. People in the integrated project reported much more interracial contact than those living in the segregated buildings. As a result, there was a positive shift in their attitude toward their neighbors. This did not occur among the segregated groups.

If equal status contact does not happen, people sometimes learn new attitudes by seeing examples of integration at work.

Change models. For a number of reasons, the models are already changing. More and more people of different races and ethnic groups are being elected to Congress, or to other public offices. Members of minorities have been appointed to high government posts, including the Supreme Court and the United Nations, and have become prominent in education. The sports world, virtually colorblind, has shown

that people of different races can compete, coexist, and cooperate right before the eyes of millions of people. People's attitudes are more likely to be influenced by what they see than what they read, so the mass media have become a mechanism for the social support Allport believed was essential in lessening prejudice. In this sense, the media take over where legislation leaves off, showing us successful working models of integrations that go beyond just compliance with the law. Attitudes can change with the help of media models, from compliance to internalization. Increasing numbers of people now *believe* in equality.

As more and more minority group people occupy positions of prominence in business, government, education, and other areas of American life, stereotypes begin to breakdown, and prejudice can be reduced. Members of the Congressional Black Caucus are shown above.

Too much cheering would be unrealistic. Breaking out of segregated housing patterns and subtler forms of discrimination will be difficult as long as poverty adds to the weight of prejudice. Yet in spite of adverse conditions, the victims of prejudice are gradually forging a sense of their own identity, gaining power and self-respect, and winning increased respect from others.

Section Review

1. Explain the scapegoat theory of prejudice.
2. Why is changing behavior first more effective than changing attitudes?
3. How does integration lessen prejudice?
4. Why are role models effective in combating prejudice?

Chapter 15 Review

Section Summaries

1. Behavior of Groups

Social psychology is the study of how people influence each other. People join groups for influence, achievement, and affiliation. Groups affect individual behavior through group goals, group pressure, group identity, and group perceptions. Group dynamics is a process in which collective behavior results from individual interactions. Groups seem to be most effective in solving specific problems, and less effective at creative tasks. "Groupthink" can increase the risk of group decisions. Social status can also influence group dynamics. Leadership power grows out of expert power, reference power, legitimate power, reward power, and coercive power. Leadership styles are classified as autocratic, democratic, or laissez-faire.

2. Persuasion and Conformity

Social norms, which provide a general framework for acceptable behaviors, create pressures to conform. This was confirmed by Stanley Milgram's work, in which subjects projected blame upon authority figures, dehumanized the "learner," and became so absorbed in the experiment that they lost touch with reality. Milgram's findings have been duplicated in real world situations in Vietnam and Nazi Germany. Solomon Asch showed that group pressure made some subjects give answers they knew were false. Group conformity is affected by prior commitments, self-esteem, the makeup of the group, and its attractiveness. Research in this area can explain interactions with friends, as well as the power of religious cults.

3. Being Consistent; Dissonance Theory

Cognitive dissonance refers to the discomfort that results when we hold two opposing beliefs. Dissonance reduction reduces this discomfort by using external justification, by internal justification, and by public statements and actions.

4. Attitudes

Attitudes are made up of (a) beliefs and knowledge, (b) emotions, and (c) action, or readiness to respond. We hold attitudes at three levels—compliance, identification, and internalization. Attitudes can be influenced by source characteristics, message characteristics, and by audience characteristics. Attitudes can also be changed by changing behavior patterns.

5. Understanding Prejudice

Prejudice is an attitude that is unsupported by reasonable evidence, that persists over time, and is based on an emotional feeling. Prejudice usually implies that the target group is somehow inferior. Prejudice leads to discrimination and sometimes persuades the targets of prejudice that they are inferior. Social factors in prejudice include physical appearance, differences in beliefs and lifestyles, conformity to social norms, and early learning. Prejudice can be unlearned, however. Personality factors that play a part in prejudice include a low tolerance for frustration and inflexible thinking. Harsh and punitive child-rearing practices may encourage these personality traits. Strategies for overcoming prejudice include changing attitudes, changing behavior, changing laws, changing social contacts, and changing models.

Psychology Skill Activities

1. Watch several commercials on television. Analyze them as to source, message, and audience characteristics. **easy**
2. Observe your class or one of your after-school activities. What leadership styles and basis of power do you observe? **challenging**

Testing for Understanding

Knowing Key Terms

Define these terms in your own words.

Section 1

social psychology
group dynamics
expert power
referent power
legitimate power
reward power
coercive power
autocratic
democratic
laissez-faire

Section 2

social norms

Section 3

cognitive dissonance
dissonance reduction
external justification
internal justification

Section 4

attitude
compliance
identification
internalization

Section 5

prejudice
discrimination

Reviewing Main Ideas

Section 1

1. What are the reasons for group formation?
2. Explain the process of group dynamics.
3. What are the sources of leadership power and the styles of leadership?

Section 2

1. How do social norms affect our behavior?
2. What factors seem to foster and encourage group conformity?
3. How do research findings about conformity apply to the real world?

Section 3

1. Explain cognitive dissonance.
2. How can dissonance be reduced?

Section 4

1. What are the components of an attitude?
2. How three levels are used to describe the strength of an attitude?
3. What variables can influence attitudes?

Section 5

1. How is prejudice different from other types of attitudes?
2. What are the causes of prejudice? What are its effects?
3. What are some strategies that have been proposed for reducing prejudice?

Thinking Critically

1. *Making Applications.* If your close friend has habits you do not like, how might you resolve this dissonance? **easy**
2. *Problem Solving.* If you were on a jury, what could you, as one person, do to get each person to do their best thinking in coming to a just decision? List as many ideas as possible. **challenging**

Demonstrating Psychology Skills

Analyze the advertisement below according to the source, message, and audience characteristics. Be specific.

Chapter 16

The Quality of Life

Today I had my final exam in history. I was not nervous before the test, because I had really studied hard, and I felt I knew the material well. Also, I had gotten easy "Bs" on the other tests in the class and hadn't studied nearly as hard for them as I did for the final. I felt as though I was really going to knock'em dead. But when I got to the classroom, and sat down, waiting for the test to start, I couldn't help being affected by the nervousness of the other kids in the class. They were moving around restlessly in their seats and talking nervously about what might be on the exam. I began to get nervous myself. My stomach started churning as I tried to recall the material I studied the night before.

Have you ever had a similar experience? Have you ever been in a situation where the mood of the crowd affected your mood? Have you ever found yourself in a crowd behaving in a way that you normally wouldn't? In this chapter, we will look at how individual behavior is influenced by the crowd. We will look at **collective behavior** or the way a group thinks, feels, or acts as a unit in response to an irrational process such as the power of suggestion.

1. Crowd Behavior

There was nothing about the concert at Cincinnati Monday night that could have led one to predict an incident such as the one that occurred. All 18,358 tickets for the *Who* concert had been sold several weeks before the concert, but only 3,000 to 4,000 of them were for the reserved seats; the remainder were 'festival tickets,' for general admission on a first-come, first-serve seating basis. Ticketholders had begun lining up by mid-afternoon and within an hour of the 8:00 p.m. show time the line was blocks long.

At about 7:00 p.m. the band, running behind schedule, began final checks of its equipment, prompting some of the waiting ticketholders to believe that the concert had begun without them. At one set of doors, restless fans smashed several windows. The doors flew open. Then, as though propelled by a slingshot, the crowd at that door stampeded.

PREVIEW

In this section, read to find out:

1. how one sociologist classifies crowds.
2. how mobs form.
3. some of the theories used to explain crowd behavior.

A rock concert in Woodstock, N.Y. in 1969 was expected to draw 120,000, but 400,000 showed up. The weather was bad; the facilities, terribly inadequate. The massive crowd, left a sea of litter behind, but not a single violent incident occurred.

David Hack described his recollections, "It started getting crowded and crowded and crowded and nobody'd let up. A few times we were up in midair and were getting turned around backwards. All I could do was to keep both arms around my wife and just fight people off and elbow a few people in the gut and get a little nasty with them. Really, it was the only thing I could do. Then my wife said she was standing on someone and I tried to let her back, and let people get back. We got away, but the guy on the ground couldn't get up. We got pushed away from him and we couldn't help him and all the people just ended up going back over him." ■

Eleven people died that night, according to the *New York Times* report, in the crush to get in. What caused the stampede? The crowd erupted. It was transformed from a group of separate individuals into a single wave of humanity. Psychologists have categorized crowd behavior and developed three main theories to explain it.

Theories of Crowd Behavior

An audience is not necessarily a crowd. People in an audience are attuned to the speaker or performer. The **crowd** is less organized. It moves and shifts. The people interact with each other, verbally and nonverbally. They share comments and suggestions with each other or offer approval or disapproval. They experience similar emotions. Gestures and comments and emotions stimulate similar behavior in others. This stimulation results in spontaneous feelings and actions that move in waves through the crowd.

Sociologist H. G. Blumer has classified crowds into four types. The *casual crowd* is one like the group of curiosity seekers who form around a police officer arresting someone for disorderly conduct. They come

Street performers attract the casual crowd, one that gathers spontaneously to "see what's going on."

together spontaneously without premeditation. Spectators at a football game form what Blumer calls the *conventionalized crowd*. The *acting crowd* has an objective to carry out and, more than likely, follows a self-appointed leader. A protest meeting or a group of striking picketers are examples of acting crowds. The *expressive crowd* engages in physical activity such as dancing in a religious sect. An example of this type of crowd might be members of the Hare Krishna cult who sometimes gather on city corners.

If the crowd resorts to disorderly, aggressive behavior, it becomes a **mob.** Often there is some event which triggers this step. Something as minor as the *Who's* final equipment check turned a frustrated, impatient crowd into a dangerous mob. Social psychologist M. Brown established four categories of mobs which form for different reasons. *Aggressive mobs* are those which engage in physical violence. Examples of these are lynch mobs and riot mobs like the one that formed at New Mexico State Penitentiary in 1980 and caused the death of 33 persons. *Escape mobs* are infected by fear and panic in the face of some disaster or emergency. The stock market crash of 1929 in which people rushed to withdraw their money from banks is an example of an *acquisitive mob*. People rush to acquire something which they believe is in short supply. An *expressive mob* is one that is caught up in physical fervor as in a religious revival.

For whatever reason a crowd or mob forms, three general theories are often used to explain crowd behavior and the individual's role in it.

Contagion theory. Social psychologist Gustave Le Bon noted that in a crowd an individual ceases to be an individual. According to **contagion theory,** the crowd engulfs its members. Individual morals and restraint give way to a collective mind almost by way of an hypnotic contagion. People's personalities dissolve into the unified personality of the crowd. People's normal thought processes, emotions, and behavior are no longer guided by individual will. Their behavior and will become that of the crowd. Le Bon described three characteristics of this phenomenon.

First, in a crowd, the individual is anonymous. **Anonymity** is not being known by others. It frees the individual from personal responsibility for his or her actions. With the shedding of responsibility comes excitement and a feeling of power. This sense of power makes the crowd feel invincible. It feels it can do or accomplish almost anything it wants.

Le Bon also believed that the feelings and behavior circulating in a crowd are contagious. People become afflicted with a heady sense of power. They contract the aura of the crowd as though they had fallen

When prisoners are given ample space and privacy, prisons are generally orderly and quiet. Overcrowding breeds violence and can lead to riots, like the one that occurred at the extremely overcrowded New Mexico State Penitentiary in 1980, in which 33 people lost their lives.

victims of a contagious disease. According to Le Bon, people in a crowd become highly receptive to being led. As though under hypnosis, they are in highly suggestible states and will follow nearly any course of action the crowd may undertake.

Convergence theory. Whereas contagion theory holds that normal, respectable citizens are transformed by the crowd, **convergence theory** suggests that people come together because they share common interests. They are not transformed by the crowd, but remain distinct, separate individuals. However, their behavior is very much the same. The crowd appears to be a single working unit because these people share common emotions, thoughts, and backgrounds. The crowd has attracted them for the same reason. They come to the crowd with the same desires and mentality. For example, it was found that lynch mobs were composed of "frustrated people from the lower socioeconomic class."

Emergent-norm theory. Convergence theory stresses the idea that people come together in a crowd for common reasons. **Emergent-norm theory** stresses the opposite—that people come together in a crowd for different reasons. People have different motives, desires, attitudes, and backgrounds that they bring to the crowd. These differences remain intact and allow members of the crowd to play different roles in the

The people in this crowd have joined the peace rally for various reasons—as their posters indicate. They probably will never see each other again, and they follow no leader. Which theory best describes this type of crowd?

crowd. Some people are leaders. Some are active followers; some are only passive followers. Some are dissenters; some are opportunists. They bring to the crowd all their differences, but they follow the crowd because it represents a *norm*.

The behavior of leaders establishes the norm, the course of action followers will take. The same phenomenon was demonstrated in the experiments conducted by Solomon Asch that you read about in Chapter 15. Subjects conformed to group consensus in judging the lengths of lines, even when it meant giving a false answer and discounting their own perceptions.

Once the norm is set, crowd members defend and enforce it. Even though the behavior of the crowd may not be personally acceptable to the individual, conforming to the group is more important. There is more immediate pressure from crowd members to conform. If an individual disagrees with action taken, but remains silent on the issue, it is the same as conforming. The norm of the crowd is unchallenged. To observers on the outside, the crowd appears unified. Some believe this was the case in Nazi Germany. Many might have recognized the injustices endured by the Jews, but they stood by as passive observers when Jewish homes and businesses were attacked. The risk of nonconforming was too great.

What happened at the rock concert? Now that you've read about crowd behavior theory, what labels would you assign to the Cincinnati rock concert? Blumer might have classified the Monday afternoon gathering as a conventionalized crowd. They were certainly not a casual

Rev. Sun Myung Moon, head of the Unification Church formed in Korea in the 1950s, is said to have a hypnotic hold on young people. His indoctrination methods have been labeled "brainwashing" by parents of many of his recruits, who are mostly in their early twenties and referred to as "Moonies." Some of the conversions have been explained by the emergent-norm theory, as the young people with unlike views are carried along with the thinking of the crowd following the norms set by the leader.

The *Who* (left) performing at the Cincinnati concert after eleven people had died in the crush to get in through the concert doors (right).

group—they did not come together spontaneously. Nor were they an acting crowd. They had no objective but to listen; an obvious role of a spectator in a conventionalized crowd. Were they expressive? Perhaps. But the crowd turned angry and unruly and grew into a mob. What kind of mob? Certainly aggressive, and maybe for some like David Hack who witnessed the stampede, the crowd took on characteristics of an escape mob—a group of people fearful for their own safety. And, because they were scrambling for first-come, first-serve seating, you might say they were an acquisitive mob.

What theory best explains their collective behavior? The people came to the concert with an identical goal—to hear a rock concert. The participants probably shared common interests and backgrounds—they were young people who like rock music. The facts that the doors weren't opened in advance and that the seats weren't reserved created a group of highly frustrated people. These factors point to convergence theory and yet can anyone deny that an infectious contagion spread through the ranks? Or was there a norm operating?

The point is that no one theory or definition clearly fits any one situation. Collective behavior often escapes solid classification. Pay attention the next time you're in a crowd. See if you can determine what forces are operating.

Section Review

1. How does a crowd differ from an audience?
2. How does a mob differ from a crowd?
3. What are three characteristics of a crowd, according to Le Bon's contagion theory?
4. How is the role of the individual different in emergent-norm theory from that in convergence theory?

2. Too Many People, Too Little Space

You're on a jammed commuter bus. You're elbow to elbow with a lot of people; you're much closer than you care to be. The bus stops and even more people get on. Now you're really jammed together. How do you feel?

Now try putting yourself in this situation. You're in a packed disco. Again, people are elbow to elbow. Everyone is moving to the music, even those who aren't dancing. People and music seem to merge together. How do you feel?

Your feelings and reactions in these two settings are probably quite different. You probably can't wait to get out of the bus, while being in the disco might be considered a pleasure.

How Does It Feel to Be a Sardine?

Your reaction to a crowd depends upon your perception of the event. Social psychologist J. L. Freedman describes three variables that influence your perception. (1) Who is crowding you? You may not mind being crowded if the people are friendly—if you are at a party, for example. (2) What activity is going on? You probably do mind being crowded if others interfere with your comfort. For example, your reaction might not be favorable if you're trying to watch a parade and others shove in front of you. (3) What is your previous experience with crowding? Up to a point, people get used to crowds, as they get used to many other stresses. Although you may not enjoy commuting in a packed bus, you learn to endure it.

PREVIEW

In this section, read to find out:

1. some ways people respond to crowding.
2. how people's reactions depend upon their perceptions.
3. about some of the studies done on crowding.

The effects of crowding depend on many factors—the purpose of the crowd, the length of time people have to spend in it, and whether they joined the crowd voluntarily. People generally can tolerate subway crowds for example, because they know to expect them, how long they'll be in them, and because they are in them for a specific purpose—to get home or to work.

But suppose you're not used to it. Suppose you do mind being crowded. Suppose you feel your choices for action are blocked and you experience a sense of feeling trapped. Under these conditions people typically respond in one or more of the following ways:

1. *Psychological stress.* Your heart rate increases. You begin to sweat, and your muscles tense. These reactions can occur even when the crowded situation is perceived positively.

2. *Leaving the scene.* This is the flight response. Assuming that you are free to do so, you get away from the crowd.

3. *Frustration and aggression.* If you can't get away, your frustration might push you to respond aggressively. This fight response can mean that you give others threatening looks or even push and shove others out of your way. Social civility breaks down.

4. *Withdrawal.* You may turn off the crowd by retreating psychologically. You begin to daydream or indulge in fantasy. This permits you to exist (temporarily, at least) "outside" the crowd.

5. *Adaptation.* You make a positive adjustment to the crowded situation. Extreme politeness and consideration for others might be one way to adapt. Or you might decide to enjoy the crowd by becoming involved in people-watching.

When Is Too Many People a Crowd?

Did you feel uncomfortable at the thought of being in a crowded disco? Or would you feel uncomfortable in a packed stadium at a football game? There are many situations in which we actually choose and enjoy the excitement of a large crowd. When does a crowd become uncomfortable? When does it have a negative effect? It depends upon many factors including the individual's perception of the crowd and his or her ability to adjust and cope.

Freedman pointed out the need to distinguish between high density and crowding. **Density** is a measurement of population. It is the number of people in a certain amount of space. **Crowding** is a psychological phenomenon, the perception of too many people in too little space.

The degree to which you feel crowded depends on why you are there, what you are trying to do, your cultural background, and other factors in addition to the actual density. Psychologist W. H. Ittleson concludes that the key element in feeling crowded is not merely the number of people or the density, but the feeling that the presence of others interferes with the achievement of some purpose.

Does density affect performance? Freedman studied the effects of both **spatial density** (the same number of people in large or small rooms) and **social density** (the same size room with different numbers of people in it). In one study, subjects listened to tape-recorded court cases and were then to act as juries in passing judgment on the cases. Interestingly, males and females reacted differently. In an all-male group, men gave more severe judgments in the small, crowded room than in a large, less crowded one. Women showed no difference in severity of judgment under the two conditions. When they did their judging in a mixed-sex group, the men gave less severe judgments than they had in the all-male group.

In another experiment, subjects were given tasks of varying complexity to perform under these different conditions. Again, males and females reacted differently. Males tended to react to high density with aggression and competitive behavior; women seemed to enjoy it and were more likely to develop cooperative strategies. However, the performance by either men or women in completing complex tasks did not suffer under high density conditions. Freedman concludes that high density does not necessarily cause stress, but intensifies what the individual is already feeling. He believes this holds true in the community as well—that crowding in itself does not directly cause crime or other social problems.

To what extent do Freedman's high-density laboratory

It's Your Turn

Think back to a time when you were in a crowd. What was the occasion? How did you feel? Now *It's Your Turn*. Be a psychologist and tell which theory (contagion, convergence, or emergent-norm) best explains your behavior and the behavior of the crowd.

experiments represent high-density conditions in the city? Even in the most dense conditions, his subjects were not really very uncomfortable, and the conditions were temporary. The subjects did not have to compete for scarce resources or struggle with threatening problems of life-and-death importance to them. One person's success did not mean another's failure. Perhaps most importantly, the experiments had no social significance for the subjects. What they did in these rooms would have no effect on their lives tomorrow. Consequently we do not know how far Freedman's findings can be meaningfully applied to city crowding.

The Effects of Crowding on Animal Populations

Over two decades John Calhoun of the National Institute of Mental Health conducted an investigation of the relationship between population density and social-emotional disorders in animals. Colonies of wild or tame rats or mice were reared in artificial environments where the effects of increasing population could be observed over several succeeding generations.

In one experiment, living quarters of the mice were arranged as "high-rise apartments" around an open area. They were provided with ample food and nesting materials and were free from germs, predators, and bad weather. Social breakdown began when all the desirable physical spaces and social roles were filled. Worn out from defending their territories, some males became extremely aggressive, engaging in unprovoked attacks. Others withdrew and became passive. Females ignored nest-building and chased their young out of the nests early. Young adults stopped struggling for territory of their own. Eventually breeding ceased in the community. The last mouse died less than five years after the start of the study.

But can these findings from animal studies be carried over to the human situation? Calhoun thinks that they can. Overcrowding has been linked to both physical and social disorders. Higher rates of death and disease, higher rates of mental illness, and more antisocial behavior such as fighting and rioting are found in the more crowded areas of our cities.

Does this mean then that high population density is directly responsible for these physical and social disorders? How do we separate the effects of crowding from the effects of poverty, high mobility, alienation, and other conditions that are also typical in crowded urban areas? These are topics for continued study.

Mice lived together peacefully in these high-rise apartments until the complex became overcrowded; then social breakdown occurred.

Section Review

1. According to Freedman, what three variables influence a person's perception of a crowd?
2. What is the difference between density and crowding?
3. Summarize Freedman's findings on the effects of crowding.
4. Summarize Calhoun's findings on the effects of crowding on animals.

PREVIEW

**In this section,
read to find out:**

1. how high density
   breeds anonymity and
   alienation.
2. some of the effects of
   anonymity.
3. some of the effects of
   alienation.

3. The Effects of the Urban Environment

In the previous section, you saw that the effects of crowding depend upon many factors—the purpose of the crowd, whether one joined it voluntarily, and whether the crowded situation is permanent or temporary. In the animal population when crowding was not voluntary and was permanent, social order broke down. To what extent do these effects apply to natural settings, to dense human life in cities? How much of the crime, social alienation, and physical and mental disorders associated with large cities can be attributed to the sheer numbers of people? Here the problem becomes complicated by several variables. Certainly poverty, low education, and high mobility also contribute to the ills of society along with high density. Consequently the relationship between population density and social disorders is never simple or direct. We do know, however, that lack of privacy and a feeling of anonymity do cause stress and tax the individual's ability to cope. How are these feelings unleashed?

The Destructive Power of Anonymity

Living among strangers with whom you have only superficial, impersonal, and often unpleasant contacts can lead to apathy, alienation, and cynicism. Partly, this is a means of coping with the stress by psychologically distancing oneself. Partly, it is a self-defense.

Big-city living nibbles away at one of people's most precious possessions—a sense of personal identity and uniqueness, being recognized and appreciated by those around them. Though surrounded by people, the individual becomes anonymous. It is easy to get the feeling, "No one knows or cares who I am, so why should I care about anyone else?" Jane Jacobs, author of *Death and Life of Great American Cities*, describes what it means to be an anonymous child: "On the old-city side, which was full of public places, the children were being kept well in hand. On the project side of the street across the way, the children, who had a fire hydrant open beside their play area, were behaving destructively. They were drenching open windows of houses, squirting water on adults who walked on the project side of the street, throwing it into the windows of cars as they went by. Nobody dared to stop them. These were anonymous children; their identities were unknown. What if you scolded or stopped them? Who would back you up over there? Would you get, instead, revenge? Better to keep out of it. Impersonal city streets make anonymous people . . ."

Being anonymous decreases the chances of being either approved or punished or even noticed. Emotions, or impulses that would

In 1977, a severe electrical storm knocked out all of New York City's electrical power for a day and a half. During the black-out, looting was widespread by people of all ages, races, and socio-economic levels.

otherwise be held in check for fear of disapproval may be released under the mask of anonymity. Feelings of anonymity often take the form of **vandalism,** the destruction of property and life without any apparent goal beyond the act of destruction itself. Such behavior seems to be unreasonable and without motive. Vandals put a lot of effort into an activity that seems to have no real value to them.

Making sense of senselessness. If vandalism were indeed senseless, we could never hope to reduce it, because we could never find the cause for it. Fortunately, it is possible to make sense of even apparently senseless vandalism. History can give us some clues, as can talking to gang members and observing the behavior of those engaged in acts of destruction. In the eighteenth century, when a group of workers called Luddites destroyed factory machines, they were stereotyped as "frenzied" and "mad," their actions as "pointless." But they were part of a movement aimed at the betterment of their society. They were protesting against the evils of the industrial system. Similarly, the property destruction that occurred during the racial disturbances in Watts, Newark, and other American cities in the late 1960s appeared "mindless"

Graffiti might be seen as vandals' way of gaining recognition—their response to the anonymity of the city.

until it was noted that the targets chosen were not random but appeared to be deliberate attacks on white-owned businesses believed to be unfair or disrespectful toward members of the black community.

Analysis of the behavior of gangs reveals several factors related to their violent acts. Gang members, like many individuals in lower socio-economic groups, typically lead lives with little hope of change or improvement. Social conditions have limited their chance of "making it," of gaining status, prestige, and social power. They have reacted by becoming outsiders, forming a counterculture with its own norms for gaining recognition. One gang member said, "If I would of got the knife, I would have stabbed him. That would have gave me more of a build-up. People would have respected me for what I've done and things like that. They would say, 'There goes a cold killer.' It makes you feel like a big shot."

Vandalism may be the outlet for powerless people to rebel and become controllers. It might be the result of feeling rejected by society: "All right, I've been rejected by you, now you will have to fear me."

Who becomes a vandal? In an effort to find out who the people are who actually vandalize automobiles on the street and what conditions are associated with such vandalism, social psychologist Philip Zimbardo performed an experiment which took place in New York City and Palo Alto, California. Two used automobiles in good condition were abandoned on the streets with their license plates removed and their

In Zimbardo's experiment on the relationship between anonymity and vandalism, a "respectable" middle-class family were the first to begin stripping the car. Adult vandals systematically removed the rest of the usable parts, eventually leaving the battered remains to be picked over by young people.

hoods raised. One was placed a block from the New York University campus in the Bronx, the other a block from the Stanford University campus. Hidden observers watched, photographed, and took notes on all those who came into contact with the "bait." The researchers expected to find that the greater anonymity in New York City would lead to a greater incidence of vandalism to the New York car and that most of the vandals would be adolescents and young children.

The first prediction was confirmed; the second was certainly not. Only ten minutes after the New York car was planted, the first auto strippers appeared—a mother, father, and young son. The mother acted as lookout while father and son emptied the trunk and glove compartment, then hacksawed the radiator, and pulled out the battery. Soon after they drove off, another passing car stopped and its adult driver jacked up the abandoned car and removed the best of its tires. By the end of the day, a steady stream of *adult* vandals had removed every removable part of the car.

Then random destruction began. Other passers-by stopped to examine the car, then cut up a tire, urinated on the door, broke all windows, and dented in the hood, fenders, door, and roof.

"In less than three days what remained was a battered, useless hulk of metal, the result of twenty-three incidents of destruction. Most of the destruction was done in the daylight hours, not at night as had been anticipated. The adults were all well dressed, clean-cut whites who would, under other circumstances, have been mistaken for mature, responsible citizens demanding more law and order."

In the town of Palo Alto, not a single item was stolen, nor was any part of the car vandalized during the full week it was left abandoned. Instead, one man passing by in the rain protectively lowered the hood, preventing the motor from getting wet! Did anonymity play a part in the outcome? The anonymity of the vast population of New York City may have been a major factor in the unleashing of antisocial behavior as compared with the social consciousness of Palo Alto, California, a community of little over 50,000 where people are likely to know one another.

Alienation and City Life

To what degree is vandalism a symptom of a more serious problem of city life called alienation? **Alienation** is a sense of feeling detached from society. In a big city a person is surrounded by literally hundreds of thousands of people, hears them on radio, sees them on television, eats with them in restaurants, sits next to them in movies, waits in line with them, gets pushed around in subways with them, touches them— but remains unconnected. Alienation can leave an effect on people that is the opposite from what takes place in mob behavior. Alienated people become bystanders, accepting no responsibility for others. They act as if others do not exist. For a woman in New York City, they did not exist, when she most needed them.

For more than half an hour, thirty-eight respectable, law-abiding citizens in Queens (New York) watched a killer stalk and stab a woman in three separate attacks in Kew Gardens.

Twice the sound of their voices and sudden glow of their bedroom lights interrupted him and frightened him off. Each time he returned, sought her out and stabbed her again. Not one person telephoned the police during the assault; one witness called the police after the woman was dead.

This *New York Times* account of the murder of Kitty Genovese shocked a nation that could not accept the idea of such apathy on the part of its responsible citizenry.

When will bystanders intervene? Why don't bystanders intervene in cases like this? What would make them more likely to do so? A classic study of bystander intervention was carried out soon after the Kitty Genovese murder.

TIME | TEMP | QUALITY OF LIFE
1:16 | 58 | 23%

Two social psychologists, J. M. Darley and B. Latane, created a bystander-intervention situation in the laboratory. Subjects were each placed in rooms by themselves. Some were led to believe they would be communicating with only one other person via an intercom. Others were told they would be communicating with two others; some believed they were talking with five others. In reality, there were no others. They were listening to tapes. During the course of a discussion about personal problems, subjects heard what sounded like one of the other persons having an epileptic seizure and gasping for help.

During the "fit" it was impossible for the subject to talk to the others to find out what, if anything, *they* were doing about the emergency. What was tested was the speed with which the subjects reported the emergency to the experimenter.

It turned out that the likelihood of intervention depended on the number of bystanders the subject thought were present. The more

As you can see by the graph, everyone in a two-person situation intervened within 160 seconds, but nearly 40 percent of those in the larger group never bothered to inform the experimenter that another student was seriously ill.

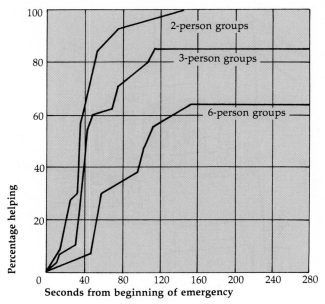

Adapted from Darley & Latané, 1968

there were, the slower the subject was in reporting the seizure, if he or she did so at all.

More hope in the real world. Psychologists I. Piliavan, J. Piliavan, and J. Rodin conducted a similar investigation on a New York subway train. A man on the moving train suddenly collapses and falls to the floor. This event is witnessed by a number of bystanders. The experimenters vary the characteristics of the "victim"—an invalid with a cane, or a drunk smelling of liquor, or, in a companion study, the invalid seemingly bleeding (or not bleeding) from the mouth. They then record the bystander responses to these emergency situations.

Despite the newspaper stories of the callous city folk, one or more persons responded directly to almost every emergency (81 out of 103) and did so with little hesitation. Help was slower for a bloody victim than for a simple collapse. But still help came, even if it was indirect, by asking a question such as: "Is there a doctor in the subway?"

Why the difference? Helping may be inhibited in the laboratory setting for the following reasons: (1) the subjects had already adopted the passive role of "the subject"; (2) they assume that the experimenter in charge is ultimately responsible for everything that occurs during the experimental session; (3) they did not actually see the victim in distress; and (4) they felt an obedience to an unstated rule: —"You stay in your seat and follow instructions until told otherwise."

C L O S E ——— U P

Culture and Crowding

Street scene, Hong Kong

What parallels can we draw between the effects of overcrowding among animals and human beings? How many of our social ills are due to crowded conditions? The best evidence that over-crowding in itself does not cause physical and social disorder comes from so-cial psychologist R. C. Schmitt, who correlated social effects with density in the most crowded city in the world—Hong Kong. This predominantly Chinese community is, figuratively, a "beehive," accommodating some 2,000 persons per acre (.4 hectares) of ground space. (By comparison, high-density cities like New York and Boston seldom exceed 450 persons per acre (.4 hect-ares).) In comparing Hong Kong with American cities, Schmitt found that it was a much healthier and safer place to live! The death rate is about two-thirds of that in the United States. Mental disturbances that required hospitalization ran about one-thirtieth of the U.S. rate. Serious crime in Hong Kong was less than half what it is in America, and mur-der and manslaughter cases were only one-sixth as numerous.

Sociologists explain this difference by pointing to the differences between Chinese and American culture. Chinese family life is highly organized and tightly controlled. There is respect for authority and a tradition of social etiquette. The city administration was also efficient, and social services were extensive. All this helped to lessen the effects of crowding.

When these conditions change, however, we can expect to see a change in social behavior. Gangs in the Chinatowns of San Francisco and New York now engage in crime and street wars that are "typically" American. As Hong Kong itself has become more permissive in the last few years, the crime rate has increased. It would seem that crowding, in itself, is not the factor affecting the health of a society.

Despite the higher rate of helping on the subway train, however, the fact remains that many people do not help. The setting seems to make a difference. For example, when the man on the crutches put on his act in an airport, the percent of those who helped was much lower than in the subway—41 percent as compared with 83 percent. The important factor may have been familiarity with the environment; the subway riders may have felt more at home in the subway and thus were more likely to deal with the trouble that arose. Or the factor might have been time. People in the airport were undoubtedly rushing to catch or meet planes. The people on the subway were "trapped" bystanders.

Section Review

1. How is vandalism related to anonymity?
2. Summarize the results of the Zimbardo experiment which took place in New York City and Palo Alto, California.
3. How is alienation a result of high density?
4. Judging from the results of two experiments, what factors seem to influence alienation in helping others?

4. Is Urban Design the Answer?

PREVIEW

In this section, read to find out:

1. how urban renewal can help solve urban problems.
2. some of the problems of urban renewal.
3. what was learned from designing New Towns.

Urban sociologist A. L. Schorr studied residential dwelling space in relation to a number of the ills of urban society. Specifically, he was able to relate crowded dwellings with emotional stress, poor physical health, and feelings of anonymity and alienation. While these conditions are undoubtedly economic in origin, the "cruel" environment becomes both the symbol of frustration and a target for destruction. Schorr points out that merely coping with the dilapidated housing and a lack of privacy contributes to fatigue, irritation, and ultimately alienation.

If this is the case, it should be possible, given money and commitment, to reduce social alienation by improving housing conditions. Such efforts, however, have met with only partial success.

The Dos and Don'ts of Urban Renewal

The Pruitt-Igoe public housing project in St. Louis, Missouri, was conceived as a model development. To many designers, it was considered a breakthrough in efficient, contemporary design, a blessing for cramped slum dwellers. The complex consisted of forty-three eleven-story buildings. The buildings were efficient and modern; rents were

Skyscraper housing projects can leave residents without space to socialize.

partially paid by the government. A few years later the buildings were either abandoned or demolished. Why did the project fail?

First, compare the Pruitt-Igoe complex with another low-income public housing project which proved more successful—Marcus Garvey Square in San Francisco. This development consisted of two-story attached townhouses that were dotted with gardens and other semi-public open spaces. Before completion of the project, the designer organized a discussion group in which prospective tenants, architects, and urban planners came together to discuss the life-styles of those who would occupy the buildings. Tenants also participated in choosing the decorations and color schemes for their homes.

What spelled failure for one project and success for another? What factors made the difference? The problems of the Pruitt-Igoe project stemmed primarily from the planners' lack of knowledge of spatial behavior. Environmental psychologist W. L. Yancey cites three design problems which contributed to the project's failure. The first problem was the image of Pruitt-Igoe; with its forty-three buildings, all alike and clustered together, it felt like an impersonal institution. Tenants had no sense of belonging. Second, there was no open space for children to play in or for residents to meet and form friendships. Third, because of the layout of stairwells and hallways, the project was unsafe. These areas, along with rooftops and parking lots, were difficult for parents and housing authorities to supervise. They became a no-man's land for vandals and muggers. Much of the crime that had formerly been spread

Architects and governments have learned some expensive lessons in how *not* to build an urban renewal project. The massive Pruitt-Igoe development in St. Louis (at left above) was partially demolished and abandoned as a failure when it became apparent that its residents did not have access to the right kind of space. The Marcus Garvey Square project in San Francisco (at right above) has been much more successful. The two-story townhouses give residents their own territory but also make it easy to contact their neighbors.

& & &
See Exercise 9, **Drawing Conclusions from Statistics,** pages 493–496 of the *Psychology Skills Handbook,* for more information about how to interpret statistical data.

out over many blocks now became concentrated within a single building.

How was Marcus Garvey Square different even though the density and the types of tenants were the same? O. Newman, author of *Defensible Space,* outlines the reasons for this difference. Instead of being "piled up," the tenants lived next door to each other. The pockets of open space provided a means for getting to know their neighbors while preserving the privacy of individual families. This arrangement also allowed for surveillance; all sections of the project were easily visible to the residents. Consequently vandalism was quite low. (Newman notes that in public housing, the taller the building, the higher the crime rate.) Another factor was image. Living in Marcus Garvey Square felt less like living in a housing project than did Pruitt-Igoe.

What conclusions can be drawn? There are several. First of all, urban planners learned that when planning an **urban renewal** project (a design for restoring part of a city), the life-styles of those who will live there must be taken into consideration. Unlike middle- and upper-class residents, those who are cramped in the more crowded, lower-economic parts of the cities do much of their living on the streets and out of open windows. Boundaries between houses or other dwellings and the immediate environment are not distinct. Their life-styles include much visiting back and forth. Also, there is a strong sense of neighborhood loyalty. Neighborhood and kinship ties grow and remain over several generations. It was extremely important to design housing complexes that did not alter this life-style or sense of "neighborhood." The Pruitt-Igoe complex did not provide space for companionship. People were isolated in their own units. In Marcus Garvey Square, the patches of public space encouraged social interaction. The life-styles residents were accustomed to did not have to be altered to a great degree.

Housing facilities must allow for personalization. All people have a strong sense of territoriality about where they live, potholes or no potholes. The Pruitt-Igoe was too impersonal and cold. People couldn't sink roots down where they didn't feel a part of their environment. This was not a problem in Marcus Garvey Square. Living in two-story townhouses, people developed a greater personal, territorial feeling about their living units. They could individualize the exteriors. The townhouses were more humanly scaled. They fit more into the residential neighborhoods surrounding them, unlike the tall, bleak towers of Pruitt-Igoe which had no relationship to the rest of the community.

Perhaps the most important factor to emerge from these projects and others like them was the issue of choice—the right to control the significant aspects of one's life. Being relocated without consent, even from "bad" to "good" housing, can breed social disaster in the form of vandalism and alienation. Although planners might have assumed otherwise, people were not necessarily unhappy with their lives just because they lived with crowded, run-down housing conditions. In fact, studies have shown many residents were quite satisfied. So when forced relocation occurred, people were often unhappier than before. The fact that tenants of Marcus Garvey Square were given an opportunity to talk with designers and to express their opinions and preferences surely added to the success of the project.

Creating Good Environments for People

If it is possible to design residential complexes to relieve crowding and stress and still meet people's physical and psychological needs, then is it possible to do the same for entire cities? Some urban planners believed it was. This idea was tested in the development of "new towns."

New Towns were to be ideal cities, modest in size (population under 100,000) and unified in design. There would be no slums and no crowding. A good social "mix" would be promoted by locating diverse groups in close proximity. The community would be largely self-sufficient, with the emphasis on local participation in civic affairs.

It's Your Turn

You've read about the possible effects of crowding. Now *It's Your Turn*. Give an example of crowding in your school. Suggest a way to lessen the effects of the crowding.

What shape will our cities take in years to come? In a project that began on the Arizona desert in 1970 (see above), architect Paolo Soleri is trying to demonstrate that we can rearrange the structure of our cities in a very different way. Working solely with volunteers, Soleri is building his dream city, Arcosanti, *up*. His plan is to preserve open land, ban the automobile, and conserve energy through the use of greenhouses that trap heat and provide food for the city. Arcosanti is based on the idea that humans of the future will want or need to live in 3-D cities where neighbors, libraries, schools, and hospitals will be an elevator away.

New Towns proved to have many advantages. However, they have come under considerable criticism, mainly for being *too well* planned. Although physical and intellectual needs were well provided for, the need for spontaneity was not. The unified architectural style and "visual order" of the communities lacked variety and interest. Moreover, the ideal of "classless" communities did not work out, largely because socioeconomic groups preferred identification with a territory of their own. New Towns became havens for the middle class.

Another objection to New Towns was that life, lived according to a master plan, lacked stimulation. This point was made in a study by psychologist L. Fellows in West Germany. The paintings and drawings of young children in three New Towns were compared with those produced by a similar age group in traditional cities. The planned nature of the New Town environment encouraged little natural curiosity and tended to blunt creativity in the children. By contrast, the work of city children was fresher and more imaginative.

But New Towns weren't the only cities to take a fresh approach to

Case Study

Fighting Poverty

Research is useful for describing the damage caused by poverty and for suggesting solutions. Yet, these findings are useless if no one acts upon them.

This is the mission of Jonathan Kozol. Kozol's latest book, *Rachel and Her Children,* is a study of the nation's homeless children. In it Kozol describes the plight of the almost 500,000 children who are never sure where they will be sleeping that night. Their parents, usually single women on welfare, are regularly shunted from welfare hotels to shelters. By touching people's hearts, Kozol hopes to win public support for programs that will help these children.

Marian Wright Edelman, author of *Families in Peril,* shares Kozol's mission. However, her weapons are facts and figures and thousands of pages of reports. Edelman, the daughter of a black Baptist minister and a former civil rights lawyer, is founder and president of the Children's Defense Foundation, a lobbying organization in Washington, D.C. By bombarding Congress with statistics and reports, Edelman has won continued funding for programs that fight childhood poverty. For every dollar spent on prenatal care, child nutrition, and early education, her statistics show, the nation will save three dollars in welfare costs.

The needy are also getting direct help from students. Estimates are that as many as 25 percent of college students regularly volunteer for public service projects. At many universities, special coordinators match volunteers to local projects. At others, student-run service organizations write detailed proposals for funding and managing social service projects in their communities. In the late 1980s, for example, the city of Cambridge, Massachusetts, awarded students a $23,000 contract to run a shelter for the homeless.

urban development. Toronto, Ontario, Canada, for example, the largest city in Canada, adopted a plan to control its growth strictly, develop an efficient transportation system, and maintain parks every few blocks for people enjoyment. Some cities in the United States have done the same.

Whether urban planners make mistakes or not, in their efforts they keep reminding us that we do not have to *just adapt* to our environment, but can change our environment to make it provide what we need. We do not have to wait until we are overwhelmed by stress and then get help; we can change what causes the stress before it happens. As a society, we can work to change systems that give people only unacceptable choices or that trap them in self-defeating behavior. We can try to build a nourishing environment that makes it possible for people to achieve the life they want.

Section Review

1. What were the problems of the Pruitt-Igoe project?
2. Why was Marcus Garvey Square more successful?
3. What were the advantages and disadvantages of New Towns?

5. Psychology with a Human Face

PREVIEW

**In this section,
read to find out:**

1. why psychology has entered a new era of social responsibility.
2. how, in this era, psychologists are not only analyzing problems but are inventing solutions.

In adding their input into the design and planning of entire communities, behavioral scientists have taken on a new role in psychology. Psychology has come a long way since Pavlov's dogs salivated at the sound of a bell, and Skinner's pigeons learned to bowl. The study of behavior has traced increasingly complex stages of learning and adaptation. The needs, drives, perceptions, biological components, abnormalities, and social behaviors have been fitted together into a psychological being that we recognize as human. Now that this being has been thrust from the laboratory into the free-for-all world of "real life," where does psychology go next?

There is a Greek myth about Pygmalion and Galatea. George Bernard Shaw adapted the story into a play, *Pygmalion*, which later became the musical, *My Fair Lady*. If you saw either the stage or movie version, you recall that Professor Henry Higgins was an expert in spoken languages. He took a cockney flower girl from the streets of London and performed an interesting experiment. Higgins believed that the flower girl, Eliza Doolittle, could be taught "good English" as well as the social graces that would transform her into a lady—in short, he was a "behavior modifier" who was ahead of his time. He wanted to create a "new person," but only in the external, "behavioristic" sense.

Unwittingly, Higgins also created an inner person, a young woman with high spirits, the capacity for love, and ideas of her own. Shaw's point was that when someone creates a new person, it follows that the creator must be responsible for the inner self as well—the meanings and values, the hopes and disappointments and visions that go with being human. In a figurative sense, psychologists today find themselves in this uneasy position. Traditionally, they have been content to identify what conditions lead to what results, letting someone else (anyone else) decide how the results could or should affect society for the better. Their subjects have learned to "speak good English," but the task of putting it to good use has been left to others.

But the evidence is all around us that the era of the scientist who is aloof from social responsibility is coming to an end. A number of hardy souls—the environmentalists, the behavior modifiers, and the social psychologists—have ventured across the frontier that separates pure research from its practical consequences. More will follow. Whether it is unethical treatment of the mentally disturbed, the psychological "dirty tricks" used on occasion by government and business, or the abuses of educational testing, psychologists can no longer afford to stand by indifferently. They are being challenged to concern them-

This mural expresses the artist's hope for a future of peace and brotherhood for all people.

selves with values as well as explanations, to distinguish what is humanly desirable from what is humanly possible.

More and more psychologists are coming to realize that the information they have been gathering all these years and their methods for understanding the hows and whys of human behavior are valuable and worthwhile. They are starting to have faith in their discipline and are gaining new respect for their subject matter—people. As psychologists become aware of what they have to offer and what their community needs, they are even beginning to redirect their research efforts. Many more psychologists are designing *applied research.* That is, they are evaluating the impact of social and personal change strategies and not just applying the results of basic research to real-life problems. In the process of seeing the vital connection between the fundamentals of theory and the realities of practice, psychologists are ultimately developing a new sensitivity to the challenge that is posed by being human. In this respect, their work, like that of the puzzled Professor Higgins, is just beginning. We hope you will join in their venture and apply your psychological knowledge to help improve the quality of our lives and those of future generations.

Section Review

1. How is *Pygmalion* a comparison of social responsibility in psychology?
2. List some ways psychologists are *applying* research.
3. How can you use your knowledge of psychology to improve the quality of life?

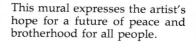

Chapter 16 Review

Section Summaries

1. Crowd Behavior

Collective behavior refers to the way a group reacts as a unit in response to an irrational process. A crowd—a large, unorganized group of people—can be classified as a casual crowd, a conventionalized crowd, an acting crowd, or an expressive crowd. A mob—a crowd that resorts to disorderly, aggressive behavior—can be classified as an aggressive, escape, acquisitive, or expressive mob. According to social psychologist Gustave Le Bon's contagion theory, the anonymity of a crowd makes people vulnerable to contagious feelings and behaviors. In contrast, emergent-norm theory holds that the crowd comes to represent a norm, which members come to defend and enforce.

2. Too Many People, Too Little Space

According to social psychologist J. L. Freedman, your perception of crowding will depend on who is crowding you, the activity involved, and your previous experience with crowding. Crowding can cause stress and a flight response. If flight is not possible, people may react with frustration and aggression, they may withdraw, or they may adapt. Density is a measure of population, but crowding is a psychological phenomenon. Although the idea is still under study, John Calhoun thinks that lasting, uncontrollable overcrowding can cause social breakdown.

3. The Effects of the Urban Environment

Feelings of anonymity often encourage vandalism. Analysis of gang behavior reveals that vandalism is related to hopelessness caused by limited opportunities and to the norms of a counterculture. Vandalism may also be a symptom of alienation. The murder of Kitty Genovese led social psychologists J. M. Darley and B. Latane to study bystander intervention. Their laboratory research showed that subjects responded more slowly or not at all if they thought others were present. However, a later study conducted in the New York subway showed that 81 of 103 bystanders responded.

4. Is Urban Design the Answer?

Urban sociologist A. L. Schorr related crowded urban dwellings to emotional stress, poor physical health, and feelings of anonymity and alienation. Comparing the failure of the Pruitt-Igoe high-rise project to the success of the low-rise Marcus Garvey Square project has shown that it is important to design housing complexes that allow for social interaction, personalization, and a sense of control. New Towns were to be ideal cities, modest in size, and unified in design, that would eliminate slums and crowding and encourage civic participation. New Towns have been criticized because they do not allow for spontaneity and stimulation. However, the work of urban planners helps us realize that, instead of just adapting, we can change our environment.

5. Psychology with a Human Face

The era of the scientist who is aloof from social responsibility is coming to an end. Ethical issues are a growing concern, and more psychologists are designing applied research. In this way, psychologists hope to improve the quality of life.

Psychology Skill Activities

1. Over the next week, observe a number of different types of crowds. Take notes about the way the crowd seems to affect individual behaviors.   **easy**

2. Working with two to four classmates, write a report explaining how you would better the physical environment of your local community.   **challenging**

Testing for Understanding

Knowing Key Terms

Define these terms in your own words.

Section 1
collective behavior
crowd
mob
contagion theory
anonymity
convergence theory
emergent-norm theory

Section 2
density
crowding
spatial density

Section 3
vandalism
alienation

Section 4
urban renewal
New Towns

Reviewing Main Ideas

Section 1
1. What types of crowds has sociologist H. G. Bruner identified?
2. According to social psychologist M. Brown, what kinds of events create aggressive, escape, acquisitive, and expressive mobs?
3. Explain the main psychological theories of crowd behavior.

Section 2
1. What variables can influence an individual's perception of crowding?
2. What are some typical responses to unpleasant, uncontrollable crowding?
3. What conclusions can be drawn from Calhoun's studies of crowding in rats?

Section 3
1. Why does crowding breed anonymity and alienation?

2. What are some of the factors associated with vandalism?
3. What causes people to become bystanders in emergencies?

Section 4
1. What is the reasoning behind urban renewal?
2. Why did the Pruitt-Igoe housing complex fail?
3. What are some of the criticisms that have been made of New Towns?

Section 5
1. Why is it said that psychology has entered a new era of social responsibility?
2. How are psychologists trying to improve the quality of life?

Thinking Critically
1. *Drawing Conclusions.* Is graffiti a form of vandalism? If so, what sense can you make of it? **easy**
2. *Making Applications.* Besides urban renewal, what could be done in cities to lessen the negative effects of crowding? **challenging**

Demonstrating Psychology Skills
Imagine that you are a psychologist hired to create a prison environment that would help turn prisoners into responsible, law-abiding citizens. How would you design the prison—physically, socially, and psychologically? Specify any useful principles that you have learned in your study of psychology.

Experimenting with Psychology

An Observation of Personal Space

As we have seen in this unit, one of the areas of interest to social psychologists is personal space. Personal space is the amount of space an individual keeps between him- or herself and another individual. This distance may vary depending upon a number of factors such as the relationship with the other person, the situation, or the sexes of the persons involved. Many studies indicate the importance of this phenomenon in human relations. You can conduct your own study.

Using the research method of observation (see pages 480-482 of the Psychology Skills Handbook), you will be collecting data on how much personal space people require when standing in lines. First, you will need to select a place where people commonly stand in lines. The school cafeteria, a movie theater, a ball park, or a bank are good places to choose. The dependent variable (see pages 473-474 of the Psychology Skills Handbook for more information on dependent variables), or behavior, that you are measuring is the distance people leave between themselves and the person in front of them in the line.

You might also want to focus on a specific factor about the person in front of the line. For example, does the behavior change for different sexes or if the other person is wearing loud or flashy clothing? Choose one of these, or a similar factor, and determine how it will be measured so it stays the same for each subject.

During the observation, choose people at random in line and estimate their distance from the person before them in line. Record this in a table such as the one below. Choose other people that reflect our specific factor (sex, clothing, etc.) and record their distances in the chart as well. Try to get as large a sample as possible.

Record of Results

Control Group (random)	Distance to Person in Front
subject 1	
subject 2	
subject 3	

Experimental Group (loud clothing, etc.)	Distance to Person in Front
subject 1	
subject 2	
subject 3	

Conclusions:

1. What is the average (mean) distance for the control group?
2. What is the average distance for the experimental group?
3. How do you explain the difference between these two groups, if any?
4. How do these results compare with what you thought would happen before you did this study?
5. What general conclusions can you state about personal space based on this observation?

Unit 5 Test

Matching (25 points)

Match each phrase with a term below.
1. distance in personal business
2. being liked by a group
3. contradictions between verbal and nonverbal behavior
4. tends to follow a self-appointed leader
5. fulfilling each other's needs
6. theory accounting for attitude change
7. really believing in an attitude
8. failure to thrive syndrome
9. being able to punish others in a group
10. stage of talking honestly

a. common response to neglect
b. coercive power
c. social distance
d. cognitive dissonance
e. mutuality
f. double messages
g. need complementarity
h. acting crowd
i. internalization
j. referent power

Multiple Choice (25 points)

Circle the choice that best completes the statement or answers the question.
1. Which is *not* a reason people seek privacy? (a) personal autonomy, (b) self-evaluation, (c) discrimination, (d) emotional release
2. Which is *not* an example of nonverbal communication? (a) congruence, (b) social distance, (c) matching phenomenon, (d) personal distance
3. Which was *not* a conclusion of Aronson's study of likability? (a) Competent people are well-liked. (b) Competent people who make mistakes find their likability increased. (c) Competence is unrelated to liking. (d) Attractiveness is not the only factor related to liking.
4. All of the following are major reasons for group formation except (a) personal autonomy, (b) influence, (c) achievement, (d) affiliation.
5. Psychologists seem to think the best style of group leadership is (a) authoritarian, (b) democratic, (c) laissez-faire, (d) none of these.
6. Stanley Milgram's famous experiment was a study of (a) territoriality, (b) dissonance, (c) obedience to authority, (d) sexuality.
7. Our attitudes come from (a) verbal learning, (b) modeling, (c) experiences, (d) all of these.
8. LeBon believes that in a crowd (a) anonymity frees the individual from personal responsibility, (b) behavior is contagious, (c) people are in highly suggestible states, (d) all of these.
9. Density is (a) a large crowd, (b) the degree to which a person feels crowded, (c) related to a high incidence of divorce, (d) the number of people in a certain amount of space.
10. To relieve cognitive dissonance, a person must (a) decrease social contact, (b) change attitudes or behavior, (c) change others' attitudes, (d) become anonymous.

True-False (25 points)

Decide whether each statement is true or false. Correct any false statements.
1. When deprived of privacy, people retreat.
2. Humans need both human contact and personal privacy.
3. Congruence is a form of territoriality.
4. The matching phenomenon is explained by the effect of proximity.
5. Saying "I did it because they pressured me," is an example of an internal justification.
6. Compliance is forming an attitude in order to avoid rejection or win approval.
7. The My Lai massacre did not come as a great shock to social psychologists.
8. Prejudice is learned.
9. Convergence theory holds that people come together for different reasons.
10. Urban design can help cure society's ills.

Critical Thinking Essay (25 points)

Write a one-page essay called, "The Psychologically Healthy Person's Relations with Others." Describe how the psychologically healthy person relates to friends, strangers, and family members, citing research as appropriate.

Psychology Skills Handbook
Table of Contents

Psychology Skills Handbook

Introduction

"First the sentence," [said the Queen,] "and then the evidence!"

"Nonsense!" cried Alice, so loudly that everybody jumped, "The idea of having the sentence first!"

As Alice did in Wonderland, most psychologists insist on having the evidence *first*—and then coming to conclusions about behavior. Psychologists gather and analyze evidence, or data, in a variety of ways following basically the same methods of research as other scientists.

The Exercises in this Psychology Skills Handbook give you a step-by-step description of the procedures psychologists follow in gathering and analyzing data. Each Exercise includes an Application section that allows you to try your hand at real psychological research and data analysis. But, first, a few general comments about how psychologists gather and analyze data.

How Psychologists Gather Data

The question a psychologist is asking about behavior will largely determine the method of research he or she will choose to find the answer. For example, suppose a researcher wanted find out whether a group of college students would deliver stronger electric shocks to a subject if they were anonymous than if they were face-to-face with the "victim." The researcher probably wouldn't choose to *survey* the group of college students on this question—although the survey method of gathering data is often used by psychologists. Why not? We all have a natural tendency to want to "look good" to others. And, often, we don't believe ourselves capable of doing things we might actually do under certain conditions. For these reasons, if the researcher chose the survey method in this case, he or she probably would get pretty inaccurate results and wouldn't end up knowing much more about the effects of anonymity on shocking than he or she did to start with. The researcher might be better off setting up an experiment to find out the answer to his or her question. Surveys and experiments are just two of many methods of gathering data described in this Handbook. Exercises in this Handbook that deal with methods of gathering data are marked with this symbol 🌀

How Psychologists Analyze Data

After the reactions of all the participants in an experiment have been tested or all individuals have been surveyed on a topic, a researcher must analyze the data he or she has collected. For most researchers in psychology this is an exciting step. This is the point at which they find out if their results contribute to a better understanding of a particular aspect of behavior or if they are going to have to go back to the drawing board and redesign their research (as our shock researcher would have had to do after analyzing the results of a survey on the effects of anonymity on shocking).

Some methods of data analysis can be surprisingly simple and straightforward. Others require a bit of statistical technique. Don't let "math anxiety" make you stop reading here, however. You don't have to be "good in math" to understand the concepts presented in the data analysis exercises that follow. You only have to understand what an equation is and be able to see mathematical symbols for what they are—a shorthand way of representing ideas and arithmetic operations. Exercises in this Handbook that deal with methods of analyzing data are identified with this symbol ❓

Exercise 1   Experiments

The work of B. F. Skinner, described in Chapter 5, is a good example of one of the most important methods of collecting data—the **experiment.** In an experiment, the researcher is able to *control* what is going on, making it much easier to see which factors cause a particular pattern of events. This method is useful when a researcher is investigating a behavior or process that might be affected by many different factors. For example, the researcher you encountered in the Introduction to this Handbook, who was interested in the effect of anonymity on subjects giving shocks to a "victim," did develop an experiment to study this question. The experimental method enabled him to control factors that he wouldn't have been able to control in a survey situation—such as the conscious or unconscious desire on the part of subjects to want to make their motives "look good" to an interviewer or the subjects' possible unawareness of their true motives.

Most experiments are carried out to test a new hypothesis or refine an old one. A **hypothesis** is a statement indicating what the researcher thinks will happen in the experiment. A hypothesis is usually stated in an if → then form. The experimenter is stating that *if* a certain thing happens *then* it will cause another thing to happen. For example, Skinner hypothesized that *if* behavior is reinforced (rewarded) *then* it will continue to occur. Skinner tested this hypothesis with pigeons in his Skinner box. If the pigeons pecked at a disk in the box, they received a food reward. Pecking at other parts of the box was not reinforced or rewarded. Soon the pigeons gave up pecking at other spots in the box and pecked only at the disk. Skinner proved his hypothesis that behavior that is rewarded is more likely to occur.

When a psychologist sets up an experiment, he or she usually decides to study the effects of one specific factor, or variable, on another. One factor in the experiment is changed, or varied, in order to study its effects on another factor, or variable. The factor that is changed by the experimenter is called the **independent variable;** the other factor is called the **dependent variable.** The independent variable may or may not cause changes in the dependent variable. This is basically what the experimenter aims to find out.

In Skinner's experiment described above, the food reward is the independent variable, and the pecking behavior is the dependent variable. Skinner found that by giving the food reward (the independent variable) only when the pigeons pecked at the disk, he could influence their pecking behavior (the dependent variable)—the pigeons would only peck at the disk and nowhere else in the box. In another experi-

Rat in a Skinner box

ment, Skinner wanted to see if pigeons could be conditioned to peck at a disk only when a green light was on. The green light became the independent variable, and the dependent variable was their pecking behavior.

To test the variables in an experiment it is necessary to state them in specific terms that can be measured. This concrete, measurable statement of the behaviors expected in an experiment is called an **operational definition.** Operational definitions help reduce the vagueness of the terms used to describe behavior—like "learning," "creativity," "anxiety," "cooperation," and so on. An operational definition of "learning" as it might apply to the first of Skinner's experiments described above is: the pigeons show "learning" if they "continue to peck only at the disk for a period of three minutes and ignore all other parts of the box."

One way of determining if the independent variable has indeed caused the dependent variable is to use two groups of subjects in the experiment. One group called the **experimental group** receives the independent variable; the other, called the **control group,** does not. It is important, however, that the two groups be equal in all ways except for the independent variable being tested. This procedure allows the researcher to compare the reactions of the two groups to see if the independent variable alone accounts for differences in behavior between the two.

Here is how the procedure works. In Skinner's green light experiment described above, he divided his pigeons into two groups. The experimental group received the food reward for pecking when the green light was on. The control group received nothing. Skinner then compared the behavior of the two groups and found that the control group, which wasn't rewarded, didn't show an increase in pecking behavior when the green light was turned on. The experimental group, which was rewarded, on the other hand, showed increased pecking activity when the light was turned on.

Experimental bias. Researchers have to guard against possible sources of bias that may contaminate, or invalidate, the results of their experiments. For example, no matter how objective researchers try to be, they have a natural tendency to want to *prove* their hypotheses. So, they might unconsciously overlook evidence that doesn't support their views and exaggerate evidence that does.

In conducting experiments with human subjects, psychologists have to guard against the kind of bias that may result from the way the researcher behaves during the course of the experiment. Through his or her tone of voice or manner, a researcher may "suggest" the kinds of responses he or she wants the subject to give. *Subjects* can bias the results of an experiment by trying to "second-guess" the experimenter. A subject might not respond naturally or might even try to "help" the experimenter by responding in a way he or she thinks the researcher wants. To guard against this bias, experimenters often go to great lengths to provide subjects with a false or incomplete description of the experiment's purpose.

Application

Suppose that you wanted to investigate the effect of electric shock on the pecking behavior of pigeons in a Skinner box. Describe the procedure you might use to set up an experiment for this purpose. What could be your hypothesis? How would you define your variables? What groups of subjects would you use? What procedures would you set up to guard against producing biased results?

After deciding which research method to use, next the researcher must define the population, or group of people, to be studied. From that, he or she chooses a smaller **sample population** to actually observe. It is usually impossible to observe an entire population of subjects. And observing or testing an entire population is usually not necessary. If a sample population is chosen correctly, and if the experiment is designed and run properly, not much more information is gained from observing the whole population than from observing a sample.

Suppose, for example, that you wanted to study the effect of imitation on language learning, a topic discussed in Chapter 6. It wouldn't be possible or necessary to study *all* the children in the United States to draw valid conclusions about this subject. You would need to use only a representative sample of children in the United States.

How would you go about selecting a representative sample? A sample should be selected so that each member of the population has an equal chance of being chosen. A sample picked in this way is called a **random sample.** If you were to sample the population of students at a particular high school, for example, you could achieve a random sample by drawing names out of a hat containing separate slips of paper with the names of all the students. Your sample would not be random, however, if you chose all your subjects from one particular homeroom or from those students who happened to be in the cafeteria at a particular time of day. The same thing would be true if you were to sample children for a study of language learning. You wouldn't want all the children to be from the same part of the country, the same economic, racial, or ethnic group, or from families with the same structure.

The 1948 presidential election was a close race, so pollsters needed a very large sample to make a reasonable prediction of the outcome. The *Chicago Daily Tribune* based its prediction of the outcome on early returns, and was in the embarrassing position of announcing the wrong "winner"—to President Harry Truman's obvious delight.

A random sample assures you that the sample is representative of the population. Researchers who think they are using random sampling methods sometimes end up with very unrepresentative samples. For example, in the 1936 election, pollsters randomly selected names from telephone books and asked those people whom they preferred in the presidential race. Their prediction: Alf Landon, the Republican candidate would win. Unfortunately, the pollsters overlooked the fact that many more Republicans than Democrats had telephones at that time. Their sample was not wisely selected. Roosevelt won by a landslide. Researchers who choose children for a study of language learning from an upper-class area of a city might find quite different results from those studying children in other settings. In comparing two groups of subjects on a particular difference researchers must also be sure that this difference is the *only one* that exists between the two groups. All other aspects of the sample groups must be equal.

How large should the sample be? That depends on what results the experimenter expects to find. Consider again the problem of predicting the outcome of an election. If one candidate does, in fact, win by a landslide, a relatively small sample would have allowed the pollster to predict the results. But in a close race, the pollster will need a much larger sample to make any kind of reasonable prediction. An election might simply be too close to call, no matter how large the sample (short of selecting a sample as large as the population itself).

The same principle applies when a researcher is doing an experiment or survey in psychology. A researcher who believes that the effect he or she wishes to demonstrate is weak will need a large sample to detect it. If the effect is expected to be quite powerful, a smaller sample will do. If you were comparing, for example, the language development of children raised in isolation versus children raised in a close family setting, a small sample might be sufficient since a powerful effect would be predicted. On the other hand, if you were comparing children raised by one parent to those raised by two parents, you might want a larger sample, as a more subtle difference might be expected.

Application

Suppose you were asked to do a study of the rate of language learning among children who attend nursery school or are in daycare with those who are not. Describe the type of sample population that would be needed. How would they be selected? What steps would be necessary to avoid bias in the sample?

? Exercise 3 Summarizing Data in Tables and Graphs

In Chapter 4, you encountered a graph showing the number of people in the population who receive the various ranges of IQ scores. Psychologists often do this with the results of their research. They summarize the data they've gathered in graphs and tables to give a clearer picture of their results.

To illustrate the advantage of showing data in these ways, look below at the list of raw data obtained from a hypothetical IQ test on a sample population (Table 1). (*Raw data* are the results of research just as they are recorded by the researcher—before they are interpreted.) What do these scores tell you about the intelligence levels of the subjects? It's difficult to tell, isn't it, when material is presented in this way?

To get a clearer picture of these results we need to find a way of summarizing the data. One way to do this is to draw up a **frequency distribution** for this data. This will tell us how many subjects scored at each IQ level. The first step in drawing up a frequency distribution is to **rank order** the scores from lowest to highest. Rank ordering is shown below in Table 2. The second step is to construct a frequency distribution table. In some cases the researcher may want to group the scores in intervals (70–85; 85–100; 100–115). This is shown in Table 3. Each interval is listed followed by the number of people who scored in that range.

Table 1 Raw Data, IQ Scores

subject #	IQ score	subject #	IQ score
1	100	11	105
2	86	12	67
3	70	13	88
4	115	14	120
5	140	15	110
6	90	16	92
7	75	17	125
8	95	18	103
9	98	19	122
10	78	20	112

Table 2 Rank Order, IQ Scores

lowest:	67
	70
	75
	78
	86
	88
	90
	92
	95
	98
	100
	103
	105
	110
	112
	115
	120
	122
	125
highest:	140

Table 3 Frequency Distribution, IQ Scores

IQ scores	frequency
55–69	1
70–85	3
86–100	7
101–115	5
116–130	3
131–145	1

A graph would make the frequency distribution of the scores shown in Table 3 even clearer. Psychologists often use **histograms** to show research results. A histogram is similar to a bar graph. On a histogram, the bars are directly next to one another, and number categories are on the horizontal axis (across the bottom). The frequency of scores is shown on the vertical axis (along the side). The histogram below shows the data from our hypothetical IQ test shown in Table 3. A quick glance at the histogram shows that the scores of most of the subjects are clustered at 86–115 intervals.

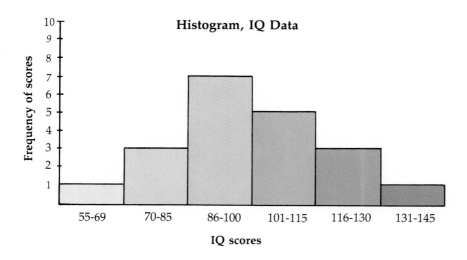

The normal curve. When graphing some data such as the IQ scores for a whole population, the measurements are known to follow a normal curve. (See the normal curve on page 187.) This is also referred to as a **bell curve.** Along the horizontal axis are the scores, while the height of the curve above the axis indicates the frequency of score, or the number of people who obtained each score. Given the results of enough subjects in such an area as IQ scores, a pattern of scores distributed in the shape of a bell curve will emerge. Other data, such as the height or weight of a population may also take on this shape. The middle of the curve represents the most frequently occurring score, the one most people achieve. As the scores get higher or lower (farther from the middle) there are fewer and fewer people at each score. Not all research data fit this pattern, however.

Application

These techniques of summarizing data in tables and graphs may be applied to other data as well. Below is the raw data from psychologist Stanley Milgram's experiment on obedience to authority, described on pages 408–410 of your text, in which Milgram tested how far subjects would go in giving electric shocks to a person if ordered to keep on giving the punishment. Construct the following from the Milgram data: (1) a rank order (2) a frequency distribution (3) a histogram.

Table 4 Raw Data from Stanley Milgram's Experiment on Obedience to Authority

Subject #	Max. Shock (volts)	Level	Subject #	Max. Shock (volts)	Level
1	135	9	21	450	30
2	450	30	22	450	30
3	285	19	23	150	10
4	300	20	24	450	30
5	450	30	25	450	30
6	165	11	26	150	10
7	450	30	27	450	30
8	315	21	28	450	30
9	450	30	29	315	21
10	315	21	30	450	30
11	450	30	31	450	30
12	450	30	32	150	10
13	360	24	33	450	30
14	450	30	34	450	30
15	150	10	35	450	30
16	450	30	36	345	23
17	450	30	37	450	30
18	150	10	38	450	30
19	450	30	39	450	30
20	180	12	40	450	30

Exercise 4 Observational Studies

Observation is a method of gathering data often used by psychologists and other behavioral scientists. There are three major types of observational studies:

1. **Natural observation** involves watching and recording how organisms (persons or other living things) behave in their natural environments. Some of the best known examples of natural observations in psychology were those done by Jean Piaget, whose theories you studied in Chapter 1. Piaget watched his own children in their nurseries, took notes on what they said and how they behaved, and later used his observations as the basis for a theory of cognitive development.

2. **Controlled observation** occurs in a laboratory setting. Here the researcher knows in advance what will be observed. For example, a

Psychologist Jean Piaget is shown here observing children.

researcher may observe how several pairs of children interact with a single toy.

3. **Participant observation** is a method used mostly by anthropologists and sociologists, but some psychologists also employ this method. When a researcher is involved in participant observation, he or she lives with a group of people, interacts with them, and observes how they behave and what they say.

Each method has its advantages. Natural observation can be used effectively by a psychologist who starts with a general area of interest but no specific hypotheses. "Just looking" can lead one to form hypotheses which can later be tested through controlled observation or other methods. Participant observation is most effective in studying human interaction, since interaction in a laboratory setting will often be artificial.

Some critics of observational studies believe it is easy for researchers who use this method to find out only what she or he wants to find out. Say, for example, the researcher wanted to convince the public that two-year-olds can play together in daycare centers. A statement in an observational study might read, "Most of the two-year-olds played together well." But "most" and "played together well" are imprecise terms. Experiments and surveys are usually more precise than observational studies. Often, too, observees can bias an observational study by changing their behavior when they are being observed.

Those who conduct observational studies believe biases and imprecision can be avoided, or at least minimized. They argue that observational data is the only "true" data—that is data not affected by artificial laboratory conditions.

Application

Propose an observational study involving young children. Describe what you would want to find out and what method of observation you would use. How would you keep your research free from bias?

Exercise 5   Surveys

Another important way psychologists collect data is through surveys. Psychologist Lawrence Kohlberg, for example, whose theories you studied in Chapter 2, based his findings about the development of moral reasoning on surveys of people of all ages. Surveys are a useful way of gathering information on the practices and opinions of large numbers of people.

Surveys can be carried out through questionnaires or face-to-face interviews. Questionnaires usually are filled out by the people surveyed—almost always anonymously. (Some psychologists believe that people will give more honest answers when they don't have to give their names.)

Questionnaires must be written carefully to provide researchers with valid results. Below are a set of guidelines for writing a questionnaire. Some are self-explanatory; others require a bit of thought.

1. Use simple vocabulary, and keep your questions short and to the point.

2. Ask for only *one* bit of information per question. For example, in the sample survey on page 484, if question 9 had been phrased like this: "Do you have someone to talk to? Who is it?" the researcher would be asking respondents to answer *two* questions instead of one.

3. The response you want should be in agreement with the question. Suppose, for example, that item 1 in the sample survey read: "If you were working and you inherited enough money to live on for the rest of your life, would you continue to hold a job or would you take a trip around the world?   a._____Yes   b._____No."

In this case, the response would not fit the question.

4. Avoid using value-laden words that suggest the answer you think is appropriate. For example, if item 3 in the sample survey read: "If you found a wallet containing $300, would you do the right thing and return it?" the respondent could guess which response the researcher thought was the right one.

5. The best type of survey uses *closed* questions that require *specific* responses. All the questions in the survey below are closed questions. If the researcher had structured question 5 like this: "What do you worry about most?" he or she would have gotten responses ranging from one to 500 words. Open-ended questions make it difficult for researchers to tally and compare results of questionnaires.

6. Make sure that all the possible answers to questions are provided for. Most of the questions in the sample survey provide the respondents with a wide variety of responses. This is the mark of a

Sample Survey

1. Wealth: If you were (are) working, and you inherited enough money to live on for the rest of your life, would you continue to hold a job?
_____ a. Yes. _____ b. No.

2. Spending: What would you do with *most* of this new-found money? (You may pick up to THREE choices.)
_____ a. Buy things for myself and my family (such as cars, homes, clothing, and trips).
_____ b. Set aside the money for education (for example, pay for college for me and my brothers or sisters).
_____ c. Give the money to my family to open up a business of our own.
_____ d. Try to make more money by investing in a business.
_____ e. Put the money in a savings account.
_____ f. Give the money to groups that do things to help people.
_____ g. Other.

3. Honesty: Part 1: If you found a wallet containing $300, what would you do? (Check ONE.)
_____ a. Try to return the money and wallet.
_____ b. Keep the money, mail wallet to owner.
_____ c. Keep money and wallet.

4. Honesty: Part 2: A store clerk gives you too much change after you have paid for a purchase. What would you do?
_____ a. Return the money.
_____ b. Keep the money.

5. Fears: What do you worry about the *most*? (You may pick up to THREE choices from the list below.)
_____ a. School.
_____ b. Friends.
_____ c. Money.
_____ d. Being attacked or robbed on the street.
_____ e. Losing a close relative.
_____ f. Finding a job after graduation.

6. Drugs: What is the *main* reason you think some teenagers use drugs? (Check ONE.)
_____ a. They are unhappy and want to escape their problems.
_____ b. To get "high."
_____ c. To go along with their friends.
_____ d. To rebel against adults.
_____ e. To experiment, out of curiosity.
_____ f. Other.

7. You: Which THREE of the following are *most important to you personally* for *you* to have? (Check up to THREE.)
_____ a. Intelligence.
_____ b. Good looks.
_____ c. Athletic ability.
_____ d. Popularity.
_____ e. Sense of humor.
_____ f. School achievement.
_____ g. Honesty.
_____ h. Loyalty to friends.
_____ i. Closeness to family.
_____ j. Money.
_____ k. Other.

8. Friends: Which THREE of the following do you value *most* in choosing *your friends*? (Check up to THREE.)
_____ a. Intelligence.
_____ b. Good looks.
_____ c. Athletic ability.
_____ d. Popularity.
_____ e. Sense of humor.
_____ f. School achievement.
_____ g. Loyalty to friends.
_____ h. Honesty.
_____ i. Money.
_____ j. Having opinions that agree with mine.
_____ k. Other.

9. Talking: Part 1: Do you feel you have someone to talk to when you have a problem?
_____ a. Yes. _____ b. No.

10. Who?—Part 2: Who is the person with whom you are *most* likely to discuss your problems? (Check ONE.)
_____ a. Mother.
_____ b. Father.
_____ c. Sister or brother.
_____ d. Girlfriend or boyfriend.
_____ e. Teacher.
_____ f. Member of the clergy (such as Priest, Minister, Rabbi).
_____ g. Guidance counselor.
_____ h. Other.
_____ i. Don't want to talk to anyone.

good survey. If, in making up a survey, you feel there might be some responses you haven't provided for, it's always good to provide an "other" category as in question 6 in this survey.

Some psychologists prefer the interview method of surveying. In an interview situation, the interviewer can modify questions the subject doesn't understand or doesn't think are valid. Also, because interviews allow for more open-ended questions, they can provide more insights into the "why" of a behavior or a feeling.

There are drawbacks to the interview approach however. Sometimes interviewers consciously or unconsciously influence the subject to answer questions a certain way. And, it is easy for the subject to give the answers he or she thinks the researcher wants to hear or he or she may even be unaware of his or her true motives and behavior.

Finally, surveys don't have to be given to every person in a group. A random sample of a group can be chosen. A description of how you arrive at a random sample is included in Exercise 3, pages 476–477.

Application

Write a questionnaire survey of 5 to 10 questions on a topic of your choice.

Sample Survey Results

percent

1. Would you hold a job, though rich?

Yes.	78
No.	22

2. How would you spend an inheritance (multiple choice)?

Spend on yourself and family.	68
Set aside money for education.	57
Put the money in savings account.	56
Invest in a business.	24
Give money to charity.	22
Open a family business.	14
Other.	23

3. If you found a wallet with $300, here's what you'd do:

Try to return money and wallet.	71
Keep money and wallet.	18
Keep money; mail wallet to owner.	11

4. What you would do if store clerk gives you too much money, in change?

Keep the money.	51
Return the money.	49

5. What three things do you worry about most?

School.	53
Losing close relative.	47
Friends.	39
Money.	38
Finding job after graduation.	36
Being attacked or robbed on street.	26

6. The main reason you think some teenagers use drugs:

To go along with their friends.	42
To escape their problems.	24
To get high.	22
To experiment.	6
To rebel against adults.	2
Other.	4

7. Which three do you value most in yourself?

Intelligence.	42
Honesty.	33
Loyalty to friends.	32
Good looks.	32
Athletic ability.	30
Closeness to family.	29
Sense of humor.	24
School achievement.	20
Popularity.	16
Money.	16
Other.	6

8. Which 3 do you value most in your friends?

Loyalty to friends.	58
Honesty.	56
Sense of humor.	50
Having opinions agreeing with mine.	26
Intelligence.	22
Athletic ability.	11
Good looks.	11
Popularity.	9
Money.	6
School achievement.	5
Other.	20

9. Do you feel you have someone to talk to about your problems?

Yes.	81
No.	19

10. You are most likely to discuss your problems with:

Girlfriend or boyfriend.	29
Mother.	27
Sister or brother.	12
Father.	9
Guidance counselor.	1
Teacher.	1
Member of the clergy.	1
Other.	12
Don't talk to anyone.	8

? Exercise 6   Figuring Averages

As you saw in Exercise 3, tables and graphs give a good picture of how scores are *distributed*. But it is also useful to know what the *average*, or typical, score is. This is true of all types of research data whether it is IQ scores or the average amount of time adults spend in REM sleep, a topic discussed in Chapter 10. There are three different kinds of "average" scores—the mode, the median, and the mean.

The **mode** is the easiest score to determine. It is the score in a distribution that occurs more often than any other. Look at the frequency distribution in Table 5 below, showing the amount of REM sleep recorded for a hypothetical group of adult subjects. You can see that 100 minutes is the score that occurred most often. Seven subjects spent this amount of time in REM sleep.

In some cases, however, instead of being interested in the most frequently occurring score, you might want to know the **median,** the score that separates the upper half of the scores in a distribution from the lower half. Fifty percent of the scores are larger than the median, and fifty percent are smaller. To find the median for the data shown in Table 5 below, first rank order the scores, then find the score which is in the exact middle of the distribution. Eighty minutes is the median score. Exactly 50 percent of the scores are higher (12); and 50 percent are lower (12).

**Table 5   Frequency Distribution,
Time Spent in REM Sleep**

score (minutes)	frequency
20	2
40	4
60	2
80	5
100	7
120	1
140	1
160	1
180	2

The median, however, is often not a good reflection of the typical subject. The median is "insensitive" to extreme scores. It does not reflect them properly in terms of the total distribution.

The third type of average score, the **mean,** is what most people think of when they hear the word *average* such as *average* IQ and *average* amount of time spent in REM sleep. It is the statistic most typically used to describe a set of data, because it gives a better picture of the total scores of a group of subjects. In most cases, the mean is a much more accurate and useful measure than the mode or median. But the kind of average score a researcher uses depends on his or her purpose in calculating the average and upon the research data involved. (See Exercise 9, *Drawing Conclusions from Statistics* for more discussion about when to use these different types of "average" scores.)

To calculate the mean, you add up all of the scores and then divide by the total number of scores. This operation is summarized by the following formula:

$$\overline{X} = \frac{\Sigma X}{N}$$

In this formula, X stands for each individual score, and the symbol Σ *(sigma)* means "sum all." This means you add all the scores together. N represents the total number of scores. In this case, there are 25 scores. $\overline{X}$ ("X-bar") is another way of saying the mean. To calculate the mean for the sleep data, you would add up all the scores and then divide by the total number of scores. It would look like this:

$$\overline{X} = \frac{2200}{25} = 88$$

The mean, or *average* amount of time these adults spent in REM sleep was 88 minutes.

Application

Using the data from Milgram's experiment shown in Exercise 3 in Table A, calculate the following: (1) the mode (2) the median (3) the mean.

⑥ Exercise 7 Case Studies

A **case study** is an intensive investigation of an individual or small group of individuals. In psychology, many of the best case studies have shared two characteristics: (1) they are longitudinal (done over a long period of time); and (2) they are written by a clinical psychologist or a psychiatrist who has treated the subject as a patient. In order to treat a patient with unusual psychological difficulties, the therapist may need to use a variety of therapeutic techniques, which will then be reported in the case study. Let us see how one psychiatrist, Dr. Cornelia Wilbur, treated Sybil, a patient with multiple personalities, a disorder you studied in Chapter 12.

Sybil eventually displayed sixteen different personalities during her years of therapy with Dr. Wilbur. It took Dr. Wilbur several sessions with Sybil and much research in the psychological literature on multiple personality just to arrive at a *diagnosis* of Sybil's disorder. Cases of multiple personality are extremely rare, and it would have been possible for Dr. Wilbur to attribute the different kinds of behavior exhibited by Sybil's many selves to some other disorder—such as manic depression.

Multiple Christmas greeting sent by six of Sybil's personalities to her psychiatrist, Dr. Cornelia Wilbur.

After arriving at a diagnosis, Dr. Wilbur worked many months trying to discover the *cause* of Sybil's disorder. As a psychoanalyst, Dr. Wilbur was convinced that the source of Sybil's disorder, and the key to her treatment, lay in her past. Dr. Wilbur believed that Sybil had gone through childhood experiences so traumatic and threatening to her ego that massive dissociation of her personality was the result. Through psychoanalysis, observations of the patient outside her office, and interviews with Sybil's father and other family members, Dr. Wilbur discovered the source of Sybil's problems. As a child, Sybil had been tortured and abused by her disturbed mother.

After years of therapy, Dr. Wilbur was able to reintegrate Sybil's personality through hypnosis. Other therapists have described how play therapy, psychoanalysis, behavior modification, family therapy, and other techniques have been used to treat patients with difficult problems. This is the chief value of the case study method. Although case studies don't provide information on the behavior of large numbers of people as experiments and surveys do, they do give detailed descriptions of therapeutic techniques that can aid psychologists in treating patients with similar problems.

Application

Read one of the following books and write a short report describing the patient's background, the therapist's diagnosis, the cause of the problem, and the method(s) of therapy:

Baruch, Dorothy. *One Little Boy*. New York: Delta Books, 1952.

Greenberg, Joanne. *I Never Promised You a Rose Garden*. New York: Holt, Rinehart and Winston, 1969.

Henry, Jules. *Pathways to Madness*. New York: Vintage Books, 1965.

Lorenz, Sarah. *Our Son, Ken*. New York: Dell, 1969.

Rubin, Theodore Isaac. *Jordi, Lisa and David*. New York: Ballantine Books, 1962.

Schreiber, Flora. *Sybil*. Chicago: Henry Regnery Company, 1973.

Exercise 8   Determining Variability and Relatedness

You saw in Exercise 6 that determining "average," or typical, scores is useful to researchers. But to describe research data even more completely, it is helpful to know how closely scores are clustered around that average. This is what is known as determining the variability of data. In finding the variability of a distribution, we really are asking, "How much *spread* is there in the distribution? Are the scores widely scattered (many scores far away from the average) or tightly clustered (many scores close to the average)?"

The most basic way to describe the variability of a distribution is to subtract the lowest score from the highest score. This measure is called the **range.** See if you can calculate the range for the data from Milgram's experiment on obedience to authority shown in Exercise 3, Table 4 (page 480). The range for the Milgram data is 21 (level 30–level 9), or 315 volts.

The main disadvantage of range as a measure of variability is that a single high or low score tends to throw off the answer. Extreme high or low scores carry too much weight, and you don't get a true picture of the actual distribution of scores. A much more useful statistic is the **standard deviation** (SD). This measure lets you know how spread out the scores really are in a distribution. To calculate the SD, all you need to know is the individual scores and their mean. Standard deviation is calculated using the following formula:

$$SD = \sqrt{\frac{\Sigma d^2}{N}} = \sqrt{\frac{\Sigma(X - \overline{X})^2}{N}}$$

This formula might look a bit more complicated than the one used to calculate the mean, but the arithmetic is just as simple. As before, X is the symbol for the individual scores, and $\overline{X}$ represents the mean. The total number of scores is represented by N and Σ is the summation sign, which means to add all the numbers together. $(X - \overline{X})$ can also be represented by d. This is called the *deviation score,* or "deviation from the mean." It is found by subtracting the mean from each individual score.

Table 6 on page 492 shows how the standard deviation is computed for the Milgram data you worked with in Exercise 3 (page 480). If you follow these steps in order, the process is not complicated. First, take each individual score and subtract the mean from it to get the deviation score (d). (The mean is 24.53, but for simplicity's sake, use 24 as the mean.) Next square each deviation score; then add all 40 squared scores together. Next divide that sum by 40 (because there are 40 subjects, $N = 40$). Finally, take the square root of the whole thing. This gives us the standard deviation (SD)—in this case 7.88.

The standard deviation tells us how variable a set of scores is. The larger the standard deviation, the more spread out the scores are. A smaller SD indicates scores clustered more closely together.

Correlation

Another useful statistic is the correlation coefficient, which indicates the degree of relationship between two variables (such as height and age or IQ scores and school grades). It tells you if, in general, high scores on one measure go with high scores on another measure. If high scores on one variable tend to be matched with high scores on the other variable, the correlation coefficient will be "positive." If, however, high scores on one variable tend to go with low scores on another variable, the correlation will be "negative." If there is really no consistent relationship between scores, the correlation will be close to zero.

As it is calculated, the correlation coefficient can range from -1.00 to $+1.00$. For example, you might expect that IQ scores would be highly correlated with scores on the Scholastic Aptitude Test (SAT). In general, you would expect a person with high IQ scores to do well on the SAT, and a person with low IQ scores to do poorly. Of course, there would be exceptions for certain individuals, but overall, you would expect this pattern to hold true. If you actually computed the correlation coefficient, you would probably get a correlation of $+.85$. This

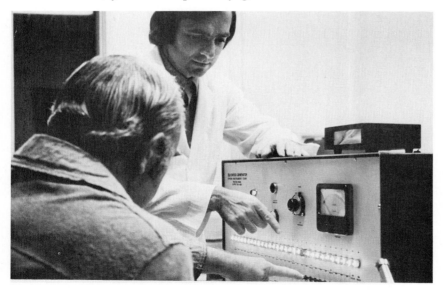

Psychologist Stanley Milgram explaining his experiment to a participant.

TABLE 6
Computation of Standard Deviation for Milgram's Data

Subject #	Score	d (X−X̄)	d²
1	9	−15	225
2	10	−14	196
3	10	−14	196
4	10	−14	196
5	10	−14	196
6	10	−14	196
7	11	−13	169
8	12	−12	144
9	19	−5	25
10	20	−4	16
11	21	−3	9
12	21	−3	9
13	21	−3	9
14	23	−1	1
15	24	0	0
16	30	6	36
17	30	6	36
18	30	6	36
19	30	6	36
20	30	6	36
21	30	6	36
22	30	6	36
23	30	6	36
24	30	6	36
25	30	6	36
26	30	6	36
27	30	6	36
28	30	6	36
29	30	6	36
30	30	6	36
31	30	6	36
32	30	6	36
33	30	6	36
34	30	6	36
35	30	6	36
36	30	6	36
37	30	6	36
38	30	6	36
39	30	6	36
40	30	6	36
			2487

total (Σd^2)

$$\frac{2487}{40} = 62.17 = \frac{\Sigma d^2}{N}$$

$$\sqrt{62.17} = 7.88 = SD$$

Note: for convenience we have used 24 as the mean.

would be a very high positive correlation, and it would mean that there is a close correspondence between those two scores.

It is important to keep in mind, however, that correlation does not prove *causation*. Even if two items are found to be highly correlated, you cannot be sure that one caused the other. More research would be needed. You might find that a third factor had caused the other two, rather than one causing the other. It is important to remember that correlation shows only relatedness, not necessarily cause and effect.

In Milgram's experiment, for example, you might want to gather information on the subjects' age, sex, background, or occupation. Then you could see if there is any correlation between these factors and the level of shock administered in the experiment.

The procedures we have outlined so far—from forming frequency distributions to calculating correlation coefficients—are examples of what are commonly known as **descriptive statistics.** These statistics help us describe overall results and tell us where a particular score stands in relation to other scores. They give us a good grasp of what the numbers are, but they do not tell us what conclusions we can draw.

Application

Table 7 below contains a frequency distribution from another possible version of Milgram's experiment. Using this data calculate the following: (1) range (2) standard deviation. (Remember you will have to calculate a mean first, to use in finding the SD.)

Table 7
Hypothetical Milgram Data

Shock	Level	Frequency
150	10	2
180	12	2
285	19	1
300	20	9
345	23	6
360	24	2
450	30	3

? Exercise 9 Drawing Conclusions from Statistics

Although statistics are very important in helping psychologists to analyze data, they can also be tricky. They can give valuable information, but they can just as easily confuse people with misinformation. For example, a man learned that most fatal accidents occur within thirty miles of home at speeds under fifty miles per hour. After learning this he was careful, when driving close to home, to keep his speed over fifty. Obviously, he has been confused by statistics. He has drawn a false conclusion.

Many areas of psychological study are susceptible to this problem. In Chapter 16, for example, we discussed the phenomenon of urban environments and crowding. Many studies in this field use statistics to try to prove a point or influence a reader. You need to be sure these statistics are being properly used and properly interpreted. How much can you really tell from them? How can you be sure you are not being deceived?

A common confusion in statistics is the distinction between rates and total numbers. Consider this record of deaths in motor vehicle accidents in cities shown in the graph below. The graph shows a definite trend toward more and more deaths in car accidents.

Deaths in Motor Vehicle Accidents

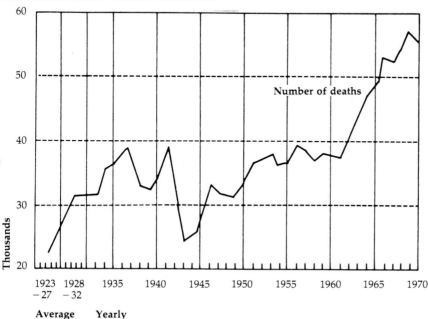

However, if a line is added to the graph showing the motor vehicle death *rate*, that is, the number of deaths per miles driven, we get a different picture. (See below.) While the number has increased, the rate has actually decreased. It is therefore important to note carefully whether a study is talking about rates or total numbers.

Motor Vehicle Death Rate

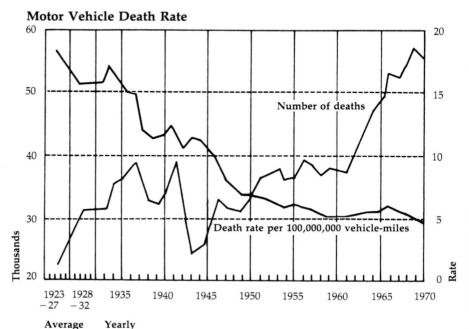

Averages are another area of statistics that needs careful consideration. You have already studied the three types of averages—mode, median, and mean. Depending upon which is used in a study the effect on the reader could be very different. For example, how would you explain this apparent contradiction? "The Sweet Nothings rock group gave six performances in six nights at the Civic Center. They drew an average of three thousand people a night. However, by their third performance the word had gotten out that the Sweet Nothings were unfortunately only as good as their name. They drew one hundred ushers, twenty policemen, and eight custodians." The key to this contradiction is the word *average.* If the mean was used, this would explain a 3000-person average even if they drew 18,000 on the first night and no people after that. Perhaps the mode would have been a fairer statistic in this case.

Knowing gross statistics, or total amounts, can be helpful, but there is a danger that people will confuse them with individual characteristics, and assume that the individual is the same as the mass.

Consider this news item:

It's better to marry later—at least later than 22 for grooms and later than 20 for brides. A recent Census Bureau study of divorce rates bears this out. About 28% of the men who wed before 22 were divorced within 20 years. But the divorce rate was only half that for men who waited. As for brides, 27% of those who wed in their teens saw their marriages break up within 20 years. Again, the picture was only half as bad for those who went to the preacher after they were twenty.

Does it follow from the above statistics that the marriage of Andy, age 21, and Rachel, age 19, is unwise? Not at all. Andy and Rachel are distinct human beings, not statistical slaves. They may well possess the maturity and self-knowledge to assure a happy marriage.

But isn't it true that Andy and Rachel stand a 28 percent and 27 percent chance of getting divorced in the next twenty years? Again, no. The 28 percent and 27 percent are gross statistics; they refer to the total population, not to any two individuals.

Finally, as we have seen, statistical reports are often presented as graphs. While graphs can be a definite aid to understanding, they can also misrepresent the truth. For example, using figures or pictures can make a change seem greater than it is, as in the graph below. It would take more than four of the little 1968 students to equal the big 1980 student, even though the number of students was only double.

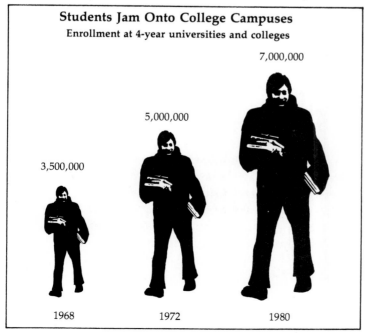

Students Jam Onto College Campuses
Enrollment at 4-year universities and colleges

7,000,000

5,000,000

3,500,000

1968   1972   1980

Graphs can also be deceitful if they are not carefully labeled. Note that the graph below tells nothing! No numbers are written to tell you the amount of tourists involved. Beware of this trick!

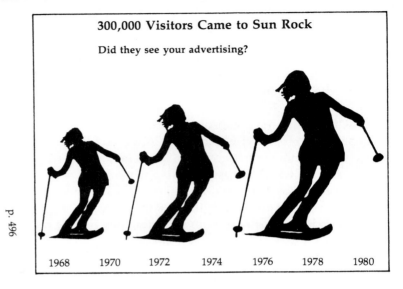

300,000 Visitors Came to Sun Rock

Did they see your advertising?

1968   1970   1972   1974   1976   1978   1980

p. 496

Application

Test your ability to draw correct conclusions from statistics in the following problems.

(1) What additional information would you need to know before accepting the following conclusions:

(a) *Statement:* Ed Maloney has dropped only one pass all season.

Conclusion: Ed must be a great pass catcher.

(b) *Statement:* The number of unemployed people in the United States is nearly as great today as during the Great Depression.

Conclusion: We are in a depression.

(2) A scientific study indicates that people born in France are more apt to become alcoholics than people born in Greece. You are personnel director for a large ad agency and are looking for someone to fill the position of art director. Two people apply, and both are equally qualified. One is French and the other Greek. Should the study influence your choice? Explain.

Conclusion: Doing Your Own Research and Reporting on It

Doing your own research can be an exciting and valuable learning experience. When picking a topic, make sure you choose something which interests you. Nothing is worse than doing research because you have to do it. Your topic should not be too large ("The Effects of Positive Reinforcement of the People of Houston and Dallas") or too small ("How Purebred Cocker Spaniels React to an Eclipse of the Sun"). Of course, your topic must be feasible. Here are some suggestions:

(1) The Effects of Positive Reinforcement on Sharing Among Two-Year-Olds

(2) Conditioning the Family Dog to Fetch the Newspaper: The Effects of Biscuits

(3) Overcrowding and Rat Behavior

(4) The Effects of Environment on How Much Students Study

You may be expected to write reports on research you have done. Others may want to know what you did and what your results were. The following suggests the sections to be included in a research report:

Title Page: Write the title in the center of the page. Include both dependent and independent variables in the title. (See Exercise 1.) For example, you might call your experiment, "The Effect of Good Student Behavior on Their Grades." (Here good student behavior is the independent variable, while grades is the dependent variable.) Write your name and the date in the lower right-hand corner of the page.

Background: Do research to find out what experiments have been previously performed on the topic you chose. Summarize the earlier research. Then tell why you chose to conduct the research and how your experiment differs from previous ones.

Hypothesis: A hypothesis is an educated guess. Tell what you expect your experiment to show and why. State your hypothesis in the *if, then* format described in Exercise 1 (page 473). But remember an experiment which disproves a hypothesis can be just as good as an experiment which supports the hypothesis. Don't be discouraged if no number of dog biscuits will convince your dog to fetch the evening paper. Try to condition another dog if you wish, but don't think your research has been a failure.

Procedures: Tell exactly what you did—in order. Include information on the materials you used and/or the directions given to human subjects. Check **Experimenting with Psychology** on pages 124, 210, 276, 370, and 468 for examples of good research procedures. Your teacher will help make sure your research follows all American Psychological Association guidelines.

Results: You may write out your results or present them in graphs charts, tables, and figures. The **Experimenting with Psychology** pages contain examples of how to record the results of research.

Conclusions: Here you discuss your results in detail. Tell how your results prove or disprove your hypothesis. Mention unexpected results as well.

Bibliography: Mention all the sources you used. Give the author, article title, source, year, and pages for each source. Don't forget to indicate the source of each direct quote in your report.

Application

Perform an experiment or conduct a survey, and write up the results.

Glossary

Pronunciation Key

hat, āge, fär; let, ēqual, tėrm; it, īce; hot, ōpen, ôrder; oil, out; cup, put, rüle; ə represents *a* in about, *e* in taken *i* in pencil, *o* in lemon, *u* in circus.

Page numbers on which a term is defined in the text are included for each Glossary entry.

A

abnormal behavior a term used by mental health professionals to describe behavior that is not psychologically healthy and that prevents a person from functioning effectively in everyday life. p. 309

ad dic tion (ə dik′shən), *n.* a physical dependence on a drug. p. 270

ad o les cence (ad′l es′ns), *n.* a period of development between childhood and adulthood. p. 54

adrenal glands two glands located at the upper end of the kidneys which release hormones in times of stress or emergency. p. 231

al ien a tion (ā′lyə nā′shən), *n.* being cut off from society and not accepting society's norms, or standards of behavior. p. 67, 454

am ne sia (am nē′shə), *n.* partial or total loss of memory. p. 325

anal stage a stage which occurs during the second and third years of life, according to Freud. It centers on the elimination of waste and toilet training. p. 291

an o nym i ty (an′ə nim′ə tē), *n.* not being known by others. p. 441

antisocial personality disorder new APA term for psychopath; characterized by antisocial behavior with no remorse for criminal action. p. 333

anxiety disorder a type of neurosis in which the anxiety itself or the coping efforts are the central symptoms. p. 320

ar che types (är′kə tīps), *n.* according to Carl Jung, universal ideas held in the collective unconscious that reflect the common experiences and beliefs of humanity. p. 295

ar ter i o scle ro sis (är tir′ē ō sklə-rō′sis), *n.* hardening of the arteries. p. 83

at ti tude (at′ə tüd), *n.* a learned tendency to respond in a certain way because of deeply held beliefs or feelings. p. 420

au to crat ic (ô′tə krat′ik), *adj.* absolute in power or authority; a style of leadership in which the leader acts as a dictator. p. 406

autonomic nervous system part of the peripheral nervous system that controls involuntary biological processes like digestion, breathing, heartbeat, and glandular secretions. p. 226

aversion therapy an approach in which an aversive or painful stimulus that increases anxiety is associated with an act that is undesirable. p. 356

a ware ness (ə wer′nes), *n.* the first step toward verbal communication, initial interest in another person. p. 385

B

be hav ior (bi hā′vyər), *n.* the actions or activities of living things. p. 4

be hav ior ism (bi hā′vyə riz′əm), *n.* a theory of psychology in which behavior is viewed as the product of outside forces. Environment and experience are seen as the most important factors influencing behavior. p. 10

behavior modification methods developed to increase the frequency of desirable behavior or to decrease behavioral problems. p. 153

behavior modification therapy a treatment which applies theories of conditioning to abnormal behavior. The approach uses principles of learning to change undesirable behaviors such as addictions, fears, or compulsions. The change is brought about by substituting new patterns of reinforcement. p. 354

bell curve a pattern of scores in the shape of a bell which will emerge when graphing certain data. p. 479

biological motivations inborn motivations necessary for survival, such as hunger, thirst, and the need to sleep. p. 240

bipolar disorder new APA term for manic depression; characterized by extreme highs and lows in moods. p. 331

body language a form of communication conveyed by movements of the body (shrug, raised eyebrow, slump, eye expressions). p. 384

bright ness (brīt′ness), *n.* an aspect of color which refers to the lightness or darkness of the color. p. 107

C

case study an intensive investigation of an individual or small group of individuals. p. 488

central nervous system one part of the two-part nervous system made up of the brain and the spinal cord. p. 225

cer e bel lum (ser′ə bel′əm), *n., pl.* **-bel lums, -bel la** (bel′ə). a part of the brain which helps the body maintain balance, posture, and eye-hand coordination. p. 221

ce re brum (sə rē′brəm), *n., pl.* **-brums, -bra** (brə). the part of the brain, together with the cortex which covers it, that is responsible for all the active thought and planning that goes on in the brain. p. 222

chain ing (chān′ing), *n.* process of making sequences of shaped actions. p. 150

chro mo some (krō′mə sōm), *n.* particle found in a cell which carries thousands of genes that determine heredity. p. 33

classical conditioning learning by

association; involves associating different kinds of stimuli: unconditioned and conditioned. p. 137

clinical psychologist a therapist who has a Ph.D. in clinical psychology, followed by an internship in a hospital or clinic. He or she cannot prescribe any form of medication but relies on verbal and behavioral forms of therapy. p. 346

clinical studies studies based on observations of actual patients. p. 6

coercive power one of the five contributing factors to leadership— being able to punish others in the group. p. 406

cog ni tive (kog′nə tiv), *adj.* mental or intellectual activity; thinking. p. 4

cognitive dissonance the psychological discomfort that results when a person holds two opposed or conflicting beliefs. p. 415

cognitive psychology a theory of psychology which is concerned with the study of behavior from the inside. Cognitive psychologists do not believe a person is controlled by environment, but that a person's surroundings are controlled with his or her ability to reason and make decisions. They believe experience affects the way new events are perceived and that the thought processes determine behavior. p. 11

cognitive theory an approach to motivation in which a person is not driven toward a goal, but evaluates options and chooses goals which fit with his or her desires and needs and which are appropriate to a given time and place. p. 249

co li tis (kō lī′tis), *n.* an inflammation of the lower bowel, often brought on by stress. p. 206

collective behavior the way a group thinks, feels, or acts as a unit in response to an irrational force like the power of suggestion. p. 439

collective unconscious according to Carl Jung, the more influential part of the two parts of the unconscious mind. It is the same for all people and contains the memories from our ancestors. p. 295

collective perception the group's perception of an event; a person often trusts it more than his or her own perception of the event. p. 115

comparative method a method of

research in which the development of a cross-section of subjects is studied. p. 37

com pli ance (kəm plī′əns), *n.* one of three levels in forming an attitude, considered the weakest level; merely forming an attitude in order to avoid rejection or win approval. p. 421

compulsive behavior behavior consisting of repetitive, ritualistic actions that serve no rational purpose. p. 321

con cept (kon′sept), *n.* a mental category that represents objects that have similar functions or are similar in appearance. p. 165

concrete operations according to Jean Piaget, the third stage of cognitive development in which formal logic plays an increasingly more important role in thinking. p. 29

cone (kōn), *n.* a sensory cone-shaped cell in the center portion of the retina. The cones work best in bright light and provide color vision. p. 105

con gru ence (kən grü′əns), *n.* a phenomenon which takes place when two people have established a close bond and like and trust each other; their movements mirror each other's. p. 384

con scious (kon′shəs), *adj.* aware; able to feel or perceive; *n.* the part of the mind that deals with things we are aware of. p. 288

con scious ness (kon′shəs nis), *n.* the degree to which one takes in information about oneself and one's environment. p. 252

contagion theory a theory that a crowd engulfs its members and that individual morals and restraint give way to a collective mind. Personalities dissolve into the unified personality of the crowd and people's behavior and will become that of the crowd. p. 441

con text (kon′tekst), *n.* parts directly before and after a word, or sentence, that influences its meaning. p. 161

control group the group in an experiment that does not receive the independent variable. p. 475

controlled observation a type of observation which occurs in a laboratory setting. p. 481

con ven tion al ist (kən ven′shə nə-list), *n.* according to L. Joseph

Stone and Joseph Church, one of the four classifications of adolescent personality; an adolescent who does what is acceptable and socially appropriate. p. 58

convergence theory a theory which suggests that people come together because they share common interests. They are not transformed by the crowd, but remain distinct, separate individuals even though their behavior is much the same. p. 442

conversion hysteria a somatoform disorder involving the loss of function without any physical reason; a mental problem is converted into a physical symptom. p. 325

corpus callosum a pathway of nerves that bridges the hemispheres of the cerebrum in the brain. p. 223

cor tex (kôr′teks), *n., pl.* **-ti ces** (-tə-sēz′). the thin outer layer, wrinkled into thousands of tiny folds, that covers the cerebrum. p. 222

cre a tiv i ty (krē′ā tiv′ə tē), *n.* expressing one's thoughts or feelings in a new way; producing a unique product that expresses the capabilities of a unique person. p. 201

cri sis (krī′sis), *n.* a normal developmental task, which if resolved successfully will develop a positive aspect of personality. If not, a negative characteristic will result. p. 59

crowd (kroud), *n.* a large number of people who interact with each other, verbally and nonverbally, share comments and suggestions or offer approval or disapproval, and experience similar emotions. p. 441

crowd ing (kroud′ing), *n.* the perception of too many people in too little space. p. 447

cul ture (kul′chər), *n.* the total way of life of a group of people.

culture-fair lessening the language and experience bias against some minority group children in standardized tests. p. 192

custodial daycare type of child care in which only the immediate needs of the child are considered. p. 41

cyclical motivation a motivation which is repeated after a need has been satisfied and an interval of time has passed, as in hunger.

D

dead storage memory's loss of access to material. p. **176**

dec i bel (des′ə bəl), *n.* a unit for measuring the relative intensity of sounds. Loudness is measured in decibels. p. **111**

deductive reasoning reasoning from the general to the specific; starting with a general concept and proceeding to a specific conclusion. p. **167**

defense mechanism according to psychodynamic theory, a defense used by the ego against feeling anxiety about unacceptable urges. Some types of defense mechanisms are displacement, reaction, formation, denial, projection, rationalization, repression, regression, compensation, and procrastination. p. **292**

de lu sion (di lü′zhən), *n.* false belief. p. **328**

delusional disorder a type of psychosis that has one major symptom—persistent delusions. Aside from the delusions, the individual's personality remains relatively intact. p. **330**

dem o crat ic (dem′ə krat′ik), *adj.* treating other people as one's equal; a style of leadership in which all group members are allowed to exert some influence on the group. p. **406**

den si ty (den′sə te), *n., pl.* **-ties.** a measurement of population; the number of people in a certain amount of space. p. **447**

dependent variable the factor in an experiment that may or may not change as a result of changes in the independent variable. p. **473**

de pres sant (di pres′nt), *n.* a sedative which depresses the central nervous system, such as alcohol or a barbiturate. p. **270**

dep ri va tion (dep′rə vā′shən), *n.* in motivation, the interval of time after a need has been satisfied and before the need begins the cycle again, as in hunger. p. **247**

descriptive statistics data obtained from research which describe the overall results and tell where a particular score stands in relation to other scores. p. **492**

de sen si ti za tion (dē sen′sə ti-zā′shən), *n.* form of behavior therapy in which things that arouse anxiety are associated with an experience that is pleasant and the anxiety is lessened. p. **354**

developmental daycare a type of daycare that provides a wide range of developmental opportunities for children. p. **41**

developmental psychology the study of behavior as it goes through stages of growth and change. p. **18**

deviation IQ formula used to determine the IQ of an adult, calculated by determining how a person's score compares with those of other persons in the same age group. p. **186**

dis crim i na tion (dis krim′ə-nā′shən), *n.* a difference in attitude or treatment shown to a particular person, class, or group. In conditioned learning, the ability to recognize the difference between two somewhat similar stimuli, distinguish between those that have important consequences, and those that don't. p. **139, 433**

dis en gage ment (dis′en gāj′mənt), *n.* the process of shifting from an active to a relatively passive role in life. p. **85**

dissonance reduction reframing one's views to justify conflicting attitudes. p. **415**

double message a disagreement between body language and spoken language such as behaving one way but verbally communicating a different attitude. p. **385**

dream analysis a method of analysis that explores the symbolic meaning of the content of a dream, the expression of which might be unacceptable in waking life. p. **348**

drive (drīv), *n.* a force that arises from a need and pushes an organism to fulfill that need; a desire to act. p. **240**

E

eclectic approach a combination of various theories in psychology. p. **12**

e go (ē′gō), *n.* in Freud's concept, the purposeful mind that performs the conscious management of needs and drives. Part of the ego's job is to choose actions that fulfill id impulses without bad results. The ego resolves the conflicts between the id and the superego. p. **288**

e go cen trism (ē′gō sen′tris əm), *n.* according to Jean Piaget, the inability to see that the world looks different to someone else. This is characteristic of the thinking of infants and small children. p. **28**

eidetic imagery a strong visual imagery. p. **164**

emergent-norm theory a theory which stresses that people come together in a crowd for different reasons; these reasons remain intact, allowing the members to play different roles in the crowd: leaders, followers, dissenters, opportunists. They follow the crowd because it represents a norm. p. **442**

e mo tion (i mō′shən), *n.* a feeling associated with behavior. p. **234**

endocrine glands a chemical communication system that releases or secretes hormones into the bloodstream when signaled by the nervous system. These hormones greatly affect behavior, the functioning of the body, and the course of its development. p. **230**

en vi ron men tal ist (en vī′rən-men′tl ist), *n.* a scientist who emphasizes social and cultural factors in determining the way a person develops, rather than heredity. p. **33**

evaluative reasoning type of thinking which involves judging the suitability, goodness, or effectiveness of an idea, as opposed to trying to create or add to it. p. **168**

ex per i ment (ek sper′ə ment), *n.* trial or test to verify a hypothesis, to find out or discover something unknown. p. **473**

experimental group the group receiving the independent variable in an experiment. p. **475**

expert power one of five contributing factors to leadership—being seen as knowledgeable in an area of group concern. p. **406**

external justification a way of explaining things we say or do that are out of character for us by blaming our actions on some outside factor. p. **417**

ESP extrasensory perception is perception that cannot be explained by ordinary sensory means. Types of ESP include telepathy, clairvoyance, premonition, and psychokinesis. p. **126**

ex tinc tion (ek stingk′shən), *n.* the weakening or fading process after the unconditioned stimulus, or reinforcement has been withdrawn. p. **139**

ex tro ver sion (ek'strə ver'zhən), *n.* a tendency to look outward, to be outgoing and friendly. p. **295**

F

fetus (fē'təs), *n.* a rapidly developing unborn baby. p. **19**

formal operations according to Jean Piaget, the fourth and final stage of cognitive development. In this stage, a person is able to view a problem from several positions and to figure out possible directions and likely outcomes. p. **29**

free association a method of analysis in which the psychoanalyst encourages the patient to relax, let his or her mind wander freely, and give a running account of thoughts, physical sensations, and memories as they occur. p. **348**

frequency distribution a method of summarizing data which tells how many subjects scored at certain levels. p. **478**

fugue episodes a dissociative disorder in which a person escapes an unhappy past by combining amnesia with travel to another place. p. **325**

func tion a lism (fungk'shə nə- liz'əm), *n.* an approach to psychology which emphasizes the function of associations in working toward a specific goal. p. **10**

G

gene (jēn), *n.* a minute part of a chromosome that influences the heredity and development of some characteristic passed on from generation to generation by parent to offspring. p. **33**

gen er al i za tion (jen'ər ə lə- zā'shən), *n.* in conditioned learning, when two or more stimuli are similar, the response to all of them is the same. p. **138**

gen e ra tiv i ty (jen'ə rā tiv'ə tē), *n.* according to Erik Erikson, the positive outcome of the developmental crisis experienced during middle age, in which a person sees his or her role as one of guiding the next generation, with concern for the world and a better society for young people. p. **77**

ge net ic (jə net'ik), *adj.* inborn; having to do with origin and natural growth. p. **193**

genital stage in Freudian theory, a stage that begins at puberty. In girls, the average age is about ten, in boys, about twelve. During this time, sensual pleasure begins to be associated with the opposite sex. p. **291**

gen ius (jē'nyəs), *n.* having great natural power of mind; a person having an IQ of 150 or more. p. **198**

ger on tol o gy (jer'on tol'ə jē), *n.* the study of old age. p. **82**

Gestalt theory an approach to psychology that emphasizes the importance of looking at whole behavior patterns to understand individual parts; in perception, Gestalt theory holds that the whole is perceived and then the parts are fitted into it, that people are born knowing how to see things in orderly ways. pp. **11, 120**

gift ed (gif'tid), *adj.* a person with an IQ of 140 or above; having natural ability or special talent. p. **198**

group dynamics a process in which collective behavior comes from a series of individual interactions. p. **402**

group therapy a treatment under the leadership of a group therapist in which patients are encouraged to express their real feelings. They analyze the motives behind their behavior, and try to be completely honest with other members of the group. p. **350**

growth-expansion a period of early adulthood in which young adults are oriented toward the future. Self-confidence is high as they make new commitments, form new goals, and seek personal achievement. p. **184**

H

hal lu ci na tion (hə lü'sn ā'shən), *n.* perceptual distortion or the changing of actual perceptions into imaginary ones. p. **264**, p. **328**

hal lu cin o gen (hə lü'sn ə jen), *n.* a drug, such as the psychedelics—mescaline, psilocybin, and lysergic acid diethylamide, or LSD—that in many instances, for the user, alters reality and causes physiological

changes to occur. p. **272**

he don ist (hēd'n ist), *n.* according to L. Joseph Stone and Joseph Church, one of the four classifications of adolescent personality; an adolescent who makes fun his or her business in life, living for the present without regard for future consequences. p. **58**

hem i sphere (hem'ə sfir), *n.* one of two sections into which the cerebrum of the brain is divided. p. **222**

he red i ty (hə red'ə tē), *n., pl.* **-ties.** transmission of characteristics passed on to offspring from parents from generation to generation. p. **32**

highway hypnosis a kind of trance effect which can be experienced by driving for a long time on a straight highway. p. **262**

his to gram (his'tə gram), *n.* a graph on which the bars are directly next to one another and number categories are on the horizontal axis (across the bottom). The frequency of scores is shown on the vertical axis (along the side). p. **479**

ho me o sta sis (hō'mē ə stā'sis), *n.* the biological drive to regulate internal environment to keep body conditions stable. p. **240**

hor mone (hôr'mōn), *n.* a chemical formed in the endocrine glands which is released into the bloodstream and affects or controls the activity of some organ or tissue. p. **230**

hue (hyü), *n.* the family of color; the color's quality of being red, blue-green, or some other color. p. **107**

humanistic psychology an approach which stresses self-understanding, creativity, and the development of one's potential. p. **12**

humanistic theory a theory that motivations fall into a natural hierarchy. First, a person tries to fulfill the most basic biological and psychological needs. Then he or she is free to strive for personal growth and fulfillment. p. **249**

humanistic therapy an approach to treatment which emphasizes the role of the patient or client rather than the analyst. Clients are helped to clarify their own reactions. p. **353**

hy po chon dri a sis (hī'pə kon- drī'ə sis), *n.* one of the most common of the somatoform disorders in which the hypochondriac is preoccupied with health matters and has an unrealistic fear of disease, often involving imaginary illness accompanied by actual pains. p. 323

hyp no sis (hip nō′sis), *n., pl.* **-ses** (-sēz′). a condition resembling deep sleep in which a person's ability to respond to stimuli is changed and the person becomes very vulnerable to suggestions made by the hypnotist. p. 262

hypnotic amnesia a condition produced in a person under hypnosis who has been told by the hypnotist to forget something he or she knows or believes. p. 264

hy po thal a mus (hī′pō thal′ə məs), *n., pl.* **-mi** (-mī). region of the brain controlling temperature, hunger, thirst, and to some extent emotional behavior. p. 221

hy poth e sis (hī poth′ə sis), *n., pl.* **-ses.** something assumed because it seems likely to be a true explanation; a statement indicating what results are expected in an experiment. p. 473

I

id (id), *n.* in Freud's concept, one of the three elements working within the human mind in the process of thinking and feeling; it is unconscious and is the powerhouse of the body's selfish, natural urges. The id drives one to satisfy the libido and all other physical pleasure drives. p. 288

i de al ist (ī dē′ə list), *n.* according to L. Joseph Stone and Joseph Church, one of the four classifications of adolescent personality; an adolescent who has high ideals, and wants to change society and improve the world. p. 58

i den ti fi ca tion (ī den′tə fə- kā′shən), *n.* the second level of attitude formation in which a person adopts an attitude as a result of an emotional attachment to another person or group. p. 421

identity crisis according to Erik Erikson, the developmental crisis of late adolescence in which a person forms a sense of who he or she is. p. 61

il lu sion (i lü′zhən), *n.* a misperception of reality. p. 122

im age (im′ij), *n.* a mental picture; likeness or copy. p. 164

implosion therapy a therapeutic technique in which a client troubled by an intensely frightening event is made to experience the event again and again in a friendly environment until the anxiety explodes inwardly. p. 355

in born (in′bôrn′), *adj.* biologically programmed; born in a person. p. 236

independent variable the factor in research that is changed or varied in order to study its effects on the dependent variable. p. 473

inductive reasoning process in which the thinker reasons from the specific to the general; starting with specific observations and reaching general assumptions. p. 168

inferiority complex feelings of inferiority resulting from childhood feelings of smallness and helplessness. p. 294

in san i ty (in san′ə te), *n., pl.* **-ties.** a legal term used in U.S. court system to describe a person who is not able to manage his or her affairs or understand the consequences of his or her actions. The term would not be used by a psychologist unless in a legal context. p. 309

in tel li gence (in tel′ə jəns), *n.* the ability to profit from experience and to adapt to new conditions in the environment. p. 184

intelligence quotient (IQ) number that shows the rating of a person's performance on intelligence tests. It is found by dividing the mental age shown in tests by the actual age and multiplying by 100. p. 186

in ter fer ence (in′tər fir′əns), *n.* theory that an older memory stops the remembering of new material. p. 175

internal justification resolving the dissonance of a given behavior by changing an attitude internally. p. 418

in ter nal i za tion (in tėr′nl ī- za′shən), *n.* the third and strongest level of attitude formation; the new attitude is taken into one's own belief system, one likes it for one's own reasons. p. 422

interval schedule a schedule which has to do with the time that elapses between reinforcements. p. 147

in ti ma cy (in′tə mə sē), *n.* according to Erik Erikson, the positive result of the development crisis of young adulthood when a

person learns to care for and share himself or herself with another person, without being lost in the process. p. 61

intimacy crisis a period in which a person shares himself or herself by developing a supportive relationship with another person, often someone of the opposite sex. p. 73

intimate distance a range of distance from actual contact to eighteen inches, reserved for intimate relationships either between sexual partners or family members. p. 379

in tro spec tion (in′trə spek′shən), *n.* a detailed examination of one's own thinking, or reflections. p. 10

in tro ver sion (in′trə vėr′zhən), *n.* a tendency to look inward toward one's self. p. 295

islets of Langerhans a part of the pancreas, a gland in the abdomen, that secretes the hormone insulin which regulates the level of sugar in the blood. p. 230

i so la tion (ī′sə′lā shən), *n.* according to Erik Erikson, one result of the developmental crisis of young adulthood in which a person draws inside himself or herself, becomes locked in with personal concerns, goes it alone. p. 73

J

joint sex role a role that is more nearly alike for males and females. p. 50

L

lais sez faire (les′ā fer′), *adj.* a style of leadership in which members of the group are encouraged to do as they please. p. 406

learn ing (lėr′ning), *n.* a relatively permanent change in behavior that results from experience. p. 134

legitimate power one of the five contributing factors to leadership— holding an official position that carries power. p. 406

lobes (lōbs), *n.* the four regions into which each hemisphere of the cerebrum of the brain is divided. Each lobe has a specific function. p. 222

longevity index a study to predict how many years of life are left to people once they have reached old age. p. 89

longitudinal approach a type of research that follows the development of a group of children over a period of time, usually several years or decades, in order to measure the influence of both early and later experiences. p. 38

long-term memory the part of the memory system which is more permanent and continually interacts with short-term memory to provide information needed. p. 171

loud ness (loud ness), *adj.* the volume or intensity of a sound. p. 109

M

manic depression a psychotic disorder, also known as bipolar disorder, affecting the moods of a person which may alternate between extreme "highs" and extreme "lows," and also may alternate with periods of normal moods. During the manic period the person feels continually elated. The depressive phase of the disorder is the complete opposite resulting in total dejection. p. 331

mar i jua na (mar′ə wä′nə), *n.* a dried plant, *cannabis sativa*, smoked in cigarette form. Its effects vary from person to person. If the user is happy, marijuana tends to have a positive effect. If the user is unhappy or is in unfamiliar surroundings, it may invite fright, depression, or panic. p. 271

matching phenomenon a tendency for people to like, befriend, date, and ultimately marry individuals whom they consider their equals. p. 389

me (mē), *pron.* the self one sees when looking at one's self through the eyes of others.

mean (mēn), *n.* the average, or most typical, score in a distribution, calculated by adding all the scores and then dividing by the number of scores. p. 487

me di an (mē′dē ən), *n.* the score that separates the upper half of the scores in a distribution from the lower half. p. 486

med i ta tion (med′ə tā′shən), *n.* the act of concentrating on a single, unvarying source of stimulation for a certain period of time, which may result in a change of consciousness. p. 266

men o pause (men′ə pôz), *n.* a period of transition that occurs in the middle years, in which women undergo physical and psychological changes as the result of end of menstruation and loss of fertility. p. 78

mental disorder a term used by psychologists and mental health professionals to describe behavior that is not psychologically healthy and that prevents a person from functioning effectively in everyday life. p. 309

mental retardation a condition in which a person since childhood is unable to do and understand what most people his or her age can do and understand. p. 195

middle childhood a period between early childhood and adolescence which has important developmental tasks that deal with physical, cognitive, and social development. p. 46

mi graine (mī′grān), *n.* tension headaches in which the cranial arteries are dilated. p. 96

mildly retarded able to be educated to some extent; can attend school and learn basic skills, sometimes qualifying for a job in the community. p. 197

mis trust (mis trust′), *n.* attitude a child can develop in the first year, according to Erik Erikson, if the environment is not experienced as orderly and predictable. p. 23

mnemonic devices cues such as tricks, jingles, poems, or any type of associations which help us remember something more easily. p. 177

mob (mob), *n.* a crowd which resorts to disorderly, aggressive behavior. p. 441

mode (mōd), *n.* the score in a distribution that occurs more often than any other. p. 486

mod el ing (mod′l ing), *n.* a technique in behavior modification therapy in which a person watches someone else act out situations he or she is unable to cope with, and then repeats the action based on what the model has done. p. 358

moderately retarded able to take care of personal needs and avoid the basic dangers of life, but not able to be taught by ordinary teaching methods. p. 196

mor pheme (môr′fēm), *n.* the smallest unit of language that has meaning. p. 158

moral judgment a decision a person makes about behavior in a given situation. p. 51

mo ti va tion (mō′tə vā′shən), *n.* the need, desire, and thought process that causes one's behavior. p. 234

multiple personality the most extreme form of dissociation in which a person may develop two or more distinct, even radically different, personalities, each taking over conscious control of the person for varying periods of time. p. 325

N

nar cot ic (när kot′ik), *n.* a drug, such as opium, morphine, and heroin, which acts on the nervous system and is used therapeutically to ease pain. These drugs are of great value medically, but are powerfully addictive. p. 270

na ti vist (nā′tə vist), *n.* a scientist who emphasizes the importance of heredity. p. 33

natural observation a procedure which involves watching and recording how organisms behave in their natural environments. p. 481

need complementarity an interaction between two people who fulfill each other's needs. p. 389

negative reinforcement the stopping of a painful or unpleasant stimulus. p. 145

ne o cor tex (nē′ō kôr′teks), *n., pl.* **-ti ces** (-tə sez′). organs of the brain classified as the "new brain"; the thinking brain. p. 221

neur on (nür′on), *n.* an impulse-conducting nerve cell. p. 225

neu ro sis (nú rō′sis), *n., pl.* **-ses.** an emotional disturbance characterized by excessive anxiety and the overuse of defense mechanisms. p. 317

neurotic depression the most common type of affective disorder; a condition in which a person does not bounce back after a spell of being depressed, or can't account for persisting bouts of depression. p. 326

neurotic paradox a state in which the neurotic person is usually upset by his or her abnormal behavior but can't seem to change it. p. 318

New Towns cities created by urban planners, usually under 100,000 in population, and unified in design. These communities are largely self-sufficient with emphasis on local participation in civic affairs. p. **461**

norm (nôrm), *n.* in society, standards of behavior. p. **67**

normal curve graph of a "normal" distribution with the average at the center and the rest evenly spreading out to high at one end and low at the other. p. **187**

NREM sleep a period of nonrapid eye movement that takes place during the stages of sleep. p. **258**

O

ob ses sion (əb sesh′ən), *n.* a thought or mental image that won't go away; in neurosis, sometimes so insistent and disturbing it can interfere with all facets of an individual's life. p. **321**

objective test an approach to personality measurement that tries to determine basic personality traits, attitudes, interests, and ambitions; generally given as an interview or a self-inventory. p. **284**

operant conditioning theory of learning by consequences. p. **144**

operational definition a measurable statement of the behaviors expected in an experiment. p. **474**

oral stage according to Freud, a stage which begins at birth and continues for about one year, during which the mouth is the main source of pleasure and contact with the environment. p. **290**

P

parasympathetic system a system of nerves which helps the body recover from a taxing situation by slowing breathing, reducing the heart rate, returning blood vessels to normal. It is one of two sets of nerves in the autonomic system. p. **227**

participant observation a method of observation in which the researcher lives with a group of people, interacts with them, and observes how they behave and what they say. p. **482**

peer (pir), *n.* a person the same

age as another; person of the same rank, ability, etc., as another. p. **65**

per cep tion (pər sep′shən), *n.* the psychological interpretation of physical events. p. **104**

perceptual constancies things that seem the same, time after time regardless of change in other conditions, such as distance and angle of viewing. p. **118**

perceptual set the influence of past experience on what a person expects. p. **112**

peripheral nervous system a network of circuits that connects the central nervous system with muscles, glands, and other bodily parts. One of the two parts of the body's nervous systems. p. **225**

personal distance a range of distance from eighteen inches to about four feet, implying familiarity. p. **379**

per son al i ty (pėr′sə nal′ə tē), *n.*, *pl.* **-ties** the sum total of what characterizes a person as an individual. p. **280**

personality disorder a fixed and rigid pattern of behaviors that results from faulty personality development. p. **332**

personality trait a characteristic of a person's behavior in many situations. Traits reflect feelings, attitudes, motivations, and values. p. **33**

personal unconscience according to Carl Jung, the part of the unconscious mind that is made up of each individual's personal experiences that were once conscious but since forgotten. p. **295**

phallic stage according to Freud, a psychosexual stage, beginning at
· about age 3, during which children learn they can derive pleasure by exploring and stimulating their own bodies. During this stage a child may experience being jealous of a parent of the same sex. p. **291**

pho bi a (fō′bē ə), *n.* an unreasonable fear or dread of something that most people find tolerable. The fear persists even if there is no actual danger. p. **322**

pho neme (fō′nēm), *n.* the smallest unit of sound that can be recognized as a separate speech sound. p. **158**

pitch (pich), *n.* the highness or lowness of a tone or sound. p. **109**

pituitary gland an endocrine gland located almost in the center of the

brain that secretes a number of different hormones. One promotes growth; others reach other glands in the body and are released upon chemical command from the pituitary, often called the master gland. p. **230**

pleasure principle seeking pleasure and avoiding pain; the id is said to operate on the pleasure principle. p. **288**

positive reinforcement reinforcing stimulus that seems to give pleasure to the subject. p. **145**, p. **357**

posthypnotic suggestion a suggestion made to a subject under hypnosis to be carried out after the subject is awakened. p. **263**

prej u dice (prej′ə dis), *n.* an attitude that is unsupported by reasonable evidence, that persists over time, and is based on an emotional feeling about the person or group being judged. p. **427**

preoperational thought according to the theory of Jean Piaget, the second stage of cognitive development, in which the child is able to represent the outside world in his or her mind. p. **28**

primary drive a drive which stimulates the organism to fulfill its biological needs; an inborn drive. p. **247**

primary reinforcer stimulus of primary value. p. **146**

pri va cy (prī′və sē), *n.*, *pl.* **-cies.** a psychological state, more than physical isolation; seclusion; secrecy. p. **378**

productive memory a process of the memory which recalls generalized information rather than exact details. p. **172**

profoundly retarded the lowest level of functioning; a person who remains virtually helpless even in adult years. p. **196**

projective test an approach to personality measurement designed to get beneath the surface and try to draw out a person's inner dynamic qualities. p. **284**

prox im i ty (prok sim′ə tē), *n.* nearness; closeness. A Gestalt principle of organization in which the closeness of objects tends to form a pattern even though the objects are not alike. p. **121, 390**

psy chi a trist (sī kī′ə trist), *n.* physician who has completed medical school with a specialty in the field of mental, emotional, and neurological illness. Psychiatrists are permitted by law to use drugs and other physical means of treatment for mental problems, in addition to talking therapy. p. 346

psychoactive substance-use disorder a disorder involving the misuse of and dependence on drugs, such as alcohol, barbituates, stimulants, heroin, or marijuana. p. 332

psy cho a nal y sis (sī′kō ə nal′ə-sis), *n.* a method for treating mental disorders, originated by Freud, which consists of interview sessions between patient and analyst to uncover the unconscious motivations behind the patient's troubling behavior. p. 348

psy cho an a lyst (sī kō an′l ist), *n.* a specialist in the particular form of therapy developed by Freud and his followers. p. 346

psychoanalytic theory a theory in which psychologists look below the surface of observable behavior to discover the motives, forces, and experiences buried within the mind that influence behavior. p. 12

psychodynamic theory a theory of personality first developed by Freud and elaborated by his followers which is based upon the idea that personality is the outcome of conflict between the id, ego, and superego. As an explanation of motivation, the theory holds that some of our most powerful motives are unconscious and thus cannot be controlled by reason. p. 248, p. 292

psy chol o gy (sī kol′ə jē), *n., pl.* **-gies.** the scientific study of the behavior of living things. p. 3

psy cho path (sī′kə path), *n.* an individual having a personality disorder characterized by antisocial behavior, little compassion for others, no remorse for criminal action, and the capability of bizarre forms of cruelty; now called antisocial personality disorder by APA. According to L. Joseph Stone and Joseph Church, psychopath is also one of four classifications of adolescent personalitities; a bully without a conscience; an adolescent who has not developed a sense of moral concern for other people and can be dangerous. p. 58, p. 333

psychosexual disorder sexual behavior that is considered bad for the individual or for society. Three types of behavior in this classification are psychosexual dysfunction, the gender identity disorders, and behaviors that are abnormal and are also socially disapproved. p. 335

psy cho sis (sī kō′sis), *n., pl.* **-ses** (-sēz′). a severe form of mental disease involving disorientation, or loss of contact with reality. p. 328

psychosocial stages according to Erik Erikson, the series of stages a person goes through as he or she develops, during which certain characteristics of the individual's personality emerge. p. 59

psy cho so mat ic (sī′kō sə mat′ik), *adj.* illness that stems from a psychological source. p. 96

pu ber ty (pyü′bər tē), *n.* period which marks the beginning of sexual maturity. p. 54

public distance range of distance between the stage and the audience, the classroom and the teacher. p. 379

pun ish ment (pun′ish mənt), *n.* in operant conditioning, the presentation of an unpleasant stimulus after a response. p. 151

R

random sample a method of selecting a sample so that each member of the population has an equal chance of being chosen. p. 476

range (rānj), *n.* the simplest measure of variability, calculated by subtracting the lowest score from the highest. p. 490

rank order scores placed in order from lowest to highest. p. 478

ratio schedule a reinforcement schedule which involves the number of responses that must be made to gain a reward. p. 147

reality principle the gratification of impulses in a way that is allowable in the real world. According to Freud, the ego works in accordance with the reality principle. p. 289

rea son ing (rē′zn ing), *n.* thinking, or cognition, with a purpose; thinking directed toward a specific goal or task. p. 167

re call (ri kôl′), *n.* a measure of memory in which, with few clues, a subject reproduces a response learned earlier. p. 174

rec og ni tion (rek′əg nish′ən), *n.* a measure of memory in which the subject identifies items presented previously. p. 173

re dun dan cy (ri dun′dən sē), *n., pl.* **-cies.** a feature of the brain in which one region will have the capacity to take over some of the work of a damaged area. p. 224

referent power one of five contributing factors to leadership—being liked by the group. p. 406

re flex (rē′fleks), *n.* an automatic, inborn, human response. p. 134

re learn ing (rē lėrn′ing), *n.* a measure of memory in which a subject learns a task a second time (usually much more quickly) after the task has been mastered and a period of time has passed. p. 174

re li a bil i ty (ri lī′ə bil′ə tē), *n.* a person taking the same test twice should ideally score the same each time. If this is not the case, the test is not reliable. p. 191

REM sleep a period of rapid eye movement in which the eyes move wildly from side to side. This begins in the second descent of sleep and the period of time increases as the stages of sleep are repeated throughout the night. p. 258

re pres sion (ri presh′ən), *n.* the process of pushing into the unconscious mind things that are too painful or disturbing. p. 177

reproductive memory memory's ability to reproduce exactly information it has stored away. p. 171

re sponse (ri spons′), *n.* the activity of a human or animal that occurs because of a stimulus. p. 134

retinal disparity the difference between what the left eye sees and what the right eye sees. p. 117

reward power one of the five contributing factors to leadership—being able to give others in the group what they want. p. 406

rod (rod), *n.* a sensory rod-shaped cell located in the layers of tissue near the edge of the retina. These cells provide both night vision and side vision. p. 106

S

sample population a representative portion of the population of subjects to be studied. p. 476

sat u ra tion (sach′ə rā′shən), *n.* the purity of the hue, which has to do with the amount of gray mixed with the pure color. p. **107**

scale of life changes a sclae of stressful events, with stress levels assigned on the basis of average ratings. p. **95**

schiz o phre ni a (skit′sə frē′nē ə), *n.* the most common type of psychosis; the two most basic characteristics are a withdrawal from reality and a pattern of non-logical thinking; others are gross distortion of reality, little social contact, and disorganization of per-ception, thought, and emotion. p. **329**

secondary drive a social or psychological drive, which is generally learned—not inborn. p. **247**

secondary reinforcer a stimulus which has no real value in itself but is associated with a primary reinforcer. p. **146**

second-hand learning according to Bandura, learning by watching others do things. p. **297**

selective attention ability of the senses to select the important part of what we need to perceive. p. **124**

self-absorption according to Erik Erikson, one outcome of the development crisis of middle age, in which a person becomes more absorbed in himself or herself and less open to new experiences. p. **77**

self-actualization according to humanist psychologists, the realization of one's full potential; going beyond meeting biological needs and learning to get along socially, striving toward inde-pendence and autonomy. p. **300**

self-concept a composite image of how one sees one's own personality. p. **282**

sen sa tion (sen sā′shən), *n.* action of the senses; power to see, hear, taste, feel, or smell. p. **104**

sensorimotor period according to Jean Piaget, a stage in which an infant learns by touching; there is no thinking, in the abstract sense, but a great deal of sensing. p. **28**

sensory memory one of three parts of the memory system; information is held in the sensory memory just long enough to be used in perceiving, comparing, judging, etc., and to decide whether to pass the information on to short-term memory. p. **169**

serial anticipation the ability to know what item will follow in a sequence.

p. **173**

severely retarded a person who functions at the level of a child just learning to talk. p. **196**

sex role the part a person plays in life, based on being male or being female. p. **49**

sexual disorder group of sexual disorders including sexual dysfunctions, paraphilias, and other sexual disorders. p. **335**

shap ing (shāp′ing), *n.* a process of rewarding behaviors that come close to a desired response, then rewarding only closer and closer responses until the desired response is learned. p. **150**

short-term memory a part of the memory system that performs a second screening job on the information passed on to it by sensory memory. What remains will be passed on to long-term memory. p. **169**

sim i lar i ty (sim′ə lar′ə tē), *n., pl.* **-ties.** a likeness of objects in color, size, weight, or shape which the eye picks out and perceives as forming a pattern. p. **121**

social and psychological motivations motivations that are learned, not inborn. p. **240**

social clock norms society imposes for a particular time-span, by which life stages are measured. p. **73**

social density in the study of crowds, a measurement of the effect of different numbers of people in the same space. p. **477**

social distance a range of distance generally from four to seven feet in which one conducts impersonal or personal business. p. **379**

social learning theory a theory of personality development that stresses the cognitive, or thinking factors involved in learning behaviors. Social learning theorists believe people learn not only by doing but by watching others do things. p. **35**

social norms standards of conduct consisting of laws, rules, standards, and customs built into a particular society. p. **408**

social psychology the study of how people influence each other. p. **400**

somatic nervous system part of the peripheral nervous system which controls functions like walking or throwing. p. **226**

somatoform disorder a category of

neurotic behavior in which the individual complains of physical symptoms for which no physical cause can be found. p. **322**

spacial density in the study of crowds, a measurement of the effect of space on people. p. **447**

spontaneous recovery the revival of an extinguished response after a period of nonresponding. p. **140**

stabilized image one that moves as the eye moves so that it is always focused at the same point on the retina. p. **267**

standard deviation a formula-calculated statistic designed to tell, in a range of numbers for example, how spread out the numbers are. p. **490**

stim u lant (stim′yə lənt), *n.* a drug that stimulates the central nervous system. Included in this category are caffeine, a common, mild stimulant, and the stronger, more dangerous amphetamines, sometimes referred to as "uppers" or "speed." p. **271**

stim u lus (stim′yə ləs), *n., pl.* **-li.** anything in the environment that brings about a reaction in an animal or human. p. **134**

stress (stres), *n.* a reaction to the pressures of life, sometimes positive, more often negative. p. **93**

struc tur a lism (struk′chər ə-liz′əm), *n.* an approach to psychology which emphasizes the importance of how the basic units of experience—physical sensations, emotions, and images—are com-bined in human consciousness. p. **10**

sub cor tex (sub kôr′teks), *n., pl.* **-ti-ces** (-tə sez′). a group or organs in the brain called the "old brain" which are responsible for such functions as breathing, eating, drinking, sleeping, and some basic emotions. p. **220**

su per e go (sü′pər ē′gō), *n.* in Freud's concept, a dimension of consciousness that holds the id and the ego in check. It combines conscience, that tells right from wrong, with the ego ideal, that inspires one to make things better for all. p. **288**

surface contact a stage in verbal communication during which conversation becomes more long-winded; real feelings and attitudes are still disguised under smiles and politeness, and subjects discussed are general. p. **385**

sym bol (sim′bəl), *n.* something that stands for or represents something else; most words are symbols that stand for concepts. p. **165**

sympathetic system a system of nerves in the autonomic system that comes to the aid of the body when it experiences strong emotions or anxiety by supplying quick energy or sending more blood to the heart and the muscles where it is needed. p. **227**

syn apse (si naps′), *n.* a gap where a nerve signal is crossed to the next neuron. p. **225**

T

ter ri to ri al i ty (ter′ə tôr′ē al′ə tē), *n.* a claim made by persons on parts of the environment as their own, not necessarily ownership but exclusive use. p. **380**

thal a mus (thal′ə məs), *n., pl.* **-mi** (-mī). an organ in the center of the brain which recieves incoming sensory messages, sorts them, and passes them on to the appropriate parts of the subcortex and neocortex. p. **221**

than a tol o gy (than′ə tol′ə jē), *n.* the study of death.

therapeutic community an institution where patients learn to take responsibility for their own actions, within the framework of the hospital setting. The staff has authority, but carries it out in a nonauthoritarian manner. The program includes therapy, rap sessions, and social interaction. p. **361**

thyroid gland a gland consisting of two lobes located on either side and in front of the windpipe that reglates the body's metabolism. p. **230**

tim bre (tim′bər), *n.* the complexity or unique pattern of each sound wave. p. **111**

traditional sex role in our society, a practice in which the dominant male goes out to work and the dependent female stays at home. p. **50**

tran quil iz er (trang′kwə li′zər), *n.* a drug that calms anxieties and tension without depressing the level of consciousness or alertness. p. **271**

trans fer ence (tran sfėr′əns), *n.* a process during the course of therapy in which patients come to identify the analyst with someone important in their lives, and the patient's attitudes and feelings about the other person are transferred to the analyst. p. **348**

trust (trust), *n.* according to Erik Erikson, an attitude established in children by having their needs met in a comforting way. p. **33**

U

un con scious (un kon′shəs), *n.* according to Freud, the larger part of the human mind that is made-up of motives, needs, and feelings a person is unaware of. p. **288**

urban renewal a project designed to restore an area of a city. p. **460**

V

van dal ism (van′dl iz′əm), *n.* the destruction of property and life without any apparent goal beyond the act of destruction itself. p. **450**

vicarious living enjoying life through what others do; reliving the joys of life in memory. p. **85**

W

waking consciousness an alert consciousness that follows sleep and lasts about sixteen hours. It is shaped by a person's perceptions, motivations, emotions, and past experiences. p. **253**

Y

young adulthood a period of growth expansion beginning somewhere around 20 years of age and extending to 35–45 years of age. p. **71**

References

General

Hammond, A. L., and Zimtardo, P. G. *Readings on Human Behavior: The Best of Science '80-'86.* Glenview, Ill.: Scott Foresman and Company, 1988.

Chapter 1

Bandura, A., and Walters, R. H. *Social Learning and Personality Development.* New York: Holt, Rinehart and Winston, 1963.

Bowlby, J. "Separation anxiety." *International Journal of Psychoanalysis,* 1960, 41, pp. 89–113.

Bruner, Jerome. *Toward a Theory of Instruction.* Cambridge, Mass.: Belknap Press, 1966.

Byrne, S., (Ed.) "Nobody home; the erosion of the American family," a conversation with Urie Bronfenbrenner. *Psychology Today,* 1977, 10(12), pp. 40–43.

Cohen, M. D. *Day Care: Serving Preschool Children.* Washington, D.C.: U.S. Government Printing Office, 1974.

Erikson, Erik H. *Childhood and Society.* New York: Norton, 1963.

Freud, Sigmund. "Psychopathology of everyday life," in J. Strachey (Ed.) *The Standard Edition of The Complete Psychological Works of Sigmund Freud,* London: Hogarth Press, 1960. (First English Edition, 1904)

Harlow, H. F. *Learning to Love.* San Francisco: Albion, 1971.

Itard, Jean. *The Wild Boy of Aveyron.* New York: Monthly Review Press, 1972.

Malson, Lucien. *Wolf Children and the Problem of Human Nature.* New York: Monthly Review Press, 1972.

Mitchell, Grace. *The Day Care Book.* New York: Stein and Day, 1979.

Ogintz, Eileen. "Baby Talk." *Chicago Tribune,* January 26, 1988.

Piaget, J. *The Developmental Psychology of Jean Piaget.* New York: Van Nostrand, 1963.

Restak, R. "Newborn Knowledge." *Science '82.*

Sheldon, W. H. *The Varieties of Human Physique: An Introduction to Constitutional Psychology.* New York: Harper, 1940.

Silver, Nan. "How to Raise Brighter, Happier Babies" *American Health,* May 1986.

Stone, L. J., and Church, J. *Childhood and Adolescence: A Psychology of the Growing Person* (3rd ed.). New York: Random House, 1973.

White, Burton L. *The First Three Years of Life.* Englewood Cliffs, N.J.: Prentice-Hall, 1975.

Chapter 2

Anonymous. "I Wanted to Die." *Reader's Digest,* July 1987, pp. 93–(6.

Baumrind, D. "Early socialization and adolescent competence" in E. Dragston and G. Elder (Eds.) *Adolescence in the Life Cycle.* Washington, D.C.: Hemisphere Publishing Company, 1975.

Coleman, J. "Academic achievement and the structure of competition." *Harvard Educational Review,* Fall 1959, 29(4), pp. 330–351.

Erikson, E. H. *Childhood and Society.* New York: Norton, 1963.

Havighurst, R. J. *Human Development and Education.* New York: Longmans, Green, 1953.

Hesse, Herman. *Demian.* New York: Harper and Row, 1965.

Kohlberg, L. "Moral and religious education and the public schools: a developmental view," in T. Sizer (Ed.) *Religion and Public Education.* Boston: Houghton Mifflin Company, 1967.

Maccoby, E. E., and Jacklin, C. N. *The Psychology of Sex Differences.* Palo Alto, Calif.: Stanford University Press, 1974.

Stone, L. J., and Church, J. *Childhood and Adolescence: A Psychology of the Growing Person* (3rd ed.). New York: Random House, 1973.

Chapter 3

Cumming, E., and Henry, W. E. *Growing Old: The Process of Disengagement.* New York: Basic Books, 1961.

Erikson, E. H. *Childhood and Society* (2nd ed.). New York: Norton, 1963.

Holmes, T. H., and Rahe, R. H. "Short-term intrusions into the life-style routing." *Journal of Psychosomatic Research,* June 1970, 14, pp. 121–132.

Kogan, N., and Wallach, M. A. "Age changes in values and attitudes." *Journal of Gerontology,* 1961, 16, pp. 272–80.

Kübler-Ross, E. *On Death and Dying.* New York: Macmillan, 1969.

Kuhlen, R. G. "Developmental changes in motivation during the adult years" in J. E. Birren (Ed.) *Relations of Development and Aging.* Springfield, Ill.: Charles C Thomas, 1964.

Langer, E. J., and Rodin, J. "The effects of choice and enhanced personal responsibility for the aged: A field experiment in an institutional setting." *Journal of Personality and Social Psychology,* 1976, 34, pp. 191–98.

Lehner, G. F. J., and Gunderson, E. K. "Height relationships in the draw-a-person test." *Journal of Personality,* 1953, 21, pp. 392–99.

Levinson, D. *The Seasons of a Man's Life.* New York: Alfred A. Knopf, 1978.

Lieberman, M. A. "Relationship of mortality rates to entrance to a home for the aged." *Geriatrics,* 1961, 16, pp. 515–19.

Neugarten, B. L. "The awareness of middle age," in R. Owen (Ed.) *Middle Age.* London: British Broadcasting Corporation, 1967.

Neugarten, B. L. "Adult personality: toward a psychology of the life cycle," in B. L. Neugarten (Ed.) *Middle Age and Aging.* Chicago: University of Chicago Press, 1968.

Newman, B. M., and Newman, P. R. *Development Through Life.* Homewood, Ill.: Dorsey, 1975.

Palmore, E. B. "Physical, mental and social factors in predicting longevity." *Gerontologist,* 1969, 9, pp. 103–8.

Riegel, K. F., and Riegel, R. M. "Development, drop and death." *Developmental Psychology,* 1972, 6, p. 306.

Selye, H. *The Stress of Life.* New York: McGraw-Hill, 1956.

Chapter 4

Maslow, A. H., and Mintz, N. L. "Effects of esthetic surroundings: 1. Initial effects of three esthetic conditions upon perceiving energy and well-being in faces." *Journal of Psychology,* 1956, 41, pp. 247–54.

Morris, R. L. "Out of body experience." *Theta No. 41,* Summer 1974, pp. 1–3.

Puharich, A. *Uri: A Journal of the Mystery of Uri Geller.* New York: Doubleday, 1974.

Sechrest, L., and Wallace, J. "Figure drawing and naturally occurring events: Elimination of the expansive euphoria hypothesis." *Journal of Educational Psychology,* 1964, 55, pp. 42–44.

Segall, M. H., Campbell, D. T., and Herskovits, M. J. *The Influence of Culture on Perception.* New York: Bobbs-Merrill, 1966.

Sherif, M. "A study of some social factors in perception." *Archives of Psychology,* 1935, 27, p. 187.

Solley, C. M., and Haigh, G. A. "A note to Santa Claus." *Topical research papers. The Menninger Foundation,* 1957, 18, pp. 4–5.

Stratton, G. M. "Vision without inversion of the retinal image." *Psychological Review,* 1897, 4, p. 344.

Targ, R., and Puthoff, H. "Information transition under conditions of sensory shielding." *Nature,* 1974, 251, pp. 692–97.

Chapter 5

Edwards, A. E., and Acker, L. E. "A demonstration of the long-term retention of a conditioned galvanic skin response." *Psychosomatic Medicine,* 1962, 24, pp. 459–63.

Jones, M. C. "A laboratory study of fear: The case of Peter," *Pedagogical Seminary,* 1924, 31, pp. 308–15.

Skinner, B. F. "Teaching machines." *Scientific American,* 1961, 205(5), pp. 90–102.

Spears, E. M. "The use of color in industry," *The Conference Board Management Record,* 1947, 9, pp. 97–104.

Watson, J. B. "Experimental studies on the growth of emotions," in C. Murchison (Ed.) *Psychologies of 1925.* Worcester, Mass.: Clark University Press, 1926.

Watson, J. B., and Rayner, R. "Conditioned emotional reactions," *Journal of Experimental Psychology,* 1920, 33, pp. 1–14.

Zimbardo, P. G. *Psychology nad life,* (12th ed.) Glenview, Ill.: Scott, Foresman and Company, 1988, p. 280.

Chapter 6

Bartlett, F. C. *Remembering: A Study in Experimental and Social Psychology.* New York: Macmillan, 1932.

Brown, R. W., Cazden, C. B., and Bellugi, U. "The child's grammar from I to III," in J. P. Hill (Ed.) *Minnesota Symposia on Child Psychology* (vol. 2). Minneapolis: University of Minnesota Press, 1969.

Chomsky, N. *Language and Mind.* New York: Harcourt Brace, Jovanovich, 1968.

Fouts, R. S., and Couch, J. B. "Cultural evolution of learned language in chimpanzees," in M. E. Hahn and E. C. Simmel (Eds.) *Communicative Behavior and Evolution.* New York: Academic Press, 1976.

Patterson, P. "Linguistic capabilities of a young lowland gorilla," in *An Account of the Visual Mode; Man versus Ape,* American Association for the Advancement of Science. In press.

Penfield, W. *The Mystery of the Mind.* Princeton, N.J.: Princeton University Press, 1975.

Rand, C., and Wapner, S. "Postural status as a factor in memory." *Journal of Verbal Learning and Behavior,* 1967, 6, pp. 268–71.

Tresselt, M. E., and Mayzner, M. S. "Normative solution times for a sample of 134 solution words and 378 associated anagrams." *Psychonomic Monograph Supplement No. 15,* 1966, 1 pp. 293–96.

Whorf, B. L. *Language, Thought and Reality.* J. B. Carroll (Ed.) New York: Wiley, 1956.

Zimbardo, P. G. "The human choice: Individuation, reason, and order versus deindividuation, impulse, and chaos," in W. J. Arnold and D. Levine (Eds.) *Nebraska Symposium on Motivation.* Lincoln: University of Nebraska Press, 1969.

Chapter 7

Albert, R. S. "Present-day status of the concept and its implication for the study of creativity and giftedness." *American Psychologist,* 1969, 24, pp. 743–53.

Bakan, R. "Malnutrition and learning." *Phi Delta Kappan,* June 1970, vol. 51, no. 10, pp. 527–30.

Barron, F. X., and MacKinnon, D. W. *The Creative Person.* Berkeley: University of California, Institute of Personality Assessment and Research, 1962.

Dove, A. "Taking the Chitling test." *Newsweek,* July 15, 1968, pp. 51–52.

Gould, S. J. *The Mismeasure of Man.* New York: Norton, 1981.

Guilford, J. P. *The Nature of Human Intelligence.* New York: McGraw-Hill, 1967.

Jensen, A. R. "How much can we boost IQ and scholastic achievement?" *Harvard Educational Review,* 1969, 39, pp. 1–123.

Jensen, A. R. "Cumulative deficit in IQ of blacks in the rural south." *Developmental Psychology,* 1977, 13, pp. 184–91.

MacKinnon, D. W. "The nature and nurture of creative talent." *American Psychologist,* 1962, 17(7), pp. 484–95.

Terman, L. M., and Oden, M. H. *The Gifted Child Grows Up.* Palo Alto, Calif.: Stanford University Press, 1947.

Thurstone, L. L. "Psychological implications for factor analysis." *American Psychologist,* 1948, 3, pp. 402–8.

Thurstone, L. L. "Theories of intelligence." *Scientific Monthly,* 1946, 62, pp. 101–12.

Wechsler, D. *The Measurement and Appraisal of Adult Intelligence* (4th ed.). Williams & Wilkins, 1958.

Williams, R. L., and Rivers, L. W. "The use of standard and nonstandard English in testing black children." Presented at the *American Psychological Association* convention, Hawaii, September 1972.

Zigler, E. Personal communication to P. G. Zimbardo, 1975.

Chapter 8

Chavkin, Samuel. *The Mind Stealers.* Boston: Houghton Mifflin Company, 1978.

Crichton, M. *Terminal Man.* New York: Knopf, 1972.

Delgado, T. M. R. *Physical Control of the Mind: Toward a Psychocivilized Society.* New York: Harper & Row, 1969.

Kinsbourne, M. "Eye and head turning indicates cerebral lateralization." *Science,* 1972, 176, pp. 539–541.

Lashley, K. S. *Brain Mechanisms and Intelligence.* Chicago: University of Chicago Press, 1929.

Olds, J., and Milner, P. "Positive reinforcement produced by electrical stimulation of septal area and other regions of the rat brain." *Journal of Comparative and Physiological Psychology,* 1954, 47, pp. 419–27.

Penfield, W. *The Mystery of the Mind.* Princeton, N.J.: Princeton University Press, 1975.

Stevens, Leonard. *Explorers of the Brain.* New York: A. A. Knopf, 1971.

Zimbardo, Philip G. Excerpt from "Elements of the nervous system," in *Psychology and Life* (10th ed.). Glenview, Ill.: Scott, Foresman and Company, 1979.

Chapter 9

Bard, P. "The neurohumoral basis of emotional reactions," in C. A. Murchison (Ed.) *Handbook of General Experimental Psychology.* Worcester, Mass.: Clark University Press, 1934.

bash, K. W. "Contribution to a theory of the hunger drive." *Journal of Comparative Psychology,* 1939, 28, pp. 137–60.

Birch, D., and Veroff, J. *Motivation: A Study of Action.* Monterey, Calif.: Brooks/Cole, 1966.

Brown, C. *Manchild in the Promised Land.* New York: Macmillan, 1965.

Carson, R. C., Butcher, J.N., Coleman, J. E., *Abnormal Psychology and Modern Life* (8th ed.). Glenview, Ill.: Scott, Foresman and Company, 1988, pp. 261–64.

Cannon, W.B. "The James-Lange theory of emotions: A critical examination and an alternative." *American Journal of Psychology,* 1927, 34, pp. 106–24.

Darwin, Charles. *The Expression of Emotions in Man and Animals.* Chicago: University of Chicago Press, 1967.

Freud, S. "Introductory lectures on psychoanalysis," in J. Strachey (Ed.) *The Standard Edition of the Complete Psychological Works of Sigmund Freud.* London: Hogarth Press, 1963. First German Edition, 1901.

Harlow, H. F., Harlow, M. K., and Meyer, D. R. "Learning motivated by a manipulation drive." *Journal of Experimental Psychology,* 1950, 40, pp. 228–34.

Hull, C. L. *Principles of Behavior: An Introduction to Behavior Theory.* New York: Appleton-Century-Crofts, 1943.

James, W. *The Principles of Psychology* (vol. 1.). New York: Holt, 1890.

James, W. "What is an emotion?" *Mind,* 1884, 9, pp. 188–205.

Kunen, J. "The name of the game is violence." *The*

Daily Item. Port Chester, N.Y., September 18, 1976.

Landis, C. "Studies of emotional reactions: general behavior and facial expressions." *Journal of Comparative Psychology*, 1924, 4, pp. 447–509.

Lange, Carl G., and James, William. *The Emotions*. Baltimore, Md.: Wilkins & Wilkins, 1922.

Maslow, A. H. *Motivation and Personality*. New York: Harper & Row, 1954.

McClelland, D. C. "Methods of measuring human motivation," in J. W. Atkinson (Ed.) *Motives in Fantasy, Action and Society: A Method of Assessment and Study*. New York: Van Nostrand, 1958.

McClelland, D. C. *Motivational Trends in Society*. New York: General Learning Press, 1971.

Prescott, James. "Body pleasure and the origins of violence." *The Futurist*, 1975, 9, pp, 64–74.

Skinner, B. F. *Beyond Freedom and Dignity*. New York: Knopf, 1971.

Welker, W. I. "An analysis of exploratory and play behavior in animals," in D. W. Fiske and S. R. Maddi (Eds.) *Functions of Varied Experiences*. Homewood, Ill.: Dorsey, 1961.

ZImbardo, P.G., and Montgomery, K. D. "The relative strengths of consummatory responses in hunger, thirst, and exploratory drive." *Journal of Comparative and Physiological Psychology*, 1957, 50, pp. 504–8.

Zimbardo, P. G. *Psychology and Life* (12th ed.). Glenview, Ill.: Scott, Foresman and Company, 1988, p. 526.

Chapter 10

Benson, H. "Your innate asset for combating stress." *Harvard Business Review*, July-August 1974, 52(4), pp. 49–60.

Benson, H., and Wallace, R. K. "Decreased drug abuse with transcendental meditation: A study of 1862 subjects." *Drug Abuse Proceedings of the International Conference*, 1972.

Blakemore, C. *Mechanics of the Mind*. Cambridge, England: Cambridge University Press, 1977.

Bloomfield, H. H. "Transcendental meditation." *Medical Dimensions*, May 1975, pp. 41–42.

Deikman, A. J. "De-automatization and the mystic experience." *Psychiatry*, 1966, 29, pp. 324–38.

Dellinger, R. W. "Investigative hypnosis." *Human Behavior*, April 1978.

Dement, W. C. "The effect of dream deprivation." *Science*, 1960, 131, pp. 1705–7.

Faraday, A. *The Dream Game*. New York: Harper & Row, 1974.

——, *Dream Power*. New York: Coward, McCann and Geoghegan, 1972.

Freud, S. *The Interpretation of Dreams* (vol. 5) *The Standard Edition of the Complete Psychological Works of Sigmund Freud*. London: Hogarth Press, 1900.

Gallwey, W. T. *The Inner Game of Tennis*. New York: Random House, 1974.

Hirsch, S. Carl. *Theater of the Night*. Skokie, Ill.: Rand McNally & Company, 1976.

Lehmann, D., Beeler, G. W., and Fender, D. H. "EEG response during the observation of stabilized and normal retinal images." *Electroencephalography and Clinical Neurophysiology*, 1967, 22, pp. 136–42.

Leichtling, B. "Sleep and dreaming," in *Psychosources*. New York: Bantam, 1973.

Levinson, B. W. "States of awareness during general anesthesia," in J. Lassner (Ed.) *Hypnosis and Psychosomatic Medicine*. New York: Springer-Verlag, 1967, pp. 200–207.

Marsh, Caryl. "A framework for describing states of consciousness," in N. E. Zinberg (Ed.) *Alternate States of Consciousness*. New York: Macmillan, 1977, pp. 121–44.

Orne, M. T. "Mechanisms of post-hypnotic amnesia." *International Journal of Clinical and Experimental Hypnosis*, 1966, 14, pp. 121–34.

Rose, S. *The Conscious Brain*. New York: Knopf, 1973.

Singer, J. L. "Fantasy: The foundation of serenity." *Psychology Today*, 1976, 10(2), pp. 32–34.

Taub, John and Berger, R. J. "The Effects of changing the phase and duration of sleep." *Journal of Experimental Psychology*, February 1976, 2, pp. 30–41.

Webb, W. B. "Sleep behavior as a biorhythm," in W. P. Colquhoun (Ed.) *Biological Rhythms and Human Performance*. London: Academic Press, 1971.

Zimbardo, Philip. Excerpt from "Hypnosis as a cognitive control system," in *Psychology and life* (10th ed.). Glenview, Ill.: Scott, Foresman and Company, 1979.

Chapter 11

Bandura, A. *Social Learning Theory*. Englewood Cliffs, N.J.: Prentice-Hall, 1977.

Bandura, A., Ross, D., and Ross, S. A. "Imitation of film-mediated aggressive models." *Journal of Abnormal and Social Psychology*, 1963, 66, pp. 3–11.

Block, J., and Haan, M. *Lives Through Time*. Berkeley, Calif.: Bancroft, 1971.

Cooley, C. H. *Human Nature and the Social Order*. New York: Scribner's, 1902.

Freud, S. *the Interpretation of Dreams* (vol. 5) *The Standard Edition of the Complete Psychological Works of Sigmund Freud*. London: Hogarth press, 1900.

Freud, S. *Psychopathology of Everyday Life* in J. Strachey (Ed.) *The Standard Edition of the Complete Psychological Works of Sigmund Freud.* London: Hogarth Press, 1960.

Freud, S. *Introductory Lectures on Psycho-Analysis* in J. Strachey (Ed.) *The Standard Edition of the Complete Psychological Works of Sigmund Freud.* London: Hogarth Press, 1963.

Mandell, J. J. "Quarterback on the couch." *Westchester*, November, 1976.

Maslow, A. H. *Motivation and Personality.* N.Y.: Harper & Row, 1954.

Maslow, A. H. *Toward a Psychology of Being.* N.Y.: Van Nostrand Reinhold, 1962.

Mead, G. H. *Mind, Self, and Society: From the Standpoint of a Social Behaviorist.* Chicago: Univ. of Chicago Press, 1934.

Murray, H. A. *Explorations in Personality.* N.Y.: Oxford Univ. Press, 1938.

Murray, H. A. *Thematic Apperception Test Manual.* Cambridge, Mass.: Harvard Univ. Press, 1943.

Revelle, W., Amaral, P., and Turriff, S. "Introversion/extroversion, time stress and caffeine: Effect on verbal performance," *Science,* 1976, 192, pp. 149–150.

Rotter, J. B., and Hochreich, D. J. *Personality.* Glenview, Ill.: Scott, Foresman and Company, 1975.

Chapter 12

American Psychiatric Association. *Diagnostic and Statistical Manual of Mental Disorders* (III-R). Washington, D.C.: American Psychiatric Association, 1987.

Bateson, G., Jackson, D. D., Haley, J., and Weakland, J. "Toward a theory of schizophrenia." *Behavioral Science,* 1956, 8, pp. 527–44.

Cammer, L. *Freedom from Compulsion.* New York: Simon & Schuster, 1976.

Carson, R. C., Butcher, J. N. Coleman, J. C. *Abnormal Psychology and Modern Life* (8th edition). Glenview, Ill.: Scott, Foresman and Company, 1988.

Greenbaum, H. "Imitation and identification in learning behavior," in J. H. Merin and S. H. Naglar (Eds.) *The Etiology of the Neuroses.* N.Y.: Science and Behavior Books, 1966.

Hoffer, A., and Osmond, H. *How to Live with Schizophrenia.* N.Y.: University Books, 1966.

Horney, K. *The Neurotic Personality of Our Time.* New York: Norton, 1936.

Kaufman, S. S. "Economic status as a factor in the etiology of the neuroses," in J. H. Merin and S. H. Nagler (Eds.) *The Etiology of the Neuroses.* New York: Science and Behavior Books, 1966.

Rank, O. *The Trauma of Birth.* New York: Harcourt, Brace Jovanovich, 1929.

Thigpen, C. H. and Cleckley, H. A. *The Three Faces of Eve.* New York: McGraw-Hill, 1957.

Vonnegut, M. *The Eden Express.* New York: Bantam, 1975.

Chapter 13

Allen, K. E., and Harris, F. R. "Elimination of a child's excessive scratching by training the mother in reinforcement procedures." *Behavior Research and Therapy,* 1966, 4, pp. 79–84.

Eisler, R. M., Miller, P. M. Hersen, M., and Alford, H. "Effects of assertive training in marital interaction." *Archives of General Psychiatry,* May 1974, 30(5), pp. 643–49.

Ellis, A. *Reason and Emotion in Psychotherapy.* New York: Stuart, 1962.

Goffman, E. *Asylums.* Chicago: Aldine, 1961.

Hawksworth, H. D. and Schwarz, T. *The Five of Me: The Autobiography of a Multiple Personality.* Chicago: Contemporary, 1977.

Hogan, R. A., and Kirchner, J. H. "Implosive, eclectic, verbal and bibliotherapy in the treatment of fears of snakes." *Behavior Research and Therapy,* 1968, 6, pp. 167–71.

Horney, K. *Our Inner Conflicts: A Constructve Theory of Neurosis.* New York: Norton, 1945.

Ittelson, W. H., Proshansky, H. M., Rivlin, L. G., and Winkel, G. H. *An Introduction to Environmental Psychology.* New York: Holt, Rinehart and Winston, 1974.

Katz, M. P., and Zimbardo, P. G. "Making it as a mental patient." *Psychology Today,* April 1977, 10(11), pp. 122–26.

Lazarus, A. A. "Behavior therapy, incomplete treatment and symptom substitution." *Journal of Nervous and Mental Disorders,* 1965, 140, pp. 80–87.

Lovaas, O. I. "Learning theory approach to the treatment of childhood schizophrenia" in California Mental Health Research Symposium, No. 2 *Behavior Theory and Therapy,* Sacramento, Cal. Department of Mental Hygiene, 1968.

Martin, B. *Abnormal Psychology.* Glenview, Ill.: Scott, Foresman, 1973.

National Institute for Mental Health, Data on staffings for state mental institutions, 1970.

Rogers, C. R. *On Becoming a Person: A Therapist's View of Psychotherapy.* Boston: Houghton Mifflin, 1961.

Rosenhan, D. L. "On being sane in insane places." *Science,* 1973, 179, pp. 250–58.

Chapter 14

Ardrey, Robert. *The Territorial Imperative.* New York: Atheneum, 1966.

Aronson, E., Willerman, B., and Floyd, J. "The effect of a pratfall on increasing interpersonal attraction." *Psychonomic Science*, 1966, 4, pp. 157–58.

Davis, Kingsley. "Final note on a case of extreme isolation." *American Journal of Sociology*, 1947, 52:5, pp. 432–37.

Dutton, D. G., and Aron, A. P. "Some evidence for heightened sexual attraction under conditions of high anxiety." *Journal of Personality and Social Psychology*, 1974, 30, pp. 510–17.

Fast, Julius. *Body Language*. New York: M. Evans and Company, Inc., 1970.

Gagnon, John. *Human Sexualties*. Glenview, Ill.: Scott, Foresman, 1977.

Hall, Edward. *The Hidden Dimension*. New York: Doubleday, 1966.

——. *The Silent Language*. New York: Doubleday, 1959.

Hudson, J. W., and Henze, L. S. "Campus values in mate selection: A replication." *Journal of Marriage and the Family*, 1969, 31, pp. 772–75.

Ittelson, W. H., Prohansky, H. M., and Rivlin, L. G. "Bedroom size and social interaction of the psychiatric ward." *Environment and Behavior*, 1970, 2, pp. 255–70.

Levinger, G., and Snoek, J. D. *Attraction in Relationship: A New Look at Interpersonal Attraction*. Morristown, N.J.: General Learning Press, 1972.

Morris, Desmond. *Manwatching: A Field Guide to Human Behavior*. New York: Harry N. Abrams, Inc., 1977.

Murstein, B. I. "Physical attractiveness and marital choice." *Journal of Personality and Social Psychology*, 1972, 22, pp. 8–12.

Newcomb, T. M. *The Acquaintance Process*. New York: Holt, Rinehart, and Winston, 1961.

Pizer, Vernon. *You Don't Say*. New York: G. P. Putnam's Sons, 1978.

Prescott, D. A. *The Child in the Educative Process*. New York: McGraw-Hill, 1957.

Rothenberg, M. Unpublished manuscript. City University of New York, 1972.

Rubin, Z. *Liking and Loving*. New York: Holt, Rinehart and Winston, 1973.

Sarnoff, I., and Zimbardo, P. G. "Anxiety, fear, and social affiliation." *Journal of Abnormal and Social Psychology*, 1961, 62, pp. 356–63.

Seagert, S., Swap, W. C., and Zajonc, R. B. "Exposure, context and interpersonal attraction." *Journal of Personality and Social Psychology*, 1973, 25, pp. 234–42.

Walster, E., Aronson, E., Abrahams, D., and Rottman, L. "Importance of physical attractiveness in dating behavior." *Journal of Personality and Social Psychology*, 1966, 4, pp. 508–16.

Walster, E., and Walster, G. W. *A New Look at Love*. Reading, Mass.: Addison-Wesley, 1978.

Westin, A. F. *Privacy and Freedom*. New York: Atheneum, 1967.

Zimbardo, P. G. Excerpt from "What is love, anyway?" in *Psychology and Life*, 10th ed. Glenview, Ill.: Scott, Foresman and Company, 1979.

Zimbardo, P. G., and Formica, R. "Emotional comparison and self-esteem as determinants of affiliation." *Journal of Personality*, 1963, 31, pp. 141–62.

Chapter 15

Allport, G. W. *The Nature of Prejudice*. Reading, Mass.: Addison-Wesley, 1954.

Asch, S. E. "Opinions and social pressure." *Scientific American*, 1955, 193(5), pp. 31–35.

Ben, D. J. "Self-perception: An alternative interpretation of cognitive dissonance phenomena." *Psychological Review*, 1967, 74, pp. 183–200.

Berkowitz, L. *Social Psychology*. Glenview, Ill.: Scott, Foresman, 1972.

Deutsch, M., Collins, M. E. *Interracial Housing: A Psychological Evaluation of a Social Experiment*. University of Minnesota Press, 1951.

Festinger, L. *A Theory of Cognitive Dissonance*. Palo Alto, Cal.: Stanford Univ. Press, 1957.

Festinger, L., and Carlsmith, J. M. "Cognitive consequences of forced compliance." *Journal of Abnormal and Social Psychology*, 1959, 58, pp. 203–11.

"Fighting Aids, the Quiet Way." *Newsweek*. April 27, 1987, pp. 64–66

Freedman, J. L., and Fraser, S. C. "Compliance without pressure: the foot-in-the-door technique." *Journal of Personality and Social Psychology*, 1966, 4, pp. 195–202.

Goldberg, P. "Are women prejudiced against women?" *Transaction*. 1968, 5(5), pp. 28–30.

Janus, I. L. *Victims of Groupthink: A Psychological Study of Foreign Policy Decisions and Fiascoes*. Boston: Houghton Mifflin Company, 1972.

"Kids with Aids." *Newsweek*. September 7, 1987, pp. 50–59.

Milgram, S. *Obedience to Authority*. New York: Harper and Row, 1974.

Razran, G. "Ethnic dislikes and stereotypes: a laboratory study." *Journal of Abnormal and Social Psychology*, 1950, 45, pp. 7–27.

Strodtbeck, F. L., James, R. M., and Hawkins, C. Social status in jury deliberations in E. E. Maccoby, T. Newcomb, and E. Hartley (Eds.) *Readings in Social Psychology*, New York: Holt, Rinehart and Winston, 1958.

Taylor, D. W., Berry, P. C., and Block, C. H. "Does group participation when using brainstorming

facilitate or inhibit creative thinking?"
Administrative Science Quarterly, 1958, 3, pp. 23–47.

Chapter 16

Blumer, Herbert. *Symbolic Interactionism: Perspective and Method*. Englewood Cliffs, N.J.: Prentice-Hall, 1969.

Calhoun, J. B. "A behavioral sink." in E. L. Bliss (Ed.) *Roots of Behavior*. New York: Harper and Row, 1962.

———. "The role of space in animal sociology," *Journal of Social Issues*, 1966, 22(4), pp. 46-58.

———. "How the social organization of animal communities can lead to a population crisis which destroys them." Reported by M. Pines. *Mental Health Program Reports*, No. 5 (HEW) Publication N. (HSM 72-9042. Chevy Chase, Md.: National Institute of Mental Health, December, 1971.

Edelman, M. W. *Families in Peril*. Boston: Harvard University Press, 1988.

Fava, S. "The sociology of new towns in the U.S.: balance of racial and income groups." Paper presented at the meeting of the *American Institute of Planners*. Minneapolis-St. Paul, Minnesota, October, 1970.

Fellows, L. "Psychological report finds new town in West Germany boring to children." *New York Times*, March 13, 1971, p. 14.

Freedman, J. L. "The effects of population density on humans" in J. T. Fawcett (Ed.), *Psychological Perspectives on Population*. New York: Basic, 1973.

———. *Crowding and Behavior*. New York: Viking, 1975.

Ittelson, W. H., Proshansky, H. M., Rivlin, L. G., and Winkel, G. H. *An Introduction to Environmental Psychology*. New York: Holt, Rinehart and Winston, 1974.

Jacobs, J. *Death and Life of Great American Cities*. New York: Vintage Books, 1961.

Kozol, J. *Rachel and Her Children*. New York Crown Publishers, 1988.

Latane, B., and Darley, J. M. *The Unresponsive Bystander: Why Doesn't He Help?* New York: Appleton-Century-Crofts, 1970.

LeBon, Gustave. *The Crowd: A Study of the Popular Mind*. Dunwoody, Ga.: N.S. Berg, 1968.

Newman, O. *Defensible Space*. New York: Macmillan, 1972.

New York Times, articles concerning the murder of Kitty Genovese, March 13, 1964, and May 6, 1964.

Piliavan, I. M., Rodin, J., and Piliavan, J. A. "Good samaritanism: an underground phenomenon?" *Journal of Personality and Social Psychology*, 1969, 13, pp. 289–300.

Schorr, A. L. *Slums and Insecurity*. Washington, D.C.: U.S. Government Printing Office, 1963.

Stansfeld, S., and Williamson, R. C. *Social Psychology* (3rd ed.). New York: The Ronald Press Company, 1966.

Stuart, Reginald. "Cincinnati officials order inquiry into concert crush that killed 11." *New York Times*, December 5, 1979, and "For those caught in the crush, Cincinnati's nightmare goes on." *New York Times*, December 7, 1979.

Yablonsky, L. *Violence in the Streets*, S. Endleman, ed. Chicago: Quadrangle Books, 1968.

Yancey, W. L. "Architecture, interaction and social control: the case of a large-scale public housing project." *Environment and Behavior*, March, 1971, 3, pp. 3–18.

Zimbardo, P. G. "A field experiment in auto-shaping" in C. Ward (Ed.), *Vandalism*. London: Architectural Press, 1973.

Index

Acknowledgments

Text

42 From "Nobody Home: The Erosion of the American Family" by Urie Bronfenbrenner. Reprinted from PSYCHOLOGY TODAY MAGAZINE. Copyright © 1977 Ziff-Davis Publishing Company. **46** From DEMIAN: EMIL SINCLAIR'S YOUTH by Hermann Hesse. Copyright 1925 by S. Fisher-Verlag. Copyright © 1965 by Harper & Row, Publishers, Inc. Reprinted by permission of Harper & Row, Inc. and Peter Owen, Ltd., London. **87** From "How to Fight Age Bias: A Gray Panther on the Prowl," MS. Magazine, June 1975, vol. 3, no. 12. Reprinted by permission. **111** William Wordsworth. "Expostulation and Reply." **162** From "Ginny and Gracie Go to School," TIME, December 10, 1979. Reprinted by permission from TIME, The Weekly Newsmagazine; Copyright Time Inc. 1979. **179** "Six Who Came Home," LIFE © 1979 Time Inc. Reprinted with permission. **182–183** A subject protocol for "Incentive effects in children's creativity," by W. C. Ward, N. Kogan and E. Pankove from CHILD DEVELOPMENT, June 1972, 43 pp. 669–676. Reprinted by permission. **190** Reproduced from the Otis-Lennon School Ability Test. Copyright © 1979 by Harcourt Brace Jovanovich, Inc. Reproduced by special permission. **214–216** Adapted by permission of Alfred A. Knopf, Inc. and International Creative Management, from THE TERMINAL MAN, by Michael Crichton. Copyright © 1972 by Michael Crichton. **216–217** Adapted from THE MIND STEALERS by Samuel Chavkin. Copyright © 1978 by Samuel Chavkin. Reprinted by permission of Houghton Mifflin Company. **220** From EXPLORERS OF THE BRAIN by Leonard A. Stevens. Copyright © 1971 by Leonard A. Stevens. Reprinted by permission of Alfred A. Knopf, Inc. **228** Excerpts from "Elements of the Nervous System," PSYCHOLOGY AND LIFE 10th ed., by Philip G. Zimbardo. Copyright © 1979, 1977, 1975, 1971 by Scott, Foresman and Company. **239** Adapted from PSYCHOLOGY AND YOU, by David Dempsey and Philip G. Zimbardo. Copyright © 1978 by Scott, Foresman and Company. **243** from

MANCHILD IN THE PROMISED LAND by Claude Brown. Copyright © Claude Brown 1965. Reprinted by permission of Macmillan Publishing Co., Inc. **252** Adaptation from "States of Awareness during General Anesthesia" by B. W. Levinson from HYPNOSIS AND PSYCHOSOMATIC MEDICINE ed. by J. Lassner. Springer-Verlag, New York, 1967. Reprinted by permission. **256** Adapted from THEATER OF THE NIGHT by S. Carl Hirsch. Copyright © 1976 by Rand McNally & Company. Reprinted by permission. **262** Adapted from "Hypnosis as a cognitive control system," PSYCHOLOGY AND LIFE 10th ed., by Philip G. Zimbardo. Copyright © 1979, 1977, 1975, 1971 by Scott, Foresman and Company. **264** Adaptation from "Investigative Hypnosis," by R. W. Dellinger, *Human Behavior* Magazine, April, 1978. Copyright © 1978 *Human Behavior* Magazine. Reprinted by permission. **301** From "Bradshaw rose above bewilderment and tears" by Skip Myslenski from CHICAGO TRIBUNE, January 20, 1980. Reprinted courtesy of the Chicago Tribune, all rights reserved. **308** From THE EDEN EXPRESS by Mark Vonnegut. Copyright © 1975 Praeger Publishers, Inc. Reprinted by permission of Holt, Rinehart and Winston and Knox Burger Associates. **320** Adapted from "Faces from the Past–VI" by Richard M. Ketchum, from AMERICAN HERITAGE, April 1962, vol. 13, no. 3. Copyright © 1962 by Richard M. Ketchum. Reprinted by permission. **322** Reprinted with permission from BEHAVIOR RESEARCH AND THERAPY, Vol. 8, no. 3, 1970, M. D. Mather, "The treatment of an obsessive-compulsive patient by discrimination learning and reinforcement of decision-making." Copyright © 1970, Pergamon Press, Ltd. **328** Adapted from THE HORN ISLAND LOGS OF WALTER INGLIS ANDERSON edited by Redding S. Sugg, Jr. Copyright © 1973 by Memphis State University Press. reprinted by permission. **330** From "Types of Schizophrenia," ABNORMAL PSYCHOLOGY AND MODERN LIFE, 6 ed., by James C. Coleman. Copyright © 1980, 1976, 1972, 1964 by Scott, Foresman and Company. **380** Adapted from BODY LANGUAGE by

Julius Fast. Copyright 1970 by Julius Fast. Used by permission of M. Evans and Company, Inc. **382** Adapted from BODY LANGUAGE by Julius Fast. Copyright © 1970 by Julius Fast. Used by permission of M. Evans and Company, Inc. **382–383** Adapted from YOU DON'T SAY by Vernon Pizer. Copyright © 1978 by Vernon Pizer. Reprinted by permission of G. P. Putnam's Sons. **383** From BODY LANGUAGE by Julius Fast. Copyright © 1970 by Julius Fast. Reprinted by permission of the publisher, M. Evans and Company, Inc., New York, New York, 10017 and Souvenir Press Ltd. **384** Desmond Morris. MANWATCHING: A FIELD GUIDE TO HUMAN BEHAVIOR. Elsevier Publishing Projects SA and Jonathan Cape Ltd., 1977. **385–386** Adapted from ATTRACTION IN RELATIONSHIP: A NEW LOOK AT INTERPERSONAL ATTRACTION by G. Levinger and J. D. Snoek. Copyright © 1972 by General Learning Press. Copyright © 1978 by G. Levinger and J. D. Snoek. Reprinted by permission. **394** Adapted from D. A. Prescott, "The child in the educative process." Copyright © 1957 McGraw-Hill Company. Used with permission of McGraw-Hill Book Company. **397** Adapted from "Beyond the pleasure principle," PSYCHOLOGY AND LIFE 10 ed., by Philip G. Zimbardo. Copyright © 1979, 1977, 1975, 1971 by Scott, Foresman and Company. **397** Adapted from HUMAN SEXUALITIES by John Gagnon. Copyright © 1977, Scott, Foresman and Company. **439–440** From "Cincinnati Officials Order Inquiry Into Concert Crush That Killed 11" by Reginald Stuart from THE NEW YORK TIMES, December 5, 1979 and "For Those Caught in the Crush, Cincinnati's Nightmare Goes On" by Reginald Stuart from THE NEW YORK TIMES, December 7, 1979. Copyright © 1979 by the New York Times Company. Reprinted by permission. **442** S. Stansfeld Sargent and Robert C. Williamson. SOCIAL PSYCHOLOGY, 3rd ed. New York: The Ronald Press Company, 1966. **448–449** Adapted from "Crowding among animals," PSYCHOLOGY AND LIFE 10 ed., by Philip G. Zimbardo. Copyright © 1979, 1977, 1975, 1971 by Scott, Foresman and

Company. Adapted from a "behavioral sink," by J. B. Calhoun in E. L. Bliss, ed., ROOTS OF BEHAVIOR. New York: Harper & Row, 1962 and "Scientific quest for a path to the future," by J. B. Calhoun from POPULI, SPECIAL SECTION, 1976, vol. 3, no. 1. **450** from DEATH AND LIFE OF GREAT AMERICAN CITIES by Jane Jacobs. New York: Vintage Books, 1961. Copyright © 1961 by Jane Jacobs. Excerpt reprinted by permission of Random House, Inc. **452** L. Yablonsky. VIOLENCE IN THE STREETS, S. Endleman, ed. Chicago: Quadrangle Books, 1968. **452–454** Adapted from a field experiment in auto-shaping from C. Ward ed. VANDALISM by Philip G. Zimbardo. London: Architectural Press, 1973. **454** From THE NEW YORK TIMES, March 13, 1964 and May 6, 1964, concerning the murder of Kitty Genovese. Copyright © 1964 The New York Times Company. Reprinted by permission. **455** Adapted from "Bystander intervention in emergencies: Diffusion of responsibilities" by J. M. Darley and B. Latane from JOURNAL OF PERSONALITY AND SOCIAL PSYCHOLOGY, 1968, 8(4). **456** Adapted from "More hope in the real world," PSYCHOLOGY AND LIFE 10 ed., by Philip G. Zimbardo. Copyright © 1979, 1977, 1975, 1971 by Scott, Foresman and Company. From THE UNRESPONSIVE BYSTANDER: WHY DOESN'T HE HELP? by B. Latane and J. M. Darley. New York: Appleton-Century Crofts, 1970. Reprinted by permission of Prentice-Hall, Inc., Englewood Cliffs, New Jersey. Adapted from "Good Samaritanism: An underground phenomenon?" by I. M. Piliavan, J. Rodin and J. A. Piliavan from JOURNAL OF PERSONALITY AND SOCIAL PSYCHOLOGY, 1969, vol. 13 and "Effect of blood on reactions to a victim" by J. A. Piliavan and I. M. Piliavan from JOURNAL OF PERSONALITY AND SOCIAL PSYCHOLOGY, 1972, vol. 23. **471** Lewis Carroll. ALICE'S ADVENTURES UNDERGROUND. **484** Adapted from "NISO Poll No. 4: This Survey's About You!" Senior Scholastic, March 1979. Copyright © 1979 by Scholastic Magazines, Inc. **485** Adapted from "What Teenagers Said in NISO Poll No. 4." Senior Scholastic, Teacher's Edition, May 1979.

Illustrations

Cover: (left, center) Ric Ferro/Florida Fotobanc (right) Jim Bradshaw

Positions of photographs are shown in abbreviated form as follows: top (t), bottom (b), center (c), left (l), right (r). Unless otherwise acknowledged, all photos are the property of Scott, Foresman and Company.

3 © Focus on Sports **5** Mitch Kezar, *Life Magazine* © 1980, Time Inc. **7** Paul Conklin **9** The Bettmann Archive **11** The Bettmann Archive (tl), Association for the Advancement of Psychoanalysis of the Karen Horney Psychoanalytic Institute and Center, New York (tc), UPI (tr), Wide World (bl), The Bettmann Archive (bc), Ken Heyman (br) **13** FALLING MAN/MANSCAPES 1969 by Ernest Trova, 10 silkscreen prints, Edition of 175, 1969, 28"×28"/Pace Editions, Inc., New York **16** © Rice Sumner Wagner **17** FAMILY GROUP, 1948–49. Bronze. By Henry Moore. Photograph by David Finn from *Henry Moore Sculpture and Environment*, published by Harry N. Abrams, Inc., 1976. **19** Anderson/Magnum **20** Alice Kandell/Photo Researchers **21** George S. Zimbel/Monkmeyer **22** Anna Kaufman Moon/Stock Boston **24** Dr. Harry F. Harlow, University of Wisconsin Primate Laboratory (l,r) **26** Christopher Vail **29** Lisa Ebright **30** Suzanne Szasz **32** NASA (bl,br) **33** Courtesy Dr. Henry L. Nadler, Genetics Department, Children's Memorial Hospital, Chicago, IL **41,42,43** Christopher Vail **45** Sidney Harris **48** Ken Heyman **49** Elizabeth Hamlin/Stock Boston (l), J.P. Laffont/Sygma (r) **50** Suzanne Szasz **52** (t) © Marcia Weinstein **52** (b) © Marcia Weinstein **54** Paul Conklin **55** (r) © Bob Daemmrich **56** Robert Ragland **57** Ginger Chih/Peter Arnold **60** George Gardner **62** (l) © Dan Chidester/The Image Works Joel Gordon (1), Richard Stromberg (r) **65** Owen Franken/Stock/Boston **66** © Charles Gatewood/The Image Works **71** © Bob Daemmrich **71** Charles Gatewood **74** Courtesy The Chicago Jaycees **75** Robert Lerner in *Think Magazine* **76** (c) © Jim Bradshaw **77** Elderly man and woman, painting by David Wilcox, courtesy of Champion International Corp. **80** Richard Stromberg **82** Yoichi R. Okomoto/Photo Researchers (l) **83** Paul Conklin (l), John Loengard, *Life Magazine*, © Time Inc. (r) **85** Vito Palmisano (l), Susan Meiselas/Magnum (r) **86** Elliot Erwitt/Magnum (l), Jill Freedman/Sygma (r) **87** © Kenneth Jarecke/Contact Press Images **88** Abigail Heyman/Magnum **91** Michael Hayman/Black Star **92** Owen Franken/Sygma **93** Suzanne Szasz **94** Charles Gatewood **95** Charles Biasiny-Rivera **102** © Joseph A. DiChello, Jr. **104** "Symmetry Drawing B"/Collection Haags Gemeentemuseum-The Hague **106** Photo by Lennart Nilsson from *Behold Man* © 1974, Little, Brown & Company **108** Courtesy Macmillan Science Co., Inc. **110** © Helmut Werb/Shooting Star **113** Peter Jordan/Liaison Joel **114** © Elizabeth Crews/The Image Works **115–116** William Vandivert Robert Amft **119** Photos by Alan Ross **123, 124–125** Murals by Greg Brown, © 1976 City of Palo Alto, CA Wide World **125** (b) From STREET MURALS by Volker Barthelmeh, Copyright © 1982 by Alfred A. Knopf, Inc. Reprinted by permission of publisher. **127** The Bettmann Archive **136** N. Wayne Hansen, Pittsfield, Mass. **141** Historical Pictures Service (t), Erika Stone/Peter Arnold (b) **142** Photo by G. Paul Bishop **143** United States Navy **144** Reprinted by permission of Jester of Columbia **145** Will Rapport/courtesy of Prof. B. F. Skinner **146** Own Franken/Stock Boston **149** Bohdan Hrynewych/Stock Boston (l), Tony Triolo/*Sports Illustrated* (r) **157** Erika Stone/Peter Arnold **160** Courtesy John Tracy Clinic, Los Angeles, CA **162** Courtesy Children's Hospital of San Diego, CA **163** Dr. Beatrice Gardner, University of Nevada, Reno **166–167** University of Arizona **176** Catherine Ursillo/Photo Researchers **178** Wide World (l,r) **179** Brian Lanker, *Life Magazine* © 1979, Time Inc. **185** Culver Pictures **186** Sidney Harris The Psychological Corporation, New York, NY **192** Robert Ragland **196** Wide World **197** Bill Hurter/Leo de

Wys **198** Cover of *Flowers for Algernon* written by Daniel Keyes. Copyright © 1959, 1966. Used by permission of Bantam Books, Inc. All rights reserved. **199** Copyright © 1980, Chicago Tribune (l), Courtesy of Ruth Slenczynka (r) **200** Courtesy Robert L. Williams **201** Courtesy of the Estate of Mrs. Georgia O'Keeffe, Photo by Malcolm Varon, National Gallery of Art **202, 203** Wide World (l), Burk Uzzle/Magnum (r) Courtesy of Davis Caves, Inc., P.O. Box 102, Armington, IL 61721 (t), Robert Amft (b) **204** Leonard Freed/Magnum (l), Owen Franken/Stock Boston (r) **205** Gustav Freedman **206** John Oldenkamp/Photophile **212–213** Scott, Foresman photograph **212** © Ric Ferro/Florida Fotobanc, Inc. **214–215** Reproduced by special permission of *Playboy* Magazine; Copyright © 1972 by *Playboy*; illustration by Ron Bradford **218** EEG courtesy University of Illinois Medical Center (l), Michael Alexander (b) **219** Dr. Jose M. Delgado (t,b) **222** Courtesy Pfizer Medical Systems, Inc. **229** Lou Merrin/Monkmeyer **236** Elizabeth Hamlin/Stock Boston **237** UPI (b) **238** Elizabeth Hamlin/Stock Boston **243** Christo's "Running Fence" © 1980 Gianfranco Gorgoni/Contact 244 NASA **246** Leo de Wys **249** The Bettmann Archive **253** Robert Amft **255** Pierre Boulat **258** Courtesy University of Chicago Sleep Lab **259** From P. Hauri, *The Sleep Disorders*, Kalamazoo, Michigan, Upjohn Company, 1977. **260** "The Melancholy and Mystery of a Street," 1914 Giorgio de Chirico. Private Collection, Photo by Allan Mitchell **261** "Ontogenetic Development of the Human Sleep-Dream Cycle," Roffwarg, H., et al., *Science*, Vol. 152, pp. 604–619, Fig., 29 April 1966. Copyright 1966 by the American Association for the Advancement of Science. **262** Collection of The Newark Newark Museum **263** Arthur Grace/Stock Boston **265** Photographer, Jonathan Wright, National Geographic Society from their film "Journey to the Outer Limits" **267** The Bettmann Archive **268** Wide World **271** Robert Footorap/Jeroboam **273** Dr. Albert Hofman **278** © Joseph A. DiChello, Jr. **286** Reprinted by permission of the publishers from

Thematic Apperception Test by Henry A. Murray, Harvard University Press. Copyright 1943 by The President and Fellows of Harvard College; copyright renewed 1971 by Henry A. Murray **290** Film Stills, Archives, Museum of Modern Art **291** © Elizabeth Crews/The Image Works **292** DeJean, Gianini, Atlan/Sygma **293** Wide World **294** Courtesy W. Clement Stone (t), Photo by Ron Green. Courtesy *Redbook* Magazine (b) **295** The Bettmann Archive **297, 298, 299** Courtesy Dr. Albert Bandura **300** Courtesy University of Wisconsin **301** Heinz Kluetmeir/*Sports Illustrated* **302** Brown Brothers **309** Allan Bruce Zee **310** Culver Pictures **312** © Dennis Brack/Black Star **313** © Bob Daemmrich/The Image Works **319** Yan Lukas/Photo Researchers **320** Culver Pictures (l), Brown Brothers (r) **321** Courtesy of Al Vercoutere, Camarillo State Hospital, Camarillo, CA **323** Arthur Tress **324** Wisconsin Center for Film and Theater Research **325** UPI **326, 327** Courtesy of Chris Costner Sizemore, author of *I'm Eve*, Doubleday, 1977 **328** From Redding S. Sugg, Jr., *A Painter's Psalm: The Mural in Walter Anderson's Cottage*, Memphis State University Press, Copyright © 1978 by Redding S. Sugg, Jr. **330** Elinor Beckwith/Taurus **333** UPI **337** Courtesy Travenol Laboratories, Inc., Artificial Organs Division, Deerfield, IL **340** © 1979 Eric A. Roth/The Picture Cube **341** "World War II—Terror," montage by Richard Saholt, Photo courtesy of the artist **345** Los Angeles Exceptional Children's Foundation Paintings/Charles Conrad photo **347** Historical Pictures Service (t), Van Bucher/Photo Researchers (b) **349** From "Acute Schizophrenia" by Dr. Howard I. Levene, Archives of General Psychiatry, Vol. 25, September 1971. Reprinted by permission **350** Robert Ragland **351** Rick Winsor (l) **352** Michael Alexander **353** Rick Winsor **354** National Library of Medicine, Bethesda, Maryland **355** Dan Hogan Charles/New York Times **356** Dr. Philip Zimbardo (l), Curt Gunther/Camera 5 (r) **358** Alex Webb/Magnum **360** Los Angeles Exceptional Children's Foundation Paintings/Charles Conrad photos (l,r) **361, 362** James H. Karales/Peter Arnold **365** Lily Solmssen/Photo

Researchers **366** Joel Gordon **367** © David R. Frazier Photolibrary **373** © Joseph A. DiChello, Jr. **375** "Thanksgiving," by Norman Rockwell Courtesy Old Corner House **376** Joel Gordon **377** © Brent Jones **378** Barbara Renan/FPG **381** Donald Dietz/Stock Boston **383** Paul Conklin **387** Courtesy Comdates, Chicago **388** © David R. Frazier Photolibrary **392** Alex Webb/Magnum **395** Courtesy Marriott's Great America **396** Jay Hoops/Leo de Wys **401** Courtesy Keith Jay and the Apollo Chorus of Chicago **406** Sovfoto (t), Peasant painting from Huhsien County of the People's Republic of China/U.S.-China Peoples Friendship Association of New York City (b) **407** 12th Air Force Photo **409** Dr. Philip Zimbardo **411** UPI **413** Richard Kalvar/Magnum (l), Constantine Manos/Magnum (4) **414** Jean-Claude Lejeune **416** UPI **418–419** Owen Franken/Stock Boston **419** Vahan Shirvanian **420** Robert Amft **421** Jean-Claude Lejeune **423** UPI **424** Wide World **425** Wide World **426** Wide World **428** © *Look Magazine*/Library of Congress **429** Brian Lanker, *Life Magazine* © 1980, Time Inc. (l), Sidney Harris (r) **430** Library of Congress **431** H. Roger Viollet **432** Earl Dotter/Magnum **433** Paul Sequeira **434** John R. Rosenberger/FPG **435** UPI **438–439** Bill Eppridge, *Life Magazine* © 1969, Time Inc. **440** Robert Amft **441** UPI **442** Paul Sequeira **443** Andy Levin/Black Star (l), Dennis Brack/Black Star (r) **444** UPI **446** Donald Dietz/Stock Boston **447** Danelo Nardi/FPG **449** Wide World **451** UPI **452** Mike Mazzaschi/Stock Boston **453** Dr. Philip Zimbardo **455** Sidney Harris **457** United Nations **459** Archie Lieberman **460** UPI (l), Courtesy of Whisler-Patri/Jeremiah O. Bragstadt (r) **463** Jack Gillette **471** From *Alice's Adventures in Wonderland* by Lewis Carroll. Illustrated by John Tenniel **474** Dr. Philip Zimbardo **476** UPI **481** Yves de Braine/Black Star **488** Reprinted from *Sybil* by Flora Rheta Schreiber, copyright 1973. With permission of Contemporary Books, Inc. **492** Dr. Philip Zimbardo.